THE FUR TRADE IN CANADA

THE
FUR TRADE
IN CANADA

An Introduction
to Canadian Economic History

REVISED EDITION

BY HAROLD A. INNIS

University of Toronto Press

TO

MARY QUAYLE INNIS

Foreword to the First Edition

THE history of the fur trade here presented by Doctor Innis may be regarded as an introduction to the analytic study of that industry which appears in another volume, *The Fur Trade of Canada* (Toronto, 1927). The two volumes together are intended to give a conspectus of the industry, showing against the historical background the social and economic significance of the fur trade, the rôle which it has played and continues to play in the general life of the country.

At the same time this volume is complete in itself. It is an interpretation of the historical record of a primary industry whose growth was a vital factor in the expansion of Canada. As such it is a contribution to the economic history of Canada. It is only through such investigations that an adequate economic history becomes possible.

Doctor Innis has made himself personally familiar with the fur trade territories of Canada, and has also gone to the original historical documents containing the record of the fur trade. The work is throughout a piece of original research animated by the spirit of interpretative scholarship.

R. M. MacIver

Toronto
June, 1929

Foreword

Harold Adams Innis was Canada's foremost historian, and it was *The Fur Trade in Canada* which, more than any of his other books, set him on the path to international fame. Not nearly so well known outside its scholarly circle as it deserves to be, the book is that rare thing, a truly original work of synthesis, firmly based on careful and extensive research, dazzling in its almost pointillist way of amassing pages of meaningful facts and at last, seemingly from a height, drawing from the facts a pattern of searching and sweeping conclusions. The book is of the greatest significance because of Innis' fundamental reinterpretation of North American history and because of the effect of that reinterpretation on subsequent scholarship.

Innis' family background embodied much of the history of Canada. The family was established in North America by a British soldier who, having fought against the rebellious American colonists in the Revolution, chose to take up a grant of land in New Brunswick at the end of the war. Both the second and third generations moved westward, beginning life anew in the midst of unbroken forest land. By the time Harold was born, on November 5, 1894, at the tag end of the century's long "great depression," the family had come to rest in Oxford County, Ontario. Young Innis was to grow as Canada grew, attaining his majority during the same collective experience—World War I—that brought a form of maturity to his nation. The family farm was close to the still-existent Canadian frontier, and the years of his early schooling also were the years when wheat declined as a cash crop in Ontario, when the newly opened prairie lands to the west were exploited and the farmers of the eastern province slowly and hesitantly became aware of the often migratory nature of a staple economy. As an adult Innis was to look back and realize the full significance of some of his childhood experiences in a way few of us can, drawing added insights into his magisterial studies of the Canadian economy, and in particular of economic dependency.

From the outset Innis enjoyed being a student, and once begun he permitted few digressions from his pursuit of knowledge. After attending rural schools he moved on to the Woodstock Collegiate Institute, where he completed a two-year course in half the time, and then to McMaster University in Toronto (and now in Hamilton). He also went on his first trip across Canada in order to teach summer school in northern Alberta.

There he discovered, unknowing, the land of which he one day would write. He joined the Canadian army upon completing his degree and was seriously wounded at Vimy Ridge. With a rather natural desire to put his experiences to use for scholarly advantage, he came back to write an M.A. thesis on "The Returned Soldier."

Innis early realized that the surest way to be the best man at the top is to concentrate on being the best man while at the bottom. His rise to fame and position was extremely rapid, his scholarly productivity prodigious, the expansion of his mental horizon nearly constant. He clearly was a man who ran and thought hard all his life. Donald G. Creighton, his biographer and friend, has observed that his farm days gave him a capacity for continuous work and an instinct for simplicity; that in his early career he was constantly hounded by financial need, driven to adding evening courses and extra writing to his already heavy work load; and that he was always "extremely, exhaustingly busy."[1] But Innis probably would have spent his energies with the same apparent abandon even had he been urban bred and well to do, for his dedication to his scholarship, his love of bringing interpretative order out of the factual chaos produced by his own massive research, and his quest for an explanation of Canada's existence, would have driven him on in any case.

Innis took his doctorate at the University of Chicago, teaching there while finishing work for the degree. He offered a 600-page manuscript (published in 1923 as *A History of the Canadian Pacific Railway*) at a time when short and often shallow essays were far more common as dissertations. In 1920 he was appointed to a lectureship at the University of Toronto, and his undoubted abilities and hard work, combined with the upward thrust of a changing and growing department, brought him rapid promotion to assistant professor in 1925, associate professor in 1929, full professor in 1936, and head of the Department of Political Economy in 1937. In 1947 he became dean of the Graduate School. While still in his forties he had become, as Creighton has noted, Canada's "senior academic statesman."

Innis' research already had led to eleven solid books, with three more to come before his death. His published dissertation was followed in 1927 by a slim volume on the contemporary economics of the fur trade; in 1929 by the first adequate collection of documents relating to Canadian history; and in 1930 by *Peter Pond: Fur Trader and Adventurer*. These three books were by-products of the research which led, also in 1930, to *The Fur Trade in Canada*. In 1936 he wrote *Settlement and the Mining*

---

[1]*Harold Adams Innis: Portrait of a Scholar* (Toronto, 1957), p. 19.

Frontier, and in 1940 he completed his second truly outstanding work, *The Cod Fisheries: The History of an International Economy*.

But Innis also was to discover that he enjoyed helping establish and administer policy and that success brought new responsibilities. He was elected president of the Canadian Political Science Association, of the Economic History Association, of the Royal Society of Canada, and of the American Economic Association; he received honorary degrees from the universities of New Brunswick, McMaster, Laval, Manitoba, and Glasgow; he was visiting professor at the universities of California, Chicago, and British Columbia; he served on a Nova Scotian commission to examine the economy of the province and in 1949 on an especially tiring Royal Commission on Transportation; he lectured at the universities of Oxford, London and—as Cust lecturer—Nottingham; he assembled from his essays, addresses, and learned articles three more books, *Empire and Communication*, *Changing Concepts of Time*, and *The Bias of Communication*; and he continued to serve as head of his department and dean of the Graduate School. Too busy and ever tired, he fell ill, briefly survived an operation, and died on November 8, 1952.

The last seven years of Innis' life had seen a notable change in his scholarly interests. Devoted to Canada and to Canadian history, worried that Canadian survival as a separate political entity on the North American continent was threatened by the wave of popular or mass culture sweeping in from the United States, Innis turned more and more to broad questions relating to communications, language, and space-time relations. His interest in communications led him, in 1945, to the U.S.S.R. as a guest of the Academy of Sciences. His sympathy for the Russian people was coupled with a growing dislike for the United States, which to him seemed to be the champion of conservatism in the face of the needs of a hungry, shattered world. He spoke out for the formation of a third force, for a bloc of uncommitted or neutral nations which might stand between the polarized powers. He feared the all too-friendly hand of American "cultural imperialism" in all its "attractive guises," and he recognized the need for Canadians to develop a distinctive culture of their own. But he never became, contrary to his biographer's apparent view, an automatic anti-American.[2] He admired many Americans and had married one, Mary Quayle, while at the University of Chicago. To those who attacked the United States in a reflex way he could have said, as he did in another context, "let me warn you that any exposition by any economist which

[2]For another contrary and, I believe, confused view, see Daniel Drache, "Harold Innis: A Canadian Nationalist," *Journal of Canadian Studies* (1969), pp. 7–12. Drache sees Innis as "resolutely anti-American."

explains the problems and their solutions with perfect clarity is certainly wrong."

During these years he began work on yet another major project, a history of the written and spoken word from Greece to the present. Although he did not live to complete it, he had worked out his major ideas before his death and had incorporated his research and philosophy into his last three volumes. (A fourth volume, *Essays in Canadian Economic History*, was edited by his wife after his death.) He had moved from western, Canadian, and North American history to the larger world stage, and when he died he was a major international figure in historical scholarship, one of the very few that Canada (or the United States) has produced.

At his death Innis was not known outside the world of scholarship, however, and then only to historians and economists. It would not be until 1969 that a youthful (and unsuccessfully anonymous) reviewer for *The Times Literary Supplement* would reveal Innis's name to the British reading public by citing him as one of Canada's few intellectual giants. The slow public awareness of Innis—still slight when measured against what Innis attempted or even against what he achieved—grew out of the very rapid expansion of public interest in the ideas of Marshall McLuhan, Canada's widely-read and much-discussed theorist of the mass media.[3] McLuhan, hailed by no less an authority in how to communicate than *Playboy* magazine as "the high priest of popcult and metaphysician of media", frequently acknowledged his debt to Innis. This debt—most clearly evident in McLuhan's *The Gutenberg Galaxy* (1962)—was to the Innis of the later years, however: to the man who wrote *The Bias of Communication*, to the reprint edition of which McLuhan contributed an Introduction. In it he remarked upon the "perpetual entertainment of surprises and of intellectual comedy" to be found between the interstices of Innis's darting insights. When is a *non sequitur* not a *non sequitur*? McLuhan was asking. The answer appeared to be, when it was written by Harold Adams Innis. One could not be certain, however, whether McLuhan's fame would lead to a re-examination of Innis's theories or merely to a new and more sophisticated way in which the media could overlook the historian who lay in wait behind McLuhan's metaphysics. (Significantly, *Playboy* saw no reason to mention Innis.)

Still, Innis was the quintessential historian. He never wrote an inadequately researched or a thoughtless book; he knew that he should use

[3]See, in particular, chapter 2 of Dennis Duffy, *Marshall McLuhan* (Toronto, 1969), pp. 14–19; and the essay by James Carey, cited in note 5, which is reprinted in Raymond Rosenthal, ed., *McLuhan: Pro & Con* (New York, 1968).

maps as well as documents, that human beings are a kind of living document in themselves, that multi-archival research is basic and travel essential. He was not content to stop his queries with the obvious questions
or his research with the obvious collections; and his massive documenta-
tion, his lengthy and discursive footnotes, his great masses of sometimes
almost undigested facts which sprawl across his pages were among his
strengths—strengths that would have been weaknesses had he not usually
gone on to interpret the facts brilliantly and persuasively, to show the
theoretician, the philosopher, and the historian below the antiquarian and
bibliographer at the surface. Some early reviewers, perhaps irritated by
Innis's obvious fascination with detail, which he often pulled about himself like a cloak, found that *The Fur Trade in Canada* suffered from "a
surfeit of information," that the arguments were "occasionally too in-
genious." But scholarly reviewers almost at once, and to an increasing
degree in later years, recognized the book for what it was, a landmark in
western and Canadian history.

Nor did Innis make the mistake, common in 1930 and increasingly
common since, of thinking that history could be written exclusively from
archives and libraries, from one's study, comfortable and essentially
untravelled. Like Parkman and Trevelyan before him, he realized that
he must see the country of which he wrote. In 1924 he journeyed in an
eighteen-foot canvas-covered Hudson Bay canoe (although river steamers
were available to him) to the Mackenzie River basin, the last major sur-
viving region of the fur trade, and the diary which he kept on that trip—
loaned to the present writer by Dean Mary Quayle Innis—infused life
into the documents he studied so closely during the next five years. He
repeatedly travelled thereafter to make certain he had the feel of a place
before he wrote of it, for he knew that there are sources of knowledge to
be gained only by going to the spot and seeing with one's own eyes. In
1926 he went to the Yukon to investigate Canadian mining; in 1927 he
toured the mines and mills of eastern Canada; in 1928 he visited the
mining towns of northern Ontario; in 1929 he reached Churchill, even
now remote on Hudson Bay; in 1930 he was in Newfoundland; and in
1932, in Labrador. His knowledge of the landscape of which he wrote
was unparalleled.

To this great outburst of research, to his evident eagerness, his untiring
interest, his willingness to subject himself to the rigors of northern travel
before the railway and highway, Innis added several qualities of mind
which helped him in his role as historian. Creighton feels that he was "a
born historian, with a tremendous irrepressible interest in the facts of
experience" (p. 59). Even as a child he knew the farm land of his home

with an "affectionate particularity." He could "tell by a glance at a particular chestnut or hickory nut what tree it had come from; he could almost
infallibly identify the source of a bucket of maple sap by its distinctive
flavour" (p. 9). He was naturally skeptical, so he emphasized the irre-
futable fact over the vague supposition, but he also had a generally
philosophical, modest turn of mind. Perhaps memories of his early
economic hardships strengthened his tendency to espouse an economic
interpretation of history; certainly his quiet agnosticism would not have
lessened this predilection. Even his interest in communications and especially in language was preconditioned by his earlier work on technology
as a factor in social change. But his modesty and his skeptical, common-
sense approach to his subject kept him from becoming doctrinaire about
economic man. He never became a Marxist, and although greatly influenced by Veblen he was not uncritical of him. Innis often spoke of his
dislike of "monopoly situations" in fields of knowledge, situations in
which the ideas of one man, be he Charles Beard, Frederick Jackson
Turner, Veblen, or Innis himself, came to dominate. Although he became
Canada's greatest national historian, he always knew, as historians must,
that his work had only begun.

The Fur Trade in Canada is several often detailed histories in one, yet
Innis seldom loses sight of the broad view. What he has told is an old
western story: the clash between sophisticated and primitive cultures, a
westward movement that pushed forward over the dead bodies of beaver
—a story of western development as a result of eastern and European
needs. But his book is more than this. It is Indian history in its evidence of
how the Hurons and the Ottawas became middlemen in the fur trade. It is
transportation history in its account of how the canoe was displaced by the
York boat. It is imperial history in its exploration of the ways in which an
American empire began to displace a British one. It is diplomatic and
international history in its interpretation of the nature of French and
British rivalry and in its comments on the American Revolution. It is
business history in its detailed account of the operation of the Hudson's
Bay and Northwest companies. It is Canadian, western, and American,
and primarily it is economic history.

The historiography of the fur trade probably begins with Edward
Umfreville's The Present State of Hudson's Bay, published in London in
1790. Thereafter would flow hundreds of books and thousands of articles,
for although there never has been a boom in fur-trade history, there is
abundant evidence of steady interest. In 1939 Stuart Cuthbertson and
John S. Ewers listed some 1700 titles in their Preliminary Bibliography on
the American Fur Trade (St. Louis), and in 1947 Joseph P. Donnelly

noted, with little duplication, 500 titles dealing with a much more limited subject.[4] The Toronto Public Library also found nearly 1,000 titles on *The Canadian North West*, with particular reference to the fur trade and the Hudson's Bay Company, in 1931. Yet Innis's volume remains one of the very few indispensable works. It is marred, to be sure, by his failure to obtain access to the closed archives of the Hudson's Bay Company, at Beaver House in London, by his persistent failure to distinguish between beaver and other pelts, and by his disconnected literary style, which relies upon the reader to see the order he is imposing even when that order is not demonstrated, as in a "psychedelic delicatessen."[5]

But the chief significance of this book is not that it is a nearly definitive history of the economics of the fur trade. It is more than that; it is the beginning of an entire reorientation of Canadian (and therefore of North American) history. Contrary to those historians who insist that Canada is a nation despite her geography, Innis asserted that Canada is a nation because of it. Rather than a series of regions each of which has more natural affinity with a like region in the United States than with other Canadian regions, she is a single, coherent unit, created by an east-west line of imperial communications, a line based on the St. Lawrence River, the Great Lakes, and the western waterways and trails, penetrating via the natural extension of the Atlantic Ocean into the capitals of Europe. Until European settlement the material culture of the Indians on the Canadian Shield was based on the white-tailed deer; the fur trade made the non-migratory beaver far more important, and since the beaver was easily discovered and even more easily killed, the fur frontier receded into the Laurentian empire and beyond with particular rapidity. (Thus a study of methods and routes of transportation also became basic to understanding the trade.) Canada was not created, Innis and his followers showed, in reaction to American expansionism; it emerged because of French and British dependence on a series of geographically determined staples. The Canadian economy has been based on fishing, the fur trade, lumbering, and wheat growing, roughly in that order, and each of these staples has flowed along a portion of the inland empire created by the St. Lawrence to tie British North America to the Mother Country with strong cables of coins.

Geographical determinism mixes with economic determinism in Innis' account, for there is another side to those coins. The nature of the com-

---

[4]*A Tentative Bibliography for the Colonial Fur Trade in the American Colonies, 1608–1800*, Saint Louis University Studies, monograph series, 2.

[5]The phrase is from James W. Carey's perceptive article, "Harold Adams Innis and Marshall McLuhan," *Antioch Review* (1967), pp. 5–39.

munications system which developed from the fur trade tied the north first to France and then to Britain, and the distinctive economy of the fur trade was to separate the north from those colonies to the south that were to become the United States. Champlain already was trading well into the interior while Englishmen were clinging to the Virginia coast. The French had pushed on through the Great Lakes to the Rocky Mountains when the more numerous British barely had reached the Piedmont. By contrasting the trading, semi-nomadic society of the North, dependent on Indian trappers and middlemen—rapidly exhausting the area's resources and forging westward again—with the organized agricultural society of the South, which found the Indian a hindrance, Innis shows how the "hostility of beaver and plough" made it inevitable that Canada should remain British when the agricultural region broke away.

He also argues that the unified, centralized fur trade made it easy for Canadian industry, finance, and transportation to be centralized at a later date under either private or mixed enterprise. The fur trade both shaped and permeated Canadian history. It was basic to the history of the North American continent.

The Fur Trade in Canada originally was published in 1930 by the Yale University Press. In 1956 the University of Toronto Press issued a revised edition which, through the efforts of Mary Quayle Innis, Samuel D. Clark, and W. T. Easterbrook—all members of the University of Toronto—incorporated Innis's corrections, marginal notations, and suggestions for rearrangement of material. Since his method of citation was somewhat quixotic, a list of references was prepared and fifty-two post-1930 titles were added. This revised edition was reprinted in 1962 by the Yale University Press with most of the various prefaces and the several appendices omitted. They are restored here for this reprint edition.

Other writings on the fur trade by Innis include material in the *Canadian Historical Review, 7* (1926), 302–20; *8* (1927), 308–21; and *9* (1928), 157–60; also "Interrelations between the Fur Trade of Canada and the United States," *Mississippi Valley Historical Review, 20* (1933), 321–32; and a lengthy foreword to Murray G. Lawson's *Fur: A Study in English Mercantilism, 1700–1775* (Toronto, 1943).

ROBIN W. WINKS

New Haven, Conn., December 1961
London, December 1969

Author's Preface

A N interest in this subject has followed from a study on the Canadian Pacific Railway. A sense of the incompleteness of that volume and of all volumes which have centred on that subject and on the subject of Canadian confederation is the occasion for this work. A history of the fur trade is complementary to a history of the recent industrial growth of Canada.

The work owes much to Professor R. M. MacIver, since with his encouragement it was undertaken as a special research subject. I am indebted also to Professor W. S. Wallace for much valuable advice; to Professor V. W. Bladen who read the early chapters and made numerous valuable suggestions; to Professor Louis Allen who gave me the advantage of his criticism on the chapters dealing with the French period; to Professor T. McIlwraith; and to Professor A. S. Morton, who has generously placed at my disposal information on different phases of the subject. The staff of the Dominion Archives has done much to facilitate the work, and I am under heavy obligations to the University of Toronto. Large numbers of men engaged in the fur trade especially men of the Hudson's Bay Company and men in the Mackenzie River district have been extremely generous in giving me information, but I should be very ungrateful should I fail to mention the kindness of Capt. L. Morten of the *Liard River* in 1924 in making it possible for me to gain an intimate knowledge of the trade, and the co-operation of my friend, Mr. John Long, who accompanied me on an extended trip throughout that district.

H. A. I.

University of Toronto
June, 1929

Preface to the Revised Edition

OVER a period of years, Professor Innis made it a habit to write on the margin of his copy of *The Fur Trade in Canada* new references which he had come across, notes or even abstracts of material he was reading which bore on the subject, and questions or comments of his own which made a new point or elaborated an old one. He undoubtedly planned to bring out a new edition of *The Fur Trade in Canada* which had been out of print for years, and would have incorporated much of this new material in the revised text.

The editors were therefore faced with material some of which was cryptic, much ambiguous or uncertain in its bearing on the text, and all very nearly indecipherable. The material, as has been suggested, was of two sorts: references, either alone or with quite copious notes, to books or articles most of which had appeared after the publication of the work in 1930, and Professor Innis's own questions and comments which had occurred to him since the book was published.

The latter, it was felt, would be of considerable interest to the readers of the revised edition, but their cryptic style made impossible their inclusion as regular footnotes without extensive editing. To avoid such editing, which would have destroyed their character as general comments, they have been collected and are published as Appendix H. The number of the page on which each comment was originally written is given so that each can readily be related to its context. These notes are printed exactly as Professor Innis wrote them except where a word or two has been suggested which might make the meaning clearer.

The great bulk of the new material consisted of references and notes. Sources which were not given have been tracked down; all sources have been checked and the quotations have been verified. In some cases sentences have been filled out and the content of some notes has been rearranged in chronological order. Two or three notes, of a few words each, have been omitted either because they were redundant or because the appearance of new material since they were written had made them seem unnecessary. Nothing has been added.

One of the most difficult problems, when the notes had been deciphered and checked with their sources, was to find the place in the text to which they might most appropriately be attached. In a few cases this had been indicated but in many, notes appeared to have been written in where space was available and with only a general application to the subject on the page. The editors have placed the notes in two ways, either as additions to footnotes already present or as new footnotes. To avoid confusion, they have been blended with the old footnotes, which they serve to widen in scope and to elaborate, sometimes at considerable length.

The original text of the first edition remains unchanged except for two dates which Professor Innis had corrected and a rearrangement of the material between former pages 44 and 48 which he had indicated explicitly. Quotations have been checked, wherever this was possible, and in some cases their arrangement has been altered to secure greater clarity and precision. Bibliographical information contained in old and new references has been transferred to a List of References.

The Fur Trade in Canada was published in 1930 by the Yale University Press on the Oliver Baty Cunningham Memorial Publication Fund. Its republication in revised form has been made possible by a generous grant from the Canadian Social Science Research Council.

A large part of the work of revision was borne by Professor S. D. Clark and Professor W. T. Easterbrook who studied every added note and weighed the problem of placing it in the text. The work of reconstructing and arranging the notes has depended on their knowledge and judgment. To them and to Professor D. G. Creighton and Mrs. Jane Ward who gave valuable advice and encouragement, the editor is deeply grateful. The University of Toronto Press and especially Miss Frances Halpenny have been most helpful and co-operative.

MARY Q. INNIS

Contents

I   INTRODUCTION

     1. The Beaver   **3**

II   THE FRENCH RÉGIME

     2. Beginnings of the Fur Trade on the Atlantic Coast (1497–1600)   9

     3. The Struggle for the Ottawa (1600–1663)   23

     4. The Struggle for the Great Lakes and Hudson Bay (1663–1713)   43

     5. The Expansion of Trade to the Saskatchewan and the Northwest (1713–1763)   84

     6. A Century of Trade on Hudson Bay (1670–1770)   119

III   FROM THE ATLANTIC TO THE PACIFIC (1763–1821)

     7. The Hudson's Bay Company   149

     8. The Northwest Company   166

     9. The St. Lawrence Drainage Basin versus Hudson Bay   263

IV   FROM HUDSON BAY TO THE PACIFIC (1821–1869)

     10. The Northern Department   283

V   THE INDUSTRIAL REVOLUTION AND THE FUR TRADE (1869–1929)

     11. The Decline of Monopoly   341

VI   CONCLUSION   383

     APPENDICES   405

     REFERENCES   421

     INDEX   443

PART ONE

INTRODUCTION

1. The Beaver

THE history of Canada has been profoundly influenced by the habits of an animal which very fittingly occupies a prominent place on her coat of arms. The beaver[1] (*Castor canadensis* Kuhl) was of dominant importance in the beginnings of the Canadian fur trade. It is impossible to understand the characteristic developments of the trade or of Canadian history without some knowledge of its life and habits.

Numerous descriptions of this animal are available in early French accounts and in later treatises. Le Clercq wrote: "The Beaver is of the bigness of a water-spaniel. Its fur is chestnut, black, and rarely white, but always very soft and suitable for the making of hats."[2] According to Denys[3] "they are usually of a dark brown, leaning towards black or even red. They occur sometimes black, and even white." Early French writers agree that the colour variation is largely the result of climate and that the fur becomes darker in more northerly latitudes. North of the St. Lawrence the fur was regarded as being much better and the skin much thinner than in more southerly and warmer areas. Champlain wrote in 1616: "As for the country south of this great river, it is very thickly populated, much more so than on the north side . . . but, on the other hand, there is not so much profit and gain in the south from the trade in furs."[4] And Champlain was interested in furs. The fur of more temperate regions was described as brown in colour and of the Illinois country as almost yellow or straw-coloured. The age of the animal also had an effect on the colour, and the young or cub beaver with dark chestnut and

[1]See the map of the range of the American beaver in E. T. Seton, *Life Histories of Northern Animals*, I, 449, also pp. 447–479; L. H. Morgan, *The American Beaver and his Works*; A. R. Dugmore, *The Romance of the Beaver*; E. A. Mills, *In Beaver World*; E. R. Warren, *The Beaver: Its Work and its Ways*; V. Bailey, *Beaver Habits, Beaver Control and Possibilities in Beaver Farming*, U.S. Dept. of Agriculture Bulletin, no. 1078; and Appendix A.

[2]Father C. Le Clercq, *New Relation of Gaspesia*, ed. W. F. Ganong, p. 277.

[3]Nicolas Denys, *The Description and Natural History of the Coasts of North America (Acadia)*, ed. W. F. Ganong, pp. 362–363.

[4]*Voyages and Explorations of Samuel de Champlain*, ed. E. G. Bourne, II, 118.

occasionally black fur above, and lighter fur underneath, was regarded as the most valuable. As with other animals the fur is much thinner and poorer in summer.

The fur of the beaver, like that of other animals, may be divided into two parts: the guard hair, up to two inches in length, and the underhair or fur, at most an inch. According to Lahontan, "a beaver has two lays of hair; one is long and of a shining black color, with a grain as big as that of Man's Hair; the other is fine and smooth, and in Winter fifteen lines long. In a word, the last is the finest Down in the world."[5] Examined through a microscope the fur has numerous small barbs. It was these barbs which made it unusually suitable for the manufacture of felt and of felt hats.[6]

The animal weighs from thirty to sixty pounds. David Thompson states that "the average weight of a full-grown male is about fifty-five pounds. His meat is agreeable to most although fat and oily: the tail is a delicacy."[7] The pelt of the average adult weighs from one and one-half to one and three-quarters pounds although Lahontan gives two pounds.[8]

The beaver is a monogamist. The young are born in May and average from two to five in number. "These animals are more prolific than our sheep in France the females bearing as many as five or six every year."[9] They are weaned in six weeks, but stay with the mother for one year. They mate at two, and are fully grown at two and one-half years. A beaver lodge has generally about nine animals of varying ages. It has been estimated that the beaver population increases by about 20 per cent per year, and that previous to the coming of Europeans the total beaver population of North America was ten million. In years of abundance the number varies from ten to fifty per square mile according to the country. Apparently it suffers from disease at varying intervals, and large numbers are wiped out.[10]

The animal migrates very little and travels over land very slowly.

[5]Lahontan, *New Voyages to North-America*, ed. R. G. Thwaites, I, 173.

[6]For a description of the manufacture of beaver hats see J. H. Hawkins, *History of the Worshipful Company of Feltmakers of London*, and Savary des Bruslons, *Dictionnaire universel de commerce* (1723-30), 3 vols., under "Chapeaux."

[7]*David Thompson's Narrative*, ed. J. B. Tyrrell, pp. 198–199.

[8]Lahontan, *New Voyages*, I, 173.

[9]*Jesuit Relations*, ed. R. G. Thwaites, VIII, 57.

[10]See E. T. Seton, *Life Histories of Northern Animals*, p. 476, where there is a reference to the disappearance of large numbers in the upper Red River district about 1800.

It does not hibernate and has adapted itself with great elaboration to the seasonal changes of a northern climate. Dams are built ensuring a supply of water, and lodges of twenty feet across the base and three to five feet high are made of sticks and branches cemented with mud. Within the lodges a circular chamber about two feet high and six feet across is built with its floor about four inches above water level. Two entrances from one and one-half to two feet wide and from five to ten feet long are built to this chamber, both being from two to three feet below the water on the outside. One is used for an ordinary runway, the other to bring in the supply of wood for food. Besides this lodge the beaver has burrows along the banks which have entrances under water. These are extended upward and sufficient soil is left on the top to provide ventilation. Wood is stored for the winter under water at convenient distances from the lodge. The food in winter is chiefly birch, cottonwood, poplar, willow, and the young bark and twigs of hardwoods, and in summer the roots of various water plants. The habitat is to a large extent determined by the deciduous forest area. The range extends northerly to a line drawn northwest from the mouth of the Churchill River to the mouth of the Mackenzie River. Territory south of this boundary, which is well wooded with poplar and willow, and which abounds in small lakes and sluggish, continuous streams, is especially favourable.

The significance of the habitat of the beaver in the development of the fur trade may be suggested. Since the beaver was an amphibious animal, its fur was thick and abundant and it could be hunted in summer, although the fur was then much less valuable. The length of time required for it to arrive at maturity was an important factor in the destruction of the supply of fur and its non-migratory tendencies and elaborate housing facilities made destruction certain. In the language of the economists, the heavy fixed capital of the beaver became a serious handicap with the improved technique of Indian hunting methods, incidental to the borrowing of iron from Europeans. Depreciation through obsolescence of the beaver's defence equipment was so rapid as to involve the immediate and complete destruction of the animal. David Thompson has described the result.[11]

Formerly the Beavers were very numerous, the many Lakes and Rivers gave them ample space, and the poor Indian had then only a pointed stick shaped and hardened in the fire, a stone Hatchet, Spear and Arrowheads of the same; thus armed he was weak against the sagacious Beaver who on the banks of a Lake made itself a house of a foot thick or more;

[11]*David Thompson's Narrative*, pp. 112–113, 199.

composed of earth and small flat stones, crossed and bound together with pieces of wood; upon which no impression could be made but by fire. But when the arrival of the White People had changed all their weapons from stone to iron and steel and added the fatal Gun, every animal fell before the Indian . . . the Beaver became a desirable animal for food and clothing, and the fur a valuable article of trade; and as the Beaver is a stationary animal, it could be attacked at any convenient time in all seasons, and thus their numbers soon became reduced.

For the furrs which the Natives traded, they procured from the French, Axes, Chissels, Knives, Spears and other articles of iron, with which they made good hunts of furr-bearing animals and procured woollen clothing. Thus armed the houses of the Beavers were pierced through, the Dams cut through, and the water of the Ponds lowered, or wholly run off, and the houses of the Beaver and their Burrows laid dry, by which means they became an easy prey to the Hunter.

The range extended to the northwest, following the isothermal lines, the deciduous forest area, and the Pre-Cambrian shield with its wealth of waterways, and the best fur was obtained from the more northerly portions. With destruction in the easterly part of North America came the necessity of pushing to the westward and northwestward to tap new areas of the more valuable furs. The problem of the fur trade became one of organizing the transport of supplies and furs over increasingly greater distances. In this movement the waterways of the beaver area were of primary importance and occupied a vital position in the economic development of northern North America. It is the purpose of this volume to trace the history of the trade as it spread across the continent.

PART TWO

THE FRENCH REGIME

2. Beginnings of the Fur Trade on the Atlantic Coast (1497-1600)

THE contact of Europeans with the Indians was essential to the development of the fur trade. In the area tributary to the St. Lawrence River this contact was in the beginning subsidiary to the fishing industry. The long return voyages from Europe to America in small sailing vessels with relatively large crews involved a dependence on trade in a commodity which brought immediate and large returns. Codfish was such a commodity available in large quantities, and having a ready market in Europe with its primitive agricultural methods and scarcity of meat. Increasing demands for improvement in handling fish led to the development of dry fishing which reduced the outlay on such commodities as salt, and economized shipping. Extension of the market to the Mediterranean and the demands of that area for the better grades of dry fish encouraged fishing along the coast for the smaller cod. Dry fishing stimulated the search for harbours suitable for drying and preferably with ample supplies of bait. With competition for the better harbours and the increasing scarcity of timber available for staging came a constant search into the remoter areas of the coast. The prosecution of whaling and the hunting of walrus as carried out by the Basques and others, the work of official explorers such as Cartier, and the probable growing importance of the fur trade were other factors contributing to the movement to the interior. On the other hand, the location of important codfish banks at an appreciable distance from the coast and at definite points on the coast line as, for example, at Ile Percée, and the existence of a serrated shore line with numerous harbours greatly retarded the growth of fishing settlements in the interior.

The early fur trade along the coast was limited. The existence of large numbers of fur-bearing animals presupposes a sparsely populated area with consequent limited development of transportation facilities and a general dependence on water transportation. Fur trade development on a large scale assumes a vast territory drained by great rivers such as characterize the north temperate climates, and a population with cultural traits peculiar to a hunting economy. The general physiographical and topographical background of the Appalachians and of the Laurentians along the Atlantic Coast and the Gulf of St. Lawrence, in what is now New England and the Maritime Provinces, precluded the existence of long rivers and limited the trade to large numbers of fishermen who frequented the harbours of the coast. The tribes of Indians in this area were limited in their movements by the short rivers, and they depended to a large extent on fishing.

Although of minor importance, the fur trade in the area tributary to the Gulf of St. Lawrence began at an early date. Cartier, in his voyage of 1534, describes the two fleets of Indian canoes (a total of forty or fifty) in the neighbourhood of Chaleur Bay.[1] The Indians, probably Micmacs, "made frequent signs to us to come on shore, holding up to us some furs on sticks." Later "they sent on shore part of their people with some of their furs; and the two parties traded together. . . . They bartered all they had to such an extent that all went back naked without anything on them; and they made signs to us that they would return on the morrow with more furs." These statements suggest that the trade was carried on in irregular fashion on the meeting of the Indians with European fishermen. Denys' description of the later trade on this coast was probably applicable to this period:

For as to the establishments, no one will ever give them [the Indians] so much that they are able to drink to the point of killing one another, and one sells to them dearer than do the ships. It is the captains and sailors who supply it to them, to whom it costs no more than the original price. Through this they do not fail to make great gain. For all the expenses and charges of the ship, these are upon the owner, besides which the crew trades or bargains with the Indians using biscuit, lead, quite new lines, sails, and many other things at the expense of the said owners. This allows them to give the Indians two or three times more than they are given at the establishments, where there is nothing on which the freight or carriage alone does not cost sixty livres a ton, aside from purchase price and leakage. And aside from this there is given the Indians every time they come to the establishments a drink of brandy, a bit of bread and of tobacco as they enter, however many they may be, both men and women. As for the children they are given only bread. They are again given as much when they go away. And in addition it is necessary to keep up a crew under wages aside from their keep.[2]

Contact was made, however, in the fishing areas not only with the Indians of the Gulf territory but also with the Indians of the St.

[1]H. P. Biggar, *The Voyages of Jacques Cartier*, pp. 49 ff.
[2]Nicolas Denys, *Description of the Coasts of North America*, p. 445.

Lawrence River.[3] Cartier, in his voyage of 1534, describes his meeting with more than three hundred Indians in the neighbourhood of Gaspé,[4] who had come from the vicinity of Stadacona to fish for mackerel. But these Indians belonged to tribes which grew "Indian corn like pease . . . which they eat in place of bread, and of this they had a large quantity with them." They were members of the Huron-Iroquois family and possessed cultural traits adapted to the forest area south and southeast of the Canadian shield. With favourable soil and climate, agriculture with the cultivation of maize, squash, and beans was important.[5] Pottery was more strongly developed, residences were more permanent, government was more elaborate, and the general characteristics of agricultural economy were in evidence. Consequently the trade in furs was not extensive with these Indians. In 1534 Cartier writes, "the whole lot of them had not anything above the value of five sous, their canoes and fishing-nets excepted." In his account of the voyage of 1535 under the guidance of two of these Indians to Stadacona and of the voyage to Hochelaga and of his return in 1541, furs are not mentioned with any special emphasis. The wealth of the river was in fish[6] and possibly in minerals. There is evidence indeed that these agricultural Indians imported their furs from the Saguenay country since Indians of that area gave Donnacona "three bundles of beaver and seal-skins, with a large copper knife from the Saguenay."[7]

From the standpoint of supply, therefore, the early possibilities of rapid development of the fur trade were limited. Nor was demand important. The early trade in fur was not confined to beaver since Cartier makes no specific reference to this animal. Indeed, according to Lescarbot,

in the time of Jacques Cartier, beavers were held in no esteem; the hats made thereof are in use only since that time; though the discovery thereof is not new, for in the ancient privileges of the hat-makers of Paris, it is said that they are to make hats of fine beaver (which is the same animal); but whether for the dearness or otherwise the use thereof had long since been left off.[8]

[3]G. T. Hunt, *The Wars of the Iroquois: A Study in Intertribal Trade Relations.*
[4]H. P. Biggar, *Voyages of Cartier*, pp. 60 ff.
[5]C. Wissler, *The American Indian* (2nd ed.), pp. 235–237.
[6]H. P. Biggar, *Voyages of Cartier*, pp. 198–199.
[7]*Ibid.*, p. 233.
[8]Marc Lescarbot, *The History of New France*, ed. W. L. Grant and H. P. Biggar, III, 117. To the effect that the making of felt hats appears to date from 1456 on the Continent and from 1510 in London, see George Unwin, *Industrial Organization in the Sixteenth and Seventeenth Centuries*, p. 131.

The early trade was presumably concerned with fancy fur or the fur which is used with and on the pelt and which is valued because of its beauty, lustre, and warmth rather than with staple fur which, because of its special barbed character, was admirably suited for felting as in the case of the beaver. With fancy fur, the development of a new marketing organization would be necessarily slow. The large numbers of small purchases of fur in a trade incidental to fishing and the intensely technical character of the commodity requiring knowledge of the characteristics of fur on the part of the purchaser, combined to retard the development of a trading organization on a large scale. Moreover, the Indians were interested primarily in beaver. The entry of furs to new ports and by new channels into Europe would call for an extension and modification of the existing fur trade organization which would develop slowly and in response to the gradually increasing supplies of fur.

The fur trade in the first half of the sixteenth century was of minor importance and incidental to fishing. By the end of the century a revolution had occurred and the agricultural Indians of the Huron-Iroquois family had been driven from the St. Lawrence valley apparently by hunting Indians. From Champlain's descriptions the hostilities incidental to this catastrophe were still being prosecuted in 1603. The Algonquins, Montagnais, and others were at war[9] with the Iroquois.

The causes of this revolution are difficult to determine, but certain facts deserve consideration. In the latter part of the century the fashion of wearing beaver hats spread rapidly, especially as beaver was used only in the more expensive hats. This demand was responsible for the development of the trade in beaver fur which apparently expanded from the mouth of the Saguenay, which as we have seen had been noted by Cartier as an important area in the production of beaver.[10] Champlain in 1603, on his way from Tadoussac to Gaspé, met Indians on their way "to barter arrows and moose-flesh for the beaver and marten of the other Montagnais, Etechemin, and Algonquin Indians."[11] The Indians of the vast area drained by the Saguenay had developed cultural traits along specific lines dependent as ever on historical background and on geographic environment. Throughout the forest

[9]See Champlain's description of the victory of the Etechemins, Algonquins, and Montagnais in 1603, *The Works of Samuel de Champlain*, ed. H. P. Biggar, I, 103 ff., and of the Montagnais in the same summer, *ibid.*, pp. 141, 178.

[10]H. P. Biggar, *Voyages of Cartier*, p. 233.

[11]*The Works of Samuel de Champlain*, I, 166.

areas of the Canadian shield,[12] to which the Saguenay gave access, hunting was the predominant occupation. Small game, fish, and especially the beaver, moose,[13] and deer were important items in the supply of food, clothing, and shelter. Generally life in these areas involved movement to fishing waters in the summer and to widely scattered hunting areas in winter. A description dated August, 1626, states:

These [Indians] where we now are [Quebec] with the French, they are wanderers only during six months of the year, which are the six winter months, roving here and there, according as they may find game, only two or three families erecting their cabins together in one place, two or three in another, and so on. The other six months of the year, twenty or thirty come together upon the shore of the river near our settlement, part at Thadoussac, and the same number forty leagues above us; and there they live upon the game which they have captured during the Winter; that is to say, on smoked moose meat, and food for which they have traded with the French.[14]

The absence or weak development of pottery and basketry, the use of snowshoes[15] and toboggans in winter and of the birch-bark canoe[16] and the pack line[17] in summer, and the skin or bark shelter were characteristic cultural features. In hunting during the winter, definite territories were assigned to specific bands or families,[18] but government was generally weak. A thorough knowledge of the territory was a necessary part of their cultural equipment as was also a thorough knowledge of the habits of animals upon which they were dependent for livelihood. The importance of the beaver because of its fur, its size, and its abundance, as a source of supply for food and clothing had occasioned the development of elaborate and effective hunting methods

[12]See C. Wissler, *American Indian*, especially pp. 229–237. See also *Handbook of Indians of Canada* (Canada, Geographic Board); J. G. Kohl, *Kitchi-Gami*; and H. R. Schoolcraft, *The American Indians*.

[13]See the map of the range of moose in E. T. Seton, *Life Histories of Northern Animals*, I, 151; and that of various species of deer, *ibid.*, pp. 37 ff.

[14]*Jesuit Relations*, IV, 203.

[15]For a description of snowshoes, see Lahontan, *New Voyages*, I, 103–104.

[16]For the northern limit of the canoe birch (*Betula papyrifera*), see the *Atlas of Canada* (Ottawa, 1916), pp. 19–20. Descriptions of the manufacture and handling of birch-bark canoes will be found in *David Thompson's Narrative*, pp. 57–58, 115–116.

[17]The use of the pack line is described in G. M. Grant, *Ocean to Ocean*, p. 34; and E. Coues, *New Light on the Early History of the Greater Northwest*, II, 478–479.

[18]See F. G. Speck, *Family Hunting Territories of the Ottawa Valley*.

for that animal.[19] The skin of the beaver had been adapted successfully to clothing and was especially important in the colder and more
northerly areas. "They wear no other clothes than a moose skin or a
Beaver robe, which consists of five or six Beaver Skins sewed together."[20]

The rapid development of trade with these Indians was dependent on their methods of treating the fur and on the character of the
felting process. The pelts were taken by the Indians when prime and
the inner side scraped and rubbed with the marrow of certain animals.
After this treatment each pelt was trimmed into rectangular shape
and from five to eight were sewn together with moose sinews into
robes which were worn by the Indians with the fur next to the body.
The scraping of the inner side of the pelt loosened the deep roots of
the long guard hair, and with wearing, this hair dropped out leaving
the fur. With constant wearing for fifteen to eighteen months the skin
became well greased, pliable, and yellow in colour and the fur downy
or *cotonné*. These furs taken in winter when prime were known later
as *castor gras d'hiver*. It was this fur which was most valuable to the
hatmaking industry. The guard hairs had largely disappeared and the
fur was especially suited to the felting process.

The length of time required to produce this fur necessitated a constant movement to the interior to meet new tribes of Indians and to
secure new supplies. The intertribal trade organization from the Saguenay became especially important. The character of this organization
is difficult to determine, but certain evidence has been made available. The trade in copper which, apparently, came from the Lake
Superior district gives an important clue. Cartier notes that "a large
copper knife from the Saguenay" was given to Donnacona by the
Indians of that area.[21] At Hochelaga "the Captain showed them some
copper . . . and pointing towards the said region [the Ottawa], asked
by signs if it came thence? They shook their heads to say no, showing
us that it came from the Saguenay, which lies in the opposite direction."[22] Apparently trade with the Indians up the Ottawa at this
time either in copper or in furs was slight since they were regarded
as "bad people, who were armed to the teeth" and who "waged war
continually." Probably therefore the French at Tadoussac traded with

19For descriptions of beaver hunting see Lahontan, *New Voyages*, II, 481–482,
485, and Appendix A.
20*Jesuit Relations*, IV, 203.
21H. P. Biggar, *Voyages of Cartier*, p. 233.
22*Ibid.*, p. 171.

the Montagnais who, in turn, traded by the Saguenay route with the Algonquins and the latter with the good Iroquois (Hurons). Champlain writes, "there is toward the north a mine of pure copper, of which they showed us some bracelets obtained from the good Iroquois."[23] During the occupation of the St. Lawrence valley by the agricultural Indians, the fur trade was carried on through the Indians of the Saguenay. Certainly in 1603 Champlain describes the Montagnais as trading up the Saguenay and Lake St. John and its tributaries with other Indians.[24] The route between the headwaters of the St. Maurice and the Saguenay was known. The St. Maurice "almost connects with the Saguenay river, according to the report of the Indians."[25] Trade between the headwaters of the St. Maurice and the headwaters of the Ottawa was certainly in evidence at a later period and, doubtless, existed in the earlier period.

The development of trade[26] into the Canadian shield by way of the Saguenay, the headwaters of the St. Maurice and the Ottawa, which was the country most productive of excellent northern beaver and in which the hunting Indians were found, gave those Indians a pronounced advantage. The penetration of European commodities by this route led to a shift in cultural traits which enabled them to make war with greater effectiveness on the agricultural Indians of the St. Lawrence valley who, because of the scarcity of furs incidental to denser population and the pursuit of agriculture, were unable to command those commodities. It is suggested that the upheaval in the St. Lawrence valley was the result of the development of the fur trade at Saguenay and the remote interior accessible by the Saguenay route.

This suggestion is open to numerous objections and since it rests chiefly on the effects of the penetration of European goods on Indian economy it is necessary at this point to describe these effects in detail. The evidence for the period prior to 1600 is lacking, but a study of the following period is suggestive. The fur trade was the line of contact between a relatively complex civilization and a much more simple civilization. The complex European culture had reached a stage industrially in which technological equipment essential to specialized production had been accumulated. Ships capable of undertaking long ocean voyages, a manufacturing system which demanded large quanti-

[23]*The Works of Samuel de Champlain*, I, 164.
[24]*Ibid.*, pp. 123–124.
[25]*Ibid.*, p. 136.
[26]See H. P. Biggar, *The Early Trading Companies of New France*, chaps. i–ii; also J. P. Baxter, *A Memoir of Jacques Cartier*, pp. 376 ff.

ties of raw material, and a distributing organization which absorbed the finished product without difficulty were typical products of European civilization. The heavy overhead cost of long voyages limited the trade to commodities which were highly valuable, to commodities demanded by the more advanced types of manufacturing processes of that period, and to commodities available on a large scale. The fur of the beaver was pre-eminently suited to the demands of early trade.

Heavy overhead costs incidental to the conduct of trade were an important cause of its rapid growth. The trade in furs was stimulated by French traders who rapidly acquired an intimate knowledge of the Indian's language, customs, and habits of life. The trader encouraged the best hunters, exhorted the Indians to hunt beaver, and directed their fleets of canoes to the rendezvous. Alliances were formed and wars were favoured to increase the supply of fur. Goods were traded which would encourage the Indian to hunt beaver. In addition to the efforts of the local traders and of the monopoly, the marketing organization in Europe had improved, technique in manufacture of beaver hats had improved, the number of workers had increased, and the demand for beaver for the manufacture of beaver hats had increased. The industries engaged in supplying European goods—hatchets, ironware, clothing materials—had also responded to the stimulus of the demand.

But important as the pressure from a more complex civilization must have been, the position of the Indian cannot be neglected. French traders were seriously limited in their trading activities among the Indians. Tribes as middlemen resented attempts to destroy their monopoly position. Monopolies[27] attempted to control the price of beaver and to raise the prices of goods to the Indians. These factors tended to lessen the pressure of a complex civilization. Indeed, in the final analysis, the pull of a relatively simple civilization on the resources of a complex civilization may be regarded as of paramount importance. No monopoly or organization could withstand the demands of the Indian civilization of North America for European goods. The task of continuously supplying goods to the Indian tribes of North America, of maintaining the depreciation of those goods, and of replacing the goods destroyed was overwhelming. As Cartier noted of

[27]See the discussion in H. P. Biggar, *Early Trading Companies*, pp. 63–64, on the effects of monopoly prices on the demand for hats and the complaints of the Hatters Corporation of Paris. Later (1634 in France, 1638 in England), laws were passed forbidding the use of other fibres in the manufacturing of beaver hats. See H. T. Martin, *Castorologia*, pp. 123–124.

the Micmacs(?), "the savages showed a marvellously great pleasure in possessing and obtaining these iron wares and other commodities, dancing and going through many ceremonies," and later of the St. Lawrence Indians, "we gave them knives, glass beads, combs and other trinkets of small value, at which they showed many signs of joy, lifting up their hands to heaven and singing and dancing in their canoes." The presents given by Cartier were uniformly received with "wonderful pleasure."[28] Champlain was the object of continual requests. In 1615 "they hoped that we would furnish them some of our number to assist them in their wars against our enemies, representing to us that they could with difficulty come to us if we should not assist them; for the Iroquois, they said, their old enemies, were always on the road obstructing their passage."[29] Sagard refers to a meeting of the Hurons "where I was entreated that the traders of the Company should be kindly disposed to the captains of the trade, that they should be given necessary articles of merchandise at a reasonable price and that on their side they would exchange very good furs."[30]

This demand for European goods was persistent and cumulative since penetration of European goods was relatively slow, largely because of the rapid depreciation of the goods and of the vast areas involved. In 1615 Champlain gave a hatchet to the chief of the Cheveux Relevés "who was as much pleased and delighted with it as if I had given him some rich present."[31] With regard to the expedition against the Iroquois in the same year, he wrote, "there were only four or five who were acquainted with the handling of arms, while in such an expedition the best are not too good in this particular."[32] At the time of Sagard's visit, the Hurons were in possession of kettles and knives, although many were anxious to borrow his utensils. They had planted peas secured at Quebec. Skinning knives, awls, and axes were in use. But iron utensils were constantly wearing out because of the intense work to which they were put; they were traded to other peoples or they were destroyed at burial feasts.[33] Once they had

[28]H. P. Biggar, *Voyages of Cartier*, pp. 53, 60, 125.
[29]*Voyages of Samuel de Champlain*, ed. W. L. Grant, p. 276.
[30]Father Gabriel Sagard-Théodat, *Le Grand Voyage du Pays des Hurons*, p. 238.
[31]*Voyages of Samuel de Champlain*, ed. W. L. Grant, p. 282.
[32]*Ibid.*, p. 278.
[33]See Father Gabriel Sagard-Théodat, *Le Grand Voyage*, pp. 197 ff. The French were successful in dissuading them from these practices. E. H. Blair, *The Indian Tribes of the Upper Mississippi Valley and Region of the Great Lakes*, I, 88.

secured access to a source of iron supplies, more primitive implements disappeared and the methods of making them were forgotten. Guns displaced bows and arrows. They required periodic mending and ammunition was in constant demand. As old cultural traits fell gradually into disuse and old ways of getting a livelihood were forgotten, the Indian became increasingly dependent on the products of the specialized equipment of Europe and increasingly dependent upon his supply of furs. In the *Jesuit Relations* of 1647–48, it was written: "The Hurons . . . did not come down last year to the French through fear of the enemies who, on the one hand threatened the country, and on the other beset all the roads. But the necessity of obtaining hatchets and other French goods compelled them to expose themselves to all those dangers."[34] The importance of iron to a culture dependent on bone, wood, bark, and stone can only be suggested. The cumbersome method of cooking in wooden vessels with heated stones was displaced by portable kettles. Work could be carried out with greater effectiveness with iron axes and hatchets, and sewing became much less difficult with awls than it had been with bone needles. To the Indians iron and iron manufactures were of prime importance. The French were the *gens du fer*.[35] "The Hurons think that the greatest rulers of France are endowed with the greatest powers and having such great powers they can make the most difficult things such as hatchets, knives, kettles. They infer from this that the King makes the largest kettles."[36]

The effect of European goods may be shown among the Indians of the Gulf territory who had been among the first to acquire possession of them. Denys in his work of 1672 writes:

They have abandoned all their own utensils, whether because of the trouble they had as well to make as to use them, or because of the facility of obtaining from us, in exchange for skins which cost them almost nothing, the things which seemed to them invaluable, not so much for their novelty as for the convenience they derived therefrom. Above everything the kettle has always seemed to them, and seems still, the most valuable article they can obtain from us. This was rather pleasingly exemplified by an Indian whom the late Monsieur de Razilly sent from Acadia to Paris; for, passing by the Rue Aubry-bouché, where there were then many coppersmiths, he asked of his interpreter if they were not relatives of the King, and if this was not the trade of the grandest Seigniors of the Kingdom. . . .

[34]*Jesuit Relations*, XXXII, 179; see L. P. Kellogg, *The French Régime in Wisconsin and the Northwest*, pp. 137–138.
[35]Father Gabriel Sagard-Théodat, *Le Grand Voyage*, p. 67.
[36]*Ibid.*, p. 174.

But they practise still all the same methods of hunting, with this difference, however, that in place of arming their arrows and spears with the bones of animals, pointed and sharpened, they arm them to-day with iron, which is made expressly for sale to them. Their spears now are made of a sword fixed at the end of a shaft of seven to eight feet in length. These they use in winter, when there is snow, to spear the Moose, or for fishing Salmon, Trout, and Beaver. They are also furnished with iron harpoons, of the use of which we have spoken before.

The musket is used by them more than all other weapons, in their hunting in spring, summer, and autumn, both for animals and birds. . . . With the arrow it was necessary to approach an animal closely: with the gun they kill the animal from a distance with a bullet or two. The axes, the kettles, the knives and everything that is supplied them, is much more convenient and portable than those which they had in former times, when they were obliged to go to camp near their grotesque kettles, in place of which to-day they are free to go camp where they wish. One can say that in those times the immovable kettles were the chief regulators of their lives, since they were able to live only in places where these were.

With respect to the hunting of the Beaver in winter, they do that the same as they did formerly, though they have nevertheless nowadays a greater advantage with their arrows and harpoons armed with iron than with the others which they used in old times, and of which they have totally abandoned the use.[37]

Some of the unfortunate effects are suggested by Biard who wrote in the *Relation* of 1616:

Nevertheless the principal cause of all these deaths and diseases is not what they [the Indians] say it is, but it is something to their shame; in the Summer time, when our ships come, they never stop gorging themselves excessively during several weeks with various kinds of food not suitable to the inactivity of their lives; they get drunk, not only on wine but on brandy; so it is no wonder that they are obliged to endure some gripes of the stomach in the following Autumn.[38]

The effects of the increasing dependence on European goods and, in turn, on the beaver were far reaching. Such cultural traits as the canoe, the pack strap, the knowledge of animal habits enabling them to hunt for food and for fur, acquaintance with plants as food and medicine, their agricultural development, and the knowledge of the country, were stressed because of their importance in enabling the Indian to cover a wider territory and to get more furs. To cite the

[37]Nicolas Denys, *Description of the Coasts of North America*, pp. 440–443.
[38]*Jesuit Relations*, III, 107.

example of the canoe, Champlain wrote of the Lachine Rapids in 1603:

The water here is so swift that it could not be more so, . . . so that it is impossible to imagine one's being able to go by boats through these falls. But any one desiring to pass them, should provide himself with the canoe of the savages, which a man can easily carry. For to make a portage by boat could not be done in a sufficiently brief time to enable one to return to France, if he desired to winter there. Besides this first fall, there are ten others, for the most part hard to pass; so that it would be a matter of great difficulty and labour to see and do by boat what one might propose to himself, except at great cost, and the risk of working in vain. But in the canoes of the savages one can go without restraint, and quickly, everywhere, in the small as well as large rivers. So that by using canoes as the savages do, it would be possible to see all there is, good and bad, in a year or two.[39]

Furs had to be collected, stored, packed, and carried for long distances in the spring and summer to the trader. Increasing stress was placed on the beaver, and energies were directed to the capture of that animal. Commodities were in demand which made it possible to spend more time for that purpose, guns, kettles, knives, awls, and axes. Among the agricultural Indians to the south and among those Indians in closer proximity to the French, the supply of beaver decreased rapidly and greater dependence was placed on the existing trading organization with the northern hunting Indians. Longer distances were covered and knowledge of the country was increased among the Indians. These factors hastened the decay of old cultural traits, the acquisition of new cultural traits, and general instability of life. Since the trade was carried on in the summer, agriculture was neglected or shifted to a greater extent to the care of the women. Sagard refers frequently to the work of the Huron women in grinding corn with which the men were able to go to more distant nations to trade. The nation was, consequently, increasingly exposed to the inroads of the Iroquois with larger numbers of men absent in the summers. The persistent and increasing demand for European commodities led to the more rapid extermination of the beaver, to increased hostilities, especially between Indian middlemen such as the Iroquois and the Hurons, to the westward flight of the Indians, to the spread of new cultural traits, and to a further expansion of the trade. This pressure of tribes on the territory of the Indians to the interior was an additional and important cause of renewed Indian wars and destruction. Wars between tribes, which with bows and arrows had not been strenuous, conducted with guns were disastrous.

[39]*Voyages of Samuel de Champlain* (Prince Society), I, 269.

Increase in trade furthered improvements in the technique of the trade.[40] Sagard wrote that the Hurons "expostulated against the methods of our merchants in completing the trade in an hour," but this attitude became less evident. According to Perrot

in point of hospitality, . . . it is only the Abenakis, and those who live with the French people, who have become somewhat less liberal, on account of the advice that our people have given them by placing before them the obligations resting on them to preserve what they have. At the present time, it is evident that these savages are fully as selfish and avaricious as formerly they were hospitable.[41]

Elaborate bargaining called for a higher development of ideas of contract and barter, for more extended development of government for the enforcement of these conceptions, and for a remarkable period of intrigue and diplomacy among Indian tribes. Indian middlemen were able to exercise greater bargaining power over more remote tribes with the use of European weapons. Consequently, they were extremely jealous of any attempt of the French or the Dutch to trade guns with these remote tribes. On the other hand, a supply of guns for more remote tribes enabled the European trader to break the monopoly of the middlemen. The net result was continuous and destructive warfare. The disastrous results of these cultural changes were shown further in the spread of European diseases, especially smallpox, and the decimation of the Indians.

This analysis of the cumulative effects of European goods on Indian economy during the period after 1600 supports the suggestion that the centre of disturbances in the latter part of the sixteenth century was the Saguenay. The Indians of the Saguenay, and of the Ottawa and Georgian Bay regions, the Montagnais, Algonquins, and Hurons who traded across the headwaters of the Ottawa, the St. Maurice, and the Saguenay demanded larger and cheaper supplies of beaver. The far-reaching changes in the cultural background, especially of the Montagnais and the Algonquins, made the demand for beaver more insistent and the struggle for control of the St. Lawrence route inevitable. With access to European goods these hunting Indians were in a position to attack with increasing effectiveness the agricultural Indians of the St. Lawrence valley, to drive them out, and to open the St. Lawrence route to the interior. With the opening of the seventeenth century Champlain found the struggle practically at an end with the

[40]Father Gabriel Sagard-Théodat, *Le Grand Voyage*, p. 130.
[41]E. H. Blair, *Indian Tribes of the Upper Mississippi Valley*, I, 134.

Montagnais still carrying on war with Iroquois. The Hurons and Algonquins supported[42] the Montagnais and were able to come down the Ottawa, certainly the St. Maurice, to the St. Lawrence to trade their furs with the French at Three Rivers and at Tadoussac. The kingdom of Saguenay[43] which had been, apparently, the source of copper for St. Lawrence River agricultural Indians was at an end. The declining importance of the long and difficult Saguenay route became evident in the recommendations of Champlain in 1603 for a proposed establishment at Three Rivers, the mouth of the St. Maurice.

Moreover, a settlement at Three Rivers would be a boon for the freedom of some tribes who dare not come that way for fear of their enemies, the said Iroquois, who infest the banks all along the said River of Canada; but if this river were inhabited we might make friends with the Iroquois and with the other savages, or at the very least under protection of the said settlement the said savages might come freely without fear or danger, inasmuch as the said Three Rivers is a place of passage.[44]

[42]"The Hurons, who then were our enemies, drove our Forefathers from this country. Some went toward the country of the Abnaquiois, others toward the country of the Hiroquois, some to the Hurons themselves and joined them. And that is how this island [Montreal] became deserted." *Jesuit Relations*, XXII, 215. See W. J. Wintemberg, "Was Hochelaga Destroyed or Abandoned?"

[43]H. P. Biggar, *Voyages of Cartier*, pp. 200–201.

[44]*The Works of Samuel de Champlain*, I, 136–137.

3. The Struggle for the Ottawa
(1600-1663)

DURING the preceding period, fishing had been carried on in the more remote parts of the Gulf of St. Lawrence and near the mouth of the river. Contact was made at Tadoussac with a large river draining a vast extent of territory and with peoples of a civilization dependent to a pronounced degree on hunting. Seasonally and locally fishing and whaling were carried on in the narrower waters of the St. Lawrence by both Indians and Europeans. With the Europeans fishing and whaling were more restricted and the dependence on such commodities as fur more necessary. With the Indians more dependent on hunting and on closer relations with other tribes throughout a larger territory, larger supplies of fur were available. Toward the end of the century a fur-trading organization had slowly been built up, and the demand for beaver to furnish material for the spreading fashion of beaver hats increased rapidly. A knowledge of the language and of the customs and habits of the Indians on the part of the traders, and a gradual spread of the knowledge of European commodities among the Indians, were also factors which helped to explain the rapidity of the development of the trade in the seventeenth century. The fur trade became less and less subsidiary to fishing as progress was made along the St. Lawrence,[1] and eventually it emerged as independent. With the opening of the century, the ground had been cleared for an extension of the fur trade up the St. Lawrence and the Ottawa. The St. Lawrence valley had been opened to the Algonquins, the Hurons, and the Indians of the *pays d'en haut*, and furs could be brought down by the Ottawa rather than by the difficult route of the Saguenay.

The prevailing note of the first half of the seventeenth century was a continuation of the struggle between the Iroquois, and the northern Indians and the French for the Ottawa River as a route for furs. In 1613 Champlain, in passing the mouth of the Gatineau on his way up

[1]Grey Owl, *Pilgrims of the Wild*, has an excellent description of differences between areas north and south of the St. Lawrence—northern Ontario and Témiscouata in Gaspé.

the Ottawa, noted that "sometimes these tribes go by way of this river
to avoid meeting with their enemies, knowing that these will not seek
for them in places so difficult of access."[2] In 1615 he noted that the
Indians went up the Ottawa (not the Gatineau) "to the Saguenay to
barter their furs for tobacco."[3] Sagard, on his return from the Huron
country in 1624, stopped on the shore of Georgian Bay "in a *cul-de-
sac*" with other Indians who were going to Saguenay.

Their canoes were very small and easy to upset. The largest could carry
three men and the smallest two with their provisions and merchandise. I
asked them the reasons for the smallness of the canoes and they told me
that they had such a long and difficult road and the passages between the
rocks were so difficult with the rapids from seven to eight leagues in length
where it was necessary to portage everything, that they could not use
large canoes.

At the end of Lake Nipissing he found "a number of Hurons who
were going to the Saguenay country." To the mouth of the Mattawa
"which comes from Saguenay and goes to Quebec . . . the Hurons
descend . . . to go to the Saguenay and proceed upstream."[4] By the
end of the period, the route was used only in cases of emergency. It
may be inferred that the Hurons ceased to go to the Saguenay from
the statement in the *Jesuit Relations* of 1647:

We have already said . . . that there are many small nations back in the
country, situated North of Three Rivers. . . . They have trade with the
Hurons, and some of them with the French. Their rendezvous takes place
in certain months of the year, at a spot which they have agreed upon; and
there, the Hurons bring them corn and meal *from their country*, Nets and
other small wares, which they exchange for skins of deer, elks, beavers, and
other animals.[5]

After the routing of the Hurons by the Iroquois in 1649–50, the
Indians, according to Radisson,[6] again came down the St. Maurice
and the Saguenay.

On the whole the Ottawa and the St. Lawrence was the route
generally followed throughout the period. On Champlain's arrival
in 1603 he found that the Montagnais, the Algonquins, and the

[2]*The Works of Samuel de Champlain*, II, 267.
[3]*Voyages of Samuel de Champlain*, ed. W. L. Grant, p. 279.
[4]Father Gabriel Sagard-Théodat, *Le Grand Voyage*, pp. 240, 243, 248.
[5]*Jesuit Relations*, XXXI, 209–211.
[6]*Early Narratives of the Northwest*, ed. L. P. Kellogg, pp. 34–35; see also A. E.
Jones, *Old Huronia*.

Etechemins were celebrating a victory over the Iroquois on the Richelieu River.[7] Later in the same season the Montagnais scored another
victory in the same region.[8] The route had been practically cleared,
and the Algonquins knew at this time the Lake Erie, Lake Ontario,
and lower St. Lawrence territory. Between 1603 and 1608 the Hurons
appeared on the St. Lawrence, and in 1609 Champlain met them on
the river on their way to Quebec.[9]

The problem of keeping the route open was incidental to the
strength of the Iroquois position. In the opening of the Ottawa route
the French had been obliged to form alliances with the hunting Indians
against the Iroquois, and Champlain was engaged in helping to fight
their battles. The *Jesuit Relations* of 1611 describes the situation:

> The remaining four tribes [Algonquins, Montagnais, Souriquois, and
> Etheminqui] appear already to be united in firm friendship and intimacy
> with them. They stay over night with us; we rove about with them and hunt
> with them and live among them without arms and without fear; and as has
> thus far appeared, without danger. This intimacy arose partly from asso-
> ciation while fishing for Cod . . . and partly from trading in furs. For the
> savages, who have neither copper, iron, hemp, wool, vegetables, nor manu-
> factured articles of any kind, resort to the French for them, giving in return
> the only thing of value they have, namely, furs.[10]

In the fight between the Iroquois and the Montagnais, Algonquins,
and Hurons in 1609 on Lake Champlain, the importance of European goods was shown in the use of guns by Champlain and it is noted
"they [Iroquois] began to fell trees with the poor axes which they
sometimes win in war, or with stone axes." On the other hand, the
struggle was not uneven and Champlain says "they barricaded themselves well."[11] In 1610 the Iroquois again offered determined resistance
near the mouth of the Richelieu against the Montagnais and the Algonquins aided by Champlain and the French, but were defeated
through the effective use of firearms.[12] In 1615 Champlain and the
Indians were obliged to withdraw in the fight with the Iroquois south
of Lake Ontario.[13] The advantages of the Iroquois in warfare came
from the existence of ample food supplies which the Montagnais as

[7]*The Works of Samuel de Champlain*, I, 103.
[8]*Ibid.*, p. 178.
[9]*Ibid.*, II, 67.
[10]*Jesuit Relations*, II, 71.
[11]*The Works of Samuel de Champlain*, II, 96.
[12]*Ibid.*, pp. 128 ff.
[13]*Voyages of Samuel de Champlain*, ed. W. L. Grant, pp. 290 ff.

hunters did not possess, from a greater density of population, and from close central control. With hunting Indians and with tribes allied but separated by great distances, elaborate plans were difficult to carry out. The Hurons arrived too late for the fight in 1610. These disadvantages offset to some extent the advantages incidental to a supply of European goods.

The opening of the St. Lawrence route to the Hurons facilitated the spread of European goods to the country tributary to the Ottawa and beyond. But expansion of trade to Georgian Bay and the interior necessitated the development of a technique by which trade could be carried on over long distances. An important feature of this technique was the existence of a base of supplies in the interior. The semi-agricultural activities of the Indians of the interior, and especially of the Hurons, gave them a decided advantage in the trade. The raising of corn by the Hurons and, to a less extent by the Algonquins, gave them a commodity of high food value, easily cultivated, of heavy yields, and of light weight which could be carried long distances in canoes and which, used with the fish and game taken on the journey, gave them sufficient strength to overcome the difficulties of long voyages. The importance of corn is suggested by Radisson who at the beginning of a journey from Lake Huron to the French settlement wrote, "We wanted nothing, having good store of corne and netts to catch fish, which is plentyfull in the rivers."[14] Sagard, in his journey to the interior in 1623, describes the difficulties of the canoe route up the Ottawa to Georgian Bay and the Huron country.[15] Corn cooked in kettles was the staple food throughout the journey, varied with fish which the Indians could sometimes get by trolling a line behind the canoes on crossing the lakes. Fish were more important on the downstream trip and caches of corn in birch baskets were made on the way down for use on the return. Moreover, because of the position of the Hurons at the edge of the Canadian shield, they rapidly extended the trade in foodstuffs with the northern hunting Indians. Champlain in 1615 described them as "clothed in deer and beaver skins which they obtain . . . in exchange for Indian corn and meal," and later remarked on "their dress . . . made of the skins of wild beasts, both those which they capture themselves, and others which they get in exchange . . . from the Algonquins, Nipissings and other tribes which are hunters, having no fixed abodes."[16] These hunting peoples in turn became

[14]*Early Narratives of the Northwest*, ed. L. P. Kellogg, p. 57.
[15]Father Gabriel Sagard-Théodat, *Le Grand Voyage*, pp. 45 ff., and 92 ff.
[16]*Voyages of Samuel de Champlain*, ed. W. L. Grant, pp. 285, 317.

traders. The Nipissings went up the Sturgeon River from Lake Nipissing "to barter the merchandise which we give them in exchange for their peltry, with those who live on it, and who support themselves by hunting and fishing, their country containing great quantities of animals, birds and fish."[17] They also went to regions north of the Huron country to trade in buffalo skins. "This journey requires forty days as well in returning as in going."[18] At a later date, 1623, Sagard, on his journey to the Huron country, mentions the trade of goods obtained at Quebec by the Hurons with the Nipissings at Lake Nipissing[19] and with the Poils levés on Lake Huron and these, in turn "go by troops in many regions and countries distant more than four hundred leagues where they trade their merchandise and exchange for furs, paint, porcelain and other rubbish."[20] Furs were collected over wide areas to be taken down chiefly in the hands of the Hurons.

The effects of the trade up the St. Lawrence and the Ottawa and of the emergence of the Hurons as middlemen were of considerable importance to the Indians who had previously depended on the trade at Tadoussac. Their control of the trade disappeared, and they were forced to rely to an increasing extent on their own activities as hunters for their supply of food and of furs for trade. Now that they were equipped with European weapons, their supply of food in the larger animals began to disappear. Le Jeune wrote regarding these people in 1637:

This year I have been present in some of their councils; they urged me to aid them with men; they also asked Monsieur, our Governor, to do this, saying that their country was being stripped of Elk and other animals, and that consequently, if the land could not furnish them a living, they would be utterly lost. In reply to this, they were told that the country was not yet in such condition that we could take away our Frenchmen for them, since we had not, as yet, enough cleared land for so many as we have here, which is very true. In other respects we are doing all we can to aid them.[21]

Beaver continued the chief source of profit:

It is the great trade of New France. The Gaspesians say that the Beaver is the beloved of the French and of the other Europeans, who seek it greedily; and I have been unable to keep from laughing on overhearing an Indian,

[17]*Ibid.*, pp. 280–281.
[18]*Ibid.*, p. 307.
[19]Father Gabriel Sagard-Théodat, *Le Grand Voyage*, p. 50.
[20]*Ibid.*, pp. 53–54.
[21]*Jesuit Relations*, XI, 143.

who said to me in banter, . . . "In truth, my brother, the Beaver does everything to perfection. He makes for us kettles, axes, swords, knives, and gives
us drink and food without the trouble of cultivating the ground."[22]

With improved hunting equipment, the beaver was rapidly worked
out in the areas adjacent to the St. Lawrence, and without beaver,
European goods were not available. According to the *Jesuit Relations*
of 1635 the beaver were disappearing around Three Rivers[23] and the
supply of beaver was obtained to an increasing extent from more
remote areas.

But when the savages find a lodge of them, they kill all great and small,
male and female. There is danger that they will exterminate the species in
this region finally [around Three Rivers] as has happened among the Hurons, who have not a single beaver, going elsewhere to buy the skins they
bring to the storehouse of these Gentlemen.[24]

With the decline of food supply and of beaver, the position of the
Montagnais and the Algonquins became more difficult. The Algonquins
became jealous of the Hurons and attempted to secure larger returns
by virtue of ancient rights which entitled them to a toll on traders
passing through their territory. "Finally there are among the Indians
certain rights to pay in the places of passage when they go on a voyage
to engage in trade and when they pass through the territory of another
tribe among whom they do not wish to stop."[25] Sagard, on his journey
down the Ottawa in 1624, describes the difficulties with the Hon-
queronons, who forced the Hurons to trade their furs for flour and
wheat.[26] Later he met an Algonquin, who reported that the French
fleet had been lost at sea, and attempted to discourage the Hurons from
going to trade.[27] At Cap de Victoire "I heard the complaints of the
interpreter Bruslé and of his people who were prevented by the Montagnais and the Algonquins from going further."[28] The extent to which

[22]Father C. Le Clercq, *New Relation of Gaspesia*, ed. W. F. Ganong, p. 277.

[23]Lahontan mentions the profitable character of the beaver trade, in 1684, at
Three Rivers. Lahontan, *New Voyages*, I, 50–51.

[24]*Jesuit Relations*, VIII, 57. Most descriptions of beaver hunting stress the fact
that at least two beavers were left in a lodge to breed. Increasing scarcity appears
to warrant the conclusion that this ceased to be the case and that the beaver were
annihilated.

[25]P. Lafitau, *Mœurs des sauvages ameriquains comparées aux mœurs des
premiers temps*, II, 334–335.

[26]Father Gabriel Sagard-Théodat, *Le Grand Voyage*, pp. 251 ff.

[27]*Ibid.*, p. 257.

[28]*Ibid.*, p. 260.

the Hurons survived this antagonism and the importance of the middlemen trade is suggested in their efforts to check French competition.
The methods are suggested by a letter from Père Joseph describing the
difficulty of opening communication with the Neutrals in 1626.[29]

But the Hurons having discovered that I spoke of leading them to the
trade ran to all the villages where they spread rumours about me that I was
a great magician; that I poisoned the air in their country and poisoned
many, that if they did not destroy me shortly I would burn their villages,
and make their children starve. Finally these Hurons always spoke so badly
of the French that they might divert them from trading with us,—that the
French were unsociable, rude, sad, melancholy people who lived only on
serpents and poison, that we ate the thunder, that we have a tail like the
animals, and that the women have only one breast located in the middle of
the bosom, that they carry five or six children at a time, and a thousand
other senseless things to make them suspect us.

The shift of the trade from the Saguenay to the St. Lawrence[30] had
significant results for the French as well as for the Indians. Navigation
was seasonal and the longer distances traversed by vessels from Europe
and the difficulty of sailing in uncharted and comparatively narrow
waters entailed an increasing overhead expense in the conduct of the
trade. Vessels were sent to Tadoussac; the goods were unloaded and
forwarded in small barques to Quebec and to such rendezvous as
Three Rivers, the mouth of the Richelieu, or the Lachine Rapids. The
vessels were sent out to an increasing extent[31] to engage only in the
fur trade so that the trading of large quantities of furs for a return cargo
was essential. Closer contact with larger numbers of Indians was a
necessity. As already suggested, various devices were adopted to induce the Indians to devote more of their time to the hunting of fur.
Missionaries were advised to encourage the Indians to leave their
children for the winter in order to ensure the return of the parents the

---

[29]Coppie ou abbregé d'une lettre du V. Pere Joseph de la Roche Daillon,
Mineur Recollect escrite du pays des Hurons à un sien amy, touchant son voyage
fait en la Contrée des Neutres, où il fait mention du pays etc. des disgraces qu'il
y encourut; Gabriel Sagard-Théodat, *Histoire du Canada*, III, 798 ff. The missionaries encountered similar opposition from the Hurons in their visits to the
Neutrals. See *Jesuit Relations* of 1640–41, XXI, 205, 211. For a reference to
objections of the Tadoussac Indians to visits of the missionaries to interior tribes
see *ibid.*, pp. 99–101; see also W. C. Macleod, "Trade Restrictions in Early
Society."

[30]For an excellent description of the St. Lawrence region see E. Salone, *La
Colonisation de la Nouvelle-France*, première partie.

[31]H. P. Biggar, *Early Trading Companies*, chaps. iii f.

following summer, and religious activities were regarded as important aids in the promotion of the trade. The *Jesuit Relations* of 1642 noted that

in order that this new vine may bear good fruit, a House should be erected at Tadoussac, to which two Fathers of our Society would go down in the Spring, and return only in the Autumn. They would do as much good to the French, who are there all Summer, as to the savages. . . . Moreover, the savages of Tadoussac, those of the Sagné, the Bersiamites, and the Papin-achiwekhi, earnestly beg that it be built—asserting that the more distant tribes will come in from all sides to receive instruction, and, by the same means, to trade with the French.[32]

Young men were sent back with the Indians to spy out the land, to learn their language and customs, and to encourage them to bring down more furs. Champlain wrote in 1610:

I had a young lad [probably Brulé], who had already spent two winters at Quebec, and who was desirous of going with the Algonquins to learn their language. Pont Gravé and I concluded that, if he entertained this de-sire, it would be better to send him to this place than elsewhere, that he might ascertain the nature of their country, see the great lake, observe the rivers and tribes there, and also explore the mines and objects of special interest in the localities occupied by these tribes, in order that he might inform us, upon his return, of the facts of the case.[33]

On his return in 1611 "I saw also my servant, who was dressed in the costume of the savages, who commended the treatment he had received from them. He informed me of all he had seen and learned during the winter, from the savages."[34] In the same year Bouvier, a competitor, sent a youth with the Algonquins,[35] and Champlain dispatched another young man (probably Vignau) with the Hurons. In 1613 Champlain asked the Indians "to take with them two young men, in order to keep the Indians friendly, learn something of their country, and place them under the obligation of coming back to us."[36] In 1615 at least one French interpreter was in the Huron country with Champlain. Sagard

[32]*Jesuit Relations*, XXII, 219. The importance of religious activities to the development of the fur trade is commonly noted throughout its history.

[33]*Voyages of Samuel de Champlain* (Prince Society), II, 246–248.

[34]*Ibid.*, III, 20. See B. Sulte, "Le Haut-Canada avant 1615"; C. W. Butterfield, *History of Brulé's Discoveries and Explorations, 1610–1626*.

[35]*The Works of Samuel de Champlain*, II, 201 ff.

[36]*Ibid.*, p. 307.

in 1623–24 mentions the names of several Frenchmen.[37] He writes: "One of our Frenchmen having gone to trade with an Indian on the north shore, located a copper mine about one hundred leagues from us." French traders were among the Neutrals and the Tobacco nations. Etienne Brulé, as we have seen, came down in 1624 with Indians to trade. Nicolet had penetrated to Green Bay on Lake Michigan as early as 1634.[38] Groseilliers and Radisson were in the Lake Michigan and Lake Superior country in the decade from 1650 to 1660. Exploration was carried on with the hope of discovering new tribes. Wars were engaged in to weld the alliances. In 1615 Champlain wrote:

> Whereupon I perceived that it was very necessary to assist [the Hurons to make war with the Iroquois], not only to make them love us more, but also to pave the way for my undertakings and discoveries which, to all appearances, could not be accomplished except by their help; and also because this would be to them a first step and preparation to coming into Christianity.[39]

Sagard writes:

> I had hoped to promote a peace between the Hurons and the Iroquois so that Christianity could be spread among them and to open the roads to trade with many nations who were not accessible but some members of the Company advised me that it was not expedient since if the Hurons were at peace with the Iroquois, the same Iroquois would lead the Hurons to trade with the Dutch and divert them from Quebec which is more distant.[40]

These devices involved, on the other hand, a further increase in the general overhead cost of the trade. They could only be effective with a united policy. Large overhead costs in this industry, as in other industries, involved severe competition in the beginning and a combination in the end. For the fur trade, competition was rendered more severe by its particular characteristics. To the rendezvous was brought down each year what is called, in the parlance of economics, an inelastic supply of furs which was to be exchanged for an inelastic supply of European commodities. It was unprofitable for either party to return with the goods brought. Under competitive conditions the supply of

[37]Father Gabriel Sagard-Théodat, *Le Grand Voyage*, pp. 124, 131, 185–188, 240.

[38]C. W. Butterfield, *History of the Discovery of the Northwest by John Nicolet in 1634*, and L. P. Kellogg, *The French Régime in Wisconsin*, chap. v.

[39]*The Voyages and Explorations of Samuel de Champlain*, ed. E. G. Bourne, II, 59–60.

[40]Father Gabriel Sagard-Théodat, *Histoire du Canada*, III, 811.

European goods tended to be larger, furs were obtained at greater cost, and profits disappeared. In 1608 De Monts had secured a monopoly of one year but was obliged to recognize that it was impossible to enforce it at Tadoussac because of the Basques' opposition.[41] In 1610 Champlain complained that he had taken the most active part in the fight with the Iroquois but that his competitors got most of the furs.[42] In 1611 at Tadoussac the Indians "wanted to wait until several ships had arrived in order to get our wares more cheaply. Thus those people are mistaken who think that by coming first they can do better business; for these Indians are now too sharp and crafty."[43] Considerable competition developed in the same year at the rendezvous at Lachine Rapids, and Champlain again complained of the work of bringing down the Indians to trade and the reward which went to his competitors although he appears to have profited through secret presents.[44] In 1612, during Champlain's absence, the situation became more serious. He summed up the whole problem:

But several others who had forsaken their former traffic at Tadoussac, came to the rapids [St. Louis and Lachine Rapids] with a number of small pinnaces, to see whether they could carry on barter with these tribes, to whom they affirmed that I was dead, whatever our men might say to the contrary. Thus does jealousy steal into bad natures in opposition to worthy objects. They only want people to run a thousand risks in discovering nations and countries, in order that they may keep the profits and the others the hardships. It is unreasonable, when one has caught the sheep for another to have the fleece. Had they been willing to share our explorations, use their resources, and risk their persons, they would have shown that they possessed honour and a love of renown; but, on the contrary, they clearly show that they are driven by pure malice to seek to enjoy equally with us the fruits of our labours.[45]

The losses of the merchants as a result of competition eventually led to a demand for some form of monopoly control. In 1610 Champlain wrote:

At Tadoussac I saw the loss which many merchants must suffer, who had taken on board a large quantity of merchandise, and fitted out a great number of vessels, in expectation of doing a good business in the fur-trade,

[41]*The Works of Samuel de Champlain*, II, 11 ff.
[42]*Ibid.*, p. 135.
[43]*Ibid.*, p. 171.
[44]*Ibid.*, pp. 188 ff.   [45]*Ibid.*, pp. 217–218.

which was so poor on account of the great number of vessels, that many will for a long time remember the loss which they suffered this year.[46]

And again in 1613:

Greediness of gain . . . causes the merchants to set out prematurely in order to arrive first in this country. By this means they not only become involved in the ice, but also in their own ruin, for, from trading with the savages in a secret manner and offering through rivalry with each other more merchandise than is necessary, they get the worst of the bargain. Thus, while purposing to deceive their associates, they generally deceive themselves.[47]

Through a gradual realization of the numerous difficulties of competition, Champlain was able to arrange for monopoly control. Co-operation was apparently essential even under conditions of competition. Some of the traders joined forces with Champlain in his fight with the Iroquois in 1610.[48] In 1611 a *patache* brought a supply of provisions to Lachine Rapids for all the competitors.[49] These intangible forms of co-operation preceded the loose association of 1613 and the later monopolies.[50] Undoubtedly the result was the first trust in North America, and the honor of being the first successful trust promoter must be given to Champlain.

The success of monopoly control in contrast to competition is shown in a description of August, 1626.

Before the time of the association of those Gentlemen to whom the King gave this trade for a certain time in consideration of certain conditions mentioned in the Articles, the Savages were visited by many peoples, to such an extent that an Old Man told me he had seen as many as twenty ships in the port of Tadoussac. But now since this business has been granted to the association, which today has a monopoly over all others, we see here not more than two ships which belong to it, and that only once a year, about the beginning of the month of June. These two ships bring all the merchandise which these Gentlemen use in trading with the Savages; that is to say, the cloaks, blankets, nightcaps, hats, shirts, sheets, hatchets, iron arrowheads, bodkins, swords, picks to break the ice in Winter, knives, kettles, prunes, raisins, Indian corn, peas, crackers or sea biscuits, and tobacco; and what is necessary for the sustenance of the French in this

[46]*The Voyages of Samuel de Champlain* (Prince Society), II, 250.
[47]*Ibid.*, III, 44. See especially H. P. Biggar, *Early Trading Companies*, chap. v.
[48]*The Works of Samuel de Champlain*, II, 126 ff.
[49]*Ibid.*, p. 207.
[50]For the numerous grants and cancellations of charters see H. P. Biggar, *Early Trading Companies, passim.*

country besides. In exchange for these they carry back hides of the moose, lynx, fox, otter, black ones being encountered occasionally, martens, badgers, and musk-rats; but they deal principally in Beavers, in which they find their greatest profit. I was told that during one year they carried back as many as 22,000. The usual number for one year is 15,000 or 12,000, at one pistole each, which is not doing badly. It is true their expenses are very heavy as they keep here forty persons and more, who are paid and maintained; this in addition to the expense of the crews of two ships, which consist of at least 150 men, who receive their wages and food.[51]

On the other hand, the succession of monopolies brought its own difficulties. Changes in control and reorganizations, the attitude of the home government, and effective enforcement of monopoly privileges involved problems absorbing the energies of the various associations concerned. As with most monopolies, lobbying with the home government was expensive. Charter privileges involved certain returns and in most cases the government insisted that settlers should be brought out. The cost of carrying out the agreements or of evading them became an important item. Enforcement of charter privileges necessitated expenditure at military posts such as Quebec and other strategic points which effectively kept out interlopers. The expense of maintaining an open route on the St. Lawrence for the Hurons and the Indians of the interior became more burdensome. Champlain wrote in 1620 regarding Quebec:

I employed the workers to build in stone and wood and everything was so well managed that in a short time we were able to support a lodge for the few workers, part of whom began to build a fort [St. Louis], for checking the dangers which might develop since without it there was no security in a country situated so far from all help. I established this building in a very good situation on a mountain which commands the traverse of the Saint Lawrence, which is one of the narrowest places in the river.[52]

The situation became serious with the establishment of settlements by the Dutch on the Hudson River. The Iroquois had available a supply of European goods which enabled them to take the offensive. The mouth of the Hudson River was open throughout the year. Moreover, it was distant from the fishing banks, and commercial development was closely dependent on the fur trade. The immediate necessity

[51]*Jesuit Relations*, IV, 207. See H. P. Biggar, *Early Trading Companies*, chaps. iv, vi–viii; also on the period prior to 1632, E. Salone, *La Colonisation de la Nouvelle-France*, deuxième partie; L. P. Kellogg, *French Régime in Wisconsin*, chap. iv.

[52]C.-H. Laverdière, *Œuvres de Champlain*, tome V, *Seconde partie des voyages du Sieur de Champlain*, livre premier, pp. 6 ff.

of developing the fur trade[53] and the shortness of the river made necessary the penetration of the more northerly richer fur-bearing country of the St. Lawrence. Indian alliances on the part of the Dutch with tribes of an agricultural civilization marginal to the hunting civilization of the fur-bearing areas as with the Iroquois were the result. The Iroquois country was deficient in its supply of the best northern furs, and the Iroquois, through possession of an adequate food supply as agriculturalists, were obliged to engage as middlemen in the fur trade to the north. Champlain in his journey of 1615 found that the Dutch were already engaging in the development of the fur trade through the Iroquois:

The savages there, assisted by the Dutch, make war upon them, take them prisoners, and cruelly put them to death; and indeed they told us that the preceding year [1614], while making war, they captured three of the Dutch, who were assisting their enemies [the Iroquois], as we do the Attigouautans [Hurons], and while in action one of their own men was killed.[54]

The development of the fur trade to the north could only be accomplished in competition with the French and the Hurons and their allies, which served to intensify the earlier struggle. With penetration to the northern country furs could be obtained by the Iroquois through the use of firearms. Guns and ammunition were the chief items of trade between the Dutch and the Iroquois. As descriptive of this trade, a document of the latter part of the period (1664) states that "full 600 lbs. alone were in the hands of a certain person, a merchant at Fort Orange, who declared that his supply was very small compared with that of other traders. The reason of this is that . . . the trade at Fort Orange for beaver and other peltry must be carried on chiefly by means of gunpowder. . . ."[55] The effectiveness with which firearms were used by the Iroquois is shown in the *Jesuit Relations* of 1642:

Moreover, when our Hurons go down to the Three Rivers or to Kebek to convey their Beaver skins there, although the whole length of the road is full of rapids and precipices, on which they are frequently wrecked, they

[53]See J. R. Brodhead, *History of the State of New York*, I, and E. B. O'Callaghan, *History of New Netherland; or, New York under the Dutch*, I and II; and H. L. Babcock, "The Beaver as a Factor in the Development of New England."

[54]*Voyages of Samuel de Champlain* (Prince Society), III, 122–123.

[55]*Documents relative to the Colonial History of the State of New York*, ed. E. B. O'Callaghan, II, 496. See a discussion of the situation in 1640, J. R. Brodhead, *History of the State of New York*, I, 308.

nevertheless fear the dangers of water much less than those of fire. For every year the Iroquois now prepare new ambushes for them, and if they take them alive, they wreak on them all the cruelty of their tortures. And this evil is almost without remedy; for, besides the fact that when they are going to trade their furs, they are not equipped for war, the Iroquois now use firearms which they buy from the Flemings, who dwell on their Shores. A single discharge of fifty or sixty arquebuses would be sufficient to cause terror to a thousand Hurons who might be going down in company and make them the prey of a hostile Army lying in wait for them as they pass.[56]

Competition of the Iroquois with the tribes allied to the French led inevitably to robbery and warfare to the point of exhaustion and annihilation and reached its conclusion in the extermination and the westward flight of the Hurons in 1649–50.

The routing of the Hurons from the country around Georgian Bay had various effects for monopoly control. It involved the disappearance of the Hurons as middlemen on whom the French had depended to bring down furs. These Indians no longer had an adequate supply of corn with which they could support themselves in the prosecution of the trade. The fur trade devolved upon the French to an increasing extent and it became increasingly expensive. French traders, as in the case of Radisson and Groseilliers, found it necessary to penetrate to the more remote regions around Lake Michigan and Lake Superior to stimulate new interest in the fur trade and to encourage the growing of corn so that the longer journeys to the colony could be undertaken. According to Radisson, "my brother stayed where he was welcome and putt up a great deale of Indian corne that was given him. He intended to furnish the wildmen that weare to goe downe to the French if they had not enough."[57]

The constant inroads of the Iroquois and the innumerable difficulties attendant upon a reorganization of the trade in the interior led to a serious interruption, the results of which were described in the *Jesuit Relations* of 1652–53:

Never were there more Beavers in our lakes and rivers, but never have there been fewer seen in the warehouses of the country. Before the devastation of the Hurons, a hundred canoes used to come to trade, all laden with Beaver-skins; and each year we had two or three hundred thousand livres' worth. That was a fine revenue with which to satisfy all the people, and defray the heavy expenses of the country. . . .

The Iroquois war dried up all these springs. The Beavers are left in peace

[56]*Jesuit Relations*, XXII, 307.
[57]*Early Narratives of the Northwest*, ed. L. P. Kellogg, p. 53.

and in the place of their repose; the Huron fleets no longer come down to trade; the Algonquins are depopulated; and the more distant Nations are withdrawing still farther, fearing the fire of the Iroquois. For a year, the warehouse of Montreal has not bought a single Beaver-skin from the savages. At Three Rivers, the little revenue that has accrued has been used to fortify the place, the enemy being expected there. In Quebec warehouse there is nothing but poverty; and so everyone has cause to be dissatisfied, there being no means to supply payment to those to whom it is due, or even to defray a part of the most necessary expenses of the country.[58]

The numerous portages on the Ottawa gave the Iroquois exceptional opportunities for raiding.[59] Visits were made by the Indians at intervals by the roundabout routes of the St. Maurice and the Saguenay and under the direction of traders such as Radisson and Groseilliers, but trade was not established on a permanent basis until new efforts were made to suppress the Iroquois.[60]

The effect of these burdens on the monopoly was shown in the slow development of the colony and in the chequered history of monopoly organization. The monopolists were interested in the fur trade and, as far as possible, evaded the tax laid down in their agreements which required them to promote settlement. In so far as agriculture benefited the trade, it was encouraged. Sagard writes that at Quebec the Company "kept a number of animals which they brought from France. They sow also every year Indian corn and peas which they trade with the Indians for furs" but later he explains that

the country is still sparsely populated and deserted and this through the negligence and lack of interest of the merchants who have been content to gather in furs and profits, without engaging in any expense for the cultivation, settlement or progress of the country. This is why they are scarcely more advanced than on the first day, for fear, they say, that the Spaniards would destroy them if they found that the country was valuable.[61]

The added expense of supporting the settlers in new territory not immediately adaptable to European agriculture, and the prospect of competition from these settlers were deterrent factors. Champlain knew the situation when he wrote in 1618:

[58]*Jesuit Relations*, XL, 211.

[59]See the skirmishes with the Iroquois of Radisson and Groseilliers on the Ottawa, *Early Narratives of the Northwest*, pp. 34 ff., 58 ff.

[60]The fur trade was wiped out in the south, 1652. See H. A. Innis, *Select Documents in Canadian Economic History, 1497–1783*, pp. 286–288. Trade was apparently revived in 1660 with the arrival of a large number of canoes belonging to the Ottawas, sixty canoes with over 140,000 livres of beaver.

[61]Father Gabriel Sagard-Théodat, *Le Grand Voyage*, pp. 37–40.

I saw that a greater fear held them; that if the country were settled their power would diminish, not making in this place all that they wished, and loosing the greatest part of the furs which would fall into the hands of the settlers of the country who would hunt by themselves and who would be brought out at a heavy expense.[62]

The consequent weakness of the colony was shown in the loss of Quebec[63] to the English from 1629 to 1632.

The energies of the colony were directed to defence against the inroads of the Iroquois and to the problem of keeping open the St. Lawrence and the Ottawa route. A fort was established at Three Rivers in 1634 and a settlement was made at Montreal in 1641–42. To protect Montreal, Fort Richelieu was built at the mouth of the Sorel River in 1642. To carry out these militaristic measures, the colony was subjected to a centralized policy in all its activities. Trade, agricultural development as in the seigniorial tenure, and even religious activities,[64] as shown in the exclusion of the Huguenots and later control of the Jesuits, reflected the influence of centralized control. The relation of centralized policy to the fur trade was shown also in the revenue of the government. Profits and revenue were obtained from the fur trade. Monopoly profits stimulated competition from the Iroquois and necessitated further outlays in military expenditures. The vicious circle continued since heavier outlays required additional revenue and furthered competition. The dependence of the governing authorities on the fur trade for revenue gave the trade a crucial importance.[65]

These difficulties incidental to the struggle for the St. Lawrence had a pronounced effect on the character of internal monopoly organization. Control shifted in spite of the fears of the monopoly into the hands of the local traders who were intimately acquainted with the problems of the trade. With penetration to the interior, and the increasing difficulties of the trade especially after the routing of the Hurons, the local trader became more important. The Company of New France was granted a monopoly on April 29, 1627. The capture of the Company's fleet by the English involved a direct loss of 300,000 livres. With the return of Quebec to France an arrangement was made in December, 1632,

[62]C.-H. Laverdière, Œuvres de Champlain, tome V, p. 317.

[63]See H. P. Biggar, Early Trading Companies, chap. ix; also G. P. Insh, Scottish Colonial Schemes, 1620–1686, passim.

[64]See Mack Eastman, Church and State in Early Canada, for the effects on religious policy, in the supremacy of the Jesuits, chaps. ii, iii; also E.-M. Faillon, Histoire de la colonie française en Canada, I, 268 ff.

[65]"All is well if only the fur trade is secure; the profits go to the shareholders and to us are left the hardships." The Works of Samuel de Champlain, V, 268.

in which the monopoly was leased for five years to a group of associates in return for 10,000 livres (covering the administration expenses of the colony) and one-third interest in the association. This subordinate Company, which disappeared in 1637 after earning a profit of 300,000 livres, was followed by an agreement with a new group of six of the members of the Company of New France—Chaffault, Rozée, Berrenger, Fouquet, Castillon, Lauzon—for four years of which Chatelets was appointed a representative at Quebec. Under this arrangement the Company of New France lost 70,000 livres and in 1641 was obliged to subscribe 103,500 livres to carry on the trade. By 1645 the Company had realized a profit of 85,000 livres but increasing difficulties with the Iroquois and jealousies regarding the profits necessitated a new arrangement and the trade was vested in the hands of the local traders, in an agreement[66] ratified March 6, 1645, between the Company of New France and "le député des habitans de la Nouvelle France," by which the Company relinquished its exclusive rights in the fur trade to the more powerful inhabitants (De Repentigny, Godefroy, DesChatelets, Giffard, Boulard) as a community with the right to make its own regulations. In return the community agreed to bring out twenty colonists annually, to bear the expenses of the government of the country and to pay one thousand pounds of assorted beaver skins annually to the Company. Following the immediate large returns of the new Company in 1645 (320,000 livres' profit in that year) dissatisfaction on the part of the colonists led to the adoption on March 27, 1647, of specific regulations[67] in the organization of the community, by which general freedom of trade was permitted within the colony,

all the French inhabitants of the said country to trade in skins and furs with the Indians, with the products of the country only, and on condition and not otherwise of carrying to the common warehouse all the skins and furs which they shall have traded with the said Indians to be exchanged at the price regulated by the said council on penalty of confiscation and arbitrary fine.[68]

Complaints of the unduly heavy costs of administration on the part of representatives of the *habitans* led to new adjustments in the Arrest[69] of March 5, 1648, with lower charges and greater freedom to trade.

[66]Can. Arch., C11A, I, 407–426.

[67]*Ibid.*, pp. 438 ff.

[68]Article 8, Arrest, March 27, 1647, *ibid.*, p. 441.

[69]See also Article 9—"Veut et entend Sa Majesté qu'à l'avenir les dits magazins ne serviront plus que pour les Sauvages et ne seront fournis que des choses necessaires à la traicte seulement." Can. Arch., Coll. Moreau Saint Méry, III, 180.

The increase in the scarcity of beaver after the disruption of the trade led to a decline in the annual returns from 250,000 livres to 65,000 livres in 1652 and to further regulations. In 1653 the *habitans* were given permission[70] to retain three-fourths of the beaver taken to the *Magazin* instead of one-half as had been the rule, the Company was released of the charge of one thousand beavers and on October 20, 1653, the district of Tadoussac was set aside to meet the general charges. In 1656 the *habitans* were given permission[71] to trade for one year at Tadoussac. Continued difficulties[72] of the monopoly were in evidence as the following statement and ordinance suggests.

[We are] under obligations for many expenses incurred in managing the trade as a result of lack of experience in which many debts had been contracted and few had been paid, [and have] difficulty in meeting the public and necessary charges for the upkeep of the colony especially since for some years the trade has been permitted indifferently to all the inhabitants, and the inhabitants [are] well instructed in all the means of profitting from the trade. . . . They no longer trade at the public warehouse and some individuals have drawn all the profit to themselves. Henceforth to commence from the present year all the merchandise for the trade in furs with the Indians which shall be sent to New France shall be taken to the public warehouse and consigned by the merchants or their factors into the hands of the clerk of the said warehouse who shall be appointed by the Council.

Complaints[73] were also made that labourers broke their contracts and deserted to the fishing boats at Ile Percée, paying for a return passage to France with smuggled furs. The problems of control by a monopoly became overwhelming. In 1660 the Company of the Habitans ceded the trade to the Company of Normandy for a payment of 10,000 livres to creditors and 50,000 livres for beaver duties. Finally the Company of New France disappeared in 1663. The period witnessed the emergence of the local trader[74] as independent from monopoly control in the internal trade.

Essential to the trade under all conditions but especially under conditions of competition was the personal relationship of the trader with the Indian. The fur trade demanded a long apprenticeship on the part

---

[70]Can. Arch., C11A, I, 494–495.

[71]*Ibid.*, pp. 512–513.

[72]See Relation of 1646, *Jesuit Relations*, XXVIII, 155–157; also March 7, 1657, Arrest du Conseil d'Etat portant Reglement sur le commerce et traitte.

[73]Arrest, March 12, 1658, Can. Arch., C11A, I, 514.

[74]*Ibid.*, pp. 529–530.

of its personnel in dealing with Indians.[75] With competition from the Iroquois it was increasingly necessary that the trade should centre with the local traders and that a large monopoly with headquarters in France should become inadequate. In the St. Lawrence and especially beyond Lachine and up the Ottawa, the trade was carried on by small boats and by canoes and was consequently in the hands of local traders. Expansion in the interior and competitive conditions tended to shift the control of the trade and to break up the control of monopoly over internal trade. Another cause of the increasing importance of local traders was the introduction and extension of the use of money[76] and the price system. With the weakening of monopoly control, and the increase in the number of traders and the amount of trade, barter was no longer adequate. The increasing use of currency stimulated individual initiative and strengthened the position of the trader as against the monopoly. Following the increase in currency came a change in the methods of collecting revenue. The conditions of the charters which insisted on the settling of the country were changed to the definite payment of a certain sum. Expenditures and revenues became items to be balanced in livres and sols. The tax-collecting mechanism was further adjusted to the transportation facilities of New France and taxes were collected on furs, deposited in the *Magazin*, and sent to France in large vessels over which due control could be exercised.

The period of the development of the fur trade on a large scale and as an independent industry[77] witnessed the evolution of distinctive organizations. Typical European institutions of the period such as the monopoly were adapted and modified according to the demands of a new environment. The inherent dependence of the trade on its personnel and the increasing stress on this dependence with the exhaustion

[75]Many authorities have insisted that the trade required little experience. On the other hand it is contended here that nothing stands out more clearly than the continuity of its personnel. With all the changes of the period prior to 1632 it is significant, for instance, that Champlain was continuously the important figure. The traders also changed little.

[76]See Adam Shortt, *Documents relating to Canadian Currency, Exchange, and Finance during the French Period*, I, *passim*; also G. Lanctot, "Les Premiers Budgets de la Nouvelle-France."

[77]For an excellent description of the place of the fur trade in the activities of New England leading to the conflict with the Dutch on the Hudson, see A. H. Buffinton, "New England and the Western Fur Trade, 1629–1675"; also *An Abridgment of the Indian Affairs* [1678–1751] by Peter Wraxall, ed. C. H. McIlwain, chap. i. On the period 1628–63 in New France, see L. P. Kellogg, *French Régime in Wisconsin*, chap. v.

of the supply of beaver led to the development of an internal organization in which the individual traders took an increasingly important part. There was heard in this early period of the trade a cry of exultation which will be heard again during its history, *Le commerce est libre*. The dominance of the local trader in internal organization was not carried to the external organization for the trade between Quebec and France. A limited number of vessels necessary for the conduct of the trade and the heavy overhead costs incidental to seasonal navigation were responsible for the continuation of monopoly control in this part of the trade. On this organization was built up the control of the home government. Through this organization was registered the decline in the trade following the destructive competition of the Iroquois and with it came the necessity for active intervention which developed in the following years. This committed the French government directly to the task of repairing its revenue from the fur trade by waging war more directly and more effectively on the Iroquois and indirectly on the European allies of the Iroquois.

During the period from 1600 to 1663 the fur trade emerges independent from fishing. This growth was dependent on the opening of the St. Lawrence to the interior. The organization of the trade shifted from a state of competition to monopoly as a result of the overhead costs incidental to movement to the interior. This monopoly organization was later modified to meet the new demands of the trade.

The fur trade was a phase of a cultural disturbance incidental to the meeting of two civilizations with different cultural traits. The demand for a more efficient route to the interior, the struggle with the Iroquois, the modification of trade organization, the limited growth of the colony, and the disappearance of native peoples were phases of the catastrophe which swept over the northern fur-producing areas of North America. The rapid destruction of the beaver had an important influence on the spread of the disturbance to the interior and the fur trade was fundamental in determining the lines followed but it was incidental to the driving forces of the demand for European goods.

4. The Struggle for the Great Lakes and Hudson Bay (1663-1713)

THE first half of the seventeenth century was characterized by a continuous struggle for control of the St. Lawrence and Ottawa route to the interior. The period ended with the break-up of the Huron middlemen organization and the destruction of the trade. In the early part of the second half of the century the French were engaged in establishing new connections and making a successful and determined effort to defeat the Iroquois and gain firm control over the route. As a result the period after 1663 was characterized by a rapid expansion of trade.

Expansion of trade was stimulated by the dispersal[1] of the Hurons and the tribes around Georgian Bay to the area around Lake Superior and Lake Michigan. The Ottawa tribes, which had, apparently, occupied the areas around Manitoulin Island and Michilimackinac, the Hurons of Georgian Bay, and other neighbouring tribes, and the Saulteurs of the Sault were driven to the southern shores of Lake Superior, especially near Chequamegon, and to the shores of Green Bay on Lake Michigan. These scattered tribes came in contact with more remote tribes of the interior, trespassed on their lands, introduced them to European goods, and engaged with them in new wars.[2] The Ottawas, crossing from Green Bay to the Mississippi, came in contact with the Potawatomi, the Sioux, and other tribes. Perrot wrote:

The Sioux, who had no acquaintance with the firearms and other implements, which they saw among the strangers—for they themselves use only knives and hatchets of stone and flint—hoped that these new peoples, who had come near them would share with them the commodities which they possessed; and, believing that the latter were spirits, because they were acquainted with the use of iron . . . conducted them . . . to their own vil-

[1]See L. P. Kellogg, *French Régime in Wisconsin*, chap. vi.
[2]See Nicolas Perrot, *Mémoire sur les mœurs, coustumes et religion des sauvages de l'Amérique Septentrionale*, ed. le R.P. J. Tailhan, and Charles Claude le Roy, Sieur Bacqueville de la Potherie, *Histoire de l'Amérique Septentrionale*. Important sections of these have been translated and reprinted in E. H. Blair, *Indian Tribes of the Upper Mississippi Valley*.

lages. . . . The Sioux returned to their own country with some small articles
which they had received from the Outaoüas . . . and they entreated the
strangers to have pity on them and to share with them that iron, which they
regarded as a divinity. . . . They [the Ottawas] gave to the envoys a few
trifles such as knives and awls; the Sioux declared that they placed great
value on these, lifting their eyes to the sky, and blessing it for having guided
to their country these peoples, who were able to furnish them so powerful
aid in ameliorating their wretched condition.[3]

The Ottawas, settling at Chequamegon, learned from the Saulteurs
of the Nipissings, who had fled to Lake Nipigon, and of the Crees
to the north of Lake Superior. According to Perrot:

At these tidings [of abundant beaver] the Outaoüas went away to the
North, and sought to carry on trade with those tribes (1662), who gave
them all their beaver robes for old knives, blunted awls, wretched nets and
kettles used until they were past service. For these they were most humbly
thanked; and those people declared that they were under great obligations
to the Outaoüas for having had compassion upon them and having shared
with them the merchandise which they had obtained from the French. In
acknowledgment of this they presented to them many packages of peltries,
hoping that their visitors would not fail to come to them every year, and to
bring them the like aid in trade-goods. They assured the Outaoüas at part-
ing that they would go on a hunting expedition (to make ready) for their
coming; that they would be present without fail at the rendezvous agreed
upon.[4]

This demand of Indian tribes in the western territory for European
goods occasioned a rapid increase in trade. The tribes of the territory
adjoining Lake Michigan, which were not familiar with the canoe,[5]
such as the Sauks, Fox, and Illinois, became the hunters of beaver to
be traded with middlemen who were thoroughly acquainted with the
Ottawa route and expert canoemen like the Ottawas and the Saulteurs[6]
(who were even better canoemen than the Hurons). The Miamis and
the Sioux ceased roasting the beaver for food, and began a search for
skins. Indian tribes limited to the restricted returns incidental to trade
with middlemen who held a monopoly were obliged to search far afield
and to war on other tribes for a supply of beaver. In the early part of
the period the Ottawas were joined on their journeys to Montreal and

[3]E. H. Blair, I, 159–163.
[4]*Ibid.*, pp. 173–174.
[5]"Father Allouez's Journey to Lake Superior, 1665–1667," *Early Narratives of
the Northwest*, ed. L. P. Kellogg, pp. 128 ff.
[6]E. H. Blair, *Indian Tribes of the Upper Mississippi Valley*, p. 157.

New France by other tribes. Hurons, Algonquins, Chippewas, Beavers, Sioux, and Kishkakon accompanied Radisson on his voyage. In 1670 Saulteurs, Missisaugas, and Crees were among the Indians[7] going to the French settlement. Du Chesneau, in his memoir on the western Indians dated November 13, 1681, suggested that at that time the Ottawas were in control. The profitable trade of the middlemen had passed from the hands of the Hurons to the Ottawas.

The Outawas Indians, who are divided into several tribes, and are nearest to us, are those of the greatest use to us, because through them we obtain Beaver; and although they, for the most part, do not hunt, and have but a small portion of peltry in their country, they go in search of it to the most distant places, and exchange for it our Merchandise which they procure at Montreal. . . .
They get their peltries, in the North, from the people of the interior . . . and in the south, ...
Some of these tribes occasionally come down to Montreal, but usually they do not do so in very great numbers, because they are too far distant, are not expert at managing canoes, and because the other Indians intimidate them, in order to be the carriers of their Merchandise and to profit thereby.[8]

The re-establishment and expansion of trade was limited by competition on two sides, from the north on Hudson Bay, and from the south by the Iroquois. The weak points of control of the fur trade in the St. Lawrence drainage basin were the low heights of land which separated the tributaries of the St. Lawrence from the rivers of the Atlantic—the Richelieu and the Hudson—and from the northern tributaries and rivers flowing into Hudson Bay—the Albany, the Moose, and Rupert rivers.

In the south, competition from the Iroquois, the Dutch and the English provoked similar aggressive measures. The decline and continued interruptions of the fur trade with its effect on revenue[9] and on settlement had brought an *impasse* which provoked the attacks of the French on the Iroquois. The raids into Iroquois territory in 1665 and 1666 were effective in securing peace and in reopening the Ottawa route. The *Jesuit Relations* of 1667–68 notes that:

The Savages, our allies, no longer fearing that they will be surprised on the road, come in quest of us from all directions, from a distance of five

[7]*Ibid.*, p. 211.
[8]*Documents relative to the Colonial History of the State of New York*, ed. E. B. O'Callaghan, IX, 160–161.
[9]See *ibid.*, IX, 59.

and six hundred leagues,—either to re-establish their trade, interrupted by the wars; or to open new commercial dealings, as some very remote tribes claim to do, who had never before made their appearance here, and who came last Summer for that purpose.[10]

The position of the French colony was strengthened and new possibilities for the fur trade realized by the construction of Fort Frontenac at the foot of Lake Ontario in 1673. This was followed by the tentative construction of a fort at Niagara[11] in 1679. The hauling of large bateaux up the difficult waters of the St. Lawrence impressed the Iroquois with the weakness of their position.[12] The establishment of Fort Frontenac[13] also opened a new route to the interior by the Great Lakes and the use of boats capable of much more efficient transportation than canoes became a reality. La Salle's construction of four barques on Lake Ontario by 1677 and of the *Griffin* in 1679 at Niagara marked the beginning of Great Lakes navigation.

On the north the Hudson's Bay Company was a disturbing factor. The effects of the dispersal of the Huron and allied tribes in bringing more remote Indians in contact with European goods have already been noted. The Assiniboines were mentioned by Father Gabriel Dreuillettes in the *Jesuit Relations* as early as 1656 as having been discovered by the early French traders.[14] Father Allouez met Indians who had been at the mouth of the Assiniboine River in 1666.[15] The Assiniboines, a part of the Sioux confederacy, had been pushed back

[10]*Jesuit Relations*, LI, 169.

[11]See F. H. Severance, *An Old Frontier of France*, I, esp. chaps. iii f.; also extract of memoir on the present state of Canada, November 12, 1685, P. Margry, *Découvertes et établissements des Français*, V, 9–11; and memoir on the advantage of the establishment of a fort at Niagara, *Documents relative to the Colonial History of the State of New York*, IX, 399.

[12]*Documents relative to the Colonial History of the State of New York*, IX, 65, 75–85, and especially 79–80; see also B. Sulte, "Guerres des Iroquois, 1670–1673," and "Le Fort de Frontenac, 1668–1678"; also extract of letter from Denonville to the Minister, May 8, 1686, on the importance of Niagara, P. Margry, *Découvertes et établissements des Français*, V, 15–19, and "Mémoire sur le Canada" advising the construction of an establishment on Lake Ontario to check the Iroquois, dated October 10, 1670, Can. Arch., C11A, III, 108.

[13]Fort Frontenac was built to check the Iroquois in the Ontario region, following expulsion of the Hurons, from going along the north shore to trade with the English. Attempts were made to meet competition by going along the south shore and to the end of the Toronto portage (Teiaiagon) particularly with the development of Oswego. See P. J. Robinson, *Toronto during the French Régime*, chap. iii.

[14]*Jesuit Relations*, XLIV, 249.

[15]*Early Narratives of the Northwest*, p. 133.

by the Indians more fortunately located in relation to European goods. These Indians and other hunting Indians, such as the Crees in the neighbourhood of Hudson Bay, being farthest distant from the French, possessed beaver in the greatest abundance, valued European commodities most highly, and secured the least favourable rate of exchange. They traded with the French through Indian middlemen, the Sioux, and in turn the Ottawa and the Saulteurs, and because of the monopoly of these middlemen and the great distances covered, obtained restricted supplies of goods.

The newly established Hudson's Bay Company (1670) began an immediate and effective competition which was felt on the Saguenay and at Sault Ste Marie. In the *Jesuit Relations*, dated September, 1671, referring to the Saguenay trade, it was noted that:

On the 17th, five canoes bearing Attikamegues, or poissons blancs, and Mistassirinins, came and joined us, bringing word that 2 vessels had anchored in Hudson's Bay and conducted extensive trading with the Savages, having taken their station there for purposes of traffic. They showed us a hatchet and some tobacco, which they had obtained from a Papinachois, who had been on a trading trip toward the North sea that very summer. [The Papinachois were regarded as a very profitable tribe.]
 . . . And, to that end [says the Frenchman to the Indian] abandon the plan of carrying on commerce with the Europeans who are trading toward the North sea, among whom prayer is not offered to God; and resume your old route to Lake St. John, where you will always find some black gown to instruct and baptize you.[16]

In a letter dated "Ste Marie du Sault," May 29, 1673, Father Nouvel wrote to Monseigneur the Governor:

Some of the savages of these regions, who saw during the winter the Savages from the interior who made their trade last autumn with des groisiliers and the english, have assured us that two ships had arrived at that great bay, and that they were annoyed by a third, which followed them, and from which they apprehended shipwreck. They added that about two hundred men were put ashore, and that in four days they had erected a large House, which they fortified with several pieces of cannon. The savages greatly praise their liberality.[17]

The monopoly of Indian middlemen in the French trade was immediately broken by the Hudson's Bay Company; goods were obtained on a large scale, and, with access by sea, at much more favourable rates.

[16]*Jesuit Relations*, LVI, 157, 177.
[17]*Ibid.*, LVII, 21–23.

The Assiniboines had apparently retreated to the area surrounding Lake Winnipeg, and in 1673 they were among the numerous tribes of Indians taking advantage of the opportunity of throwing off the monopoly control of middlemen trading with the French, by resorting to the new posts of the Hudson's Bay Company on James Bay.[18] Trade with the English on Hudson Bay continued, and after the establishment of Fort Nelson in 1682 grew rapidly. In 1683 French traders at Green Bay had met Indians who had traded for hatchets at the mouth of the "Assiniboie" River (Ft. Nelson).[19] In a letter dated Quebec, November 10, 1686, it was pointed out that:

We know comparatively little about the routes which could be followed to the bottom of the Bay by land but we have proved that the route by Temiskaming and Abitibi is a terrible road and of such great difficulty that it would only be possible to carry provisions for going and returning. It is believed that the route from Nemisco by Tadoussac is less difficult but in truth it is also too long and very difficult . . . these Monseigneur are the only two known routes to the bottom of the bay. . . . All the commerce of the Bay in a word is of no value except as it could be carried on by sea since it saves the infinite expense of carrying provisions and merchandise by land. But our merchants are in no position to compete with the English in this way since they have good seagoing boats well armed and well equipped. It is much to be feared that our company could not be successful in saving the best furs of Canada since certainly the greater part of "castor gras" comes from the North and besides the fur there is very much finer.[20]

Competition from Hudson Bay tapped the sources of the best beaver of the French,[21] and the effectiveness of competition was greatly enhanced by the location of the posts at the mouths of the rivers flowing into James Bay. James Bay and the territory north of the tree line were of strategic importance to the fur trade, since from these areas the French had drawn large quantities of the best northern furs, and the length and

[18]Beckles Willson, *The Great Company*, I, 133.

[19]E. H. Blair, *Indian Tribes of the Upper Mississippi Valley*, I, 364.

[20]Can. Arch., C11A, VIII, 258–259; see also petition against the *fermier* of Tadoussac regarding the inability to meet English competition, *ibid.*, VII, 323; also a statement to the effect that the French could compete effectively with tobacco and hatchets, November 5, 1683, *ibid.*, p. 270.

[21]"There are many beavers in this country better than those which come from Canada," Jérémie, *Relation du Détroit et de la baie d'Hudson*, p. 22; *Recueil d'arrests et autres pièces pour l'établissement de la Compagnie d'Occident*, pp. 38–39; see also E. A. Preble, *A Biological Investigation of the Hudson Bay Region*.

difficulty of the rivers of these regions gave the Hudson's Bay Company an advantage.

Immediate steps were taken to check competition. Father Albanel was dispatched in 1674 to go to Hudson Bay by way of the Saguenay,[22] and to attempt to win back Groseilliers[23] and Radisson whose co-operation was so important to the English, and he was in part success-ful. Northwest of Lake Superior, measures were also taken. Crees adja-cent to Hudson Bay posts secured commodities, especially guns, and carried on war with the neighbouring Assiniboines. The Assiniboines were consequently located between the Sioux in the south who obtained European goods from the French, and the Crees on the north who ob-tained goods from the English. An alliance between the Assiniboines and the Crees favoured the Hudson's Bay Company.[24] To offset the effects, Duluth in 1679 arranged a peace at the head of Lake Superior between this alliance and the Sioux,[25] which facilitated trade in French goods. Moreover, posts were established north of Lake Superior, and in 1678 a fort was built at the entrance to Lake Nipigon.[26] By 1681 French traders were carrying on trade to the north of Lake Superior at Lake Nipigon, Kaministiquia, and toward the head of the lake.[27] Fort La Toruette at the mouth of the Ombabika on the north of Lake Nipi-gon was built in 1684,[28] and Fort de Français near the forks of the Kenogami and the Albany in 1685. Finally the French were successful in the capturing of Forts Albany, Moose, and Rupert in 1686. Fort Nelson, however, remained in control of the English, but an attempt was made to dissuade the Assiniboines and the Crees from going to that post by trading through the Kaministiquia route. As early as 1680 traders had apparently crossed the height of land at this point to trade

[22]See John Oldmixon, "The History of Hudson's-Bay" in *Documents relating to the Early History of Hudson Bay*, ed. J. B. Tyrrell, p. 393.

[23]"Mémoire qui presentent . . . les interessez dans la Compagnie de la Baye d'Hudson establi en conséquence des ordres de Sa Majesté, Paris, 6 fevrier, 1685," Can. Arch., C11A, VII, 315; also for a description of the activities of Father Albanel in luring Radisson and "Groselyer" from the Hudson's Bay Company, see Can. Arch., Colonial Office Records; Hudson Bay state papers 1673–96, pp. 6 ff.

[24]P. Margry, *Découvertes et établissements des Français*, VI, 82.

[25]L. P. Kellogg, *French Régime in Wisconsin*, p. 330.

[26]See A. J. McComber, "Some Early History of Thunder Bay and District," pp. 13 ff.

[27]P. Margry, *Découvertes et établissements*, VI, 5.

[28]*Ibid.*, pp. 51–52.

with these Indians.[29] In 1688 Noyon wintered at Rainy Lake,[30] or the Lake of the Crees, and the country to Lake Winnipeg, or the Lake of the Assiniboines, was known. This route had obvious difficulties, and attempts were made as a result to reach Fort Nelson by sea. The "Compagnie du Nord," including several Quebec merchants, was given a charter on May 20, 1682,[31] to carry on trade in Hudson Bay, and its success was furthered through an aggressive military policy. M. de Denonville, in a memoir on the state of Canada dated November 12, 1685, wrote:

If not expelled thence [from Hudson Bay] they will get all the fat beaver from an infinite number of nations at the North which are being discovered every day; they will attract the greatest portion of the peltries that reach us at Montreal through the Outaouacs and Assinibois, and other neighboring tribes, for these will derive a double advantage from going in search of the English at Port Nelson—they will not have so far to go, and will find goods at a much lower rate than with us. That is evident from the fact that our Frenchmen have seen recently at Port Nelson some Indians who were known to have traded several years ago at Montreal.

The posts at the head of the Bay, adjoining the rivers Abitibis and Nimisco can be reached through the woods and seized; our Frenchmen are acquainted with the road. But in regard to the posts occupied by the English in the River Bourbon or Port Nelson, it is impossible to hold any post below them, and convey merchandise thither except by sea. Some pretend that it is feasible to go there overland, but the river to reach that quarter remains yet to be discovered and when discovered, could only admit the conveyance of a few men and not of any merchandise. The best informed on this subject agree herein.[32]

The capture of Fort Nelson in 1697 by the French led to the partial disappearance of the Kaministiquia routes.[33] The history of the latter part of the period in Hudson Bay is one of charges and countercharges[34]

[29]George Bryce, *Remarkable History of the Hudson's Bay Company*, p. 78.

[30]P. Margry, VI, 496–497.

[31]B. Sulte, *Histoire des Canadiens-français, 1608–1880*, V, 97–98; also *Bulletin des recherches historiques*, XXIV, 275–276. It is unfortunate that the documents relating to this company are exceedingly rare. See Sloane MSS, 2716, "Mémoire de la Compagnie Française Hudson Bay," 1689; also 2902, "The French in Hudson Bay," and R. Douglas and J. N. Wallace, eds., *Twenty Years of York Factory, 1694–1714: Jérémie's Account of Hudson Strait and Bay*, Introduction. Chesnaye is said to have subscribed 100,000 francs—see *La Presse*, Montreal, November 18, 1899; also P.-G. Roy, *La Famille Aubert de Gaspé*.

[32]"Memoir of M. de Denonville on the State of Canada, November 12, 1685," *Documents relative to the Colonial History of the State of New York*, ed. E. B. O'Callaghan, IX, 286.

[33]See *Twenty Years of York Factory*, ed. R. Douglas and J. N. Wallace.

[34]See Beckles Willson, *The Great Company*, I, chaps. v ff.

in which, on the whole, the French were most successful. Competition from Hudson Bay was largely eliminated by military aggressions.

The temporary control over the Iroquois permitted an extensive development of the trade. The effectiveness of the Ottawa middlemen organization was enhanced by the assistance of French traders and missionaries who followed the Indians to Chequamegon and to Green Bay, to the head of Lake Superior and to the Mississippi. The French penetrated to the Sioux country and came in contact with the Miamis, the Fox, and neighbouring tribes. Jolliet and Marquette in 1673 explored the Mississippi.[35] La Salle extended his activities along the south shore of Lake Michigan and the headwaters of the tributaries of the Mississippi.[36] Duluth in 1679 and 1680 explored the area west of Lake Superior to the Mississippi and established posts on the north of Lake Superior, at Kaministiquia and on Lake Nipigon.[37]

On the other hand, the scarcity of beaver in the Iroquois country and the ever present demand for European goods necessitated constant hunting on the part of Iroquois bands in the territory north of Lake Ontario and Lake Erie, and constant attempts to establish trade with northern and western tribes allied to the French. This problem was recognized by the French; in the narrative of Governor de Courcelles' voyage to Lake Ontario in 1671 it was noted:

It is well known that the Iroquois nations, especially the four upper ones, do not hunt any beaver or Elk. They absolutely exhausted the side of Ontario which they inhabit, that is the South side, a long time ago . . . to get any they are obliged to cross to the North of the same lake, formerly inhabited by the Hurons.[38]

Talon, in a memoir dated November 10, 1670, wrote:

If the observations that I have myself made and caused others to make, be correct, the English of Boston, and the Dutch of Manatte and of Orange, who are subject to them, attract, by means of the Iroquois and other Indian tribes in their neighborhood, over twelve hundred thousand *livres* of Beaver, almost all dry and in the best condition, part of which they use in their trade with the Muscovites, either themselves or through the Dutch.[39]

[35]"The Mississippi Voyage of Jolliet and Marquette, 1673," *Early Narratives of the Northwest*, ed. L. P. Kellogg, pp. 226 ff.

[36]See Francis Parkman, *La Salle and the Discovery of the Great West.*

[37]"Memoir of Duluth on the Sioux Country, 1678–1682," *Early Narratives of the Northwest*, pp. 329 ff. For a description of exploration activities see L. P. Kellogg, *French Régime in Wisconsin*, chap. x.

[38]*Documents relative to the Colonial History of the State of New York*, IX, 80.

[39]*Ibid.*, p. 65.

War with the Ottawas as middlemen was, consequently, as inevitable to the Iroquois as it had been during the earlier period with the Hurons. The memoir of La Barre, dated November 4, 1683, stated:

That nation [the Iroquois], the bravest, strongest and shrewdest in all North America, having twenty years ago subjugated all their neighbours, turned their attention to the trade with the English of New York, Orange and Manatte; and, finding this much more profitable than ours, because the Beaver (exempt from the duty of one-fourth which it pays here) is much higher there than with us, they sought every means to increase it; and as they perceived that they could not succeed better in that than by destroying the Outaouax, for thirty years our allies, and who alone supply us with two-thirds of the Beaver that is sent to France. . . .

You perceive hereby, my Lord, that the subject which we have discussed is to determine who will be master of the Beaver trade to the south and southwest; and that the Iroquois, who alone supply the English with considerable beaver, have a deep interest in despoiling us of that advantage by applying it to their own benefit; and that, therefore, no matter what treaty we make with them, the cause always continuing, they will not fail to seize on the most trifling occasions to endeavour to render themselves masters of those people and those posts, and, by robbing us, destroy the Colony of the King of France in Canada.[40]

Moreover, there was reason to believe that, as in the case of the Hurons, peace between the Iroquois and the Ottawas was not encouraged by the French. Lahontan wrote:

Those who alledge that the destruction of the *Iroquese*, would promote the interest of the colonies of *New-France*, are strangers to the true interest of that country; for, if that were once accomplished, the Savages who are now the *French* allies, would turn their greatest Enemies, as being then rid of their other fears. They would not fail to call in the *English*, by reason that their Commodities are at once cheaper, and more esteem'd than ours; and by that means the whole Commerce of that wide Country, would be wrested out of our hands. . . .

I conclude, therefore, that 'tis the interest of the *French* to weaken the Iroquese, but not to see 'em intirely defeated.[41]

The effectiveness of English and Iroquois competition was partly a result of geographic background, and partly a result of more efficient manufactures in England. Cheaper and superior English goods,[42] and a

[40]*Ibid.*, pp. 201–202.

[41]Lahontan, *New Voyages*, I, 394; also "Memoir on the War against the English and the Iroquois, 1690," P. Margry, *Découvertes et établissements*, V, 48–49.

[42]See a table of prices of goods at Montreal and Orange, 1689, *Documents relative to the Colonial History of the State of New York*, IX, 408–409; also

favourable route from the Hudson to Lake Ontario were the important factors. "It is a fact that the Iroquois have more esteem and inclination for us than for the English, but they are carried away by the influence of the low prices of goods they require, combined with the higher rate the English pay for Beaver."[43] The English trade was especially advantageous in guns and ammunition, in rum from the West Indies, and in clothing and blankets. The *coureurs de bois* were attracted by the favourable prices, as well as the Iroquois. La Barre wrote in 1683:

There are at present over 60 of those miserable French deserters at Orange, Manatte and other Dutch places under English command, more than half of whom deserve hanging, who occupy themselves all spring and summer only in seeking out ways to destroy this Colony. If strenuous efforts be not made to cut off this road, and to chastise those wretches, they will be the cause of the ruin of this country before the expiration of four years.[44]

Smuggling[45] was carried on by Fort Frontenac and Fort Chambly in spite of ordinances prohibiting the trade, and carrying the death penalty.[46] Fort Frontenac was erected as a "refuge and entrepôt for Coureurs de bois scattered among all the Ottawa nations, and to carry on thence a trade in beavers with the Dutch and the English."[47]

With the aid of cheaper goods, the Iroquois were able to compete effectively and to trade with tribes around Lake Erie and the Ohio, the Wabash, and the southern shores of Lake Michigan. The English were

---

cost of transportation Quebec to Montreal, *ibid.*, pp. 36–37, and an elaborate and valuable statement of the cost of moving goods from Montreal to Fort Frontenac, 1684, *ibid.*, pp. 144–146, 218–221; and *An Abridgment of the Indian Affairs* [1678–1751] by Peter Wraxall, ed. C. H. McIlwain, Introduction, chaps. i, ii.

[43]M. de Denonville to M. de Seignelay, January, 1690, *Documents relative to the Colonial History of the State of New York*, IX, 441. See for the advantages of the English in rum, powder, and *draperies*, Can. Arch., C11A, X, 595; also XIV, 398.

[44]*Documents relative to the Colonial History of the State of New York*, IX, 203.

[45]Extract of the "Memoir addressed to messrs. the partners of the society *en commandite* of the farm and trade of Canada, on the means of preventing the smuggling of beaver," *ibid.*, pp. 211–212.

[46]"Ordinance prohibiting all Frenchmen removing to Manatte, Orange and other places belonging to the English and Dutch, on pain of death against those who will not be domiciliated. Versailles, the 10th April, 1684." *Ibid.*, p. 224. See "Opinion de Monsieur de Meulles sur les congés qui se donnent en Canada," Mémoires Généraux, 1686, Can. Arch., C11A, CXXI, 1–5, and Lahontan, *New Voyages*, I, 90–91.

[47]*Documents relative to the Colonial History of the State of New York*, IX, 211.

able to engage in intrigues with the Ottawas and the Hurons, and with the tribes of Lake Michigan. In 1686 a trading expedition was sent to Michilimackinac by "the flemings and the English of New Yorck,"[48] but it was summarily checked. The problems of the French in combating competition from the Iroquois and the English were extremely complicated. The French trader, for example Perrot, was a diplomatist of the first order. As competition became more severe he was obliged to engage in diplomacy to prevent the Ottawas trading with the Iroquois.[49] His task was accomplished in part, as suggested, by encouraging hostility between these two tribes, but it was necessary also to maintain peace with the Iroquois. To maintain influence among the tribes, and to acquire a share of the profits of Indian middlemen, larger numbers of traders penetrated to the interior, and these traders incurred the jealousy of the middlemen whose profits were reduced. The monopoly of the middlemen was broken by the French who traded in guns and ammunition to more remote tribes. The Potawatomi discouraged trade by the French with the Maskoutech.[50] The Hurons attempted to prevent trade between the French and the Sioux.[51] The Fox prohibited French trade with the Sioux.[52] The Nipissings in 1666 tried to prevent trade with Montreal by spreading rumours of disease.[53] According to La Potherie,[54] the Ottawas were alarmed at the appearance and possibilities of La Salle's boat, and were instrumental in its destruction. Lahon-

---

[48]Letter of Rev. Father Beschefer to M. Cabart de Villermont, Quebec, September 19, 1687, *Jesuit Relations*, LXIII, 281–283; see also Lahontan, *New Voyages*, I, 98–99, 127, and L. P. Kellogg, *French Régime in Wisconsin*, chap. xii. In 1685 an expedition led by a Dutchman from Albany went by the Niagara Portage to Mackinac to trade. A second party in 1686 wintered near Oswego and went in 1687 by the Niagara route to Michilimackinac but were unsuccessful in trade. Col. Patrick MacGregorie, one of the leaders, had to change the route to avoid the fort at Detroit.

Denonville built the fort at the mouth of the Niagara in 1687 after his raid against the Senecas but was obliged to abandon it in 1689. In 1687 Denonville met Duluth who had brought Indians by Lake Huron and Erie. With a post at Niagara it would have been necessary to fortify Toronto, but the massacre at Lachine in 1689 seriously impaired French influence among the Indians. It was restored by the return of Frontenac and his energy in re-establishing Fort Frontenac. P. J. Robinson, *Toronto during the French Régime*, chap. iv.

[49]L. P. Kellogg, *French Régime in Wisconsin*, chaps. xi, xiii.

[50]E. H. Blair, *Indian Tribes of the Upper Mississippi Valley*, I, 322 ff.

[51]*Ibid.*, pp. 366 ff.

[52]*Early Narratives of the Northwest*, ed. L. P. Kellogg, p. 344.

[53]E. H. Blair, *Indian Tribes of the Upper Mississippi Valley*, I, 340–341.

[54]*Ibid.*, I, 352–353.

tan in his letter dated Montreal, November 2, 1684, described the speech of the Iroquois during the negotiations of that year:

You must know, *Onnontio,* we have robb'd no *French-Men,* but those who supply'd the *Illinese* and the *Oumamis* (our Enemies) with Fusees, with Powder, and with Ball; These indeed we took care of, because such arms might have cost us our life. . . .

We fell upon the *Illinese* and the *Oumamis,* because they cut down the trees of Peace that served for limits or boundaries to our Frontiers. They came to hunt Beavers upon our Lands; and, contrary to the custom of all the Savages, have carried off whole Stocks, both Male and Female. They have ingag'd the Chaouanons in their interest, and entertain'd 'em in their Country. They supply'd 'em with Fire-arms, after the concerting of ill designs against us.[55]

In addition to the problems incidental to diplomacy among the Indians, the French traders competed among themselves,[56] for instance at Green Bay and Chicago, and the south shores of Lake Michigan. The breakdown of diplomacy under these tremendous demands was shown in the revival of the Iroquois wars after 1684, and especially after the massacre of Lachine in 1689. It was necessarily followed and strengthened by military measures. Fort Frontenac was re-established in 1694 after its abandonment in 1689, Fort St. Joseph was built on the Detroit River in 1686 and supplanted by Fort Detroit in 1701.

The penetration of European goods among the western Indians, the emergence of the Ottawas as middlemen, and the long period of diplomacy and warfare had important effects on Indian life, and in turn on the organization of the fur trade. An immediate result was the settlement of Indians who were unable to go to Montreal, because of lack of experience with canoes, at points, especially near Green Bay, which gave them direct access to trade in European commodities brought by middlemen. The concentration about Green Bay is suggested in the following extract. The Potawatomi after the first visit to Montreal (1668)

sent deputies in every direction to inform the Islinois, Miamis, Outagamis, Maskoutechs, and Kikabous that they had been at Montreal, whence they

[55]Lahontan, *New Voyages,* I, 81–82. Lahontan noted that Fort Frontenac was practically impossible of defence because of the St. Lawrence rapids (*ibid.,* pp. 69–87). The Iroquois refused to abide by La Barre's demands in refraining from war. The French were anxious to open the lake route; Duluth sent support to La Barre in 1684.

[56]E. H. Blair, *Indian Tribes of the Upper Mississippi Valley,* II, 13–14.

had brought much merchandise; they besought those tribes to visit them and bring them beavers. Those tribes were too far away to profit by this at first; only the Outagamis came to establish themselves for the winter at a place thirty leagues from the bay in order to share in the benefit of the goods. . . . Their hope that some Frenchmen would come from Chagoua-mikon induced them to accumulate as many beavers as possible. . . . Those people had only five or six hatchets, which had no edge, and they used these by turns for cutting their wood; they had hardly one knife or one bodkin to a cabin and cut their meat with stones which they used for arrows; and they scaled their fish with mussel shells. . . . The Miamis, the Mas-koutechs, the Kikabous and fifteen cabins of Islinois came toward the bay the following summer, and made their clearings thirty miles away, beside the Outagamis . . . they had seen knives and hatchets in the hands of the Hurons, who had dealings with the French, which induced them to asso-ciate themselves with the tribes, who already had some union with us.[57]

Settlements were also made near French posts built to protect the Indians against the Iroquois and other enemies. At Fort St. Louis in 1683 "they established themselves to the number of 300 lodges . . . Islinois and Miamis and Chaouanons." They also settled about Michili-mackinac and Sault Ste Marie. As a result of the congregation of Indian tribes about specific points, and the entrance in the trade of French traders, control shifted from the hands of the Ottawa middlemen. As already shown the large profits of the Ottawas were incidental to the trade with newly discovered tribes who were insistent on European goods, and who possessed heavy robes of beaver skins which com-manded the highest prices, and whose beaver fields were not depleted. Because of the large profits of this trade, French traders, such as Radisson and Groseilliers, became interested in the western tribes.[58] As Radisson wrote, "for where that there is lucre, there are people enough to be had." These traders furthered the work of the Ottawas and others in spreading European goods, and in stimulating the fur trade. La Potherie wrote:

While we were waging war with the Iroquois, those tribes who dwelt about Lake Huron fled for refuge to Chagouamikon . . . they came down to Montreal only when they wished to sell their peltries, and then, trembl-ing. . . . The name of the French people gradually became known in that region and some of the French made their way into those places where

[57]*Ibid.*, I, 316–322.

[58]On the work of such pioneers as Groseilliers and Radisson, see *Voyages of Peter Esprit Radisson*, ed. G. D. Scull, and B. Sulte, "Les Coureurs de Bois au lac Supérieur, 1660"; and later, B. Sulte, "Les Français dans l'Ouest en 1671," and especially L. P. Kellogg, *French Régime in Wisconsin*.

they believed they could make some profit; it was a Peru for them. The savages could not understand why these men came so far to search for their worn out beaver robes; meanwhile they admired all the wares brought to them by the French, which they regarded as extremely precious. The knives, the hatchets, the iron weapons above all, could not be sufficiently praised. . . .

The old man struck two pieces of wood together to obtain fire from it; but as it was wet, he could not light it. The Frenchman drew forth his fire-steel, and immediately made fire with the tinder. The old man uttered loud exclamations about the iron which seemed to him a spirit.

[In presenting goods to the Maskoutechs] I see this fine village filled with young men . . . who will, without doubt, not fear their enemies if they carry French weapons. It is for these young men that I leave my gun. . . . It will also be more satisfactory in hunting cattle and other animals than are all the arrows that you use. To you, who are old men, I leave my kettle; I carry it everywhere without fear of breaking it. . . . Throw aside your bone bodkins, these French awls will be much easier to use. These knives will be more useful to you in killing beavers and in cutting your meat than are the pieces of stone that you use.[59]

As a result of the increasing importance of the French trader in the interior, of the settlement of the Indians at definite points, and of the longer journeys and the increasing costs, the trading organization suffered material changes. The rendezvous on the St. Lawrence and its successor, the annual fairs at Montreal and other points,[60] became less important. Attempts were made to restore the trade to Montreal, Three Rivers, and Quebec as early as 1676, but without material results.[61] Small traders, creditors, and interpreters at Montreal protested in vain against the decline of the fairs.[62] The smaller number of Ottawas was noted in 1686. M. de Meulles wrote:

It is good to know that being obliged to go to hunt the beaver up to seven or eight hundred leagues from Quebec, it is only the French who are cap-

[59]E. H. Blair, *Indian Tribes of the Upper Mississippi Valley*, I, 307, 326 ff.

[60]For descriptions of the general methods of carrying on the fur trade at fairs and through the *coureurs de bois* see Le Jeune's Relation, 1633, *Jesuit Relations*, V, 265, and especially for the later developments, Lahontan, *New Voyages*, I, 92–94.

[61]Ordonnance, October 8, 1676, Can. Arch., Coll. Moreau Saint Méry, II, 809–811, and C11A, XXXIV, 201–202; also see *Jugements et délibérations* [New France], II, October 5, 1676, pp. 73–76, April 26, 1677, pp. 124–125. Foreign traders were rigorously limited to certain places; see, for a brief survey of regulations as to these traders, *ibid.*, March 23, 1676, pp. 56–57.

[62]P. Margry, *Découvertes et établissements*, V, 185.

able of overcoming the difficulties, which is so true that these are the only ones who have discovered the Sioux who are eight hundred leagues distant and the other countries from which they draw the beaver and it is true also that the Ottawas who came many times to the number of two hundred canoes come no more except in very small numbers and it is a large number when we see forty or fifty canoes of Ottawas in a summer and it is certain that the small profits which are made in the fairs fall into the hands of four or five large merchants who trade in twenty-four hours all their furs and very few of the inhabitants benefit from the trade.[63]

The decreasing importance of the Ottawa middlemen hastened concentration of the trade in the colony. The trade carried on in the interior involved for the merchant a heavy outlay in goods, and large interest charges incidental to the slower turnover.[64] As a result it became concentrated in the hands of a small number of large merchants. Lahontan wrote regarding Montreal in 1685: "Almost all the Merchants of that City act only on the behalf of the Quebec Merchants, whose factors they are. . . . All the Merchants have such a perfect good understanding one with another, that they all sell at the same price."[65] And regarding Quebec:

The Merchant that has carried on the greatest trade in *Canada* is the Sieur Samuel Bernon of Rochel, who has great Warehouses at Quebec, from which the Inhabitants of the other Towns are supplied with such Commodities as they want. 'Tis true, there are some merchants at Quebec, who are indifferent rich and fit out Ships upon their own bottom, that ply to and again between France and Canada; and these merchants have their Correspondents at Rochel, who send out and take in every year the Cargoes of their Ships.[66]

The heavy overhead charges incidental to the trade with France were an additional cause of concentration. Beaver skins were light, and the goods which were brought out from France bulky and heavy. "Most of the Ships go laden to Canada and return light or empty."[67] In the "Mémoire sur la ferme du Domaine d'Occident" dated December 28, 1698, the net results were described.

In other times the Indians brought only the furs to the inhabitants of Canada who gave in return the provisions and merchandise from France

[63]"Opinion de Monsieur de Meulles sur les congés qui se donnent en Canada," Mémoires Généraux, 1686, Can. Arch., C11A, CXXI, 2–3.

[64]Lahontan saw about June 7, 1684, twenty-five to thirty canoes of *coureurs de bois* arrive after a year and eighteen months. Lahontan, *New Voyages*, I, 54; also H. A. Innis, *Select Documents in Canadian Economic History*, pp. 311–313.

[65]Lahontan, *New Voyages*, I, 96–97.

[66]*Ibid.*, p. 374.   [67]*Ibid.*, p. 373.

used by the Indians, the French did not go to the woods and everyone made a trade in furs but from time to time the principals became masters of this trade of which the profit in consequence ceased to be common, the other inhabitants spread out on all sides, penetrated the depths of the woods and have for the most part no other returns than what they receive in the price of furs.[68]

Moreover, the effects of English competition became more conspicuous in the later part of the period. In a letter from M. de Clairambault d'Aigremont to M. de Pontchartrain dated November 18, 1710, it was pointed out that:

The Coureurs de bois are useful in Canada for the fur trade, which is the sole branch that can be relied on, for it is certain that if the articles required by the Upper Nations be not sent to Michilimackinac, they will go in search of them to the English at Hudson's Bay, to whom they will convey all their peltries, and will detach themselves entirely from us, which would inflict a notable prejudice on that Colony. Experience sufficiently proves that it is not to be expected that these nations will come in quest of them to Montreal; witness the few canoes that have come down within eight or nine years, except in 1708, when about 60 descended. When these Indians will be obliged to go to a great distance to get their necessaries, they will always go to the cheapest market; whereas, were they to obtain their supplies at their door, they would take them, whatever the price may be.[69]

The organization of the internal trade under French control was rapidly extended. Ordinarily the *coureurs de bois* left Montreal in the spring, or about the middle of September. Arriving at Michilimackinac[70] they re-equipped with food and left for Lake Superior to the north or for Lake Michigan to the south. They returned to Michilimackinac the following spring about the middle of July, and left for Montreal. This journey[71] involved an absence of at least a year, but occasionally from two to three years were required for effective prosecution of the trade in the interior. M. Du Chesneau in a letter to M. de Seignelay, dated November 13, 1681, wrote:

And in order, My Lord, that you may be convinced of it, permit me to inform you that there are two sorts of Coureurs de bois. The first go to the original haunts of the Beaver, among the Indian tribes of the Assinibouets,

[68]Can. Arch., C11A, CXXV, Pt. I, 398.

[69]*Documents relative to the Colonial History of the State of New York*, ed. E. B. O'Callaghan, IX, 852–853; cf. W. B. Munro, "The *Coureurs de Bois.*"

[70]For a description of the difficulties of the trip to Michilimackinac see Lamothe Cadillac, in P. Margry, *Découverts et établissements*, V, 83–85.

[71]Can. Arch., C11A, VI, Pt. I, 212.

Nadoussieux, Miamis, Illinois and others, and these cannot make the trip in less than two or three years. The second, who are not so numerous, merely go so far as the Long Sault, *Petite Nation*, and sometimes to Michili-mackinac, to meet the Indians and French who come down, in order to obtain, exclusively, their peltries, for which they carry goods to them, and sometimes nothing but Brandy contrary to the King's prohibition, with which they intoxicate and ruin them. The latter can make their trips in the time indicated to you, nearly, and even in a much shorter period. It is not easy to catch either the one or the other, unless we are assisted by disin-terested persons; and, if favoured but ever so little, they easily receive intel-ligence and the woods and the rivers afford them great facilities to escape justice. This has occurred within four years.[72]

Traders penetrating to the interior were dependent upon an ample food supply, and on contact with a large number of Indians. Sault Ste Marie became important not only as a gateway to Lake Superior, but also, as Galinée noted in 1670, as an important supply point for whitefish.

This fish is so cheap that they give ten or twelve of them for four fingers of tobacco. Each weighs six or seven pounds. . . . Meat is so cheap here that for a pound of glass beads I had four minots of fat entrails of moose, which is the best morsel of the animal. . . . It is at these places that one gets a beaver robe for a fathom of tobacco, sometimes for a quarter of a pound of powder, sometimes for six knives, sometimes for a fathom of small blue beads etc. This is the reason why the French go there, notwithstanding the frightful difficulties that are encountered.[73]

La Potherie described Michilimackinac as

the general meeting place for all the French who go to trade with stranger tribes; it is the landing place and refuge of all the savages who trade their peltries. . . . When they choose to work, they make canoes of birch bark which they sell two at three hundred livres each. They get a shirt for two sheets of bark for cabins. The sale of their French strawberries and other fruits produces means for procuring their ornaments. . . . They make a profit on everything.[74]

Lahontan described it in his letter dated "Missilimackinac," May 26, 1688:

The *Coureurs de bois* have but a very small settlement here; though at the same time 'tis not inconsiderable, as being the Staple of all the goods

[72]*Documents relative to the Colonial History of the State of New York*, IX, 131, 152–153.
[73]*Early Narratives of the Northwest*, ed. L. P. Kellogg, p. 207.
[74]E. H. Blair, *Indian Tribes of the Upper Mississippi Valley*, I, 282.

that they truck with the South and the West Savages; for they cannot avoid passing this way, when they go to the Seats of the *Illinese* and the *Oumamis,* or to the *Bay des Puants,* and to the River of *Missisipi.* The Skins which they import from these different places, must lye here some time before they are transported to the Colony.[75]

Green Bay became more important as a gathering place for the agricultural and hunting Indians. Lahontan wrote:

This is a place of great Trade for Skins and *Indian* Corn, which these Savages sell to the *Coureurs de bois,* as they come and go, it being the nearest and most convenient Passage to the river of *Missisipi.* The Soil of this Country is so fertile, that it produces (in a manner without Agriculture) our *European* Corn, Pease, Beans, and several other Fruits that are not known in France.[76]

At a later date with the increasing importance of the Great Lakes route, a similar depot was established at Detroit. In 1714 its importance was described.

The preservation of this post is of importance for the proposed establishment at Michilimakina, since, from the commencement of the present year up to this time, more than 800 *minots* of Indian corn have been exported from Detroit; and the more Michilimakina will augment, as the land there is poor and does not produce corn, of the more consequence is that some Indians remain at Detroit to cultivate the soil, which is good thereabouts, particularly for Indian corn.[77]

The policy of concentration of posts, which developed after 1696, gave a direct stimulus to the growth of these depots.

The method of carrying on trade to the interior and to these depots, has been described by Lahontan in his letter dated Boucherville, October 2, 1685.

The merchants put into the two Canows stipulated in the License, six Men with a thousand Crowns-worth of Goods, which are rated to the Pedlars at *fifteen per cent.* more than what they are sold for in ready money in the Colony. When the Voyage is perform'd, this Sum of a thousand Crowns commonly brings in seven hundred *per cent.* clear profit, and sometimes more, sometimes less; for these Sparks call'd *Coureurs de Bois* bite

[75]Lahontan, *New Voyages,* I, 146; also *Jesuit Relations,* LXIII, 283, and P. Margry, *Découvertes et établissements,* V, 76.

[76]Lahontan, *New Voyages,* I, 168.

[77]*Documents relative to the Colonial History of the State of New York,* IX, 866. See I. A. Johnson, *The Michigan Fur Trade,* and A. E. Parkins, *The Historical Geography of Detroit,* chaps. ii, iii.

the savages most dexterously, and the lading of two Canows, computed at a thousand Crowns, is a Purchase for as many Beaver-skins as will load four Canows. Now, four Canows will carry a hundred and sixty packs of skins, that is, forty apiece; and, reckoning each pack to be worth fifty Crowns, the value of the whole amounts to eight thousand Crowns. As to the Repartition of this extravagant Profit, 'tis made after the following manner: In the first place, the merchant takes out of the whole bulk six hundred Crowns for the Purchase of his License; then a thousand Crowns for the prime Cost of the exported Commodities. After this, there remains 6400 Crowns of Surplusage, out of which the merchant takes forty *per cent.* for Bottomree, which amounts to 2560 Crowns; and the remainder is divided equally among the six *Coureurs de Bois*, who get little more than 600 Crowns apiece and indeed I must say 'tis fairly well earned; for their fatigue is inconceivable. In the meantime, you must remark, that over and above the fore-going profit, the merchant gets 25 *per cent.* upon his Beaver-skins by carrying them to the Office of the Farmers General, where the Price of four sorts of Beaver-skins is fixed. If the Merchant sells these Skins to any private Man in the Country for ready Money, he is paid in the current Money of the Country, which is of less value than the bills of Exchange that the Director of that Office draws upon Rochel or Paris; for there they are paid in *French* livres, which are twenty Sols, whereas a *Canada* livre is but fifteen sols. This advantage of 25 *per cent.* is called *Bénéfice*; but take notice, that 'tis only to be had upon Beaver-skins.[78]

Local merchants supplied commodities for the trade, and received a proportion of the profits. In the earlier period, the proportion was as much as one-half, but later[79] this share diminished. The trader was a partner directly concerned in the conduct and success of the trade.

The development of a trading organization in the interior had important effects on the colony, and on the external organization of trade.

[78]Lahontan, *New Voyages*, I, 100–101.

[79]See contract cited L. P. Kellogg, *French Régime in Wisconsin*, p. 123, also "Congés et permis déposés ou enregistrés à Montréal sous le régime français," *Rapport de l'archiviste de la Province de Québec pour 1921–1922*, pp. 190 ff. The latter includes references to transactions of 1681, 1682, 1683, 1685, 1686, 1694, 1708, and 1715 dealing with the issue of *congés* by the governor and by the lessees of posts such as Detroit to trade chiefly with the Ottawas and involving in most cases one canoe and three men. They also include references to the sale of *congés*, to agreements between owners of *congés* and others for supplying the outfit and engaging in the trade. In 1715 the *congés* involved permission to trade after participating in the Fox wars. Evidence exists to show that more than one *congé* was issued to one person and that they were sold to partnerships of from two to six. The same interests were also successful in securing more than one *congé* through purchase or through issue to individual partners. Merchants occupy a prominent place in the transactions.

The effects on the colony were shown directly in the increasing number of men necessary for its prosecution, and for the wars incidental to the checking of competition from Hudson Bay, and from the English and the Iroquois. The trade was carried on in the summer and seriously restricted the supply of labour for agriculture. In M. Du Chesneau's letter to M. de Seignelay, dated November 13, 1681, he complained that: "Two years absence of five hundred persons [coureurs de bois] (according to the lowest calculation), the best adapted to farm work, cannot increase agriculture; and this is confirmed by the complaints I have received from proprietors of Seigniories who do not participate in the profits of the Coureurs de bois, that they cannot find men to do their work."[80]

The close dependence of the colony on the fur trade was also evident in the problems which appeared following expansion to the interior, and the marked increase in the supply of furs. The difficulties of the trade at the beginning of the period were evident in the bankruptcy of the Company of the Habitans.[81] To meet the situation the "Conseil souverain," which had been established in April, 1663, recommended that the rights to one-fourth of the beaver and one-tenth of the orignaux, and the trade of Tadoussac should be granted for three years to the highest bidder.[82] These rights were consequently sold after considerable competition to Aubert de la Chesnaye for 46,500 livres on October 23, 1663.[83] The establishment of the Company of West Indies in May, 1664,[84] made no immediate change in the arrangement, but on April 8, 1666, these rights were transferred to it.[85] The Company began with an attempt to exercise the full rights of the charter in the control of trade, but, because of complaints from the habitans and the activity of Talon, it was unsuccessful and free trade within the colony continued to be the rule.[86] The success of the military activities against the Iroquois, and the increase in the supply of fur which occasioned a fall in price brought serious problems to the Company of West Indies. M. de la Chesnaye[87] wrote in 1670 that prices had fallen in five or six years

[80]Documents relative to the Colonial History of the State of New York, IX, 154; see Amnistie pour les Coureurs des bois de la Nouvelle France, mai, 1681, Edits, I, 249–250.

[81]See the report of liquidators of the Company, June 25, 1665, Can. Arch., C11A, II, 360.

[82]Jugements et délibérations, I, 14.

[83]Ibid., pp. 38–40.   [84]Edits, I, 41–48.   [85]Ibid., pp. 60–61.

[86]Can. Arch., C11A, II, 172; also E. Salone, La Colonisation de la Nouvelle-France, pp. 206 ff.

[87]Appendix B.

from 14 to 4 livres per *livre*. Expenditure in the colony for fortifications increased rapidly,[88] and the revenue secured from furs declined. It had been estimated that the right to one-fourth of the beaver and one-tenth of the *orignaux* would produce annually 46,900 *livres*, and it actually produced 34,000 *livres*. In 1674 the Company had accumulated a debt of 3,523,000 livres, and, as a result, disappeared.[89] To prevent the decline in price it was planned to place the trade under a single hand and to fix the price at a certain level; probably the first valorization scheme in North America thus came into effect. The trade was sold to Nicolas Oudiette on May 24, 1675, for 350,000 livres.[90] He was obliged to accept all beaver at 4 livres 10 sols *la livre*, and to sell in France at not more than 10 livres.

The payment of a fixed price for all grades of beaver encouraged the sale of grades of beaver which were beginning to come on the market as a result of exploration, especially in the south and southwest, following the activities of La Salle. The beaver was of a poorer quality than that in the northern Wisconsin district, and the Indians were not accustomed to wearing beaver robes for a great length of time and making *castor gras*. Larger supplies of *castor sec* came on the market. The guard hair was still on them and the fur lacked the downy character of *castor gras*, the result of long wear. With a fixed price other poorer grades became more conspicuous. *Demi-gras d'hiver*, or robes which the Indians were beginning to wear, and of which the skins were beginning to turn yellow; *castor gras d'été*, or robes which were made of skins taken in summer with very little fur, and thick pelts; *castor veule*, or robes which had been scraped thin and treated, but not worn, of which the skins were white and very light; *castor sec d'hiver* or *bardeau*, or beaver skins taken in winter which had not been made into robes, because of holes and imperfections and which were, as a result, badly prepared and very coarse; *castor sec d'été*, or skins taken in summer; *mitaines* and *rognures*, or small pieces used for making sleeves and mittens, were among the grades appearing on the market. Large quantities of *castor sec* seriously affected the price in the home market, since the hatmakers used only one-fourth of *castor sec* to mix with three-fourths of *castor gras*. The sale of surplus dry beaver in Holland and

[88]See a statement April 6, 1667, regarding the heavy drain of the Iroquois wars on revenue, *Documents relative to the Colonial History of the State of New York*, IX, 59.

[89]Edit du Roi portant révocation de la Compagnie des Indes . . . du mois de décembre, 1674, *Edits*, I, 74–78.

[90]*Ibid.*, p. 87.

other markets reduced the price and prejudiced the position of the *fermier*. Since beaver was purchased by weight the thick skins and lighter fur of the poorer grades were sold more advantageously than the light skin and thick fur of the *castor gras*, which was in demand among the hatmakers. Fraudulent practices, such as keeping the beaver in damp cellars to increase the weight, were prevalent. There followed a protest from Oudiette, and a plea for a revision of prices. The arguments put forward by the *fermier* and the traders are shown in the following extracts from the "Procès verbal touchant le prix des castors et orignaux qu'il fault examiner" of Du Chesneau, dated October 20, 1676.[91]

We have learned from the unanimous voice of the inhabitants after a conference with them, that it would be very prejudicial to the country to diminish the "castor sec" since it was this variety which made the greatest commerce being three fourths more than the "castor gras." The Iroquois took only the "castor sec" either from what they had hunted on their own lands or from what they traded with other nations having no use for the "engraisser." If "castor sec" was refused and suffered any diminution the Indians would carry it to the English and the Dutch who esteem it more than the "gras," and they would deprive this country of their commerce. With the other neighbouring nations they are invited by continual presents and ambassadors sent to them by the English and the Dutch, who if they succeeded in their design would not fail to engage these people to make war on this colony. The "castor gras" is very much lighter than the "sec" since for "l'engraisser" they are obliged to make it into robes and trim it squarely so that more than a third is lost for "rongneures." If they were to "engraisser" the beaver the Indians would not be able to come down for four or five years since under orders of Messieurs de Tracy, Courcelles and Talon, formerly governors and intendants, the French who had been among the distant nations had exhorted them no longer to "engraisser" the beaver as the "sec" was more valuable. And we have requested that permission should be given the inhabitants to place a controller from their side in charge of the receipt of the beaver with the clerk of the "fermier," offering themselves to pay the wages it shall be judged proper to offer, and that the beaver shall be taken for all its weight by the "fermier" and not taken only for a pound and a half although it sometimes weighs up to two pounds.

The *fermier* replied on the other hand

that by his trade he was obliged to supply 60,000 of beaver of which three quarters must be "gras" and that he had had much difficulty in meeting this order this year, that this has been the cause of much alarm having only

[91]Can. Arch., Coll. Moreau Saint Méry, II, Pt. I, 72–80.

three to four thousand "castor gras" and a surfeit of forty thousand of "meschant sec," that diminishing the "meschant castor sec" will not prejudice the country since it would force the Indians to prepare their skins better and to clean them which they neglect doing because they sell by weight and that this diminution would be recompensed by the increase which they should give for "castor gras," that if they do not diminish the "meschant castor sec" the manufacturer of hats is ruined since they could not be made from "castor sec" alone.

A compromise was reached in 1677 in which the price of *castor gras* was raised to 5 livres 10 sols; *Muscovie veule* and *demi-gras* remained at 4*l*. 10*s*., and *castor sec ordinaire* was reduced to 3*l*. 10*s*.[92] *Muscovie veule* included beaver skins taken in winter without damage, which had large excellent fur and long hair, and was carefully prepared for the trade in Russia. In that country the fur was taken out and the remaining hair left on the skins for wear. This grade was placed on the same basis as *castor demi-gras*.

The chief problem of the valorization scheme, however, was that of controlling supply. Regulations were enacted as early as 1673 to prevent traders going to the interior. It was planned to limit trade[93] and after the new price arrangement a fresh crop of legislation appeared. The number and frequency of the regulations were indices of their ineffectiveness. In many cases they defeated their own ends by outlawing the traders and increasing the trade with the English. The failure of prohibitions was shown[94] in a "Memoir of M. Du Chesneau on Irregular trade in Canada," dated November 13, 1681.

The King, having been informed that all the families in Canada were

[92]*Edits*, I, 87–89; also Can. Arch., C11A, IV, 270 (May 16, 1677); see a list of prices of various furs in Lahontan, *New Voyages*, I, 379.

[93]See Ordonnance du Roi au sujet des Vagabonds et Coureurs de bois, 5 juin, 1673, *Edits*, I, 73–74; Ordonnance du Roi qui défend d'aller à la traite des Pelleteries dans les habitations des Sauvages, 15 avril, 1676, *ibid*., p. 86; Ordonnance du Roi qui défend d'aller à la chasse hors étendue des terres défrichées et une lieue à la ronde, 12 mai, 1678, *ibid*., pp. 105–196, modified later "si ce n'est qu'avec la permission du gouverneur et qu'entre le quinze janvier et le quinze avril de chaque année," 25 avril, 1679, *ibid*., pp. 230–231; Edit du Roi qui défend d'aller à la traite des pelleteries dans la profondeur des bois et les habitations des Sauvages du mois de mai, 1681, *ibid*., pp. 248–249. For evidences of punishment on violation of these regulations see *Jugements et délibérations*, November 2, 1678, II, 260–261.

[94]See Ordonnance, 2 mai, 1681, Can. Arch., Coll. Moreau Saint Méry, VI, 5–6; see also Ordonnance, 1er 8bre, 1682, *ibid*., p. 44, *and Documents relative to the Colonial History of the State of New York*, ed. E. B. O'Callaghan, IX, 159.

engaged with the Coureurs de bois; that it was to be feared that the latter will become refugees among the English, which would be an irreparable loss to the Colony, inasmuch as they might convey their peltries thither, they being the best qualified to defend the country; and as it is for the advantage of Canada that a certain number of Frenchmen should go to the Far Indians, in order to prepare and attract them to us; oblige them to bring us their beaver; discover, ourselves, their designs, and finally to support, by these voyages, such families as may be in need:

His Majesty was graciously pleased to grant an amnesty to the disobedient, with authority to issue twenty-five licenses, yearly, to twenty-five canoes, having each three men, to trade among the savages.

Amnesties were passed, the regulations were modified, and, in general, the attempts at control broke down. The system of licences, which permitted twenty-five canoes to go to the trade, proved inadequate. Three men were permitted to each licence, giving a total of seventy-five *coureurs de bois*. This number increased to nearly four hundred including men going out, men in the country, men returning, and men allowed to go on special permits.[95] The licences became a source of political corruption, and a method of control over the trade of advantage to the ruling authorities. Prices of *congés* declined to 30 crowns.[96] In 1696 in an attempt to further control supply, all *congés* were abolished.[97] "We have absolutely suppressed all licences and permissions to trade with the Indians." The trade was restricted to certain important posts, and troops stationed to ensure enforcement of the regulations. The troops and commandments became interested, and the fur trade continued.[98]

Price and trade regulations were scarcely more effective in limiting

[95]Can. Arch., C11A, XXI, 189–192.

[96]*Ibid.*, XXXI, 270–271; see also Lahontan, *New Voyages*, I, 96–101.

[97]Déclaration du Roy, 21 mai, 1696, Can. Arch., Coll. Moreau Saint Méry, VII, Pt. II, 851–854. For a discussion of the restriction of trade see L. P. Kellogg, *French Régime in Wisconsin*, chaps. xii–xiii; see also Déclaration du Roy portant defenses d'aller en traitte en la profondeur des terres avec terme de deux ans à ceux qui y sont pour revenir en la colonie du Canada ou celle de Mississippi du mois de juin de l'annee 1703; also amnesty, May 10, 1710, Can. Arch., Coll. Moreau Saint Méry, IX, Pt. I, 248.

[98]See "Remarks concerning the Tadoussak Mission . . . since 1671," by Father François de Crepieul, April 7, 1686, *Jesuit Relations*, LXIII, 265, and especially letter from Rev. Father Etienne de Carheil to Monsieur Louis Hector de Callières, governor of Michilimackinac, August 30, 1702, *ibid.*, LXV, 195–203; see also the objections of the *fermiers* to the establishment of Detroit intended as a check to the English and Iroquois, but used by Lamothe Cadillac for control of the trade, P. Margry, *Découvertes et établissements*, V, 182–185.

supply. Regulations became more numerous after 1690, and took a variety of forms. In 1691 restrictions[99] were placed on the marketing of poor beaver from *pais des Illinois*, and prohibitions were enacted against the falsifying of weights with oil, or by leaving the beaver in damp cellars. Certain customs had grown up protecting the *fermier*.[100] *Sec d'hiver* or *bardeau* skins were accepted on the basis of *une livre et demie* although weighing much more. In weighing other furs 2 per cent was allowed the *fermier*. On May 30, 1695, the following prices and grades were established[101] to be effective July 1, 1697:

> Beaver will be received at the office of the "fermes" at Quebec in three grades and qualities only, "bonnes, loyales, et marchandes," that is to say, 1st—"Castor Veule, gras" or "demi-gras"; 2nd—The "castor gras d'été et mitaines"; and 3rd,—"castor sec d'hyver et Moscovie." Such beaver will be purchased by Pointeau [the *fermier*]—the first at 5 l, 5 s. "la livre poids de marc," the second at 2 l, 12 s, 6 d. and the third at 3 l, 5 s.

Complaints were made that the "castor sec d'hyver" was badly prepared and generally full of dirt which spoiled the other grades with which it was packed and an ordinance was passed to the effect that the "castors secs d'hyver" should be well and carefully cleaned.[102] It was also specifically stated that furs not falling within the three grades mentioned—*les castors illinois ou bardeaux, ceux du bas automne ou du printems et les rogneurs*—should be rejected. By the rejection of *castor sec d'été* it was expected[103] that the Indians would make the beavers into robes and wear them, thus converting them into *castor gras d'été*, and that they would tend to leave off hunting in summer, and consequently get only the best furs. The regulation of 1695 appears to have been enacted partly as a result of complaints against too close grading. Beaver brought down as *gras* was graded by the *fermiers* as *veule*, and for the *habitant* there was no alternative but acceptance of the low grade. Because of this uncertainty the Indians were not encouraged to make *castor gras* because the trade in *castor sec* was found

[99]Règlement de Monsieur de Champigny pour les fermes, 30 avril, 1691, Can. Arch., Coll. Moreau Saint Méry, VII, Pt. I, 65–66.

[100]"Mémoire sur les affaires de Canada en leur état present au 1er mai, 1696," Can. Arch., C11A, XVI, 431.

[101]Ordonnance de Monsieur de Champigny, 27 septembre, 1696.

[102]Quebec, August 9, 1697, Can. Arch., Coll. Moreau Saint Méry, VIII, Pt. I, 41–46. Hours for receiving beaver were seven to eleven in the morning and two to seven in the afternoon.

[103]Letter of Champigny, November 6, 1695, Can. Arch., C11A, XIII, 416–417.

to be more substantial, better regulated, and more certain. To avoid this difficulty *castor gras* was received at the same rate as *castor veule* in the *arrêt* of 1695. The new regulation brought its own problems. Since *castor veule* weighed much less than *castor sec* the *habitant* lost on weight more than he gained in price, and *castor sec* continued to come on the market. In 1696 a reduction appears to have been made[104] and *le gras* and *demi gras* were quoted at 5*l.* 10*s. la livre*, and *le veule* at 4*l.* 10*s.* This reduction brought on the same difficulties[105] as existed prior to 1695. In 1700 prices were again regulated—beaver received in 1699 and 1700: *castor sec quitte du quart 2l. 0s. 0d.; Le Moscovite et robes neuves 3l. 0s. 0d.; le gras, demi-gras et veule 3l. 18s. 9d.; le gras d'été 1l. 19s. 4d.*; and hereafter: *du castor sec en robes neuves qui n'auront pas été portées, le quart ôté 2l. 5s; Du Moscovite 2l. 10s; Du gras, demi-gras, et veule 3l. 5s; castor gras d'été* and *castor sec d'été* were rejected.[106] On May 28, 1701, a new regulation[107] reduced the price of *le castor sec et robes neuves* to 40 sols or 2 livres and raised the price of *le Moscovite* to 60 sols or 3 livres.

Continual price adjustments and regulations for control brought further difficulties which were especially evident in the period following 1700. During the early period every effort was made to reduce the amount of *castor sec*. In the period after 1700, a complete change had occurred in which every effort was made to reduce the amount of *castor gras*. The probable causes of this extraordinary reversal may be indicated. The difference in price between *castor gras* and *castor sec*, and the greater restriction of *coureurs de bois* after 1696 were important considerations. The English were unable to compete for *castor gras* and bought larger quantities of the other varieties. In transportation "a canoe loaded with two thousand weight of *castor sec* was valued at only 4,000 livres, whereas if it had been loaded with *castor gras* it would have been valued up to 6,500 livres." Moreover, with fewer *coureurs de bois* the Indians were given more time to produce *castor gras*. Of greatest importance, the success of the French on Hudson Bay increased the supply of this grade. In 1697 this district supplied 19,487 pounds and in 1701 approximately 40,000 pounds. The net result was

[104]"Mémoire sur les affaires de Canada en leur état present au 1er mai, 1696," Can. Arch., C11A, XIV, 431.

[105]See memoir addressed to Count Maurepas, P. Margry, *Découvertes et établissements*, V, 139 ff.

[106]*Edits*, I, 282.

[107]*Ibid.*, pp. 285–286.

the flooding of the market with *castor gras*.[108] In 1706 prices were reduced, *castor sec* to 30 sols *la livre*, and *castor gras* forbidden for six years. In 1710 the price of *castor sec* was raised to 34 sols *la livre*, and *castor gras* again prohibited. With the Treaty of Utrecht the demand for *castor gras* increased, and on October 8, 1714, it was decreed that the company of Neret and Gayot would receive *castor gras* at 40 sols.[109] The agreement of 1710 was revoked, and the original agreement of 1706 restored and continued to 1717, the date of expiration of the lease.

With successful naval and military campaigns to check competition, and an increasing demand for European goods which followed, and especially with the discovery of new tribes with ample supplies of beaver, attempts to check supply were doomed. The average annual supply[110] of beaver from Canada from 1675 to 1685 was 89,588 pounds, and from 1685 to 1687, 140,000 pounds whereas the consumption of beaver in France averaged forty to forty-five thousand pounds. The surplus was sent to Holland and Europe to compete with supplies from New England and Hudson Bay. In 1685 Oudiette, *fermier du droits*, was obliged to transfer the control of the trade to Fauconnet. The hatmakers were loaded with furs at the beginning of Fauconnet's *régime*, and the increase to 1687 necessitated the appointment of Domergue. In 1692 Pointeau was appointed. In the failure of each successive appointment of men in charge of the *ferme* the problem remained unsolved. It was complicated by violent fluctuations in supply largely occasioned by the wars. In 1689 and 1693 large quantities of fur were brought down which had accumulated during the Iroquois wars. The flood of *castor sec* from the south continued as shown by Champigny in his "Mémoire pour le castor à Québec," dated October 26, 1694.[111]

It is necessary to dispose of four times the "castor sec" that were disposed of before they had developed the trade from Illinois, Miamis and

[108]"Mémoire sur les congés de faire la traitte des pelleteries chez les nations sauvages de Canada," April 12, 1703, Can. Arch., C11A, XXI, 188 ff.; see also Appendix C for an explanation of the surplus of *castor gras*.

[109]Adam Shortt, *Documents relating to Canadian Currency*, I, 195–197.

[110]See "Return of Beaver received from Canada from 1675 to 1685," *Documents relative to the Colonial History of the State of New York*, IX, 287; also "Mémoire touchant le commerce du Canada," Can. Arch., C11A, IX, 400 ff.; and "Mémoire concernant les affaires de Canada, avril, 1689," *ibid.*, X, 595; and H. A. Innis, *The Fur Trade of Canada*, Appendix A.

[111]Can. Arch., C11A, XIII, 274–276.

neighbouring places, of which the beaver taken to the south are not so well furnished with hair nor so fine as those of the north, they are also badly prepared and have thick skins and the"fermiers" found themselves loaded with this quantity of large beaver of which they only dispose in proportion to "le gras" and not having a quantity in conformity to the "sec" means that in the sale to the hatmakers less of the "gras" and more of the "sec" is used so that the hatmakers cannot make good hats without ruining themselves. If they ask why at other times there was more of the "gras" than the "sec" it was that the French traded the merchandise with the Indians according to the manner in which they killed their beaver. When they could not make it themselves, they did not carry so much merchandise to the Indians who made the robes of their beaver which they "engraissoient" in order to cover themselves and did not take the trouble to accumulate as many of the dry and brought only those which were well prepared and the great part suitable for the Russian trade.

The reason that these last discovered nations of the coast of the south did not prepare their beaver better was that they had never worn the skins since they had been of no value to them before they traded with the French, whereas the Algonquins which were one of the first nations discovered wore the beaver at all times for clothing. "Les fermiers" delude themselves in saying that they could not choose the beaver as they had in other times; they have never chosen it; they have always taken all that the country produced but they could say that before the trade in beaver with the southern nations and, from the liberty which they have given to the French of going to search in all the distant tribes, they brought here only the good beaver, well sorted and more of "gras" than of the others. Since the English were masters of the beaver trade of Hudson Bay especially of Fort Nelson they had sufficient to furnish Holland, Germany and Spain; fifty thousand of beaver from these quarters gave more material for the hatmakers to manufacture good hats than two hundred thousand of those brought from the nations of the south; since they obtained more fur on a small beaver of the north than on a large beaver of the south which might weigh two pounds—this is the reply which they would make to the demands of "Mes. les Fermiers generaux" since the English have better beaver than us, the country being much colder, and the source of better and finer furs. By the agreement which "Mes. les fermiers" have made for the beaver trade of this country they are obliged to take for different prices all the beaver which the inhabitants purchase from the Indians—if they find today such a large number of bad skins it is only since they have traded with the nations of the south.

On January 1, 1697, the *fermier* had on hand 850,185 *livres* of beaver which it was estimated could be consumed in ten years. On February 10, 1696, the following estimate was made:

150,000 castors at 3 *l.*	450,000	
Price of farm from King	120,000	
Returns of Canada in France at 12%	54,000	
Expense of bureau at Quebec	12,000	
Transportation and storage in France	10,000	
Total	646,000	
Returns 150,000 castors at 100 sols		750,000
Duty at Quebec, wines, etc.		25,000
Tadoussac		12,000
1/10 orignaux and domain		3,000
		790,000
		646,000
Profit		144,000

A comparison of the actual receipts from 1697 to 1699 shows the inadequacy of the estimate. In 1697 over 200,000 *livres* were received, in 1698, 103,000, and in 1699, 296,000. In four years[112] 696,923 *livres* had been received, of which 373,271 *livres* were *castor sec*. The following contemporary account outlines the problems of the period:

From this information the Council recognizes two things which serve to influence the future of this commerce. The first is that the beaver trade in France and Europe is limited to a certain consumption beyond which there is no sale and the beaver remains a pure loss to those charged with the conduct of the trade. If this trade could be extended beyond these limits all those through whose hands it passes successively and the King should not suffer these losses. The second is that the interests of Canadians consist in being able to sell yearly the greatest amount possible since unfortunately for them it is the only trade to which they are attached and from which they can obtain the greatest profit for themselves and the state, but it is not sufficient to Canadians to have the desire to sell, it is necessary that they should find at the same time people who wish to purchase and to pay and this does not appear to be possible.

A final experiment[113] was inaugurated in the formation of the Company of Canada (October 15, 1701)[114] which included among its

[112]Can. Arch., C11A, XIII, 441 ff., also XXXV, 285; see Appendix C.

[113]"Sur un mémoire contenant trois manières pour la disposition du castor de Canada," Can. Arch., C11A, X, 549–552. On the general difficulties of "les fermiers du Roy" see "Sur le mémoire de M. de Champigny concernant le castor," n.d., *ibid.*, XIII, 277–280.

[114]*Edits,* I, 280–283. See "Beaver Trade Agreement," between Guigue and the colony of Canada, in Canada, Public Archives, *Report,* 1928, pp. 32–44.

shareholders the important merchants of New France. It was expected that regulations for control would be more effectively enforced by enlisting their support. It was arranged that the beaver already in the hands of the *fermier* should be taken to Lyons, Marseilles, Nantes, and Saint-Malo, manufactured in those cities, and the product sold in all countries except Holland, Sweden, Denmark, the Hanseatic towns, and the ports of the Baltic Sea, and Russia. The new company was given control of those countries and of the remaining areas of France. La Rochelle was named as the *entrepôt* of the trade to which the furs were to be imported, and from which they were to be exported free of duty.[115] The company also entered into an agreement[116] with Gayot, Bouélet, and Pasquier, a Paris firm, to sell its furs. It began with about 700,000 *livres* of beaver for which it had paid 470,000 livres (about 15 sols per *livre*), plus 456,900 livres worth of beaver left over from 1699. In five years, including 1704, it had received beaver valued at 1,020,338 livres at Quebec, and 335,870 livres from Detroit, Fort Frontenac, and Hudson Bay. The total cost was therefore 2,283,108 livres. Of this, 889,065 *livres* had been sold in France, and 1,045,340 *livres* in Holland, making total receipts 1,934,405 livres, of which commissions, expense, and interest had absorbed 835,260 livres. Moreover, the Company had lost on its farming rights during the period.[117] At the beginning of 1705 there were bills of exchange outstanding against the Company to the extent of 1,607,249 livres,[118] and it was obliged to sell its right to Aubert, Neret, and Gayot, May 10, 1706— confirmed by Arrêt du Conseil, July 24, 1706. This company agreed[119] to take over all the obligations and rights of the Company of Canada for twelve years, ending December 31, 1717. The trade in *castor gras* was forbidden during the first six years, and permitted to the extent of thirty thousand per year during the last six years at 40 sols *la livre*. Since the company was unable to dispose of its supply of *castor gras* during the first six years, a new arrangement[120] was made May 19, 1710, by which the company was not obliged to receive *castor gras* during the last six years, but in compensation the price of *castor sec* was raised from 30 sols to 34 sols per *livre*. With these measures the supply was, to some extent, brought under control.

[115]Arrest du Conseil d'Etat du Roy du 9 fevrier, 1700, Can. Arch., Coll. Moreau Saint Méry, VIII, Pt. II, 50–54.

[116]November 9, 1701, Can. Arch., C11A, XIX, 1701, 230–231.

[117]P. Margry, *Découvertes et établissements*, V, 202.

[118]See a detailed statements of accounts, "Raisons du mauvais état des affaires de la Colonie de Canada, à Paris de 27 janvier, 1705," Can. Arch., C11A, XXIII, 5 ff.

[119]*Edits*, I, 302–304. [120]*Ibid.*, pp. 321–322.

The problem of the fur trade in restricting supply was greatly complicated by changes in the home market in France in Europe. With a marked increase in the supply of poorer grades of beaver,[121] there was a decline in demand. Denys in *The Description and Natural History of the Coasts of North America*, published in 1672, noted a falling off in the demand for beaver hats.[122] "Those skins have had formerly a great vogue when the beaver hats were popular but they are not so much (in fashion) at present." Attempts had been made as early as 1634 to regulate the use of beaver in the manufacture of hats.[123] The *demi-castor* was prohibited and provision made for the increasing consumption of beaver in regulations of October 13, 1664; June 21, 1666; April 15, 1673; April, 1690; October 13, 1699; August 10, 1700. These regulations were evaded in numerous ways, and in 1706 the ban against *demi-castors* was lifted. On February 8, 1685,[124] an agreement (confirmed April 12, 1685) for one year was made by "le fermier du Domaine d'Occident et Nouvelle France" in which all beaver was sold to the "Maistres Chapeliers" of Paris, to enforce closer supervision of the manufacture. In 1697 the *ferme* was transferred to Guigues (representing a Paris corporation), who planned to increase demand by manufacturing woollen clothing from beaver fur.[125] These plans were indices of the seriousness of the problems rather than remedies.

The increasing use of larger proportions of poor, dry beaver in the manufacture of hats seriously injured the trade. Changes in style, which favoured smaller hats, decreased consumption. The *demi-castor* hat had come into favour in spite of regulations.[126]

Besides the decline of the sale caused by beaver coming from foreign countries there has developed the fashion of small and light hats and

[121]By the 1650's because of the expense of beaver fur from Canada, it became customary to make "half-beaver" hats, of a mixture of half beaver and half a cheaper fur. In 1664 the manufacture of such adulterated hats was forbidden under penalty of a fine of 200 livres and confiscation of wares. In June, 1666, a further penalty of loss of the status of Master, and later other penalties, followed. A new decree of April 15, 1673, levied a penalty against adulteration of 3,000 livres. C. W. Cole, *Colbert and a Century of French Mercantilism*, II, 413–414.

[122]Pp. 362–363.

[123]*Les Chapeaux de castor.*

[124]Can. Arch., Coll. Moreau Saint Méry, VI, 290–291.

[125]The *Dictionnaire de commerce* gives the date of this experiment as 1699. A factory was set up at Faubourg St. Antoine but the product was found to be unsatisfactory for various reasons.

[126]"Mémoire touchant le commerce de Canada," Can. Arch., C11A, IX, 400 ff.

especially those which prejudice the rules of the hat trade, the small hat-makers (bastimers) who along with the trimmers mix in the beaver hats prohibited material such as the fur of rabbit, "lièvre" and others.

Substitutes became more popular and occasioned a decline. Champigny, in a letter dated September 23, 1699, wrote of

the great quantities of hats of vigogne, palatine and other species which they have invented and manufactured for nearly twenty years which are sold at a much lower price and of which they have made a very large trade in France and in foreign countries which prohibit the entrance of beaver.[127]

During the wars of the Spanish Succession (1700 to 1713) *laine de vigogne*, a wool[128] from a species of llama in Peru, was used instead of *castor gras* to mix with *castor sec* for the manufacture of hats.

The effect of a decline in the consumption of beaver for the manufacture of beaver hats on the price of beaver was especially marked because of the high percentage of the cost of raw material to the total cost. In 1696 it was estimated[129] that the total cost of manufacture of a hat was 14 livres 10 sols, including 30 to 35 sols per hat to the workers who fashioned the hat from the felt, 20 to 25 sols to the dyers, the cost of from eight to ten ounces of beaver fur, of which five to six ounces were obtained from each pound of beaver, 5 livres per pound, or a maximum of 10 livres per hat, and the cost of cleaning the felt, removing the guard hairs, preparing the hides, shearing and sorting the fur for the felting machine, or about 4 livres 10 sols per hat. The hats were sold wholesale and retail by the master hatmakers and netted 24 livres, giving a profit of 9 livres, 10 sols per hat. Roughly one-third of the final sale price was absorbed in profits, one-third in the price of raw material, and the remainder for labour and manufacture. The pronounced fall in the price of beaver in 1700[130] was a result of these factors.

The market suffered also from the effects of the revocation of the Edict of Nantes in 1685[131] The position of La Rochelle, an important depot of the trade, and of France, received a severe blow. Beaver was

[127]Can. Arch., Coll. Moreau Saint Méry, VI, 297.
[128]Can. Arch., C11A, XIV, 1696, 438.
[129]Can. Arch., C11A, XIV, 444–446.
[130]*Documents relative to the Colonial History of the State of New York*, ed. E. B. O'Callaghan, IV, 789.
[131]"Mémoire au sujet du castor," October 26, 1722, Can. Arch., C11A, XLIV, 202–206; also *ibid.*, XXXIV, 206.

sent from France to La Rochelle and distributed to various markets. In this city, hats of the best qualities, smooth, glossy, and *à poil*, were made and sold to the French. After being worn, they were returned and filled with gum, making them hard and short haired, and sold to Spain. They were again returned and put up in small styles, sent to Lisbon, and thence to Brazil. Finally, worn full of holes, they were taken to the African coast by the Portuguese. The migration of skilled work-men[132] from France was a direct loss to France, and a gain to the fur trade and the hatmaking industry of other countries.[133] In 1701 it was found necessary to import workmen from England to make fine hats.

The foreign markets were not adequate to absorb the increasing surplus following the decline in consumption in the home market. Indeed, these foreign markets also became less profitable. *Castor sec*, which arrived in the autumn in France, was usually sold in the follow-ing spring, a portion to the hatmakers of France, a portion to Russia, and a portion, the heavy skins with flat hair, to Germany for the manufacture of sleeves and furs. Denys wrote:

[Beaver skins] are used, nevertheless, for furs in Germany, Poland, Russia, or other cold countries to which they are sent. Although there are some of them in Russia, the hair is not so beautiful nor so long. Besides they have a secret in that country which we have not yet in France, that of removing from a skin of beaver all the down without injuring the long hair. Thus the skin is used for fur with the long hair; and they send the down to France, and it is that which is called Russian Wool. In France the long hair is cut from the skin in order to obtain the down, and the long hair is lost. But the skin is used to make slippers or *mules* of the Court-

---

[132]G. Martin, *La Grande Industrie sous le règne de Louiv XIV*, p. 296. For a general discussion of the decline of French manufactures at this period, see Henri Sée, *L'Evolution commerciale et industrielle de la France sous l'ancien régime*, pp. 148 ff. For advantages to England see *The Victoria History of the County of Surrey*, ed. H. E. Malden, II, 363. On the effects of the disruption of the trade in England through the oversupply of furs in France, the Courtbooks of the Company of Feltmakers in the Guildhall Library, London, are suggestive. On the French guilds, René de Lespinasse, *Les Métiers et Corporations de la ville de Paris*, Histoire Générale de Paris, tome III, and E. Levasseur, *Histoire des classes ouvrières en France depuis la conquête de Jules César jusqu'à la Révolution.*

[133]Hatmakers moved from Caudebec to Wandsworth, England. R. C. Poole, *A History of the Huguenots of the Dispersion and the Recall of the Edict of Nantes*, p. 92. Within ten or twelve years before 1698 the great export of hats to Holland from Rouen disappeared. Many hat manufacturers had moved to Holland and England from Rouen and Caudebec and production was only equal to the wants of the country (*ibid.*, p. 172). The Edict of Nantes was significant to the fur trade of Canada in injuring the industry in France.

house at Paris [also for covering boxes, trunks and cut into strips for making sieves for grain].

Muscovie beaver was sold in Amsterdam or Rotterdam either directly, or on commission to Russia. This grade was sold by the skin although bought by the pound in Canada. The first vessels in April and May, and later *la grande flotte* in June and July, took the furs to Russia. An elaborate organization had grown up as shown in the specialization of the market. Special grades were sent to various countries, for example, white fur to England where white hats were in demand. The underneath fur of the beaver skins was used in Holland and the backs sent to Russia. Following wars with Spain, the Indies market was closed, and wars with Holland, England, and the northern countries destroyed the organization of the trade. Through competition of furs from England the sale of beaver to Russia declined from twenty-five to thirty thousand skins per year to fifteen to eighteen thousand skins. The cheaper *Muscovie* or Russian wool or fur, returned from Russia, entered into competition with the fur sold direct to the hatmakers of France. Holland became an important competitor, especially with the stimulus of heavy import duties in France, and the low prices of furs. England also shared in the trade with large shipments of furs.

The serious effects on the colony of the failure to control supply were accentuated through the decline in demand, and the disorganization of the trade in Europe, and were seriously complicated with the increasing trade of the English. The misfortunes of New France and France were the opportunities of the English colonies and England. As already suggested, in the earlier part of the period prior to the valorization scheme of 1675 the tax of one-fourth was a direct incentive to smuggling especially with the decline in prices.[134] The *fermiers* complained of evasion of the taxes:

Saying that by the liberty they have permitted to the foreign merchants for some years to receive the furs in their warehouses for better facilitating the trade with the inhabitants; under the good faith by which they brought the said furs to the bureau of the said company to have them acquitted of the accustomed rights when they wished to load them for France in the boats; that nevertheless many of the said merchants and others serving them send their furs to distant habitations to load them for France after the boats have raised anchor in this road . . . which robs "la ferme" of the said rights and the commerce. These miscreants could sell the furs at a better

[134]See "Mémoire du Sr. de la Chesnaye sur le Commerce du Canada—sur l'impossibilité de former une Nouvelle Compie parere qui puisse se soustenir et secourir le pays" (1667).

price in France not having paid the duties of those who religiously observed the payments.[135]

In the latter part of the period, with a further decline in prices, smuggling to Gaspé became more pronounced. A letter from Pontchartrain, dated Versailles, July 7, 1690, stated:

When the voyageurs have unloaded the returns of their trade in beavers at Montreal, which they have brought from the Indians, with the merchants of Quebec who come to meet them at Montreal the voyageur suffers as well as the "fermier" since the merchants who come to Montreal take the beaver in payment of debts of the voyageurs and not at their true value (since they have nearly always been under the necessity of borrowing from them they are forced to take a loss in giving often "castor gras" for "castor veulle") and instead of the merchants carrying all their "castors" to the bureau at Quebec they trade them and send them to l'isle Percée where they are sent to Bilbao and elsewhere in fraud.[136]

Smuggling to the English, however, was a more serious cause of complaint. The English strengthened their hold on the Indians through the sale of cheaper goods.[137] English manufacturers were improved following the migration of craftsmen from Europe to England. A decline in the supply of beaver made necessary a greater dependence of the Indian on European cloth for wearing apparel, and the growing importance of the woollen industry in England gave the English a decided advantage in the Indian trade. In 1707 a report as to the causes of the growing trade with the English[138] made the following comment:

It is necessary to consider first the cause which makes them go there. The chief cause is that they do not find with us certain "draps rouge et bleu d'aulne et un cart de large" or they are forced to purchase them more dearly than from the English, and also powder and lead,[139] these three chief articles our resident Indians make a pretext to go to find among the English and by the same means purchase also other merchandise which they could get from us.

[135]"Requeste du Sr. Bazire, commis de Messieurs de la Compagnie des Indes Occidentales presentée à Monsieur Talon, Intendant de la Nouvelle France," Can. Arch., Coll. Moreau Saint Méry, IV, Pt. I, 167–168; see also a reply of the merchants denying the charge, *ibid.*, p. 174.

[136]Can. Arch., C11A, XI, 216.

[137]*Ibid.*, XXVII, 1707, 76–77.

[138]"Mémoire où l'on propose à la cour les moyens de retablir de commerce avec les sauvages de Canada pour les empeschers de porter leurs castors et pelleteries à la colonie Anglaise," Can. Arch., C11A, XXVII, 76–77.

[139]Lead was imported by France from Germany.

In a joint letter from Vaudreuil and Bégon, dated Quebec, November 15, 1713,[140] the growing importance of English manufactures was apparent.

The fur trade is also considerably diminished by the excessive prices of the merchandise, the English profit from this disagreeable circumstance, draw among them the Indians as much by the cheap prices as by the character of the merchandise which they supply them especially "des draps de Limbourg et Ecarlatines." You informed us last year that His Majesty had given orders to have goods manufactured in the kingdom to imitate them which is very much to be desired for this country or if they would not suffer the entrance of any foreign goods, since necessity has no law, Srs. de Vaudreuil and Bégon believe that if they could not be obtained in France of this quality it is important for sustaining the Colony that His Majesty should permit them to be sent from England to France to be loaded on the armed vessels for this colony.

The Indians insisted upon "un drap bleu, une raye blanche large comme le petit doigt proche de la lizière, et a l'écarlatine rouge une lizière plus noire."[141] In 1714 *écarlatines* of English manufacture were sent out, and in 1715 an imitation manufactured in Languedoc. The imitation was immediately detected. "They are neither as strong nor as closely knit as those of England. They are lighter and consequently have less wool." The Indians became as expert in judging cloth as "les plus habiles negotians."[142] The superiority of English woollen goods which was regarded as partly a result of the policy of the English government toward the industry,[143] and the more rapid turnover of goods traded through Fort Orange, were factors which stimulated trade between Montreal and New England.[144] This superiority was characteristic of other manufactures, and in 1716 it was held[145] that the French were superior only in powder, but the English woollen industry was

[140]Can. Arch., C11A, XXXIV, 7–8.

[141]"Mémoire sur les Ecarlatines," Can. Arch., C11A, XXXV, 331.

[142]"Réponses aux propositions du député du commerce de Languedoc sur les Escarlatines, 9 octobre 1716," *ibid.*, XXXVI, 144–145.

[143]"Mémoire sur la fabrique des Escarlatines et sur le commerce qui s'en fait en Canada et celuy des Castors 11 mai 1716," *ibid.*, pp. 370–372; see also H. Heaton, *The Yorkshire Woollen and Worsted Industries from the Earliest Times up to the Industrial Revolution*, chap. viii.

[144]See a letter dated Quebec, November 7, 1715, Can. Arch., C11A, XXXV, 53–55; also a letter dated May 23, 1719, *ibid.*, XL, 231; also *ibid.*, XCIII, 8–9.

[145]February 1716, *ibid.*, XXXVI, 119. For a general discussion of English superiority in strouds, rum, and other commodities, see Cadwallader Colden, *History of the Five Indian Nations of Canada*, pp. 31–32.

of fundamental importance to the fur trade, and eventually to the control of Canada by England.

Smuggling was further encouraged by the various changes in prices and grades. The refusal to accept *castor gras* after 1706 in order that the large supply of this grade on hand should be absorbed had un-expected results on the trade. The Indians formerly encouraged to secure *castor gras* regarded this change as an act of bad faith. Since considerable time was necessary to produce this grade, and since the announcement of its rejection required considerable time to spread to the remote interior, the Indians were left with supplies of fur which had formerly been regarded as the most valuable grade.[146] The results are suggested in the following extract.

In this country the entire exclusion of "castor gras" in their receipts dur-ing a certain number of years has appeared unfortunate since this is the best quality of beaver which could not be refused from the Indians without persuading them that it was bad faith. These Indians have remembered that in previous years everyone had recommended them most particularly to bring their "castor" after it had been made "gras." The Canadians have then been under obligations to receive the "castor gras" from the Indians but at the same time it was necessary to suffer loss. This has resulted either in selling fraudulently in France and from there in Holland or in carrying to New England in all sorts of ways. What has been pernicious for the commerce of France is that in this way they have furnished to foreigners the best material for the hats as well for the quality as the fashion, which has produced a good merchandise, which has given them the preference in the sale so much that our French manufacturers have failed since they have had only the old on hand which has made our hatmaking of a bad quality and the cause of complaint.

Clandestine trade grew up with New England, and other European countries[147] gained a fresh supply of the best beaver fur, whereas France was obliged to consume the supplies of old beaver, much to the detriment of manufacturers.[148]

For many years Portugal and Spain (which have a great market for hats in the trade to the Indies), Germany and other countries drew their hats from manufacturers in England. The Company when it wishes to fix the price of beaver in Canada proportionally to that which the English give would have in its hands all the beaver which Canada could produce, it

[146]"Chefs concernans le Canada pour l'année 1707," Can. Arch., C11A, XXVII, 94–95, also XXXIV, 206.

[147]See "Délibération faite au Bureau au Corps des Maîtres Chapeliers de Paris le janvier 1715," *ibid.*, XXXV, 388.

[148]*Ibid.*, XCIII, 10–11.

might hold the price in France on the basis of a profit and procure to the manufacturers of France the real advantage of finding in Spain, Portugal and Germany and in the other countries the same consumption which they had at other times, and which the English enjoy today to their prejudice, and which they should enjoy no more since their colonies could produce very few beaver and their manufactures of hats would decline through a lack of supply of material if they could not draw from Canada the greatest part.

With the exhaustion of the old supplies of beaver, and the falling off in the supply of *vigogne* after 1713, the hatmakers complained of the lack of *castor gras* and it was even found necessary to import this grade from England.

Prohibitions were enacted, dated June 25, 1707, and later July 6, 1709, against trade with English localities. In the latter ordinance jurisdiction over violations of these prohibitions was placed in the hands of the Conseil supérieur de Québec. Continued violations were the occasion for a regulation of May 6, 1715,[149] giving jurisdiction only to the Intendant or his representative. It was practically impossible to dissociate smuggling from political corruption. Seizures of *écarlatines* and beaver[150] traded with New England were responsible for a later ordinance of April 2, 1716,[151] prohibiting trade with Orange, Boston, Manhattan, and other English centres. Numerous records of seizures[152] and ordinances were indices of ineffective enforcement. New ordinances dealing with various features of smuggling were enacted on June 4, 1719,[153] June 2, 1720,[154] May 15, 1722,[155] and May 22, 1724.[156] On May 25, a regulation was put into effect requiring the registration of all bark canoes. But complaints[157] of illicit trade continued.

[149]*Edits*, I, 347.

[150]Notice of seizure of twenty *paquets* of beaver and *écarlatines*, September 24, 1715.

[151]Can. Arch., Coll. Moreau Saint Méry, XXXIX, Pt. II, 493 ff.

[152]Notification of seizure of foreign goods (cloth and kettles) in the hands of Sr. Dauteuil du Mousseaux; also Procès verbal de seizure d'un canot à Niagara (belonging to a Detroit *habitant*), dated October 1, 1727.

[153]Arrêt du Conseil d'Etat du Roi au sujet des fraudes du castor, *Edits*, I, 401–403.

[154]Arrêt du Conseil d'Etat du Roi concernant les marchandises étrangères, *ibid.*, pp. 404–405.

[155]Arrêt du Conseil d'Etat, *ibid.*, pp. 463–464.

[156]Déclaration du Roi au sujet des voyages qui se font de Canada en la Nouvelle Angleterre, *ibid.*, pp. 489–491.

[157]See complaints of illicit trade at the King's posts on Lake Ontario and Lake Erie, September 24, 1726, Can. Arch., Coll. Moreau Saint Méry, VIII, 378–380.

The period witnessed a continuation of the effects of the insatiable demand of the western Indians for European goods. These Indians were largely unacquainted with the canoe, with the result that an efficient organization of middlemen grew up, transporting the furs and trading goods over wide areas. Following expansion of the trade with increasing costs incidental to longer journeys, competition from the north and the south became more serious. Warfare and diplomacy were the most effective weapons. Increase in military expenditure, demand for larger numbers of men to carry goods and furs over longer distances, and for effective military control, and greater dependence of the colony on furs were inherent features of the fur trade. On the trade was based the life of the colony. The intense activity of the missionaries among the Indians, the violent disputes over the brandy question,[158] the marked interest of the governmental authorities, the break-up of paternalism in the internal trade and its continuation in the external trade, the notorious lack of control over the traders, and the colony's lack of development[159] were essential characteristics of a community dependent on furs. The problems of the colony were co-incident with the domination of the larger merchants in its regulation policy. The concentrated control of the trade enabled them to protest effectively against changes in the price level which endangered their interests.

The success of the military policy of the French had within itself the seeds of failure. The persistent demand of the newly discovered tribes of Indians especially to the south greatly increased the supply of poorer furs, and reduced prices, in the face of increasing costs incidental to longer distances to be covered in transporting commodities and furs. Moreover, the revenue which depended primarily on the fur trade declined with the fall in the price of furs while the need for revenue with new military ventures became more urgent. The inflation policies of the government were an inevitable result. Finally inflation, decline in the price of furs, and cheaper goods of the English made

[158]See Mack Eastman, *Church and State in Early Canada*, passim; W. B. Munro, "The Brandy Parliament of 1678"; *Documents relative to the Colonial History of the State of New York*, IX, 131, 144, 441. See a later memorial as to the effects of the sale of liquor to Indians, Father Lafitau, *Jesuit Relations*, LXVII, 41–45.

[159]For a description of the economic development of the colony see E. Salone, *La Colonisation de la Nouvelle-France*, quatrième, cinquième et sixième parties; also F. Parkman, *The Old Régime in Canada*, chap. xx; but more especially L. Gérin, "Le Gentilhomme français et la colonisation," pp. 81–85.

competition more serious, and military ventures more necessary. From the vicious circle of the fur trade the colony had no escape.

The demand of the Indians for European goods and the marked increase in the supply of furs was significant for France as well as for New France. The supply of furs fluctuated violently as new tribes were discovered or as campaigns were lost and won. The demand for the finished products, chiefly beaver hats, as a luxury, gave in the beginning a favourable market, and produced large profits. But, with the vagaries of fashion, the demand fell off and profits disappeared with disastrous results to the colony. Commodities to exchange for furs were manufactured on a larger scale, and served to stimulate the economic life of France. On the other hand fluctuations in the market for furs reacted on industrial life and affected her position. The economic and institutional life of Europe had reached a period of comparative adjustment and balance previous to the discovery of the New World. The economic and institutional life of France undoubtedly suffered material disarrangement through the importation of furs on a large scale from New France. It was the contact between the Indian civilization of North America and the European civilization, as brought by the French, which produced a disturbance disastrous to the Indian peoples and of profound importance to the French and to Europeans. The contrast between diverse cultures produced a disaster for which no remedy was adequate.

5. The Expansion of Trade to the Saskatchewan and the Northwest (1713-1763)

THE Treaty of Utrecht in 1713 deprived the French of the forts in Hudson Bay, and reopened competition with the Hudson's Bay Company in that area, while in the south competition continued and became more effective.

The smuggling organization which had grown up with the English on the south in the earlier period, and especially during the war, persisted. Colden describes this organization as centring around the Iroquois who had deserted to the French at the instigation of the French priests. These "Praying Indians" were chiefly interested in the trade between Albany and Montreal, and the importance of the organization was shown in unsuccessful attempts of the English to further direct Indian trade, rather than indirect trade through the French. An Act passed in New York in 1720, for encouragement of the Indian trade, prohibited all trade between New York and New France for three years since it was claimed that the French had engrossed the Indian trade through English goods. The result[1] was a marked decline in New York trade, and an increase in the number of European goods coming directly to New France.

The success of the smuggling organization was largely dependent on the cheaper and superior English goods which continued to exercise an important influence throughout the period. In the manu-

[1]See a Petition of the Merchants of London to His Majesty against the said Act (Extract of the Minutes of the Right Honourable the Lords Commissioners for Trade and Plantations, July, 1724); Papers relating to an Act of the Assembly of the Province of New York for Encouragement of the Indian Trade, Cadwallader Colden, *History of the Five Indian Nations of Canada*, pp. 7 ff.

On the other hand, proponents of the Act contended that the policy of prohibition of trade with the French had the effect of bringing Indians to trade with the English. Cheaper lines of English goods were regarded as a determining factor. See especially the Report of the Committee of Council of the Province of New York in answer to the said Petition, November 6, 1724 (*ibid.*, pp. 12 ff.). For an excellent discussion of the effects of the policy and of its final breakdown, see Peter Wraxall, *An Abridgement of the Indian Affairs*, ed. C. H. McIlwain, pp. lxv ff.; also E. J. Devine, *Historic Caughnawaga*, chaps. v-vii.

facture of staple goods for the fur trade the English had improved their position. La Galissonière and Bigot reported in a joint letter dated Quebec, October 20, 1748, that:

The English have the better of us in the quality of merchandise in two important articles. The first is kettles—the second is cloth. They believe that up to the present the Indians wish only English cloth and they have become so well accustomed to it that it would be difficult to introduce others, but it is well to observe that it is the French contraband traders who have given them this opinion.[2]

A year later in a letter dated Quebec, November 8, 1749, complaints were made as to French kettles. "They have asked for kettles of yellow copper in bales of one hundred pounds each, the one in the other, assorted by size each bale of twenty-five to thirty kettles. Those which they have sent are almost all of the same size, badly made and too heavy for the Indians."[3] Again protests were made in the same year, in a letter dated Quebec, October 1, 1749, as to cloth as well as kettles.

The red cloth is brown and "point battu"; the blue is equally of a very inferior quality to that of England and it is not surprising that when they send envoys among the Indians they find no favour. The Company consents to supply the kettles; "Mrs. de la Galissonière et Bigot" do not propose to engage them; they desire only that they shall give orders for kettles of a good quality and not with iron "dans le tour du chaudron et aux oreilletes"; these must be supplied by the traders who suffer if the Company makes them.[4]

The advantage of a cheap supply of rum obtained by the English from the West Indies was a source of frequent comment in the documents of the period. The effects of English competition were serious.

The English pay for the beaver on the basis of 4l. 12s. "la livre" in letters of exchange on London payable in crowns at 48 to the mark to the profit of merchants and voyageurs from Montreal. They exchange beaver with the Indians on the same basis in merchandise which gives them a better return than the French could give them, while the Company paid in letters of exchange at long terms at 52s. 3d. "la livre" deduction from the profit of 5% for tare. It is reasonable that the difference in price should act as a powerful incentive to engage the Indian, the merchant and the voyageur to carry beaver to the English colonies.[5]

[2]Can. Arch., C11A, XCI, 47–48.
[3]Can. Arch., C11A, XCIII, 371.
[4]Ibid., p. 4.
[5]Ibid., pp. 8–9.

The successful competition of the English became especially disastrous during the Seven Years' War. The situation was summarized in a document discussing escarlatines, dated presumably about 1758.

Escarlatines from England are an indispensable necessity for the beaver trade in Canada. To get these escarlatines, which they have up to the present tried in vain to imitate in France, the Company is obliged to bring them from England to Holland and from Holland to France on neutral boats. . . . But to bring them from France to Canada the Company ships up to the present in merchant boats. It has sustained more severe losses than the trade could support and it cannot expect that the risks will become less than they have been in the past. In 1756 it lost 300 pieces in a total of 1160; in 1757, 370 pieces in 660. The increase in freight which in ordinary times is only around 65 per ton for escarlatines, and the loss which the Company sustains on this trade (and to the exhorbitant price is added insurance of 60 to 80%) place it under the indispensable obligation of increasing the price of escarlatines from 50 to 100. The escarlatines are paid for by the Company before leaving Europe. It must create a fund for the beaver it receives in return, its agents deprived of these funds are obliged to draw on them in letters of exchange payable in March, April and May following, with the result that the Company requires double and triple the funds and without any new increase in the sale price in proportion to the prejudice which they suffer through the delay in the return of funds.[6]

The position of English trade was strengthened not only through the growing importance of a smuggling organization, and cheaper and superior goods, but also through the increasing numbers of experienced English traders. In order to develop trade in the interior by way of Lake Ontario the English found it necessary to establish posts at strategic points. The establishment of Oswego in 1722 gave access to Lake Ontario, and stimulated Indian trade.[7] The importance of this move was recognized by the French as shown in the following extract from a letter of May 25, 1725.

The Marquis de Vaudreuil observes, that he received intelligence on the eighth of December, that the English and Dutch had projected an establishment at the mouth of the Choüaguen river [Oswego], on the banks of Lake Ontario, and pretty convenient to the post we have at Niagara.

The news of this establishment on territory which has been considered, from all time, to belong to France, appeared to him so much the more important as he was sensible of the difficulty of preserving Niagara, where there is no fort, should the English be once fortified at Choüaguen, and that

[6]*Ibid.*, CIII (2), 542–546.
[7]Oswego was re-established in 1759 by Henry Van Schaak of Albany. F. W. Barnes, "The Fur Traders of Early Oswego," p. 134.

the loss of Niagara would entail at the same time that of the entire Indian trade of the Upper Country; for these nations go the more readily to the English, as they obtain goods much cheaper, and as much Rum as they please, from them.[8]

The fears of the French on the establishment of this post and other posts were justified.[9] In a letter dated May 7, 1726, it was noted that Sr. Longueuil

has found 100 English at the portage of the river Oswego with more than 60 canoes at four leagues from Lake Ontario who forced him to exhibit his passport and showed him an order from the Governor of New York requiring them not to let any Frenchman pass without a passport. . . . He has seen in his voyage more than 100 Indian canoes which carried furs to the English to exchange for "l'eau de vie." He has also met many canoes of Nipissing and Saulteur Indians coming from Lake Huron to trade with the English. From the proceedings of the English, it is known that they wish to make an establishment at Niagara to prevent one which he had proposed to make there. They have been in the same summer a league and a half from Fort Frontenac and have drawn from there nearly all the Indians through the attraction of "l'eau de vie," which is a considerable loss to these two posts. He has learned from the other side that the English from Carolina have built two houses and stores on a small river which discharges into the Wabash where they trade with the Miamis and the Ouyatanons and other Indians of the "pays d'en haut."[10]

In 1727 it was reported that 57 canoes with 738 packs of beaver and deerskin arrived at Oswego. A letter dated Quebec, November 12, 1736, stated regarding the trade on Lake Ontario:

As for the commerce now carried on at Fort Frontenac and Niagara, it becomes every year more inconsiderable in comparison to the expenses the king incurs there. These two posts which produced some years ago as much as 52,000 lb. of peltries, have these four years past returned only 25 @ 35,000 lb. [11]

[8]Documents relative to the Colonial History of the State of New York, ed. E. B. O'Callaghan, IX, 949.

[9]See argument regarding probable establishment of control at Toronto 1720–30, in P. J. Robinson, Toronto during the French Régime, chap. v.

[10]Can. Arch., C11A, XLVIII, 360–365.

[11]Documents relative to the Colonial History of the State of New York, IX, 1049.

The decline in the trade of Fort Frontenac and Fort Niagara was evident in a comparison of returns from these posts. See "Etat de la vente des Pelleteries provenantes de traittes faittes du Fort Frontenac, 1716, 1717, and 1718," Can. Arch., C11A, XXXVIII, 155–158, with a detailed account of expenses

Following the construction of posts in the interior, English traders became thoroughly experienced in dealings with the Indians. By 1740 a letter to London noted that:

The Indian Trade, to the great Advantage of this Province, is now divided into several hundred Hands, and there have been for many Years past upwards of one hundred young Men of this Province, who have gone yearly among the Indians, to supply them with our Goods.

By this means, at a modest estimate, I am assured, that the Indian Trade of this Province is now far above five times as much as when Governor Burnet began to put his Scheme in execution.

And this is not all the Advantages reaped thereby, but a much more considerable one to this, and all the other English Colonies is, that not only our own six Nations, but also many far and remote Indian Nations are drawn off from their Dependance on the French, and made, by Trade and Intercourse, dependent on the English; but this means a great Security and Protection is acquired by the English, in case of a War with France; and by this trade our Settlements in this Province are extended up to the Onondagues Carrying-place, which is now well attended with waggons, for the more commodious transporting of Goods to trade in the Lakes.

And they are now settling on the Branches of Sasquehanah River; and from the western branches of this river, there is but a small land-carriage to Allegheny, a branch of that great River Mississippi; which branch extending a thousand Miles from its Mouth, where it enters the said River; and which joins so near to our Settlements, as is above taken notice of, opens as a Trade to that vast Country, called by the French Louisiana, which they possess on the Mississippi.[12]

To offset the effects of competition from the English on the south, the French followed a consistent policy of erecting military posts. In 1726 a strong fort was established at Niagara to check the trade at Oswego. A letter of May 7 of that year noted:

To prevent this establishment [Oswego] which he regarded as of dangerous consequence he proposed in concert with M. Bégon to build a stone house at Niagara and also to construct two boats to load with materials and afterward to trade and prevent the Indians from carrying their furs to the English.[13]

---

involved in carrying on the trade, 1718, *ibid.*, pp. 159–160, and "Etat de la vente des Pelleteries provenant de traittes faittes aux forts Frontenac et Niagara la présente année, 1742," *ibid.*, LXXVIII, 29.

[12]From J. A., Esq., to Mr. P. C. of London, showing the success of the measures taken at that time, New York, 1740, Cadwallader Colden, *History of the Five Indian Nations*, pp. 43–44. See V. D. Harrington, *The New York Merchant on the Eve of the Revolution*, pp. 232–233. James Alexander claimed the fur trade of New York increased five times from 1729 to 1740.

[13]Can. Arch., C11A, XLVIII, 360–365.

Detroit continued to prevent penetration to Lake Huron and Lake Michigan, and Fort Vincennes was built on the Wabash route in 1727,[14] to check trade with the Indians of Lake Michigan, and the Mississippi. At various points this line of forts gave signs of weakening and new forts were constructed.[15] In a letter dated Quebec, October 9, 1749, the dangers of the Toronto portage and the establishment of Fort Rouillé were described:

> On the advice that we have had that the Indians of the North ordinarily passed at Toronto on the west coast of Lake Ontario 25 leagues from Niagara, and 75 leagues from Fort Frontenac, to go to Oswego with their furs, we have felt that it would be advisable to establish a post in this place and send an officer there, fifteen soldiers and some workmen for constructing a small staked fort.[16]

It was found during the same period that Lake Superior Indians were trading at Oswego, and in 1751 a post was established at Sault Ste Marie as a safeguard. The establishment of posts on the Ohio to control the Ohio route precipitated the final struggle.

On the south the French were checking Iroquois and English competition by military measures. On the north, competition from the English in Hudson Bay presented a more difficult problem. The Crees and the Assiniboines secured goods from three routes: first from Fort Nelson; second, Kaministiquia; and the third, Green Bay through the Fox and the Sioux. With the renewal of competition from the English at Fort Nelson, after the Treaty of Utrecht, fresh attempts were necessary to regain the furs from these Indians. In 1710 the Assiniboines came to Kaministiquia when not prevented by the Crees and "quelques François ont pénétré dans leur pays."[17] The route to Lake Winnipeg was known in great detail in 1716[18] and Jérémie knew of the through connection from Dog Lake to Fort Bourbon during his residence at the latter point.[19] The advantages of the route by Grand Portage are mentioned as early as 1722. In a memoir dated February 3, 1717, the possibility of discovering the Western Sea through the

[14]See E. J. Benton, *The Wabash Trade Route*, esp. chap. i.

[15]Fort Toronto 1750? See P. J. Robinson, *Toronto during the French Régime*, chap. vi. See J. Macdonell's reference to ambush of Iroquois in 1743 or 1753 on the French River, in *Five Fur Traders of the Northwest*, ed. Charles M. Gates, p. 85.

[16]Can. Arch., C11A, XCIII, 46.

[17]For this memoir and the letter mentioned below, see P. Margry, *Découvertes et établissements*, VI, 14, 510.

[18]*Ibid.*, pp. 495–496.

[19]*Twenty Years of York Factory, 1694–1714: Jérémie's Account of Hudson Strait and Bay*, p. 35.

construction of three posts at Kaministiquia, Rainy Lake, and Lake Winnipeg was stressed, but it was noted that the expenses of these posts would be met by the profits of the trade, and also

by means of these posts they should prevent the Indians carrying their furs to the English, which are the most beautiful on the continent, beaver and other skins of Hudson Bay; which might force them to abandon their post, not having any other trade than with these Indians.

It is believed that these people would prefer our trade since they would find the merchandise carried to them instead of being obliged to go to Hudson Bay where they find almost no hunting or fishing and suffer very much taking more than two months to ascend the river . . . because of rapids. . . .

It is certain that these posts would prevent many Indians carrying furs to Hudson Bay and in this way the French would profit. . . .[20]

The supply of *castor gras* had declined as a result of the severe restrictions on this commodity prior to 1713, but with the Treaty of Utrecht of that year, markets were rapidly opened up. The Northwest became a promising field to support recovery in this grade. Vaudreuil in a letter dated Quebec, November 4, 1720, wrote:

If they could establish a post [Rainy Lake] it would be very advantageous for the trade of this colony, with the "castor gras" which they would obtain and which is there in abundance. This quality of beaver being necessary for the consumption of the hat-trade, they would have their furs which consist principally in the most beautiful martens and "loups cerviers," and they should engage [the Indians] imperceptibly to come to trade at Kaministiquia and turn them from going to trade at Hudson Bay.

Moreover, the supply of furs at the southern posts was on the decline, especially as a result of the Fox wars. M. Pachot in a letter dated Quebec, October, 1722, wrote regarding the establishment of two posts at Rainy Lake and among the Sioux: "These two establishments appear to be a very great necessity for the colony of Canada in that the beaver . . . is being all destroyed in all the other posts."[21] With the Sioux, and the Crees and Assiniboines at war, it was proposed that one post should be established among each, and that command should be gained over the important fur-producing area to the Northwest. La Vérendrye suggested the urgency of establishing a post among the Sioux to permit the development of trade among the Crees and the Assiniboines.[22] The second Fox war, which lasted from 1727

[20]P. Margry, *Découvertes et établissements*, VI, 501–502.
[21]*Ibid.*, VI, p. 514.   [22]*Ibid.*, p. 568.

to 1738, shut off the route to the Mississippi by the Fox River portage and Green Bay, and led to the establishment of a post among the Sioux (1727–37) as a source of trade west of Lake Superior, and as a war measure to withdraw support from the Fox. It remained to establish posts among the Crees and Assiniboines, and, as already shown, there was only one route by which these Indians could be prevented from going to Hudson Bay—the route from Kaministiquia.

The first post at Kaministiquia after 1713 was established by Sr. de la Noüe in 1717,[23] and was under his command until 1721. His successor was Sr. Deschaillons,[24] who also commanded the post of Nipigon. His wife, according to a *congé* dated June 2, 1723, sent three canoes to Kaministiquia, and in the same year a canoe and five men were sent to Nipigon. In 1724 and 1725 Madame Verchères sent a canoe and five men to Sr. de Verchères, in command at Kaministiquia at that time. In 1727 La Vérendrye was sent to the post at Nipigon. In 1728 *la dame de Varennes* was given permission to send three canoes and sixteen men to Kaministiquia, and in the following year permission was given to La Vérendrye to take two canoes with six men each with no reference to destination. In the same year (1729) Sr. Verchères returned to Nipigon with two canoes and ten men, and in 1730 his wife sent a canoe and six men to him. La Vérendrye wrote in his journal in 1729 that the territory between Lake Superior and Lake Winnipeg "is the country of moose and marten while beaver is so plentiful that the savages place little value on it and only collect the large skins which they send to the English." He apparently came down to Montreal in 1730,[25] and returned for his first trip to the interior in 1731. When they arrived at Grand Portage, La Jemeraye[26] was sent to establish Fort Saint Pierre on Rainy Lake while La Vérendrye wintered at Kaministiquia. La Jemeraye returned to Kaministiquia in 1732[27] and Jean Baptiste, the son of La Vérendrye, was dispatched to dispose of the furs at Michilimackinac and to return with the outfit from that point. La Vérendrye proceeded to Lake of the Woods and established Fort St. Charles. Jean Baptiste arrived with the outfit in November, 1732, after navigation had closed. In 1733 the canoes

[23]*Ibid.*, pp. 504 ff.   [24]*Ibid.*, p. 512.

[25]For a list of *congés* from 1681 to 1730 see "Congés et permis," *Rapport de l'archiviste de la Province de Québec pour 1921–1922*, pp. 190–223.

[26]"Vérendrye," *South Dakota Historical Collections*, VII, 133–134.

[27]*Ibid.*, pp. 137 ff.; see also *Journals and Letters of Pierre Gaultier de Varennes de la Vérendrye and his Sons*, ed. L. J. Burpee, and A. S. Morton, "La Vérendrye: Commandant, Fur-Trader and Explorer."

arrived with few supplies. On June 18, 1734, at the insistence of the Crees and the Assiniboines, La Vérendrye dispatched Sr. Cartier, a trading partner, and later his son Pierre, to establish Fort Maurepas near the mouth of the Red River. These men were later followed by La Jemeraye. La Vérendrye returned to Montreal in 1734 and came back in 1735. In that year he arranged to farm the posts to some merchants for three years, and dissolved his partnership with those who furnished supplies. In 1736 news arrived from Fort Maurepas and Roseaux, an outpost on Red River, of the death of La Jemeraye. Sr. Le Gras arrived with two loaded canoes at Fort St. Charles from Kaministiquia on June 17, 1736.

In 1736 the gap between Lake Superior and Lake Winnipeg had been bridged, but the representatives of the trading company were very reluctant to push trade farther west and were disposed to increase the trade at more convenient localities such as Fort Vermilion. Moreover, the organization of the trade to the Crees and the Assiniboines of Lake Winnipeg had destroyed the monopoly position of the Sioux, and not without protest, as was shown in the massacre[28] of La Vérendrye's son, Jean Baptiste, Father Aulneau, and nineteen *voyageurs* on Massacre Island, in the Lake of the Woods in 1736. It was necessary for the French to consolidate their position by a more aggressive policy. In 1737 Sr. La Marque, apparently one of the chief partners in the trading company, went in to assume direct control. In the same year La Vérendrye returned to Montreal, and secured support for further penetration to the interior in 1738. Documents show that he became indebted on May 31, 1738, to François Marie Soumande de Lorme, a trader of Montreal, for 6,693*l*. 12*s*. 6*d*., payable in August, 1739, and on May 27, 1738, to Louis d'Ailleboust, Sr. de Coulonges, for 2,787*l*. 4*s*. 2*d*., payable, contrary to custom, at Michilimackinac. On his journey from Kaministiquia in 1738[29] he tried to prevent war against the Sioux, and prevailed upon the Indians "to take good care of their lands, so that the French, who came from so great a distance to supply their wants, should always find the road open . . . to continue very faithful to the French . . . to hunt well, so as to satisfy the traders." Arriving at the junction of the Red and Assiniboine Rivers,

I found ten Cree huts and two war chiefs, who expected me, with a quantity of meat, having been notified that I was coming. . . . I sent for the two chiefs to my tent. I knew that they went every year to the English. . . . I told the one who had been accused of everything that had been said of

28L. P. Kellogg, *French Régime in Wisconsin,* chap. xv, esp. p. 337.
29"Vérendrye," *South Dakota Historical Collections,* VII, 324–328.

him. . . . He answered . . . "I have not been to the English for more than six years. I sent, indeed, during the last years that the French abandoned us, and it was necessary to have our wants supplied."

Later La Vérendrye informed these people that he wished "to increase the number of our children to learn to hunt on the Assiniboine and to give them intellect. I . . . recommended him to encourage these people to hunt well, to bring provisions to the French forts and to keep their word not to go to the English." In October on the way up the Assiniboine he was advised to build a fort "at the portage which goes to the Lake of the Prairies, for this is the road of the Assiniboines in going to the English. . . . Being here thou wilt stop everyone." Fort La Reine was accordingly built, and he was joined by M. de la Marque with the Sr. Nolan his brother. M. de Louvière had left Fort Maurepas to come to the Forks of the Red River and the Assiniboine to build a fort for the people of Red River. In the spring of 1739 La Vérendrye sent his son to "endeavour to prevent the Indians from going to the English."[30]

The importance of the fur trade to La Vérendrye was constantly emphasized in his journals and was the occasion for suspicion on the part of the governmental authorities in France.[31] Maurepas in a letter to Beauharnois dated Versailles, April 22, 1737, wrote "that the beaver trade had more to do than anything else with the Sieur de la Vérendrye's Western Sea expedition"—a view which he continued to hold in spite of La Vérendrye's protestations of heavy losses. La Vérendrye constantly urged the Indians to hunt for furs. In a speech to the Cree and Monsoni warriors at Fort St. Charles on May 9, 1734, he said:

"I am going down to Michillimackinac and perhaps to Montreal to carry your message to our Father and to get a supply of things that we are short of here, such as tobacco, guns and kettles, which you will get in exchange for martens and lynxes, and not for beaver, which you will use for your other needs as I promised you in the winter." [He continues in his journal:] My object in saying this was to oblige them to hunt those smaller animals which they are not accustomed to do, and at the same time to get the women to take it up and also the children of from ten to twelve, who are quite capable of it.[32]

Contrasting the advantages of trade with the French, who granted credit in the autumn, with the treatment of the English, he said:

[30]*Ibid.*, p. 347; also P. Margry, *Découvertes et établissements*, VI, 591.
[31]See *The Aulneau Collection, 1734–1745*, ed. A. E. Jones, esp. pp. 67 ff.
[32]*Journals and Letters of La Vérendrye*, ed. L. J. Burpee, pp. 179–180.

When you deal with them [the English] you have to do it as if you were
their enemies; they give you no credit; they do not allow you inside their
fort; you cannot choose the merchandise you want, but are obliged to take
what they give you through a window good or bad; they reject some of your
skins, which become a dead loss to you after you have had great trouble
in carrying them to their post. It is true that our traders sell some things
a little dearer, but they take all you have; they reject nothing, you run no
risk, and you have not the trouble of carrying your stuff a long distance.[33]

The importance of *castor gras* was constantly urged. The traders
"receive your robes after you have used them which previously were
lost. . . . I warn you not to kill beaver in summer for the traders will
not take it."

In the latter part of the period the district to the north of Lake
Winnipeg became more important. With the end of the Fox wars, and
the re-establishment of trade by the Fox portage route, the trade to
the south of Lake Winnipeg declined. Difficulties between the Sioux
and the Assiniboines were constantly in evidence. Two posts built
under La Vérendrye, one on Red River "à cinque lieues du lac" (Fort
Maurepas), and the other "à la fourche de la rivière des Assiniboels"
(Fort Rouge), had been abandoned[34] (apparently in 1739) because
of the proximity of Forts La Reine and Maurepas, the latter having
been moved to the mouth of the Winnipeg River in the same year.
In 1747 Pierre de la Vérendrye found Fort La Reine in ruins and Fort
Maurepas burned by the Indians. In 1752 LeGardeur de Saint-Pierre
found Fort La Reine burned and he was obliged to winter on Red
River.[35]

Meanwhile new posts were being established in the north. In 1737
the Crees urged the establishment of a fort at the end of Lake Winnipeg
at the entrance of the great English river (the Nelson), since there
would be a very large trade in lynx and marten "et surtout en castors
gras que l'Anglois ne reçoit point." La Vérendrye relates:

On April 10th [1739], I sent my son le Chevalier to locate some favorable place for the construction of a fort on the Lac des Prairies, following
the request which the Crees of this place have made of me, and then to
proceed to the Rivière du Poskoioac and examine below, at the entrance
at the end of Lake Winnipeg and see if he could not find an advantageous
place to construct a second post. . . .

[33]*Ibid.*, pp. 183–184.
[34]P. Margry, *Découvertes et établissements*, VI, 617; see N. M. Crouse, "The
Location of Fort Maurepas."
[35]P. Margry, *Découvertes et établissements*, VI, 630, 648.

On the 22nd [April] . . . I learned from an Indian that a large band of Assiniboines had drawn up on the Lake of the Prairies who were working on their canoes to go to the English. On the 24th, I sent Sanschagrin with a hired man to bring them here so as to turn them from going to the English.[36]

Fort Dauphin was built in 1741 on the northwest point of Lac des Prairies, and also Fort Bourbon, "dans le fond du lac Nepigon, à la décharge de la grande rivière du Poskoyac."[37] A licence was made out to Lac Bourbon in 1745. According to Prud'homme[38] Fort Dauphin was reoccupied and strengthened, and a small post called Fort Bourbon built at the mouth of Red Deer River on Lake Winnipegosis by Le Chevalier de la Vérendrye in 1748. A memorandum of La Vérendrye's, dated 1749, gives Fort Bourbon as located on Rivière aux Biches close to Lake Bourbon[39] (Cedar Lake), and another fort located at the mouth of the Saskatchewan which was abandoned in winter. The first post apparently disappeared with the later permanent occupation of the latter. In 1748 Le Chevalier built a tentative post near the forks of the Saskatchewan. A more permanent post was built in this locality in 1753 called Fort St. Louis or Nipawi. Fort Paskoyac was built at the mouth of the Carrot River on the Saskatchewan apparently after 1750.[40] A temporary fort was built up the Saskatchewan within sight of the Rocky Mountains (Fort La Jonquière), possibly near Calgary, in 1751. Hendry[41] in his journey in 1754 and 1755 found Fort à la Corne established as an outpost to Fort Paskoyac. In 1754 he found two Frenchmen at Paskoyac, the master and men having gone down to Montreal, and in 1755 he found the master and nine men—the complement of one canoe—the master and seven men having arrived in the fall. At Fort à la Corne he found six men. The effect which these posts had upon the trade of the Hudson's Bay Company was vividly described

[36]Ibid., p. 591; also Journals and Letters of La Vérendrye, ed. L. J. Burpee, p. 358.

[37]P. Margry, Découvertes et établissements, VI, 594.

[38]For a full but not entirely satisfactory discussion of western occupation, see L.-A. Prud'homme, "Pierre Gaultier de Varennes, sieur de La Vérendrye, 1685–1749" and "Les Successeurs de La Vérendrye, 1743–1755"; "The Journal of Anthony Hendry, 1754–55," ed. L. J. Burpee; B. Sulte, Mélanges historiques, X, 138–142.

[39]See a list of posts established in the Northwest in which Fort Bourbon is located at "la rivière aux Biches" about thirty leagues from the Saskatchewan; P. Margry, Découvertes et établissements, VI, 616–618.

[40]See A. S. Morton, The Journal of Duncan M'Gillivray, pp. xxiv-xxv.

[41]"The Journal of Anthony Hendry," pp. 321 ff.

by Hendry. Fort à la Corne served to supply the Indians from the North and South Saskatchewan, Fort Pasquia or Paskoyac from Cumberland Lake and Churchill River, and Fort Bourbon, the Indians from Lake Winnipegosis.

Extension of the trade to the Northwest involved an increase in the costs of transportation and greater difficulty in competing with the English. Evidence of this increase in costs of transportation, and of its effect was shown in several directions. As early as 1724 complaints were made of the expensiveness of trading in heavy and coarse skins of low value, such as bearskins.[42] In the Northwest abundant evidence existed to show that heavy furs were sent to the English in Hudson Bay. Robson claimed that attempts were made to secure heavy goods from the English for the trade. He wrote:

I have also frequently seen in the governor's hand, a letter addressed to him from the chief factor at the French settlement on Nelson river. It was written in French and Indian; and the purport of it was to establish a trade between them and the English at York-fort, for those heavy goods which the French stood in great need of, but could not bring from Canada, such as guns, kettles, tobacco, &c. and the English were desired to say, how much beaver they expected in exchange for these articles. The governor told us, that he had sent a copy of the letter to England; and added that if the Company consented to such a treaty, we should get no furs but what came through the hands of the French, who would soon have huts all the way down Nelson-river. . . . The French by kind offices and liberality in dealing, which we think of no consequence, have obtained so much influence over almost all the natives, that many of them are actually turned factors for the French at our settlements for heavy goods. This the Indians openly acknowledged to the linguist in the year 1746, just before I left York-fort.[43]

And again:

But he thinks, that the Beavers which are brought down to the Company, are refused by the French, from their being a heavy Commodity; for the Natives who come to trade with the Company, dispose of their small valuable furs to the French, and bring down their heavy Goods to the Company, in Summer when the Rivers are open, which they sell, and supply the French with European Goods, purchased from the Company.[44]

[42]See a statement as to the heavy freight charges for bearskins, November 2, 1724, Can. Arch., C11A, XLVI, 186.

[43]J. Robson, *An Account of Six Years Residence in Hudson's-Bay, from 1733 to 1736, and 1744 to 1747*, pp. 62–63.

[44]Evidence of J. Robson, *Report from the Committee Appointed to Inquire into the State and Condition of the Countries Adjoining to Hudson's Bay, and of the Trade Carried on There, . . . 24th April, 1749*, p. 216.

The Report of 1749 contained considerable evidence[45] to the same effect. Not only were the heavier furs brought to the Bay, but the heavier goods—guns, ammunition, hatchets, iron tools, Brazil tobacco —were imported from the English through the Indians. The French were obliged to accept only the lighter more valuable furs, otter and marten, and to rely increasingly on their influence among the Indians, on the use of brandy, and of conjury. Anthony Hendry[46] on his journey from Hudson Bay in 1754 and 1755 obtained an accurate picture of the situation:

May 24. The natives received from the Master [of Fort à la Corne subordinate to Fort Paskoyac] ten Gallons of Brandy half adulterated with water and when intoxicated they traded Cased Cats, Martens and good parchment Beaver skins, refusing Wolves and dressed Beaver. In short he received from the Natives nothing but what were prime Winter furs.

25 . . . It is surprising to observe what an influence the French have over the Natives. I am certain he hath got above 1000 of the richest Skins.

May 30. Paskoyac—Thin Birch rind Canoes will carry as much as an India Ships Long boat and draws little water; and so light that two men can carry one several miles with ease; they are made in the same form and slight materials as the small ones; only a thin board runs along their bottom and they can sail them when before a wind, but not else. The French talk Several Languages to perfection; they have the advantage of us in every shape; and if they had Brazile tobacco, which they have not, would entirely cut off our trade.

May 31. . . . The Indians would not set out; they have kept a continued trading with the French; and I believe many would trade all if they could persuade the French to take their heavy furs.

June 1. . . . Several Asinepoet Natives distributed their heavy Furs and Pelts that the French have refused, amongst our Indians with directions what to trade them for.[47]

An increase in the supply of furs from the new areas was consequently less important through the growing inability to compete for furs because of increasing costs of transportation.

The extent of the trade to the Northwest is suggested by the number of *congés*.[48] Following up the work of La Vérendrye, Ignace Gamelin,

---

[45]See Mr. Richard White's evidence, *ibid.*, p. 218; Christopher Bannister's evidence, *ibid.*, pp. 224–225; Alexander Browne's evidence, *ibid.*, pp. 226–227; H. Ellis, *A Voyage to Hudson's-Bay*, pp. 212–213.

[46]The name is now spelled Henday.

[47]"The Journal of Anthony Hendry," pp. 352–353.

[48]See "Congés de traite," 1739–1752, *Rapport de l'archiviste de la Province de Québec pour 1922–1923*, pp. 192–265. See also later volumes.

a partner of M. de la Marque, secured two *congés* in 1739, one for three canoes and eighteen men, under Sr. Neveu, and one for four canoes and twenty-eight men under Sr. Maugras for the "poste de l'Ouest." In 1740 the same individual dispatched five canoes and thirty-two men, under Baptiste Pomainville. It is difficult to follow the relationship of La Vérendrye to the traders La Marque and Gamelin, but apparently an agreement continued after the expiration of La Vérendrye's farming lease in 1738. On November 12, 1740, La Vérendrye contracted to pay La Marque and Gamelin seventy-five packages of beaver but it was claimed he only delivered nine. On September 9, 1742, Sr. La Marque & Company was paid fifty-six bales by Sr. Verchères on La Vérendrye's account and twenty-four more were sent to Sr. Le Gras on account of goods left by that Company in the west. In the same years the general policy of leasing posts was changed, and all the posts were farmed out to traders reserving a certain allowance for the officers, but apparently the *fermiers* or traders were given little encouragement by the officers in full control. In any case La Vérendrye was not required to pay the assessment of 3,000*l*. on his *ferme* in that year, and it was claimed that he was 50,500*l*. in debt. In 1743 Sr. Maugras for La Vérendrye secured two *congés*, one for two canoes and twelve men, under Joseph Laviolette, and one for six canoes and forty-six men. In 1744 La Vérendrye was replaced by Sr. Noyelles. In the same year Sr. Maugras purchased the farm of Kaministiquia for three years for 3,000 livres. In 1745 the same individual secured three *congés*, one to Lac Bourbon with three canoes and twenty men, under Phillippe Leduc, one to Forts Maurepas and St. Charles with three canoes and eighteen men, and one to Forts La Reine and Dauphin with five canoes and thirty men. In the same year he secured three *congés* with one canoe and six men each for Kaministiquia. In 1746 three *congés* were issued for the *Mer de l'Ouest*, one to J. Huno, a canoe and five men; one to Mathurin Laroche, a canoe and six men; and one to Sr. Maugras, four canoes and twenty men, under Pierre Primot and J.-Bte. Ladouceur. The following year Sr. Noyelles was displaced by La Vérendrye and Sr. Maugras secured two *congés*, one for Fort Dauphin with two canoes and twelve men under Ladouceur and Boyer; one for the *Mer de l'Ouest* with two canoes and twelve men under Mathurin Laroche; and La Vérendrye one *congé* of four canoes and twenty-four men, under Beaumois and Gonneville. In 1748 La Vérendrye secured another *congé* for four canoes and twenty-four men under F. Sauvage; and Ignace Gamelin, for Forts La Reine and Maurepas with two canoes and fourteen men, under J. Durivage. In 1749 Ignace Gamelin sent two canoes and twelve men to Forts Maurepas and La Reine under J.-B. Ladouceur, and Sr. Maugras (for La Véren-drye), four canoes and twenty-four men to Forts Dauphin and Bour-bon, under J.-B. Rapin. With the death of La Vérendrye on December 6, 1750, M. de Saint Pierre succeeded to the charge of the post, and in 1751 and 1752 Sr. L'Echelle sent eight canoes and forty-eight men both years. On June 2, 1745, Sr. Monière sent two canoes and twelve men to Lac la Pluie. In 1746 Pierre Royer was the *fermier* of the post, and sent one canoe and six men. In 1748 and 1749 Lac la Pluie and Lac du Bois were under control of Gonneville Rupalais who sent three canoes and twenty-three men the first year, and three canoes and eighteen men the second.

By the end of the French *régime*, posts had been established in the Lake Winnipeg district to prevent the Indians from going to Hudson Bay. The Vérendryes had systematically organized the fur trade of the Northwest in the strategic location of posts to the south, and later, to the north of Lake Winnipeg. In spite of the numerous difficulties, a chain of posts had been established across the difficult stretch between Lake Superior and Lake Winnipeg, and trade with the Crees and the Assiniboines of that locality had been established. The portages and trails had been improved; food supplies, fish, game, and wild rice, were organized to support these distant trading posts; the depots at Michili-mackinac, Kaministiquia and probably Grand Portage, had been ex-tended to facilitate the transport of goods from Montreal in the short season; and financial arrangements had been concluded by which advances could be made which would not involve a yearly settlement. The opening of this route ensured for the French an established control over the rich fur-bearing territory of the Northwest, and enabled them to compete with the English in Hudson Bay. Moreover, it relieved them from the uncertainties which had prevailed for the trade by the Fox portage to the Sioux on the upper waters of the Mississippi, and to the Assiniboines beyond. The problems incidental to wars with the Fox, and the difficulties involved in maintaining forts among the Sioux as in the period from 1727 to 1737 were avoided. A road had been opened to the heart of the rich fur country as a check to competition from Hudson Bay and a relief from the difficulties of the south.

Total production[49] throughout the period in the north and in the south tended to reach comparative stability. The highest point in the number of *livres* of beaver received by the Company was 221,000 in 1733, and the lowest point 94,000 in 1737. Statistics for the period begin with 146,395 *livres* in 1717, and end with 148,998 *livres* in 1755. On the whole, production was not characterized by the pronounced in-

[49]See H. A. Innis, *The Fur Trade of Canada*, p. 77, also Appendix A, pp. 149 ff.

crease of the preceding period, and greater stability was in evidence. The relative importance of different areas may be shown from varied data. The posts established in the west were responsible for an immediate increase in supply. "Ces deux nouveaux postes [*Les Scioux, La Mer de l'Ouest*] en ont produit cette année [1735] près de 75 milliers [625 packs], et il n'en arriva l'année dernière à Montreal que 15 à 20 milliers de ces deux postes."[50] Another account gave a total production from these posts in 1735 of 100 *milliers* and a total from all posts of 170 *milliers* or 1,400 packs.[51] La Vérendrye wrote that 600 packages were secured in the west but only 400 were sent down in 1735. In 1750[52] the two posts produced 300 to 400 packs—an indication that production from this area had remained comparatively stable or declined slightly. Of the remaining posts in 1750 Lac Alepimigon or Nipigon produced 80 to 100 packs; Caministigoya 60 to 70; La Pointe de Chagouamigon 250; Michilimackinac 600 to 700; La Baye 500 to 600; Temiscamingue and Tadoussac were of decreasing importance. By rough calculation about 800 packs were produced in the district tributary to Lake Superior and 1200 packs in the district tributary to Lake Michigan. Approximately 500 packs were taken from the area north of Lake Superior. The relative importance of the posts in the latter part of the period is shown in a statement[53] dated Albany, August 10, 1761, giving an estimate of the Indian trade in the French period.

The value of the Merchandise sold at the following Posts.

Le Detroit the Illinois Commerce Exclusive . . .	350000 Livres
Les Miamis	80000
Les Wutanous	60000
Michilimackinac the Illinois exclusive	250000
La Baye et Les Sioux	100000
Le Nepigon	30000
La Pointe de Chagouamigon	80000
St. Joseph	60000
The Trade at Niagara was in the King's Hands and not so well known but Supposed	440000
Livres	1500000

[50]Can. Arch., C11A, LXIII, p. 61.

[51]P. Margry, *Découvertes et établissements*, VI, 574.

[52]See memoir by Father Coquart, April 5, 1750, *Jesuit Relations*, LXIX, 95 f.; also Can. Arch., C11E, XIII, 193 ff.; and L.-A. Prud'homme, "Les Successeurs de La Vérendrye."

[53]"An Account of the Indian Trade in the Upper Country," Can. Arch., Hardwicke Papers, vol. 35915, Pt. I, 173.

The above is the Value of Goods at Montreal, when sold at 30 p.ct. advance for Freight and Charges.

I find the French computed the Value of all kinds of Skins Imported from Canada to amount to 135000 Sterling p. ann.

The trend of production throughout the period is indicated in the number of canoes and men dispatched to various posts. In the decade from 1720 to 1730 the number of canoes sent to southern territory varied from sixteen to thirty-nine, and generally more than twenty-five canoes were sent each year, whereas in the Lake Superior and northwest areas the number varied from two to eight, and generally more than five canoes were sent. In the period from 1739 to 1752 the numbers fluctuated from twenty-five to sixty-six, and generally more than forty canoes were sent to the southern territory, whereas in the Lake Superior and northwest areas the numbers varied from eight to twenty-seven, and generally more than fifteen were sent. The number of canoes in the district tributary to Lake Superior increased rapidly throughout the period, but reached a peak in 1745. In the territory to the south the number of canoes also increased, and reached a peak in 1750. Allowing for discrepancies in the statistics the conclusion is more or less sustained that the production had reached its highest point in the period 1740 to 1745, and following the effects of the high prices of goods of the latter date declined. The northern territory was more directly affected by competition from Hudson Bay, and the south could not be expanded because of the growing importance of the English trade.

Consumption remained practically stationary throughout the period. It was estimated that in 1716 France consumed 600 *ballots* (72,000 pounds) of beaver of which one-half was *gras* and one-half *sec*. Holland purchased in addition 50 *ballots* of *gras* and 200 *ballots* of *sec*—a total of 850 *ballots* at 120 *livres* each or 102,000 *livres*. For this amount a steady market was found. A later estimate[54] stated that France absorbed 50,000 to 60,000 *livres* annually. The large quantities of bad *castor sec* which came on the market at certain periods were generally disposed of in Holland, often under unfavourable circumstances. At the end of the period (1749) English products[55] had made substantial inroads on the French market in Spain, Portugal, Italy, and Germany. On the other hand, prices of beaver had increased, and the marketing problem of the early period was not in evidence.

[54]Can. Arch., C11A, XXXVII (bis), 494. This estimate gives a production of from 100,000 to 120,000 beaver annually.

[55]*Documents relative to the Colonial History of the State of New York*, ed. E. B. O'Callaghan, X, 199 ff.

As a result of the tendency toward stability in the supply of beaver, the problem of restricting production, prevalent in the earlier period, was not apparent. Violent fluctuations of a short-run character were still in evidence. Indian wars incidental to the destruction of the beaver, and the westward movement of the Iroquois continued to cause marked changes in supply. During the second Fox war[56] (1727–38) it was reported in a letter[57] of October 13, 1735, that

the wars . . . for some years in the upper country have prevented the Indians from hunting especially those of the Baye, of the folles avoines, the Miamis, and the Indians of Detroit; those of Lake Huron, the Ottawas and Saulteaux have unfortunately continued to go to Oswego through the attraction of "eau de vie" which is distributed without measure, and the good market of this English post.

And later:

. . . the commerce of the upper country is not favorable since the troubles have occurred; the Indians have made no hunts since the war, or if some of them have hunted since the war they use the pretext of the war for not paying their debts and carry their furs to Oswego.

Changes in the prices of furs and of goods had the usual effects. With high prices the supply of furs increased. A letter dated October 24, 1746, noted:

I shall observe that as long as the beavers are at a high price, the voyageurs redouble their industry to encourage the Indians to winter in beaver country; they know that "les fermiers du poste de la Baye" obtain a great profit when the Indians winter among the Sioux where there is beaver instead of remaining on the borders of the Wisconsin and la Rivière à la Roche hunting only the bear, "cerf, chevreuil" and cat; the same at the post of Pointe de Chagouamigon if they do not engage the Indians to winter on the tongue of land which is between this post and the Sioux or in that which separates the country of the West from Lake Superior, and which is frequented by the Crees and the Sioux, they will remain to hunt in the places more convenient or they will live on moose and bear.[58]

Prices were chiefly regulated as in the preceding period by monopoly control, and represented a compromise between the merchants who demanded high prices and the Company which was obliged to sell the furs on the European market, but the tendency toward stability of

[56]L. P. Kellogg, *French Régime in Wisconsin*, chap. xv; see also Can. Arch., Collection de Mémoires et de Rélations.
[57]Can. Arch., C11A, LXIII, 61.
[58]*Ibid.*, LXXXV, 403–404.

production greatly simplified the problems of price control. The early part of the period was characterized by uncertainty incidental to postwar adjustment and to the difficulties of the trade in the earlier period. The treaty with Srs. Aubert, Neret, and Gayot expired with the end of 1717. In August, 1717, the Compagnie d'Occident was given a monopoly of the beaver trade from January 1, 1718, to December 30, 1742.[59] Opinion in the colony was not unanimously in favour of monopoly control, and various arguments were advanced in support of freedom of trade.[60] Company control was regarded as the cause of all previous misfortunes; the directors failed to take sufficient interest in the Company's affairs; failure of the Company involved the whole colony; loss by fire in the Company's depot would occasion a loss for the colony. These dangers would be avoided with freedom of trade. On the other hand economy in storage, demurrage, commissions, and other expenses with a commodity particularly liable to damage, and the difficulties of the surplus being disposed of advantageously in foreign markets unless it was under the control of a single hand, were considerations favouring monopoly control. The expenses of handling beaver were important items. Freight from Canada to France was per *livre* of beaver, 2 sols; insurance 10 per cent, or 4 sols; packing 2 sols; commission and transportation from La Rochelle to Paris, 2 sols; a total of 10 sols *la livre*.[61] The Compagnie des Indes claimed that a capital of 800,000 livres was necessary to carry on trade between Quebec and France. The net result of the arguments and complaints against Company control was the Arrest of May 16, 1720, which made the trade in beaver free. The exclusive privilege of the Company was exchanged for a tax on importation to France of 9 sols per *livre pezant* of *castor gras* and 6 sols per *livre pezant* of *castor sec*. On January 23, 1721, an attempt was made to check the frauds incidental to free trade by permitting the import of furs to France through certain ports. The privilege of the Company was re-established on May 30, 1721, but on the protest of the merchants,[62] was revoked again on July 20, 1721. It was re-established on January 28, 1722. The complications in-

[59]*Edits*, I, 378.

[60]See "Mémoire sur la Necessité de laisser aux negotians du Canada la liberté du Commerce du Castor," Can. Arch., C11A, XXXV, 449–455.

[61]See "Mémoire addressé au Comte de Toulouse pour prouver que la liberté du Commerce demandée par les Canadiens est très préjudiciable à ce commerce et la colonie," *ibid.*, XXXVII, 494.

[62]See "Mémoire concernant la colonie de Canada et le Commerce des Castors" by "Les Negotiants de la Rochelle et de Canada," 8 juillet, 1721, *ibid.*, XLIII, 93–94.

cidental to these numerous changes proved detrimental to the trade.[63]

Following the establishment of the Company in 1718, *castor gras d'été* and *de bas-automne* "seront entièrement rejetés." So too were *castor sec d'été* and *de bas-automne* "chargés de chair ou de trop gros cuirs." *Castors gras* and *demi-gras* "de bonne qualité" only, were accepted as *castor gras*. "Toutes les robes neuves ou celles qui n'auront été portées que du côté de la peau seront mises avec le sec." Only *castor sec d'hiver* and *de beau poil* were accepted. No distinction was made between *Moscovites* and *castor sec*. *Castor gras* was purchased at 3 livres *la livre poids de marc* in letters of exchange drawn by the Company's agent in Quebec, for six months' sight on the Company in Paris, and *castor sec* at 30 sols *la livre* in letters of exchange, one-half at six months' sight, and one-half at two months' sight. Beaver was delivered to the Company in bales of 120 *livres pesant*, 5 per cent[64] deducted for good weight. It was urged that the price paid for *castor gras* was insufficient to secure a supply, especially since the Indians had ceased to produce it, and since it was claimed that three years were necessary for making this grade,[65] but apparently without effect. In 1719 the price of *castor sec* was raised from 30 to 34 sols *la livre* to check fraud. It was also suggested that *castor sec d'hyver* with *gros cuir* should be received on the basis of 2 livres, that *castor veule* should be paid 40s. *la livre* since being "gratté pour en faire du castor gras" it weighed much less than *castor sec*,[66] but apparently without effect. The strict attention to grades and the rejection of the poorer grades favoured increased smuggling.[67] After the period of free trade (1722), prices were regularly charged as provided in the charter of the Company: "We reserve the right to regulate, on the basis of information sent to us from the country, on the quantities of the different species of *castors* which this Company receives each year from the *habitans* of Canada, and the prices which it will be required to pay them."

In 1722 the price of *castor gras* and *demi-gras* was 4 livres, of *castor sec* 2 livres; in 1725 *castor sec* was increased to 3 livres, and the following year[68] more energetic steps were taken to check smuggling by accepting the lower grades. *Castor gras* and *demi-gras* were given

[63]*Edits*, I, 441–442.

[64]See Arrêt du Conseil d'Etat du Roi portant Règlement pour la recette des Castors du 11 juillet 1718, *ibid.*, pp. 395–399.

[65]Can. Arch., C11A, XXXVII, 435–436.

[66]January 6, 1720, *ibid.*, XLI, 16–17.

[67]*Ibid.*, XLIV, 202–206.

[68]Arrêt du Conseil d'Etat, 30 mars 1726, *Edits*, I, 504–505.

separate prices—*le gras* 4 livres, *le demi-gras* 3 livres, *le sec* 2 livres, *le veule* 50 sols, and *engraissé* 2 livres. *Castor d'été et bas automne tant gras que sec* and *le veule d'été et bas automne* were received at one-half the price of *castor* of good quality as fixed on July 11, 1718. *Castor chargé de chair* of good quality was received as *castor sec* with a quarter reduction in weight, *castor gros cuir* as *castor de bonne qualité*. In 1726 the distinction between *castor gras* and *demi-gras* continued as a source of complaint. The bureau graded too low and in turn the trader was obliged to grade lower for the Indian. These difficulties again encouraged smuggling and the distinctions were abolished on July 21, 1727.[69] The price of *demi-gras* and *veule* was changed to 50 sols *la livre* and *castor engreissé* to 30 sols. In 1728 *castor gras* and *demi-gras* were raised to 4 francs *la livre* and *castor veule* remained unchanged. On January 1, 1730, *castor gras* and *demi-gras* were reduced to 3*l*. 10*s*., and *castor veule* to 48 sols.[70] The Company complained of fraud through falsification of weight with grease and oil and also that the better grades of beaver were smuggled to the English.[71] In turn the hatmakers complained.[72] Following these complaints arrangements were made January 4, 1733, to receive dry summer beaver for the following year at 20 sols, and fat summer beaver at 35 sols *la livre*. Thereafter summer beaver was to be received at 10 sols *la livre*, and burnt. The industry was subsidized[73] to that extent to prevent furs going to the English.

On December 20, 1735, *castor gras esté* and *sec esté* were ordered to be received beginning January 1, 1736, on the same basis as existed prior to the regulation of 1733.[74] On July 11, 1738, all beaver (fat and dry of good quality) was to be received at 55 sols *la livre*, and all other beaver of summer and late autumn at 20 sols *la livre* (ordinary deduction of 5 per cent). On June 6, 1746, as a result of the war, prices of beaver were increased; fat winter beaver 55 sols to 4 livres; dry winter beaver 55 sols to 3 livres 15 sols; all other beaver, summer and late autumn, 20 sols to 30 sols *la livre*.[75] Provision was made for reduction after the war to pre-war prices. In 1749 *castor gras* and *sec*

[69]Ordonnance, 21 juillet 1727, Can. Arch., Coll. Moreau Saint Méry, II, 146–147; also C11A, XLIX (bis), 415.

[70]Ordonnance, 20 octobre 1728, Can. Arch., Coll. Moreau Saint Méry, II, 283–284.

[71]Réponse de la Compagnie des Indes, 6 février 1729, Can. Arch., C11A, LI, 357.

[72]*Ibid.*; also *Edits*, I, 504–505.

[73]Can. Arch., Coll. Moreau Saint Méry, X, 109–111.

[74]*Ibid.*, pp. 197–198.   [75]*Ibid.*, II, 287–290.

of good quality were reduced after August 21 to 3 livres, 10 sols *la livre*, and in 1750 to 3 livres, 5 sols *la livre*.[76] During these years of rapid price changes the problems of grading became more serious. A letter dated September 29, 1748, complained:

> It is not possible to create other grades to this species than those which are established and which are known under the names "castor gras, hyver, castor veule, et sec hyver, castor esté, bas automne, et autre rebuté du gras et du sec"; if they wish to fix grades for all the different species of beaver they would be infinite, since there is no month of the year where the beaver does not change slightly in quality and this multiplies again the disputes without counting the varieties which come from different climates.[77]

The period was characterized by the usual difficulties of controlling the supply of poorer grades of beaver. Under conditions of competition the lower grades could not be rejected, and remained as an embarrassment for the European market. But it is significant that prices at the end of the period were higher than at the beginning. According to a statement of prices of various grades sold to the hatmakers in Paris[78] *castor gras* was quoted at 5 livres 10 sols in 1716, and at 7 livres 10 sols in 1751, and *castor sec* at 3 livres 10 sols in 1716, and 7 livres 10 sols in 1751. In England beaver increased from 5s. 5¼d. in 1739, to 7s. 6½d. in 1748. The supply of furs had apparently reached a point of stability.

The tendency toward stable production also simplified the problems of regulation of trade in the interior. Following the withdrawal of traders from the west in 1696 and attempts to concentrate trade at posts in charge of commandants, and the failure of those attempts because of Iroquois competition and wars, the colony returned to the old policy of issuing licences. Preparatory to the inauguration of the policy an amnesty was granted in 1714.[79] The licensing system was introduced with the issue of fifteen permits in 1715. Another amnesty[80] was granted in March, 1716, for the benefit of those who had not taken advantage of the earlier one, and on April 28 of the same year, the

[76]See a list of prices for 1749 in Peter Kalm, *Travels into North America*, 2nd ed., II, 397.

[77]Can. Arch., C11A, XCI, 32–33.

[78]See *ibid.*, CXXI, Pt. I, 124.

[79]Ordonnance du Roi qui accorde une amnistie entière aux habitans de la Nouvelle France qui ont été sans congé parmi les nations sauvages et ce sous certaines conditions du 19e mars 1714, *Edits*, I, 342–343.

[80]Lettres Patentes en forme d'Edit portant amnistie pour les Coureurs de bois et qui établit de nouvelles peines et la forme de procéder contre ceux qui n'en profiteront point, mars 1716, *ibid.*, pp. 350–352.

licensing system was extended to twenty-five permits.[81] The restrictions were nullified to a certain extent through articles permitting traders to proceed into the interior to carry supplies for wars among the Indians, especially against the Fox. Traders were permitted to take merchandise for trade to pay for the expense. Regulations were difficult to enforce under conditions of competition. An additional problem followed the establishment of a separate jurisdiction in Louisiana to which traders escaped.[82] The licensing system established in 1715 and 1716 was revoked in 1719, and no further permits were issued after 1720. Licences were restored after 1728 and a varied system grew up which included the licence, the leasing of posts, and the handling of posts directly through the King's account. From 1728 to 1742 the licensing[83] system was dominant. As usual an amnesty had to be granted to the *coureurs de bois* in 1737. On April 20, 1742, regulations were enacted to control the trade through leasing of various posts. The revenue raised by this source became a tax to the trade borne chiefly by the traders. Posts were leased to *fermiers* giving the largest bids and again subleased. On March 26, 1743,[84] Temiscamingue was auctioned for 5,600 livres (leased for 6,000 livres in 1724), Michipicoten 3,750 livres, Ouiatonons 3,000, and La Baye 8,100, giving a total of 20,450 livres. In the following winter[85] Kaministiquia was farmed for three years for 3,000 livres and Miamis for 6,850 livres. The disadvantage of the leasing system became especially apparent during a period of high prices of goods. Posts which were leased or subleased were usually centres of complaint from the Indians, who were anxious to get higher prices such as competition made possible. The boundaries of the posts were not carefully limited and disputes occurred between lessees of adjoining posts. With leases for short terms (as for instance three years), the lessees sold large quantities of rum, and generally carried on the trade with reference to the largest possible profit irrespective of the welfare of the Indians. In 1747, as a result of high prices, the

---

[81]*Documents historiques*, pp. 116–117.

[82]L. P. Kellogg, *French Régime in Wisconsin*, pp. 302 ff.; also "Congés et permis," *Rapport de l'archiviste de la Province de Québec pour 1921–1922*, pp. 190–223; P. F. X. de Charlevoix, *Journal of a Voyage to North America*, I, 131; P. Margry, *Découvertes et établissements*, VI, 510–511. For a general description of the trade of the Mississippi see N. M. M. Surrey, *The Commerce of Louisiana during the French Régime, 1699–1763*.

[83]Déclaration du Roi portant amnistie pour les Coureurs de bois du mois d'avril mil sept cent trente-sept, *Edits*, I, 551–552.

[84]"French Régime in Wisconsin," *Wisconsin Historical Collections*, XVII, 434–435.　　　　[85]*Ibid.*, p. 444.

fermiers asked to be discharged.[86] "The *fermiers* of all these posts have made representations to be discharged from payment of their taxes; they allege considerable losses." In that year nine canoes were sent to Detroit, but only on condition that they should receive licences free of charge. The returns[87] in furs were very small and it was estimated that the Company received only 100,000 to 120,000 beaver skins. In 1749 the licensing system again became important. Temiscamingue, Nipigon, Kaministiquia, and Chagouamigon were farmed out and the remaining posts exploited by licences.

The arrangements were in part adjusted to what the traffic would bear—licences were issued to posts in which English competition was felt in order that prices should be reduced through competition of licence holders. Under competitive conditions taxation of the posts in the interior was practically impossible. In posts in which competition was not felt, monopoly control was continued. The King's posts such as Niagara and Frontenac were not profitable, and were subsidized to check English competition. They were apparently the subject of mismanagement. Complaints were made that the late arrival of the King's vessels made it impossible to forward the season's goods from Montreal to Fort Frontenac. During periods of war with heavy burdens on revenue, the leasing system was favoured as more remunerative. The financial exigencies of the government were an important factor in regulation policy.

The general situation in the latter part of the period was described as follows:[88]

Nearly all the posts of the trade are privileged—that is to say those who obtain the privileges are allowed to trade exclusively. These posts are given, sold or farmed and in all these cases the trade suffers equally. Those which are sold or are farmed are commonly for three years. They expect in this short space to make a rapid and considerable fortune; the means which they employ for success are to sell as dear as possible the merchandise which they bring and to purchase the furs at the lowest price possible in which they cheat the Indians by making them drunk. In 1754 they had in the post of la Mer d'Ouest a skin of beaver for four grains of pepper and they

[86]Quebec, October 7, 1747, Can. Arch., C11A, LXXXVII, 280–281.
[87]"French Régime," *Wisconsin Historical Collections*, XVII, 472.
[88]Can. Arch., Collection de Mémoires et de Rélations; also "French Régime," *Wisconsin Historical Collections*, XVIII, 25–26, and *passim* (Memoir of Bougainville, pp. 167–195). See a list of *congés* May 6, 1739, to June 8, 1752, giving date of issue, name of governor, number of *canots*, place of departure, number of men, destination, purpose of voyage, and in most cases a role of *engagés*, in "Congés de traite," *Rapport de l'archiviste de la Province de Québec pour 1922–1923*, pp. 191–265.

charged up to eight hundred francs for a pound of vermilion. At the same time the merchandise was valued no higher at Detroit than at Montreal since these posts were free and the voyageurs went there through licences. . . . There is ordinarily an officer who commands in each post and who is regarded by the Indians as their partner, to whom they address themselves for counsel in their affairs, and so on. This officer is successful if he is a man of spirit and disinterested. The canoes go with the *congés* from M. le General viséd by the Intendant; the outfitters pay for these *congés* 500 francs which are destined to meet the expenses of the wall around Montreal and the remainder is distributed by the General of the country to poor families. He returns an account of the distribution. The arrangement which is practised sometimes and which is preferable is that the trade of each post is farmed to the merchant who pays a price in proportion to the number of canoes sent up and who engages besides to pay to the officer command-ing a sum to cover the expenses. . . . This arrangement is more convenient to an officer who exploits as a merchant the fort which he commands; he is able to command the friendship and respect of the Indians by this alone.

Revenue from the fur trade was shown in part in the prices paid for various *fermes* in the latter part of the period. Leases expiring 1758 were purchased for Chagouamigon 8,000 livres, La Baye 9,000, Nipi-gon 3,000, Kaministiquia 4,000, La Mer de l'Ouest 8,000.

The period from 1713 to 1763 witnessed the expansion of the fur trade from Montreal in northern North America beyond the St. Lawrence drainage basin, and into the heart of the Hudson Bay drain-age basin on the Saskatchewan. With this expansion the limits of the fur trade from a geographic point of view under prevailing technique had been practically reached. Competition from Hudson Bay became more effective, costs of transportation increased, and profits declined in spite of a rise in price. Competition from the English from the south also became more effective. The effects of these developments on the colony, and their importance as factors in the downfall of the French *régime* in Canada have been in part suggested and may be summar-ized.

European goods were in greater demand among the Indians as old cultural traits disappeared. The beaver disappeared as a result of per-sistent trapping to meet this demand. Peter Kalm at the end of the period noted the ever prevalent manner in which European goods had become a part of Indian economy.

The *Europeans* have taught the *Indians* in their neighborhood the use of firearms, and they have laid aside their bows and arrows, which were formerly their only arms, and make use of muskets. If the *Europeans* should now refuse to supply the *Indians* with muskets, they would be starved to death; as almost all their food consists of the flesh of animals, which they hunt; or they would be irritated to such a degree as to attack the *Europeans*. The *Indians* have hitherto never tried to make muskets or similar fire-arms; and their great indolence does not even allow them to mend those muskets which they have got. They leave this entirely to the Europeans. . . .

Hatchets, knives, scissors, needles, and a steel to strike fire with. These instruments are now common among the *Indians*. They all take these instruments from the *Europeans* and reckon the hatchets and knives much better than those which they formerly made of stones and bones. The stone hatchets of the ancient *Indians* are very rare in *Canada*.

Kettles of copper or brass, sometimes tinned in the inside. In these the Indians now boil all their meat, and they have a very great run with them. They formerly made use of earthern or wooden pots, into which they poured water, or whatever else they wanted to boil, and threw in red hot stones to make it boil. They do not want iron boilers because they cannot be easily carried on their continual journies, and would not bear such falls and knocks as their kettles are subject to.[89]

The fur trade demanded larger quantities of bulkier goods as the Indians became more dependent on European goods, and the trade was less profitable to the French.

With reduced profits it was necessary to pay greater attention to new and cheaper supplies of fur. Exploration and penetration to new areas were results. In turn this involved higher costs of transportation, slower rate of turnover, and heavier interest charges. With longer distances, primitive methods of transportation confined to the waterways, and the essentially more expensive costs of transportation of commodities up the rivers, the effectiveness of competition from adjoining drainage basins increased. The Mississippi River became a more important highway competing for furs along its heights of land with the St. Lawrence. The Hudson Bay drainage basin had appreciable advantages. Resort to new tribes with cheaper supplies of fur became less remunerative. Wars with intervening Indian middlemen were a result and these wars became increasingly expensive, as in the case of the wars[90] with the Fox Indians. The vicious circle, in which cheaper English goods and more efficient English traders in the south necessitated greater expenditure on military measures to check competition, and the burden of increasing expenditures falling chiefly on the fur trade reduced the prices offered by the French to the Indians and encouraged further competition, has already been noted. Trade with France was interrupted

[89]Peter Kalm, *Travels into North America*, II, 391 ff.

[90]See an interesting and detailed statement, "Etat de la défense qui a este faite a l'occasion de la guerre des Renards Anneé 1716," Can. Arch., C11A, XXXVIII, 163 ff.; "French Régime," *Wisconsin Historical Collections*, XVI, 400 ff.

and the Indians became more dependent on cheaper English goods. Increasing trade in furs on the part of the English seriously weakened the French position in the European market. The dependence of the colony of New France on Europe occasioned by the characteristics of the fur trade seriously weakened its position in time of war. The military organization which had grown up because of the exigencies of the fur trade, though long effective, eventually collapsed. The institutional organization of the colony adapted to the characteristics of the trade failed to adjust itself with sufficient rapidity to the demands of a diversified economic growth essential to independent survival.

At the end of the period a trading organization had been built up which because of its efficiency did much to offset the results of English competition. The equipment had improved materially. In the licences of 1680 references were made to the canoe and three men. With extension of trade to the interior the size of the canoe steadily increased, and at the end of the period the licences referred to canoes with seven or eight men. Supplies of provisions had been organized with greater effectiveness. Detroit became an important agricultural depot supplying corn to Michilimackinac as a provision post. Lead mining[91] was carried on in the west, and the products of the country utilized to an increasing extent. Depots for the supplying of provisions had apparently been established in the Northwest, but to a very limited extent. The establishment of Fort La Jonquière was an indication that arrangements had been made for a more elaborate organization for supplying provisions in the interior. On the whole, however, it was the rule for French posts tributary to Lake Winnipeg to send men to Grand Portage or Michilimackinac to meet men from Montreal. The evidence is not conclusive but guides mentioned in the *congés* at Montreal for *La Mer de l'Ouest* are mentioned in succeeding years and it is scarcely probable that men went to the Northwest and returned in the same season. J.-Bte. Ladouceur and Mathurin Laroche are mentioned as guides in 1746 and in 1747, and Jos. Durivage in 1748 and 1749. Posts had been established on the Saskatchewan, large numbers of men and guides knew the route to the Northwest, an organization had been built up and connections had been made with the Indians. The trail had been adequately blazed for the development in the Northwest under the English in the later period. The foundations had been laid by the French.

As has been shown, with constant penetration to the interior, the trade became increasingly dependent on the individual trader. Furs

[91]See L. P. Kellogg, *French Régime in Wisconsin*, pp. 359 f.

were collected over wide areas and the ability of the trader in dealing with Indians was of dominant importance. With increasing distances and heavier commodities large numbers of *voyageurs* were essential to the trade, heavy expenditure was involved in wages and supplies, in the purchase of goods in France for the trade, and in the increasing slowness of the turnover. The element of distance necessitated the residence of traders in the interior who prosecuted the trade and communicated its demands to merchants in Montreal. At the end of the period a stable organization had grown up in which traders in Quebec and in Montreal were represented by correspondents at Detroit and other points. These traders purchased the necessary commodities in Europe for the trade in the interior. The result was essentially a type of organization in which profit sharing or partnership developed between the trader in the interior and the Montreal merchant. Devices giving the trader the greatest possible responsibility and offering the largest possible rewards were necessary to secure whole-hearted co-operation between the trader and the merchant, since the trader was far removed from surveillance. Under monopoly conditions, the result of the farming of various posts, control tended to shift to the hands of the merchants and the necessity for individual initiative in the trader was not so great. Under competitive conditions, such as developed under the licensing system and followed the inroads of the English, control tended to shift to the hands of the trader. With monopoly the trader became more of a manager hired by the merchant, whereas with competition the merchant became a creditor. But even with monopoly conditions as shown in the farms and sub-farms of posts the trader was of crucial importance.

In the shipping of furs from New France to Europe the organization was designed from the standpoint of control of the home government. Fixed prices were paid and adjusted to the merchants and traders for the furs, and the overhead and expense of handling shifted to this organization. The difficulties of the organization with the traders were indicated in the charges and countercharges which illuminated documents of the French period and in numerous failures of organizations concerned. Discontent with prices, oversupply of furs, inadequate marketing facilities, smuggling to the English, and fraud, were among the complaints registered.

Through this organization, built around the characteristics of the trade, control of the home government became effective. The difficulties of the trade were brought before the home government immediately. A decline in revenue through English competition brought direct results in the fortification of new posts, in new appointments of colonial officers, and in military measures. The ever present character of this competition necessitated an ample military organization for the colony, and the development of institutions of militaristic importance.

Through these organizations—the trading organization of the interior and the monopoly organization of external trade—there developed in the colony a highly centralized system of administration. This centralization was shown in agriculture, in industry, in the church, and in colonial government. The tendency toward centralization was responsible for the development of paternalistic government. But this tendency was most conspicuous in external control. In the internal trade it tended to disappear especially as the possibilities of competition increased as was shown in the ineffectual legislation against trading with the English, and in the charges of participation in the trade brought against the colonial officers. As the trade extended to the interior and the supply of beaver was exhausted such control became more effective, but on the other hand the individual trader became of more vital importance. On the side of the trader was the growth of individual responsibility among the people against which the colonial officers found occasion to complain. Individual responsibility has been regarded as incompatible with paternalism, but its growth largely explains the manner in which the French people embraced and extended responsible government in the later period. Externally, the fur trade fostered paternalism, but internally the drift was undeniably in the opposite direction.

These institutions enabled the fur trade to continue long after its geographic limitations had been reached, although these limitations were eventually decisive. The advantages of the St. Lawrence drainage basin were sufficient to promote the growth of institutions and organizations which effectively checked competition from other drainage basins. When these advantages had disappeared through the exhaustion of the supply of beaver, these institutions continued effective. From the standpoint of the trader, long experience in dealing with native populations, knowledge of Indian economy and Indian life were of crucial importance in checking outside competition. From the standpoint of centralized monopoly, a highly developed militaristic organization in erecting fortified posts and in carrying on effective campaigns was able to supplement the influence of the trader.

The breakdown of these institutions was inevitable. Increasing competition from outside stressed the necessity of increasing dependence on these institutions. Greater distances to be covered rendered the trade increasingly expensive. Military organization played a more important part and became to a larger extent more expensive. Heavier drains[92] were made on the resources of the home government, and more especially on the resources of the colony. The French power in New France collapsed of its own weight. Institutional development characteristic of the fur trade was not adequate to the new economic conditions.

The effects of war on the fur trade were singularly disastrous. In the interior, native wars were responsible for the decimation of the Indians and for the unusual fluctuations in the supply of furs during war years. External wars were even more destructive. The fur trade was necessarily carried on through the production of manufactured commodities in Europe and the transportation of those commodities to native populations who demanded them to an increasing extent as older cultural traits disappeared. Areas dependent primarily on the fur trade were dependent on the regular transportation of manufactured products from Europe. This was especially evident in a country which adhered to the mercantile policy. Numerous statements of this policy are available, and the following extract from a letter of October 20, 1726, may be cited:

It is quite contrary to the principles and maxims of colonies—that of consuming only the manufactures of the country to which they belong, and it is necessary to realize that the money paid to the English for escarlatines either for those bought from them in the colony or for those furnished by the Company, is always a considerable loss of money which leaves France or the Colony, which is the same thing.[93]

Industrial development within the colony even as related to the fur trade was rigidly scrutinized and prohibited[94] and control over manufactures, if not over internal trade, was effective through the centralization of authority which the fur trade encouraged. Interference with transportation and a failure in manufactured goods, therefore, had immediate and serious results for the trade. The capture of a season's shipload of furs, or of goods, was disastrous to the colony. Immediately the French were unsuccessful in war with the English, attempts were made to supply commodities from adjoining areas, and the routes by the Hudson River and by Hudson Bay became of increasing importance.

[92]This has been brought out very clearly in Adam Shortt, *Documents relating to Canadian Currency, passim* but especially II, 869.

[93]Can. Arch., C11A, XLVIII, 69.

[94]See the rigid enforcement of regulations prohibiting the manufacture of any type of beaver hat in the colony, Can. Arch., Coll. Moreau Saint Méry, X, 423–424.

For the colony of New France, essentially dependent as it was on the fur trade, war was of further consequence. A decline in the supply of fur immediately affected the revenue which was drawn primarily from the most important commodity. Revenue derived from import duties on goods used in the trade was reduced as well as revenue derived directly from the furs.[95] War, on the other hand, involved increased expenses. The direct relation between the fur trade and the colonial administration as carried out from France, or in the colony, was unique. The paternalism of the French *régime* was characteristic of a colony dependent on the fur trade.

On the other hand, in the internal trade in which the furs were obtained to an increasing extent from more distant areas, the control of the administration inevitably broke down. The trade stressed individual initiative, resource, and general freedom from restraint. With greater cost of transportation involved in the extension of the trade to more distant areas, with falling prices incidental to trade expansion, and an increased burden of taxation to support militaristic ventures, the colony was more vitally affected by fluctuations in the trade, control was more difficult, and the tendency toward an increase in trade with other areas more pronounced. Dependence on the fur trade and a military organization was not compatible with agricultural and industrial development and large external trade.[96] It was recognized in many quarters and at an early date that the fur trade had very serious effects on the economic life of the colony but it is significant that despite attempts to stimulate other activities,[97] the fur trade continued as a dominant factor.

La Potherie described the general effects of war in the preceding period:

Misery is ordinarily inseparable from war which is often followed by famine; Canada relieved by the retreat of the English finds herself reduced to a pitiable state and with a deficit of all the necessaries of life. Wheat is valued at ten to fifteen francs per minot, wine a hundred crowns per barrel, brandy six hundred francs and all its other merchandise in proportion.

[95]E. Salone, *La Colonisation de la Nouvelle-France*, pp. 212 ff.

[96]W. B. Munro, "The *Coureurs de Bois*," suggests that the fur trade had an additional influence in weakening the colony by lowering its moral standards. For an instructive article on the relation of the fur trade to war especially in connection with internal administration, see L. Gérin, "Le Gentilhomme français et la colonisation du Canada."

[97]See Raudot, Mémoire sur les affaires présentes du Canada, 7 août 1706; also Le Jeune's *Relation*, P. Boucher's *Canada in the Seventeenth Century*, the activities of Talon, and later the very able work of Hocquart.

Monsieur de Champigny seeing that the storehouses of the King had only sufficient food for a month billeted the troops among the inhabitants who were obliged to feed them. This public calamity which lasted for six months prevents sending parties against the English and the Iroquois, and we are left in a spirit of lethargy.[98]

During the war which ended with the Treaty of Aix-la-Chapelle in 1748 the supply of French goods was practically cut off, with serious effects on the trade. In a letter of June 19, 1745, the high cost of merchandise and its results were noted.

The exploitation of the posts has been made very difficult this spring and there have been very few *congés* issued compared with last year, the scarcity as well as the high price of merchandise has been responsible for this decline in trade, which can be regarded as totally lost next year if our vessel does not arrive in good time. It is to be feared that this year the small quantity of merchandise sent to Niagara as well as to the other posts will discourage the Indians and cause them to go to the English to supply their needs.[99]

In the following year a letter of October 22, 1746, described a more serious situation:

I shall find myself obliged to give the Indians beaver skins instead of goods to make their clothing; this well demonstrates our poverty; it will produce a bad effect among them; they are naked; they have neither hunting nor cultivated land because they have been occupied in war. One other consideration, this is the sadness and discontent of the people who could not secure their requirements from the merchants, there is only a small number who could purchase the most necessary things but the price has been so exhorbitant, 120 to 130%. This dearness has its influence on the produce of the country which increases to double its ordinary value. We have scarcely any salt which is necessary to salt the provisions of the country. There is scarcely any trade with the "pays d'en haut" and it is necessary to abandon it. All the traders as well of Quebec as of Montreal do not know what to do with their furs, there being no armed boat to escort them or to load them.[100]

[98]Bacqueville de la Potherie, *Histoire de l'Amérique Septentrionale*, III, 125. For further illuminating accounts of the effects of war on a colony which was not consistently self-sufficient in its food supply, see *Documents relative to the Colonial History of the State of New York*, X, 898–899, 933, 1129–1133; see lists of increased prices, *ibid.*, pp. 711, 865–866, and "Exposition du prix des denrées en Canada, 1759," Can. Arch., C11E, X, 253–260; also L. Dussieux, *Le Canada sous la domination française d'après les archives de la Marine et de la Guerre*, pp. 365–367.

[99]Can. Arch., C11A, LXXXIII, 161.

[100]*Ibid.*, LXXXV, 393.

A letter of October 22, 1748, noted that "the traders purchase at Montreal at least 150% dearer than during the peace and they sell in proportion and in spite of this they are ruined since the Indians will not pay."[101] The wars of the period seriously weakened the position of the French in the fur trade and contributed to the downfall of the French *régime* in Canada.

The effects of the fur trade on the home government were important in other ways. A marked increase in the supply of beaver fur[102] necessitated a pronounced improvement in the manufacturing organization and in the marketing organization for the finished product. The increase in supply assumed also an increase in the production of commodities suitable for exchange with the natives. The rapid growth of this new trade called for realignment of European economic organization. New markets were essential to absorb the increased production of the finished product. The increased production of commodities for the trade[103] still further complicated the problem, and called for an increase or a redistribution of energy for these new tasks. In the new world the characteristics of the fur trade which were of significance to economic development were the dependence on native population, the distinct cultural differences of the Indians and the Europeans, the geographic background with especial emphasis on seasonal variations and on numerous waterways, and the rapid exhaustion of beaver incidental to these factors. The native population and the French community were increasingly absorbed in the task of bringing furs, and of taking commodities for exchange from and to more distant areas.

The fur trade through its dominant importance weakened the position of the colony and of the mother country. It stressed dependence on such geographic factors as a northerly location and the forest areas of the Pre-Cambrian shield with their native hunting populations. The fur trade was prosecuted most successfully in areas not suitable to agricultural and industrial development, and eventually colonies dependent on the fur trade were destined to take a subordinate position to those geographic areas which gave a more diversified economic development. But the organization of the fur trade adapted to its specific geographic

101*Ibid.*, XCII, 46–47.

102In 1663 Great Britain imported "in bever, demicaster and felt hats made in the city, and suburbs of *Paris*, besides many others made at *Roven, Lions,* and other places, for about one hundred and twenty thousand pounds a year." S. Fortrey, *Englands Interest and Improvement*, p. 25.

103See B. Sulte, "Le Commerce de France avec le Canada avant 1760"; also "Les Chambres de Commerce de France et la Cession du Canada," *Rapport de l'archiviste de la Province de Québec pour 1924–1925*, pp. 199 ff.

areas persisted with unusual tenacity. The fur trade was vitally dependent on manufactured goods from Europe. The organization never took an independent position from the old world such as an organization with diversified economic growth could afford. Canada remained in the first instance subordinate to France and in the second place subordinate to Great Britain chiefly through the importance of the fur trade and its weak economic development.[104] It was significant that La Vérendrye had laid down the boundary of Canada in the search for the better beaver of the northern areas.

[104]For a description of the economic development of New France see H. A. Innis, *Select Documents in Canadian Economic History, 1497–1783*, Pt. II.

6. A Century of Trade on Hudson Bay (1670-1770)

TRADE on Hudson Bay[1] began with the establishment of Charles Fort on the Nemisco or Rupert's River in 1668.[2] Groseilliers and Radisson, experienced French traders,[3] had been responsible for the venture of English capital, and Groseilliers was of special importance in securing favourable returns which arrived in England in 1669. On May 2, 1670, a charter was granted to the Company and a new voyage undertaken with Radisson and Groseilliers. Voyages were made along the coast to the mouths of Moose River[4] and of Albany River during the summer to carry on trade.[5] The chief post on the Bay was removed from the east to the west side, on the transfer from Rupert's House to

[1]The details of the early history of the Hudson's Bay Company may be found in George Bryce, *The Remarkable History of the Hudson's Bay Company*; A. C. Laut, *The 'Adventurers of England' on Hudson Bay*; A. C. Laut, *Pathfinders of the West*; A. C. Laut, *The Conquest of the Great Northwest*. Miss Laut deposited numerous transcripts with the Newberry Library at Chicago (*Papers of the Bibliographical Society*, XVI, 1923, p. 25), but it is still necessary to write as did John Oldmixon, "Notwithstanding the pressing Instance I made to the concerned in the *Hudson's-Bay* Trade for Information to continue the Account of it down to this time; it not being yet come to Hand, I am obliged to be short therein." A valuable contemporary account is given by Oldmixon in *The British Empire in America*, I, 542–567.

[2]D. E. Long, "English Interest in the Fur-Trade of Hudson Bay before 1670."

[3]See John Oldmixon, "The History of Hudson's-Bay" in *Documents relating to the Early History of Hudson Bay*, ed. J. B. Tyrrell, pp. 386–387. "The French us'd many artifices to hinder the Natives trading with the English; they gave them great Rates for their Goods, and oblig'd Mr. *Baily* to lower the Prices of his. . . . The French, to ruin their Commerce with the Natives, came and made a Settlement"—eight days' journey up the Moose River from the English. Also the French competed with Indians trading at Rupert's (p. 393).

[4]An abridged journal of 1673–74 of the fort at Rupert's River is given in John Oldmixon, *British Empire in America*, I, 549 ff.

[5]"From Albany River they had generally 3500 Beavers a Year"; ten thousand beavers "in all their Factories was one of the best Years of Trade they ever had" (Oldmixon, "The History of Hudson's-Bay," pp. 381, 401). *Albemarle's* visit was in 1680; see J. B. Tyrrell (ed.), *Documents relating to the Early History of Hudson Bay*, p. 12.

Albany, in 1683. Posts were established at Port Nelson in 1682, and at the mouth of the Churchill in 1688. Within fifteen years from the founding of the Company,[6] forts had been established at Albany River, Rupert's River, Moose River, Port Nelson, and New Severn. In 1676 merchandise exported to the Bay was valued at £650 and furs imported at £19,000.[7] In 1679 the returns of furs included 10,500 beaver, 1,100 marten, 200 otter, 700 elk, and smaller furs.[8] Rupert and Moose were supplying about 5,000 beaver each, and Albany 3,500. As a result of this expansion the Company was in a position to declare its first dividend[9] of 50 per cent in 1684, its second dividend of 50 per cent in 1688, and a third of 25 per cent in the following year; to treble its capital in 1690; and to declare in the same year a dividend of 25 per cent on the new capital.[10]

The effects of this expansion on the French trade have already been described. In 1686 a French expedition was successful in capturing Rupert, Moose, and Albany forts, and holding them until 1693. But the trade at Fort Nelson and New Severn continued to increase, and it was estimated in 1690 "that our Returns in Beaver this year (by God's Blessing) are modestly expected to be worth 20,000 *l.*"[11] Limited to Fort Nelson the Hudson's Bay Company attempted to develop trade in the interior to offset the losses incidental to French control of the posts in James Bay. In 1688 attempts were made to develop the trade to the north, and orders were given that Henry Kelsey should be sent to Churchill River;[12] on June 17, 1689, he left with the Hopewell shallop to proceed along the coast.[13] Because of slow progress he left the boat and went by land finding only the difficult tundra country. He returned to Fort Churchill to find that it had been burned, and leaving this point, arrived at Fort Nelson on August 8.

With little success in the direction of Fort Churchill, Kelsey was sent into the Assiniboine country in 1690, "to call, encourage, and invite, the remoter *Indians* to a trade with us."[14] He left on June 12, and after

[6]George Bryce, *Remarkable History*, pp. 21–22.

[7]Beckles Willson, *The Great Company*, I, 215.

[8]A. C. Laut, *Conquest of the Great Northwest*, I, 162.

[9]George Bryce, *Remarkable History*, pp. 24–25.

[10]Trade at York Fort amounted in 1716 to 47,000 skins value, in 1717 to 22,600 skins value; James Knight's journal, *Founding of Churchill*, pp. 151–153.

[11]*Papers Presented to the Committee Appointed to Inquire into the State and Condition of the Countries adjoining to Hudson Bay, and of the Trade carried on there, 1749*, p. 26.

[12]*Ibid.*, p. 54.

[13]*The Kelsey Papers*; see also *Founding of Churchill*.

[14]*Papers Presented to the Committee . . . 1749*, p. 55.

travelling six hundred miles and crossing thirty-three portages reached a point which he called Deering's Point. In 1691 he sent a letter by the Indians to George Geyer, in charge of York Fort, who, in turn, sent by these Indians a new commission and necessary instructions including a request that he should return in 1692, and apparently that he should keep a journal. Kelsey had reported "that the Indians are continually at war within land, but have promised to get what Beaver they can against next year, others not before the next Summer come twelve-months when they promise to come down."[15] Kelsey received his instructions from the Governor[16] and left Deering's Point on July 15, 1691. He travelled 43 miles by canoe to reach the Saskatchewan, and 20 miles on that river before caching his supplies preparatory to going to the interior. After travelling 147 miles he came in contact with the buffalo. An additional 174 miles brought him to the edge of the spruce country and 40 miles farther to the edge of the woods. Altogether he apparently travelled 542 miles to reach the Naywatamee Poets.[17] He found the usual disturbances, following the introduction of European goods and especially guns, and incidental to war on the part of the middlemen (the Crees and the Assiniboines accustomed to canoes), against the more remote and less fortunate Indians of the Plains. Kelsey's task was to check the wars between the tribes of the interior in order that they might hunt more beaver. On September 6, 1691, he wrote that he had advised the Indians,

telling ym yt they must Imploy their time in Catching of beaver for yt will be better liked on then their killing their Enemies when they come to ye factory neither was I sent there for to kill any Indians but to make peace with as many as I could but all my arguments prevailed nothing with ym for they told me wt signified a peace with those Indians considering they knew not ye use of Cannoes and were resolved to go to wars so I seeing it in vain I held my peace.[18]

Eventually reaching the Naywatamee Poets on September 12, he persuaded the chief to go down to the Fort, but during the course of the winter new trouble broke out in which the Crees killed two of them, and prevented them going down. These Indians (Crees) were no more

[15]C. N. Bell (ed.), *Journal of Henry Kelsey*, p. 3. On the location of Deering's Point see Bell; also *The Kelsey Papers*, pp. xxxviii-xxxix.

[16]*Papers Presented to the Committee . . . 1749*, pp. 58 ff.

[17]Mr. J. B. Tyrrell identifies these Indians as the Mandans but unfortunately gives no reasons for his conclusions. "Poets" was a name for the Sioux. See J. F. Kenney, "The Career of Henry Kelsey," p. 47.

[18]Kelsey's Journal, *The Kelsey Papers*, p. 16. The two printed journals of 1749 omitted several items of the original. Also see J. F. Kenney, "The Career of Henry Kelsey."

anxious in Kelsey's period than in the later journey of Hendry to give up their position as middlemen. Whether or not the Naywatamee Poets of Kelsey were the same as the Archithinue of Hendry, in each case the problem of getting them to come to Hudson Bay was the same and practically insoluble.

In 1692 "Henry Kelsey came down with a good fleet of Indians." The London authorities in a letter dated 17 June, 1693, wrote:

To Governor Geyer *and Council*, at York Fort.

We are glad that *Henry Kelsey* is safe returned, and brought a good Fleet of *Indians* down with him; and hope he has effected that which he was sent about in keeping the *Indians* from warring one with another, that they may have the more Time to look after their Trade, and bring a larger Quantity of Furs, and other Trade, with them to the Factory; which you also may dissuade them from when they are with you, by telling them what Advantages they may make; that the more Furs they bring, the more Goods they will be able to purchase of us, which will enable them to live more comfortably, and keep them from Want in time of Scarcity.[19]

In 1690 the French captured Fort Severn, and in 1694 Fort Nelson. The latter was lost in 1696 to the English, but regained in the following year, and held to 1714. The English were restricted during this period to Fort Albany and Moose Factory on James Bay. In these posts they attempted to stimulate trade, but they were in direct competition with the French to the south as at Temiscamingue and Nipigon.

During the period prior to the Treaty of Utrecht, the English were seriously interrupted by the naval and military ventures of the French, but they had built up an important trading organization. In the establishment of this organization French experience which had been gained in a long apprenticeship on the St. Lawrence was of fundamental importance. The knowledge of French deserters was drawn upon with the greatest possible advantage to the English. Although the location of posts on James Bay was determined in the first instance by the knowledge of the country gained in earlier explorations,[20] a knowledge of the requirements of the trade was scarcely less important, and in this the services of Radisson and Groseilliers were invaluable. The minutes of a committee meeting of the Hudson's Bay Company for November 12, 1671, are illuminating in this connection:

That Capt[n] Guillam give in an inventory of all the stores and provisions of both Shippes, and that hee bee called to give his advise in writeing of

[19]*Papers Presented to the Committee* . . . *1749*, p. 56.
[20]See L. J. Burpee, *The Search for the Western Sea*, chaps. i, ii; also L.-A. Prud'homme, "La Baie d'Hudson."

what cargo is needful to bee provided for the next expedition and an estimate of what charge may bee requisite for one or two shippes and what els may bee expediente and Mr. Radison and Mr. Goosbery and Mr. Bailey to give theyr advise in writeing also thereabouts.[21]

The reliance on French experience was even more in evidence in the purchase of trading goods.

Committee meeting 8th February 1671/2. That Mr. Millington bee desired to take care for provideing one thousand biscay hatchets, one halfe of three poundes and one halfe of two poundes a piece, to bee sure that they bee such as are for trade with indians and not such as are for the inhabitants of Canada. . . .[22]

Committee meeting March 4, 1671. That Mr. Radison, Mr. Groselyer and Mr. Bailey wth the assistance of Mr. Gorst or any two of them doe take a stricte view of the returned cargo belongeing to the Company. . . . That Mr. Bailey with the advise of Mr. Radison and Mr. Groselyer treate with such persons as they thinke fitt for such goods as may bee needful for suplyeing a cargo for the next yeares expedition for Hudsons Bay, that is to say, two hundred fowleing pieces and foure hundred powder hornes with a proportionable quantity of Shott fitt thereunto first bringeing patternes of the gunns to bee bought, unto the next committee, and more two hundred brasse kettles sizable of from two to sixteene gallons a piece, twelve grosse of french knives and two grosse of arrow heads and about five or six hundred hatchets. . . .[23]

27th November 1673. . . . That Mr. Raddison attende Mr. Millington forthwith with a patterne of biscay hatchetts to be provided for this company, such as are usually sent from thence for France to serve the Indians in and about Cannada, and that Mr. Millington bee desired to give order for two thousand hatchetts to bee brought from Biscay by the first opportunity, and that Mr. Kirke bee desired to treate for provideing such french goodes as may be necessary, and give reporte thereof to the Committee. . . .[24]

The disposal of furs and general conduct of the trade were similarly dependent on the experience of Radisson and Groseilliers. "That Mr. Bailey with the assistance of the two frenchmen and Mr. Kirke and Mr. Heatley doe forthwith take care to see all the beaver equally allotted in about li. 100 . . . to a Lott."[25] With the advantages of this experience, the English succeeded in building up a trading organization adapted to the demands of the trade in Hudson Bay.

---

[21]Can. Arch., Hudson's Bay Company Minute Book commencing 24 October, 1671, p. 15.

[22]*Ibid.*, p. 28.

[23]*Ibid.*, p. 30.

[24]*Ibid.*, p. 72.

[25]*Ibid.*, p. 16.

The fur trade to that area began under a monopoly sanctioned by the Crown,[26] as was typical of European methods of developing distant foreign trade. Around the Hudson's Bay Company was built up a trading organization which was the core of later development. According to the stockbook of 1667, Sir James Hayes held £1,800; Carteret[27] (one of the proprietors of Carolina in 1663), £770; Shaftesbury, £600; Albemarle, £500; Prince Rupert, £470; the Duke of York, Craven, Viner, Colleton, Hungerford, Sir John Kirke, Lady Margaret Drax, £300 each; Arlington, £200; and other minor amounts making a total capital of £10,500.[28] On February 13, 1673, a regulation was passed permitting new members to join on the payment of £300, but no new member could purchase above £1,500 of stock. In 1675 there were thirty-two shareholders. Transfers of stock were carefully noted. One hundred pounds of stock gave one vote, and voting could be conducted by proxy. The annual meeting was held generally in November. The management was under the control of the governor (a member of the Royal Family), a deputy governor, and a committee of seven (including the treasurer). The governor was regarded as an individual of great value in dealings with the English government and for diplomatic purposes. His reward was a part of the overhead of monopoly. A member of the committee was required to hold at least £200 stock (in 1673, £300), and only four members were allowed to continue in office, the remaining three being chosen from the shareholders from year to year. Weekly committee meetings tended to be the rule especially during the rush season—departure and return of boats. Attendance at committee meetings was paid at 6/8 per meeting. The government of the company was concentrated in the hands of the larger shareholders, and arrangements were designed to promote continuity, concentration of authority, and government patronage.

With the development of trade new arrangements in internal organization were necessary. On November 7, 1671, Mr. Rastel was appointed to take charge of all papers, commissions of commanders and factors, costs of setting out ships for each year, accounts of receipts, payments, sales of beaver and goods, bills of lading, and accounts of factors. A temporary committee was appointed to take account of homeward and returned cargo; and the captains were directed to take

[26]The Royal Charter for incorporating the Hudson's Bay Company granted by His Majesty King Charles the Second in the 22nd year of His reign A.D. 1670, *The Canadian North-West*, ed. E. H. Oliver, I, 135 ff.

[27]See *Voyages of Peter Esprit Radisson*, Introduction.

[28]A. C. Laut, *Conquest of the Great Northwest*, I, 124.

charge of the ships, provisions, and stores. Notices of the minutes were to be sent to the people concerned. The characters of the employees were noted and filed. Usually minor committees of two or three were appointed for specific duties. These committees chosen with reference to experience tended to become more or less permanent. They dealt with such matters as purchases of supplies, ships, inventories, sales of furs, returned cargo, accounts presented, wage adjustments, and private trade. On November 28, 1672, three members of the committee, of whom one was to be governor or deputy governor, were given power to manage affairs of the company. The tendency toward concentration of control was shown in the minutes of April 10, 1672, in which Sir John Robinson, deputy governor, was made responsible for all bargains for provisions, goods, and beaver. On the other hand it was later found necessary to pass a resolution to the effect that four members of a committee constituted a quorum in the event of the deputy governor's absence. As late as 1679, a minute directs the secretary to write all orders of committee in books of orders. Permanent appointments became the rule with the increasing size of the business—accountant, purchasing agent, ship's husband, and warehouseman.

Wage schedules were planned and adopted—a difficult problem since wages varied with occupation, experience, and location. For voyages to the Bay captains were paid £200 or for a yearly period £8 per month for a year of thirteen months. The wages for officers and seamen varied: mates, £3.10 to £5 per month; carpenter, £3.10 to £4.10; boatswain, £2.10 to £3.10; gunners, £2 to £2.10; seamen, 30/ to 36/. Usually 10/ to 20/ per month was added to these rates, provided the crew returned the same year. In the Bay the governor was paid £200 per year; the deputy governor, £100; the chief factor at Rupert River, £40. Agreements were arranged for three and four years' (occasionally longer) service—the wages increasing each year and dating from arrival in the Bay. Gunsmiths were paid 40/ per month; blacksmiths, £15 to £25 per year; carpenter, £15 and over; bricklayers, £10 to £20; tailors, £6 to £15; surgeon, £3 per month; coopers, £15 to £20 per year; cook, £10 to £20; shipwright, 30/ to 45/ a month; warehousekeeper, £20 per year; and bookkeeper, £10. Craftsmen were needed in the Bay for the construction of new posts and for the reduction of transportation costs, e.g., guns were mended by a gunsmith in the Bay, rather than sent back to England for repairs. Seamen were paid 25/ to £3 per month, for three years, or £6, £8, £10, £12, consecutively for four years; labourers, £6, £9, £12, for three years up to £16 per year. Young men twenty to thirty and bachelors were preferred.[29] From fifteen to thirty men were needed for each post. In 1710[30] the policy of introducing Orkneymen was begun at rates for five years of £8, £10, £12, and £14 for the last two years. Wages were commonly stated as for men at Fort Nelson, or men in the Bay or at the Bottom of the Bay but it is extremely difficult to draw conclusions as to variations based on these differences in location.

Insurance rates were determined. The *Prudent Mary* was insured in 1680 for £2,000 outward bound and £6,000 homeward bound. Financial connections were established.[31] Loans were made in some cases from individual capitalists, from the shareholders, or money was acquired by calling on each shareholder for a *pro rata* subscription. In the event of the ships not returning the same year this problem became serious.

A sales organization was elaborated. The difficulties involved in the development of this organization were related to the technical character of the commodity, and the seasonal character of the trade. The first auction sale was announced on November 17, 1671, for the disposal of three thousand pounds of beaver.[32] Prior to this date furs had been sold by private agreement. The arrival of the vessels was followed by the sale of the products. Grading of furs was an important operation. Furriers were hired to carefully separate the skins and place them in piles of approximately two hundred skins. This task occupied ten to twelve days for which twenty guineas was paid. In the early period the company appears to have set a price on the fur, and to have sold the lot to one individual. There is also evidence that beaver was sold abroad by commission agents or factors for the Company as at

[29]*Spectator*, no. 164, for Friday, September 7, 1711, carried this notice: "The Governour and Company of Adventurers of England trading into Hudson's-Bay give Notice, That they having divided the Sum of 1977*l*. 12*s*. 6*d*. pursuant to their Proposals for enlarging Marriage Portions amongst such who were married before the 24th of June last; and that the second Dividend on Marriages will be made the 1st of January next unto such who shall be married before the 23d of December next, pursuant to the said proposal. They also give further Notice, That a Dividend will be made on the 6th of October next, pursuant to their Proposal, for enabling Apprentices to set up their Trades, unto such whose Contract or Indenture expire on or before the 26th of this Instant September." Lawrence Lewis, *The Advertisements of the Spectator*, p. 105.

[30]Beckles Willson, *The Great Company*, I, 241–242.

[31]For details on financial policy, dividend payments, and capital see W. R. Scott, *The Constitution and Finance of English, Scottish and Irish Joint-Stock Companies to 1720*, II, 228–237; and also *Report from the Committee . . . 1749*, Paper no. XXII.

[32]Beckles Willson, *The Great Company*, I, 59.

Genoa. But with an increase in the number of buyers the auction sale was a logical development. Rules of selling were laid down. Definite prices for certain lots were set and a certain advance made at each bidding as, sixteen lots beaver, each two hundred skins, at 11/ per pound to advance 2d. each bidding. Definite hours, nine to twelve, and two to five, were set apart on the date advertised for the sale. To prevent buyers holding off, statements were commonly added to the effect that no more beaver would be sold for twelve months, and none would be sold under existing prices. The sales were advertised through printed bills sent to merchants, furriers, and hatters. Purchasers were usually allowed 1 per cent discount with payment before a certain date, and were given the right to drawbacks on furs exported to Russia and other markets.[33] Parchment skins, fit for the Russian market, were reserved and sold direct. In the sales, bonds were usually made for separate lots of furs, and placed in the hands of separate goldsmiths. To these goldsmiths the purchasers transferred the funds. Matters of dispute in the sales were settled by the committee. Beaver was of greatest importance and was sold as coat beaver corresponding to *castor gras*; parchment beaver or *castor sec*; and as half-beaver, or stage beaver, or poorer quality beaver. Size and colour were also important desiderata. Occasionally old and new beaver were mixed. The fur was put through a cleaning process and every care taken to ensure a good quality. Other furs—mink, marten, otter, and cat— and skins—moose and deer—were sold in the same auction and in separate auctions. For beaver the sand of the warehouse was usually sifted and the hair sold as well. The sales policy of the Company was such as to get the largest possible return in the shortest possible time. The overhead was reduced through avoidance of a policy of integration in control over the furriers, manufacturers, or middlemen. This policy, however, had certain modifications. A reserved price was usually made for furs to ensure at least a favourable return. During a period of low prices, such as occurred in England around 1700 through a change in fashion, the Company was left with furs on hand. Changes in fashion and in the supply of individual species of fur through wars or natural fluctuations were important factors in determining the sales policy.

Private trade was a serious problem in the enforcement of monopoly, and devices for its restraint were worked out. The value of the commodity and the ease with which it could be smuggled made enforcement difficult. The Company censored the letters, inserted clauses in the agreements of the men prohibiting private trade, searched the men and

[33]*Report from the Committee . . . 1749*, pp. 229 ff.

the ships on their arrival, called for sworn affidavits, imposed fines, and placed officers and men under bonds for varying sums.[34]

Control methods and an adequate cost system were established. The unit of control and accounting was the year. Each outfit for the year was given a different mark, and the goods were consigned to each post. Not only were new and more effective methods of packing goods and stores for the voyage to Hudson Bay developed, but the goods for different posts in the Bay were given separate marks, and loaded on the vessels in such a way as to permit unloading of each post's consignment with the least possible delay and confusion. The furs were likewise marked as from different posts and the sales allocated accordingly. With the establishment of Fort Nelson the system appears to have been elaborated into two districts, Fort Nelson and the Bottom of the Bay. This arrangement followed the short season and the necessity of sending two cargoes, one to the upper part of the Bay and the other to the lower part. The internal organization of the Bay developed from these demands. A governor, deputy governor, and chief factor constituted the important governing body. Such centralization was necessary to prevent overlapping of different posts, to arrange for transfer of supplies from posts with surplus to those deficient, and to arrange an exchange of country produce. Mooseskins, for instance, were sent to Fort Nelson because of its deficiency, to make snowshoes. Communication was, therefore, maintained between the posts. As shown, in the Bottom of the Bay, small vessels were necessary to navigate the shallow waters, to bring the furs from various posts to a single depot, and to distribute the goods from this depot to the posts. Charlton Island came into favour and still remains the central depot. The whole organization involved the use of bills of lading, indents, instructions, and other devices for control.

Purchasing policies were worked out. In the beginning, reliance was placed on French experience, and goods for the trade were bought in France. Arrangements were made, however, by the use of samples, for the manufacture of most commodities in England at an early date. In purchasing, samples of commodities were examined, offers were accepted, goods were finally inspected, and careful reports made on their suitability for the trade. Gradually considerable experience was acquired; a manufacturing organization and a purchasing organization were built up. Trade-marks were used as a check an manufacturers; generally old firms were given preference and various connections were established. Estimates were gradually worked out on the basis

---

[34]See Beckles Willson, *The Great Company*, II, 35–39.

of experience for the year's supply. Attention was constantly paid to the possibilities of cheaper markets, as in the arrangement for the purchase of corn from Virginia. The Company was obliged to exercise direct control over some processes of manufacturing, i.e., hiring their own shot cast, but as a rule there was very little evidence of integration. The policy was primarily that of reducing overhead to a minimum. Warehouses were usually hired. Permanent offices were acquired, although the policy of long-term leases was followed. Hiring of the vessels not only ensured reduced overhead but an early return voyage. Boats of seventy-five tons were hired at £7 to £7.10 per ton. Small vessels for the Bay were purchased outright or the pieces were purchased, carried to the Bay, and set up there. These boats were built at a cost of £4.10 per ton, while pinnaces, long boats, and shallops varied in cost from 8/, 12/, to 24/ a foot.

The ships[35] were dispatched from Gravesend, usually in June, loaded with supplies for the trade, provisions for the voyages and the posts, and building supplies for new posts. Supplies for the trade which had been carefully chosen included knives, awls, hatchets, guns, gunpowder, powderhorns, shot, kettles, tobacco, and cloth. "The principal things necessary for the support of an Indian and his family, and which they usually trade for, are the following: a gun, a hatchet, an ice chisel, Brazil tobacco, knives, files, flints, powder and shot, a powder horn, a bayonet, a kettle, cloth, beads and the like."[36] Estimates were worked out for the posts from year to year on the basis of previous experience. Supplies for 1684 were made up from the following order.

Dec. 6, 1683, 300 guns for Bottom of the Bay, 100 guns for Pt. Nelson etc., to be made by 3 different gunsmiths. Dec. 7, 1683, 1000 hatchets from 10 d. to 14 d. each, 1800 long knives at 2/9 per doz., 900 long small knives, 1000 Rochbury large knives, 500 Rochbury small knives, 1000 Jackknives.[37]

The extent of the provision supplies was shown in various items:

1674—32 men two ships out and home (160) days, 17 men passengers— 10 outwards and 7 homewards,—20 men to stay in country,—59 quarters malt, 221 cwt. bread, 40 cwt. flour, 84 cwt. each of beef and pork, 10 cwt. currans and other fruit, 20 quarters peas, 928 lb. butter, 1856 lb. cheese.

[35]See a list of the ships 1739–48, *Report from the Committee . . . 1749*, pp. 253–254; and also J. B. Tyrrell, "Arrivals and Departures of Ships, Moose Factory, Hudson Bay, Province of Ontario, 1751–1880," pp. 163 ff.

[36]E. Umfreville, *The Present State of Hudson's Bay*, pp. 64–65.

[37]For a complete list of articles used in the trade, see Indent and Invoice of September 7, goods arriving at York Factory, Can. Arch., Journal of York Fort, 1714.

[Again for one year's supplies] 25 cwt. beef, 18 cwt. pork, Hayes Id., 4½ cwt. beef, 8 cwt. pork, Rupert River, 26 cwt. beef, 14½ cwt. pork, Chyche-wan [Albany], 17½ cwt. beef, 12 cwt. pork Pt. Nelson.

Supplies for building purposes included bricks, tiles, glass, and lumber.

Altogether an important organization had been built up prior to 1713. This organization was maintained throughout the period of the struggles with the French, and suffered little depreciation during the years in which the Company was restricted to James Bay.[38] The experience of the trade and the manufacturing and trading organizations which had been acquired[39] were invaluable to later development. The organization grew up in definite relation to the technical demands of the trade in Hudson Bay. The general character of the trade involved, as in New France, heavy overhead costs incidental to a one-way traffic with an outgoing cargo of heavy and bulky trading goods and supplies, and a return cargo of light valuable furs. Large quantities of ballast were necessary for the return voyage. The importance of these overhead costs is shown in a comparison of the expenses of carrying on business with the cost of trading goods. For the period from 1739 to 1748,[40] the value of the trading goods varied from a low point of £3,143.18.4 in 1747, to a high point of £4,152.16.11 in 1744, while the cost of carrying on the trade and maintaining the factories varied from £11,757.10.6 in 1741, to £21,702.0.5 in 1745.

Contributory to these costs were the heavy expenses incidental to defence against French attacks. In 1718 stone bastions were planned for posts at Moose, Albany, Nelson, and Churchill. In the same year the fort was strengthened at East Main. In 1733 an expensive programme was carried out in strengthening Prince of Wales Fort. Richmond Fort was built in 1749 on the east coast, but abandoned in 1758. A new post was built at Severn River in 1756. Other expenses were involved in carrying out voyages of exploration,[41] not only for the development of new trade, but also to convince the home government that the Company was encouraging the search for the northwest

[38]For an indication of the extent of the trade to Hudson Bay, see the value of goods exported 1698–1738, A. Dobbs, *Account of Countries adjoining to Hudson's Bay*, p. 202. The value of these statistics is limited since they are obviously extracted from customs records.

[39]The information given under various topics has been obtained from transcripts of Hudson's Bay Company Minute Books in the Can. Arch.

[40]See *Report from the Committee . . . 1749*, pp. 262–266.

[41]See "A List of Vessels fitted out by the Hudson's-Bay Company on Discovery of a North-West Passage," *Papers Presented to the Committee . . . 1749*, pp. 3–4.

passage. Captain Knight sailed along the west side in 1719, and was followed by others, and Captain Coats sailed along the east side in 1750, with consequent losses in lives and in money. Hendry penetrated the interior in 1754.

As with the monopolies of New France the costs of monopoly privilege were not light. To the costs involved in military fortifications[42] and preparations, and voyages of discovery were added expenses necessary to check attacks on its charter rights. In 1690 the Company secured an Act of Parliament[43] confirming its charter for seven years. The Felt-makers Company secured a stipulation obliging the Company to hold at least two sales of coat beaver annually, and not exceeding four. "These should be proportioned in lotts of about £100 sterling each, and not exceeding £200. In the intervals of public sales the Company should be debarred from selling beaver by private contract, or at any price than was sett up at the last Publick sale." At the end of seven years the Skinners Company and the Felt-makers Company petitioned against a confirmation of the privileges, but without effect.[44] In 1749 a more determined attack was made which led to an investigation by Parliamentary Committee, but to no change in the Company's status.[45]

The problem of the Company was the reduction of overhead costs incidental to the character of the trade and to the possibilities of competition. An immediate task was the increase in the size of the return cargo and the reduction of the attending expense of long voyages. New lines of trade were encouraged. At Churchill, whaling was relatively important. Mining was prosecuted, although with little success. Trade was developed in various commodities, deer horns, rabbit skins, quills, feathers, and other products. Attempts to reduce the amount of outgoing cargo accompanied the measures taken to increase return cargo. Supplies for the Bay were limited as far as possible and the personnel in the Bay were urged to develop an economy enabling them to live off the country. Lack of agricultural development made inevitable a dependence on hunting and fishing, and in turn on Indian experience. Partridges and rabbits were staple products. Père Silvy, during the

42J. Robson, *Account of Six Years Residence in Hudson's-Bay, passim.*

432 W. and M., c. 15; Beckles Willson, *The Great Company*, I, 184.

44*Ibid.*, p. 211.

45The long controversy over the validity of the charter gave rise to Parliamentary investigation, to the publication of the 1749 Report, of A. Dobbs's *Account of the Countries adjoining to Hudson's Bay*, Henry Ellis's *A Voyage to Hudson's-Bay*, and other works; see Beckles Willson, *The Great Company*, I, II, chaps. xxii, xxiii.

winter at Port Nelson, wrote that sometimes two hundred partridges were killed in a day.[46] Jérémie estimated that a company of eighty men wintering at that point in 1709–10 consumed ninety thousand partridges and twenty-five thousand hares.[47] Geese[48] and fish were added to these staples, and some deer were caught in snares. At Churchill (Prince of Wales Fort) whitefish and salmon were caught and salted down, and deer meat was brought in by the Indians. In a journal of Prince of Wales Fort, dated March 9, 1723, it was written:

Our patt^d Hunters came home to day brin^g· 150, . . . brought home in all 5000 besides what was Eaten by the Hunters abroad, Spent for them, 130 li. of powder, 590 li. of Shott, 154 flints and Worms 3.[49]

And again on May 29:

Richd Norton says they have 1500 Geese in salt theer, so I ordered them to salt no more there.[50]

On June 13:

Wee having left of Goose Hunting for this Spring having killed in all 2132 Geese, for which wee have expended 150 li. of powd^r 620 li. of Shott and 225 flints.[51]

At Albany Fort fishing was very important, and whitefish were salted or frozen according to the season of the year.[52] Geese and partridge were also taken here. At Moose River fish and geese were staples.[53]

They have Pike, Trout, Perch, and white Trout in great Perfection in all their Rivers; but the principal Fish they take is a little larger than a Mackarel, of which 13 or 14000 are taken at *Albany* in a Season, which supplies them and their *Indian* Friends in Winter; these they take after the Rivers are frozen over, keeping Holes open in the Ice, in a streight Line at proper Distances, through which they thrust their Nets with Poles, and the

[46]"Journal du P. Silvy depuis Bell'isle jusqu'à Port Nelson," *Relation par lettres de l'Amérique Septentrionalle* (1709–10), ed. Le P. Camille de Rochemonteix, p. liii.

[47]R. Douglas and J. N. Wallace (eds.), *Twenty Years of York Factory, 1694–1714: Jérémie's Account of Hudson Strait and Bay*, p. 38.

[48]For a description of the hunting of geese at Churchill and York Forts see *An Account of a Voyage for the Discovery of a North-West Passage by Hudson's Streights to the Western and Southern Ocean of America performed in the Year 1746 and 1747 in the Ship California*, II, 31 ff.; and for the hunting of partridge and rabbits, *ibid.*, I, 174–175; also Can. Arch., Journal of York Fort, 1714.

[49]Can. Arch., Journal of Prince of Wales Fort, 1722–23, p. 32.

[50]*Ibid.*, p. 49.   [51]*Ibid.*, p. 55.

[52]Can. Arch., Journal of Albany Fort, August 29, 1730, to August 8, 1731.

[53]Can. Arch., Journal of Moose River, August 17, 1732 to August 18, 1733.

Fish coming there to breathe, are mask'd or entangled in the Net; these they freeze up for Winter without Salt. The wild Geese come to these Rivers from the Southward in the middle of *April*, as soon as the swamps are thawed, at which time they are lean; they stay until the Middle of *May*, when they go Northward to breed; they take at *Albany* in that Season about 1300 for present Use; they return again with their young about the Middle of *August*, and stay until the Middle of October, when they go farther Southward; they save generally about 3000 of these, which they salt before the Frost begins, and what they take afterwards they hang up in their Feathers to freeze for Winter Store, without Salt; the Natives shoot them in the Swamps. There are three Kinds, one a grey Goose, which without Giblets weighs from 6 to 10 Pounds, another which they call Whaweys, are from 4 to 6 Pounds; they have also Swans, grey Plover exceeding fat, white Partridges as big as Capons, in Abundance all Winter and Spring, which feed upon the Buds of Spruce, Birch and Poplars.[54]

The importance of country produce was indicated in the evidence brought before the Committee of 1749.

And being asked, What the Allowance was? he said, They had Six pounds of Flour a Week; that one Day they had Three Quarters of a Goose (which Geese weigh a Pound, a Pound and a half, and some Geese Three or Four Pounds,) together with half a Pint of Pease, and small Beer, when in the Factory, and water when up in the Woods, with what Brandy the Governor pleases to give them; that, another day, they had Three Partridges, of the same Size as ours, with Peas, as aforesaid, the Cheese and Butter is a Day's Allowance by itself, and they have no Brandy up in the Woods, that when a Goose is boiled, it will not weigh a Pound, and they make no Difference as to the Size. And being asked, How many Partridges, he thinks would be sufficient for a Man a day? he said, He thought, Four.[55]

The dangers of dependence on a supply of food from the country were evident. A warm autumn was the occasion for the loss of quantities of frozen fish and meat. Fluctuations in the supply of game were frequent. But these dangers were in themselves a spur to greater activities in developing food resources.

Dependence of the Company on the Indian was closely related to the problem of reducing overhead. Indians were encouraged to hunt for the Company, especially during the goose season, although they required considerable training in the use of guns and were at first wasteful of powder. They made snowshoes for the men of the Company.

[54] A. Dobbs, *Account of Countries adjoining to Hudson's Bay*, pp. 52–53.

[55] Mr. John Hayter's evidence, *Report from the Committee . . . 1749*, p. 222; see C. D. Melville and A. R. M. Lower, N. A. Comeau, *Reports on Fisheries Investigations in Hudson and James Bays and Tributary Waters in 1914*.

Knowledge of the interior[56] and of other tribes was gained from them. Kelsey, Hendry, and Hearne travelled with the Indians on their journeys of exploration. Methods of hunting deer and other animals were also learned from the natives.

> There are *Indians* who are at all Times near the Factories, for which they kill Provision and go Hunting, just as the Governor gives them Direction. There are others who come at the Time the Geese are going Northward, in order to shoot Geese for the Factories, continue there in the Summer, fishing; kill Geese again, when going to the South; and, the Season being over, return up the country.[57]

Constant reference to the Homeguard Indians in various journals was an indication of the dependence of the Company on the native population. The difficulties with which the English adapted themselves to new conditions were shown in the amount of sickness and the mortality rate. The borrowing of Indian cultural traits was important to the elimination of these particular difficulties and to the success of the Company.

The policy of the Company stressed increasing self-sufficiency.[58] Building supplies were obtained as far as possible from the country, and sawyers, carpenters, and men were engaged in cutting, squaring, whipsawing, and hauling timber for the construction and repair of the forts. The personnel problem was developed in relation to the same problem of heavy overhead. Agreements covered a period of three to five years giving sufficient time to adapt the labour to new conditions.[59] If men proved unsatisfactory "Company may recall them home at any time without satisfaction for their remaining time." The labourers were generally required to perform a variety of tasks. Cutting and hauling wood and timber, hunting partridge and other game, setting deadfalls for fur, fishing, packing furs, storing goods, and brewing beer were among the routine tasks of the posts.[60] The skilled workmen—smith, cooper, tailor, and other craftsmen—manufactured and mended various

[56]For an illuminating instance of the dependence of exploration on the Indians and especially on Indian women, see journals of various forts and especially *A Journey from Prince of Wales's Fort in Hudson's Bay to the Northern Ocean ... in the Years 1769, 1770, 1771, and 1772*, by Samuel Hearne, ed. J. B. Tyrrell.

[57]*An Account of a Voyage . . . ,* I, 180–181.

[58]The importance of this dependence on the country may be shown by comparing the accounts of a later date; see E. Umfreville, *Present State of Hudson's Bay*, pp. 38–39; and *David Thompson's Narrative*, pp. 35–37, 43–51, 99.

[59]George Bryce, *Remarkable History*, p. 109.

[60]See J. Robson, *Account of Six Years Residence*, pp. 11–12.

trading goods. The smith was engaged in making steel traps, retempering, grinding, and making hatchets, making and filing ice chisels, and making scrapers; the tailor was employed making up coats; the armourer mending guns, and the carpenter in building boats and repairing the posts. The various journals are most illuminating on these details. The regulations for the labour force were designed to the same end. Families were not encouraged. The activities of the men were rigidly controlled. The regulations included in the Governor's orders for the men's behaviour, dated September 26, 1714, illustrated the problems.

1. All persons to attend prayers.

2. "To live lovingly with one another not to swear or quarrel but to live peaceable without drunkenness or Profaneness."

3. No man to meddle, trade or affront any of Indians, nor to concern themselves with women which Frenchmen did thereby cutting themselves off through jealousy. Men going contrary to be punished before Indians.

4. No man to go abroad or to hunt without obtaining leave.

5. No person to embezzle powder or shot entrusted to them to hunt with or to keep defence of factory.

6. Not to carry fire about warehouse, nor smoke tobacco on any of the flankers but to be always careful. To have but one lamp that the watch lamp burning for public.

7. No man to go off duty until he sees the next one up, not to suffer drinking.

8. To live lovingly and do things with cheerfulness.

9. People who go hunting trapping for fox, marten, wolf or any skin—company lays claim to one-half as they find victuals, drink and wages,—other half to do with as they please. All such skins to be registered and account set home as those skins were not traded.

The arrangement and organization of executive officers under a single head[61] was a step in the same direction in the reduction of overhead. The governor superintended the general activities, and the deputy governor and postmasters were under his supervision.

The policy of the Company as in all organizations with heavy overhead costs was that of developing trade from the standpoint of what the traffic would bear. The amount which the traffic would bear varied with different posts and at different periods, depending primarily on the extent of competition from the French. In the north the Churchill

[61]See letter from York Fort to Albany Fort asking for men, building supplies, and specified trading goods to be sent by the East Main sloop, Can. Arch., Journal of York Fort, 1714.

River[62] tapped areas beyond French competitive territory. The policy of the Company was one of pushing trade to the north to the beaver limits, and encouraging trade among new tribes of Indians in that area who had little acquaintance with European goods.[63] The re-establishment of Prince of Wales Fort was a first step. Richard Norton, the chief factor, wrote encouragingly of a prospective increase in trade with the Northern Indians and of trade with the Upland Indians in 1724.[64] In 1733 he reported regarding the Northern Indians, "I have traded more than twice the Quantity of Furs this Year than ever was traded in one Year from them, since this Factory has been settled."[65] The authorities in London constantly urged that every effort should be made to increase the trade. In the instructions dated London, May 17, 1739, they wrote:

To Mr. Richard Norton and Council at Prince of Wales' Fort. We confirm our Orders of last Year, to encourage as much as possible, the Indians, that are to the Northward of your Factory, and to endeavour to increase your Trade with them; which we hope you will be able to effect.

We do order and direct, that the *Churchill Sloop* be launched, and fitted out every Year, as early as possible, in the spring, to sail to *Pistol Bay*, *Whale Cove*, along the Western Coast, trading with the Natives that are there, and among the islands, in *June* and *July*.

And for the Master of the Sloop's Encouragement, and the Sailors Incitement to do their Duty, the Committee will order to be carried to the Account, in Credit of the Master of the Sloop, five *per cent* of the neat Produce of the Profit of the said Trade, and another five *per cent* of said Profit to be divided equally among the Sloops Company, and carried to their respective Accounts, and paid them when they come home.[66]

[62]Churchill was the point to which Eskimos came to get wood for boats, etc. Knight's journal, *Founding of Churchill*, p. 135.

[63]See *ibid.*, chap. iv, for a description of Knight's attempts to open trade with the northern Indians, the importance of a woman slave as interpreter, and difficulties in overcoming hostility of the Home Indians (Crees). Captain Davis returned to England in 1715 without landing at York Factory and thus caused great inconvenience to the fort and hampered trade with the northern Indians (*ibid.*, p. 60). In 1717 Indians came from Slave Lake down the Churchill. They preferred to come down the Churchill rather than the Nelson as less difficult, but the Company was anxious to keep them going to Nelson rather than Churchill to avoid difficulties with the northern Indians. Moose skins were scraped too thin because they were carried long distances. The Company attempted to encourage the Indians to hunt marten (*ibid.*, p. 166).

[64]*Papers Presented to the Committee . . . 1749*, p. 47.

[65]*Ibid.*, p. 48.   [66]*Ibid.*, p. 50.

From year to year solicitous instructions were forwarded to encourage the trade in the northern districts "without taking any from York Fort" to the south. The success of the Company is indicated by Dobbs.

As to the Trade at *Churchill* it is increasing, it being at too great a Distance from the *French* for them to interfere in the Trade. The Year 1742 it amounted to 20,000 Beavers: There were about 100 Upland *Indians* came in their Canoes to trade, and about 200 Northern Indians, who brought their Furs and Peltry upon Sledges; some of them came down the River of *Seals*, 15 Leagues Northward of Churchill, in Canoes, and brought their Furs from thence by Land.[67]

Trade from York Factory to the interior was rapidly developed after 1713, with no competition from the French in the interior. The Assiniboines and Crees were obliged, as in Kelsey's time, to depend upon Hudson Bay for a supply of European goods, and they became middlemen trading between the Plains Indians, who had no knowledge of canoes, and the post at the mouth of the Nelson River. These middlemen hunted buffalo in the Plains areas during the winter season and in the spring arrived at a rendezvous where canoes were built, and the furs, caught and traded, taken down to Hudson Bay.

In the month of March, the Upland Indians assemble on the banks of a particular river or lake [Cedar Lake during the voyage of Joseph La France], the nomination of which had been agreed on by common consent, before they separated for the winter. Here they begin to build their canoes, which are generally compleated very soon after the river ice breaks. They then commence their voyage, but without any regularity, all striving to be foremost; because those who are first have the best chance of procuring food. During the voyage, each leader canvasses, with all manner of art and diligence, for people to join his gang; influencing some by presents, and others by promises; for the more canoes he has under his command, the greater he appears at the Factory.[68]

Trade on the part of the middlemen[69] was stimulated by various devices, but the demand for European goods was of fundamental importance. The best hunters were rewarded with various favours and

[67]A. Dobbs, *Account of Countries adjoining to Hudson's Bay*, p. 47; W. Coats, *Geography of Hudson's Bay*, notes an increase from 8,000 to 18,000 skins.

[68]E. Umfreville, *Present State of Hudson's Bay*, pp. 56 ff.; see the account of Joseph La France, in A. Dobbs, *Account of Countries adjoining to Hudson's Bay*, pp. 37 ff.

[69]See Can. Arch., Journal of York Fort, 1714, for evidence of the importance attached to an Indian slave woman from whom the Governor hoped to learn of the possibilities of trade to the north.

promotions. "The governors make titular officers of those who are accounted the best huntsmen and warriors, and most esteemed for their understanding by the rest of the party. To each of these they give a coat, a pair of breeches and a hat, appointing him captain of a river."[70] These measures became more essential following the penetration of La Vérendrye and French traders to the area about Lake Winnipeg. The middleman organization which had grown up with the trade to Hudson Bay became a decided advantage to the posts of the French on the Saskatchewan. Success of the French traders involved a direct blow to one of the most important sources of fur tapped by Nelson River. Joseph La France estimated the Indians brought to York Fort in 1742, 130,000 beavers and 9,000 marten. Ellis wrote in 1746: "This [York Factory] is looked upon to be in all Respects the most valuable of the *Hudson's-Bay Company's* Settlements; because the most considerable Part of their trade is carried on here, where it is computed they deal for between forty and fifty thousand rich Furs annually."[71]

The result of French competition was a decline in supply of the better furs. In the period from 1738–39 to 1747–48, the total number of pounds of beaver received by the Company declined from a high point of 69,911, to a low point of 39,505 in 1746–47, and to 52,716 in 1747–48. On the other hand, the price of beaver rose from 5*s* 5¼*d.* in 1738–39, to 7.6½ in 1747–48, and the value rose from £19,007.0.9 in 1738–39 to £19,878.6.6 in 1747–48. Marten declined in number from 15,196 in 1738–39 to 8,485 in 1747–48, although the high point of 18,992 was reached in 1744–45. Prices declined from 6.5¼ in 1738–39 to 5.1¼ in 1746–47, but rose to 6.8 in 1747–48. The value declined from £4,891.4.3 in 1738–39, to £2,887.10.0 in 1747–48. Other furs increased in value from £6,049.19.7 in 1738–39 to £7,394.9.5 in 1746–47. The total value of furs increased from £23,328.5.11 in 1738–39, to £30,150.5.11 in 1746–47, but the decline in numbers was unmistakable.

As a result of this decline Anthony Hendry was sent to the interior in 1754 to persuade the Plains Indians to come down to the forts, to encourage the middlemen to trap more extensively, and to check the competition of the French. His success was similar to that of Kelsey. The Blackfeet presented the same objections as had the Naywatamee Poets.

[70]J. Robson, *Account of Six Years Residence*, p. 53. For a later description of the methods of the Company and their effectiveness in increasing trade see E. Umfreville, *Present State of Hudson's Bay*, pp. 56 f.

[71]H. Ellis, *Voyage to Hudson's Bay*, p. 212.

[Oct.] 15. Tuesday [1754]. . . . I was invited to the Archithinue [Black-feet] Leader's tent: when by an interpreter I told him what I was sent for, and desired of him to allow some of his young men to go down to the Fort with me, where they would be kindly received, and get guns etc. But he answered, it was far off, and they could not live without Buffalo flesh; and that they could not leave their horses etc.: and many other obstacles, though all might be got over if they were acquainted with a Canoe, and could eat Fish, which they never do. The Chief further said they never wanted food, as they followed the Buffalo and killed them with the Bows and Arrows; and he was informed the Natives that fre-quented the Settlements, were oftentimes starved on their journey. Such remarks I thought exceeding true.[72]

The attitude of the middlemen was also one of hostility to the develop-ment of direct trade with the Blackfeet.

[May] 15. [1755]. . . . One hundred and twenty seven tents of [Black-feet] came to us: I bought 30 Wolves' skins from them, and the Indians [middlemen] purchased great number of Wolves, Beaver and Foxes etc. . . . I did my Endeavour to get some of them down to the Fort; but all in vain: and altho' the Indians [middlemen] promised the Chief Factor at York Fort to talk to them strongly on that Subject, they never opened their mouths; and I have great reason to believe that they are a stoppage: for if they could be brought down to trade, the others would be obliged to trap their own Furs: which at present two thirds of them do not.[73]

Hendry was successful, however, in persuading the Eagle Indians to come down, but from the standpoint of the Hudson's Bay Company the problem was solved temporarily with the Seven Years' War, which led to the abandonment of the posts by the French in the Northwest.

In the southern posts on James Bay competition was more serious. Albany Fort was third in importance in Hudson Bay, and competition from the French was met by the establishment of a subpost on the Albany River at Henley House in 1720. Competition was met in the south by a reduction of prices. The extent to which this practice was followed is difficult to determine in spite of the establishment of a standard of trade by the authorities in London. In 1678 a standard was worked out for Albany,[74] but was apparently not applied. According to Willson a standard was filed with the Council of Trade in 1695 which included forty-seven articles. The standard presented in the 1749 report included sixty-five general items.[75] Several articles of the earlier

[72]"The Journal of Anthony Hendry," ed. L. J. Burpee, p. 338.
[73]Ibid., pp. 350–351. [74]Beckles Willson, *The Great Company*, I, 216.
[75]*Papers Presented to the Committee . . . 1749*, pp. 16–19.

standard are included in Bryce,[76] and the prices are higher than in the later standard. A discussion of these standards must be undertaken with caution. In the first place the Company's servants at the Bay apparently charged rates different from those set in the standard. Joseph La France complained of prices very much higher than those of the standard at Fort Nelson in 1742.[77] Robson complained:

> That the present Method of carrying on Trade is for the Indians to bring down their Goods to the Fort, and deliver them through a Window or Hole. . . . He was acquainted with the Company's Standard of Trade; . . . the Method is, to appoint Two Traders, and no other of the Company's servants are admitted to trade. . . .[78]

> This over-plus trade is big with iniquity; . . . The Company have fixed a standard for trade, as the rule by which the governors are to deal with the natives. According to this they raise upon some of the goods, which they know the natives must or will take, a gain of near £2000 *per cent.*, computing by the value of a beaver-skin, which is made the measure of everything else: so that a beaver-skin which is often sold for eight shillings, is purchased at the low rate of four-pence or six-pence. . . . Yet not content with this, the governors add to the price of their goods, exact many more furs from the natives than is required by the standard, and sometimes pay them not equally for furs of the same value; and I wish it could not be said, that taking advantage of the necessities of this abused people, who as they have no other market to go to are obliged to submit to any terms that are imposed upon them, they derive some gains also from weights and measures. This they call the profit of the over-plus trade, part of which they always add to the Company's stock for the sake of enhancing the merit of their services, and apply the remainder to their own use, which is often expended in bribes to skreen their faults and continue them in their command. It is this trade that is the great bond of union between the governors and captains.[79]

Not only was there variation from the standard but also in the character of the goods. The Indians were alleged to have complained of various shortages, "to the following purport":

> You told me last year to bring many Indians to trade, which I promised to do; you see I have not lied; here are a great many young men comes

[76]G. Bryce, *Remarkable History*, pp. 22–23. This standard is apparently taken from John Oldmixon, *British Empire in America*, I, 547. The standard was said to have been established twenty-five years before 1708, or about 1683. J. B. Tyrrell (ed.), *Documents relating to the Early History of Hudson Bay*, pp. 380–1.

[77]A. Dobbs, *Account of Countries adjoining to Hudson's Bay*, p. 43.

[78]Evidence of J. Robson, *Report from the Committee . . . 1749*, p. 216.

[79]J. Robson, *Account of Six Years Residence*, pp. 39–40.

with me; use them kindly, I say; let them trade good goods; let them trade good goods I say! We lived hard last winter and hungry, the powder being short measure and bad; being short measure and bad, I say! Tell your servants to fill the measure, and not to put their thumbs within the brim; take pity on us, take pity on us, I say! We paddle a long way to see you; we love the English. Let us trade good black tobacco, moist and hard twisted; let us see it before it is opened. Take pity on us; take pity on us, I say! The guns are bad, let us trade light guns, small in the hand, and well shaped, with locks that will not freeze in the winter, and red gun cases. Let the young men have more than measure of tobacco; cheap kettles, thick and high. Give us good measure of cloth; let us see the old measure; do you mind me? The young men loves you, by coming so far to see you; take pity, take pity, I say; and give them good goods; they like to dress and be fine. Do you understand me?[80]

Under these circumstances an analysis of existing standards cannot be regarded as final. The standard presented in 1749 shows that the prices for small articles, files, gunworms, needles, scrapers, scissors, thimbles, fire steels, twine, and even for brandy and wine, were the same at all posts. Thread, and two-gallon runlets, were the only items dearer in the south than in the north. The largest proportion of items was dearer in the north than in the south, in some cases twice and treble the southern prices. All items of clothing, weapons, ammunition, and hardware were dearer in the north. Some items were apparently traded only at southern posts—black lead, brown sugar, worsted binding, cargo breeches, goggles, and three-gallon runlets—and a few items only in the north—fine blue broadcloth, brass kettles, barrel boxes, and three-quart runlets. Churchill River had a smaller number of items for trade than other posts—yarn gloves, pistols, barrel boxes, and broad Orris lace were omitted from its list. The analysis supports the conclusion that higher prices were charged, and a smaller stock of goods carried in the north (Churchill and York Fort) than in the south (Moose River and Albany River). Through meeting competition in the south[81] and lowering prices the Company increased prices and extended trade in the north.

In 1770 at the beginning of fresh competition with Canadian traders in the interior the Company had at Prince of Wales Fort[82] or Churchill a chief factor and officers and sixty servants, and tradesmen giving a return of 10,000 to 40,000 Made Beaver; at York Factory a comple-

[80]E. Umfreville, *Present State of Hudson's Bay*, pp. 63–64.

[81]See W. Coats, *Geography of Hudson's Bay*, pp. 41, 50, on competition in the south.

[82]George Bryce, *Remarkable History*, pp. 108–110.

ment of forty-two men and returns from 7,000 to 33,000 Made Beaver;
at Severn Fort, eighteen men, 5,000 to 6,600 Made Beaver; at Albany
Fort (including two subposts at East Main, twelve men and 1,000 to
2,000 Made Beaver; and Henley House), thirty men and 10,000 to
12,000 Made Beaver; and at Moose Factory, twenty-five men and
3,000 to 4,000 Made Beaver. Another estimate[83] gives beaver receipts
of the posts in the period after 1770 as roughly in the following proportion: Albany Fort, 21,454; Moose Factory, 8,860; East Main,
7,626; York Factory and Severn River, 37,861; and Churchill River,
9,400. The trade centred about the mouths of the large rivers which
drained the vast areas of the interior, especially the Albany, the Nelson,
and the Churchill.

The success with which the Company had solved the problem of
overhead costs by various devices was shown in profits. In 1720 the
stock was trebled[84] and a subscription of 10 per cent taken, making an
increase from £31,500 to £103,950. Sales of fur increased according
to Laut from £20,000 to £30,000 and £70,000 a year.[85] Dividends
on the new capital of 5 per cent were paid in 1721; 8 per cent, 1722;
12 per cent in 1723–24; 10 per cent from 1725 to 1737; 8 per cent in
1738; and 10 per cent in 1739.[86]

During the century of occupation of Hudson Bay the English had
built and elaborated an organization remarkably adapted to control of
the trade in that area. As contrasted with the trade in the St. Lawrence,
in which control was impossible, effective control of trade by a centralized body in England was the dominant characteristic. This control
had disadvantages which became evident in many directions. Complaints were made by the governors and other officers of Hudson Bay
that the indents were disregarded in many particulars. In many cases
the men were not altogether loyal to the Company and *esprit de corps*
was weak. Matthew Sarjeant gave evidence:

That the Company understand a great deal of their affairs; but are frequently advised by their Governors and Factors, whose Interest is not
always the same with that of the Company; for they have settled Salaries;
and if the trade is ever so much increased, he never knew any further
encouragement given to them.[87]

[83]A. C. Laut, *Conquest of the Great Northwest*, I, 386.
[84]*Papers Presented to the Committee . . . 1749*, pp. 27–28.
[85]A. C. Laut, *Conquest of the Great Northwest*, I, 148.
[86]*Ibid.*, p. 315.
[87]*Report from the Committee . . . 1749*, p. 221.

Instructions authorized in the central organization and sent out yearly were not sufficiently flexible to meet all contingencies of a local character. But, on the whole, these disadvantages were slight and central control was shown to be adapted to the Hudson Bay area.

The success of control from London was the result of several factors. In the first place the geographic features were important. With the expansion of competitors to the interior as in the case of the French by river transportation and its limited facilities, distances increased, cost of transportation was greater, heavier goods were demanded by the Indians, available supplies of fur were exhausted, and the advantage of cheap transportation to the interior by ocean-going vessels, as in Hudson Bay, became more conspicuous. The evidences of this advantage were shown most plainly in Forts York and Churchill which tapped regions most distant from the St. Lawrence. Again this control was more effective through the competition of the Hudson's Bay Company with advantages incidental to the growing supremacy of Great Britain in manufactures. Moreover, the cultural traits of the Indians were important factors. On the St. Lawrence the agricultural developments of the Indians in the growth of Indian corn proved of fundamental importance to the prosecution of the trade over wide areas. In Hudson Bay agricultural development was limited, and exploration and penetration of the interior without a supply of Indian corn was practically impossible. The Company was dependent on the Indians, especially at Forts Nelson and Churchill, to make their canoes in the interior, and to obtain their food supply by hunting on their way to the Bay. Without a supply of food adaptable to transportation in canoes,[88] and without a supply of birch bark, penetration to the interior was undertaken with difficulty and chiefly through dependence on the Indians. The heavy overhead cost of trade in the Bay forbade additional expense in this direction. As a result of these difficulties, as well as of monopoly control, the penetration of European goods to the interior was less rapid and had less disastrous effects to the Indians than on the St. Lawrence. Changes in Indian economy were made more gradually. The heavy overhead of the trade in Hudson Bay increased the import-

[88]Weakness of men in the Bay, poor food, and resulting scurvy were bitterly complained of by Captain Knight in 1717. See his journal, *The Founding of Churchill*, pp. 168, 173–175, 180–182. Philip Turnor was turned back twice going up from Moose River (see *Journals of Hearne and Turnor*, pp. 264–265) and Samuel Hearne also turned back twice on his journey to the Coppermine. These men, largely on a diet of fish, furnish a contrast with the energy of Mackenzie, depending on pemmican.

ance of the Indian as a fur hunter. With a more limited population characteristic of a typical hunting occupation the welfare of the Indian was an important factor. Realization of the importance of the Indian was shown in support given to the Indian especially during a period of famine and difficulty. A surplus supply of fish and meat was drawn upon to feed Indian families.[89]

. . . the Indians come to Churchill River in July, and stay Three Weeks or a Month; . . . some few come after Christmas, when they come down upon the Ice, and carry home Powder and Shot in Exchange for Furs; . . . he [Robson] never knew any Goods returned on the Indians hands; and he has heard the chief Factor say, That if the Indians bring down a Quantity of Goods insufficient to purchase Necessaries for their Subsistence, the Company will (if they know them) trust them with Goods, which the Witness Looks upon as an Encouragement: . . . there are generally Six or eight Indians stay about the Fort all the Year round, who, when they can't get Provisions, are allowed half a Pint of Oatmeal a Day.[90]

The saying that the only good Indians were dead Indians never applied to the fur trade. It was the swiftness of the change in the cultural situation which made competition in the fur trade intolerable to native populations in the south. A similar development has followed in the present century with the rapid introduction of European goods among the Eskimos and their threatened destruction.

With advantages of geographic location, a supply of cheaper goods, and monopoly control over trade with the Indians, the Hudson's Bay Company developed an organization in relation to the definite area of Hudson Bay. The fixed standards of trade and of wages, and definite rules for the trade determined in London would have been impossible in the St. Lawrence where all attempts to enforce control of the trade defeated their own ends. The success of various devices for control was a factor explaining the lack of advance[91] in the interior and the failure

[89]See especially Can. Arch., Journal of Albany Fort, 1730–31.

[90]*Report from the Committee . . . 1749*, p. 216.

[91]See L. J. Burpee, *Search for the Western Sea*, chaps. iii–vii; Beckles Willson, *The Great Company*, II, chap. xxiii. The journeys of Kelsey, of Anthony Hendry in 1754–55, and of Hearne to the Coppermine in 1770, and the establishments of Henley House on Albany River in 1720, and of Fort Cumberland on the Saskatchewan in 1774, were the most important features in the movement to the interior during a period of more than a century. See "Journal of Matthew Cocking," ed. L. J. Burpee; also a general discussion, L.-A. Prud'homme, "La Baie d'Hudson"; also citation of Andrew Graham's account of the Hudson's Bay Company's forts in 1771 in George Bryce, *Remarkable History*, chap. xiii; also the criticisms of E. Umfreville, *Present State of Hudson's Bay*.

to establish posts. The end of this state of affairs began with a termination of the wars, renewed activity in the development of the trade in distant territories, more effective organization of competitors, and the necessity for a more aggressive policy. The difficulties involved in a change of policy were responsible for the relatively slow progress of the Hudson's Bay Company in the interior.[92] But this belongs to the following period.

[92]L. H. Gipson, *The British Empire before the American Revolution*, III, chap. ix shows the extent of exports of fur from Great Britain to France. Hatters migrated from England to France, for instance in 1727, 1750, and 1764. The Hat Act, 1732, was a result of the claim of the feltmakers that American hatmakers used cheaper beaver and the making of hats was restricted in the colonies. This Act of 1732 restraining the export of hats from the colonies and limiting the number of apprentices in the trade was a handicap to colonial hatmakers who had access to the chief supplies of fur. The Revolution removed such handicaps but the supply of furs was cut off and musquash skins were actually imported from London. "Letters of Phineas Bond," *American Historical Association Report*, 1896, pp. 632–633.

PART THREE

FROM THE ATLANTIC TO THE PACIFIC
(1763-1821)

7. The Hudson's Bay Company

THE fur-trading organization of Hudson Bay had been adapted after a century's experience to the demands of that area. The problem of the Hudson's Bay Company in the later period was the modification of this more or less rigid organization, closely controlled from London, to the demands of trade as carried on in the interior under radically different conditions where close control was impossible.

Competition after the conquest began in the territory south of James Bay on the Moose and Albany rivers, and was met indirectly through a continuation of attempts to develop trade in the northern, remote, noncompetitive districts. As in the previous period trade to the north from Churchill promised to offset the decline in the south. The northern Indians had been encouraged to develop trade as middlemen with the Dog-ribs, Copper, and Athabasca Indians to the west. They made visits to Churchill taking furs from the Indians who lived on caribou along the edge of the barren-ground country. About 1760 Matonabbee was chosen by the governor of Churchill to make peace between the Northern Indians and the "Athapuscow" Indians, and after several summers was successful in establishing trade.[1] To encourage this trade Samuel Hearne was instructed in 1769 to visit them and

2ndly, Whereas you and your companions are well fitted-out with every thing we think necessary, as also a sample of light trading goods; these you are to dispose of by way of presents . . . to such far-off Indians as you may meet with . . . in order to establish a friendship with them. You are also to persuade them as much as possible from going to war with each other, to encourage them to exert themselves in procuring furrs and other articles for trade, and to assure them of good payment for them at the Company's Factory.[2]

After two unsuccessful attempts he left Fort Churchill on December 7, 1770, in company with Matonabbee and other Indians. Hearne describes the difficulties of bringing furs across this country to the forts, and suggests the extent to which European commodities had penetrated to the interior. The Eskimos on the Coppermine were dependent on copper and had almost no iron. At the date of his visit, copper was

[1]*A Journey from Prince of Wales's Fort in Hudson's Bay to the Northern Ocean in the Years 1769, 1770, 1771, and 1772, by Samuel Hearne*, ed. J. B. Tyrrell, pp. 328 ff.   [2]*Ibid.*, pp. 52–53.

preferred by the Copper Indians except for hatchets, knives, and awls made of iron, although it was becoming of less importance, and the paths to the copper fields were overgrown with vegetation. The superiority of iron gave the northern Indians a decided advantage.

When they barter furrs with our Indians, the established rule is to give ten times the price for every thing they purchase that is given for them at the Company's Factory. Thus, a hatchet . . . is sold to those people at the advanced price of one thousand *per cent*; they also pay in proportion, for knives, and every other smaller piece of iron-work. For a small brass kettle of two pounds, or two and a half weight, they pay sixty martins, or twenty beaver in other kinds of furrs. . . . It is at this extravagant price that all the Copper and Dog-ribbed Indians, who traffic with our yearly traders, supply themselves with iron-work, etc.

From these two tribes our Northern Indians used formerly to purchase most of the furrs they brought to the Company's Factory; for their own country produced very few of those articles, and being, at that time, at war with the Southern Indians, they were prevented from penetrating far enough backwards to meet with many animals of the furr kind; so that deer-skins, and such furrs as they could extort from the Copper and Dog-ribbed Indians, composed the whole of their trade; which, on an average of many years, and indeed till very lately, seldom or ever exceeded six thousand *Made Beaver per annum*.

At present happy it is for them, and greatly to the advantage of the Company, that they are in perfect peace, and live in friendship with their Southern neighbours. . . . Within a few years the trade from that quarter has increased many thousands of Made Beaver annually; some years even to the amount of eleven thousand skins. . . .

Several attempts have been made to induce the Copper and Dog-ribbed Indians to visit the Company's Fort at Churchill River, and for that purpose many presents have been sent, but they never were attended with any success. . . . It is a political scheme of our Northern traders to prevent such an intercourse, as it would greatly lessen their consequence and emolument.[3]

Under these circumstances the penetration of European goods was restricted. The Dog-ribs west of Slave Lake had no iron.[4] Even among the northern Indians not more than half had brass kettles, and many were still obliged to boil water with heated stones in birch-rind vessels.[5] At the date of Hearne's journey the "Athapuscow" Indians were making trips to Churchill Factory by the difficult route of the barren grounds. They were probably[6] also engaged in taking furs to Churchill

[3]*Ibid.*, pp. 199–201.   [4]*Ibid.*, p. 267.   [5]*Ibid.*, p. 305.
[6]*Travels and Adventures in Canada and the Indian Territories between the Years 1760 and 1776 by Alexander Henry, Fur Trader*, ed. J. Bain, pp. 326 ff.

by canoes through the long and difficult route by Portage la Loche and through the hostile territory of the Crees.

These attempts to develop trade to the north were destined to failure with the penetration of the Canadian traders. The route of these traders from Montreal and Grand Portage was directly across the head-waters of the important rivers flowing into Hudson Bay. They pushed steadily to the northwest along the headwaters of the Albany, the Nelson, the Churchill, and later the Mackenzie rivers, and tapped the sources of the Hudson's Bay Company's internal trade. It was necessary for the Company to take active measures in establishing forts in the interior.[7] Thomas Curry penetrated to the Saskatchewan in 1771, and before Hearne had returned to Churchill, Matthew Cocking was dis-patched to persuade the Indians to refuse to trade with the Canadians and to come to Hudson Bay.[8] The difficulties incidental to developing a trade which would interfere with the profit of Indian middlemen, and to persuading Indians unaccustomed to canoes to come to the Bay, which were evident in Kelsey's and in Hendry's journals, were no less evident in that of Cocking.

[July] 23. [1772.] . . . The Pedlar, Mr. Currie (who intercepted great part of the York Fort trade this year) is . . . at Cedar Lake. . . .

[Aug.] 23. . . . The Natives all promise faithfully to go down to the Forts next year and not to trade with the Pedlars: but they are such notorious liars there is no believing them. . . . I find they consider an Eng-lishman's going with them as a person sent to collect Furs; and not as an encouragement to them to trap furs, and come down to the Settlements. . . .

[Sept.] 19. . . . Smoked with the Asinepoet Strangers: I advised them to be diligent in trapping furs, and to go with me to the Company's Forts, most of them being strangers: but they seemed unwilling, saying, they were unacquainted with the method of building Canoes and paddling: However they would send their furs by their friends who yearly visit the forts. . . .

[Dec.] 3. . . . I endeavoured to persuade two of them [Blackfeet] to accompany me on my return to the Fort . . . but they said that they would be starved and were unacquainted with Canoes and mentioned the long dis-tance: I am certain they can never be prevailed upon to undertake such journeys.[9]

Cocking was not more successful in securing the services of French traders. "Louis primo tells me he is going down also, to see his friends:

[7]William Pink went inland from York Factory to winter in 1767. *Journals of Hearne and Turnor*, pp. 6–7.

[8]"Mr. Currie's encroachment was the reason I [Andrew Graham, York Factory] sent Mr. Cocking inland"; "Journal of Matthew Cocking," p. 99.

[9]*Ibid.*, pp. 99 ff.

I told him that he was doing wrong as he was under a written contract to serve the Company: but all to no purpose."[10] Failing in attempts to bring the Indians to the Bay, Cocking returned to York Factory in 1773 and Hearne established Cumberland House in 1774.[11]

There is evidence that the Frobishers engaged in trade with Indians from the Athabasca district, on the way down the Churchill to Hudson Bay in the same year,[12] but certainly this plan was carried out in 1775, and a most successful trade[13] was prosecuted at Portage de Traite in 1776 with two bands of Indians from the Athabascan territory who had joined to protect themselves against the Crees on their way to Cumberland House.[13] One canoe continued the journey to procure, according to Alexander Henry, drugs and nostrums. In the same year Matonabbee made extraordinary and successful demands of Hearne at Churchill River by threatening to go to the Canadian traders.[14] In 1777 Frobisher again secured large returns from these Indians after wintering at Isle à la Crosse. Pond was most successful in Athabasca in 1778–79. A final blow to the Hudson's Bay Company's trade from Athabasca followed the smallpox epidemic of 1781–82, in which large numbers of the Athabascan Indians, and according to Hearne,[15] nine-tenths of the Northern Indians were wiped out. Canadian traders penetrated to Slave Lake and established trade with the Copper and the Dog-rib tribes. Finally in 1782 Fort Churchill was captured by La Pérouse. In the same year Matonabbee, at that time the leader of

[10]*Ibid.*, p. 119.

[11]"Pedlars by this time has too much influence and that I ware too late in coming." Hearne, 1774; see *Journals of Hearne and Turnor*, p. 105. The pedlars were said to give for nothing knives, steels, worms, flints, awls, needles and paint. Guns, kettles, powder, shot, cloth, gartering they were said to sell much cheaper than the Hudson's Bay Company. The only Company goods among the Indians were "a few guns and hatchets, the latter of which the Canadians brings but few and sell them dear."

[12]Louis Primeau and seventeen others wintered in 1773–74, commanded by Joseph Frobisher, in "the little house" about ten miles east of Cumberland (*ibid.*, pp. 106, 121). Frobisher went to Grand Portage in the spring of 1774 and sent Primeau to intercept Indians on their way to Churchill (*ibid.*, pp. 106–107). The Frobisher brothers with six canoes passed Cumberland House on October 9. On December 16, 1774, five Frenchmen coming from the Frobishers' house passed on their way to Paterson, Holmes and Francois' house, "being in great distress for want of Provisions" (*ibid.*, p. 131). On May 16, 1775, the same five men passed Cumberland in a canoe on their way north to Frobishers' (*ibid.*, p. 150).

[13]*Travels and Adventures . . . by Alexander Henry*, pp. 329 ff.

[14]*A Journey from Prince of Wales's Fort . . . by Samuel Hearne*, p. 285.

[15]*Ibid.*, p. 200.

all the Northern Indians, committed suicide and the disruption of the Churchill trade was complete.[16] Alexander Mackenzie wrote:

Till the year 1782, the people of Athabasca sent or carried their furs regularly to Fort Churchill, Hudson's Bay; and some of them have, since that time, repaired thither, notwithstanding they could have provided themselves with all the necessaries which they required. The difference of the price set on goods here and at the factory, made it an object with the Chepewyans to undertake a journey of five or six months, in the course of which they were reduced to the most painful extremities, and often lost their lives from hunger and fatigue.[17]

The Hudson's Bay Company had depended upon an organization of Indian middlemen who traded at profitable rates with Indians, unable, because of cultural traits, to resist the extortion by going to the forts themselves. In little more than a decade the Canadians had been able to establish trade with these Indians at favourable rates to themselves, and in a remarkably short period of time to break up the organization of the Company.

To retrieve these losses it was necessary for the Hudson's Bay Company to assume a more aggressive policy in the interior. At Cumberland House the establishment was enlarged and included fifty-one men. In 1779 bonuses of £2 per year were paid to traders to stimulate interest and Frenchmen deserting from the Canadians were paid £100 per year. In 1776 Hudson's House was established farther up the river above the present site of Prince Albert. In 1782 the Company suffered from the loss of York Factory to the French. After recovery from these losses Manchester House was built in 1786.[18] This post was destroyed in 1793, as was also South Branch House, which had been built on the South Saskatchewan, in the following year.[19] The latter was replaced by Chesterfield House built in 1800. Angus Shaw complained of Hudson's Bay Company competition at Lac d'Orignal in 1789,[20] and Alexander Mackenzie mentioned the hostility of Hudson's Bay traders in a

[16]*Ibid.*, p. 334.

[17]Alexander Mackenzie, *Voyages from Montreal through the Continent of North America*, I, cxxxviii–cxxxix.

[18]For the dates of establishment of various posts see *David Thompson's Narrative*, Introduction.

[19]Turnor was anxious to learn of a short cut across from Lake Athabasca and Slave Lake to Hudson Bay to compete with the Canadian route. He learned of Wager Inlet, Chesterfield Inlet, Churchill. *Journals of Hearne and Turnor*, pp. 327–433.

[20]L.-R. Masson, *Les Bourgeois de la Compagnie du Nord-Ouest*, I, 32.

letter dated "Rivière Maligne," September 1, 1787.[21] In 1790 Turnor was sent on a survey to Lake Athabasca.[22] In 1795 Edmonton House was built and at about the same time Carlton House. The Company constructed a post on Reindeer Lake (Fairford House 1795, Bedford House 1796), and in the latter year David Thompson carried out a survey from Reindeer Lake to Lake Athabasca. Peter Fidler[23] was sent to the Athabasca territory in 1802 and established Nottingham House on Lake Athabasca and Mansfield House on Peace River, but the latter was abandoned. In 1803 Chiswick House was built on the Slave River twenty-five miles above Slave Lake, and in 1804 a post was built on Moose Island in Slave Lake. In 1806 the Company was forced to abandon the Athabasca district.

On the Albany River, Martin's Falls House was built as a depot for further expansion in 1782. Activities of Canadian traders such as Mr. Shaw, John Long, and Duncan Cameron in the Nipigon territory were offset by the establishment of Osnaburg House in 1786.[24] In 1790 a post was established between Rainy Lake and Lake of the Woods,[25] but later abandoned. According to Bryce another post was established on Red Lake in the same year. At the mouth of Winnipeg River, a post was built in 1795 as a relay station for the boats which came from Martin's Falls.[26] According to Henry[27] "their boats carry about 45 packages of unequal weights, but averaging 80 pounds each, and are conducted by four oarsmen and a steersman." In 1794 Brandon House was built at the mouth of the Souris River, and two years later a post was built near old Fort la Reine. In 1804 the Company was competing on the Assiniboine and the Red River, and among the Mandans on the Missouri.[28]

In its expansion to the interior the Hudson's Bay Company suffered

---

[21]*Ibid.*, p. 19.   [22]*Ibid.*, p. 37.

[23]J. B. Tyrrell, "Peter Fidler, Trader and Surveyor, 1769–1822." Peter Fidler had been assistant to Turnor in 1790. See *Journals of Hearne and Turnor*, p. 237.

[24]*John Long's Voyages and Travels in the Years 1768–1788*, ed. M. M. Quaife; and L.-R. Masson, *Les Bourgeois*, II, 243.

[25]George Bryce, *Remarkable History*, chap. xiii.

[26]The first party from Hudson Bay by Albany to Lake Winnipeg came in 1793 headed by Donald McKay, late of Pointe Clair, and a Mr. Sutherland with three boats and two canoes; J. Macdonell in *Five Fur Traders*, p. 106. On the problems of the Albany route, see *Journals of Hearne and Turnor*, pp. 271–272 and contrast with Cumberland House, pp. 273–275. For requirements of Albany in provisions, see p. 280.

[27]Elliott Coues, *New Light on the Early History of the Greater Northwest*, I, 36, 46.   [28]L.-R. Masson, *Les Bourgeois*, I, 329 ff.

materially through the rigidity of the organization which had been adapted to Hudson Bay. For example the Northwest Company during its period of expansion was able to attract by its elastic organization such able men as Umfreville and David Thompson. A letter from David Thompson to Joseph Colen, who was in charge of York Factory, dated "Deers River," June 1, 1797, illustrates the lack of *esprit de corps.*

My friends belonging to York inform me that you are very desirous to find out who was the author of those letters that were wrote to H. B. Co. and militated against you 1795. I will give you that satisfaction. When I came down that year the other gentlemen were waiting my arrival in order to assist them in drawing up their grievances; as you were then absent I accepted the office with some hesitation, but as the letters were to be delivered to you on your landing at York for your inspection, and that you might have time to answer them, I considered you in a manner as present. Those letters were drawn up by me, assisted by my friend Dr. Thomas, and not one half of the evils complained of were enumerated.[29]

The personnel policy was inadequate to effective competition in the interior. As late as 1768 the seamen of the Company struck for higher wages.[30] Clandestine trade continued as a source of loss. In 1770 a slight change in wage policy was made which involved an increase in salary to the chief factors, and a gratuity of three shillings to the chief factor, and of one shilling and sixpence to the captains on every score of made beaver "brought home to the Company's account."[31] Bonuses above salaries from 1779 to 1799 often exceeded to the chief factors £200, to the traders £40, and to the traveling servants £80.[32] But these changes were inadequate. Harmon wrote in 1800 regarding the abandonment of the Company's post in Swan River district: "As they [Hudson Bay men] have nothing to expect from the Company, but their salaries, they seem so far as I can learn, to make but little exertion to extend their trade, and, thereby, to benefit their employers."[33] Complaints[34] were made that servants of different posts of the Company were competing with each other. The rigid control of the Governors over the interior posts was the cause of discontent and desertion.

The handicaps of the Company in Hudson Bay during the period

[29]*David Thompson's Narrative*, pp. xlii-xliii.

[30]Beckles Willson, *The Great Company*, II, 35 f.   [31]*Ibid.*, p. 39.

[32]A. C. Laut, *Conquest of the Great Northwest*, I, 381.

[33]D. W. Harmon, *A Journal of Voyages and Travels in the Interior of North America*, p. 30.

[34]Letter from the Company to William Tomison, 1802; see Tomison's journal, *Beaver*, October and December, 1920.

immediately following the development of competition in the North-west from the Northwest Company were well illustrated in the Journal for York Factory for 1786 and subsequent years.[35] The technique of conducting the trade under such conditions as the Bay imposed had been elaborately worked out, and the limitations of this technique for the conduct of the trade in the interior were striking.

Its policy of reducing the imports of provisions and supplies to cut down the overhead expense incidental to a heavy one-way traffic continued. The men were engaged in fishing, hunting, preparing and salting partridge, geese, rabbits, and deer, and trapping fur-bearing animals; in brewing, and in cutting and rafting down firewood and timber for repairs and building; and in gathering limestones and burning lime. They were engaged in growing vegetables, and making hay for the cattle, and tending the swine which the Company had imported for the consumption of the Fort. The provisions were packed in sawdust, or stored for preservation in ice in the "victual hole" and in the cellars during severe winters. The tasks of the craftsmen—cleaning and mending guns, making and repairing kegs and runlets, squaring and sawing timber, making sleds and snowshoes, making suits of clothing, turning out ironworks, including hatchets and other implements, became more onerous. The work involved in storing the goods, setting out and taking up buoys, drying, stretching, and pressing skins, grinding oatmeal, making bread, cleaning out the snow, picking oakum, and collecting stones for ballast, had increased. Penetration to the interior involved new tasks. Additional supplies were unloaded from the Company's boats, stored, and repacked for transport to the interior in the following year. Throughout the winter, various boxes were packed, gun flints were collected, stored, and sorted, shot was weighed and put into bags, gunpowder was packed in runlets, tobacco was prepared, bundles of cloth and goods made up, kegs were filled with brandy, and with the appearance of the inland brigade these goods were loaded and sent to the interior. The inland furs were brought down, stored, and sent to England on the arrival of the boats. As a result of the additional work complaints were numerous. The keeping of live-stock was not economical since men were employed making hay when other work of greater importance was neglected. Insufficient time was given to collect stones for ballast and the captain of the vessel collected those immediately available in front of the fort, with the result that the banks wore away very quickly and imperilled the buildings.

[35]"A Diary of Occurrences at York Factory . . . commencing August 29, 1786," notes in possession of the late Mr. C. W. Jeffreys.

Consequences of a more serious character were attendant on the apparent decline in efficiency which developed during the period of monopoly control on the Bay. It was astonishing, in view of the long experience which the Company had, and in view of the precautions characteristic of the early history of the organization, that scurvy should develop on a large and serious scale in the Fort because of the bad quality of the meat sent from England. One finds in this Journal of 1786 a statement that:

> This putrid state of the meat was too well evinced by the eye alone setting aside the sense of smelling—when the knife was put into it we had often—very often the disgusting sight of the remains of a heap of maggots which had gone through the double purgation of salt and boiling, for it must be plain to common reason that such appearances in meat could not be produced at any other time than prior to being put into pickle.

Brazil tobacco—an important commodity—was found in bad condition because of being placed in a damp place, and in spite of mixing with oil and molasses was found unsuitable for the inland trade. Runlets sent out from England were full of worm holes. Cheese and butter were so bad that they could not be sent inland. Trading goods obliged to face competition with Canadian goods in the interior were unsatisfactory.[36] One-half of the gun-flints—a commodity about which the Indians were most particular since their lives depended on them— were found unfit in contrast to the black and clear flints of the Canadians which never missed fire. Kettles were apparently contracted for in England by weight, with the result that they were too heavy for the trade, and could not compete with those of the Canadians. The Hudson's Bay Company was certainly not in a position to meet the Northwest Company under the handicap of this lack of organization.[37]

As a result of these disadvantages the Company's fortunes reached a low ebb during the period of the continental system,[38] when, in

[36]See Turnor's journal, 1779. He said York Fort buildings were too small to accommodate the men and complained of poor workmen, carpenters, bricklayers, poor guns, too few men. *Journals of Hearne and Turnor*, pp. 256–258. On June 7, 1791, Turnor reports: "Our pilot had burst a new 4 foot gun he had of Mr. Malcolm Ross for Piloting us, about 18 inches from the breech; it appeared the worst I ever saw bust; it was not thicker than a very thin counterfeit halfpenny, was exceeding brittle and had never been close welded but appeared double" (*ibid.*, p. 375).

[37]On July 3, 1790, at Cumberland House, Turnor says of Indians from the north: "these Indians formerly traded at Churchill but now trade with the Canadians" (*ibid.*, p. 318).

[38]Beckles Willson, *The Great Company*, II, 122 ff.

addition to its difficulties in North America, the European market was destroyed and sales reduced. In 1808 dividends were passed.

On the other hand in spite of these disadvantages the Company maintained its advantages of cheap transportation from England, and in the long run these advantages proved decisive. Even at an early stage the Company was able to gain control over less remote areas. John Macdonnell complained that the district tributary to Rivière Tremblante

has been almost ruined since the Hudson Bay Company entered the Assiniboil River by the way of Swan River, carrying their merchandise from one river to the other on horseback—three days' journey—who by that means and the short distance between Swan River and their factory at York Fort, from whence they are equipped, can arrive . . . in the Assiniboil River a month sooner than we can return from the Grand Portage, secure the fall trade, give credits to the Indians and send them to hunt before our arrival. . . .[39]

Alexander Mackenzie wrote regarding the country south of the Churchill and east of the route through Cumberland House:

Its inhabitants are the Knisteneaux Indians, who are called by the servants of the Hudson's Bay Company, at York, their home-guards.

The traders from Canada succeeded for several years in getting the largest proportion of their furs, till the year 1793, when the servants of that company thought proper to send people amongst them, (and why they did not do it before is best known to themselves), for the purpose of trade, and securing their credits, which the Indians were apt to forget. From the short distance they had to come, and the quantity of goods they supplied, the trade has, in a great measure, reverted to them, as the merchants from Canada could not meet them upon equal terms.[40]

These geographic advantages enabled the Company to survive and permitted a reorganization of its policies sufficient to compete with greater effectiveness in the interior. Several factors contributed to hasten the reorganization. Transportation facilities were fundamentally important, and the Company improved its position materially by abandoning the use of canoes and adopting boats suitable for hauling larger quantities of goods up the wide stretches of the Hayes River and the Saskatchewan. The men became more expert in handling canoes and boats. W. Auld wrote from York Fort, on October 3, 1811:

[39]L.-R. Masson, Les Bourgeois, I, 275.
[40]Alexander Mackenzie, Voyages from Montreal, I, cxviii.

We began in 1774 to settle this River [Saskatchewan] on a very humble scale hiring Indians to embark a man in each of their canoes with a small triffle of goods, this was continued for years no doubt the canoes would become a little bigger and when one of our men thought he could manage one he naturally would choose a small one, in process of time they became more experienced, they came in contact with Canadians (those natural water Dogs), emulation winged onwards tho but slowly for being commanded by Mr. Tomison it was not until 15 years ago that the Canoes were made as big as they now are; in 1795 while he was in England the person in charge Mr. George Sutherland launched boats into the Saskatchewan and the bold experienced Canoeman who knew the Rapids had nothing to learn but exchanged his paddle for an oar, descended in triumph to the sea.[41]

The policy of keeping the canoes at York Fort until the arrival of the boats from England and its frequent serious results was gradually modified. The disputes of the early period which were incidental to the small number of expert canoemen disappeared with these improvements. Combinations of these men insisting on higher wages and refusing to enter into contracts were less prevalent. The men were, at first, inexperienced in packing and handling freight, and large numbers of goods were damaged. "I have frequently met with boats belonging to the Hudson's Bay Company with 35 pieces goods and I am certain I shall speak within compas when I say that the Company's property did not exceed 11 pieces of merchandise."[42] These wasteful methods were slowly eliminated. Boats were apparently improved, especially in the first decade after 1800.[43] The type of boat in use on the Albany-

[41]Can. Arch., Selkirk Papers, I, 81 f. Hearne complained of the serious problem of getting canoes made by Indians in 1774–75. *Journals of Hearne and Turnor*, pp. 118, 157. "The greatest obstacle that is likely to prevent the Company from getting goods inland is the want of proper canoes, to procure which I am much at a loss what measures to take, as I find that no payment or promises can induce the natives to make a sufficient quantity." Turnor, 1779, notes the loss of a man going down to York Fort through careless handling of canoes. He advised that boats be built at Cumberland House to go up the Saskatchewan as canoes were cut by ice and damaged very easily. It was difficult to use boats from York Factory to Hill River, twelve days, because of heavy portages. Boats could be used to bring down provisions to Cumberland. There were too few experienced men to handle canoes. *Ibid.*, pp. 254–256.

[42]Can. Arch., Selkirk Papers, I, 327.

[43]Northwest Company canoes were towed fully loaded or half loaded up the Grand Rapids on the Saskatchewan. (1808): "This is upward of a mile long, but would be a very good road, were it not that the H. B. Co. from York

Oswego route, and later on the upper St. Lawrence, apparently exercised considerable influence in the evolution of the York boat. These boats were more suitable for heavy freight and lake travel, and gave the Company a decided advantage in the area immediately tributary to Lake Winnipeg. Their difficulties on long river hauls were noted in 1810 by Henry: "These poor fellows [H. B. men] have suffered much in cold water, snow, and ice having had to track continually [up the Saskatchewan]. Their boats are not constructed for pulling up the current as our canoes are."[44]

As a result of the increasing use of boats, York Factory became the chief depot from which goods were sent to the interior. Larger numbers of men were necessary, and the Orkney Islands were drawn upon to an increasing extent. According to Willson[45] the number of men at York Factory increased from twenty-five to one hundred. Supply depots were organized on the Saskatchewan and the Assiniboine.[46] A system of communication was established similar to that of the Northwest Company. David Thompson wrote: "There is always a Canoe with three steady men and a native woman waiting the arrival of the annual Ship from England to carry the Letters and Instructions of the Company to the interior country trading houses."[47]

Along with the improvement in transportation facilities, changes were made in personnel policy. It was necessary to abandon the policy of control from a centralized body in London, and to stress the development of individuality, self-reliance, and bargaining ability among the traders. To reorganize the arrangements of a century required a long period. A stable organization adapted to Hudson Bay changed slowly to meet the radically different conditions of the interior.[48] In the change of personnel policy, the Hudson's Bay Company reaped the advantage of Northwest Company experience. The policy of the Northwest Company was adapted to a period of rapid expansion, and with increase in numbers, especially after the amalgamation with the XY Company

Factory, with large boats, are in the habit of laying down a succession of logs from one end to the other for the purpose of rolling their boats over." Elliott Coues, *New Light*, II, 463.

[44]*Ibid.*, II, 654.

[45]Beckles Willson, *The Great Company*, II, 78.

[46]See the diary of Tomison, October and December, 1801, *Beaver*, October and December, 1920; and compare with E. Coues, *New Light, passim*. For a description of the dependence of numerous posts on fishing and of methods of fishing see *David Thompson's Narrative*, pp. 38–51, 110–112, 157–158.

[47]*David Thompson's Narrative*, p. 134.

[48]E. Umfreville, *Present State of Hudson's Bay, passim*.

in 1804, and the disappearance of new territory, it faced a crisis. Whereas, in the years of expansion, men had been drawn from the Hudson's Bay Company, with the disappearance of new territory men were later becoming disappointed through lack of advancement and were deserting to the Hudson's Bay Company. Moreover, the weakness of the Hudson's Bay Company in 1809, and its rigid organization subordinate to London, facilitated a change of control to outside interests. The alternative possibilities of settlement in the Northwest became more attractive and Selkirk was able to purchase a controlling interest in the Company[49]—a control which would have been impossible with the Northwest Company at that date. Under these conditions Selkirk secured a block of land in the Red River district,[50] and Colin Robertson,[51] who had been dismissed from the Northwest Company, was engaged to propose remedies for improvement. The changes suggested for reform of personnel policy were determined by his experience in the Northwest Company.

In a memorandum headed "Suggestions for the Consideration of the Honourable Hudson Bay Company," dated 1812, Colin Robertson wrote:[52]

One great obstacle to your inland commerce, is a want of men, and even those you employ are but ill calculated for the country. When an Orkneyman engages in your service it is more from necessity than inclination; he can find employment nowhere else, and when he has accomplished his darling object of gathering a few pounds, he bids farewell to a country that affords him no pleasure; this often obliges you to abandon Posts until a supply of men arrives from those Islands, so that when you reestablish these Posts, you find yourselves Strangers to the country and almost forgot by the Natives. Another thing Orkney men are unacquainted with the manner of voyaging in Canoes, by which the Northern business is conducted. . . .

I would warmly recommend to your notice the Canadians.—It is from these active, subordinate men that the North West Company derives their greatest profit.

They would rather prefer paying a Canadian Forty pounds a year, not in Money but in goods, at the following prices; for a common shirt 30/, a yard of strouds 30/, for a Pint of high wines or Brandy 12/, and all

---

49See Chester Martin, *Lord Selkirk's Work in Canada*, chap. ii, and A. S. Morton, "The Place of the Red River Settlement in the Plans of the Hudson's Bay Co., 1812–1825."

50See review by H. A. Innis of J. P. Pritchett, *The Selkirk Purchase of the Red River Valley, 1811*, in *North Dakota Historical Quarterly*, VI, 1932, 171–173.

51A. C. Laut, *Conquest of the Great Northwest*, II, 114 ff.

52Can. Arch., Selkirk Papers, II, 167 ff.

other articles in proportion. It would require but few such articles as these to pay a man his wages, even were he allowed Sixty Pounds a year, yet these poor people, notwithstanding the extravagant price they pay for their necessaries, are so much attached to the country that they seldom or ever complain. . . . But here it must be understood that those jealousies between your officers inland which have been so prejudicial to your interests in that country, must be put a stop to, and this can only be done by empowering your governor of Churchill with the sole direction of your inland officers.

Now Gentlemen, the only substitute for the shares which are held up by the North West Company, to their young men, is allowing the clerks in your service a commission on the profits arising from their exertions. This in my opinion with a salary would have the desired effect. As to your standard by which your accounts are at present settled in the interior it is so preju-dicial to your interest that a stranger would be apt to conclude, from such a manner of keeping accounts, that wolves, skins, and Parchment were the only articles in demand in London, while the Beaver and the Musk-rat were of little or no value. The abolishing the standard and adopting that of Accounts Currents, which ought to be kept with the different departments and Posts inland would considerably improve the value of your returns, and shew you at once the trader who is most worthy of being [promoted] or rewarded in your service. . . .

The circumstance to which I principally allude is the peculiar and acrimonious hostility, which the N.W. Co. systematically exert against those of our trading posts, which are most advanced towards the valuable beaver country of which we had a remarkable instance in their conduct towards Mr. Fidler at Isle a la Crosse. . . .

It is evident that the posts against which our adversaries direct their peculiar hostility, cannot be expected to carry on a very advantageous trade, yet they must be maintained as a barrier to defend the rest of our establishments; and it is of essential consequence, that the very best of our officers should be selected to command these advanced guards. But accord-ing to the arrangements which now subsist, the Factors and Traders who manage these frontier posts, will have the smallest emoluments. In the Factories which are situated near the coasts of the Bay and out of reach of the Canadians, a profitable trade may be carried on with little exertion; and if the Officers of every Factory receive a share of the profits of their own separate trade, those who are placed in the easy situations will be highly paid while no adequate remuneration will come to those who with the greatest ability and exertion maintain those frontier establishments, by which the profits of the rest are secured.

In order to obviate this difficulty without departing from the principle of the new arrangement, the most feasible plan appears to be, that the profit of all the Factories should be thrown into our aggregate fund, out of which shares should be distributed among the officers of our whole establish-ment in various proportions according to the importance and difficulty of the station assigned to each individual.

He suggested that an agency should be established at Quebec to hire the men required and to secure other advantages.

Another great advantage of having a House in Canada would be the purchasing of high Wines, Tobacco and Provisions for the Bay. These articles can be found there from 50 to 60% cheaper than in the London Market; but this would require one of your ships to touch at Quebec in the Spring or a small vessel in Canada for that voyage; and I am strongly of opinion that the returns would defray her expenses as your officers in-land are frequently under the necessity of trading Buffalo robes and dressed Skins besides several kinds of Peltries, which would find a good market in Canada, whereas if they were sent to England would be a dead stock.

W. B. Coltman was accordingly appointed as a representative in Quebec.

It was suggested in 1813 that the share principle should be adopted as follows: two superintendents, ten shares, twenty; nine chief factors, four shares, thirty-six; nine seconds, two shares, eighteen; twelve seconds, one share, twelve; making a total of eighty-six shares.

Miles MacDonnell, another Northwest Company man, gave further advice:

It is surprising the Coy. never encouraged men to bring out their families to this country. A few families might be well accommodated at each of the different Factories. The women could find sufficient employment in making and mending clothes, washing, cooking, etc. Were this the case, the men would be more contented and feel more attached to the country than they do. The children growing up here would be fitter to serve in carrying out the trade than those men imported, and a great deal of the iniquitous and scandalous connection with Indian women would be at an end.[53]

As a result of these suggestions direct and fixed payments were abolished[54] and wages, based in part on individual returns, were substituted. As early as 1810 barter was abolished[55] and accounts kept. The factor was made responsible for each year's outfit. The net profits were divided—one-half to the servants, i.e., one-sixth to the chief factor, one-sixth to the travelling traders, and one-sixth to the general labourers. General superintendents were given £400 a year, factors £150, traders £100, and clerks £50. Servants were given "thirty acres of land, ten extra acres for every two years they serve." Alexander MacDonald, in a letter dated Callander, January 26, 1812, wrote following the regulations of March 27, 1811:

The terms that the Honourable Company of Merchants trading to Hudson Bay allow their servants are as follows:—In the first place they are to

---

[53]*Ibid.*, II, 17–18.   [54]See Appendix D.
[55]A. C. Laut, *Conquest of the Great Northwest*, II, 120.

be bound and indented for Three Years at the expiry of which they have it in their choice, either to come home (passage free) in the Honble Company's ships, or to remain in their Service upon new terms, their wages and appointments being sure to be advanced after the Three Years if they at all deserve it. . . .

The terms are Twenty pounds per annum of wages or £ 17 a year with the following allowance in Clothes Yearly viz—a good Jacket, vest, Trousers, Blanket and Hat with two warm coverings for their neck and a good strong great coat once in Three Years, and as much Leather as will keep them in shoes in the old Highland way.

They are to be allowed travelling charges at the rate of 3/6 for every Thirty miles to the place of embarkation and 2/ p day after arriving there until they go aboard; as soon as any of them are equal to the task of steering a Boat down the rapids of Rivers he will get £ 5 a year additional.[56]

With this reorganization competition after 1810 became more effective. The Company had established a base at York Factory from which it attacked the long line of the Northwest Company.[57] In the earlier period energy was dissipated in maintaining three depots at Churchill, York Factory, and Albany. Dependence on York Factory and the shorter route to the interior gave the Company a decided advantage in transporting heavier goods at a lower cost. The demand for heavier goods increased with the gradual disappearance of Indian cultural traits, and the position of the Hudson's Bay Company was strengthened. The establishment of a settlement at Red River under Lord Selkirk threatened the supplies of the Northwest Company from that district. In the second decade of the nineteenth century the Company was in a position to support more effectively expeditions to the Athabasca country. In 1815 Colin Robertson and John Clarke[58]

[56]Can. Arch., Selkirk Papers, I, 285–286.

[57]The great problem of the Hudson's Bay Company was the large number of men, spreading out in the interior, high cost of transport, and large quantities of supplies. "The Canadians have greatly the advantage . . . in getting goods inland as five of their men with one canoe will carry as much goods as ten of the Honourable Company's servants can with 5 canoes." "The track they [the Canadians] go is much better than the track near York fort, and . . . they come before the current into Sea Lake [Lake Winnipeg] which is when they have the heaviest cargo, but they seldom come in with the loss of less than one tenth of their canoes, and often lose goods and all." *Journals of Hearne and Turnor*, pp. 222–223. See especially Turnor's recommendations, pp. 252–258.

[58]John Clarke was with Astor on his second expedition in 1811 to Astoria; he started back from Astoria in 1813, joined Selkirk and the Hudson's Bay Company in 1815. He met Franklin at York Factory and Fort Garry and was on Labrador. Adèle Clarke, *Old Montreal: John Clarke, His Adventures, Friends and Family*, pp. 10–28.

assembled canoes at Terrebonne, Robertson leaving the expedition at Lake Winnipeg, and the remainder continuing the journey to Athabasca. In spite of disastrous results Colin Robertson led a fresh attack in 1818, and from that date difficulties between the Companies became intolerable.[59]

The agreements of 1802 and 1804 of the Northwest Company ended "with the returns of the outfit of the year one thousand eight hundred and twenty-two." Plans for a succeeding agreement led to the amalgamation of 1821. The organization which had grown up under the Northwest Company and which extended from the Atlantic to the Pacific acquired a charter, which protected it from further attacks on its legal position, and a direct route through York Factory which had become of crucial importance to effective prosecution of the trade. The Hudson's Bay Company, by a competition which was always ruinous, successfully demanded a larger share of the trade.

[59]See G. C. Davidson, *The North West Company*, chap. vii, for a full description. Also see description of voyage of Abbé Dugas, *Un Voyageur des pays d'en haut*, chap. ii.

8. The Northwest Company

A. Reconstruction

THE conquest of New France was largely the result of the efficiency of English manufactures combined with the control of shorter routes to the interior from New York and Hudson Bay. As a result of the conquest English manufactures completely dominated the fur trade and goods were no longer brought from France. Except for temporary success in smuggling[1] the external organization of the trade shifted to the hands of English traders. The advantages of the English in manufacturing organization which became increasingly obvious toward the end of the preceding period were enhanced through the possibilities of increased production for a new market.[2] Specialization in the production of goods suitable to the fur trade, described in the following extract of a later date,[3] had already reached an important stage, and was rapidly extended.

Principal articles exported from Great Britain, for the Indian trade by the North West Company are:—

Blankets, manufactured at Witney, Oxfordshire.

Woollens, ditto in Yorkshire namely: Strouds, Coatings, Moltons, serges, and Flannel, common Blue and Scarlet cloths.

Cotton manufactures, from Manchester: Striped Cottons, Dimities, Janes, Fustians, Printed British Cottons, Shawls and Handkerchiefs, Gartering and Ferretting.

Hardware in large quantities.

Irish linens, Scotch sheetings, Osnaburgs and Linens, Nets, Twine, Bird-lime, Threads, Worsted yarn, large quantities.

Brass, Copper and Tin kettles.

Indian fusils, Pistols, Powder, Ball, Shot and Flints.

Painters' colors, Vermillion, etc.

[1]See references to the checking of smuggling by the French from St. Pierre and Miquelon, Can. Arch., Q, I, *passim*.

[2]In 1781 at Michipicoten it was claimed that the Canadians could not get as good cloth, blankets, or guns as the Hudson's Bay Company but had good tobacco. Turnor's journal, June 26, 1781; see *Journals of Hearne and Turnor*, p. 301.

[3][Nathaniel Atcheson,] *On the Origin and Progress of the North-West Company of Canada*, p. 14; see also Alexander Mackenzie, *Voyages from Montreal*, I, li; and G. C. Davidson, *North West Company*, pp. 220–223.

Stationery, Beads, Drugs and Large parcels of all kinds of Birmingham manufacture, with other articles of British manufacture.

Moreover, the English had been successful in elaborating an organization for carrying on the trade in the interior and there had been an increase in the number of experienced traders. The English traders were able to follow up the advantage of the conquest with amazing rapidity.

On the other hand, the supremacy of the French during the earlier *régime* had depended on organization, personnel, and long experience with the trade. The technique of the trade which had been elaborated by the French in relation to Indian cultural traits was of fundamental importance to the newcomers. The experience of Alexander Henry is illuminating.[4] He had apparently been connected with the fur trade of the English at Albany and during the war was engaged in supplying the British army at Oswego, and followed it down the St. Lawrence to Montreal. With the surrender of Montreal, "proposing to avail myself of the new market, which was thus thrown open to British adventure, I hastened to Albany, where my commercial connections were, and where I procured a quantity of goods." In 1761 on a journey from Fort Levis, where he had sold his goods to the garrison, he met M. Leduc, who had been engaged in the fur trade of Michilimackinac and Lake Superior. Through him he became acquainted with a guide, and after again proceeding to Albany for goods and securing the assistance of Etienne Campion, left in 1761 from Lachine for Michilimackinac. On the way up the Ottawa he noted the methods of carrying on the trade, the character of the canoes, ways of handling them, the number of portages, and other details. He described Michilimackinac as "the place of deposit, and point of departure, between the upper countries and the lower. Here, the outfits are prepared for the countries of Lake Michigan and the Missisipi, Lake Superior and the north-west; and here, the returns, in furs, are collected, and embarked for Montreal." He noted the importance of fish and maple sugar as staples at Michilimackinac and the significance of corn, the canoe, and the French *voyageur* to the fur trade.

The village of L'Arbre Croche [twenty miles west of Fort Michilimackinac] supplies, as I have said, the maize, or *Indian corn*, with which the canoes are victualled. This species of grain is prepared for use, by boiling it in a strong lie, after which the husk may be easily removed; and it is next mashed and dried. In this state, it is soft and friable, like rice. The allowance, for each man, on the voyage, is a quart a day; and a bushel,

[4]*Travels and Adventures . . . by Alexander Henry*, ed. J. Bain, *passim*.

with two pounds of prepared fat, is reckoned to be a month's subsistence. No other allowance is made, of any kind; not even of salt; and bread is never thought of. The men, nevertheless, are healthy, and capable of performing their heavy labour. This mode of victualling is essential to the trade, which being pursued at great distances, and in vessels so small as canoes, will not admit of the use of other food. If the men were to be supplied with bread and pork, the canoes could not carry a sufficiency for six months; and the ordinary duration of the voyage is not less than fourteen. The difficulty, which would belong to an attempt to reconcile any other men, than Canadians, to this fare, seems to secure to them, and their employers, the monopoly of the fur-trade. . . . I bought more than a hundred bushels, at forty livres per bushel. . . . I paid at the rate of a dollar per pound for the tallow, or prepared fat, to mix with it.

Having purchased his supplies and assorted his goods he "hired Canadian interpreters and clerks, in whose care I was to send them into Lake Michigan, and the river Saint-Pièrre [among the Sioux] . . ., into Lake Superior, among the Chipeways, and to the Grand Portage, for the north-west."

In the same year (1761) "Messrs. Stanley Goddard and Ezekiel Solomons" from Montreal were also engaged in trade. In 1763 Henry mentions Mr. Bostwick who had obtained a permit in 1761, and a Mr. Tracey who was killed. Although Henry and other traders suffered serious losses because of the Indian wars, they rapidly became acquainted with the methods of the trade as conducted from Michilimackinac and assumed active direction. In 1765 Henry secured the exclusive trade of Lake Superior from the Commandant at Michilimackinac. He purchased goods to the extent of 4 canoes, at twelve months' credit for 10,000 pounds of beaver (two and sixpence per pound), engaging 12 men for 1,200 pounds of beaver, and bought 50 bushels of maize for 500 pounds. Entering a partnership with M. Cadotte at Sault Ste Marie he wintered at Chequamegon sending a clerk with two canoes to Fond du Lac and through the great scarcity of European goods secured 150 packs of beaver or 15,000 pounds of beaver besides 25 packs of otter and marten skins. The success of the partnership of Henry and Cadotte was symbolic of the necessary combination between English capital and French experience. In 1767 there arrived at Michilimackinac "a hundred canoes from the northwest laden with beaver."

The technique of the fur trade built up by the French remained practically intact. Carver noted at Grand Portage in 1767 the effectiveness of the French traders with the Northwest Indians as contrasted with the English traders on Hudson Bay.[5] Bases for the production of agricultural supplies in the interior had been established and the *voyageur* with his knowledge of the rivers and of navigation remained. During the period of disturbance supplies of beaver had accumulated and the Indian had been left without European goods. Under these conditions recovery of the fur trade was rapid.

It was the centralized organization which had grown up in connection with the external trade to France which suffered most. French merchants in Montreal accustomed to purchase goods from France were forced to turn to England and in this change they were handicapped through language and a lack of knowledge of English connections. The French trader in the interior was forced to seek out new sources for supplies and to make new arrangements with English merchants or French merchants who had adapted themselves in the short time to the new situation by establishing connections with English houses. An interesting letter in French by Dick Van der Heyden dated London, April 23, 1767, in the *Quebec Gazette* of August 27, 1767, suggested the general problem as an attempt to establish connections with French merchants. The writer claimed to be thoroughly acquainted with the American Indian trade at Albany and also with the trade in London, having arrived there in 1752. He also claimed a large share of the Albany trade and solicited commissions to sell furs and to buy trading goods for Montreal merchants. He stressed chiefly his ability to grade furs and to sell privately rather than through the public auction and at a better advantage. The organization of external trade with England was rapidly extended first through the trade conducted through Albany and later through direct relations between Montreal traders and England. In England increasing supplies of fur led to modifications in the trade and increasing demands for goods occasioned the growth of new connections and a new organization.[6] The early existence of a

[5]J. Carver, *Travels through the Interior Parts of North America in the Years 1766, 1767 and 1768*, pp. 107 ff.; see also the "Journal of Matthew Cocking," *passim*, and L. J. Burpee, *Search for the Western Sea*, pp. 302 ff. For the contrast between the effectiveness of the methods of trading with the Indians, of the French and of the English, and for the consequent partiality of the Indians for the French, see B. Roberts to Lord Dartmouth, June 9, 1773, Can. Arch., Dartmouth Papers, No. 632.

[6]*Quebec Gazette*, August 23, 1764–65. I am also indebted to Mrs. K. B. Jackson for notes on the Minutes of the Board of Trade, C.O. 391, LXXI, and on Pownall, Secretary of the Board of Trade, to Jenkinson, March 2, 1764, C.O. 324, XXI.

new organization was shown in the agitation carried on against the duties on beaver skins imported from His Majesty's Dominion. After several consultations with the London merchants trading to Canada, a policy was outlined by the Board of Trade during January, February, March, and April, 1764, and practically accepted in detail in 4 Geo. III, c. 9. The Board of Trade recommended the entire abolition of the import duties on beaver skins, but the Act imposed a nominal duty of 1d. on each skin. The pressure of hat manufacturers who complained that the increasing supply of furs had occasioned a larger re-exportation of fur, was successful in securing measures levying an export duty of 7d. on every beaver skin and 1s. 6d. on every pound of beaver wool. Further evidence of the virility of the organization was shown in the appointment of Fowler Walker on April 19, 1765, at £200 per year as an agent to represent the interests of the traders of Montreal and Quebec.[7]

The influence of this organization was also shown in the colony. The French military organization, which included alliances with influential Indian tribes, had broken down[8] and the road was opened for the expansion of English trade. As shown in the case of Alexander Henry,[9] the trade to the interior began in 1761 with the issue of a small number of licences. Following the restoration of order in the interior, regulations were issued following the Proclamation of October, 1763, and the trade was placed under the control of Sir William Johnson, superintendent of the northern districts. These regulations were to the effect that,

Whereas His Majesty by his Royal Proclamation given at St. James the seventh Day of October, one thousand seven Hundred and sixty Three, in the third year of his Reign, hath thought fit to declare and enjoin, that the Trade with the several nations or Tribes of Indians, with whom he is

[7]See *The Maseres Letters, 1766–1768*, ed. W. S. Wallace, Appendix 9, p. 123, and for an indication of Walker's influence, see *ibid.*, p. 11. It is interesting to note that Montreal merchants were becoming more independent of the Quebc traders and protested against an appointee of Quebec; see Petition of Merchants of Montreal, April 1, 1764, Can. Arch., C.O. 42, I, 364; also C.O. 391, LXXI, 416. See R. A. Humphreys, "Governor Murray's Views on the Plan of 1764 for the Management of Indian Affairs."

[8]For an account of the causes of the Indian wars I am indebted to Mrs. K. B. Jackson; see an article by this author (as M. G. Reid), "The Quebec Fur-Traders and Western Policy, 1763–1774"; also P. C. Phillips, "The Fur Trade in the Maumee-Wabash Country"; and for a general treatment, C. E. Carter, *Great Britain and the Illinois Country, 1763–1774*, esp. chap. v.

[9]*Travels and Adventures . . . by Alexander Henry*, ed. J. Bain, pp. 183–184.

connected, and who live under his protection should be free and open to all his Subjects whatever . . .

Provided that no Person or Persons whatsoever, until his Majesty's further Pleasure is known, do trade or Traffic, vend or dispose of any goods, wares, or Merchandize of any kind whatsoever, to any Indian by Royal Proclamation except in such Forts or Posts already, or which hereafter shall be established by His Majesty and garrisoned by His Troops, for which purpose Licenses will be granted at the Secretary's office in Quebec and at that of His Deputy at Montreal; For the due observance whereof, every Trader is required to enter into Bond for double the value of their goods upon oath, and specify the Quantity of arms and ammunition they shall carry with them.

A proclamation of April 13, 1764, permitted freedom of trade to everyone at the posts of Carillon (on the Ottawa) and the Cedars (on the St. Lawrence) but trade beyond these points was carried on through licences.[10] In the regulations of January 24, 1765, every trader was allowed to take out a licence but was obliged to give security. Commandants were placed over important posts, and the licensees required to take out a bond to obey their orders. The importance of the organization to the trade was shown in numerous protests against these forms of control.[11] In a statement dated February 20, 1765, it was noted that:

[10]Can. Arch., C.O. 42, I, Pt. II, 196–197; II, Pt. II, 403–404; also Q, II, 339, and the proclamation of January 31, 1766, Q, V, Pt. II, 295–298.

[11]Objections were raised against the regulation requiring bonds of double the value of the goods to ensure obedience of the traders to the Michilimackinac commandant, Can. Arch., Hardwicke Papers, 35,914, pp. 166–167; also copies of letters from merchants to Walker, ibid., pp. 177–191; and Robert Rogers to Fowler Walker, March 4, 1771, ibid., 35,915, Pt. II, pp. 237–281; see the Memorial of sundry merchants of the city of London interested in the trade of the Province of Quebec (signed fifteen names), Can. Arch., Q, III, 420–423; also Hardwicke Papers, 35,915, Pt. II, pp. 356–381 (which includes a striking account of the necessity of the traders constantly urging the Indians to hunt for furs); and letter of French merchants at Michilimackinac, July 2, 1765, ibid., Pt. I, p. 177; also address to Captain Howard by merchants, with his answer and letter to Sir Wm. Johnson dated Michilimackinac, July 5, 1765, asking for free trade, letter of H. S. Conway to Commandant at Michilimackinac, March 27, 1766, charging favouritism, and letter from the merchants of Montreal, March 30, 1766, and letter of J. Murray, April 1766, replying to the merchants and agreeing to change the character of the licences lengthening the time from twelve to eighteen months and proposing to sign them himself to prevent favouritism. Sir Wm. Johnson on May 3, 1766, continued to insist on merchants trading only at posts. The merchants petitioned on August 22, 1766, for redress from undue punishment for violation of agreements in 1765, and again in a letter dated Montreal, April 2, 1767, protested against possi-

Michilimackinac being the chief Post to the northward where nothing is produced but Indian corn, the Traders cannot Winter there for want of Provisions but have always been obliged to quit that Place to winter with the Indians in their Villages at the distance sometimes of six hundred Leagues to the North West, by this means they cultivate a friendship with the savages and Excite a desire in them to have the commodities of Europe in order to cloath themselves and their Families, which by the abundance at their own doors, they get at a cheap Rate, and is a spur to their Industry without which they would not kill a quarter Part of the Beaver etc. but only hunt for sustenance and a few skins to make themselves cloathing.

The nations Inhabiting near the Bay des Puans, St. Joseph, and the Point of Chagouamigon whose Hunting grounds lie between there and the Mississipi on whose Banks they usually Winter will by the communication of the River Illinois carry their Furrs and Peltries to New Orleans or Truck them with such Traders as will be sent up from thence; and should that city pass into the Hands of the Spaniards their allies the French will nevertheless supplie them with suitable goods at a cheaper Rate than the English can do by reason of the high price of Labour among our Manufactures to wit, especially in Gunns, coarse cutlery etc. . . .

It is well known that the Indians have no magazines of Furrs they must therefore come to the Forts and Posts almost empty handed to get credit for their winter hunt. When they shall have Furrs instead of coming a great distance to pay their Debts, 'tis to be feared they will rather carry them to some other Posts to Truck them for new goods.[12]

The dangers of competition from the Mississippi[13] were continually stressed. A letter in the *Quebec Gazette* of August 18, 1768, ran as follows:

Extract of a Letter from Michillimackinac, to a Gentleman in this city, dated 30th June.

Trade is very dull here, tho' we have many Traders. . . . All those who wintered between this and the River Missisippi, complain of the French and Spaniards, of New Orleans, having undersold them considerably in every Article; in Consequence whereof the Indians, bordering on that River, us'd our Traders very ill, plundered many, kill'd several Englishmen

---

bilities of too rigid enforcement of the regulations. A further plea for freedom of trade was made by merchants at Michilimackinac on June 30, 1767. On July 18, 1767, Rogers at Michilimackinac wrote to Dobie and W. Grant asking that his plans for freeing the trade be sent immediately to England because of the jealousy of Roberts. In 1767 licences were granted under Roberts permitting freedom of trade from Michilimackinac. Can. Arch., Baby Collection, I.

[12]Can. Arch., C.O. 42, II, Pt. II, 363–364.

[13]See Pond's description of French trade at Prairie du Chien from New Orleans in 1773–74, "Journal," *Wisconsin Historical Collections*, XVIII, 338 ff.

and one Canadian, for which Violences we have two Hostages of the Suak nation who are to remain here till the rest of their Tribe bring in the Offenders.

Charges of favouritism were made against commandants who allowed some traders to winter among the Indians and refused others, and who exacted undue charges and engaged in trade in their own interests. Petitions asked for changes on many grounds. A memorial on the Indian trade to His Excellency Guy Carleton, dated Montreal, September 20, 1766, and signed by fifty-seven names, included new objections and reiterated old ones.[14]

We think that the Trade with the Indians should be free and open, to all His Majesty's Subjects without Exception, and that no one should avail himself of any Advantage more than another. . . .

Unless there is a Permission for all Persons to winter with the Indians on their hunting Grounds, that the Trade must every year diminish, for many Nations of Indians, and those too who have always made the greatest Consumption of our British Manufactures, and have brought the largest Quantity of Furs and other Peltries to our Market, are at so great a Distance from any Fort, that it is impossible they should supply themselves, and return again to their hunting Grounds in the same Year; Consequently if it was their determination to be supplyed from the English, yet every second Year of their hunting must be lost, which would prevent the consumption of our British Manufactures, stop the Current of our Trade, hinder us from making proper Remittances to our Correspondents, and in the end entirely break the Chain of our Commerce; but this is not all, for to our Mortification, we every day see French Traders from the Missisipi who have Permission to trade with the Indians wherever they have Inclination, and the Peltries that would, if we had equal Liberty to trade, come through this Government, are now sent to the Missisipi and go to France, from whence they have French Manufactures in return; we are well assured great Quantities passed that way last year, which we apprehend is the Reason why peltries in England are so much Lower in their value and as long as we are restrained in our Trade, the French from the Missisipi, by having freer access than we have, will always have it in their Power to carry the Trade from us; to the great Detriment of our Manufactures in Great Britain, and the utter Ruin of this our Province of Quebec. . . .

It is well known that the Support of an Indian and his Family is his Fusee; now if any Indian Family who perhaps Winters at the Distance of five or six hundred Miles from one of these Established Forts, should by

[14]Copy of a Memorial upon the Indian trade . . . to His Excellency Guy Carleton, Esq., Can. Arch., Shelburne MSS, L (1754–66), 137–139; also in Q, IV, 201 f.

any Misfortune either break his Fusee, or the least screw of his Lock be out of Order, or want Ammunition, where could that Indian Family be supported from, or how get their Sustenance? they must either perish with Hunger, or at least loose their Hunting that year, which will be so much Peltries diminished from the Publick Quantity: and unless that family is relieved by some persons in the Fort giving them Credit, the ensuing year they will not be able to return to their hunting Ground, and so be lost for ever. . . .

These Persons who have never had Commerce with the Indians, may think any Indian coming from so great Distance, tho' he should not have it in his Power to return to his own hunting Ground, yet may always get his living by hunting on his way: but those who have been acquainted with them, know the Indians are so tenacious of their Property, and Jealous of other Nations, that they will not suffer them in passing through their Lands, to hunt for their Support; therefore these Nations at the greatest Distance will never be able to come to the Post established. . . .

Without the Indians have Credit given them, 'tis impossible to carry on a Trade to Advantage. And when we are on the Spot to winter with them, we have always an Opportunity of knowing their Dispositions, pressing them to exert their Diligence, and are ready in the Spring to receive what is due.

The increasing quantity of goods[15] which was being sent by the Albany route[16] was a further cause of alarm among the Quebec merchants.[17] Benjamin Frobisher, an important trader, and others again, pointed out in a memorandum dated Quebec, November 10, 1766,[18] the difference in the type of country to the north around Michilimackinac with its scarcity of provisions and the country to the south where there was plenty of game for subsistence about the forts and complained that the regulations were not adapted to the northern trade. Complaints became more specific that the policy of control was favourable to the interests of New York and hostile to the interests of the Province of Quebec. New York favoured restriction of trade to the posts whereas the northern traders demanded freedom of trade.[19]

[15]Toronto Public Library, Letters and Accounts, North-West Company; see also the complaints of Albany merchants, especially Simon McTavish, against the Quebec Act as a probable interference with the importation of rum and other commodities *via* Albany.

[16]For a description of the Albany route in 1768 see *Journal of [John Lees] of Quebec, Merchant*. Also see V. D. Harrington, *The New York Merchant on the Eve of the Revolution*, pp. 232 ff.

[17]H. T. Cramahé to the Earl of Hillsborough, Can. Arch., Q. VI, 82; also Dartmouth Papers, No. 713.

[18]"Observations on the Indian trade," Quebec, November 10, 1776, Can. Arch., Shelburne MSS, L, 160–164.   [19]*Ibid.*, pp. 137–139.

The Province of New York desire the Trade may be continued to the Forts, for say they, the People in Canada having a better Navigation than we have, if they are permitted, can send among the Indians, and carry most of the Peltries through the Province of Quebec.

The following extract from the Minutes of Council of the Province of Quebec[20] brought out the complaint more forcibly.

And here we think we do not speak the Language of persons improperly devoted to our own Province, when we say that this has much better pretensions to give the law upon this head to those countries, than any other Government upon the continent. Our Traders are more Numerous, they Exchange more of the British Manufactories (the others those from Albany in particular, only carrying up Rum) and have besides such a free communication with the Posts by means of the great Rivers which fall directly into the St. Lawrence, so must make them the carriers of, by far the greatest and most valuable produce of those Countries to the European Markets. . . .

To shew a Disposition on our Parts for forming some Plan to this purpose was my only Inducement to comply with the Governor of New York's Requisition; The Interests of the two Provinces in regard to the Indian Trade differ too widely, to expect they will ever perfectly agree upon general Regulations for carrying it on; and tho' some trifling matters may be settled here, the great difficulty, under which the Traders at present labour, the means of recovering and securing their Property in the upper country, as well as of apprehending fugitive Debtors, I believe, can only be remedied at Home.

The numerous complaints led to a change in policy[21] and served as an illustration of the strength of the organized fur trade. Sir William Johnson, who was in charge of the northern district, claimed that the measures were necessary from the standpoint of military precaution although he admitted that they were not effective.[22] A policy was inaugurated in 1768 which extended the powers of the provinces, and

[20]Minutes of Council, William Hey, P.C., Guy Carleton, Can. Arch., Q, VI, 82, 90.

[21]See the minute instructions as to details in the issue of licences in a letter from Geo. Allsopp, Quebec, April 13, 1769, Can. Arch., S. 717, p. 132; also *Quebec Gazette*, September 29, 1769.

[22]W. Johnson to Lieutenant Governor Carleton, January 27, 1767, Can. Arch., Q, IV, 118–119. This was answered by renewed complaints of the regulations, and of French and Spanish competition. Quebec, March, 1767, *ibid.*, pp. 123–126; also Appendix E, and Memorial from the merchants and traders of Montreal respecting Indian trade, January 15, 1768 (signed twenty-two names), Can. Arch., Q, V, Pt. I, complaining of the regulations of Sir William Johnson and their rigid enforcement. *The Papers of Sir William Johnson*, ed. A. C. Flick, especially IV and V, give valuable information on the problems of regulation.

especially of Quebec and New York, allocating more or less definite areas to them. The outcome was competition between the provinces, and general confusion. On October 31, 1771, Quebec merchants protested against resolutions of the New York Assembly taxing rum and dry goods.[23] The traders of Quebec formulated a demand for an extension of the jurisdiction of the province and control of the trade, and the final result was shown in the boundaries laid down in the Quebec Act of 1774.

The fur traders of Montreal and Quebec with the organization in London and their connections with English supply houses exercised a powerful influence in breaking the control of Albany and New York and in the establishment of legislation securing control of the trade within the boundaries outlined in the Quebec Act of 1774. The centralization of control in external trade in the French *régime* and the sensitiveness of the home and colonial governments to changes became characteristic of the trade as conducted by the English. The vital dependence of a colony, from which furs were the chief export, on English manufacturers made this development inevitable. In the short period of less than fifteen years, the English merchants and traders had found it necessary to develop an organization which had features strikingly similar to those of the French *régime*.[24]

The technical demands of the trade were of fundamental importance. The vastness of the country tributary to the St. Lawrence drainage basin, as it had been covered by the French, made inevitable the adoption of French methods of conducting the trade. The merchants from Albany accustomed to carrying on the trade within relatively narrow limits prior to the end of the war were faced with vastly different

[23]A regulation prohibiting rum in the fur trade led Albany merchants to protest in 1764 and was relaxed in 1766 when a licence system was introduced. *Documents relative to the Colonial History of the State of New York*, ed. E. B. O'Callaghan, VII, 613–615. It was suggested in 1768 (*ibid.*, VIII, 19–31) that management of the trade be left to the colonies. Suggestions of the New York Assembly in 1771 were opposed by Quebec but the Quebec Act provided a solution. See *ibid.*, VII, 15 ff, 40–41, 571–572, 657–660. On the importance of Canada to the New York fur trade and relation to the treaty of 1763 see Harrington, *New York Merchant*, pp. 167, 309–310. Co-operation as to taxing was impossible as Quebec had no assembly and no taxing power in contrast with New York and Pennsylvania. A. L. Burt, *The United States, Great Britain and British North America*, pp. 19–20.

[24]John Lees was in business in Quebec and had accounts with Chabert in Detroit which he went to collect in 1768. In 1768 Detroit supplied flour and Indian corn to the surrounding region.

conditions.[25] Illustrating the advantages of French experience in Montreal, Peter Pond, in beginning trade from Michilimackinac in 1773, obtained the bulk of his goods from New York but "I wanted some small articles in the Indian way to compleat my assortment which was not to be had in New York. I there took my boate . . . to Montreal where I found all I wanted." Methods of control and regulation adequate to the English trade were inadequate to the new demands. Merchants of Montreal and Quebec, becoming adapted to the new situations, found their interests differing materially from the interests of the traders of New York and the other provinces.

The effectiveness and rapidity with which the break between Quebec and New York was made was another result of the trade. The importance of the fur trade in the St. Lawrence drainage basin in the French *régime* led to a centralization of policy and organization in external affairs and to an increasing dependence on the trader in the interior. The furs were collected over a wide area on the numerous tributaries and brought down to the main trunk of navigation.[26] Control was easily

[25]John Lees writes: "In this place [Albany, 1768] are severall Dutch people of Considerable Estates, before the Reduction of Canada many of them made a great deal of money in a Contraband Trade with that country [in] furrs." *Journal of [John Lees] of Quebec, Merchant*, p. 14. "Schenectady is greatly increased in building since last War; Its only support is the Indian Trade, and its chief Inhabitants . . . are bateau-men, that are employed by those concerned in the Indian Trade" (*ibid.*, p. 15). "The South side of the Lake is always used by Batteaus and Canoes bound up being much safer for them than the North side, which is full of Shoals, Rocks, and Islands; this however was the side of the Lake used always by the French in time of War, but in time of peace, they often came by the South Side having, it is said, then Carried on a good deal of Contraband Trade with our Indian Traders at Oswego" (*ibid.*, p. 24). In regard to Phyn and Duncan, merchants, see note, p. 14 of Lees' *Journal* and R. H. Fleming, "Phyn, Ellice and Company of Schenectady."

[26]Travelling along the south shore from Oswego toward Niagara in July, 1768, Lees met Gamelin from Detroit with 2 canoes of 70 packs, also 2 canoes for Mr. Baby, 1 for Cazeau, 1 for M. Mouton, 2 canoes with Mr. Rameau, 2 for Mr. Berthelot of Montreal, and 2 batteaus for Phyn of Schenectady. "Very few Canoes had gone up this year from Canada; but a good many had gone loaded down, rather more than last year." At Niagara, he relates (p. 26), "the Bank is . . . so high, that all the Kings provisions, and Traders goods are hauled up by a Windlass from the Shore between 90 and 100 feet," and hauled by horses and oxen to Fort Schlosser.

John Stedman had a contract in 1763 to widen the portage at Niagara. Lees describes in 1768 (pp. 27–28) Stedman's contract paying £100 and 17 rations of provisions for carrying over all the King's stores. He was paid £3 York currency for carrying over an empty batteau and 3/10 York currency for taking

built up in a district limited in transportation facilities by geography and climate, but was difficult to effect in widely scattered territory. The merchants in Canada and London were able to build up a strong organization with great rapidity in external policy. As late as 1794 Simcoe in a letter to the Board of Trade dated September 1, noted the influence of this organization. "The Fur Trade has hitherto been the Staple of Canada and the protection of it, untill the Establishment of the Government of Upper Canada, seems to have been the primary object of all the Military Arrangements and consequent Settlements in the Upper Country."[27]

The immediate reasons for the importance of the fur trade were reflected, as in the French *régime*, in the financial policy of the colonial government and in the adaptation of the fur trade to the mercantile policy. The shipment of furs from Quebec involved payment of a duty which brought in a revenue of £20,267.16.9 in 1784 and an average of £22,021.15.4 for the nine years from 1793 to 1801.[28] In 1808 duties paid averaged £20,000. Goods exported for the trade were valued at £40,000 annually. Although smuggling was prevalent[29] as in the French *régime* the fur trade remained important to the financial position of the government.

The growth of an organization in a territory with interests of pronounced difference from those of the remaining English provinces had significant effects in the struggle which later developed in the American Revolution. It was a contributing cause of the Revolution, and also an important element in the determination of the final results. To a very large extent the American Revolution and the fall of New France were phases of the struggle of settlement against furs. The war against New France was a war against an organization which had been built up on the fur trade, and which checked westward expansion of the English colonies. Similarly, the Revolution was a struggle against an organiza-

---

over each pack. Canoes were carried over on men's shoulders. A cart load was carried up for £5 New York currency, a canoe being 2½ cart loads. Stedman cut hay for his stock on a large meadow near the river.

On Lake Erie (pp. 31–35) Lees met two batteaus belonging to Edgar of Detroit and Cuyler of Albany; "Mr. Adhemar" with 4 canoes; 3 batteaus belonging to Schenectady carrying G. Meldrum, T. Williams, and two Dutchmen named Visscher; 1 batteau of Felix Graham of Detroit; 2 canoes with 70 packs aboard "mostly Catts, Bears and Deer Leather," and 2 Albany batteaus from Detroit.

See also Mrs. Anne Grant, *Memoirs of an American Lady*.

[27]*The Correspondence of John Graves Simcoe*, ed. E. A. Cruikshank, III, 52–53.   [28]Can. Arch., Q, CVIII, 59–61.

[29]*Correspondence of Simcoe*, II, 297; and III, 55, 190, 220.

tion which had been built up on the fur trade, and which also threatened westward expansion. The final struggle between the English colonies and New France was precipitated by the French occupation of the Ohio valley. The American Revolution was also in part precipitated by a policy shown in the proclamation of 1763 which forbade the settlement of Indian territories and in the Quebec Act which made the Ohio valley the southern boundary of the Province of Quebec. The final results witnessed the supremacy of settlement and after a period of negotiation the establishment of a boundary line which followed roughly the southern boundary of the more important navigation routes of fur-trading northerly districts. The diversified economic development of the English colonies supported by the manufacturing efficiency of Great Britain gave sufficient strength to defeat a colony weak through dependence on the single staple of fur, even though supported by the energy of a powerful mother country. But the manufacturing efficiency of Great Britain in support of the fur trade area directly dependent upon it was in turn sufficient to defeat the diversified economic growth of the colonies and to maintain control of Canada. From the standpoint of the English colonies, the conquest of New France and the American Revolution were struggles favouring the progress of settlement and industrial growth as against the demands of the mercantile policy of Great Britain. The Quebec Act of 1774 and the retention of Canada after the American Revolution were partly the result of a mercantile policy since they guaranteed a continuation of the fur trade and the continued wide consumption of British manufactures. The long and difficult negotiations prior to the Jay Treaty involved a continuation of the same policy.[30]

The fur trade organization was supported in addition by the advantages outlined in a memorandum on the "State of the Trade with the Indian Countries" written in Montreal in 1785, in which the following statement was made:

But supposing that the United States should insist on our abandoning the Posts and that Great Britain should not be in a situation to dispute their claim, yet with proper management, more than two thirds of the furr Trade would center in this province, having at present and will (for a number of years to come) have every advantage over them that we could wish, which advantages (they will never surmount unless we in this Province permit them) such as experienced Guides, expert Canoe men and able interpreters, to those may be added the facility of procuring Birch Canoes and above all

[30]For a valuable survey of the influence of the fur trade on the negotiations of the period see W. E. Stevens, *The Northwest Fur Trade, 1763–1800.*

the Knowledge which our Traders have of the various articles necessary for the many Indian Nations.[31]

Even after the surrender of the forts under Jay's treaty, it was possible to write:

To talk, therefore, of their acquiring possession of three-fourths of the fur trade by the surrender of the posts on the lakes, is absurd in the extreme; neither is it likely that they will acquire any considerable share of the lake trade in general, which, as I have already pointed out, can be carried on by the British merchants from Montreal and Quebec, by means of the St. Lawrence, with such superior advantage.[32]

B. THE AMERICAN REVOLUTION

Since the American Revolution was an evidence of the supremacy of settlement it was destined eventually to have important effects on fur trade organization. The immediate consequences of the American Revolution were shown in a scarcity of commodities and a disruption of the trade. Powder was scarce and blankets were difficult to obtain because of the demands of the troops. Trade was impossible in the war areas.[33] The trade from New York was cut off and traders, such as Peter Pond, who had obtained goods from New York and Albany, were forced to depend on Montreal. Simon McTavish, the firm of Phyn and Ellice, and others were obliged to leave Albany and move to Montreal.[34]

Fears were entertained that the enemy was benefiting from the trade.[35]

The Augmentation in Furrs to Canada, of late years, may be owing to the encroachment on the Hudson's Bay Company and the Trafic with the Spanish Traders on the other side of the Mississippi. The consumption of British Articles of Commerce may probably have been augmented by the

[31]Can. Arch., Shelburne MSS, LXXXVIII, 20.

[32]Isaac Weld, *Travels through the States of North America and the Provinces of Upper and Lower Canada, during the Years 1795, 1796, and 1797*, p. 306; see also *Correspondence of Simcoe*, I, 216.

[33]See an account of an expedition in 1780 from Mackinac to Prairie du Chien for furs stored at that point, *John Long's Voyages and Travels in the Years 1768–1788*, ed. M. M. Quaife, pp. 185–190.

[34]*Minutes of the Albany Committee of Correspondence 1775–1778*, II, 1065, and R. H. Fleming, "Phyn, Ellice and Company of Schenectady."

[35]See Invoice of goods, presents to Indians in America, . . . August 8, 1775, Can. Arch., Q, XI, 210 ff.; also Requisition of Lieutenant Colonel John Campbell, Superintendent of Indian Affairs, for presents to the Indians for the year 1781, *ibid.*, Q, XVII, Pt. II, 712; Pt. I, 255–257.

large presents given to Indians, and by some of the articles sliding into the Rebel Colonies. . . .

The labour and Difficulty in conveying supplies to the enemy by way of Lake Superior are not great . . . they may reach them by the Mississipy from that Lake by three different Routes; disaffected Traders have done, and can do much mischief in that Lake by fomenting the quarrels long subsisting between the *Scioux* and *Chippawas*, and consequently preventing the former who are the most powerful and most attached of all Indian Allies, from leaving their country to attend our calls.

More rigid control was exercised and the number of passes restricted.[36] Private vessels were banned from the lakes and goods for the trade were carried only on the King's vessels.[37]

Haldimand in a letter to Lord George Germain dated Quebec, October 25, 1780,[38] wrote:

The great demand for passes to the upper Countries since the commencement of the Rebellion, but particularly the last two years, at a time when the natural Trade must necessarily diminish from the Indians being employed in war, created suspicions that means were found to convey supplies much wanted by the Rebels, into their country. . . . I conceived the most effectual means to prevent the Evil, would be by permitting no more than a sufficient quantity of goods, for the use of each Post, to be sent up; in this however I have not been able to succeed, the number of Traders and quantity of goods to that country increasing every year.

. . . The inconsiderable number of troops thinly distributed amongst the Posts, and (until very lately) their weak state of defence, render it imprudent to Risk the large Quantities of goods which the clamour of the merchants obliged me, contrary to my Judgment, to acquiesce in their sending up, the capture of which, must have essentially militated against the King's Service. These considerations had their Force at all the Posts, yet the merchants continued to solicit for passes, particularly to Michilimackinac and for the North West Trade. . . .

. . . The Fur Trade is not the object . . . it is the great consumption of Rum and Indian Presents (manifested by the amazing sums drawn for on those accounts) purchased at a most exorbitant price from the traders.

The effects of these regulations were shown in numerous complaints[39]

---

[36]*Ibid.*, Haldimand Papers, B.99, pp. 173–175.

[37]*Ibid.*, Q, XXV, 299–300. [38]*Ibid.*, Q, XVII, Pt. I, 142–146.

[39]See Memorial of merchants trading to Lake Superior and the Northwest praying that licenses be granted to allow goods to leave La Chine without delay, May 1, 1779, Can. Arch., Haldimand Papers, B.217, pp. 73–77; also a List of passes for the immediate relief of the trade to Lake Superior and the Grand Portage, May 21, 1779—26 canoes, 208 men, 3,640 gal. of rum, 260 gal. of wine, 50 arms, 64 cwt. of powder, 100 cwt. of ball and shot, *ibid.*, p. 79.

and petitions from the merchants for relief. It was the continuation of the regulations after the war to check clandestine trade with the United States, however, which occasioned the more vehement protests. Haldimand in letters of instruction to Brigadier General St. Leger dated Quebec, September 14, 1784,[40] wrote:

> If the Transport of any merchandise upon those Lakes, except in King's Vessels was permitted, a Door would be opened for a clandestine illicit Commerce which would be very hurtful to the Trade of this Province, as a great part of the Furs from the Upper Country would be introduced to the American States by means of numberless small Rivers running from the Lakes, but particularly by the great Route of Oswego, directly to Albany. Injurious as this species of commerce must be to the Fair Trader, we have had very recent instances of it's being practised over Lake Champlain by some of the most considerable merchants in Montreal, who are connected with great Houses in London; it is attended with another Evil, upon the Upper Lakes, that of introducing the Americans into the interior parts of the country, and giving them opportunities to debauch our friendly Indians, and supplant us in the Fur Trade.

Complaints of favouritism, of restriction of trade, and of pilfering on the part of soldiers[41] became more numerous.

> Goods have been detained 6, 12 and 16 months at the Landing places, and on their arrival at their destined Markets the unfortunate Traders have found Individuals possessed of the Governor's *privilege* for vending their Cargoes at the Forts in preference to other Traders. It is natural to conjecture that such preferences are granted through interested motives, when we consider to whom they are given. . . . And I cannot help observing that the French Traders in general have mostly suffered by this pernicious conduct, which has given rise to a just saying amongst them. "It is a Specimen of English Liberty."[42]

A memorial of the merchants trading to the upper country dated Montreal, April 2, 1785,[43] complained:

---

[40]Can. Arch., Q, XXIV, Pt. I, 145; see also a protest signed by Hamilton & Cartwright, John Thompson, Samuel Street & Co., and Douglas & Symington, merchants of Niagara, against the importation of American goods from Schenectady, Niagara, August 1, 1783, Can. Arch., Q, XXI, 428–430; and a letter prohibiting Ellice & Co. shipping furs to the United States, February 2, 1784, Can. Arch., Haldimand Papers, B.62, p. 70; also *ibid.*, B.64, p. 131. The effectiveness of these restrictions was shown in part in *John Long's Voyages and Travels in the Years 1768–1788*, pp. 217 f.

[41]Can. Arch., Q, LI, Pt. I, 117.

[42]*Ibid.*, Shelburne MSS, LXXXVIII, 11–12.

[43]*Ibid.*, Q, XXIV, Pt. II, 330.

That the partiality shewn to Individuals in forwarding goods by preference passes last year, hurt exceedingly the Trade in general, and prevented
those who had to depend on the Rotation from getting their goods to
market, great part whereof are still lying on the communication to the
detriment and injury of the Proprietors.

That as the vessels on the Lakes are generally so much employed in
transporting stores and provisions for Government as to occasion the
merchants effects to remain a very long time on the communication subject
to waste, damage and pilfering, and as a heavy expense is incurred by
sending up in the Vessells men who are engaged to winter in the interior
parts of the country, Your Memorialists most earnestly represent these two
objects as being exceedingly detrimental and expensive, and therefore they
pray that they may be allowed to carry their Goods across the Lakes in
Batteaux or Canoes Which will not only assure to them a certainty of
getting to market in time, but save them from a burthensome charge: . . .
and they are the more hopeful of obtaining this request, as they are
particularly . . . that all their Peltries should be brought down in the Kings
Vessells so that there may not be the smallest temptation to carry them
into Alien States.

Constant protest eventually brought relief. The Northwest Company
in a petition dated Montreal, October 4, 1784,[44] asked for a release
from the regulation banning private vessels:

Such provisions especially Indian corn must necessarily be purchased
about Niagara, at Fort Erie, when it cannot be had in the settlement of
Detroit, and all the company wishes for is to have the preference in the
transport to Michilimackinac in the King's vessels, if ready in point of time;
if not, to suffer a private vessel to be *commanded by a King's officer* if his
Excellency thinks fit, to take their provisions forward from Fort Erie or
Detroit, and thence to Michilimackinac.

The Company have further to request that his Excellency will be pleased
to permit them to build a small vessel at Detroit to be sent to St. Marys
early the next spring with a part of their provisions for the purpose of
getting her up the Falls, to transport the same over Lake Superior, and to
remain upon that Lake to be employed every summer in the same service;
as the men sent in their canoes from Montreal are by no means adequate
to the heavy transport of goods and Provisions over that Lake to the Grand
Portage.

Permission was given at Quebec on November 10, 1784, to the Northwest Company to build a vessel in Detroit.[45] The vessel[46] (34-foot keel,
13-foot beam, and 4-foot hold costing £1,843 York currency) could

---

[44]*Ibid.*, Haldimand Papers, B.217, p. 479.
[45]"North West Trade," *Report on Canadian Archives*, 1888, p. 72.
[46]"North-Western Explorations," *ibid.*, 1890, pp. 59–60.

not be taken up the Falls because of its size, and permission was asked that it might be used in transporting provisions from Fort Erie and Detroit to Michilimackinac. In this and in other ways resistance was broken down. Following further protests[47] merchants were permitted in 1785 to take goods from Montreal to Niagara in their own boats and canoes.[48] On August 23, 1786, trade was declared free and open subject to licence regulation[49] but private navigation was still prohibited. In 1787 permission was given to navigate private vessels on Lake Ontario under securities but it was still withheld on Lakes Erie and Huron. Private navigation was extended throughout the Great Lakes in 1789. A letter to Hon. W. Grant, Chairman of the Committee of Inland Commerce and Navigation, from Phyn, Ellice & Co., Forsyth, Richardson & Co., McTavish, Frobisher & Co., John & Andrew McGill, William Robertson, Dobie & Badgeley, and A. Auldjo dated October 26, 1790, asked for every freedom in inland navigation to enable them to compete with the Americans and the Spaniards. Regulations of April 30, 1788, May 4, 1789, and July 5, 1790, and tightening of the provisions of 28 Geo. III, c. 6., permitting free construction and navigation of merchant vessels, obviated all difficulty.

The net effects of the American Revolution however were more

---

[47]See numerous letters and memorials asking for the return of free navigation, Can. Arch., Haldimand Papers, B.61, *passim*; also Memorial of the merchants and traders of Montreal trading to the upper posts, to the Hon. Henry Hamilton, July 11, 1785, asking for aid in transporting the goods which had accumulated at Fort Erie up the Lakes, *ibid.*, Q, XXV, 89–91; James McGill to Hon. Henry Hamilton, August 1, 1785, "North-Western Explorations," pp. 56–58; James McGill to Hugh Finlay, August 8, 1785, *ibid.*, pp. 58–59; also further correspondence between the merchants and the government asking for removal of restrictions on lake navigation, *ibid.*, pp. 61 f.; also Can. Arch., Shelburne MSS, LXXXVIII, 10 f.; and the Memorial of the merchants and traders of Montreal trading to the upper countries in behalf of themselves and their correspondent traders at the several posts on the upper Lakes, April 10, 1786, Can. Arch., Q, XXVI, 300–301, against exorbitant charges; also protest of William Robertson, Detroit, against undue freight charges and preferences to Macomb, Edgar and Macomb, and others, *ibid.*, Q, LI, Pt. I, 101–121. As a protest merchants refused to pay the freight on His Majesty's vessels, see *Quebec Gazette*, March 28, 1782. "Notice that accounts must be paid for 1777–8–9 before any goods would be shipped past Carleton Island that year." In 1785 these debts were estimated at £20,500. Letter from Dorchester to Lord Sydney, Quebec, November 9, 1787, Can. Arch., Q, XXVIII, 184–185; see also *ibid.*, Q, XXVI, Pt. I, and Pt. II, *passim*, for aspects of the disputes. It was alleged that exorbitant freight charges were made on goods going from Niagara to Detroit or Michilimackinac, "Marbois on the Fur Trade, 1784," p. 735.

[48]Letters . . . St. Leger, May 7, 1785, Can. Arch., Q, XXIV, Pt. II, 326–327.

[49]Can. Arch., Q, LI, Pt. I, 91 ff., also pp. 122–124.

serious with the development of regulations prohibiting trade on American territory[50] and especially after the Jay Treaty and the abandonment of the British posts.[51] The extent and character of the trade is suggested in the following extracts. Writing on Detroit on September 1, 1784, Evan Nepean stated:

And I think if the post [Detroit] is not given up to the Americans it will increase, for the Spaniards can not send coarse Woolen manufactures up the Mississippi to supply their Trade near so cheap as the English by their communication, as a proof of which they have this Year Bartered several Cargoes of Peltry with our Traders for these commodities, and in short cannot carry on their Trade without them, while we keep possession of the Lakes.[52]

On July 28, 1793, Captain Doyle of the Twenty-fourth Regiment stationed at Michilimackinac wrote to Governor Simcoe:

The most considerable Trade from this Post is to and beyond the Mississippi by the rout of La Prairie du Chien, from which place the Traders descend with facility to the American Settlements at the Illinois who are all affected to the British Government. The trade to that Country is much in our favour, as they consume a great quantity of British manufactures particularly Cottons, and not having a sufficiency of Peltries to give in return the balance is paid in cash which they receive from their neighbours the Spaniards. . . .

There is also a considerable trade carried on from hence to the Spanish Post of Pain Court, (or St. Louis) upon the Mississippi, which is considerably in our favour, but cannot be depended upon for two reasons, first, the admission of goods from this Post, being contraband tho' not rightly observed, secondly, should an enterprising Merchant send Goods from New

[50]For a discussion of the trade in Michigan during the Revolutionary War and later, see I. A. Johnson, *The Michigan Fur Trade*, chaps. v, vi; also A. E. Parkins, *Historical Geography of Detroit*, chaps. v, vi; S. F. Bemis, *Jay's Treaty, a Study in Commerce and Diplomacy*, chap. iii, and *passim*; and A. C. McLaughlin, "The Western Posts and the British Debts," on the efforts of the Americans to gain control of the fur trade (1783–96). For protests of the fur traders and of the Northwest Company against the delivery of the posts to Americans, see Memorial to Simcoe, December 9, 1791, Can. Arch., Q, CCLXXVIII, 136–145; Memorial of April 23, 1792, *ibid.*, pp. 146–162; also on the dangers of losing Mackinac, *ibid.*, XLIX, 314; see Charles Stevenson to George Hammond, New York, March 6, 1792, on protest against the damage which the trade would incur through the transfer of Grand Portage to the Americans, *Correspondence of Simcoe*, I, 117; also J. G. Simcoe to H. Dundas, Quebec, April 28, 1792, protesting interference of Americans with the trade of the Indians, *ibid.*, pp. 139–140.

[51]See G. S. Graham, "The Indian Menace and the Retention of the Western Posts."   [52]Can. Arch., Q, LVI, Pt. II, 569.

Orleans up the River, he could undersell the Traders from this Post, but this traffic which has been thus open to them for years, they have not attempted. . . .

. . . There are also a chain of British Traders, extending from the Illinois, up the Mississippi, to the Mouth of the River St. Peter, which River they ascend to its very source, it is the most valuable branch of commerce belonging to this Post, and capable of being improved to a great degree, that extensive Country abounding in valuable Furs, and there being no danger of interruption. . . .[53]

Trade had been carried on in the Mississippi territories by French interests and in a general union for three years after 1785. Evidences of difficulties appeared in the trade with the Spanish at St. Louis when the Spanish authorities protested against the illicit trade of English traders with Indians under Spanish dominion.[54] Following the Jay Treaty regulations steadily became more exacting.[55] Efforts were made to evade these regulations as shown in an agreement of the Northwest Company dated July 25, 1796, for five years with J. Bte. Cadotte to carry on trade tributary to Fond du Lac.[56] On July 16, 1803, another agreement was made for three years with M. Cadotte for the trade of Point Chagouamigon, Rivière du Sauteux and Lac des Courts Oreilles.[57] So successful were these efforts that after 1796 trade with the American posts continued and actually increased. In 1797 goods passing the Niagara Portage from Montreal to Detroit included 43,668 gallons of liquor, 1,344 minots of salt, and merchandise valued at £55,220, and furs (5,826 packs, 2,616 from Detroit, 3,210 from Michilimackinac)

[53]Ibid., Q, CCLXXX, Pt. II, 374–375; Correspondence of Simcoe, I, 403–404.

[54]See letters, August 21, 1794, Dorchester to the Duke of Portland, and June 12, 1795, Governor of Louisiana to Dorchester.

[55]See document as to the establishment of rendezvous within the British frontier for trade, April 17, 1796, Can. Arch., Q, LXXV, Pt. I; John Richardson to Thomas Forsyth, February 17, 1810, Q, CXIII, 243. For complaints of British traders of treatment by Americans, see the Memorial of the merchants of Montreal carrying on trade to Michilimackinac and the Indian country within the territory of the United States, Montreal, October 20, 1808, and estimate of the cost of eight boats, £26,842.5.6, property of the Michilimackinac Company seized at the entrance of the Port of Niagara on May 21, 1808, signed by Forsyth, Richardson & Co., McTavish, McGillivrays & Co., James & Andrew McGill & Co., Parker, Gerrard, Ogilvy & Co.; also Forsyth, Richardson & Co., to Inglis, Ellice & Co., Montreal, August 4, 1808, Can. Arch., Q, CVII, 3–20; also R. Hamilton to McTavish, McGillivrays & Co., Niagara, May 21, 1808, Can. Arch., C, CCCLXIII.

[56]See a copy of this agreement in C. N. Bell, The Earliest Fur Traders on the Upper Red River and Red Lake, Minnesota (1783–1810).

[57]Can. Arch., Minutes of the Northwest Company.

valued at £87,390 were sent in return. Packs from Detroit increased from 1,910 in 1796 to 2,616 in 1797 and to 2,704 in 1798.[58] Following the Louisiana Purchase of 1803, British traders suffered further prohibitions and the Michilimackinac Company was formed for ten years as a result. On December 3, 1806, an agreement for ten years defining the boundary lines between the trade of the Northwest Company and of the Michilimackinac Company was arranged to prevent misunderstanding and collision of interests with the Americans.[59] Arrangements were planned in 1811 between the Michilimackinac Company and the American Fur Company (Astor's company) for a working agreement as to territory, the purchase of supplies, and the disposal of furs. With the Non-Intercourse Act forbidding the ingress and egress of supplies and returns from the United States, arrangements were made for the sale of the Northwest Company interests in the Michilimackinac Company.[60] The withdrawal of the Northwest Company from American territory[61] had been followed by the development of American organization chiefly under the direction of J. J. Astor.

The effects of the American Revolution and of these incidental regulations on the fur trade were contributory to the general movement which was conspicuous in the history of the trade during the French *régime* and which continued with unabated force in the later period. The exhaustion of the beaver fields and the necessity of moving to new areas were of fundamental importance. The constant westward movement of the trade continued and was accelerated with the American Revolution and its effects.

Fur was becoming scarce in the southern areas and increasing competition following settlement became more serious. A letter from Alexander Henry to Edgar, dated Montreal, September 1, 1785, stated, "The Detroit trade has been very bad and John Askin as bad as any." And again reporting from Montreal, March 5, 1786, he wrote, "The great loss on furs has hurt the merchants much and our friend Askin must suffer most." On November 12 of the same year his letter stated:

The trade of that country [Mackinac] is much altered for the worse since I left it, all the merchants in that trade has made a general concern

[58]*Ibid.*, Q, CCLXXXVI, 123–124.

[59]For a full statement of the agreements see Can. Arch., Minutes of the Northwest Company in the Baby Collection.

[60]Extract of letter from Thomas Forsyth, London, February 17, 1810 to John Richardson advising sale of interests to Mr. Astor. Can. Arch., Q, CXIII, 243.

[61]For a description of the final retreat of Canadian traders from American territory see J. W. Pratt, "Fur Trade Strategy and the American Left Flank in the War of 1812."

and I left a sufficient quantity of goods for two years, the loss on furs has been very great the last year and no prospect of its mending. I came down by Detroit, the same complaints are made there of the badness of trade, they also have made a general partnership.

A year later, October 22, 1787, conditions had not improved. "The upper country is worse than ever from the great quantity of merchandise sent into it by the King's presents a part of which is carried to the most distant parts and traded for furs by the agents and interpreters." In 1789 Detroit supplied less than 1,900 bales and in 1790 returns were unusually low because of the mild winter. The decline was most evident in beaver and the more valuable furs and greater dependence was placed on muskrat and raccoons.

C. THE NORTHWEST TRADE

Contact with the Northwest country inland from Grand Portage appears to have continued with little interruption throughout the war period.[62] Statements with considerable authority claim that French and English traders went to Rainy Lake in 1761 and remained until 1763. Henry states in 1761 that he sent Canadian clerks and interpreters "to the Grand Portage, for the northwest."[63] On the other hand, this trade must have been carried on with considerable uncertainty until after the Pontiac wars. According to some accounts[64] the first adventure left Michilimackinac for the Northwest in 1765 but the canoes were plundered at Lac la Pluie by the Indians and returning in the following year met a similar fate. Matthew Cocking in 1772 notes that François the French Pedlar was in the Northwest country seven years earlier, or in 1765, since he met a Frenchman among the Assiniboines on the Saskatchewan who had deserted from François at that time.[65] The identity of François is difficult to establish but he was apparently the same man Cocking met at a settlement below the Forks of the Saskatchewan in 1773, and was also referred to as Saswee.[66] One might

[62]"North-Western Explorations," pp. 50 f.; see S. J. Buck, "The Story of the Grand Portage"; also G. C. Davidson, *The North West Company*, chap. iii, L.-R. Masson, *Les Bourgeois de la Compagnie du Nord-Ouest*, I, Esquisse historique; and E. Cruikshank, "Early Traders and Trade-Routes in Ontario and the West, 1760–1783."

[63]*Travels and Adventures . . . by Alexander Henry*, p. 48.

[64]Benjamin and Joseph Frobisher to General Haldimand, Montreal, October 4, 1784, "North-Western Explorations," p. 50; see also "Sketch of the Fur Trade of Canada, 1809," *Report of the Public Archives*, 1928, pp. 58–73.

[65]"Journal of Matthew Cocking," p. 105.   [66]*Ibid.*, p. 118.

hazard the conjecture that François Sassevillet,[67] one of the canoemen mentioned in the licence granted to Maurice Blondeau for Grand Portage in 1772, was François the Pedlar but it was more probably Lafrance Bourbonois who from his position at the head of the list was apparently a guide. The same individual was in charge of the canoes of Blondeau in 1770 and probably returned to Montreal in 1771, which appears to warrant the conclusion that Blondeau was interested in the Northwest trade at any early date.

Matthew Cocking also states that Mr. Finlay from Montreal wintered not far below old Fort à la Corne five years earlier, or in 1767.[68] This date is supported in the Memorial of B. and J. Frobisher to General Haldimand dated October 4, 1784, where it is stated that an attempt to reach the Northwest in 1767 was successful in having canoes penetrate beyond Lake Ouinipique, but it is more probable that Finlay wintered at this point a year later, or 1768.[69] A note signed by B. Roberts, superintendent at Michilimackinac, on the fur returns for 1767, states: "This being the first year the traders were permitted to winter amongst the Indians at their villages and hunting grounds it was found necessary they should enter into fresh security with the Commissary, of this, the only post they had liberty to winter from."[70] A few of those given licences to go by Lake Superior appear in the accompanying table.

[67]Can. Arch., Licence returns. Professor A. S. Morton argues Le Blancell, i.e., Le Blanc.   [68]"Journal of Matthew Cocking," p. 101.

[69]See Robert Campbell, *A History of the Scotch Presbyterian Church, St. Gabriel Street, Montreal,* p. 111, in which 1768 is given. Professor Morton argues 1769. James Finlay is also reported as wintering at "Fort Prairie" 1768–69; *Papers of Sir William Johnson,* VII, 953–954. He was said to have cleared £3,000 one winter. With 12 Frenchmen in 3 canoes Finlay came up to Finlay's House. One canoe with one Englishman and 5 Frenchmen were left at Basquia to stay the summer of 1769. W. S. Wallace, "The Pedlars from Quebec," p. 392. Finlay was supported by Hunter and Bailey, London merchants. See also *Johnson Papers,* VI, on Finlay.

[70]"Fur-Trade Returns, 1767," ed. C. E. Lart, p. 353. This copy differs slightly from that of the Dartmouth Papers. Roberts made a return of Canadian trade to Lord George Germain, "first of the kind ever attempted in that country, can give but an imperfect state of a few months trade . . . for untill I open'd the trade to the Indian villages, no person whatsoever was permitted to barter his goods but under the cannon of the establish'd posts." Trade increased rapidly but merchants "strove as much as possible to underrate it being fearfull that a tax was intended." Letter from Roberts to Nepean, February 5, 1783, C.O. 267, no. 7, Gambia series, British Museum. (B. Roberts, Secretary for Moorish affairs, resigned as commissary of stores and artillery in Senegambia and became Captain in Africa Corps, retaining his employment as Secretary.)

CANOES GONE OUT WINTERING FROM MICHILIMACKINAC

July 7, 1767 Traders' names that go in canoes	Names of those who enter into security for the good be-haviour of those going out	No. of canoes	Places of wintering	Value of mer-chan-dise
Blondeau	Spicemaker,[71] Blon-deau, Jun.	2	Fort la Reine and Fort Dauphin	£700
Le Blancell[72] [François?]	Alexander Baxter	6	Fort Dauphin and La Prairie	£2400
Campion	Groesbeeke [apparently from Albany]	1	Lac de Pluie and Lac Dubois	£400

Thos. Corry with security from Isaac Todd, had a licence for two canoes valued at £1,000, to go to Kaministiquia. According to the returns from other posts Finlay's name appears as security to different canoes but not as a trader. In the same year Clause penetrated beyond Lake Nipigon.[73] The evidence suggests convincingly that Grand Portage was an important rendezvous from an early date. Carver was at Grand Portage in 1767 and describes as a matter of routine, the route of "those who go on the Northwest trade to the Lakes De Pluye, Dubois etc." "The French having acquired a thorough knowledge of the trade of the Northwest countries, they were employed on that account after the reduction of Canada, by the English traders there, in the establish-ment of this trade with which they were themselves quite un-acquainted."[74] The French traders were engaged in leading the Crees and Assiniboines of whom Carver met a large party, from the Hud-son's Bay Company to trade with the Montreal traders. These Indians were middlemen to other Indians of the Plains, as Carver notes the Mandans,[75] and Fort La Reine was still a rendezvous for French traders. The trade of the Assiniboines with the Mandans described by La Vérendrye continued.

Benjamin and Joseph Frobisher, who had connections with Todd and McGill of Montreal, made their first venture to the Northwest in

[71]F. C. Spiesmacker succeeded Rogers at Michilimackinac 1767–68.

[72]I.e., Le Blanc.　　　　　　　[73]L.-R. Masson, *Les Bourgeois*, II, 242.

[74]Jonathan Carver, *Travels through the Interior Parts of North-America*, p. 106; also T. C. Elliott in *Oregon Historical Quarterly*, XXI, 341–368, XXII, 91–115, XXIII, 52–69.

[75]Carver, p. 111.

1769[76] but were robbed by the Indians. In that year Maurice Blondeau secured a licence for 3 canoes with 19 men for "Michilimackinac and La Mer de l'Ouest" with a cargo of 320 gal. rum and wine, 800 lb. gunpowder, 14½ cwt. ball and shot, 24 rifles, 44 bales and rolls, 14 boxes, 10 kegs, and 7 bags, valued at £1,350; and Lawrence Ermatinger sent 2 canoes with 15 men (Joseph Desfonds guide) to "La Mer du West" and a cargo of 160 gal. rum and brandy,[77] 32 gal. wine, 500 lb. gunpowder, 1,000 lb. ball and shot, and 16 rifles valued at £800. In the following year Blondeau sent to "La Mer du Ouest" 4 canoes with 20 men and a cargo of 500 gal. rum, brandy and wine, 1,100 lb. gunpowder, 17 cwt. ball and shot, 46 bales, 15 cases, 12 kegs, 17 bags, and 16 rolls, valued at £1,506, and Benjamin Frobisher and Dobie sent 3 canoes to Michilimackinac and Grand Portage with a cargo of 224 gal. beverages, 1,100 lb. gunpowder, 24 cwt. ball and shot, 24 rifles, 46 bales, 9 rolls, 8 kegs, and 10 packages, valued at £1,200. Joseph Frobisher apparently spent the winter of 1770–71 at the mouth of Nettley Creek on the Red River.[78] In the same year Antoine Bourbonnois and Hubert Le Roux sent 1 canoe to Grand Portage with a cargo valued at £80, Joseph Deloge 1 canoe valued at £250, Pierre Dumay 1 canoe valued at £350, and J. Bte. Rapin 1 canoe valued at £300. Previous to 1770 the trade was probably directed chiefly to the area south of Lake Winnipeg. Blondeau probably sent his canoes in 1769 and 1770 to Fort La Reine and vicinity. John Macdonell refers to "Blondishes" fort[79] which is apparently distinct from Adhemar's on the Assiniboine. The later history of the southern posts is obscure.[80] Peter Pond wintered at Fort Dauphin in 1775–76 but came to this post from Cumberland House. Trade with the Mandans was disrupted through raids of the Assiniboine and later hostilities of the Plains Indians necessitated the abandonment about 1780[81] of Le Fort aux Trembles which had probably displaced Fort La Reine.

[76]Apparently few canoes, if any, reached the Saskatchewan in 1769–70 and only when the Canadians got Chief Wappenassew to assist them was the trade restored. Wappenassew was a Hudson's Bay Company Indian at York Factory from 1755 to 1770. He became attached to the Canadians in 1770 and convoyed canoes to Michilimackinac. W. S. Wallace, "The Pedlars from Quebec," pp. 394–395.

[77]New England rum was regarded as very effective in trading. Hudson's Bay Company brandy was difficult to carry up rapids from New York; see *Journals of Hearne and Turnor*, pp. 122, 160, 250.

[78]Elliott Coues, *New Light*, I, 42.   [79]L.-R. Masson, *Les Bourgeois*, I, 270.

[80]George Bryce, "The Assiniboine River and Its Forts"; also C. N. Bell, *The Old Forts of Winnipeg, 1738–1927*.

[81]1781, according to J. Macdonell, *Five Fur-Traders*, p. 112.

Smallpox[82] spread from the Mandans to the Assiniboines and in turn as far as the Athabasca country in 1782. The difficulties of the trade to the south of Lake Winnipeg probably hastened the movement to the north and helped to eliminate the weaker traders who had survived through the advantages of the shorter route to the south and the supplies of corn from the Mandans.[83] In any case after Finlay's expedition in 1768 evidences of a shift to the north became pronounced.

In 1771 Thomas Corry apparently wintered at Cedar Lake[84] and "interrupted great part of York trade this year" (1772).[85] Cocking met Indians at Pasquia who had been engaged in 1771 hunting for "the pedlars to procure them food." He met several canoes on the Saskatchewan which had traded with the Canadians. The following year Henry Jeannott sent 1 canoe valued at £600 to Grand Portage; Antoine Reilhe, 1 canoe valued at £250; Hubert la Croix for Joseph Howard, 1 canoe valued at £450; Benjamin and Joseph Frobisher, 3 canoes with 32 men and a cargo of 1,400 lb. gunpowder, 22½ cwt. ball and shot, and 34 rifles valued at £1,500; Maurice Blondeau,[86] 3 canoes with 28 men and a cargo of 300 gal. rum and brandy, 30 gal. wine, 1,200 lb. gunpowder, 18 cwt. ball and shot, 30 rifles valued at £1,642; and Jos. Defond for account of Lawrence Ermatinger, 4 canoes with 28 men, and a cargo of 600 gal. beverages, 100 lb. gunpowder, 14 cwt. ball and shot, and 32 rifles valued at £1,400. Cocking found in 1773 that François had 6 canoes with him at the settlement below the Forks, that 3 more canoes were at Shallow Lake (Saskeram), 2 canoes below Moose Lake and 4 canoes to the south in the track of Indians going by the Brassy Hill River to York Fort. Trade was prosecuted by the Canadians with very great effectiveness.[87] In 1773

---

[82]Alexander Mackenzie, *Voyages from Montreal*, I, xxxvii f.

[83]See map of Peter Pond showing that the Mandans took supplies of corn for sale to Fort Epinette. "North-Western Explorations," p. 53.

[84]"Journal of Matthew Cocking," p. 99.

[85]In 1771–72 Corry took 7 canoes down and apparently returned in 1772–73 from Grand Portage. W. S. Wallace, "The Pedlars from Quebec," pp. 395–396. In the summer of 1772 John Cole and Bové, a French Canadian, deserted Corry for the Hudson's Bay Company, after apparently robbing him. It would seem Corry planned to send Askin to the Pas in 1772–73.

[86]On Red Deer River.

[87]In 1773 Frobisher was on the Saskatchewan (Cumberland House); Blondeau was "up the Saskatchewan." Another Frobisher with 6 canoes was probably at Fort Dauphin. W. S. Wallace, "The Pedlars from Quebec," p. 397. In 1772 Franceway with 15 canoes wintered at Finlay's House. William Bruce at Basquia had left the Mississippi after killing an Indian. In 1773 Bruce was at Red Deer River.

licences were granted to Maurice Blondeau for 3 canoes with 22 men and a cargo of 100 gal. beverages, 1,200 lb. gunpowder, 18 cwt. ball and shot, 30 rifles, 37 bales, 6 bales kettles, 25 bales of tobacco, 10 *caisses de feraille*, 15 barrels pork, ham, and butter; to Jean-Etienne Waden, 2 canoes, 16 men, and a cargo valued at £750; and for Lawrence Ermatinger, 3 canoes and 13 men with a cargo valued at £1,000. In 1774, Waden signed a licence for Jos. Le Clair to take 2 canoes and 13 men to go to Grand Portage and to winter in the north. James McGill and Charles Paterson secured a licence for 5 canoes and 34 men with a cargo of 8 kegs wine, 40 kegs gunpowder, 44 kegs ball and shot, 8 cases of rifles, 70 bales dry goods, 6 cases axes, 50 bales tobacco, 20 kegs pork, 20 kegs grease, and a basket of kettles, valued at £2,000; Maurice Blondeau and J. Bte. Adhemar,[88] 4 canoes and 29 men with a cargo of 280 gal. beverages, 1,500 lb. gunpowder, 24 quintals ball and shot, 50 rifles, 15 cases ironwork, 50 bales merchandise, 8 bales kettles, 45 bales and rolls of tobacco, 20 barrels of lard, butter, and ham; Benjamin Frobisher, 4 canoes, 29 men, and 60 kegs rum, wine, etc., 1,700 lb. gunpowder, 2,100 lb. ball and shot, 40 rifles, 84 bales dry goods and tobacco, 640 lb. kettles, 8 kegs and cases of merchandise; Lawrence Ermatinger, 4 canoes, 32 men, of whom 17 were wintermen, and a cargo of 500 gal. liquors, 1,500 lb. gunpowder, 16 cwt. ball and shot, and 56 rifles, valued at £1,300; and Joseph Howard, 2 canoes valued at £700, 17 men. In 1775, Edward Chinn signed a licence for 1 canoe and 5 men with a cargo valued at £125. Waden secured a licence for 2 canoes and 15 men; Gautiot and Durand 3 canoes and 18 men; Charles Sanguinet, 2 canoes with 18 men of whom 11 were winterers; Henry Bourdignon, Romant Sanscrainte, and Joseph Duchesneau, 2 canoes and 17 men; James McGill, Benjamin Frobisher, and Maurice Blondeau, 12 canoes with 3 guides and 75 men, with a cargo of 100 gal. rum and brandy, 24 kegs wine, 64 kegs gunpowder, 90 bags ball and shot, 150 rifles, 150 bales dry goods, 15 trunks dry goods, 12 boxes ironware, 12 nests brass kettles, 100 packages carrot and twist tobacco, 50 kegs hogs' lard and tallow, 60 kegs pork; and Lawrence Ermatinger, 6 canoes and 38 men, with 600 gal. beverages, 2,000 lb. gunpowder, 3,600 lb. ball and shot, 80 rifles, 85 bales dry goods, 5,500 lb. tobacco, 15 cases ironworks, and 10 cases brass kettles valued at £1,700.[89]

[88]John Lees met four of Adhemar's canoes on Lake Erie going from Detroit to Montreal. *Journal of [John Lees] of Quebec, Merchant*, p. 31.

[89]Holmes, Paterson and François with 8 canoes on October 9, 1774, were going up the Saskatchewan and Pangman with 12 canoes (*Journals of Hearne and Turnor*, pp. 120–121, 158). In June, 1775, Bruce, B. Blondeau, Tute and

The large shipment of McGill, Frobisher, and Blondeau in 1775, appears to mark the beginning of large-scale trade to the Northwest and the beginning of the Northwest Company. The names of the licensees are significant evidence of the dependence of the Northwest Company on French and English experience. Alexander Henry who was anxious to recoup his losses from a mining venture and who was also probably apprehensive of difficulties in the colonies went to the Northwest in 1775 and at Grand Portage found the traders "in a state of extreme reciprocal hostility" with "very hurtful" consequences "to the morals of the Indians."[90] On Lake Winnipeg he was joined by Peter Pond, who had left the Mississippi district in that year and who was probably also apprehensive of difficulties in the colonies, and on September 7 by Joseph and Thomas Frobisher and Mr. Paterson, "a fleet of thirty canoes and a hundred and thirty men." M. Cadotte was a partner of Henry's[91] and at Cumberland House left with four canoes for Fort des Prairies. Pond left with two canoes for Fort Dauphin. "Messrs. Frobisher retained six, and myself four." At Fort des Prairies which Henry visited during the winter, there were Messrs. Finlay, Paterson, Holmes, and Cadotte. According to Henry:

Four different interests were struggling for the Indian trade of the Saskatchiwaine; but, fortunately, they had this year agreed to join their stock, and when the season was over, to divide the skins and meat. This arrangement was beneficial to the merchants; but, not directly so to the Indians, who, having no other place to resort to, nearer than Hudson's Bay, or Cumberland House, paid greater prices than if a competition had subsisted. A competition, on the other hand, afflicts the Indians with a variety of evils, in a different form.

---

others struck south a little above Lake Winnipeg. In 1774 the two Frobishers were on the Churchill with 6 canoes.

About sixty canoes of pedlars came in from Grand Portage in 1774 and went in different directions a little above Lake Winnipeg. "The reason of their separating so wide from each other is on account of getting the furs cheaper and at the same time enables them to provide provision for the men at less expense and with greater certainty than they possibly could do if in greater bodies." *Ibid.*, pp. 122–123.

Also in the trade at this time were B. Graves, a partner of Peter Pond in 1775; Charles McCormick, who was with Pond in 1777–78; Nicholas Montour, clerk with Frobisher. *Ibid.*, p. 221n.

[90]*Travels and Adventures . . . by Alexander Henry*, pp. 235 ff. (quotation below from pp. 320–321). A licence was issued at Montreal, April 10, 1775, to Messrs. Henry and Cadotte to go to Sault Ste Marie and Grand Portage with 4 canoes, 29 men, 26 kegs rum, 18 cwt. gunpowder, 16 cwt. ball and shot, 62 rifles; total value of merchandise, £2,236.12.6.

[91]But see particularly *Journals of Hearne and Turnor*, pp. 42–47.

The following were the prices of goods at Fort des Prairies:

A gun	20	beaver-skins.
A stroud blanket	10	do.
A white do.	8	do.
An axe, of one pound weight	3	do.
Half a pint of gunpowder	1	do.
Ten balls	1	do.

but, the principal profits accrued from the sale of knives, beads, flints, steels, awls and other small articles.

Tobacco, when sold, fetched one beaver-skin per foot of *Spencer's twist*; and rum, not very strong, two beaver-skins per bottle; but, a great proportion of these commodities was disposed of in presents.

The quantity of furs brought into the fort was very great and from twenty to thirty Indians arrived daily, laden with packs of beaver skins. Thomas and Joseph Frobisher and Alexander Henry with forty men wintered on Beaver Lake. On April 12, 1776, Thomas Frobisher and six men went to Churchill River to build a fort at Portage de Traite, where he was joined by the remainder of the party on June 15. They started up the Churchill to find the Indians and met them at the entrance of Isle à la Crosse Lake. These Indians were from Athabasca and they traded "twelve thousand beaver skins, besides large numbers of otter and marten." The returns of the general joint stock of that year were apparently very successful.

Thomas Frobisher returned with the Indians in the summer of 1776 and wintered, according to Peter Pond's map,[92] on Isle à la Crosse Lake, coming out in 1777. According to the same source, Pond wintered in 1776 and 1777 on the north branch of the Saskatchewan. In that latter year licences were granted for Grand Portage to Venant Lemer St. Germain and to Charles Paterson for one canoe each and to Jean Etienne Waden and C. Chaboillez for three canoes each; to George McBeath, with Alexander Ellice guarantor, for 5 canoes, 32 men, 790 gal. beverages, 40 rifles, 1,200 lb. gunpowder, 12 cwt. of shot and ball, valued at £2,000; to F. Oakes, with L. Ermatinger guarantor, for 7 canoes, 49 men, 1,350 gal. beverages, 64 guns, 1,500 lb. powder, 18 cwt. shot and ball, valued at £2,000; to William Kay, with John Kay guarantor, 7 canoes, 41 men, 1,376 gal. beverages, 88 rifles, 2,400 lb. of gunpowder, 30 cwt. ball and shot, valued at £2,600; and J. Bte. Adhemar, with James McGill guarantor, 10 canoes, 94 men, 440 gal. beverages, 112 rifles, 3,700 lb. gunpowder, 47 cwt. ball and shot, valued at £5,100. There is evidence to show that each of these traders took out licences to Grand Portage in the previous year (1776)

[92]See map in G. C. Davidson, *The North West Company*, p. 32.

but the returns are not available.[93] According to Mackenzie, traders on the Saskatchewan in 1778 pooled their stock to send Pond to the Athabasca country following the success of Thomas Frobisher the preceding year.[94] There is no indication as to the names of the traders involved but St. Germain, Waden, McBeath, Paterson, Adhemar, McGill, Frobisher, McTavish, and Oakes were probably interested. In any case Pond crossed the height of land at Portage la Loche and wintered on the Athabasca River about forty miles above Lake Athabasca. He came out in 1779 but was obliged to return in the same year for a cache of furs he had left.

The licences for 1778[95] which were for 2 canoes each, included Charles Chaboillez, guarantors B. Frobisher and T. Corey; W. and J. Kay and D. Rankin, guarantors G. Phyn and Jas. McGill. J. E. Waden had a licence for 3 canoes guaranteed by R. Dobie and J. McKindlay; Holmes and Grant, 4 canoes, guarantors, R. Grant and Porteous; McBeath and Wright, 6 canoes, guarantors, G. Phyn and Jas. McGill; Forrest Oakes, 6 canoes, guarantors, Oakes and Ermatinger; McTavish and Bannerman, 8 canoes, guarantors, McTavish and J. B. Durocher; and John

[93]In 1777 Graves, McCormick, Bruce, Montour, Pangman, Pond and B. Blondeau were at Sturgeon River Fort. In November, 1777, Francis killed an Indian there. *Journals of Hearne and Turnor*, p. 54. Apparently St. Germain in partnership with J. B. Nolin bought Michipicoten with 1 canoe of goods in 1778 from Alexander Henry for 15,000 livres. The first winter they got 23 packs of furs. In 1779–80 they got 44 packs in which there were 34 packs of beaver, 3 of otter, 3 of cats, 1½ of marten, 2½ of bear, musquash etc. In 1780–81 the trade was not half so good. They proposed to go in 1781–82 to build a post at Me-caw-baw-nish Lake. *Ibid.*, p. 301. Turnor said that Holmes was highest up the Saskatchewan in 1776–77; *ibid.*, p. 231. Was his the house the ruins of which Turnor passed on March 13, 1779, noting that it had been built by Holmes in trust for Frobisher and Co.? *Ibid.*, p. 217.

[94]Alexander Mackenzie, *Voyages from Montreal*, I, xxxv-xxxvi.

[95]In 1778 B. Blondeau with a canoe and 6 men on Pine Island Lake got 11 packs of furs, mostly cats, beaver and marten, chiefly from Indians in debt to the Hudson's Bay Company. *Journals of Hearne and Turnor*, pp. 214, 234.

On March 7, 1779, Philip Turnor met Canadians from Blondeau's upper post going to Pine Island Lake. Turnor arrived on March 17 at two houses, one of them inhabited by Blondeau, the other by Robert Grant. His journal entry for March 19 mentions a house in possession of Gibosh (Gibeau?) in trust for Waden, one in possession of Holmes and Graves, and one in possession of Nicholas Montour in trust for Blondeau. The upper settlement on the Saskatchewan in 1779 belonged to McCormick, Graves, Pangman, Blondeau, Holmes, Grant, and Gibosh. It was first settled by Pangman, McCormick, and Gibosh. Graves, "having a great number of men, hauled his goods up as soon as the river set fast. They found they should have ruined each other had they not entered into a General Partnership." Blondeau had not entered the partnership

McGill and Thomas Frobisher, 12 canoes. In a report of Charles Grant it was stated:[96]

Last year the passes for the Indian goods were given out so late, that it was impossible to forward goods to the places of destination especially in the North-west. For that reason those concerned in that quarter joined their stock together and made one common interest of the whole, as it continues at present in the hands of the different persons or companies as mentioned at foot of this. . . .
Quebec, 24th April, 1780.

Todd & McGill	2	shares
Ben. & Jos. Frobisher	2	do.
McGill & Paterson	2	do.
McTavish & Co.	2	do.
Holmes & Grant	2	do.
Wadden & Co.	2	do.
McBeath & Co.	1	do.
Ross & Co.	1	
Oakes & Co.	1	

The North West is divided into sixteen shares all which form but one Company at this time.

The returns for the passes in the same year included George Mc-Beath, 2 canoes; St. Germain, 3 canoes; W. and J. Kay, 2 canoes; McTavish and Bannerman, 4 canoes; Porteous, Sutherland and Co.,

---

but he expected to come in. In 1778 Blondeau and Pangman were partners and Graves, Holmes, and Grant. Robert Longmoor of the Hudson's Bay Company accepted one of Blondeau's houses. (Pond linked with Graves, Holmes, and Grant?) Blondeau was interested in four sites besides the vacant house lent to Longmoor. On the Saskatchewan in 1778–79 were (*ibid.*, p. 253):

Blondeau	6 canoes		63 packs
McCormick	6		46
Gibosh (Waden)	3		31
Pangman	5		36
Graves	5	}	118
Holmes & Grant	5		
			294

Among the Canadians, Graves and Jacobs were from Great Britain, Robert Grant was a North Briton, McCormick and Holmes were natives of Ireland (*ibid.*, p. 232). Traders were driven out in the spring of 1779 by the murder of John Cole (*ibid.*, p. 224).

About 10 canoes went to Churchill 1778–79. Blondeau planned to winter in 1779–80 north of Cumberland House and leave Tute to act for him on the Saskatchewan. Graves sent 2 canoes of goods in to Athabasca in 1779. *Ibid.*, pp. 233–234.

[96]"North West Trade," *Report on Canadian Archives*, 1888, p. 61.

2 canoes; J. Ross, 1 canoe; B. and J. Frobisher, 6 canoes; F. Oakes, 2 canoes; Paterson and Frobisher, 4 canoes. It is difficult to reconcile the two returns but Grant's report includes the supply firm of Todd and McGill; and probably Waden & Co. included St. Germain; Holmes and Grant included Porteous, Sutherland & Co., and F. Oakes included W. and J. Kay. Licence returns in 1780 included J. Lecuyer, 1 canoe; Frobisher and Patterson, 8 canoes; Holmes and Grant, 5 canoes; Waden and St. Germain, 5 canoes; Peter Pond, 4 canoes; Ross and Pangman, 4 canoes; F. Oakes, 3 canoes; S. McTavish, 5 canoes; W. and J. Kay, 2 canoes; B. and J. Frobisher, 2 canoes.[97] According to one account the agreement of 1779, called "the nine parties' agreement," was renewed in 1780 for three years but discontinued in two years. The following licence arrangements tend to support that conclusion. In 1781 Todd and McGill, B. and J. Frobisher, and McGill and Paterson under one licence sent 12 canoes; S. McTavish, 4 canoes; McBeath, Pond, and Graves, 4 canoes; Holmes and Grant, 4 canoes; Waden and St. Germain, 4 canoes; B. and J. Frobisher, 1 canoe; F. Oakes, 2 canoes; 1782, F. Oakes, 1 canoe, S. McTavish, 6 canoes; Charlebois and Morel, 1 canoe; Chamailant and Dassu, 1 canoe; Waden and St. Germain, 4 canoes; Holmes and Grant, 2 canoes; B. and J. Frobisher, 10 canoes; and George McBeath and Co., 4 canoes; 1783, B. and J. Frobisher, 5 canoes; S. McTavish, 6 canoes, Holmes and Grant, 3 canoes; and Desjerlais and Plante, 1 canoe. The Northwest Company of 1783–84 probably included Peter Pond, one share (taken in 1785); McBeath, one share; Grant, two shares; and Holmes, one share; S. McTavish, three shares, with two additional shares held by Small; and B. and J. Frobisher, four shares, with two additional shares held by Montour.[98]

During the period of uncertainty following the war with the United States and the severe restrictions placed on trade, a combination of interests became inevitable. Larger numbers of traders including Pond and Henry and McTavish became interested in the Northwest trade immediately following the outbreak of hostilities. To compete with the Hudson's Bay Company it was necessary to combine as shown in the arrangements of 1775. To carry on trade across the difficult

---

[97]In 1780 no canoes had passed Michipicoten by June 26 though they usually passed in May. *Journals of Hearne and Turnor*, pp. 299–300. In 1780 Bruce and Boyer fought at Fort aux Trembles against the Indians. Bruce and Tute died of smallpox in 1781–82. *Ibid.*, p. 159n.

[98]See H. A. Innis, "The North West Company."

country between Grand Portage and the Saskatchewan,[99] depots for the production of dried meat and pemmican were essential. Co-operation had been essential to support Pond on the journey from the Saskatchewan to Athabasca. The capital requirements of this extended trade to Athabasca were an important contributing factor in the formation of the Northwest Company. In 1781 Pond was at Grand Portage and a joint enterprise was arranged for the prosecution of trade with Indians coming down the Churchill River. Waden had wintered at Lac la Ronge during the first year of amalgamation in 1779 and probably also in 1780, while in 1781 Pond was entrusted to represent other interests in a joint stock with him. In March of 1782 Waden was killed. Trade was carried on with the Churchill River Indians and they were persuaded to abandon the trip to Hudson Bay through fear of the smallpox which had been disastrous in the south. News of Waden's death probably led to a break up of the agreement in 1782. Pond may have been the trader to proceed "with one canoe strong handed and light loaded" to winter in the Athabasca country in 1782, but more probably he arrived too late at Portage la Loche and being preceded by representatives of the other interests, wintered at Clear Lake. Unfortunately smallpox had spread to the Athabasca country and returns were light in 1783 (seven packages of beaver). Pond continued to Athabasca in that year, however, and brought out large quantities of fur to Grand Portage and to Montreal in 1784. In 1785 he returned[100] to the Athabasca country and in the summer of 1786 sent Cuthbert Grant to establish a post at the mouth of the Slave River. John Ross also went into the Athabasca country in 1785[101] for the opposition company which had been formed that year at the instigation of Peter Pangman, who was dissatisfied with the arrangement of 1784, and probably sent Laurent Leroux to establish a post in opposition to Cuthbert Grant.[102] John Gregory, Peter Pangman, John Ross, Alexander Mackenzie, and Normand McLeod (dormant partner) were partners of the new company. Opposition

[99]In 1779 traders were driven out of the Saskatchewan by Indians and probably began to go to Athabasca. Large returns were expected from that area and difficulty as to the rights of the Hudson's Bay Company was overcome. *Journals of Hearne and Turnor*, pp. 224–235. Cole had left the Hudson's Bay Company (*ibid.*, p. 230) apparently to go with Graves. Frobisher was probably linked to Holmes, Grant, Graves, and Pond.

[100]L.-R. Masson, *Les Bourgeois de la Compagnie du Nord-Ouest*, I, 94.

[101]*Ibid.*, pp. 10 ff.

[102]Apparently wrong. Cuthbert Grant was with Gregory and McLeod, Leroux with the Northwest Company. *Journals of Hearne and Turnor*, p. 370.

between Ross and Pond in the Athabasca country became so severe that Ross was murdered "in a scuffle with Mr. Pond's men" in the winter of 1786-87.[103] This precipitated an amalgamation in a new concern in 1787 with the following shares: John Gregory, Peter Pangman, Alexander Mackenzie, and Normand McLeod, one share each; McTavish, Frobisher & Co., seven shares; Robert Grant, Nicholas Montour, and Patrick Small, two shares each; Peter Pond, George McBeath, and William Holmes, one share each; a total of twenty shares.

The amalgamation permitted the consolidation of interests in the trade as a basis for further expansion. General interest had been aroused at this time as to the possibilities of a northwest passage from Athabasca to Cook's Inlet. As a result of the amalgamation it was possible to explore Mackenzie River and Alexander Mackenzie was immediately dispatched in 1787 to Athabasca department to relieve Pond for that expedition. In a letter dated Athabasca, December 2, 1787, the former wrote that he had arrived on October 21. Following the amalgamation, economies were suggested in the department and Leroux was ordered to abandon Slave Lake. St. Germain arrived too late to take goods to the Peace River country and Grant, with two canoes for Slave Lake, was stopped by ice on Lake Athabasca. As a result it was decided to establish Lac la Pluie as an advance depot from Grand Portage. Alexander Mackenzie went out in 1788 to Lac la Pluie and Pond went to Grand Portage to receive final instructions regarding his voyage down the Mackenzie. Apparently it was decided that Pond's assistance would be of more value in Montreal to enlist the support of the government in the expedition and that Alexander Mackenzie should be sent down the Mackenzie in his place in 1789. On Mackenzie's return to Athabasca with Roderic Mackenzie, the latter established Fort Chipewyan on Lake Athabasca. In 1789 Alexander Mackenzie undertook the trip to Cook's Inlet.[104] Laurent Leroux accompanied him with a trading outfit[105] to the houses erected in 1786 on Slave Lake and across the lake to the north arm, where trade was prosecuted during the summer with the Copper Indians and the Slave Indians around Lac la Martre. Leroux wintered on Slave Lake. Mackenzie returned to report failure for his expedition and went out to

---

[103]The shooting of Mr. Ross "made the other company who was most powerful readily join them in partnership to prevent too great inquiry into the affair; if it had not happened Mr. Ross's party would soon have been ruined but they now trade as they please having no opposers." Philip Turnor, July 22, 1791; *ibid.*, p. 417.

[104]G. C. Davidson, *The North West Company*, p. 44.

[105]Alexander Mackenzie, *Voyages from Montreal*, I, 194.

Grand Portage in 1790 where he signed the new agreement giving him two shares out of twenty, and returned to Fort Chipewyan.[106] Determined to reach the Pacific he went to England in 1791 and returned in 1792 preparatory to the voyage up the Peace River in 1793. The earliest establishment on Peace River[107] was apparently made under Pond's direction in the neighbourhood of the present Fort Vermilion above Vermilion Falls in 1786. This was replaced by a fort below Carcajou and higher up the river at least as early as 1792. In that year Alexander Mackenzie established a post at the forks of the Peace and the Smoky[108] and in the following year continued the journey to the Pacific.

Although contrary to Pond's expectations, no feasible transport route to the Pacific had been found, Mackenzie's expeditions successfully mapped out the northern fur fields and provided for a rapid extension of trade. In the territory tributary to the Slave River and the Mackenzie River below Lake Athabasca the prospects of trade varied. Competition from the Chipewyans trading to Hudson Bay made it necessary to consider the abandonment of the post on Slave Lake.[109] On the Mackenzie, Indian tribes were found who possessed no iron and the Hare Indians were urged to hunt beaver and marten to trade with the Dog-ribs as middlemen to the Northwest Company.[110] The Eskimo were found to have traded iron presumably with the Russians. Plans were inaugurated for the organization of this district. The English chief[111] who had formerly traded to Hudson Bay was encouraged to trade with the Beaver Indians on Mackenzie River and to act as a middleman in trade with other Indians. Roderic Mackenzie wintered in 1790 at a post on a small island at the entrance of Mackenzie River and sent out his returns on the ice to be sold in England in the same season. To gain further command of Mackenzie River a post was built at Marten Lake,[112] probably in 1793. Another post was established eighty miles below Slave Lake on the Mackenzie in 1796. Three years later a fort was built at Bear Lake and in the same year Livingston in an attempt to establish trade with the Eskimo was killed. By 1804 two chief posts had been built on the Mackenzie,[113] one at the mouth of the

---

[106]H. A. Innis, "The North West Company."

[107]Alexander Mackenzie, *Voyages from Montreal*, I, 348 ff.; see J. N. Wallace, *The Wintering Partners on Peace River*, chaps. ii, iii.

[108]Alexander Mackenzie, *Voyages from Montreal*, I, 284–285; II, 160–161.

[109]L.-R. Masson, *Les Bourgeois*, I, 24, 29.

[110]Alexander Mackenzie, I, 292–293.

[111]*Ibid.*, p. 333.   [112]L.-R. Masson, I, 95.

[113]Can. Arch., "Account of Mackenzie River" with a chart, by Willard Ferdinand Wentzel, dated Fort Enterprise, Winter Lake, February 26, 1826.

Liard River (now Fort Simpson), and one on Bear Lake. In 1805 a
post was erected at the mouth of the Blue Fish River below the mouth
of Bear River (Fort Good Hope). Fort Liard was built up the Liard
River. During the period of competition with the XY Company trade
suffered directly and indirectly. After 1804 the returns increased
rapidly, doubling and trebling. Fort Nelson on the Liard produced 72
packs, The Forks, 40 packs, Great Bear Lake, 23, Fort Good Hope
over 20 packs—a total, for the district, of 170 packs of which three-
fourths was beaver. For the department a partner, 4 clerks, and 27
men, an outfit of 112 pieces, including stores for clerks and *engagés*,
and 5 canoes, were supplied.

In the territory tributary to English River, Peace River, and the
Athabasca similar plans were made. It was found that Indians on the
headwaters of the Parsnip River were receiving iron from traders on
the Pacific coast and that Indians on Peace River as in the neighbourhood of Slave Lake had acquired goods through middlemen. Both
Pond and Mackenzie reported the importance of the Crees as middlemen as Hearne had reported the importance of the Chipewyans. These
tribes with strategic middlemen positions had traded at exorbitant
prices with serious loss to the remote Indians. The Crees by virtue of
their position had driven the Chipewyans (Hearne's Northern Indians)
to the territory north of the Churchill River.[114] With European guns
they had driven back the Beaver Indians from the territory around
Portage la Loche by going up the Churchill, and they had crossed
over by the Saskatchewan to Lesser Slave Lake and the Peace River
Trail to war on the Beavers and the Indians along the Peace.[115] Mackenzie found that these Indians had even penetrated above the difficult
waters at the junction of the Finlay and the Parsnip.[116] Eventually
peace had been arranged between the Crees and the Beaver Indians at
Peace Point on Peace River near Lake Athabasca.[117] The Beavers had
in turn forced back the Rocky Mountain Indians and others on Peace
River. The Crees continued the war on other Indians, driving the Slave
Indians[118] down Slave River into the territory north of Slave Lake

---

[114]Alexander Mackenzie, I, cxxvi.

[115]*Ibid.*, II, 14–15.   [116]*Ibid.*, p. 66.

[117]*Ibid.*, I, 340–341. "The Canadians have two settlements [up the Peace
River] which are the support of this country; its there they get all their dried
provision for their journeys and without a settlement in this river they would
not be able to get their furrs out." *Journals of Hearne and Turnor*, pp. 401–402.

[118]Alexander Mackenzie, I, 215. In 1791 Southern Indians went with Philip
Turnor from Lake Athabasca "to war upon the Indians to westward of the
Slave Lake." *Journals of Hearne and Turnor*, p. 399.

(1775–77?). Mackenzie found they had been carrying on war (1782–83?) with Indians on Mackenzie River below the mouth of the Liard[119] and he also found Beaver Indians who had been driven to the neighbourhood of the Liard. War was still being prosecuted by the Crees in 1789.

Under these circumstances trade with the remote Indians proved extremely profitable through the demand for European goods, especially guns with which they could defend themselves, and which they had previously obtained at very high rates and with great difficulty. Writing in 1793 Alexander Mackenzie stated that:

All the European articles they [Beaver Indians] possessed, previous to the year 1780, were obtained from the Knisteneaux [Crees] and Chepe-wyans, who brought them from Fort Churchill, and for which they were made to pay an extravagant price.

As late as the year 1786, when the first traders from Canada arrived on the banks of this river [Peace], the natives employed bows and snares, but at present very little use is made of the former, and the latter are no longer known. They still entertain a great dread of their natural enemies, but they are since become so well armed, that the others now call them their allies.[120]

To further improve the trade to these districts,[121] Roderic Mackenzie was dispatched to search for a better route to Athabasca[122] than that by Portage la Loche. Angus Shaw built a post at Lac d'Orignal in 1789 and developed a separate district from this centre in 1790–91.[123]

There remained to be organized the territory of the Pacific coast drainage basin. The advantages of this trade had been recognized after the voyages of Captain James Cook. Alexander Henry's letters to Wiliam Edgar dated Montreal, September 1, 1785, and March 5, 1786,[124] insisted on the possibilities of a route from the Northwest to the Pacific but Pond and Mackenzie had shown that no overland route was feasible. After the amalgamation with the XY Company in 1804, however, it became necessary to find new territory for the large number of partners. Moreover, the expedition of Lewis and Clark was regarded

---

[119]Alexander Mackenzie, I, 225 ff.   [120]Ibid., II, 22–23.

[121]L.-R. Masson, Les Bourgeois, I, 30. See E.-Z. Massicotte, "Dominique Rousseau, maître orfèvre et négociant en pelleteries."

[122]L.-R. Masson, I, 31.

[123]Ibid., p. 35. For a list of the Company's arrangements in 1799 see ibid., pp. 61 ff.

[124]Toronto Public Library, Letters and Accounts, North-West Company; cited in H. A. Innis, Peter Pond.

as a forecast of the possibilities of American competition and Rocky Mountain Fort on Peace River had been established by 1799. In 1805 Simon Fraser was sent to establish Fort McLeod on McLeod Lake.[125] In 1806 posts were built on Stuart Lake (Fort St. James) and on Fraser Lake and in 1807 at the junction of Nechako and the Fraser (Fort George). In 1808 Fraser descended the river which bears his name. The department of New Caledonia was added to the Company's territory. In 1806 David Thompson was sent to establish posts across the Rocky Mountains[126] by way of the Saskatchewan and in 1807 built "Kootanae House" below Lake Windermere. Under his direction a post was built at the falls on Kootenay River in 1808. In 1809 Kully-spell House was built on Lake Pend d'Oreille and Saleesh House about sixty miles east on Clark's Fork River. In 1810 because of difficulties with the Piegan Indians he was obliged to cross the mountains by going to the north on Athabasca River. Spokane House was built probably in that year. In 1811 he went down the Columbia River and arrived at Fort Astoria. Following David Thompson's successful voyage down the Columbia in 1811 and the establishment of Astoria by the Pacific Fur Company at the mouth of that river, the Company dispatched the *Isaac Todd* from London to the Pacific coast. The purchase of the property of the Pacific Fur Company at Astoria in 1814 gave the Northwest Company control of the fur trade in that area.

Meanwhile the maritime fur trade had been profitable to numerous expeditions. Its development[127] had features similar to the trade on the Atlantic Coast. A large number of short, swift rivers, excellent harbours, a native culture with no previous knowledge of European goods, and a territory with large numbers of valuable amphibious fur-bearing

[125]A. Morice, *The History of the Northern Interior of British Columbia*, chaps. iv, v. *Report of the Public Archives*, 1929, pp. 109–159.

[126]*David Thompson's Narrative*, pp. lxxxvi ff.

[127]For a general description of the development of the trade in this area, see W. Irving, *Astoria*; H. H. Bancroft, *History of the Northwest Coast*; E. Coues, *New Light on . . . the Greater Northwest*; *David Thompson's Narrative*; *Early Western Travels, 1748–1846*, ed. R. G. Thwaites; T. C. Elliott, "Fur Trade in the Columbia River Basin prior to 1811." See also James Cook, *A Voyage to the Pacific Ocean [1776–1780]*; George Dixon, *A Voyage round the World*; John Meares, *Voyages Made in the Years 1788 and 1789 from China to the North West Coast of America*; Eliah Grimes, "Letters on the Northwest Fur Trade," ed. S. E. Morison; "Letters relating to the Second Voyage of the *Columbia*," ed. F. W. Howay; John Boit's "Log of the *Columbia*—1790–1793," ed. F. G. Young and T. C. Elliott; Kuykendall, "A Northwest Trader at the Hawaiian Islands"; *The Adventures of John Jewitt*, ed. R. Brown; and S. E. Morison, *The Maritime History of Massachusetts, 1783–1860*, chaps. iv, v.

animals, such as the sea otter, were important features. A long voyage on the part of the trading vessels and heavy overhead expense necessitated, in the beginning, a lucrative trade, and eventually, severe competition. In this competition, regulation and monopoly control of the English through the East India Company and its subsidiaries proved inadequate. Smuggling, success of competitors not subject to control, more effective methods of bargaining on the part of the traders, and on the part of the Indians, and consequent hostilities of the natives were characteristic results of the fur trade as conducted in this accessible country.[128] Rapid destruction of the more valuable amphibious fur-bearing animals, especially the sea otter,[129] along the coast, necessitated the search for more important rivers which gave access to the wide territories of the interior. The character of the Pacific coast drainage basin with its short, swift rivers gave geographic importance to a river with the largest drainage area, the Columbia. With the heavy capital investment necessary to carry on trade involving long voyages and with the prosecution of the trade in restricted areas competition was impossible and monopoly control inevitable.[130] Acquisition of this control by the Northwest Company was undoubtedly obtained through its centralized organization, its efficient and energetic personnel, and its characteristic effectiveness in dealings with the home government.[131]

[128]For a discussion of the supremacy of the Americans as against English monopolies in the trade see F. W. Howay, "Early Days of the Maritime Fur-Trade on the Northwest Coast"; also "Indian Attacks upon Maritime Traders of the North-West Coast, 1785–1805."

[129]F. W. Howay, "An Outline Sketch of the Maritime Fur Trade," emphasizes the relation of American traders to the sea otter trade.

[130]See J. B. Tyrrell (ed.), "David Thompson and the Rocky Mountains," describing Duncan McGillivray's failure in 1800 and Thompson's own trips through the mountains 1807 to 1812. See also Grace Lee Nute, "A British Legal Case and Old Grand Portage," on a lawsuit of Hervieux and McGillivray.

[131]See Alexander Ross, *Adventures of the First Settlers on the Oregon or Columbia River, 1810–1813*, ed. R. G. Thwaites; G. Franchère, *Narrative of a Voyage to the Northwest Coast of America in the Years 1811, 1812, 1813, 1814*; also "Petition of the Northwest Company to enjoy trade on the Pacific Coast and China at that time in control of the East India Company" in which it was urged that alien Americans enjoyed the trade while British subjects were prohibited, January 23, 1810, Can. Arch., Q, CXIII; and [Nathaniel Atcheson,] *On the Origin and Progress of the Northwest Company of Canada, passim*; "Letter from Simon McGillivray," asking for haste in British sanction enabling the Northwest Company to establish a settlement on Columbia River prior to the arrival of the Americans, November 10, 1810, Can. Arch., Q, CXIII; "Petition to export a quantity of goods to Columbia River," *ibid.*, CXX, 93–96; "Memorial, November 19, 1812, for an exclusive charter for the North-

The later development of the trade in the interior was dependent on the cultural background of the native populations. The existence of abundant supplies of food in the case of the salmon, the difficulties of the country which retarded movements over wide areas essential to hunting, the tribal feuds characteristic of territories involving isolation, and the general warmth of the climate were factors which prohibited the development of the fur trade on a large scale. In these areas reliance on the Indian for a supply of furs was less feasible. As a result the traders were obliged to organize bands of hunters to penetrate difficult areas and to trap the animals along the route.[132]

The effects of the expansion of the fur trade to the Northwest, to Athabasca and the Pacific, on the technique and organization of the trade were pronounced. With greater distances, costs of transportation increased and interest charges were more serious following heavier capital investments and slower turnover of the trade.

With the beginning of trade after the conquest[133] large numbers of individuals were able to engage on separate adventures. A very heavy turnover of grantees of licences is shown in the earlier returns. New grantees in large numbers appeared from year to year and individuals who returned to the same trading grounds year after year were not numerous. The heavy displacement was probably due to the taking over of the internal trade by English traders as well as to the heavy mortality rate attendant on lack of experience. In 1767 Benjamin Frobisher, Isaac Todd, McGill, Alexander Henry, Forrest Oakes, James Finlay, appear as guarantors to numbers of French traders going to various points in the interior. At this date two-thirds of the trade from Michilimackinac went to Lake Michigan and chiefly to La Baye and the Mississippi, and the remainder to Lake Superior and the Northwest. In Lake Michigan territory the trade was divided among a large number of traders (chiefly French) with one or two canoes each. The character of this trade was described in the following account:

---

west Company and for naval protection for the vessel sent to Columbia River to take possession of the country for the Company," *ibid.*; and "Bill of Sale of Pacific Fur Company to Northwest Company," G. C. Davidson,*The North West Company*, Appendix, pp. 293–296.

132See Alexander Ross, *The Fur Hunters of the Far West*, I and II, *passim*; and for later but similar methods of trading, *Journal of John Work*, ed. W. S. Lewis and P. C. Phillips, *passim*; Ross Cox, *Adventures on the Columbia River*; and G. C. Davidson, *The North West Company*, pp. 167 ff. Journals of various traders have been reprinted in the *Washington Historical Quarterly* and the *Oregon Historical Quarterly*.

133See Wayne Stevens, "Organization of the British Fur Trade, 1760–1800."

The adventurer in the Indian Trade must have his Goods ready at Montreal in the *Month of April* consequently they must be arrived from England at Quebec in or before the Month of Novem^r the preceding year, from there during the winter they must be transported to Montreal where they are prepared for the Indian Voyage by being put up in Packages, not exceeding One hundred pounds weight each, and every package is, or should be, an assortment of different species of Merchandize. These Packages are then conveyed in carts to a place call^d La Chine three leagues further up the River than Montreal, to avoid the Falls of St. Lewis situated between these two places; there the Birch canoes with their complement of 6 men each, being ready, the Goods are put on board and so they proceed (the first week in May) on the voyage by the River Ottawaes to the Post of Michilimakinac about 300 Leagues west of Montreal.

As they must unload and Land their Canoes every night and during the course of the Voyage carry them on their backs in 35 different places some of which are a league long it is generally from 35 to 40 days after their departure from La Chine before they arrive at Michilimakinac.

This Indian Post has been long famous for its convenient situation for trade between the Great Lakes and therefore the constant rendezvouz of the Canadian Traders in particular. Here they unload their large Canoes and put the Goods into lesser ones which are despatched to different places on and about the Lakes Huron, Superior and Michigan.

It is generally the middle of June before the Earliest Canoes arrives, the remainder of this Month, July, August, and September, is all the time the Traders have to dispose of their Goods and to carry their Furs to Montreal, if in this time they cannot finish their Business, and are obliged to stay all winter, they are sure to make a loseing voyage.[134]

A general survey of the organization of the trade is given in the letter books of Lawrence Ermatinger. During the earlier years importers with connections in England sold directly to the traders but this step in the organization quickly disappeared and traders purchased directly from London or importers became traders. Ermatinger purchased goods directly from English manufacturers but later discarded this arrangement as unsatisfactory and dealt with an agent or a house in England which carried out negotiations for him. Orders were sent by the last boat from Quebec in the autumn or by later post through New York.[135] The house bought trading goods from manufacturers in the United Kingdom and on the Continent (Brazil tobacco from Lisbon), insured them, usually £500 above the invoice price, and dispatched them to Quebec and Montreal merchants. Ermatinger imported goods from England in 1773 from the firm of Price and Morland, paying

[134]Can. Arch., Hardwicke Papers, 35,915, Pt. I, pp. 165–166.
[135]See a list of goods ordered by Ermatinger, Can. Arch., S. 812, pp. 283 ff.

one-third for the goods in the autumn and the remainder on twelve months' time. The death of the senior partner, Benjamin Price, and discontent with the new firm which sent unsatisfactory goods, led to a search for a new house and the establishment of connections with Davis, Strachan & Co. In a letter to this firm dated October 12, 1776, Ermatinger ordered about £9,000 worth of goods. He sent directions to them regarding the settling of minor debts for him in England, and gave orders as to the character, shipment, and insurance of goods. A later letter, November 28, asks them to use their influence in preventing a grant of exclusive trade to the Northwest Company. To the same agents or houses, furs were sent with directions to be sold, the returns being used to pay for trading goods. The credit of the London house was extended for the goods and wiped out when the furs were sold. Every effort was made to secure constant reports of changes in the prices of furs from the English agents through New York, Boston, or Philadelphia throughout the winter. A letter from Lawrence Ermatinger dated October 30, 1770, to Mr. Benjamin Price in London, gave typical instructions:

I also send you inclosed bill of loading and invoice of 5 bales of Furrs send by the Elizabeth Capt. Judge amounting to £210. 11. 1 sterling, this is the sum they have cost, and hope they may turn out well, in bale No. 5 there are 352 Raccoons and 1 fox and 3 deer in the hair which are round the bale for covering. Pray sell them by itself, deduct all the charges freight & except insurance and pay the produce to Mr. Vialars on acct. of Mr. Christoph Sanguinet they are not included in my invoice Pray don't miss them. . . .

I must beg of you to write by every vessel, which goes to New York Boston and Philadelphia particularly if you have any certain accounts of Pelletries rising and falling, which is an article much may be done by, but I once more observe to you, it much depends on good intelligence from your quarter.

Accounts of the probable returns were also forwarded to London during the same season, occasionally through New York correspondents. Ermatinger also forwarded news of the trade to a correspondent in Quebec.

Quebec, Mr. Jonas Clarke. Minot, 28th June 1773. This morning arrived the first cannoe for this season from Michilimackinac which brings us out very goods news, most of all the traders who wintered in the Mississippi have done nothing at all.

Trading goods which were urgently required for the spring trade were forwarded by the first vessel leaving London for New York rather than the first vessel leaving for Quebec. This trade, however, was limited to more or less compact goods[136] (awls, beads, thimbles, fire steels). Attempts to secure goods manufactured in New York were not successful.[137] Goods were brought, in the case of articles needed before the canoes left Lachine, by first vessel to Quebec and forwarded post-haste to Montreal. Later vessels brought the great bulk of goods to Quebec. They were forwarded to Montreal in smaller boats or bateaux,, carefully repacked during the winter and freighted to Lachine for early transportation in the spring up the Ottawa.[138] Trade was carried on between individual merchants to make up the outfits. The packing was done with great care, valuable commodities distributed throughout each piece and the whole arranged in convenient sizes of about ninety pounds for portage. The pieces were expected in most cases to withstand water in case of accident. Rum (8 gal.) and powder and shot were carried in kegs, and dry merchandise in bales. Tobacco, for example, was manufactured in carrots of one pound to two pounds and packed in ninety-pound bales. It was rolled in linen, well tied with cord line and packed in double canvas. It was also shipped in rolls of forty-five pounds each with two rolls to a bale. These goods were sent to various districts and a rough cost-accounting system was established allocating the costs to the districts as "Adventure to Nippegon, Adven-

---

[136]Lawrence Ermatinger to Thos. Woder, London, October 14, 1774, Can. Arch., S. 812, pp. 283 ff.

[137]See the difficulties of Ermatinger in getting tobacco manufactured in New York, *ibid.*

[138]"The 5 canoes sent under the care of Marchessau left Lachine the 11th May, 1765, Boyer and Bisonett." Can. Arch., S. 861.

The contents of a canoe sent to Forrest Oakes dated Montreal, August 19, 1767, included 6 bales of tobacco with 25 carrots each weighing 90 lbs. each and valued with the packing at £28.8. a bale with 25 2½ pt. blankets and 4 lbs. Bohea tea, valued with packing at £11.14.9, 2 bales with 25 2½ pt. blankets each and 5 lbs. vermilion each valued at £25.0.6, a bale of 25 2½ pt. blankets with 2 lbs. vermilion and 1 doz. knives and forks valued at £11.7.3, a bale of 18 3 pt. blankets with 9 lbs. white beads valued at £10.0.9, a bale of 16 3 pt. blankets and 9 lbs. of beads valued at £9.1.9, 3 kegs of spirits, 8 gal. each, valued at £12.12, 2 bales of kettles valued at £25; 10 kegs red port wine valued at £20, 1 barrel of loaf sugar £2.11.6, a barrel of knives valued at £4.2, 2 barrels of gunpowder valued at £7.14, 11 bags of shot and ball with 3½ hundred beaver shot, ½ hundred pichon, 2 cwt. ball, valued at £11.12.6 and a case with 2 china bowls, 1 doz. china cups and saucers, and 1 blackjack valued at £2.17, a total of 38 pieces valued at £180.15.0. For an illustration of the method of packing furs see "Recapitulation of Furs and Peltries, North West Company, 1804-5, Fond du Lac Department," *The Expeditions of Zebulon Montgomery Pike*, ed. E. Coues, I, 284–285.

ture to Missilimackinac, Adventure to the Northwest." To each district was charged the cost of goods supplied, wages of men, provisions for men, equipment, transportation for furs from districts, and other expenses, and to facilitate arrangements each piece was marked with the name of the owner, year of outfit, district, and weight of goods at Montreal.[139] Districts were marked by numbers or letters of the alphabet, the most distant department being given the first letter or number and the remainder in order. Goods were sent by the Ottawa at first cost plus expenses or they were supplied from Montreal at 50 per cent advance. The furs were put in bales marked according to department, district, number of the piece, and weight, and dispatched to Albany or Montreal and England. The freight charge on furs from Michilimackinac to Montreal was 30/ per pack of ninety pounds in 1768. Furs were also bought and sold by the merchants in Montreal and Quebec.[140]

In the interior, traders established headquarters at Michilimackinac and other points. Forrest Oakes at Michilimackinac bought the goods from Ermatinger, which had been purchased by the latter in England. Instructions[141] were sent down to Ermatinger in Montreal as to the date at which the canoes should be sent, the character of the men to be hired, route of the canoes, amount and character of goods needed, equipment and provisions, and general details. Furs were sent to Ermatinger to be sold independently or on joint account.[142]

Michilimackinac, Mr. Forrest Oakes, 3 May, 1774. A great many goods are going this year into the North, which I am afraid may hurt the ensuing years trade. However goods will not be so plenty the year after this, you may depend upon it.

I have send your peltrys to England on our joint account I have the sale of Beaver, but not yet any of the small furrs. Beaver has been sold extremely well, and hope the price will remain so.

The Montreal merchant according to instructions bought canoes, hired and arranged for the payment of wages of the men going to the interior, packed and took the goods to Lachine, and performed innumerable services. Writing to Forrest Oakes, Ermatinger requested:

139See D. W. Harmon, *Journal of Voyages*, pp. 1–16.

140See account books of Lawrence Ermatinger, 1768, Can. Arch., S. 750, pp. 9 ff.

141See a "Copy of Forest Oakes instructions given to me 30th August, 1769," also Ermatinger to Oakes, Grand Portage, Montreal, May 11, 1772, replying to charges of poor tobacco and general high prices, Can. Arch., S. 861.

142Can. Arch., S. 812.

Mr. Forrest Oakes, 25th May, 1774. Should you determine not to come this fall and your order should again amount to 4 cannoes I must insist on your giving me liberty to send all new cannoes, unless an extraordinary good one can be found amongst your own, as also to send two guides, for one guide for 4 cannoes detains them very much on the road and to putt 64 pieces in each cannoe so early in the spring believe me its more than cannoes can carry.[143]

In hiring men arrangements were made as to number of canoes sent and the number of each type of canoeman required—steersmen or "bouts," middlemen, and winterers. A statement of Ermatinger's dated May 10, 1767, gave a "Memorandum of the men which are engaged to Mr. Oakes and their price," of which an extract may be cited:[144]

Gone Pierre Bonssel St. Sulpice Gouvernal Michilimkina for	230	livres
Gone Andre Bouthillier St. Sulpice, mittel ditto "	170	"
Gone Pierre Parrent, Terrebonne to Wintre	315	"
Antoine La Lande Guide to go to the Grand Portage and return "	300	"
Settled—Aimable Rouillard Feauybourg de Ricollet to go as above, devant de Cannote "	320	"
Jean Baptiste Eltaing Brunnet, St. Genevieve, to go as above, milieu de Cannot "	250	"
Settled Jean Baptiste Bigras, Isle Jesus, to go as above, Bout de Cannote "	315	"
to go to Micilimakinac		
Robert Geanne to go and return M. "	225	"
Louis Meinard from Chambly, to Wintre "	400	"

The merchant in Montreal not only secured the goods from England, purchased the canoes and hired the men, but also directed the route of the canoes and arranged for provisions and supplies necessary for the journey. Ermatinger's "Instructions de M. Mayrand, Montreal, May 14, 1772," were as follows:

Vous conduisez les cannots dicy a Michilimakinac et si vous ne trouvez des cannots au detour qui doivent venir au devant de vous, avec des provisions vous prendrez un de vos cannots avec 14 Hommes ou plus pour aller au Michilimakinac ou vous deliverez une Lettre a M. Leonard St. Pierre qui doit vous livrer 120 sacqs de Bled lessive, suivant son obligation a vous remise si au cas le dit Sieur ne peut vous fournir cette quantite, il faut tacher de s'acheter allieurs et de tirer sur moy pour montant.

[143]*Ibid.*
[144]Can. Arch., S. 861.

La lettre pour M. Hance qui doit vous livrer suivant sa promesse a faitte a Mr. Oakes 12 Barrills de 16 Pots de Graisse et 4 Barrils de seize Pots de sucre sauvage, s'il ne peut vous les fournir il faut l'acheter absolutement M. Howard a qui vous remettrez une lettre vous assistera et vous fournira un cannot pour un porter les vivres, enfin je luy ai ecrit de vous assister ai tout ce que vous aurez Besoin jai ecrit en meme temps a M. St. Pierre et M. Hance a ce Sujet. . . .

Il y a un coutume a Michilimakinac que lors que les Hommes arrivent au dit Post, de les faire couper du Bois pour la garrison, une chose qui'il faut absolutement eviter, supposez qu'il vous couste quelque chose pour en etre exempte.[145]

Ermatinger's letters also give information to correspondents and merchants in Detroit and Michilimackinac regarding the price of furs, the purchasing of furs on his account, the possibilities of getting in touch with new traders, and the reliability of prospective merchants. Directions were sent to forwarders and agents at Niagara regarding the transport of furs and goods and provisions. Co-operation was essential between the London house, the Montreal merchant, and the trader in the interior,[146] as well as between a large number of other individuals who forwarded correspondence, prepared supplies, and contributed to the effective prosecution of the trade.

But it was a trade prosecuted by individuals, each with an eye to the largest profits. The distribution of the overhead in the trade was the result partly of custom but rather of consistent bargaining on the part of the traders concerned. Credit given by London firms was based on confidence in the judgment of the Montreal merchants and these in turn extended credit on the basis of confidence in the ability of the trader. Fluctuations in the trade were the occasion of unusual difficulty. A mild winter, inability of the Indians to return furs in payment, inability to meet the demands of the Montreal merchants and of the London agents—this was the logical sequence. Unfavourable regulation of the trade, delay in arrival of vessels from England, wars on the Continent, as in the French Revolution, Indian hostility, and competition were possible factors causing serious disturbance in the trade. Ermatinger in a letter to Mr. John Rowley, dated London, September 29, 1773, wrote:

The last winter was so very mild in this part of the world that the savages have had but a very indifferent hunt which unables them to pay

[145]Can. Arch., S. 812.

[146]Ermatinger to Oakes, September 5, 1770; Ermatinger to Howard (Michilimackinac), *ibid.*

their credit to the traders amongst them and of cours Meets every one concerned, for the Produce of Peltries is at least 2/5 less this to the quantity we had last year.[147]

Charles Grant's report, dated April 24, 1780, described the problem:

The Indian Trade by every communication is carried on at great expense, labour and risk of both men and property; every year furnishes instances of the loss of men and goods by accident or otherwise. It is not therefore to be expected that the traders in general are men of substance; indeed few of them are able to purchase with ready money such goods as they want for their trade. They are consequently indebted from year to year, until a return is made in Furrs, to the merchants of Quebec and Montreal who are importers of goods from England and furnish them on credit. In this manner the Upper Country Trade is chiefly carried on by men of low circumstances, destitute of every means to pay their debts when their trade fails; and if it should be under great restraints, or obstructed a few years, the consequences would prove ruinous to the commercial part of this Province and very hurtful to the merchants of London, shippers of goods to this country, besides the loss of so valuable branch of trade in Great Britain.[148]

Such were the organization and the problems of the trade prior to expansion to the Northwest.

The shift to the Northwest was responsible for material changes in organization. For these changes, the increasing costs of transportation were of vital importance. The canoe occupied an important position because of the shorter Ottawa route and the necessity of bringing furs down from Grand Portage to Montreal and Quebec before the boats left usually in October for England. For rapid and certain transportation[149] of the more valuable and lighter commodities into the country and of furs out of the country the canoe was essential. A general description of this trade is given in a report on the fur trade by Benjamin and Joseph Frobisher to General Haldimand, dated October 4, 1784:

The Inland Navigation from Montreal, by which the North-West business is carried on, is perhaps the most extensive of any in the known World, but is only practicable for Canoes on account of the great number of

[147]*Ibid.*; see also Can. Arch., Haldimand Papers, B.99, p. 73.

[148]"North West Trade," *Report on Canadian Archives*, 1888, pp. 59–60.

[149]"It [the Ottawa route] admits of the day of departure as well as the arrival being fixed with certainty and exactness, which point, on account of the wind, cannot be attained on passing over the lakes, and yet is of the utmost importance for the Canada merchants, as they must neither miss the period of receiving the furs from the interior of the Indian territory nor that of expediting them for Europe." *La Rochefoucault-Liancourt's Travels*, p. 113.

Carrying places. To give your Excellency some Idea of which, there are upwards of ninety from Montreal to Lake du Bois only, and many of them very long ones.

Two setts of men are employed in this business, making together upwards of 500; one half of which are occupied in the transport of Goods from Montreal to the Grand Portage, in Canoes of about Four Tons Burthen, Navigated by 8 to 10 men, and the other half are employed to take such goods forward to every Post in the interior Country to the extent of 1,000 to 2,000 miles and upwards, from Lake Superior, in Canoes of about one and a-half Ton Burthen, made expressly for the inland service, and navigated by 4 to 5 men only, according to the places of their destination.

The large Canoes from Montreal always set off early in May, and as the Provisions they take with them are consumed by the time they reach Michilimakinac, they are necessitated to call there, merely to take in an additional Supply, not only for themselves but also for the use of the Canoes intended for the Interior Country and the Consumption of their servants at the Grand Portage, but as these Canoes are not capable of carrying the whole of such Provisions it thence becomes necessary to have a Vessel or Boats upon Lake Superior for that Transport only, and the utmost dispatch is required that everything may be ready in point of time to send off their supplies for the Interior Country, for which purpose the Goods, Provisions and everything else required for the Outfits of the year, must be at the Grand Portage early in July; for the carrying place being at least Ten Miles in length, Fifteen days are commonly spent in this Service, which is performed by the Canoemen, who usually leave the west end from the 15th July to the 1st August, according to the distance of the places they are intended for.

Their general loading is two-thirds Goods and one-third Provisions, which not being sufficient for their subsistence until they reach winter Quarters, they must and always do, depend on the Natives they occasionally meet on the Road for an Additional Supply; and when this fails which is sometimes the case they are exposed to every misery that it is possible to survive, and equally so in returning from the Interior Country, as in the Spring provisions are generally more scanty. In winter Quarters, however, they are at ease, and commonly in plenty, which only can reconcile them to that manner of life, and make them forget their Sufferings in their Annual Voyage to and from the Grand Portage.[150]

The expense of canoe transportation was shown more precisely in the report of Charles Grant dated April 24, 1780. He stated that:

A canoe load of goods is reckoned at Montreal, worth in dry goods to the amount of £300 first sterling cost in England, with 50 per cent.

[150]"North-Western Explorations," *Report on Canadian Archives*, 1890, pp. 50-51.

charges thereon makes £450; besides that, every canoe carries 200 gallons of rum and wine, which I suppose worth £50 more, so that every canoe on departure from that place may be said worth £500 currency of this Province. The charges of all sorts included together from Montreal to Michilimackinac £160, and from thence to the Grand Portage £90, so it appears that each canoe at Michilimackinac is worth £660 currency; every canoe is navigated by eight men for the purpose of transporting the goods only and when men go up to winter they commonly carry ten.[151]

Itemized expenses for canoes included cost and storage. A note in the Ermatinger papers of July 25, 1764, states: "Bought a cannoe in partners with Richard Dobie for 110 livres, and 7 peices of his Barke, the same cannoe was marked R.E. and put in St. Louis LaCornes store."[152] Further items in Ermatinger's cash book of 1770 included:[153]

July 30.	Paid 3 boats carrying powder to Lachine	18/
Aug. 12	Paid pass for Oakes' canoe	£1.16
	Expenses going to Lachine to sett the cannoe of	9/
	Packers for making bales for upper country	1.4/
	Cartage to Lachine	18/
Sept. 10	Paid for 2 loads to Lachine for Oakes goods	12/
Sept. 13	Paid for Oakes canoe	£1. 3
Oct. 22	Freight from Missilimackinac 3 packs	£3.0.0
Oct. 24.	Paid guide to take canoe down Long Sault	£2.8
	" " " " " " Sault St. Louis	6/
	" freight for 4 bales for Quebec	17/
March 30 1771		
	Paid for putting 2 small canoes in the ground, 12/ and storage, 12/	£ 1. 4
April 18.	Paid for carting goods to Lachine	£ 1. 1
	" engages	2/
	taking two canoes out of hangard	6/
April 30.	Paid 2 men to bring a canoe to Lachine	6/
May 8.	New canoe	£15.

Depreciation of canoes through service was rapidly calling for almost annual replacement. Moreover, the capacity of a canoe was decidedly limited.[154] Alexander Henry wrote:

[151]"North West Trade," *ibid.*, 1888, p. 60.
[152]Can. Arch., S. 861.
[153]*Ibid.*, S. 867.
[154]With a canoe 35 feet long, 4½ feet broad, 30 inches deep, carrying 8 men and a clerk, it took 26 days from Montreal to Michilimackinac; *An Englishman*

The freight of a canoe, of the substance and dimensions which I have detailed, consist of sixty *pieces*, or packages, of merchandize, of the weight of from ninety to a hundred pounds each; and provisions to the amount of one thousand weight. To this is to be added, the weight of eight men, and of eight bags, weighing forty pounds each, one of which every man is privileged to put on board. The whole weight must therefore exceed eight thousand pounds; or may perhaps be averaged at four tons.[155]

Canoe transportation involved a heavy wages toll. According to Alexander Henry:

To each canoe there are eight men; and to every three or four canoes, which constitute a *brigade*, there is a *guide* or conductor. Skilful men, at double the wages of the rest, are placed in the head and stern. They engage to go from Montreal to Michilimackinac, and back to Montreal again, the middle-men at one hundred and fifty livres and the end-men at three hundred livres, each. The *guide* has the command of his brigade, and is

in *America, 1785: Being the Diary of Joseph Hadfield*, p. 108. See description of construction of the canoe, pp. 110–112. Hadfield lists the articles loaded in a canoe:

	Each	Total
16 bales containing each 1 pc. stroud and other dry goods	100	1600 lbs.
12 kegs rum, ea. 8 gals.	80	960
2 kegs wine, ea. 8 gals.	80	160
4 kegs pork and beef	70	280
2 kegs grease, ⅓ tallow, ⅔ lard	70	140
1 keg butter		70
3 cases iron work	100	300
1 case guns		90
6 kegs powder	80	480
4 bags shot and ball	85	340
4 bags flour	100	400
4 rolls Brazil tobacco	90	360
4 bales tobacco	90	360
63 packages		5540 lbs.
9 men	140	1260
9 bags	30	270
1 keg rum		80
6 bags bread or pease	100	600
4 kegs beef or pork	70	280
1 travelling case		80
Kettles, poles, paddles, oil-cloth, gum, bark, etc.		140
		8250 lbs.

[155]*Travels and Adventures . . . by Alexander Henry*, pp. 14–15, for this and the following quotation.

answerable for all pillage and loss; and, in return, every man's wages is answerable to him. This regulation was established under the French government.

The licence returns leave a decided impression that the turnover in labour was high, not more than one in seven or eight returning to the same point under the same grantee in succeeding years. Occasionally canoemen became interested in the trade and took out expeditions themselves or under the direction of Montreal firms. A demand for skilled canoemen led to a rise in wages and to desertion and confusion, as suggested in the following memorandum for Sir Guy Carleton, dated January 20, 1778.

2do, that it be published before the Traders and their Servants that the latter must strictly conform to their agreements, which should absolutely be in writing or printed, and before witnesses if possible, as many disputes arise from want of order in this particular.

3do It has ever been customary that a canoe man who falls indebted to his Master at the end of his voyage does (if in health) work out the debt by further service with the same master; or if he agrees with another that other to pay the debt in furrs or money as was his wages, immediately.

4th. An infamous custom has of late been practised by some, of engaging the men of other Traders whilst in actual service, and before their time was out such agreement should be declared with and any credit given on such faith be lost to the trader.

5th. It has been an unvariable custom and seems founded on equity that the last outfitter should be the first paid, after which the other creditors whether of two or twenty years ought to share alike. . . .

6th. In disputes between the Trader and Canoe man the officer ought to be the sole judge because the agreements are so explicit if properly made out, that by referring to them the decision is plain but between trader and Trader, two or four with the officer so as to give him the casting voice, will be perhaps more eligible.[156]

Some progress was made in improving this transportation and reducing costs but it was not of material importance. Alexander Mackenzie's description (in a later period) gives a larger canoe than that of Alexander Henry.

The necessary number of canoes being purchased, at about three hundred livres each, the goods formed into packages, and the lakes and rivers free of ice, which they usually are in the beginning of May, they are then despatched from La Chine, eight miles above Montreal, with eight or ten men in each canoe, and their baggage; and sixty-five packages of goods, six

[156]Can. Arch., Haldimand Papers, B.99, p. 2.

hundred weight of biscuit, two hundred weight of pork, three bushels of pease, for the men's provision; two oil-cloths to cover the goods, a sail etc., an axe, a towing-line, a kettle, and a sponge to bail out the water, with a quantity of gum, bark, and watape, to repair the vessel.[157]

The Company was able to reduce expenses by dividing a total outfit of thirty canoes into three brigades with one or two pilots to each brigade, but the number of men changed little, varying from eight to ten. With heavy upstream paddling on the Ottawa and lining up swifter stretches of water no reduction was possible. The canoe line consisting of five small lines about sixty yards in length, loosely twisted on each other, was an important part of the equipment.

The first part of the journey brought the canoes to Sault Ste Marie. It was necessary at this point to lighten them for transportation across Lake Superior and according to David Thompson they carried from forty to forty-five pieces including containers of spirituous liquors of 90 to 100 lbs. each.[158] The canoe was supplemented on the lakes by sailing vessels.

For the purpose of conveying all these things, they have two vessels upon the Lakes Erie and Huron, and one on Lake Superior, of from fifty to seventy tons burden. This [Sault Ste Marie] being, therefore, the depot for transports, the Montreal canoes, on their arrival, were forwarded over Lake Superior, with only five men in each; the others were sent to Michilimackinac for additional canoes, which were required to prosecute the trade, and then taking a lading there, or at St. Mary's, and follow the others. At length they all arrive at the Grande Portage. . . .[159]

The large canoes or *canots du maître* were important items in the trunk line from Montreal to Grand Portage.

With trade to the Northwest by Grand Portage men were hired to go from Montreal to Grand Portage and return in the same season.[160] According to contracts included in an engagement book of Ermatinger's from 1773 to 1775 they were expected to perform the following tasks:

Par ces presentes engages et s'engage volontairement au Sieur Laurent Ermatinger negotiant en cette ville pour a sa premiere requisition partir de

[157]Alexander Mackenzie, *Voyages from Montreal*, I, lvi; also G. C. Davidson, *The North West Company*, pp. 216–217; Colonel Landmann, *Adventures and Recollections*, I, 303 ff.

[158]*David Thompson's Narrative*, p. 177.

[159]Alexander Mackenzie, *Voyages from Montreal*, I, lxxi.

[160]Ermatinger to Forrest Oakes, Grand Portage, dated Montreal, May 11, 1772, Can. Arch., S. 812.

cette ville en qualite de devant de canot pour aller au Grand portage s'obligeant aussy de porter dans les dit portage six pieces en allant et six pieces en revenant, et revenir la meme annee sur les canots du dit Sieur ou autre chargeer ou alleger.[161]

The heavy expenses of the canoe and its inadequacy in handling bulky goods and supplies were responsible for a greater use of the lakes route and dependence on the larger lake boats.[162] The use of the lakes route was hastened by the closing of the Albany route which had depended on large boats rather than canoes. McTavish, Phyn & Ellice, and other Albany traders, obliged with the outbreak of the American Revolution to move to Montreal and to engage in the trade of the Northwest, hastened through their ownership of boats the adoption of the lakes route from Montreal. They introduced numerous economies of transport and gave the Albany traders an advantage in the trade which continued until the middle of the next century as the names of Mc-Tavish, Ellice, and McGillivray attest. Early recognition of the advantages of boats was shown in a letter from Ermatinger to Forrest Oakes, Michilimackinac, dated April 25, 1775:

The plan of sending the principle of your goods by way of D'Etroit I much approve of, and if you send me a memorandum for goods ere you go to the Grand Portage, or soon after your arrival there, I shall send, such as tobacco (pakd up in barrels) kettles, Guns, Powder, Shott, Strouds, and Blanketts immedially on receiving your order, and perhaps it may get to Michilimakinac this Fall, such a plan will safe you great expences, for the Men are deer and scarce to be got, I have only been able to engage about 20 Winterman, but I hope to get a few more ere the last Cannoes setts out.[163]

The extent of the reliance of the Northwest Company on the lakes route is suggested in the following extract:

One of these traders was agent for the North-West Company, receiving, storing, and forwarding such articles as come by the way of the lakes upon their vessels: for it is to be observed, that a quantity of their goods are sent by that route from Montreal in boats to Kingston, at the entrance of Lake Ontario, and from thence in vessels to Niagara, then overland ten miles to a water communication, by boats, to Lake Erie, where they are again received into vessels, and carried over that lake up the river Detroit,

[161]Can. Arch., S. 735.
[162]"Part of the company's furs are sent round the lakes in shipping, but the major part goes down the Ottawa in the Montreal canoes." J. Macdonell, 1793, in *Five Fur Traders*, p. 94.
[163]Can. Arch., S. 812.

through the lake and river Sinclair to Lake Huron, and from thence to the Falls of St. Mary's, when they are again landed and carried for a mile above the falls, and shipped over Lake Superior to the Grande Portage. This is found to be a less expensive method than by canoes, but attended with more risk, and requiring more time, than one short season of this country will admit; for the goods are always sent from Montreal the preceding fall; and besides, the company get their provisions from Detroit, as flour and Indian corn; as also considerable supplies from Michilimackinac of maple sugar, tallow, gum, etc.[164]

A heavy expenditure of capital for lake transportation became unavoidable. Bateaux were employed on the long and difficult upstream haul from Montreal to Lake Ontario. In 1775 Lake Ontario had three sloops, one of sixty tons and two of thirty tons, largely employed in the trade. Farmers were engaged[165] to haul freight over Niagara portage[166] and in 1794 were paid 1/8 New York currency per hundredweight, the wagons carrying from twenty to thirty hundredweight each trip. On Lake Erie and Lake Huron there were four sloops and two schooners with a total tonnage of 235 tons in 1775. Of the total tonnage on the Great Lakes, Grant owned 310 tons, McTavish and McBeath, 30 tons and John Askin, 15 tons. Navigation was restricted to the King's vessels during the war and to goods from Montreal. His Majesty's vessels totalled 350 tons, of which 140 were on Lake Ontario.

---

[164]Alexander Mackenzie, *Voyages from Montreal*, I, lxx–lxxi.

[165]*Correspondence of Simcoe*, III, 192. For an excellent account of transportation up the St. Lawrence and along the Lakes see I. Weld, *Travels through the States*, chaps. xxix f. See complaints of Detroit merchants regarding a contract price of £7.10 York for 13 barrels of 35 gal. each or 4/6 per 112 lb. and a charge of 6/- by John Stedman in 1778, Can. Arch., Haldimand Papers, B.217; also *Quebec Gazette*, February 17, 1780, on the difficulties of organization on the Niagara Portage; also Ernest Green, "The Niagara Portage Road," and E. A. Cruikshank, "Shipbuilding and Navigation on Lake Ontario to September, 1816"; also C. E. Cartwright, *Hon. Richard Cartwright*.

[166]Various travellers mention Philip Stedman who had a monopoly on this portage. Robert Hunter says in 1785 Stedman paid 1,000 guineas for the business and made £3,000 yearly; he charged £6 York for every bateau taken to Fort Schlosser, kept 60 oxen and 60 horses, and made 300 ton of hay a year. *Quebec to Carolina in 1785–1786: Being the Travel Diary . . . of Robert Hunter Jr., a Young Merchant of London*, ed. L. B. Wright and Marion Tinling, p. 97. Joseph Hadfield, who acompanied Hunter, reported that Stedman paid £1,500 sterling each year for his monopoly on the nine-mile portage at Niagara and realized a good £1,000 sterling per annum. He carried provisions for the government at low rates but received great rates on merchandise which was the property of private persons. *An Englishman in America, 1785: Diary of Joseph Hadfield*, pp. 92–93. See also an account of Stedman and his land on the American side of the river in J. Maude, *Visit to the Falls of Niagara in 1800*, pp. 143 ff.

During and after the war Montreal's position was strengthened against competition from Albany, and Great Lakes navigation became more important. In a memorandum dated Montreal, April 23, 1792, to His Excellency John Graves Simcoe from McTavish, Frobisher & Company, Forsyth, Richardson & Company, and Todd, McGill & Company, the supremacy of Montreal was pointed out:

It is true, that when previous to the late War, the route by the Mohawk was equally free with that by the St. Lawrence they had the principal part of the Detroit Trade because the Ports on the Atlantic, being open at all seasons, gave a decided superiority over us in the West India trade, by which means they could always undersell us in Liquors. But as *Liquors* are too bulky to form a material part of the value of distant equipments, and from the present situation of the Molasses Trade . . . we should now in that respect have the less to fear.—As to European Merchandize, we were always equal, if not superior, because the St. Lawrence admitting of larger Boats than the Mohawk, diminished our expence of Transport.[167]

The expenses of the Mohawk route were estimated in 1797 as follows:

Expenses on goods by the Mohawk river vizt.	
Use of a Boat from Schenectady to Oswego	£ 5
3 Men at £12 ea provisions included	36
For passing the locks on the river	3 12
N. York curr^cy	£44 12
Equal in Quebec "	£27 17. 6

These boats carry only 12 barrels exclusive of the men's provisions which makes £2.6.5½ per barrel to which if we add the transport from Albany to Schenectady and the storage at this latter place it will bring it to at least 10 Dollars per barrel.[168]

The supremacy of Montreal and the removal of restrictions after the war gave a stimulus to navigation in the Great Lakes from the

---

[167]*Correspondence of Simcoe*, I, 135. For a full description of the trade to Albany and of the effectiveness of the short direct routes of the Ottawa from Michilimackinac to Montreal, see Cadwallader Colden, "A Memorial concerning the Fur Trade of New York," *History of the Five Indian Nations of Canada*, pp. 25–42; also for a detailed description of the route from New York to Oswego, "Marbois on the Fur Trade, 1784"; also the advantages claimed for the St. Lawrence route over the route to Lake Ontario, Isaac Weld, *Travels through the States*, chap. xxix, *passim*. For an accurate description of the trade from Montreal see Alexander Mackenzie, *Voyages from Montreal*, I, i–xci. The journal of Peter Pond includes a valuable description of the Albany route to Mackinac and of the Montreal and Ottawa route. See also Colonel Landmann, *Adventures and Recollections*, I, 303 ff., and II, *passim*.

[168]Can. Arch., Q, CCLXXXVI, Pt. I, 124.

standpoint of the fur trade. In 1790 the Northwest Company had two vesels of 12 and 15 tons on Lake Superior. In 1793 it had the sloops *Beaver* (45 tons) and *Athabaska* (40 tons) (built August 15, 1786) on Lakes Erie, Michigan, and Huron, to bring supplies chiefly from Detroit and Mackinac to the Sault. In that year the *Athabaska* had been floated down the Sault rapids from Lake Superior, and the *Otter* (75 tons) was built on that lake to take her place. In 1800, Harmon stated that this vessel carried 95 tons of freight and made four or five trips per season to Grand Portage. By 1803 the *Invincible* had been added on Lake Superior.[169]

Various improvements in transportation were made in other directions. Canoes were manufactured for the trade at Three Rivers[170] in Eastern Canada and at the Island of St. Joseph[171] near Michilimackinac as an integral part of the organization. At Sault Ste Marie[172] locks were built:

Here [Sault Ste Marie] the North West Company have built locks, in order to take up loaded canoes, that they may not be under necessity of carrying them by land, to the head of the Rapid; for the current is too

[169]John Macdonell mentions the building of the *Otter* in 1793 by Mr. Nelson; John Bennet was sailing master. It arrived at Grand Portage August 2, 1793. *Five Fur Traders*, pp. 89, 96. See also G. A. Cuthbertson, "Fur Traders on Fresh Water." About 1805 Thomas de Boucherville saw a boat come to Niagara sent by Angus McKintosh, loaded with Northwest Company furs; "Journal, 1812–13."

[170]See B. Sulte, "Canot d'écorce"; J. Long, *Voyages and Travels*, pp. 50–51. "The birch tree is found in great plenty near the town, but it is from the more northern part of the country where the tree attains a very large size that the principal part of the bark is procured that canoes are made with"; I. Weld, *Travels through the States*, p. 255. According to Heriot these canoes were purchased for £ 12 or (La Rochefoucauld) 28 livres *d'or*. The Michilimackinac canoes were purchased for 200 to 300 livres. Macdonell speaks of buying bark, gum and watap to mend canoes from Indians at Lake of Two Mountains; *Five Fur Traders*, p. 71.

[171]George Heriot, *Travels through the Canadas*, p. 204.

[172]Nolin was in charge of the Northwest Company's business at Sault Ste Marie in 1793. White fish were salted at the Sault and sent to Detroit and Mackinac; salt cost 1/8 per lb. J. Macdonell in *Five Fur Traders*, pp. 88–89. On the way to the Sault in 1793, after reaching Lake Huron and following J. Frobisher's instructions to the brigade in which Macdonell was travelling, 45 pieces were taken from the guide's canoe and distributed in other canoes and "[we] shipped all Mr. McLeod, Le Moine, and my effects on board it and took a man out of each of the other canoes which made us a crew of fourteen paddles, and set out on our journey," leaving the brigade to await the arrival of the associate brigade under Denis.

strong to be stemmed by any craft. The Company are likewise building a saw mill, at the foot of the Rapid, to furnish boards, &c for the Grand Portage, &c . . .[173]

Roads were planned from Toronto to Penetanguishene to shorten the routes.[174] Heavy goods[175] could be received at York until the end of October, sent to Lake Huron on sleighs during the winter, and forwarded from Georgian Bay to Sault Ste Marie much earlier. Difficulties with ice on the lakes as well as the strong easterly winds of the early spring were avoided. The Company was able to secure legislation prohibiting the sale of liquor to canoemen going down the Ottawa rapids.[176]

The problem of securing cheaper transportation was closely related

[173]George Heriot, *Travels through the Canadas* wrote (p. 199): "The factory of the Company is situated at the foot of the cascades of Saint Mary on the north side and consists of store-houses, a saw-mill, and a bateaux yard. The sawmill supplies with plank, boards and spars, all the posts on Lake Superior and particularly Pine point which is nine miles from thence, has a dockyard for constructing vessels and is the residence of a regular master builder, with several artificers. At the factory there is a good canal, with a lock at its lower entrance and a causeway for dragging up the bateaux and canoes. The vessels of Lake Superior approach close to the head of the canal, where there is a wharf; those of Lake Huron to the lower end of the cascades. . . . The company has lately caused a good road to be made, along which their merchandise is transported on wheeled carriages from the lower part of the cascades to the depots."

[174]See Benjamin Frobisher to Hon. Henry Hamilton, Montreal, May 2, 1785, "North-Western Explorations," *Report on Canadian Archives*, 1890, pp. 54 f.; also *Correspondence of Simcoe*, II, 287, 358; and Can. Arch., Q, CCLXXX, Pt. II; Q, CCLXXXI, Pt. I, *passim*, and Q, CCCXIV.

[175]The cost of taking a canoe *de maître* from Lachine by the Ottawa to Michilimackinac carrying 100 pieces weighing 90 lb. each, or about 4 tons, included the canoe, £16.13.4; wages for guide, £16.13.4; wages for 2 end men, £25; for 8 men, £66.13.4; 8 cwt. of biscuit, £9.6.8; 2 cwt. of pork, £4.13.4; 2 bu. peas, 5/; gum, watap, £2.1.8.; incidentals, £50; a total of £191.6.8, or £47.16.8 per ton: while the cost of taking a bateau carrying 3 tons from Lachine, by Kingston, York, and Lake Simcoe to Michilimackinac included freight to Kingston, £18.0.0; storage, £1.5; freight, Kingston to York, £7.16.3; storage, 2 days' hire of 15 horses and 15 men to go from York to the end of the portage at the old Pine fort, £15.0.0; to portage at old Pine fort, £2.10; to canoe *de maître* from Pine fort to Penetanguishene, £16.13.4; to 10 men for 8 days at 40/ per month, £5.9.4; to provisions for men for 8 days, £5.0.0; to gum, watap, £2; to storage at Penetanguishene, £2.10; to freight to Penetanguishene, £11.14.4½; a total of £89.3.3½ or £29.14.5 per ton. The advantage in favour of York was £18.2.3 per ton. Can. Arch., Q. CCLXXX, Pt. II, 403.

[176]Minutes of Council, December 2, 1790, Can. Arch., Q, LI, Pt. I, 86.

to that of securing a cheap supply of provisions. Alexander Mackenzie suggests the character of this demand in his description[177] of Grand Portage:

The mode of living at the Grande Portage is as follows: The proprietors, clerks, guides, and interpreters, mess together, to the number of sometimes an hundred, at several tables, in one large hall, the provision consisting of bread, salt pork, beef, hams, fish, and venison, butter, peas, Indian corn, potatoes, tea, spirits, wine, etc., and plenty of milk, for which purpose several milch cows are constantly kept. The mechanics have rations of such provision, but the canoe-men, both from the North and Montreal, have no other allowance here, or in the voyage, than Indian corn and melted fat. The corn for this purpose is prepared before it leaves Detroit, by boiling it in a strong alkali, which takes off the outer husk; it is then well washed, and carefully dried upon stages, when it is fit for use. One quart of this is boiled for two hours, over a moderate fire, in a gallon of water; to which, when it has boiled a small time, are added two ounces of melted suet; this causes the corn to split, and in the time mentioned makes a pretty thick pudding. If to this is added a little salt, (but not before it is boiled, as it would interrupt the operation) it makes a wholesome, palatable food, and easy of digestion. This quantity is fully sufficient for a man's subsistence during twenty-four hours; though it is not sufficiently heartening to sustain the strength necessary for a state of active labour. The Americans call this dish hominy. [Fn.:] Corn is the cheapest provision that can be procured, though from the expense of transport, the bushel costs about twenty shillings sterling, at the Grande Portage. A man's daily allowance does not exceed ten-pence.

A full allowance to a voyageur while at this post is a quart of lyed Indian corn or maize and one ounce of grease.

(1793)[178]

The agricultural districts of the southern territories became increasingly important. Provisions and supplies moved from Fort Erie and Detroit to Mackinac.[179] Farming with especial reference to the

[177]Alexander Mackenzie, *Voyages from Montreal*, I, lxxx-lxxxi. For an excellent description of Grand Portage see a "journal" in G. C. Davidson, *The North West Company*, pp. 237–238. For the Can. Arch. copy of this journal L. J. Burpee has written an introduction in which John Macdonell is given as the author. See *Five Fur Traders*, pp. 93–95. There were 1,000 men at Grand Portage in 1793.

[178]Journal from Lachine to the Qu'Appelle, Can. Arch., Masson Papers (copies), 7 Folio 4. J. Macdonell's journal in *Five Fur Traders*, pp. 94–95.

[179]Private vessels between April 15 and November 26, 1793, carried from Fort Erie to Detroit 5,325 gal. wine, 38,952 gal. spirits, 890 guns, 19,550 lb. gunpowder, 495 cwt. ball and shot, 1,229 bales and trunks of dry goods, 1,758

demands of the fur trade as in the raising of hogs and the growing of wheat and corn, was stimulated. In 1778 the Northwest Company and Mackinac were permitted to take 13,000 hundredweight of flour from Detroit. In 1794 the Niagara district supplied annually 80,000 pounds of flour for the Northwest trade. Supplies were also brought from Milwaukee, and Michilimackinac itself was an important centre. A memorial and petition of the merchants of Montreal trading to the Indian or upper country dated Montreal, December 28, 1790, described the importance of a base of supplies.

Your Memorialists take the liberty of observing, that though the rout most generally used from Lower Canada to the Western and North West country, is that of the Ottawa, or Great River, leading immediately to a communication with Lake Huron, considerably north of Detroit yet such is the poverty of the country, that unless provisions can be procured from Detroit, the North West Trade would cease to be carried on, because of the insupportable expense that would accrue, if transported in canoes by the Great River.[180]

The forwarding of supplies and provisions became an important business. In 1778 the firm of Todd & McGill in Montreal imported goods for John Askin at Michilimackinac and Askin in turn imported supplies and provisions for Todd & McGill. He purchased corn and flour and other products on contract and later on a commission basis for his chief customer, the Northwest Company.[181] He was also an

---

cases, boxes, hogsheads of sundries, 769 packs of furs (?), 31 chests tea, 28 jars oil, 110 rolls of tobacco, 1,027½ bu. Indian corn, 24,000 lb. flour, 2 crates earthenware, 84 spades and shovels, 42 plowshares, 12 stoves, 13 ovens, 6 pots, 210 bars of iron, 1 anvil, 1 vice, 2 weights; and between April 15 and November 20, 1793, from Detroit to Michilimackinac and the Falls of St. Mary, 975 gal. wine, 22,536 gal. spirits, 280 guns, 3,350 lb. gunpowder, 69 cwt. ball and shot, 217 trunks and boxes of dry goods, 678 cases, boxes, hogsheads of sundries, 1,979 packs of furs, 3 chests tea, 2 jars oil, 17 barrels castoreum, 3,983½ bu. Indian corn, 189,172 lb. flour, 176 bu. oats, 14 packs of green hides, 9 bars of iron, 1 cable, 45 brick tiles, 80 boards, 1 anchor, Can. Arch., Q, CCLXXX, Pt. II, 395–398. See Can. Arch., the diary of John Askin, 1774–75, at Michilimackinac for references to farming and gardening and especially the raising of hogs; also *Correspondence of Simcoe*, III, 69, for return of private vessels, 1794, Province of Upper Canada.

[180]Can. Arch., Q, L, 63. It is interesting to note that Bougainville in his "Memoir" strongly urged the development of settlement and agriculture at Detroit as a support to the posts of the interior. *Wis. Hist. Coll.*, XVIII, 167 ff.

[181]For a description of Askin's activities see the letters published in "Fur-Trade on the Upper Lakes 1778–1815," *Wis. Hist. Coll.*, XIX, 234–488; and *Askin Papers, 1747–1795*, ed. M. M. Quaife. In 1778 Askin sold rum to the

important contractor for the shipment of rum and other supplies by the lakes route. Earlier (1774) Simon McTavish was engaged in forwarding rum from Schenectady for Detroit and the Northwest trade. The supply business on the lakes and the larger units of transportation required the development of an extended organization.

The development of an organization for transportation over the important and basic trunk line between Montreal and Grand Portage was accompanied by improvements in transportation routes to the interior and to Athabasca. From Lake Superior to Lake Winnipeg and to the interior the portages were more numerous, a smaller number of men was available, and the canoes were sent to the various districts in which the goods were to be traded. A small type of canoe was essential. These small canoes (*canot du Nord*)[182] were manufactured in part by the Indians along the route to Lake Winnipeg. Grand Portage was a terminus for the *canot du maître* and the *canot du Nord* at which the goods were exchanged and in the canoe yard of this depot Heriot states that seventy canoes per year were contracted for. The large number of men employed on the trunk section were engaged in carrying goods over the portage and bringing back the furs, and later in going to the depot at Rainy Lake. Increase in the quantity of goods is

---

Northwest Company when brought by the Lakes at a fixed price and, when brought by the Ottawa, at first cost plus expenses. For shipping from Mackinaw to Grand Portage he charged $2.00 per 1¼ minots or 1 barrel or 1 cwt. flour, from Mackinac to the Sault, $.75, and from the Sault to Grand Portage, $1.25. In 1789 he contracted at Detroit to deliver for three years, 600 bu. hulled Indian corn, French measure, at $2.00 a bu., 12,000 lb. French weight of flour at £1.16, N.Y. currency, per cwt. French measure (108 lb. English measure), to be delivered free on board the Northwest Company's vessel—the company supplying the bags—before the last of June. Another agreement of a similar character was made to begin 1793.

[182]E. Coues, *New Light on the Early History of the Greater Northwest*, I, chap. i. Hearne described (1774) the Canadians' "north" canoes as 24 ft. by 4 ft., 8 in. by 1 ft., 8 in. deep, each paddled by four men. The steersman of each canoe had £50 per annum, the foreman £40, the rest of the crew £20 to £25. Two men in each canoe received £5 extra for mending and carrying the canoe. At Grand Portage they embarked 65 or 70 packs and provisions for 10 weeks, each canoe holding over 2 tons. (This is larger than is generally given.) *Journals of Hearne and Turnor*, pp. 122–123. Philip Turnor in 1779 said the Canadian canoes were from 24 ft. by 4 ft., 8 in. by 21 in. deep to 27 ft. long by 5 ft. wide by 2 ft. deep. *Ibid.*, p. 222. The Canadians had partners who made canoes in their absence "and are always ready at the Grand Portage against their arrival every year, for one canoe if ever so good will not serve 2 year. The Pedlars have also some few men of their own who are handy at that kind of work." *Ibid.*, p. 157, also pp. 118, 152.

shown in the contrast of agreements of 1773 and 1775 which required men to carry six pieces going and coming across the portage, with standard, printed contract forms for men engaging with the Northwest Company in Montreal in 1798. The latter included the article:

Et passer par Michilimakinac si il en est requis passer Huit Pieces sur le Grand Portage en entrant, et quatre Pacquets en sortant, ou rabatre Six Livres ou Chelins ancien cours par chaque piece ou paquet, a l'option des dits Sieurs M'Tavish, Frobisher &'Co. ou leur representant et de travailler six jours a tous autres ouvrages, excepte de passer encore des pieces. S'oblige d'aller au Lac de la Pluie s'il est necessaire, en augmentant les gages cy apres de Cent Cinquante livres ou chelins, et avoir bien et dument soin pendant les routes, et etant au dit lieu . . . des Marchandises, Vivres, Pelleteries, Utenciles et de toutes les choses necessaires pour le voyage.[183]

Goods were carried nine miles over the portage to Fort Charlotte,[184] the terminus of the Northern canoes, the portage being divided into 16 *poses*.[185] The men were also engaged in repacking the furs and the goods for their respective destinations.

The people being despatched to their respective winter-quarters, the agents from Montreal, assisted by their clerks, prepare to return there, by getting the furs across the portage, and re-making them into packages of one hundred pounds weight each, to send them to Montreal; where they commonly arrive in the month of September.[186]

The goods were separated according to the demands of the various districts:

The Merchandise for the winter trade of the distant trading Posts was here assorted, and made up in pieces each weighing ninety pounds; the Canoes were of a less size, and the load was twenty-five pieces, besides the provisions for the voyage and the baggage of the Men; being a weight of about 2900 pounds, to which add five Men, the weight a canoe carries will be 3700 pounds.

These Canoes are formed into what are called Brigades of four to eight Canoes for the different sections of the interior countries.[187]

For the interior, separate personnel was necessary as distinct from those engaged on the route to Grand Portage.

[183]*Travels and Adventures . . . by Alexander Henry*, p. 14.
[184]Donald Ross was in charge of Fort Charlotte in 1793; Macdonell in *Five Fur Traders*, p. 97.
[185]Alexander Mackenzie, *Voyages from Montreal*, I, lxxvii.
[186]*Ibid.*, pp. lxxix–lxxx.
[187]*David Thompson's Narrative*, p. 177.

The North men being arrived at the Grande Portage, are regaled with bread, pork, butter, liquor, and tobacco, and such as have not entered into agreements during the winter, which is customary, are contracted with, to return and perform the voyage for one, two, or three years; their accounts are also settled, and such as choose to send any of their earnings to Canada, receive drafts to transmit to their relations or friends; and as soon as they can be got ready, which requires no more than a fortnight, they are again despatched to their respective departments.[188]

The canoes "are navigated by four, five, or six men, according to the distance which they have to go. They carry a lading of about thirty-five packages, on an average; of these twenty-three are for the purpose of trade, and the rest are employed for provisions, stores, and baggage."[189] Alexander Henry (the younger) has given a typical account of the contents of the canoes which left for the North in 1800:[190]

Sunday, July 20th [1800]. . . . early this morning gave out to all their respective loading, which consisted of 28 packages per canoe, assorted for the Saulteur trade on Red River, namely:

Merchandise, 90 pounds each	5 bales
Canal tobacco	1 bale
Kettles	1 bale
Guns	1 case
Iron works	1 case
New twist tobacco	2 rolls
Leaden balls	2 bags
Leaden shot	1 bag
Flour	1 bag
Sugar	1 keg
Gunpowder	2 kegs
High wine, 9 gallons each	10 kegs

With these loads they set off. "Those for the most distant trading Posts are sent off first; with an allowance of two days between each Brigade, to prevent incumberances on the Carrying Places."[191]

In 1803 the Northwest Company moved its rendezvous at a cost of at least £10,000 from Grand Portage[192] to Kaministiquia (later

[188]Alexander Mackenzie, *Voyages from Montreal*, I, lxxviii–lxxix.
[189]*Ibid.*, p. lxxxi.
[190]E. Coues, *New Light*, I, 7.
[191]*David Thompson's Narrative*, p. 106.
[192]Apparently the XY Company took over the Northwest Company fort after removal of the latter from Grand Portage in 1803. Thomas de Boucherville, "Journal," p. 8.

Fort William) since Grand Portage was within the American boundary and in 1804 the XY Company followed. Alexander Henry (the younger) describes the journey to the new post in 1803.[193] The route was more difficult with consequent complaints from the men and a smaller load (by two pieces) for the canoes. Following the removal of this depot a storehouse was established at Mountain Portage.[194] Canoes going to the interior were unable to take a full load from Kaministiquia because of the rapids. Provisions were consequently stored at this upper point.[195]

The growing importance of Athabasca demanded more extensive arrangements. Alexander Henry (the younger) described its position after 1800. "It is this vast extent of country from which the N.W. Co. may be said to draw their treasures. It is true, profits arise from the trade in other parts, eastward; but nothing in comparison to what we obtain from the Athabasca country."[196]

The cost of maintaining Athabasca district is illustrated in part by the number of pieces and the character of the goods sent from the depot. In 1806 in a total of 156 canoes, 53 belonged to Athabasca, Athabasca River, and English River; in a total of 3,290 pieces, 1,083 belonged to these departments; in a total of 1,771 provisions, 598 went to these departments. About one-third[197] of the goods, equipment, and provisions of the Company were sent to these three departments. In 1818 a total of 30 canoes and 848 pieces[198] were sent from Rainy Lake to Athabasca, Athabasca River, and English River—a decline during twelve years. The total of 848 pieces included 134 pieces of high wines, spirits (Port and Madeira), 102 bales of tobacco, 164 pieces of guns and ammunition, 200 pieces of provisions—a total of 600 pieces. Of the remainder, 24 pieces were hardware, 190 pieces baled goods and other minor items. The value of the goods sent to the Athabasca department was shown in the Athabasca scheme of 1815. At Slave Lake the goods on hand (inventory of 1815 plus outfit for 1816) were

[193]E. Coues, *New Light*, I, 217 ff.

[194]D. W. Harmon, *Journal of Voyages*, p. 113.

[195]In 1793 John Macdonell sent off from Fort Charlotte for the Red River fourteen canoes, which were smaller than the Montreal canoes and required four or five men each (four for the nearest posts); *Five Fur Traders*, p. 97. The same year Cuthbert Grant bought a canoe on his way in to Red River, when he encountered Indians, *ibid*., pp. 101–102.

[196]E. Coues, *New Light*, II, 474.

[197]An abstract of canoes for 1806 gives similar proportions, Can. Arch., Northwest Company Minutes, p. 58.

[198]Another account gives 866 pieces weighing at 90 lb. each around 80,000 lb. and giving for each canoe 2,666 lb.

valued at 10,416$\frac{1}{6}$ livres, the articles in use at 915$\frac{3}{12}$ livres, making a total of 11,331$\frac{5}{12}$ livres, to which should be added for Hay River, goods on hand 8,239$\frac{3}{4}$ livres, articles in use 317$\frac{3}{4}$ livres, a total of 8,557$\frac{1}{2}$ livres; a grand total of 19,888$\frac{11}{12}$ livres. On Peace River, Fort Chipewyan had goods on hand 29,355 livres, and articles in use 1,349$\frac{1}{6}$ livres, total, 30,704$\frac{1}{6}$ livres; Fort Vermilion, goods on hand 9,883$\frac{1}{6}$ livres, articles in use 342 livres, total 10,225$\frac{1}{6}$ livres; Dunvegan,[199] goods on hand 20,177$\frac{5}{6}$ livres, articles in use 629$\frac{3}{6}$ livres, total 20,807$\frac{1}{3}$ livres; St. John, goods on hand 4,207 livres, articles in use 524 livres, total 4,731 livres; New Caledonia, goods on hand 10,271 livres, articles in use 1,031$\frac{1}{4}$ livres, total 11,302$\frac{1}{4}$ livres—a grand total of 72,661$\frac{11}{12}$ livres. The total value of the goods on hand for the department was 96,619$\frac{3}{4}$ livres, including 4,069$\frac{5}{6}$ livres of advances and equipment; of the articles in use 5,107$\frac{11}{12}$ livres, making an investment of 101,727$\frac{3}{4}$ livres, or approximately £5,086 Halifax currency (1 livre = 1 shilling). The invoice of the Athabasca outfit for 1816 totaled £8,618.18.6, which with the men's equipment of £3,246.17.5 represented an investment of £11,865.15.11, and the invoice for 1817 totaled £9,321.7.9. If forty-two months[200] were admitted as the length of time necessary to realize on the furs exchanged for these goods at 6 per cent *per annum* the total interest charge on the 1815 outfit (a very low year) was 21,362 livres, or roughly one-fifth. Mackenzie River district would require an additional year.

The heavy costs and the importance of the department necessitated an efficient transport system. As already suggested the shortness of the season complicated the problem. As we have seen, Alexander Mackenzie complained in 1787 that the canoes arrived at Athabasca too late to be sent to Slave Lake or the Peace River country and the extension to New Caledonia made this problem more serious. Harmon[201] left Rainy Lake (Lac la Pluie) July 26, 1808, and arrived at Chipewyan, September 7, and Dunvegan, October 10. From New Caledonia it was necessary for the canoes to start from McLeod Lake immediately on the breaking up of the ice and in spite of constant travelling they were caught in the ice on Peace River on their return, and the goods were taken to their destination on sleds. The shortness of the season

[199]Dunvegan was established in 1800, abandoned in 1825, and reopened in 1826 by Colin Campbell, the grandfather of Garrioch; A. C. Garrioch, *A Hatchet Mark in Duplicate*, p. 231.

[200]Alexander Mackenzie, *Voyages from Montreal*, I, li.

[201]D. W. Harmon, *Journal of Voyages*, pp. 177–178.

and the rapid fall of the water in the autumn, characteristic of mountain streams, necessitated the greatest possible speed. As already shown, at least as early as 1788 an attempt was made to solve the problem by establishing an advance depot at Rainy Lake. Goods were taken from Grand Portage to Rainy Lake to be exchanged for furs brought down to that point. Mackenzie writes:

At this period, it is necessary to select from the pork-eaters, a number of men, among whom are the recruits, or winterers, sufficient to man the North canoes necessary to carry, to the river of the rainy lake, the goods and provision requisite for the Athabasca country; as the people of that country (owing to the shortness of the season and length of the road, can come no further), are equipped there, and exchange ladings with the people of whom we are speaking, and both return from whence they came. This voyage is performed in the course of a month, and they are allowed proportionable wages for their services.[202]

A further development followed in the establishment of Chipewyan as a depot, and the extension of the trunk line system to this point. Again Mackenzie writes:

The laden canoes which leave Lake la Pluie about the first of August, do not arrive here [Fort Chipewyan] till the latter end of September, or the beginning of October, when a necessary proportion of them is despatched up the Peace River to trade with the Beaver and Rocky-Mountain Indians. Others are sent to the Slave River and Lake, or beyond them, and traffic with the inhabitants of that country. A small part of them, if not left at the Fork of the Elk River, return thither for the Knisteneaux, while the rest of the people and merchandise remain here, to carry on trade with the Chepewyans.[203]

Harmon described Chipewyan as "the general rendezvous for all Athabasca. Here the goods are set apart for all the different posts, in this extensive department; and to this place, the greater number of persons who have the charge of these posts, come every fall, to receive their merchandise."[204]

The elaborate transportation system necessary to carry on the trade from Grand Portage to the interior and to Athabasca required a highly developed organization for the supply of provisions. An indication of

[202]Alexander Mackenzie, *Voyages from Montreal*, I, lxxviii.
[203]*Ibid.*, pp. cxxxiv–cxxxv.
[204]D. W. Harmon, *Journal of Voyages*, p. 138. "This [is] the compleatest inland house I have seen in the country . . . and I am informed they have a sufficient quantity of trading goods in this country for at least two years to come"—Turnor, June 29, 1791, *Journals of Hearne and Turnor*, p. 398.

the demands for supplies is shown in the following extract from the journal of Alexander Henry (the younger):

Sept. 13th, 1809. . . . Our expenditure of provisions for each canoe during this voyage [Fort William to Fort Vermilion, two months] was: Two bags of corn, 1½ bushel each, and 15 lbs. of grease, to Lac la Pluie; two bags of wild rice, 1½ bushel each, and 10 lbs. of grease, to Bas de la Rivière Winipic; four bags of pemmican, 90 lbs. each, to Cumberland House; and two bags of pemmican, 90 lbs. each, to serve until we came among the buffalo—generally near the Montée, or at furthest the Elbow, of the Saskatchewan. This shows the vast quantity of provisions we require yearly to carry on the trade in the N. W. Those brigades which proceed N. W. of Cumberland House require three additional bags of pemmican per canoe, and some a fourth.[205]

The difficulty of carrying large supplies of provisions in the canoes led to the establishment of provision depots. Part of the provisions for the in-going journey was supplied from Grand Portage. "Provisions for four men to Red river, 4 bags corn, 1½ bushels in each; ½ keg grease." These provisions[206] were brought from Sault Ste Marie and the south although farming was carried on to a slight extent at Grand Portage.[207] Provision posts were also established *en route* from Grand Portage to Red River as at the Athabasca depot on Rainy Lake. At this point "we saw . . . cultivated fields and domestic animals, such as horses, oxen, cows, &c. The port is a depot for the wintering parties of the Athabasca, and other still more remote, who bring to it their peltries, and return from it with their outfits of merchandise."[208] Lower down at Fort Alexander or Bas de la Rivière[209] a further supply of provisions was obtained and farming was also carried on.

This trading post had more the air of a large and well-cultivated farm, than of a fur traders' factory: a neat and elegant mansion, built on a slight

[205]This and the following quotation in the text are from E. Coues, *New Light*, II, 539; I, 8.

[206]Three sacks of corn per canoe were exhausted by Lake Winnipeg and the men caught fish; Macdonell in *Five Fur Traders*, pp. 108–109.

[207]Inventory of goods at Grand Portage, June, 1787: 6 horses, 1 3-year-old colt, 5 cows, 1 bull, 2 oxen, 2 calves, 6 sheep. Total value of goods on hand, £6,983.12.2¾. Old goods, £2,387.8. Letters and Accounts of the Northwest Company, Public Library, Toronto.

[208]"Franchère's Narrative," *Early Western Travels*, ed. R. G. Thwaites, VI, 383.

[209]Fort Alexander on the Winnipeg River was built by Toussaint Le Sieur in 1792 two leagues below the old French fort. The fort depended chiefly on fish. At Lake Winnipeg the men took boats—21 pieces in canoes and 23 pieces of the largest, clumsiest articles in three boats. *Five Fur Traders*, p. 107.

eminence, and surrounded with barns, stables, storehouses, etc., and by fields of barley, peas, oats and potatoes, reminded us of the civilized countries which we had left so long ago.[210]

Other supplies on this part of the journey such as rice and fish were obtained from the Indians.[211] Fort Alexander was the second important provision depot.

The greatest use of the Winepeg House is for a depot of Provisions, which are brought to this place by the canoes and boats from the Bison countries of the Red and Saskatchewan Rivers, and distributed to the canoes and boats for the voyages to the several wintering furr trading Houses.[212]

Provision supplies were secured by establishing posts up the Assiniboine River. Fort Espérance was built on Qu'Appelle River possibly as early as 1783 (Davidson gives 1787) but probably 1784. Fort Epinette was established possibly as early as 1784[213] as a centre of trade with the Mandans[214] and as a supply post. It was abandoned in 1794 through Hudson Bay competition and a post built at La Souris River. Fort Espérance was supported by frequent establishments at Montagne à la Bosse. In 1793 posts were also in existence at River la Coquille

[210]"Franchère's Narrative," p. 379.

[211]For an account of the use of wild rice by the fur traders see *Travels and Adventures . . . by Alexander Henry*, p. 242; *David Thompson's Narrative*, pp. 275, 296.

[212]*David Thompson's Narrative*, p. 181.

[213]See the map of Peter Pond accompanying a document dated 1785, "North-Western Explorations," *Report on the Canadian Archives*, 1890, p. 53.

[214]Canadians were apparently deflected from the Mandans and the upper Missouri trade in 1796–97 by the Missouri Company. Captain Mackay, possibly with the Northwest Company or an independent trader, was on the Catapoi River where "we find the furthermost wintering post of the English Traders from Canada" and from which they "make their unlawful Trade" on the Missouri with the Mandans. As an agent of the Missouri Company he went from the Catapoi to the Mandans in 1787. In 1793–94 the English sent traders from Assiniboine posts to the Mandans and apparently competition among them raised prices. Captain Mackay in 1795 was sent by Governor Zenon Trudeau to take possession of Missouri for the Spanish and was in the country till 1797. He sent John Evans up the Missouri from Maha village which he left June 8, 1796, arriving at the Mandans on September 23. On September 28 he took possession of the post of the Canadian traders. On October 8 several Canadian traders arrived but were forced to retreat. On March 13, 1797, Mr. Jessaume, a Canadian trader, arrived from the English traders but was also forced to leave. The British were anxious to penetrate the upper Missouri and by means of a Mandan fort to get the Rocky Mountain trade. See "Extracts from Capt. Mackay's Journal—and Others."

and River Tremblante but chiefly for trade in beaver and otter.[215] In 1795 John Macdonell[216] sent at least 275 taureaux of pemmican to Fort Alexander[217] (enlarged in 1792). The district adjoining Lake Winnipeg was organized from the standpoint of furs as well as provisions, and post were established up the Red River as well as the Assiniboine. According to Alexander Mackenzie two posts were established on Red River, four on the Assiniboine, and three on Lake Manitoba to supply this depot.[218] Longboats carrying 100 to 250 bags of provisions of 90 pounds each were brought down from the Red and Assiniboine rivers to Bas de la Rivière. Cumberland House was built in 1793 and replaced the depot near the Pas as a third post for provisions. At this point "the people who are destined to Fort des Prairies and those who are proceeding to Athabasca separate. The former go up the Sischatchwin River and the latter up the English River." Fort George was built by Angus Shaw on the Saskatchewan in 1792[219] above the post controlled by James Finlay at Fort de l'Isle. It was replaced by a fort twenty miles higher up in 1800.[220] Fort Augustus in the present vicinity of Edmonton and Rocky Mountain House were built in 1795 and in 1799.[221] A post was built on the South Saskatchewan[222] but it was destroyed by the Indians in 1794. Another post was built at the junction of the Red Deer and the Bow rivers but abandoned in favour of a better site in 1804. According to Mackenzie in 1798,[223] posts on the North and South Saskatchewan (Nepawi, South-branch, Fort George, Fort Augustus, and Upper Establishment), supplied the depot at Cumberland House for the transport to English River and Athabasca.[224]

---

[215]L.-R. Masson, *Les Bourgeois*, I, 275.

[216]*Ibid.*, p. 294.

[217]See N. McLeod's diary at Fort Alexander, 1800–1, *Five Fur Traders*, pp. 121–185.

[218]On June 21, 1790, Turnor said that 5 canoes of Canadians from the north waited two days on the Saskatchewan for people up river who supplied them "with provisions for their journey out." On June 23, Small, Mackenzie, Shaw, and McGillivray came out. *Journals of Hearne and Turnor*, pp. 316–317. On August 25, 2 canoes of Canadians came out with 10 to follow, possibly 12 canoes for the year, Mackenzie among them (*ibid.*, p. 322). Of salt on the Slave River, Turnor wrote (July 6, 1791): "The Canadians get great quantities of it from the Indians" (*ibid.*, p. 403).

[219]Masson, *Les Bourgeois*, II, 17.

[220]*Ibid.*, p. 23.   [221]*Ibid.*, p. 32.

[222]*David Thompson's Narrative*, pp. lxxvii ff.

[223]Alexander Mackenzie, *Voyages from Montreal*, I, cx.

[224]D. W. Harmon, *Journal of Voyages*, p. 115.

Transport supplies at Fort Alexander, Cumberland House, and later Grand Portage were largely dependent on the buffalo.[225] Availability of large quantities of pemmican was essential to the trade to Athabasca just as corn and grease were essential to the trade to Grand Portage. To produce pemmican on a large scale, it was necessary to employ a large staff to hunt buffalo, to manufacture the finished product and to transport it to the depots in the spring. In the production of pemmican the Plains Indians occupied a strategic position. The plains areas were not productive of the more valuable type of furs, and wolfskins were a staple export. Moreover these Indians were engaged in constant warfare with Indians of the strong woods country to the north on whom the fur trade depended. It was necessary to encourage the beaver hunters without offending the Plains Indians. The fur traders were engaged in checking warfare between the Crees to the north and the Blackfeet to the south. Failing in diplomacy they were obliged to establish strong fortified posts along the edge of the buffalo country. The Plains Indians relied largely on the buffalo for supplies of food and clothing and were less dependent on European goods with the result that trade in pemmican with them was developed slowly.

Alexander Henry (the younger) wrote: "The principal occupation of these people is making pounded meat and grease, which they barter with us for liquor, tobacco, powder, balls, knives, awls, brass rings, brass wire, blue beads, and other trinkets."[226] Rum, tobacco, firearms, and ammunition were the chief commodities traded to make them dependent on the Europeans. Ammunition was constantly in demand and McGillivray wrote: "When a nation becomes addicted to drinking, it affords a strong presumption that they will soon become excellent hunters."[227] The following extract from a statement regarding "an Enquiry into a bill for prohibiting the use of spirituous liquors among the savages of North America"—a bill which had been sponsored by Mr. Wilberforce and his supporters—dated Montreal, October 3, 1808,

[225]C. Wissler, *American Indian*, pp. 218–222. For a discussion of the importance of Indian culture, characteristic of the buffalo areas, to the fur trade, see R. O. Merriman, "The American Bison as a Source of Food: A Factor in Canadian Economic History" (Master's thesis, Queen's University, Kingston, 1925); also C. Wissler, "The Influence of the Horse in the Development of Plains Culture"; for a map of the range of the buffalo, see E. T. Seton, *Life Histories of Northern Animals*, I, 255. See also Oscar Lewis, *The Effect of White Contact upon Blackfoot Culture*.

[226]E. Coues, *New Light*, II, 517.

[227]A. S. Morton, *Journal of Duncan M'Gillivray*, p. 47. This volume gives an excellent description of the importance of the Saskatchewan plains to the trade.

and signed by John Ogilvy and Thomas Thain, agents of the North-west Company and by McTavish, McGillivrays & Company explained the situation:

. . . and although as we have observed above, these Indians, as well as their neighbours within our territory, have no valuable furs, their friend-ship and co-operation, is necessary to the support of the trade carried on with the others. *They alone supply all the food on which the company's servants subsist*; without which they could be compelled to abandon three fourths of the country, and all the valuable part of the trade. The sole em-ployment of these Indians, is to kill the large animals with which their country abounds; to select particular parts of their flesh and tallow; and prepare it in the usual manner and deposit it at the posts where the Com-pany's servants will find it, as they progress from and return to the general rendezvous; as these Indians are not like those of the cold and mountainous regions in want of manufactured goods, their principal inducement to per-form the services we have enumerated is the *present of rum*, which they receive at stated periods. These are the most independent, warlike and restless, of all the Indian tribes; and require to be managed with the greatest delicacy; more particularly as they form the link which binds in a common interest with the Northwest Company the whole Indian population of the interior country.[228]

Woollen clothing became important later.

But we now plainly, as well as the Indians, see in this climate, the great advantage of woollen over leather clothing, the latter when wet sticks to the skin, and is very uncomfortable, requires time to dry, with caution to keep it to its shape of clothing. On the contrary the woollen, even when wet, is not uncomfortable, is readily dried and keeps its shape, which quality they admire. The Indians now fully appreciate the use of woollen clothing, and every one is glad by means of trade to change his leather dress, for one of the woollen manufacture of England.[229]

On the whole, trade with the Plains Indians was not a reliable source for pemmican. Indeed their wars with the Indians of the strong woods greatly increased the expenses of the Company in necessitating the construction of fortified posts, the maintenance of a large staff for protection and the constant shifting of the posts to prevent war. The costs of maintaining a large staff were evident in numerous extracts. Harmon wrote on February 7, 1805, "Our family consists of upwards of seventy persons who consume at least four hundred and fifty pounds

[228]Can. Arch., Q, CVIII, 51–68.
[229]*David Thompson's Narrative*, pp. 421–422.

[buffalo meat] daily."[230] Franklin noted that, "At La Montée there were seventy Canadians and half breeds and sixty women and children who consumed upwards of seven hundred pounds of buffalo meat daily, the allowance per diem for each man being eight pounds."[231] Men were left in charge for the protection of the posts in the summer and to cultivate crops which would reduce the costs of provisions.[232] Indeed the transport system required the closest attention on the part of the managers of all the posts to the possibilities of self-sufficiency.[233] In Athabasca district salt was obtained from the neighbourhood of Peace River. Crops were grown at various posts along the Peace, and, in New Caledonia, Harmon depended on the supply of salmon.

An indication of the expense occasioned by the whole transportation system from Montreal to Athabasca was shown in the number of employees of the Company and general wages. The number of employees changed slightly throughout the period after 1800. In 1798 there were 50 clerks, 70 interpreters and clerks, 35 guides, and 1,102 canoemen, of which 5 clerks, 18 guides, and 350 canoemen were employed on the route from Montreal to Grand Portage and Rainy Lake.[234] For about the same period another report gives a total of 981 men in the interior, 77 men at posts on the Ottawa River, St. Maurice River, Moose River, Hudson Bay, and Temiscamingue, and 540 men on the route from Montreal to Grand Portage. In addition, 80 to 100 Canadians and Iroquois hunters[235] were hired to hunt over the country.[236] The men engaged in the trade were distributed as follows: Hudson Bay drainage basin, 630 men, Mackenzie River, 257, and the United States and St. Lawrence, 171. In 1805 one account gave a total of 803 men employed

[230]D. W. Harmon, *Journal of Voyages*, p. 103.

[231]Capt. John Franklin, *Narrative of a Journey to the Shores of the Polar Sea in the Years 1819, 20, 21, and 22*, I, 183.

[232]See D. W. Harmon, *Journal of Voyages*, for a description of experiences as a summer man in the Lake Manitoba district. Co-operation was occasionally necessary between the Hudson's Bay Company and the Northwest Company as a result of Indian attacks; see Isaac Weld, *Travels through the States*, pp. 187–188.

[233]Alexander Mackenzie, *Voyages from Montreal*, I, cxxxv ff. For an interesting description of the attempt to make posts self-sufficient see the journal of Rocky Mountain Portage on Peace River in M. O'Neil, "The Peace River Journal."

[234]Alexander Mackenzie, *Voyages from Montreal*, I, liii–liv.

[235]McLeod mentions two Iroquois hunters in 1800–1; *Five Fur Traders*, pp. 140–141.

[236]See "Courts of Justice for the Indian Country," *Report on Canadian Archives*, 1892, pp. 142–143; also G. C. Davidson, *The North West Company*, pp. 280–281.

in the interior.[237] For the same year another statement of Northwest population gave 1,610 men (of which 520 had been of Alexander Mackenzie & Company), 405 women, and 600 children.[238] The change in distribution of population was not appreciable, although departments in the plains area increased.

For the later periods statistics are available for Athabasca alone and the importance of this distant department to costs of transportation is obvious. In 1801 of a total of 981 men in the Northwest country, 257 were in the Athabasca district, 75 in English River, and 98 in the Saskatchewan River department which largely furnished supplies to the northern areas. Almost half (444) of the total number of men were dependent on the Northern territory. Of a total of 102 posts, 39 were in the same district and of a total of 18 partners, 11 were in this territory. In 1805[239] Athabasca, Athabasca River, English River, and Fort des Prairies were responsible for 459 men of a total of 1,090. From 1801 to 1805 the proportionate number of men employed in the Athabasca department declined. This decline was characteristic of English River and the Northern departments generally although from 1805 to 1818 the number employed apparently remained stationary.[240]

Wages also appear to have changed slightly after 1800. Rates were based largely on skill.

In each of these canoes are a foreman and steersmen; the one to be always on the look-out, and direct the passage of the vessel, and the other to attend the helm. They also carry her, whenever that office is necessary. The foreman has the command, and the middle-men obey both; the latter earn only two-thirds of the wages which are paid the two former. Independent of these, a conductor or pilot is appointed to every four or six of these canoes, whom they are all obliged to obey; and is, or at least is intended to be, a person of superior experience, for which he is proportionably paid.[241]

[237]See list of men at posts in 1805, Can. Arch., Masson Papers.

[238]E. Coues, *New Light*, I, 282.

[239]See an incomplete list for 1804, L.-R. Masson, *Les Bourgeois*, I, 315–413.

[240]See statement of men's agreement 1817–18, Can. Arch., McGillivray Papers.

[241]Alexander Mackenzie, *Voyages from Montreal*, I, lxxxi–lxxxii. Professor W. N. Sage of the University of British Columbia has in his possession a contract of a *milieu* to winter at English River for six years at 300 livres per year. Mr. C. N. Bell of Winnipeg has a large number of these contracts in his possession; see also the Northwest Company Accounts, Toronto Public Library, and G. C. Davidson, *The North West Company*, p. 231 n.

Agreements were signed at Montreal and at Grand Portage. Standard printed forms became the rule and included articles against private trade, and provision for the deduction of 1 per cent of the wages for a fund for disabled *voyageurs*. Accounts as to advances to each man in goods and cash were forwarded from Montreal to the upper rendez-vous. The length of time for the engagement in the interior varied and was as long as six years. The great majority of the men were middle-men and relatively unskilled. With few exceptions they were French.[242] In 1767 wages of "porkeaters" (men who were hired for the trip from Montreal to Grand Portage and return) were roughly 350 livres for a guide, 300 to 320 livres for foremen and steersmen, and 250 livres for middlemen. Winterers hired by the year received 300 to 400 livres. About 1800, "porkeaters" received: guides, 800 to 1,000 livres; fore-men and steersmen, 400 to 600; middlemen, 250 to 350; and winter-ers received: foremen and steersmen, 1,200 livres; middlemen, 800. The increase in wages for skilled canoemen was most pronounced. In 1805 winterers in the Athabasca department were paid: guide, 800 livres; foremen and steersmen, 500 to 750; middlemen, 300 to 550; in Lower Red River: guide, 600 to 750; foremen and steersmen, 450 to 600; middlemen, 150 to 350. Departments tended to vary between these extremes. In 1817–18 wages in the Athabasca department had declined very slightly. Temporary changes apparently followed amalga-mations and monopoly control, as in 1804 wages at Kaministiquia declined from the level of the previous year.[243] Each department varied as to the number of interpreters, fishermen, summermen, and hunters; some departments had a cooper and a blacksmith. Men who per-formed other work and were also interpreters received proportionally higher wages. On July 15, 1806, following monopoly control, regula-tions were passed stating definite wages and equipment for each de-partment and each occupation. Athabasca department, English River

---

[242]With John Macdonell in 1793 went men from the parish of Berthier—L. La Tourelle, foreman, P. Valois, steersman. Faignan, the favourite guide of Joseph Frobisher, was kept behind and F. Huneau from Isle Perrault went as guide of the brigade and Denis as guide of the associate brigade. Guides ran canoes down Carillon rapids and the Long Sault for $5. Later Bazil Ireland, guide, joined Macdonell with canoes from Montreal. *Five Fur Traders*, pp. 67–72, 96.

[243]E. Coues, *New Light*, I, 247. On January 18, 1800, John Askin wrote of the XY Company: "The opposition to N West has raised the price [wages] . . . very high." Young men asked much more at Montreal than at Detroit. They wanted 700–800 livres and would sign for only one year. *Askin Papers*, II, 274. Also, the price of flour was raised. *Ibid.*, p. 286.

and Rat River departments received the highest wages and other departments were scaled down.[244]

Equipment for the "porkeaters" included 1 blanket, 1 shirt, 1 pair of trousers; for winterers, 2 blankets, 2 shirts, 2 pair of trousers and tobacco; and differences in equipment for various occupations were shown usually in the tobacco item. In the regulations of July 15, 1806, men of the more remote departments as in the case of Athabasca were given additional items such as knives, beads, and vermilion. Wages were paid as a rule in goods[245] and many departments showed a pro-

[244]George Heriot, *Travels through the Canadas*, pp. 233 ff., gives an account of the trade based on Alexander Mackenzie's work. Wages in the Athabasca and English River departments were fixed at 600*l* for *devants* and *gouvernails*, and 400*l* for *milieux*. Each man received 1 3 pt. blanket, 1 2½ pt. blanket, 2 pr. leggings, 2 shirts, 2 *braillets*, 2 handkerchiefs, 3 carrots tobacco, 2 large knives, 2 small knives and the *boutes* received in addition, 1 carrot tobacco, 1 large knife, 1 small knife, ½ lb. beads, ¼ lb. vermilion; Athabasca River department gave *boutes* 700*l*, *milieux*, 500*l* and same equipment; Rocky Mountains forts were given the same except that *milieux* received 450*l*; Upper Fort des Prairies paid for the *boutes* 500*l*, *milieux* 400*l*, and the same equipment. At Lower Fort des Prairies *boutes* were paid 450*l*, *milieux* 350*l*, and a common equipment, 1 3 pt. blanket, 1 2½ pt. blanket, 2 shirts, 2 *braillets*, 2 pr. leggings, 3 carrots tobacco—the *boutes* receiving 1 carrot tobacco more; Cumberland House received not over 50*l* more. For the remaining departments a common equipment was given and at Fort Dauphin *boutes* 400 to 450*l*, *milieux* 300 to 350*l*; Upper Red River *boutes* 400 to 500*l*, *milieux* 300 to 350*l*; Lower Red River *boutes* 400 to 450*l*, *milieux* 300*l*; Lake Ouinipique *boutes* 450*l* to 500*l*, *milieux* 350 to 400*l*; Lac la Pluie *boutes* 450*l*, *milieux* 300 to 350*l*; Lac des Isles *boutes* 550*l*, *milieux* 400; Monontague *boutes* 400 to 450*l*, *milieux* 300 to 350*l*; Lake Nipigon *boutes* 400 to 450*l*, *milieux* 300 to 350*l*; Fond du Lac department 400 to 500*l*; Folle Avoine country 350 to 400*l*; Rivière de Montreal 400 to 450*l*. "It having been found that much confusion and irregularity have arisen in the wages and equipment of men throughout the Country, to the great loss and injury of the concern, it was resolved at a meeting of the N. W. Co. held at Kamm on the 15th day of July 1806, that the wages and equipment of the different Departments shall be regulated as above." Can. Arch., Northwest Company Minutes.

[245]Count Andriani has estimated that 1,400 bundles of fur received at Grand Portage sold at £40 sterling each in Montreal, and were sold in London by the Northwest Company for £88,000. For these 1,400 bundles the Company paid about £16,000 sterling, or

Cost of commodities purchased in England	354,000 livres
Pay for 40 guides, interpreters and conductors of expedition	88,000 livres
Pay 1,100 men wintering in interior, 1,800 livres each	1,980,000 livres
Pay 1,400 men Montreal to Grand Portage	350,000 livres
Price of provision consumed Montreal to Grand Portage	4,000 livres
total expense for 1,400 bundles	2,776,000 livres

The Company seems to lose 600,000 livres Tournois but all employees, except 40

nounced excess of men's debits to the Company over credits. The wage bill for the departments varied appreciably. In 1805 wages for English River totalled 35,000 livres; for Lower Red River, 20,000 livres; and for Fond du Lac, 63,913 livres. In 1817–18 total wages for Athabasca department were 76,000 livres for 215 men.

Clerks were engaged for five to seven years for £100, provisions, and clothing.[246] If no provision was made for a partnership at the end of the agreement £100 to £300 per year was paid. In 1803 clerks were allowed to purchase goods at Grand Portage and Lac la Pluie at 100 per cent on Montreal prices and at interior posts at 150 per cent on these prices. Those who "summered" inland were charged only 100 per cent on Montreal prices. Proprietors and clerks were given stipulated quantities[247] of such articles as tea, coffee, and chocolate in a regulation of July 23, 1806.

The evidence points very directly to the conclusion that a monopoly control of the trade made possible substantial reductions in wages outlay through direct control in standards of wages and indirectly through the sale of goods. Wages fluctuated as a result of competition and monopoly.[248] After the amalgamation of the XY Company and the Northwest Company, clerks' salaries were reduced from £100 per year to £60 per year for first year, £80 for second year, and £100 for third. In 1819 following competition of the Hudson's Bay Company, wages in the Athabasca district increased,—"a middleman gets now a thousand livres Halifax currency, and a *boute* fourteen hundred, interpreters from sixteen to two thousand; clerks from one hundred and fifty to two hundred pounds same currency."[249]

Disputes between the men and the Company were not unknown but appear to have been rare. In 1789 ten firms signed an agreement

---

guides and 1,400 men working between Montreal and Grand Portage who are paid half in cash and half in merchandise, are paid entirely in merchandise, which at Grand Portage yields a profit of 50 per cent. As a result of profit, 900 servants in 1791 owed the company more than the amount of ten or fifteen years' pay. The apparent loss of the Company becomes a gain. *Thirteenth Report of the Bureau of Archives for the Province of Ontario*, 1916, pp. 113 ff., in *La Rochefoucault-Liancourt's Travels*. There is some evidence to show that Andriani received his information from Peter Pond.

[246]John Macdonell was hired as a clerk on May 10, 1793, for five years at "£100 at the expiration, and found in necessaries"; *Five Fur Traders*, p. 67.

[247]See packing account of sundries to complete Athabasca and Athabasca River men's equipment, 1818, and recapitulation of Athabasca gentlemen's orders, Can. Arch., McGillivray Papers.

[248]L.-R. Masson, *Les Bourgeois*, I, 39.

[249]*Ibid.*, p. 124.

to the effect that no *voyageur* should be hired "unless he produced a certificate from his curé." The low prices of furs incidental to the French Revolution were apparently followed by a reduction in wages and D. A. Grant in a letter to S. McTavish dated St. Helen, July 10, 1794, complained of the recalcitrant character of the French[250] and of the weakness and pusillanimity of the magistrates who had allowed "a party of upper country engagés who rose and took off the pillory" to escape. On August 3, 1794, at Lac la Pluie several ringleaders demanded higher wages but without success. The more obstreperous were sent to Montreal. Sanctity of contract was an effective weapon for the company[251] and *esprit de corps* was developed to an appreciable extent. Men of the Athabasca department regarded themselves as the best travellers. Winterers looked with scorn on the *mangeurs du lard*. On arrival at the height of land above Lake Superior each recruit was initiated to the title of a northman by having water sprinkled in his face with a small cedar bow and by taking an oath that he would not allow any new man to pass that road without submitting to a similar ceremony, and that he would kiss no *voyageur*'s wife against her will.[252]

The advantages of a large-scale organization in the fur trade were shown in part in the wage policy. Wages could be paid to a limited extent on the basis of what the traffic would bear. Improvement in transportation routes made possible a reduction in personnel. The wage bill was kept to some extent under control but it remained a very important item of expense and was chiefly a cost of transportation. Alexander Mackenzie estimated that on the whole, expenses of transportation equalled one-half the total adventure of the Company and the prosecution of the trade in more remote areas following the date of his estimate (made about 1798) probably increased the proportion.[253]

The organization of the departments west of the Rocky Mountains, especially to the south, was not complete without arrangements for cheaper transportation of furs and goods than the route across the continent to Montreal. The solution of this problem was found in the dispatch of vessels from England by the Horn to the mouth of the

[250]See note in Turnor's journal of Holmes's fear that Canadians would attack them in the spring of 1779. *Journals of Hearne and Turnor*, pp. 225–228.

[251]See A. S. Morton, *Journal of M'Gillivray*, p. 7.

[252]For expressions used see *Five Fur Traders*, p. 99, also A. Simpson, *Life of Thomas Simpson*, p. 60 n.

[253]Alexander Mackenzie, *Voyages from Montreal*, I, lii–liii.

Columbia. Furs from the Columbia district were sent direct to Canton. Tea and Chinese products were taken to England on the return voyage. Difficulties with the East India Company in carrying on direct trade with China led to the arrangement in 1815 by which the furs were dispatched through a Boston house. Trade was carried on through American hands from 1816 to 1820.

The advantages in the conduct of the trade by a large organization were shown in other directions than in the elaboration of an extensive transport system. Methods of control of vital importance to the success of the Northwest Company were worked out. Systems of administration and accounting were improved and adjusted to the technical demands of the trade. The territory was divided into districts and partners placed in charge. The partner usually chose a central position for his post and established outposts in which more responsible clerks and men were stationed to trade with the Indians of the neighbourhood. Control of the outposts was maintained by periodic visits from the partner in charge. The department and the year were the units of control. It was possible to check the account of each partner in charge of the department. Accounts[254] were kept by the partner of the amount of credit given to Indian hunters in the fall and the amount returned. According to an account dated 1801 an invoice value of goods as at the rendezvous (Grand Portage, later Kaministiquia and Rainy Lake) was used as a basic cost for interior posts. To this cost was added equipment items for the personnel (proprietor, £20; clerks and interpreters, 400s.; guides and interpreters, 300s.; canoemen, 78s.) and to this total, interest at 4.66 per cent for one year plus the inventory of the previous year. Finally there was added 6 per cent interest for one year, the freight of the packs to Montreal (41s. 8d. each), and wages of the personnel. November 30 was apparently regarded as the end of the financial year. The importance of slow turnover and of the credit nature of the trade was shown in the interest items. On the other side of the sheet was placed the inventory of goods remaining at the end of the outfit, advances to men, returns from provisions supplied (1s. per pound) and returns from furs with a reduction of discount for six months at 6 per cent. Within the department the returns from individual traders were checked by the partners. The handling of goods and furs beyond the rendezvous was controlled in separate accounts and the cost of transportation allocated on a fixed basis.[255] Freight of packs to Montreal was charged at a fixed price and the freight of goods

254E. Coues, *New Light*, I, 4.
255*Ibid.*, pp. 200–201.

to the rendezvous was included in the invoice price. The tariff[256] for the sale of goods was adjusted partly on the basis of what the traffic would bear depending on the character of competition. In 1804 a more precise allocation was arranged,[257] the advance of goods at Kaministiquia on the Montreal price being 23 per cent, and the advance of price of various goods in the interior being arranged according to the character of the commodity and the location of the department. Allocation as to posts within the departments appears not to have been carried out.[258] Posts as widely separated as Fort Chipewyan and New Caledonia carried goods at the same price. On the other hand inventories were kept for each post and goods were distributed and valued for each post as separate units.

With the information available in these accounts the Company was in a position to determine matters of policy. The purchasing of commodities and the sale of furs were managed by the Montreal agents on a commission basis. These agents arranged with the partners of the Company in the interior (the wintering partners) each year at Grand Portage for the general management of the business. Questions of promotion, rotation of furlough, wages, tariffs, regulations for the trade, granting of the power of attorney to the agents, and details which affected the interest of the agents, of the partners, and of the concern were discussed often and with much energy. In order that decisions could be made with the greatest possible advantage it was necessary to have on hand adequate reports of the trade in the interior. An elaborate communication system was established over the whole of the area. Requisitions for the year in goods and men depended on the amount of trade. News of the supply of furs was placed in the hands of the Montreal merchants at the earliest possible date.

[256]See the prices of goods charged at Fort des Prairies in 1776 under monopoly conditions, *Travels and Adventures . . . by Alexander Henry*, pp. 320–321, and compare these prices with a more extended list in the Northwest Company, Fond du Lac department, at which it was stated "that the real price of goods here in exchange for peltry, is about 250 per cent on the prime cost," *Expeditions of Zebulon M. Pike*, ed. E. Coues, I, 283. Heriot suggested that the following tariff prevailed: 10 beaver skins = 1 gun, 1 beaver = 1 lb. powder = 2 lb. glass beads, 2 marten skins = 1 beaver skin, 2 beaver skins = 1 otter skin. *Travels through the Canadas*, p. 243. La Rochefoucauld in citing Andriani's journal writes that articles in Detroit are 3 times, in Michilimackinac 4 times, at Grand Portage 8 times, and at Lake Winnipeg 16 times, their usual value at Montreal. "Nay the agents fix the price still higher at their will and pleasure." *La Rochefoucault-Liancourt's Travels in Canada 1795*, p. 115.

[257]See Appendix F.

[258]See Athabasca Scheme 1815, Can. Arch., McGillivray Papers.

Angus Shaw stationed at Lac d'Orignal in 1789 received letters from Montreal, Grand Portage, and Fort des Prairies on December 15 of that year.[259] According to Roderic Mackenzie the first winter express from the Athabasca region for Lake Superior left Fort Chipewyan on October 1, 1798, and reached Sault Ste Marie on May 17, 1799, taking 229 days. The primary points of information were the extent of fall outfits in different departments, the actual state of the trade and its appearances, the quantity of goods on hand, and the quantity expected to remain in the spring, the quantity of provisions supplied by different departments, a statement of the men's accounts and engagements, the arrangements of the posts, and other details of the trade. Alexander Henry (the younger) at Lower Red River learned of the amalgamation of the XY and Northwest companies signed November 5, 1804, on January 1, 1805,[260] Harmon at Fort Alexandria, on February 8.[261] The following extract illustrates the general arrangements.[262]

MEMO TO REGULATE THE WINTER EXPRESS.

The Express to leave the Peace River on the 3rd Jan. 1807

    Ditto   "   "   Fort Augustus .... 24th   "   "

    Ditto   "   "   Isle a la Crosse ...... 12th   "   "

By this means the Athabasca and English River Express will meet at Fort Vermillion on the 30 Jan. or thereabouts.

The Express to leave Fort Vermillion on the 1st Feb. 1807

    Ditto   "   "   Fort St. Louis 14   "   "

    Ditto   "   "   Riv. qui appelle 28   "   "

    Ditto   "   "   M. Henry's .... 10 March   "

And so on without delay to Kam . . . where it ought to arrive easily in April. . . .

. . . to include every kind of general information and remarks regarding the state of the country. Signed D. McGillivray, 3 July, 1806.

Advantages of a large-scale organization were also shown in the difficult problems of marketing. In 1784 most of the furs were exported on two ships although eight ships were listed as carrying furs. The furs on reaching England were in part used in manufactures and

[259]L.-R.Masson, *Les Bourgeois*, I, 32.

[260]Elliott Coues, *New Light*, I, 255.

[261]D. W. Harmon, *Journal of Voyages*, p. 103.

[262]Can. Arch., Northwest Company Minutes, p. 54; see also D. W. Harmon, *Journal of Voyages*, p. 41. For a typical statement of the contents of an express see G. C. Davidson, *The North West Company*, pp. 301–305; also McLeod Papers and the Northwest Company agreements of 1802 and 1805 for details as to the position of the agents; also A. Mackenzie, *Voyages from Montreal, passim.*

in part re-exported. Five-eights of the beaver was consumed in manufacturing hats, one-quarter exported to Russia when that market was
open, and one-eighth to France and Holland.[263] Joseph Frobisher in a
letter dated Quebec, February 1, 1778,[264] to creditors pointed out the
numerous dangers to the trade and showed incidentally the wide range
of the marketing system.

When you consider the very bad prospect of the sale of Furrs from
the war between the Russians & Turks which shuts the communication
with China—some of the most considerable debts due to me being payable
in Furs—and our great dependance being on the demand from Petersburgh
for the sale of our best Beaver, also the risk of an interruption to our
Mississippi Trade from the Americans or Spaniards if either of them should
take an active part in the war which by report is likely to break out. . . .

Beaver and otter sent through Russia to China were dispatched on
East India Company boats with the closing of that route. As a result
of the bad market in Europe during the French Revolution furs were
sent to China in the years 1792, 1793, 1794, 1795, and 1797 in this
way but at considerable loss because of difficulties with the East India
Company in bringing return produce. To prevent these losses arrange-
ments were made in 1798 to send furs to China by way of the United
States and in that year 19,283 pounds or 13,364 skins of fine beaver,
1,250 fine otter, and 1,724 kit fox were dispatched by this route.[265]
Simon McTavish in a letter dated Montreal, June 22, 1799, wrote,
"From Hallowell's report of the China trade, we know that there is a
vent that way for a considerable quantity which taken out of the
London market will enhance the remainder."[266] The decline of the
European market during the operation of the continental system
against England rendered the China trade more important.[267] In
negotiations for better marketing facilities the importance of the English correspondents and agents was stressed and relationships with these
organizations became more stable as shown in the provisions of the
amalgamation agreement of 1804 protecting the rights of respective

[263]For a reference to the proportion of various furs re-exported to different
countries see G. C. Davidson, *The North West Company*, pp. 271–272; Can.
Arch., Q, XLIII, Pt. II, 826–828. Germany was an important purchaser while
France showed signs of decreasing importance.

[264]Can. Arch., Frobisher Letter Book, p. 43.

[265]Alexander Mackenzie, *Voyages from Montreal*, I, lii.

[266]L.-R. Masson, *Les Bourgeois*, I, 48.

[267]January 18, 1800: "Seaton Maitland & Co. who had all the China business
in hand of McTavish & Co. is shut." *Askin Papers*, II, 274–276. See also G. P.
Morris, "Some Letters from 1792–1800 on the China Trade."

agents. These agents petitioned in 1809[268] for a drawback of duties on furs and skins (excepting beaver and musquash) on re-exportation in order that they might meet the competition of American furs in Europe. These firms and the general organization by virtue of its size were in a position to present a united front to the government on matters of policy affecting their interests. They were energetic in their protests regarding disputes on the location of the American boundary.[269] The numerous petitions[270] were by no means uniformly successful but they were indices of the Company's activities.[271] They maintained an elaborate system of communication and were among the first to bring news of the declaration of war by Congress in 1812.[272] These advantages were only available with large capital and an elaborate organization.

The effects of the expansion of trade to the Northwest, to Athabasca and the Pacific and of the growth of a large organization were shown directly in the demands for larger supplies of capital. Transportation expenses for men, provisions, boats, and canoes between Montreal and the more remote districts necessitated heavy outlays of capital. As early as 1784 the report of Benjamin and Joseph Frobisher to General Haldimand dated Montreal, October 4, stated that:

The property the Company have already in that Country, exclusive of their Houses and Stores, and the different Posts, as appears by the settlement of their Accounts this present year Amounts to the sum of

[268]Petition from merchants of London trading to Canada March 10, 1809 (Inglis, Ellice & Co., Brickwood, Daniell & Co., McTavish, Fraser & Co.), Can. Arch., Q, CXI, 158–161.

[269]See memorial of the fur traders in regard to the American boundary, 1814, G. C. Davidson, *The North West Company*, pp. 296–301.

[270]See memorial of Phyn, Inglis, against a grant of land to the Northwest Company to the prejudice of other merchants, December 6, 1799, Can. Arch., Q, CCLXXXVI, Pt. II, and refusals of government to make the grant, *ibid.*, Q, CCLXXXVII, Pt. I, Pt. II. Full details of the controversy between Phyn, Inglis & Co., and their Canadian correspondents, Forsyth, Richardson & Co., Parker, Gerrard, Ogilvy & Co., and John Mure against McTavish, Frobisher & Co., over the ownership and use of the portage road and the canal at Sault Ste Marie, are available in Can. Arch., Northwest C series 363. See petitions for a charter in 1811 and 1812, G. C. Davidson, *The North West Company*, Appendices K and L, pp. 283–292.

[271]For other indications of these activities see N. Atcheson, *American Encroachments on British Rights; or, Observations on the Importance of the British North American Colonies.*

[272]See letter from Forsyth, Richardson & Co., and McTavish, McGillivrays & Co., to H. F. Ryman dated Montreal June 24, 1812, Can. Arch., Q, CXVIII, 4.

£25,303.3.6 Currency; and their Outfits for the next Spring which will be sent from Montreal as soon as the Navigation is open, will not fall much short of that sum so that the Company will have an Interest at the Grand Portage in July next of about £50,000, original Cost, in Furrs, to be sent to Montreal by the return of their Canoes, and in goods for the Interior Country. . . .[273]

A letter of John Inglis dated Mark Lane, May 31, 1790, stated:

I beg leave also to mention that the merchants in this country and in Canada, who are engaged in this adventurous Traffick, have generally a property embarked, and chiefly in the Indian Country equal to two years returns, and there is besides fixed property of considerable value at the Posts.[274]

Harmon understood the essential problem.

I am convinced, that, at this great distance from the place of market for furs, the trade cannot be profitably carried on unless it be done on a large scale, which requires a greater capital than an individual can embark in this undertaking. The experiment has been made, in a number of instances, and it has uniformly failed.[275]

The organization which provided the capital necessary for the rapid growth of the trade was unique in its close relationship to the technique of the trade. As it was extended from Grand Portage to Athabasca and the Pacific it depended for its success on the individuality, self-reliance, and bargaining ability of each man. Surveillance from headquarters was impossible. It was adapted to secure from each partner the whole-hearted interest of the concern.[276] The Northwest Company was designed to secure promotion which depended primarily on the ability of the trader to secure returns.[277] Its effectiveness depended on a trained personnel. Partners in Montreal and in the interior were in many cases experienced traders who had served an apprenticeship in the interior, for example Alexander Mackenzie, Roderic Mackenzie, and William McGillivray.

[273]"North-Western Explorations," *Report on Canadian Archives*, 1890, pp. 50–51.
[274]Can. Arch., Q, XLIX, 287.
[275]D. W. Harmon, *Journal of Voyages*, pp. 133–134.
[276]As to *esprit de corps* among the partners, see L. J. Burpee, "The Beaver Club"; also a description of the operation of the Company with especial reference to the reason for its effective organization, A. Mackenzie, *Voyages from Montreal*, I, xx f.; also copies of agreements of 1802 and 1804, L.-R. Masson, *Les Bourgeois*, II, 459–499.
[277]See Chester Martin, *Lord Selkirk's Work in Canada*, pp. 29–31; also the Earl of Selkirk, *A Sketch of the British Fur Trade in North America, passim.*

The evolution of the Northwest Company after the amalgamation of 1787 illustrated the importance of an elastic organization. The agreement of 1787 was supplanted by that of 1790 which came into effect in 1792 and ran until 1799. This agreement was supported by arrangements with various clerks and traders. In 1791 Lesieur and Simon Fraser entered into an agreement[278] with the Northwest Company to trade at Rivière des Trembles and Portage de l'Ile for five years with a guaranty of £200 profit.[279] St. Germain traded at Rivière à la Biche on the same terms. On October 28, 1795, McTavish, Frobisher & Company agreed to pay St. Germain 2,400 livres (*ancien cour*) per year to the end of the Northwest Agreement, or a total of 9,600 livres. In the same year an agreement[280] was made between Mc-Tavish, Frobisher & Company (Simon McTavish, Joseph Frobisher, John Gregory, and William McGillivray) and Alexander Mackenzie, agent for Angus Shaw, Roderic Mackenzie, Cuthbert Grant,[281] Alexander McLeod,[282] and William Thorburn for the conduct of the trade from 1799 to 1805, the firm to consist of 46 shares. This arrangement was a guaranty to a large number of traders who were in a position to become rivals, that a place would be provided at the end of the existing agreement.[283] Apparently over twenty new partners were added in 1799.[284] At a meeting dated June 30, 1801, it was provided that the following should be admitted as partners and given $\frac{1}{46}$ share, their interest to begin with outfit 1802: H. McGillis, A. Henry, J. Cadotte, J. McGillivray, J. McKenzie, Simon Fraser. At the same meeting it was agreed that every effort should be made to improve the service and to stamp out drunkenness among the partners by making it punishable by expulsion. On July 19, 1803, J. B. Cadotte was expelled, and his returns ceased with outfit 1802. Under the stress of competition a new agreement was made in 1802 in which the number of shares was increased to 92 of which McTavish, Frobisher & Company had 30 and the partners 2 shares each, leaving 16 shares vacant for further

---

[278]L.-R. Masson, *Les Bourgeois*, I, 39.

[279]John Macdonell saw Simon Fraser on his way in, 1793; *Five Fur Traders*, p. 99.

[280]Masson, II, 459.

[281]Cuthbert Grant was at Grand Portage in 1793; in charge of Red River. *Five Fur Traders*, pp. 96, 100.

[282]McLeod went with Macdonell from Montreal in 1793; he and W. Thorburn returned for reasons of health. *Ibid.*, pp. 69, 95–96.

[283]"General List of Partners, Clerks & Interpreters who winter in the North West Company's Service," *Report of Public Archives*, 1939, pp. 53–56.

[284]Masson, II, 460.

expansion. Security to the arrangement was made by extending the term to twenty years. J. D. Campbell was given $\frac{1}{92}$ share, or half the $\frac{1}{46}$ share vacated by A. McLeod in 1802, and David Thompson $\frac{2}{92}$ shares beginning with outfit 1804. The amalgamation of 1804 gave the XY Company one-fourth of the profits. On July 6, 1805, arrangements were made giving the new company 25 shares out of 100. The number of shares was increased from 92 to 100 and $\frac{2}{92}$ shares were relinquished by R. Mackenzie, A. McLeod, W. Thorburn, Simon Fraser, J. Finlay, and Cuthbert Grant, and $\frac{1}{92}$ shares by P. Grant and J. Finlay, making a total of 22 shares to which McTavish, Frobisher & Company contributed 3 shares making a total of 25 shares for the new Company.

Stress on the importance of the individual trader was accompanied by concentration in the external business of the company as conducted by the supply houses of Montreal and England and shown in the growth of McTavish, Frobisher & Company. On April 15, 1787, Benjamin Frobisher of the firm of B. & J. Frobisher, died, and in the same month in a letter dated at Montreal, McTavish suggested an arrangement by which the formation of a partnership would ensure control over the Northwest trade and prevent opposition, especially from Gregory of the firm of Gregory & McLeod.[285]

The partnership of McTavish, Frobisher & Company was arranged on November 19, 1787. The firm controlled $\frac{7}{16}$ of the trade. Mr. J. Hallowell was admitted to the new firm with 1 share on January 1, 1788. In the amalgamation of 1787 control of the trade was assured. With these arrangements the firm of Dyer, Allan & Company in England, which had supported McTavish, was given one half of the business and Brickwood, Pattle & Company the other half.

J. F. to Messrs. Brickwood, Pattle & Co.—Montreal, October 16, 1787.
The cash which we will require in the course of the winter and to send our canoes away in the Spring may probably amount to 4 or £5,000 which we propose to draw for one half on your house and the other half on Messrs. Dyer, Allan & Co., you may be assured that we shall be as sparing and draw at as long a sight as possible.

In 1788 Dyer, Allan & Company proposed to retire and it was arranged that Phyn, Ellice & Inglis should take their share. In the new agreement of 1790 at Grand Portage,[286] McTavish, Frobisher & Com-

[285]See R. H. Fleming, "McTavish, Frobisher and Company of Montreal."
[286]For a description of the various early agreements of the Northwest Company see H. A. Innis, "The North West Company."

pany held $\frac{7}{20}$ of the shares but one of the shares was given to Daniel Sutherland. In the agreement of 1802 the share of this company was increased to $3\frac{0}{76}$ and the partnership was extended for twenty years. The union with the XY Company in 1804, with the Hudson's Bay Company in 1821, and the further extension of the agreement for twenty-one years demonstrated clearly the inevitable tendency with increasing capital toward cut-throat competition and monopoly. The influence of the Montreal and London supply houses became increasingly evident. Many of the old partners had died. The Beaver Club[287] lost much of its importance. Alexander Henry alone had lived to see the whole trend of development from 1739 to 1824. Family influence became more important and the McGillivrays, nephews of Simon McTavish, and Ellice, came to hold key positions. It was possible for these interests to secure control over the Northwest Company as Selkirk had acquired control of the Hudson's Bay Company. They were able to arrange for the final amalgamation with the Hudson's Bay Company to which the wintering partners exclaimed: "Amalgamation! This is not amalgamation but submersion! We are drowned men."

The effect of these demands for large quantities of capital was shown also in the organization of the trade. The organization of the southern trade offered an important contrast. Smaller quantities of capital were necessary to carry on the trade and the geographic background made the control of any large organization difficult. For example, the general store formed at Michilimackinac on July 1, 1779,[288] was of short duration and the agreement of 1785 was a failure. Whereas in this trade a large organization failed to achieve any permanent success the tendency in the trade to the Northwest was continually toward larger organizations. In the south the formation of large organizations was unsuccessful whereas in the north the formation of small competing organizations was unsuccessful.

The success of the large organization was the result of the necessity for close co-ordination and the demand for large quantities of capital. As already suggested the first evidence of co-operation among the traders was found in the penetration to the Saskatchewan in 1775 of

[287]The Beaver Club was founded in 1786 with sixteen members; *Askin Papers*, II, 782.

[288]See "List of the proprietors of the general store at Michilimackinac, the number of canoes each person has put in, their supposed value, and the present residence of each proprietor"—32 firms, 29½ canoes, and supposed value £438,750; "The Haldimand Papers," *Report of the Pioneer Society of the State of Michigan*, IX, 658.

traders who had been forced from the southern trade and from Albany as a result of the American Revolution. These traders brought with them substantial quantities of capital in the form of large boats on the lakes and they found it necessary in carrying on trade over such distances in the interior to co-operate. An appreciation of the necessity of close organization was shown at an early date partly as a result of the difficulties of the war. In 1776 the Northwest Company was accused of sending a deputation to Congress.[289]

The North West Company are not better than they ought to be, their conduct in sending an Embassy to Congress in '76 may be traced now to matters more detrimental. I hope the General will grant them no passes without insisting on their bringing the King's stores from the Portage.

In 1778 they combined to support Pond's expedition to Athabasca. The restricted number of passes was referred to as the cause of joint-stock operation in 1779. Difficulties with the Plains Indians at posts near Eagle Hills in the Saskatchewan in 1780 and the desolation caused by the smallpox were noted by Mackenzie as a cause of co-operation. After the Revolution a threatened encroachment from the United States on the boundary line from Lake Superior to Lake of the Woods was given as a reason for concerted action. "Their first object was to prepare the necessary supplies and provide against any interruption to their business from the United States by discovering another passage from Lake Superior to the River Quinipigue."[290] In 1784 Edward Umfreville was dispatched to discover a better route than that by Grand Portage. In these cases a common task presented itself and it could only be performed by co-operative effort.

In the latter stages of development co-operation appears less important as a factor tending toward concentration, and the ruinous effects of competition under conditions of heavy overhead costs became

---

[289]Extracts of letters from Lieutenant-Governor Sinclair concerning the trade and traders to Michilimackinac and the Northwest, February 15, 1780, Can. Arch., Q, XVII, Pt. I, 256–257; see also Can. Arch., Haldimand Papers, B.217, p. 468.

[290]Can. Arch., Haldimand Papers, B.217, p. 470; also Frobisher Letter Book, p. 60; see letters to the government on the subject of the boundary line, "North West Trade," *Report on Canadian Archives*, 1888, pp. 63 f.; also petition of merchants, February 6, 1783, Can. Arch., Shelburne MSS, LXXII, 288–293. See requests for exclusive privileges and charters, Memorial of the Northwest Company, Montreal, October 4, 1784; Benjamin and Joseph Frobisher to General Haldimand, Montreal, October 4, 1784; and Memorial of Peter Pond, Quebec, April 18, 1785, "North-Western Explorations," *Report on Canadian Archives*, 1890, pp. 48–54; E. Umfreville, *Nipigon to Winnipeg*.

a driving force in favour of amalgamation. Reference has been made to the competition of the small Montreal Company from 1785 to 1787, formed at the suggestion of Pangman, Ross, and Pond following disagreement with the 1784 arrangement under the auspices of Gregory, McLeod & Company. The competition of this small organization began with the outfit of 1785.[291] In that year the Northwest Company sent to Grand Portage and Detroit, 25 canoes and 4 bateaux with 260 men in canoes and 16 men in bateaux carrying 6,000 gal. of rum, 340 gal. of wine, 300 rifles, 8,000 lb. of powder, 120 cwt. of shot, all of which was valued at £20,500, whereas Gregory and McLeod sent 4 canoes with 50 men, 400 gal. of rum, 32 gal. of wine, 63 rifles, 1,700 lb. of powder and 20 cwt. of shot, valued at £2,850, and Ross and Pangman took up the same number of canoes, 40 men, 350 gal. of rum, 32 gal. of wine, 36 rifles, 1,600 lb. of shot, 18 cwt. of shot, valued at £2,775. In 1786 the Northwest Company increased their outfits to include 30 canoes and 300 men, 2 bateaux and 9 men, 3,000 gal. of rum, 500 gal. of wine, 500 rifles, 9,000 lb. of powder, 120 cwt. of shot, valued at £25,500, whereas Gregory and McLeod sent 8 canoes, 83 men, 1,600 gal. of rum, 64 gal. of wine, 104 rifles, 2,800 lb. of powder, 45 cwt. of shot, valued at £4,500. Finally, in the year of amalgamation, the Northwest Company sent 25 canoes and 250 men, 4 bateaux and 20 men, 5,300 gal. of rum, 786 gal. of wine, 500 rifles, 7,000 lb. of powder, 106 cwt. of shot, valued at £22,000, and Gregory and McLeod sent 9 canoes, 90 men, 1,600 gal. of rum, 54 gal. of wine, 150 rifles, 3,400 lb. of powder, 45 cwt. of shot valued at £4,700.

The small company in 1785 placed John Ross in charge of the Athabasca district, Alexander Mackenzie of English River, Peter Pangman of Fort des Prairies and Mr. Pollock, a clerk, of Red River. It was obliged to build new posts at Grand Portage and in the interior. The "guides, *commis*, men and interpreters were few in number and not of the first quality." The success of Pollock against Robert Grant[292] and William McGillivray in the Red River department would probably not be important. Roderic Mackenzie describes the competition with Patrick Small and William McGillivray of the Northwest Company in the English River district in 1786 and the instructions[293] of Alexander Mackenzie who was in charge of the district are illuminating as to the

---

[291]L.-R. Masson, *Les Bourgeois*, I, 10.

[292]Robert Grant and Peter Pangman retired in 1793; *Five Fur Traders*, pp. 95–96.

[293]L.-R. Masson, *Les Bourgeois*, I, 13 ff.

character of the personnel.[294] In the Athabasca district severe competition was the cause of the death of John Ross. In the summer of
1787 the union was arranged concerning which Alexander Mackenzie
wrote, "As we had already incurred a loss, this union was, in every
respect, a desirable event to us, and was concluded in the month of
July, 1787."[295] He wrote to Roderic Mackenzie in a letter dated
December 2, 1787:

After the experience you must have of the dreadful effect the late
opposition has had upon those who were engaged in it and upon the
country, I cannot believe you entertain any thought of a repetition on
your own account. Could I, in four years of hard labour and anxiety pay
the debts I owe our concern in consequence, I should feel satisfied.[296]

A new organization was under appreciable disadvantage having little
knowledge of Indian habits, language, and economy. The best hunters
were known and traded with by the old Company and Indians who
were refused credit because of a bad reputation went to the new firm.
A more serious difficulty was the lack of capital but on the other hand
in spite of the lack of capital competition was sufficiently ruinous to
both companies to warrant an early amalgamation. Later competition
brought out similar tendencies. After 1787 traders penetrated from
Prairie du Chien on the Mississippi across the height of land to Red
River, and from the rivers flowing into Lake Superior.[297] In 1794

[294]Patrick Small took 10 canoes in by Cumberland House in 1790, left one
to go in to Grassy Lake by the Port Nelson track and one at a new settlement
near Churchill, and took four canoes to Isle à la Crosse, the rest apparently
going on to Athabasca. *Journals of Hearne and Turnor*, pp. 330, 335, 344, 350.

[295]Alexander Mackenzie, *Voyages*, I, xlv.   [296]Masson, I, 22.

[297]Apparently prior to 1792 the route by Fond du Lac was stopped by
antagonism of the Sioux and Chippewa. Reaume was the first man to break
through that year. The route was obviously difficult as John Hay, who went up
the Assiniboine and wintered on the Souris or Mouse River in 1794–95, came
out in 1795 by Winnipeg River and Grand Portage. See "Extracts from Capt.
Mackay's Journal," notes by John Hay, pp. 200–210.

In 1794–95 Hay and Laviolette found the following forts on the Assiniboine:
(1) Fort la Reine (La Prairie), about 20 leagues from Red River; (2) Pine
Fort, about 18 leagues further up; (3) Rivière à la Souris or Mouse River, 20
leagues higher; (4) Montagne à la Bosse or Hump Mountain Fort, 25 leagues
higher; (5) Catapoi River, 16 leagues; (6) Swan River, 15 leagues higher;
(7) Coude de l'homme fort (Man's Elbow), 15 leagues higher; (8) Portage of
Lake Manitou, 20 leagues—all except (1), (2), and (4) on rivers coming in
from the south. The Hudson's Bay Company, Hay reports, had forts on this
river from 1793. (He mentions Mr. Goodwin of the Company.)

Hay left Mackinaw on June 27, 1794, and went to Fond du Lac, Lake

Beaubien and Laviolette came into Red River from the south.[298] According to John MacDonald an opposition appeared[299] apparently under David Grant[300] at Sturgeon River in 1793 supported by Gregory and Robinson of Montreal and continued at that point and Nepawi the following year. Competition in Red River district meant surplus stocks of goods and ventures to more remote areas as in the Saskatchewan. In the winter of 1794–95 five different interests were trading at La Souris.[301] In 1799–1800 Alexander Henry (the younger) was opposed at White Mud River by the T. Association from Montreal.[302] In 1797 the larger interest became more important and according to Harmon established a rival depot at Grand Portage.[303] The interests concerned were apparently[304] those of John Mure of Quebec, Forsyth, Richardson & Company, Parker, Gerrard, Ogilvy & Company, Phyn, Inglis & Company, and Leith, Jamieson & Company. Forsyth, Richardson & Company appear to have been most active[305] but the two firms of Forsyth and Ogilvy sent canoes to Fort Chipewyan in 1799.[306]

Superior; one league further was Sayer's Fort (Northwest Company). His party passed J. Reaume's fort on Leaf River, built when he was stopped by the Sioux. On Red River Laviolette broke 2 canoes and wetted 20 bales. On the route was Red Lake River up which Reaume returned one year to Mackinaw. Hay and his company passed Fort du Tremble of the Northwest Company, on Red River, another Northwest fort on Mire River with no one in it, and the Pamican River where Reaume wintered in 1792.

[298]Masson, I, 290.

[299]Ibid., II, 20.

[300]David and Peter Grant planned a depot in opposition at Grand Portage, 1793. *Five Fur Traders*, pp. 94–95.

[301]Masson, I, 294. Duncan McGillivray reports seven forts of the Northwest Company and fourteen of the opponents in Red River in 1794–95. Peter Grant went with four canoes, the Hudson's Bay Company with five boats, and Michilimackinac interests, seventeen canoes.

[302]Elliott Coues, *New Light*, I, 5.

[303]D. W. Harmon, *Journal of Voyages*, p. 15.

[304]Masson, II, 498–499. For a valuable discussion see R. H. Fleming. "The Origin of 'Sir Alexander Mackenzie and Company.'"

[305]Forsyth, Richardson had a canoe wintering in Nipigon in 1792–93, competing with the Hudson's Bay Company; the latter did not get a single pack and Mr. Hudson, their chief, froze to death. Macdonell in *Five Fur Traders*, pp. 90–91. Alexander Henry (the younger) comments on the new Northwest Company in 1799, "a new rais'd corps without discipline"; he mentions Forsyth at Montreal, Sharp at the Portage. *Askin Papers*, II, 180.

[306]John Maude (*Visit to the Falls of Niagara in 1800*, pp. 142–239) met Mr. Ogilvy, partner of the new Northwest Company, when Ogilvy and Mr. Tough, his clerk, arrived in a bateau from Grand Portage on August 22, 1800. Maude sold his horses to Mr. Innis, who was on the point of setting out for Grand

Simon McTavish wrote in a letter dated Montreal, June 22, 1799, "The threatened opposition have this year made a serious attack on us, and I fear that a coalition of interests between the parties opposed to us may render them more formidable."[307] The amalgamation feared by McTavish which became known as the XY Company was formed in 1800 and was strengthened by the support of Sir Alexander Mackenzie.[308] The effects of the opposition were shown in the Red River with special emphasis beginning in 1801.[309] In 1802 they had posts on the Saskatchewan[310]; in 1803 a post was built on Peace River above the Forks[311] and in the same year they had a post on Bear Lake.[312] In 1804 Harmon mentions the XY fort at River Qu'Appelle and also a winter post at Fishing Lake.[313] In 1803 they built a post five miles above the Northwest post of Fort Alexandria in the Swan River country. The success of the XY interests is difficult to determine but it was not conspicuous.[314] In the dispute over the ownership of land

---

Portage, and left Niagara with Ogilvy and Tough, August 27, on the schooner *Governor Simcoe*. He went on in a bateau from Kingston and on August 29 passed eight of Ogilvy's bateaux going up for furs (36 bales each). On September 1, Maude dined with Parker, Gerrard and Ogilvy. He saw the steamer *Euretta*, 360 tons, and the *Montreal*, 400 tons. On September 4 he dined with J. Frobisher, Henry, and Todd, among others, and on September 5 with A. Mackenzie, "Nor'West" Mackenzie. He saw Mr. Mure, partner of Ogilvy at Quebec, on September 10. On his trip down the river, he visited the seigneury of M. Montour at Lac St. Pierre. Mrs. McTavish (Montreal) was, he said, "the only very handsome woman I saw in Canada." (Joseph Frobisher was "a native of Halifax, in Yorkshire.")

[307]Masson, I, 47.

[308]Alexander Henry (the younger) to Askin, January 18, 1800: "Frobisher and [Mackenzie] is out." "Who should be the first—McTavish or [Mackenzie]—and as there could not be two Caesars in Rome one must remove." *Askin Papers*, II, 274–275. Henry to Askin, April 18, 1802, of Mackenzie: "if these bucks had less money they would not be so anxious as they are." *Ibid.*, II, 375.

[309]E. Coues, *New Light*, I; Alexander Henry does not mention XY competition until 1801.

[310]Masson, II, 23 ff.

[311]*David Thompson's Narrative*, p. lxxxii.   [312]Masson, II, 123.

[313]D. W. Harmon, *Journal of Voyages*, pp. 75–80.

[314]In 1800 the XY Company sent six canoes with 70 pieces by the Pembina River to Athabasca; five of their men deserted to the Northwest Company. See McLeod diary in *Five Fur Traders*, p. 142.

The "Journal" of Thomas de Boucherville mentions the XY Company; apparently it was forced to depend on weak personnel for he only stayed one winter. The French Canadians Lacombe and Chenier were in charge at Rainy Lake and St. Croix River.

Thomas de Boucherville joined the XY Company as a clerk in 1803 for

for the erection of buildings at Kaministiquia and at Sault Ste Marie following the removal of these posts to British territory the handicaps of the smaller company were conspicuous. Alexander Henry in a letter dated Montreal, December 10, 1804, to John Askin, wrote: "it is said the New Company lost £70,000 since their commencing the opposition, it will be some time before they bring up that sum." On November 5, 1804, an agreement of amalgamation[315] was signed.[316] The fur trade was singularly susceptible to ruin from competition[317] and it was singularly dependent on the availability of large capital resources as well as skill and experience. Marked tendencies in the trade were the increasing importance of large quantities of capital and the increasing control which a smaller number of capitalists was able to exercise.

The weakness of the Company was a result of two conflicting tendencies incidental to the necessity for greater concentration of control and for greater reliance on the individual trader as competition increased. The internal trade as carried on by the wintering partners was conducted by men with strong personalities such as Peter Pond

---

seven years. He was then 18 years old. He left Lachine in a canoe belonging to M. Maillou; the guide was Larocque, the *gouvernail* Robillard. Other clerks who went with him were Vienne, Curotte, McMullin, Gordon, and Cameron. He saw Sir Alexander Mackenzie, who had preceded the party from Montreal, at Sault Ste Marie. He went on the XY Company boat *Perseverance*, commanded by Captain White with Mackenzie and George Moffatt on board, to Grand Portage. Over the portage Ducharme was his guide, Laporte the *gouvernail*. His party met Lacombe at Rainy Lake and Jacob of the old Northwest Company with his men at "Tête au Brochet" on Lake Winnipeg. They went to Fort Dauphin, of which McMurray was commandant, and there met Nolin of the Northwest Company. De Boucherville went *en derouine* (trading) with Clermont as interpreter and five men. De Boucherville was left ill with the Indians. He and a companion saw a white wolf. He went *en derouine* again with Clermont and the others were Boisvert, Goulet, Lauzon, and Allaire. De Boucherville was forced to return to Lower Canada because of bad legs. He met de Rocheblave on Lake Winnipeg and went from Bas de la Rivière to Grand Portage in a canoe, apparently from Athabasca. He got to Grand Portage at the end of June, met Thain, and returned with him on the *Perseverance*. He visited Michilimackinac and went with Thain down the Ottawa to Montreal.

315L.-R. Masson, *Les Bourgeois*, II, 484.

316On December 8, 1804, plans were made for valuation of the ships *Nancy*, *Caledonia*, and *Charlotte* by Forsyth, Richardson & Co. following the amalgamation. *Askin Papers*, II, 444.

317For a description of intense competition in 1804–5 at Rainy Lake and the St. Croix River see the diaries of Hugh Faries and Thomas Connor in *Five Fur Traders*.

and Alexander Mackenzie who persisted in breaking from the organization and precipitating competition. In the agreement of 1804 Isaac
Todd in a letter to Lieutenant Colonel Green dated Montreal, October
25, 1804, wrote, "Sir Alexander Mackenzie is excluded from any
interference, with him and McGillivray there will, I fear, never be
intimacy." It is significant that Todd who was interested in the supply
houses of Montreal should have been an influential negotiator for
union.

The returns on the capital of the Company were seriously affected
by the changes in organization. The sixteen-share agreement for five
years with the beginning outfit of 1784 and the two following years,
1785 and 1786, in which it suffered from competition with Gregory
and McLeod, secured average returns of £30,000.[318] Another estimate
gives the returns for 1784 as £25,303.3.6 and for 1786 as £32,403.12
based on returns of £4,175.9 for a $2/16$ share. After the amalgamation
of 1787 the shares were increased to twenty and the returns of 1788
were estimated at £40,000 and of 1789, at £53,000. The average for
the six years 1790–95 has been stated as £72,000 in spite of opposition after 1783. The Northwest Company was said to control $11\frac{1}{14}$,
the Hudson's Bay Company $\frac{1}{7}$, and the Canadian opposition $\frac{1}{14}$ in
1795. The average for four years from 1796 to 1799 increased to
£98,000 and for five years from 1800 to 1804 to £107,000 in spite
of strong opposition from 1799 to 1804. Roderic Mackenzie estimated
that the value of the adventure in 1787 was £30,000 Halifax currency
and that this had trebled in eleven years. The profits from 1784 to
1798 totalled £407,151 Halifax currency. Periods of difficulty arose
with the termination of contracts and after 1800 competition, especially from the Hudson's Bay Company, became a more important
factor. In 1802 the value of $\frac{1}{45}$ share was given as £3,288.2.5, making total returns of £147,965.8.9, and in 1803 a $2/88$ share was valued
at £4,493.1.7 or a total of £197,695.9.8. After the amalgamation,[319]
the returns of the Northwest Company, excluding the twenty-five shares
of the XY Company, declined as shown:

1804	£192,540.9.6	($2/92$ share valued at	£4,185.13.3)
1805	154,479.0.0	($2/90$ share valued at	3,432.17.4)
1806	136,133.0.0	($2/75$ share valued at	3,630.4.0)
1807	127,987.15	($2/75$ share valued at	3,415.15.0)
1808	118,118.3.8	($2/76$ share valued at	3,106.4.10)
1809	105,237.10	($2/75$ share valued at	2,806.5.10)

[318]"Sketch of the Fur Trade of Canada, 1809."
[319]E. Coues, New Light, I, 282.

1810	85,420.19.6	(²/₄ share valued at	2,308.13.6)
1811	84,225.5.5	(²/₃ share valued at	2,307.10.10)
1812	84,007.15.10	(²/₁ share valued at	2,365.18.4)

In 1813 returns from the trade increased to £150,918.11.8 (²/₁₀₀ share valued at £3,018.5.10) but declined in 1814 to £143,897.18.4 (²/₁₀₀ share valued at £2,877.19.2) and in 1815 to £133,684.15.10. Recovery was made in 1816 to £192,220.1.8 but decline followed to £153,750.0.0 in 1817 and to £70,658.19.2 in 1818. The tendency toward decline was persistent. Declining returns were of serious consequence to the organization of a concern which required a heavy capital outlay for its operations.

But although the capitalistic side was favourable to amalgamation, the amalgamation in itself brought forward the problem of placing the added men. The XY Company added approximately one-third to the personnel. To supply territory for the enlarged company and to keep pace with the necessities of larger numbers of promotions essential to ensure the efficiency of the larger organization, exploration was extensively carried out,[320] new areas were reached, and new tribes, in fur-bearing country which had not been exploited and with natives unaccustomed to European commodities, were brought into the trade.

Even before the amalgamation the Northwest Company had found it necessary to expand to new territory. On October 1, 1802, McTavish, Frobisher & Company leased the King's posts for twenty years at £1,025 per year and the Northwest Company established posts at Lake St. John and Mistassini.[321] In 1803 the *Beaver*, a vessel of 150 tons, was sent to Hudson Bay and posts were established for a short period on Charlton Island and at the mouth of Moose River. After amalgamation it was necessary to introduce new economies and to find new territory. In 1804 C. Chaboillez sent an expedition under F.-A. Larocque[322] to trade with the Mandans[323] on the Missouri. In 1805 Larocque was again dispatched to the Missouri[324] and directed to carry the trade westward to the Rocky Mountains,[325] but he met with

[320]See Alexander Mackenzie, *Voyages from Montreal*, voyages to the mouth of the Mackenzie and to the Pacific; Simon Fraser, "Journal of a Voyage from the Rocky Mountains to the Pacific Coast, 1808"; *David Thompson's Narrative*, *passim*.

[321]G. C. Davidson, *The North West Company*, pp. 78–79.

[322]L.-R. Masson, *Les Bourgeois*, I, 299 ff.

[323]See note on p. 233 on Mandan trade problem, 1796.

[324]Masson, I, 325 ff.

[325]Duncan McGillivray attempted to cross the Rocky Mountains but was forced to turn back and David Thompson therefore attempted the task. See

little success. A later expedition was sent to the Missouri in 1806[326] but the trade was not important. In the same period the department of New Caledonia was opened. The following resolution adopted in 1806 is significant.[327]

Whereas from the great number of proprietors now in this country it is impossible to place them all to advantage in the North West Departments; And whereas the business of the concern extends to other Departments out of the North West, which ought not to be neglected, and which it is conceived would be essentially benefited by the presence of a partner, And whereas the King's Post Department is of this number the present manager of it, Mr. Shaw, having it only in his power to visit the Posts annually, while the business at Quebec and along the Communication chiefly engages his attention and prevents him from paying sufficient regard to the Trade of the interior Country:

It was therefore resolved at a meeting of the North West Company held at Kamanistiquia on the 4th July, 1806, that Mr. James McKenzie now going to Montreal on his rotation should be appointed and he is accordingly appointed, to winter next year at the King's posts and there to remain until the concern shall otherwise determine.

Colin Robertson pointed out in his memorandum of 1812[328] the problem of the Northwest Company and of the fur trade:

Beaver is now become so valuable an Article in the Fur Trade that notwithstanding the total stagnation of every other Peltry in that line, it seems to meet with little or no depression in price; this in a great measure can be accounted for from the distance the European Merchants have to go in search of that useful and industrious Animal. It is not many years since the Canadian establishments of the Fur Traders in North America extended no further than the banks of Lake Superior; but now their boundaries are the Atlantic, the Pacific and Frozen Oceans; however I am afraid their ambition and enterprize have carried them too far, as these distant settlements oblige them to employ three sets of men to bring the returns of McKenzies River and New Caledonia to Montreal. . . .

F. W. Howay, "David Thompson's Account of his First Attempt to Cross the Rockies." Thompson's account is entitled, "Account of an Attempt to cross the Rocky Mountains, by Mr. James Hughes, nine men & myself, on the part of the [North West] Company; in order to penetrate to the Pacific Ocean— 1801." This disposes of Professor Morton's claim that McGillivray was the first to cross the mountains; see A. S. Morton, *A History of the Canadian West*, pp. 467–468.

[326]Masson, I, 371 ff.
[327]Can. Arch., Minutes of the Northwest Company.
[328]Can. Arch., Selkirk Papers, II, 167 ff.

Perhaps you will observe that the country is already exhausted, and of course too late for innovations. No! gentlemen were it possible for me to bring any of you to the banks of Lac Wonipicthen to see every spring from 1000 to 1200 Pack of 90 lb. each of the finest furs the North produces, and these returns the harvest of a country where you have not a single establishment, say Athabasca, Lesser Slave Lake, and the English river. . . .

For the late junction with Sir Alexander Mackenzie & Co. has so much overstocked the country that the North West Company notwithstanding they have extended their shares to One Hundred, will if the Old Partners do not retire soon, find it difficult to provide for the major part, even of the most deserving of them. . . .

When this was written the North West Company had no intention of forming establishments on the North West Coast of America but the number of young Gentlemen they were in some measure bound to provide for obliged them to extend their views, in consequence of which they formed a Partnership with one Astor of New York and sent out a vessel from that port to Nootka Sound, and I learn from Montreal that another ship is to be fitted out from London this spring for the same place. . . .

The accuracy of his remarks was shown in a letter from McTavish, McGillivrays & Company "to Messrs. McTavish, Fraser & Company, Inglis, Ellice & Company, Sir Alexander Mackenzie," dated Montreal, August 18, 1812.

The progress already made by the American party who have established themselves in the Columbia River renders this determination on our part absolutely necessary for the defence of our only remaining Beaver country, and we know from dear bought experience the impossibility of contending from this side of the mountains with people who get their goods from so short a distance as the mouth of the Columbia is from the mountains. This reason would in itself be conclusive, but there is another [of] almost equal force, viz, The great scarcity of Beaver now complained of in all the departments of the northwest Eastward of the mountains. This has been so much felt for the last two years that the country in its present state cannot support our establishments of partners, clerks and canoe-men, so that there is a necessity for extending the field, were there no intruders in the country to menace us.[329]

[329]Can. Arch., Q, CXX, 90. See also regarding the importance of Astor's proposed expedition to the Columbia in spurring the Northwest Company to immediate action, letters from McTavish, McGillivrays & Co., John Ogilvy, Thomas Thain, agents of the Northwest Company dated Montreal, January 23, 1810, to McTavish, Fraser & Co., Inglis, Ellice & Co., and Sir Alexander Mackenzie in London, from Nathaniel Atcheson, April 2, 1810, and from Simon McGillivray, November 10, 1810, Can. Arch., Q, CXIII, 221–242.

As a result of this tendency competition with other areas increased, costs of transportation increased, the necessity for finding new territory to absorb new members of the company continued and, above all, increasing profits were essential to attract new members.

The organization of the Northwest Company adapted to expanding trade over wider areas became a serious handicap with changed conditions in which new territory was no longer available. W. F. Wentzel, an unrewarded clerk, in a letter to Roderic Mackenzie dated Bear Lake, March 6, 1815, wrote: "Notwithstanding these gloomy appearances [in the Athabasca district] squires are manufactured yearly with as much speed and confidence as Captains, Lieutenants and Ensigns were in His Excellency, Sir George Prevost's time when I was two years ago in Montreal."[330]

As control within the Northwest Company became more concentrated and the inability to adapt itself to a permanent trade became more conspicuous, control in the Hudson's Bay Company became less concentrated and the ability to adapt itself to an expanding trade became more conspicuous.

By 1821 the Northwest Company had built up an organization which extended from the Atlantic to the Pacific. The foundations of the present Dominion of Canada had been securely laid. The boundaries of the trade were changed slightly in later periods but primarily the territory over which the Northwest Company had organized its trade was the territory which later became the Dominion. The work of the French traders and explorers and of the English who built upon foundations laid down by them was complete. The fur trade had pushed beyond the St. Lawrence drainage basin to the north and the northwest along the edge of the Pre-Cambrian shield and the forest regions, and had organized the bases of provisions in the more fertile territory to the south at Detroit, the Assiniboine, the Saskatchewan, the Peace, and lastly, the Columbia. The Northwest Company was the forerunner of confederation and it was built on the work of the French *voyageur*, the contributions of the Indian, especially the canoe, Indian corn, and pemmican, and the organizing ability of Anglo-American merchants.

[330]L.-R. Masson, *Les Bourgeois*, I, 115.

9. The St. Lawrence Drainage Basin versus Hudson Bay

THE decline in furs throughout the whole Northwest, the growing effectiveness of the Hudson's Bay Company's competition with its reorganized personnel policy and its initial geographic advantage and the inability of the Northwest Company to adapt its expanding organization to permanent conditions and its consequent demand for new territory led to increased hostility between the two companies.

The disappearance of beaver and the increasing costs of transportation of provisions and supplies were of vital importance. An excellent indication of the general trend is shown in statistics for the Lower Red River department of the Northwest Company from 1801 to 1808.[1] Although comparison from year to year is difficult, because of changes in the amount of territory included in the department and periods of opposition, the trend is obvious. In 1801, the department produced 1,904 pounds of beaver which increased to 2,868 pounds in 1804 and declined to 908 pounds in 1808. The total packs of furs produced showed similar tendencies varying with increases in such items as wolves, fisher, marten, and muskrat. During this period on the other hand the production of pemmican increased from 77 pieces (90 pounds each) in 1801 to 334 pieces in 1808. In addition the department had traded cheaper, more bulky, furs to the Hudson's Bay Company for pemmican. Other items of supplies were also produced during the latter part of the period—grease, sugar, beef, tongues, dried meat, salt, and gum for canoes. The whole illustrated the increasing demand for provisions to carry on trade in more remote areas and the decreasing supply of furs in older districts.

The exhaustion of the beaver fields was apparently hastened by the use of steel traps and the discovery of the use of castoreum as bait. According to David Thompson the use of steel traps for beaver dates from 1797.[2] Steel traps are heavy and it is probable that their use spread slowly throughout the West. In 1818 only two pieces of traps

---

[1]E. Coues, *New Light on the Early History of the Greater Northwest,* I, *passim.*

[2]*David Thompson's Narrative,* pp. 204–205.

(180 pounds) were sent to the Northern districts, although Harmon noted their use by the greater part of the Indians on the east side of the Rocky Mountains.[3] The disappearance of beaver was of serious consequence to the Indians.[4] It necessitated a migration to new areas and a more rapid destruction of the animal. The constant westward migration of the Indians, especially of the best beaver hunters as in the case of the Iroquois, was an important factor. Moreover trapping was prosecuted with greater effectiveness by the immediate personnel of the trading companies. On Hudson Bay[5] this development was conspicuous from an early date. The trap line[6] was also followed by the men of the Northwest Company. In the Oregon territory hunting expeditions sent out by the Company were the rule. *Castor gras* and coat beaver had lost their importance and made possible the destruction of beaver on a more rapid and extensive scale.

The importance of beaver as compared with other furs continued. Harmon estimated the relative position of the various furs:

> The following catalogue of animals will exhibit the comparative value of the furs, which are annually purchased and exported to the civilized parts of the world, by the North West Company. The animal is first mentioned, the skins of which amount to the greatest sum; and so on, in order, to the last, the skins of which, will amount to the smallest sum. . . . Beaver, otter, muskrat, martin, bear, fox, lynx, fisher, mink, wolf, buffaloe.

> The following catalogue will exhibit the comparative weight of the skins, of the different animals, which are annually purchased and exported, as above mentioned. . . . Beaver, martin, muskrat, bear, otter, wolf, buffaloe, lynx. &c.[7]

In 1784, 1789, 1801 and three years' average ending 1805, beaver equalled consistently about one-third of the total value of furs exported. On the other hand prices increased consistently during these years[8] from 8/6 to 10/2, 15/6, and 14/. The number of skins fluctuated widely but tended to decline. Deer was second in importance in 1784 and in 1789, a very close third in 1801, and second in three years' average ending 1805. Prices also rose from 4/3 to 4/10 to 6/, but de-

[3]D. W. Harmon, *Journal of Voyages*, p. 284.

[4]*David Thompson's Narrative*, pp. 76–77.

[5]For descriptions of methods of trapping see *ibid.*, pp. 49–50, 70–71, 73, 75.

[6]See descriptions of a dispute over the location of trap lines, E. Coues, *New Light*, I, 132.

[7]D. W. Harmon, *Journal of Voyages*, p. 382.

[8]These years unfortunately do not show the decline incidental to the French Revolution which became especially evident after 1792. See Henry on prices in 1800, *Askin Papers*, II, 274–276.

clined to 5/ on three years' average. Numbers fluctuated but were at
the same level in 1784 and 1801. Otter was third in 1784, in 1789,
fourth in 1801, and the three years' average ending 1805; prices
changing from 24/ to 23/10 to 28/6 and 17/6. Numbers remained
stationary. Bear was fourth in 1784, fifth in 1789, and second in 1801,
but third on the three years' average; prices changing from 26/ to
21/8 to 55/ and 40/ and numbers doubling throughout the term.[9]
Raccoon was fifth in 1784, fourth in 1789, and sixth in 1801 and fifth
on the three years' average; prices increased steadily from 2/2 to 3/4
during the period in 1801 and fell later to 2/; numbers on the whole
increased five times. Marten was sixth in 1784, in 1789, seventh in
1800, and eighth in the three-year period; prices increased slightly and
numbers fluctuated widely but decreased one-half throughout the term.
On the whole the importance of beaver was pronounced. Heavy skins,
deer, and bear were important and fine fur, especially otter, was not
insignificant. Large numbers of other less important furs were also purchased. Prices were generally rising.[10]

The decline of beaver exports is not conspicuous in the period from
1793 to 1808. From the high point of 182,346 skins in 1793 they declined to 155,599 in 1794, to 144,945 in 1795, to 130,820 in 1796,
and to 124,612 in 1797. Fluctuations characterized the remainder of
the period, a rise to 127,440 in 1798, a decline to 117,165 in 1799,
a rise to 135,043 in 1800, a decline to 119,965 in 1801, a rise to
144,189 in 1802, a sharp decline to 93,778 in 1803, a recovery to
111,448 in 1804, a new low level of 92,003 in 1805, a recovery to
119,708 in 1806, a slight falling off to 114,363 in 1807 and a rise to
126,927 in 1808. To secure a more adequate index of production,
exports to the United States should be added especially after 1798
when trade was developed with China. In that year 19,283 pounds of
beaver were sent to the United States and in 1805 exports to the United
States included 29,115 pounds beaver and 28,379 marten, 10,427
otter, 128,837 muskrat, 21,776 raccoon. With this addition little evidence existed to show a decline of beaver to 1808. A decline following

[9]Bears fluctuated widely. In 1811 a remarkable migration and destruction of
bears is recorded.

[10]"The consumption of peltry for dress has fortunately for the fur merchants,
prevailed for many years past, and several have from this cause acquired independent fortunes." George Heriot, *Travels through the Canadas*, p. 233. In
1797, beaver hats *No. 5 blacks* were made of 8 ounces beaver, 4 ounces hare, 1
ounce dressings. Best plates took 9 to 12 ounces beaver. Information Christy &
Co.

the closing of American territory to the Northwest Company was offset in part by expansion to the Northwest.

The value of furs exported[11] from Quebec in 1784 was £236,418;[12] in 1788, £258,970; and in 1801,[13] £371,139.11.4. Of a total value of £200,000 for furs[14] produced in 1790 it was estimated that of

[11]Can. Arch., Shelburne MSS, LXXXVIII, 19.

[12]Can. Arch., Q, XLIII, Pt. 11, 826; also G. C. Davidson, *The North West Company*, p. 270.

[13]Can. Arch., Q, LXXXIX, 169; G. C. Davidson, p. 283; "Courts of Justice for the Indian Country," *Report on Canadian Archives*, 1892, p. 144.

[14]G. C. Davidson, *The North West Company*, pp. 272–273; also Statement of Phyn, Ellice and Inglis, London, May 31, 1790, Can. Arch., Q, XLIX, 289–290. According to the account of the fur trade in 1791 by Count Andriani, cited by La Rochefoucauld (*La Rochefoucault-Liancourt's Travels in Canada 1795*, pp. 110 ff.), Niagara, Lake Ontario, Detroit, Lake Erie, Michilimackinac, Lake Huron, produced 1,200 bundles of mixed peltry—a mixture of fine peltry with a large number of wolves, fox, bear, buffalo, deer:

Michipicoten	40	bundles fine peltry (beaver, otter, marten,
Pic	30	"	"	"	wild cat)
Alampicon (Nipigon)	24	"	"	"
Grand Portage	1,400	"	"	"
Fond du Lac	20	"	"	"
La Pointe	20	"	"	"
Keweenaw (?)	20	"	"	"

The "Total amount of the Fur-trade" for export is given as:

Northwest Company received from Grand Portage	£ 88,000
From Bay of Chaleur, Gaspé, and Labrador	60,000
From area tributary to Michilimackinac	60,000
	£208,000

Exports in 1786 of peltry from Great Lakes, Grand Portage, and interior: £225,977.

Hadfield (*An Englishman in America, 1785*, p. 109) in 1785 gives figures for annual export of the trade:

	Packs		£	£
Detroit	3,000	(in 1784 with large quantity of deer killed, 5,000)	10	30,000
Mackinac	5,000		15	75,000
Grand Portage	700		40	28,000

These he says are confirmed by "amount of sales for the year 1777 made in London in the month of January."

The Northwest Company post at Michipicoten was passed by Macdonell in 1793; *Five Fur Traders*, p. 90. Northwest Company competition with M. Coté and associates at Pic River, 1793; see *ibid.*

£60,000 one half was obtained from the country below Montreal and one half from the country along the Ottawa between Montreal and Grand Portage. The Northwest produced £40,000 and the trade to the south of the lakes through Detroit and Michilimackinac £100,000 (3,400 packs of furs from Detroit and surrounding district at £12 each) and 3,020 packs (1,500 from Green Bay[15] and adjoining territory) at £20 each from Michilimackinac and tributary territory. The average exports of furs for three years ending 1805 totalled £263,088.13.8. In 1805 furs sent from the Northwest country[16] included 51,033 muskrat, 40,440 marten, 4,011 fine marten, 2,132 common otter, 4,328 mink, 2,268 fisher, and 100,031 pounds beaver. The beaver included 48,757 large skins and 24,840 small skins, making, with the addition of 3,903 other skins, a total of 77,500 skins, or 100,031 pounds. On the basis of 1 beaver skin equaling $1\frac{1}{3}$ pounds, 29,115 pounds of beaver or 21,838 skins were exported to the United States in that year, and 113,841 skins were exported to England and the United States. From this analysis the Northwest produced 77,500 skins of a total of 113,841 or roughly 75 per cent.

In the total production of the Northwest the Athabasca country became increasingly important. Of a total return of 2,253 packs (90 pounds each) in 1805, 1,490 packs were sent from the Northwest country, 302 from Northwest Lake Superior, and 361 from South Lake Superior. Of 1,490 packs from the Northwest country 509 packs were from Athabasca, Athabasca River, and English River, and 712 packs from Fort des Prairies, Red River, and Lake Winnipeg. The proportion of beaver from Athabasca region is difficult to estimate, but of the total 77,500 skins (100,031 pounds) it may safely be inferred that a large share came from that area. In a total of 115 packs averaging 90 pounds or 10,350 pounds of furs in the Fond du Lac department, there were 4,426 pounds of beaver. The heavier and less valuable skins undoubtedly came from the posts in the Plains areas. Expenses of transportation from most distant posts were only borne by the most valuable furs. The relative importance of the furs is shown in incomplete returns for 1801. Upper English River[17] supplied 148 packs in a total of 1,516 (almost 10 per cent) which were valued at £4,581 in a total value of £20,300 (over $22\frac{1}{2}$ per cent). Furs from Athabasca district would undoubtedly show an even higher value. Statistics as to beaver production in North America throughout the

[15]Peter Pond estimated 1,500 pelts going to Mackinac from Prairie du Chien in 1774.

[16]E. Coues, *New Light*, I, 283.

[17]*Ibid.*, p. 199.

period[18] are unsatisfactory but allowing for discrepancies, their suggestiveness is apparent. Hudson's Bay Company's sales of coat beaver declined from 14,450 in 1765 to 7,070 in 1780, 2,150 in 1802, and 281 in 1820. Parchment beaver fluctuated from 30,450 in 1765 to 35,763 in 1781, 37,187 in 1802, 15,524 in 1811, and 15,683 in 1820. Beaver from the United States and Canada fluctuated from 66,664 in 1765 to 126,600 in 1784, 140,000 in 1802, 101,100 in 1810, and 56,000 in 1820. The decline in total exports after 1800 was unmistakable.

The decline in the supply of beaver which intensified competition had serious effects on the Indians and in turn on the expenses of the trade. The effects of competition on methods of trading[19] and on the sale of rum to the Indians have been the object of attention on the part of many writers attracted by these lurid aspects of the trade. During conditions of monopoly rum was not an important item and the following description of the trade in 1790 is probably accurate:

It cannot be ascertained that much evil has hitherto resulted from the spirits distributed to Indians by the voyagers of this country; and yet it is notorious notwithstanding the restrictive laws, the passports, and the Bonds, with which the Indian commerce has been fettered, that quantities of liquors have, and must annually be carried among the nations to the remotest corners of their wintering grounds among the extensive countries they inhabit. The Trade's personal interest and safety have been the best security against abuses. It does not appear that they have given the Indians more Rum than was necessary to prevent them from carrying their Furs to a distant or Foreign market, nor has it been customary to make Rum an article of Barter in the Trade. Its use is rather confined to gifts at feasts and publick Talks, where care is taken to guard against the evil consequences of Drunkeness and Debauch. The Traders are sensible that their most permanent interests are that the Indians be induced to hunt, that they be annually supplied with necessaries, ammunition, and cloathing, in exchange for the Beaver and Furs of their chace. For, tho' Rum might procure the hunt of a year, yet if obtained only by its means future Industry would cease. Murder might result and all its concomitant evils.[20]

[18]H. Poland, *Fur-bearing Animals in Nature and Commerce*, pp. xxi ff.; also H. A. Innis, *The Fur Trade of Canada*, pp. 77–79.

[19]At Michipicoten in 1781 Philip Turnor claimed that Indians at the divide sold "Beaver Catts" to the Hudson's Bay Company at Wapiscogamy post and took beaver, otter and marten to the Canadians; *Journals of Hearne and Turnor*, pp. 288–289.

[20]Minutes of Council, December 11, 1790, Can. Arch., Q, LI, Pt. I, 95–96; also a letter dated December 11, 1790, signed by Phyn, Ellice & Inglis, and McTavish & Co. insisting on freedom of trade in the liquor traffic.

The consumption became serious as a result of competition as shown in the following items for a period including years of competition and amalgamation.[21] The consumption of rum and spirits by the Northwest Company averaged 9,600 gallons (1793–98) and 12,340 gallons (1799–1804). It increased from 10,189 gallons and 10,098 gallons in 1799 and 1800 respectively to 10,539 in 1801, 14,850 in 1802, 16,299 in 1803, declining in 1804 to 12,168. The average consumption for 1802 to 1804 was 14,400 gallons which with an average of 5,000 gallons by the XY Company gives a total for the Northwest of 19,400 gallons. After amalgamation in 1804 decline was immediate from 13,500 gallons in 1805 to 10,800 gallons in 1806, 9,500 gallons in 1807, and 9,000 gallons in 1808, an average for these years of 10,700 gallons. Statistics of importation of rum by the Northwest Company and the Hudson's Bay Company are not available for a later period but descriptions of conditions under competition are numerous.[22]

Competition was especially serious in the areas marginal to the "strong woods" and to the Plains.[23] The supply of beaver was limited and the Indians more independent. A large number of men was necessary to secure provisions, to engage in trapping furs, to go about among the Indians collecting furs *en derouine*, and to protect the forts. The list of Plains forts destroyed by the Indians was ample testimony of the dangers of this area. Indeed the hostility of the Plains Indians in many cases necessitated co-operation between competitors for protection. The Hudson's Bay Company lost heavily through the inadequacy of the personnel left in the country during the summer.[24] Rapid exhaustion of the beaver necessitated frequent removal of posts and change of routes to make unnecessary long journeys on the part of the Indians and to offset the opposition. During one year twenty-one posts were located in Red River district involving severe competition and the demoralization of the Indians. John Macdonell in a description of Assiniboine country wrote,

[21]See "Sketch of the Fur Trade of Canada, 1809"; also Petition and paper against a bill of the Imperial Parliament to prohibit use of spirituous liquors among the savages of British America, Can. Arch., Q, CVIII, 51–69. On competition see Abbé G. Dugas, *Un Voyageur des pays d'en haut*, chap. iv, also the Earl of Selkirk, *A Sketch of the British Fur Trade in North America*.

[22]For a description of competitive conditions in the latter part of the period see C. Martin, *Lord Selkirk's Work in Canada*, chap. iv ff.; G. C. Davidson, *The North West Company*, chaps. vi ff.; also W. F. Wentzel's letters, L.-R. Masson, *Les Bourgeois*, I, 96; and *A Narrative of the Captivity and Adventures of John Tanner*, pp. 181–185, 265–266.

[23]See E. Coues, *New Light, passim*, for an illuminating account of Henry's experiences as a trader first on the Red River and later on the Saskatchewan.

[24]A. S. Morton, *Journal of Duncan M'Gillivray*, p. 65.

These gentlemen [Northwest Company], when by themselves, establish as few posts as they conveniently can, in order to save property. On the contrary, when incommoded by new comers, they subdivide and divert the trade into as many little channels as they have men and clerks to occupy, well knowing that their opponents, who have but few goods generally, cannot oppose them at every place.[25]

W. Auld in a letter dated York Fort, October 3, 1811,[26] outlined the problem for the Hudson's Bay Company not only in areas marginal to the Plains but also in the fur-producing territory.

All your inland posts have a Canadian post close adjoining, each carefully watches the motions of the Indians as well as each other and instead of the Indian bringing his furs they each send parties of their men to the tents to get such furs as are due or barter what they have, this requires art, address, experience and knowledge of the language to derive the greatest benefit, where the men are most competent there the scale is favourable, now we cannot have too many men at an inland post who understand the natives, it very frequently happens that two or three parties of servts are absent on some duty while the master may be days by himself at the house, I speak here of every place in your Territories where an opposition exists, almost every fur is fetched in this manner excepting Red River and Saskatchewan where furs are of little value and the Indians, daring, brave, and never to be insulted with impunity, I dont speak of the Factories; there no opposition requires such strange interference; hence in this view of the subject you will readily acknowledge my desire for experienced men as through 19/20ths of your whole Territories the furs collected inland are obtained by the *runners*, it is no easy matter to form such and they are of the last importance. . . .

The effect of competition on the Indians was a constant source of trouble to the traders. Presents were given on a larger scale. In 1789 the Northwest Company was obliged to give first-class chiefs in competitive areas 10 measures of powder (5 handfuls), 80 balls, 3 fathoms tobacco, 3 or 4 knives, ½ dozen flints, awls, and other trinkets. The effect on Indian organization and government was pointed out by Alexander Henry (the younger):

It is lamentable that the natives in general, in this country, have lost that respect they formerly had for their chiefs. The principal cause of this is the different petty copartnerships which of late years have invaded this country from Canada; the consequences are now serious to us, as the natives have been taught to despise the counsels of their elders, have acquired every vice, and been guilty of every crime known to savages.[27]

[25]L.-R. Masson, *Les Bourgeois*, I, 274.
[26]Can. Arch., Selkirk Papers, I, 65 f.
[27]E. Coues, *New Light*, II, 550.

Duncan Cameron in the Nipigon country wrote also of these effects:

> They are all remarkably proud of being reckoned great men, but still they have little or no influence over the others, for, after making the father a chief, you are sometimes obliged to do the same with his son in order to secure his hunt, for the former has not power enough over him to secure it for you, let him be however so willing. They only have some influence when they get a keg of rum from their trader to treat the others with, and can get plenty of ammunition and tobacco to share with them.[28]

McGillivray in his journal constantly complained of the insolence of the Indians, their laziness—a result of cheap goods—the expensive provisions he was forced to purchase, and the consequent losses to the trade. With competition Indian astuteness in bargaining improved and expenses increased. Indians, becoming accustomed to wines and rum, demanded products with reduced proportions of water. They were accused of firing the plains to frighten buffalo from the forts and to increase the value of provisions.[29] On November 18, 1810, Henry (the younger) wrote, "Two Bloods and their families brought in 14 fresh beavers—the meat, but no skins; these they preserve to enhance the value of the wolves they may kill this winter."[30]

The shift in Indian cultural traits continued to make the Indian increasingly dependent on European goods, and with the decline of fur production, greatly enhanced the expenses of the trade especially as carried on under competitive conditions. Greater dependence on European commodities involved the transportation of larger supplies of heavier goods. Harmon wrote:

> The Indians in this quarter have been so long accustomed to use European goods that it would be with difficulty that they could now obtain a livelihood without them. Especially do they need firearms with which to kill their game, and axes, kettles, knives etc. They have almost lost the use of bows and arrows, and they would find it nearly impossible to cut their wood with implements made of stone or bone.[31]

A greater demand for European goods and an increasing scarcity of furs brought the usual results to the Indian population.

> The Indians with whom we trade are frequently at war with distant nations to the Westward which the Traders generally encourage, because

---

[28]L.-R. Masson, *Les Bourgeois*, II, 278.

[29]A. S. Morton, *Journal of Duncan M'Gillivray*, p. 33.

[30]E. Coues, *New Light*, II, 663.

[31]Bird Mountain, November 19, 1802, D. W. Harmon, *Journal of Voyages*, p. 73.

on their return they come over a vast tract of country and bring with them large quantities of fine furs. . . .[32]

Competition was described by Alexander Henry (the younger) and others:

[March 22, 1804.] Grosse Gueule and myself had a serious dispute; he wanted to give his furs to the X. Y., which I prevented, at the risk of my life; he was advised by them to kill me. . . .

April 1st. I went to the upper part of Tongue river to meet a band of Indians returning from hunting beaver, and fought several battles with the women to get their furs from them. It was the most disagreeable derouine I ever made; however, I got all they had, about a pack of good furs; but I was vexed at having been obliged to fight with the women. It is true it was all my neighbor's debts. . . .

April 2d. . . . the most active and capable are gone with the Indians to hunt beaver and take care of the furs.[33]

The following description is also suggestive:

Journal for 1805–6, Cross Lake. . . .

Wednesday, [September] 18. I determined to leave the Men of one Canoe to build and go down with the English Track with the others in hopes of falling in with some of the H. Bay peoples Indians &c. . . .

Monday 23 we set off and on our way down towards the long Portage I heared a gun—we fired and was answeared by the Indians—we found 2 Lodges say 13 men that was waiting for the English I given them 2 Large Kegs Rum and Clothed the chiefs and all their Childeren & prevailed on them to come up and winter with me at Cross Lak or duck Lake.

Tuesday 24 about midday I got them off we past by the English House where the Indians put Marks for the English that they mite find them on their arrivall—I sent them all off & remained behind for we was only 2 Men in the large Canoe all this day as I was obliged to put the men in the Indian Canoes to get them on as the one half of them was drunk—after they were all gone I Turned all their marks quite the other way—and did not tutch any thing in the House for if I had they would know that some of our people had been that way I got that night nier out of the Lake for I made all hast possible to get them out of the way. . . .

Thursday 26 we got them off with much ado caring all their things over the Portages and even some of them Selves—we got up that night to the Terre Blanch-Portage where we Campt. . . .

[32]Joseph Frobisher to John Brickwood, Montreal, June 30, 1788, Can. Arch., Frobisher Letter Book, p. 60.
[33]E. Coues, *New Light*, I, 239–240.

Jan. 9, 1806 the men I sent to Sipiwisk arrived and informed me that the English were there and had not seen an Indian exceptg one that came up with them—that they were all the fall looking for the Indians till the ice took them other ways they woud be up heare, but me turning the Indian Marks last fall put them astray till it was too late for them to come up &c.[34]

The abuses became more serious with the lack of legislation and even with the enacting of satisfactory legislation there remained the serious difficulty of enforcing it in these remote areas. Harmon wrote on October 16, 1803:

This jarring of interests, keeps up continual misunderstandings and occasions frequent broils between the contending parties; and to such a height has their enmity risen that it has, in several instances, occasioned bloodshed. But here the murderer escapes without punishment for the civil law does not extend its protection so far into the wilderness. I understand, however, that measures are in contemplation in England, which will remedy this evil.[35]

The net results were concisely described by Franklin:

This mode of carrying on the trade not only causes the amount of furs, collected by either of the two Companies, to depend more on the activity of their agents, the knowledge they possess of the motions of the Indians, and the quantity of rum they carry, than upon the liberality of the credits they give, but is also productive of an increasing deterioration of the character of the Indians and will probably ultimately prove destructive to the fur trade itself. Indeed the evil has already in part recoiled upon the traders; for the Indians long deceived have become deceivers in their turn and not unfrequently after having incurred a heavy debt at one post, move off to another, to play the same game. In some cases the rival posts have entered into a mutual agreement, to trade only with the Indians they have respectively fitted out; but such treaties being seldom adhered to, prove a fertile subject for disputes and the differences have been more than once

[34]Can. Arch., 2 Masson Papers, M.734.

[35]D. W. Harmon, *Journal of Voyages*, pp. 78–79; see Act, 43 Geo. III, c. 138, assented to August 11, 1803; also "Courts of Justice for the Indian Country," *Report on Canadian Archives*, 1892, note E, pp. 136–146. The problem became acute with the murder of James King by La Mothe; see McTavish, Frobisher & Co. to Major Green, Montreal, November 29, 1802, Can. Arch., Northwest series 363, and Jas. Green to McTavish, Frobisher & Co., York, December 28, 1802, enclosing an opinion by Justice Allcock as to the jurisdiction of courts in the Western district, Can. Arch., Letter Book Military Secretary's Office, No. 7, C.1210.

decided by force of arms. To carry on the contest, the two Companies are obliged to employ a great many servants, whom they maintain often with much difficulty, and always at a considerable expense.[36]

Competition[37] tended to throw the trade out of line throughout the whole of the interior. Both companies took advantage of monopoly departments to support the losses suffered in competitive areas. The Northwest Company had guarded the Athabasca department as a reserve of the best furs and as a monopoly but the effect of competition was pronounced. As a result of the reduction of supplies which made dependence on the country increasingly necessary, a failure in the supply of rabbits in 1810 was the cause of starvation in the district in which several people died and others were forced to live on beaver skins and other furs.[38] The War of 1812 enhanced the usual difficulties. In that year Alexander Henry and his family were massacred at Fort Nelson on the Liard by the Indians.[39] Clerks in the district received no promotion, and the Indians suffered severely from lack of goods. In 1815 the total number of packs from Mackenzie River was sixty-four. Wentzel gives the following account of later developments:

By this time the concern [Northwest Company] conceiving the department [Mackenzie River] incapable of defraying the expenses ordered it to be evacuated altogether, which was accordingly done in the summer 1815 to the great hazard of our lives, for the natives having obtained a knowledge of our intentions had formed the design of destroying us on our way out.

Notwithstanding that no promises had been made of returning at a future period to trade with them, I was sent the following summer with six Canadians in a large canoe and a small supply of goods to renew the intercourse. In the course of my passage down the river as far as Fort Good Hope I fell in with several parties of all the different tribes and was welcomed by them with extravagant demonstrations of joy. They danced and cryed by turns, rushing up to their knees in the water to pull my canoe ashore, begging at the same time that the whites would return to their lands and promising their utmost endeavours to render our situation with them as comfortable as possible. I explained to them that it did not depend upon myself but on the partners at Fort Chipewyan to whom

---

[36]Capt. John Franklin, *Narrative of a Journey*, I, 130–131, and *passim*; see also "Events in the Interior during the Winter of 1820–1," Fort William, April 22, 1821, G. C. Davidson, *The North West Company*, Appendix O; also J. J. Hargrave, *Red River*, Appendix B, pp. 491–496.

[37]For an account of competition at Isle à la Crosse, a key post, see Dugas, *Un Voyageur des pays d'en haut*, chaps. v, vi.

[38]L.-R. Masson, *Les Bourgeois*, I, 106 f.   [39]*Ibid.*, II, 125.

I undertook to make a report of their request and advised them to hunt furs and prepare provisions in the expectation that it would be granted; I also assured them that if we did not resume our deserted establishments a canoe would certainly go down every year to trade their furs and bring them the most useful supplies. This pacified them and they agreed to exert themselves in collecting peltries.[40]

Writing from Bear Lake on March 6, 1815, Wentzel stated:

Athabasca, which once commanded fifteen establishments, will ere the present gets to hand possess no more than eight, viz: Slave Lake, Turtle Creek, Fort Chipewean, Fort Vermillon, Hay River, Dunvegan, St. John's, and *Pierre au Calumet* in Athabasca River; being two posts in the Slave Lake, two of Fort Chipewean and four in the Peace River.[41]

Expenses of transportation and the possibilities of control led to a reduction of posts in the remote districts and the returns of furs were also reduced.[42]

The decline in beaver and increasing difficulties with the Indians and increasing competition were accompanied by an increase in expenses. Duncan Cameron wrote regarding the accessible Nipigon country in 1804:

I am, however, sorry to remark that this part of the country is now very much impoverished . . .; beaver is getting very scarce, but I have nevertheless managed to keep up the average of returns by shifting from place to place every year and increasing the number of posts, which, of course, augmented the expenses and made the trade dearer, but that cannot be helped at present. . . .[43]

Evidence of increasing costs was shown indirectly in numerous attempts of the Northwest Company to reduce transportation expenses and to introduce other measures of economy as appears in the following resolves:

Whereas the great sacrifices occasioned by the opposition carrying on against the North West Company for five years successively and other causes, have considerably diminished the profits, on the shares, and seems to point out the necessity of adopting every measure by the concerned that can tend to retrench expences and introduce a system of economy throughout the Country: And as it appears essential to the adoption of this system that certain regulations should be fixed upon, respecting the manage-

[40]Can. Arch., "Account of Mackenzie River" by W. F. Wentzel.
[41]L.-R. Masson, *Les Bourgeois*, I, 114–115.
[42]*Ibid.*, pp. 109 f., 282–283.
[43]*Ibid.*, II, 245.

ment of different Branches of the business in future—the Freight and Transport of their property and Canoes—and the proper distribution of their Engagés going into and coming out from the wintering Posts, becomes a matter of the greatest importance. The undersigned Proprietors therefore, at a general meeting held at Kamanitiquia, the fourth and afterwards the tenth day of July One thousand eight hundred and four, after due consideration have come to the following Resolves,

1st. That the practice of making use of light Canoes by Proprietors be entirely abolished throughout the North West departments.

2nd. That every Proprietor shall attend his Canoes in Person *in going into and coming out* from the wintering Grounds.

3rd. That no Proprietor shall have a less load in his Canoe than Eight pieces *under the regular load of the Canoes of his Brigade*, this to make room for the Baggage.

4th. That no Proprietor shall have more than one Man, over and above the number that are in his loaded canoes.

. . . Any Proprietor failing to conform thereto, shall forfeit to the Concern the sum of Fifty pounds for every extra man he may take into his canoe either in going in, or in coming out and the sum of ten pounds for every piece of goods he may have in his canoe less than the number above specified. . . . It being however necessary that the Company's agents at Kamanitiquia should be informed as early as possible every Spring of the occurrences at the different departments after the departure of the Winter Express, It is resolved, that one light Canoe shall be appropriated to this purpose which shall collect all the letters the Proprietors may have to forward from the respective Quarters . . . for which purpose they will have such Papers as they wish to send in readiness on the road where the Canoe passes, and as one of the proprietors of the Athabasca department should come annually to Kamanitiquia . . . it is thought necessary and proper that the Light Canoe shall come from that department only, it being otherways out of the power of such Proprietors to come out in time. . . .[44]

In 1806 further efforts were made.

Whereas it appears that much inconvenience and many unpleasant consequences arise from the practice of bringing pacquettons out of the Country on the Company's Canoes: And whereas such practice is in various ways contrary to the Interest of the Concern and even to the terms of the Mens Engagements; It was therefore resolved at a meeting of the North West Co. held at Kamanistiguia on the 17th day of July 1806 that hereafter no man . . . whatsoever shall be suffered to embark on the Company's Canoes, or bring out of the interior Country or winter-

[44]Can. Arch., Minutes of the Northwest Company. Abuse involving light canoes is reported as early as 1793; Macdonell in *Five Fur Traders*, p. 97.

ing ground to this place yearly more than two Buffalo Robes or two dressed skins, or one of each, on any pretence whatever nor will it be permitted one man to bring out any leather for another, under the penalty of 50 livres N. W. C. Y. And whereas it appears that many winterers have of late and particularly this year found means to bring out a considerable quantity of furs and peltries, with which they carry on an unlawful traffic in the Camp with petty Traders and Montreal Men; It was therefore also resolved that hereafter no Man whatsoever, under engagements to the Company shall be permitted on any pretence whatever to bring out of the wintering ground, or to this place any furs peltries whatsoever, under the penalty of forfeiting his wages. And for the due observance of these regulations every proprietor is hereby directed to apprize his men accordingly, that they may not plead ignorance of this resolve. In Witness whereof the parties present have hereto set their hands place and date above written.[45]

Measures were also introduced limiting the expenses of the personnel especially after the amalgamation of 1804.

. . . at a meeting of the Proprietors of the North West Co. held at Kamanitiquia the 14 July 1806, to take into consideration the affairs of the concern. It was suggested that the number of women and Children in the country was a heavy burthen to the concern, and that some remedy ought to be applied to check so great an evil, at least, if nothing effectual could be done to suppress it entirely. . . . It was therefore resolved that every practicable means should be used throughout the country to reduce by degrees the number of women maintained by the Company, that for this purpose, no man whatsoever, either partner, Clerk, or Engagé, belonging to the Concern shall henceforth take or suffer to be taken under any pretence, whatsoever, any woman or maid from any of the tribes of Indians now known or who may hereafter become known in this Country to live with him after the fashion of the North West, that is to say, to live with him within the Company Houses or Fort and be maintained at the expence of the Concern.

Resolved that each proprietor respectively shall be answerable for the conduct of all the people in his departments, and that they shall be answerable to him for every offence committed against this resolve, and for the more strict observance thereof, . . . resolved that every proprietor who shall transgress against this resolve or suffer any other person or persons within his immediate charge or direction to transgress it, shall be subject to the penalty of One Hundred Pounds Hx. Cy. for every offence so committed to be forfeited to the rest of the concern. It is however understood that taking the daughter of a white man after the fashion of the country shall be considered no violation of this resolve.[46]

[45]Can. Arch., Minutes of the Northwest Company, pp. 50–51.
[46]Ibid., pp. 43–44.

As early as 1794 Alexander Mackenzie had suggested the advantages of an outlet by Hudson Bay.[47] Various suggestions which
would give the Company access to this route were made at later dates
as in 1802 and 1805. In 1804 Edward Ellice offered "103,000 *l.* Navy
5 *l.* per cents" to buy out the rights of the Hudson's Bay Company.[48]
The Northwest Company agreement of 1804 (Article 6) provided for
a prospective arrangement.[49] In 1805 further suggestions were made
as shown in the following minutes of the Company:

At a meeting of the proprietors of the North West Company held at
Kamanitiquia on the 6th day of July 1805, to consider the present state
of the Negociation with the Hudson Bay Company, for obtaining a transit
for their property thro' Hudson Bay to the North West or interior country—
it was resolved that (as it appears that the said Hudson Bay Company are
not disposed to grant such a transit, without compensation, or as they
themselves express it without sufficient indemnity and security to be given
on the part of the North West Company) the agents of the concern shall
be and they are hereby authorized and directed to offer to the said Hudson
Bay Company . . . a sum not exceeding Two thousand pounds sterling (or
thereabout) a year, for such transit, for a period to be agreed upon . . .
providing they consent that the North West Company shall establish a
free communication with the interior country, by Nelson or Hayes' River,
without being subject to any interference or molestation whatever; and as
the object is of importance, the agents of the concern are also directed and
authorized (as an additional advantage to the Hudson Bay Company) to
propose withdrawing the posts of the North West Company from East
Main and Moose River, and to agree to relinquish in future the whole
trade of the coast of Hudson Bay to themselves, reserving only the right of
establishing as the concern may see fit, the communication with the inland
country by York Factory, that their property may be carried backward and
forward without hindrance or obstruction, on the part of the Hudson's
Bay Company.[50]

Thos. Forsyth and D. McGillivray apparently made an offer to the

[47]For instances of attempts to secure an outlet through Hudson Bay see
Mackenzie's report of explorations to Pacific Ocean and suggestions as to a
commercial route by Hudson's Bay, September, 1794, Can. Arch., Q, CCLXXX,
Pt. II, 358–363; also "Proposed General Fishery and Fur Company," 1802,
Report on Canadian Archives, 1892, note F, pp. 147–151; and especially Alex-
ander Mackenzie, *Voyages from Montreal* (London, 1801), pp. 408 ff., also A. S.
Morton, *Journal of Duncan M'Gillivray*, p. 65.

[48]*Report from the Select Committee on the Hudson's Bay Company*, 1857,
p. 344.

[49]L.-R. Masson, *Les Bourgeois*, II, 488.

[50]Can. Arch., Minutes of the Northwest Company, p. 36.

Company but it was rejected.[51] A later proposal[52] dated November 7, 1810, for fixing the boundary line between the two companies for twelve years beginning 1811 was made in which the Northwest Company offered to give up the following posts:

	Canoes	Men	Posts	Packs	Value	Pounds
Nipigon country	4	24	4	40–50	45–50	£ 2,250
East and North of						
Lake Winnipeg	5	28	4	40–50	45	2,250
Rat River	3	20	2	30–40	35–50	1,750
Upper Red River	5	34	3	80–90	85–30	2,550
Lower Red River	3	22	2	60–70	70–30	2,100
South Side of						
Saskatchewan	6	38	2	80–90	90–30	2,700
	26	166		330–390		£ 13,600

employing 6 partners, 25 canoes valued at £500 each (annual outfit), 27 clerks and interpreters, and 130 to 150 men. Other boundaries were proposed in 1815[53] but again without success. These attempts to gain admission to the Northwest by the shorter Hudson Bay route were finally crowned with success in the amalgamation of 1821.

As a result of the period of intense competition conditions became intolerable and amalgamation was the inevitable result. After amalgamation with the XY Company, fresh and violent efforts were made by the Northwest Company to check the Hudson's Bay Company. Haldane[54] of the Northwest Company in 1806 attempted to block the Albany route by attacks on the posts at Bad Lake, Red Lake in Minnesota, and Big Falls near Lake Winnipeg. J. D. Campbell was appointed to block the Saskatchewan route and in 1808 attacked the Company at Reindeer Lake. The approach of the Hudson's Bay Company to the Northwest territory and the threatened serious interference of Selkirk's colony with the increasingly important supply of the Northwest Company's provisions[55] precipitated difficulties which led to bloodshed at Seven Oaks. The encroachment of the Hudson's Bay

[51]Can. Arch., Selkirk Papers, I, 199.

[52]*Ibid.*, pp. 188–191.   [53]*Ibid.*, pp. 222–255.

[54]Beckles Willson, *The Great Company*, pp. 354 ff.; also A. Laut, *The Conquest of the Great Northwest*, II, 70 ff.

[55]Chester Martin, *Lord Selkirk's Work in Canada*, especially chap. v, *passim*; also Great Britain, Colonial Office, *Papers relating to the Red River Settlement*, 1819.

Company on Athabasca was an important factor in the precipitation of a struggle[56] from which there was no relief other than by amalgamation.

On March 26, 1821, the amalgamation agreement was signed.[57] The Northwest Company was given the charter privileges for twenty-one years. Of the total interest the winterers received forty shares; the Hudson's Bay Company, thirty shares; and McTavish & Company, thirty shares. The geographic advantages of the Hudson's Bay Company were merged with the advantages of the type of organization which had developed in the French *régime* and which had been elaborated with such effectiveness in the Northwest Company. Another partnership agreement was added to the long list which had characterized the history of the Northwest Company. The principle of the partnership was to persist as the dominant type of organization of the fur trade practically until the end of the nineteenth century. It was the device with which the trade could be prosecuted with greatest effectiveness over great distances in which the central authority could exercise no direct control over the individual trader.[58] On the other hand amalgamation marked in a definite way the beginning of control exercised by capital interests with headquarters in London. Heavy outlay of capital and large overhead costs were responsible for the intolerable conditions which followed competition and which led to monopoly throughout the history of the trade.

[56]See S. H. Wilcocke, "Narrative of Circumstances attending the Death of the late Benjamin Frobisher, Esq.," L.-R. Masson, *Les Bourgeois*, II, 181–226; also Wentzel's letters, *ibid.*, I, 119 f.

[57]H. McKenzie to R. McKenzie, Montreal, May 19, 1821. See deed of covenant executed by the Hudson's Bay Company and the McGillivrays and Ellice, 1821; G. C. Davidson, *The North West Company*, pp. 305–307.

[58]See statement of funds of *voyageurs* in account with McTavish, McGillivrays & Co. with a long list of people with accounts unsettled, 1817–18, *Montreal Gazette*, Feb. 11, 1819 (Thomas Thain and Pierre de Rocheblave were agents of the Northwest Company).

PART FOUR

FROM HUDSON BAY TO THE PACIFIC
(1821-1869)

10. The Northern Department

THE problems of amalgamating the organizations of the Hudson's Bay Company and the Northwest Company were exceedingly complex. The agreement provided for the bare outlines of the new organization but new lines of policy suitable to altered conditions had yet to be worked out.

Amalgamation involved several adjustments between the London houses before union was complete. The agreement for twenty-one years dated March 26, 1821,[1] of William McGillivray, Simon McGillivray, and Edward Ellice with the Hudson's Bay Company, divided the total gains into 100 shares of which 40 shares were given to the chief factors and chief traders or to those actually employed in the trade of North America. A loss in one year on the 40 shares was to be met out of the profits of the following year. Another agreement, March 28, 1821, provided that on the expiration of the partnership in 1842, the property was to be formed into a stock of £250,000 of which the Hudson's Bay Company would own £150,000 and W. and S. McGillivray and E. Ellice £100,000. The trust money accumulating from the sale of territory was to be shared ⅗ to the Company and ⅖ to the McGillivrays and Ellice. This was followed by an agreement of April 6, 1821, between W. McGillivray first part, S. McGillivray and E. Ellice second part, and members of the Northwest Company third part, in which the partners of the Northwest Company (excepting Sir Alexander Mackenzie's and John Mure's heirs)

[1]See *Copy of the Deed Poll under the seal of the Governor and Company of Adventurers of England, trading into Hudson's Bay, bearing date the twenty-sixth day of March, 1821, stating the appropriation of the forty shares reserved by the principal Deed for Chief Factors and Chief Traders, with their duties; the regulations relating thereto, and for carrying on the trade.* For further details as to arrangements see Wintering Partners of the Northwest Company to Wm. and Simon McGillivray and Edward Ellice, Esq.; Release of claims and ratification by wintering partners of the Northwest Company of the within mentioned arrangement with the Hudson Bay Company; and Letter addressed to creditors of McGillivrays, Thain & Co. who have assented to the assignment of S. McGillivray, London, 25th July, 1826, signed by Simon McGillivray, and a letter to John McGillivray from Simon McGillivray, London, 27th July, 1827, copies of which are in the Can. Arch. See also G. deT. Glazebrook, "A Document concerning the Union of the Hudson's Bay Company and the North West Company."

exonerated the McGillivrays and Ellice of all claims and gave them 30 shares subject to the deduction of profits of $1\frac{2}{100}$ shares for 14 years (expiring 1836) to the following: A. N. McLeod, 3 shares; T. Thain, 3; J. Richardson, 1; J. Forsyth, 1; H. McKenzie, 1; J. Fraser, 1; P. de Rocheblave, 1; A. Shaw, 1. Exclusive of these shares the McGillivrays and Ellice accounted for the full amount of inventory put into the Hudson's Bay Company—£164,000. On May 7, 1822, W. and S. McGillivray[2] and E. Ellice agreed to divide 30 shares held by them equally during their lives. After the death of W. or S. McGillivray the whole was to be divided into two shares, one the property of the survivor, and the other of E. Ellice. An agreement of March 26, 1824, dissolved the partnership of March 28, 1821, and the whole joint stock, £326,807, considered as £400,000, was transferred to the Hudson's Bay Company of which £225,000 became the property of the Company and £175,000 the property of the McGillivrays and Ellice, each being credited with £58,333.6.8. A deed of September 15, 1824, transferred £50,000 from the stock of the McGillivrays and Ellice to the hands of trustees, £30,000 to indemnify the Hudson's Bay Company against the claims of the holders of the 12 shares, and £20,000 to secure the Hudson's Bay Company against breaches of agreement prior to 1842. The stock of the McGillivrays and Ellice was reduced to £125,000 or £41,666.13.4 each. The fund was to be retransferred after the settlement of all claims. The agreement of May 7, 1822, was replaced with an agreement also dated September 15, 1824, providing in case of death of one of the McGillivrays that £62,500 should become the property of the survivor, and the other share of Ellice, as well as an equal share of £50,000 in the hands of the trustees. W. McGillivray died on October 16, 1825, leaving the whole to be divided equally between S. McGillivray and E. Ellice. These agreements completed the foundations of an independent organization in London.

The Deed Poll of March 26, 1821, provided that the Company should depend on the fur trade and no expense of colonization or commerce not relating to the fur trade was to be borne by it.[3] The 40 shares of the wintering partners were divided into 85 shares, of which 50 were given to the Northwest Company and 35 to the Hudson's Bay Company. Each chief factor was entitled to 2 shares and

[2]McTavish, McGillivray & Co. was dissolved, Montreal, November 30, 1822. Thomas Thain to collect debts, *Montreal Gazette*, Jan. 3, 1823 (June?).

[3]Beckles Willson, *The Great Company*, pp. 433–435; and A. C. Laut, *Conquest of the Great Northwest*, II, 232.

each chief trader to 1 share. The Northwest Company had 15 chief factors (30 shares) and 17 chief traders (17 shares) and the Hudson's Bay Company, 10 chief factors (20 shares) and 11 chief traders (11 shares). The remaining 7 shares were reserved for seven years for old servants of the companies—4 for the Hudson's Bay Company and 3 for the Northwest Company.[4] After seven years the shares were open to new appointees.

As a result of these arrangements Simon McGillivray and Nicholas Garry were dispatched by the amalgamated Company to arrange for details of organization in Canada. Governor George Simpson was placed in charge of the whole trading territory. Four departments were organized: (1) Montreal—the Canadas, the King's Posts, and later Labrador; (2) the Southern—part of the shore east of Hudson Bay and the territory between James Bay and the department of Montreal, depot at Moose Factory; (3) the Western—west of the Rocky Mountains; and (4) the Northern which included the territory between Hudson Bay and the mountains and between the United States and the Arctic Ocean. The division was based primarily on accessibility by water transportation and control. According to Bryce[5] four factors were placed in each department and in the Western or Rocky Mountain department they were subject to one chief. The departments were grouped into two districts, the north district and the south district. In the north district seven chief factors constituted a council and in the south, three chief factors. The work of the governor and councils of the departments involved the management of the fur trade "subject to the control and superintendances of the Board of Directors at home."[6] Details as to the conduct of the trade were controlled by the council[7] as well as arrangements as to the allocation to districts and posts of chief factors (including rotations of furlough), chief traders, clerks, postmasters, interpreters, and men. Recommendations were made by the council to the Home Board in London, consisting of a governor, deputy governor, and seven directors of whom the governor

[4]For the names of the partners from each Company, see H. A. Innis, "Rupert's Land in 1825," p. 303.

[5]George Bryce, *Remarkable History*, p. 396.

[6]Evidence of the Rt. Hon. Edward Ellice, *Report from the Select Committee on the Hudson's Bay Company*, 1857, p. 325. For evidence on the authority in the hands of Governor Simpson, see *ibid.*, pp. 44–45, 74–75.

[7]For Minutes of Council for different years see H. A. Innis, "Rupert's Land in 1825," pp. 304 ff., and *The Canadian North-West, Its Early Development and Legislative Records*, ed. E. H. Oliver, I, 630 ff.; II, 689 ff.; also *Minutes of Council, Northern Department of Rupert's Land, 1821–31*, ed. R. H. Fleming.

and committee of directors were elected annually, which gave final
approval and made all appointments.

The fur trade had shifted at each successive step to the west and
the northwest.[8] The struggle of settlement against furs which began
in the Conquest, continued in the American Revolution and its after-
math, and in the amalgamation of 1821 was now being pushed in
the Northwest. The organization of the trade had resisted the encroachment of settlement and in the West made its final stand in the
period from 1821 to 1869. Settlement had increased in the southern
districts—Ontario and Quebec—and control by an organization of
the trade in those areas was impossible. Of the three departments
more directly under the control of Governor Simpson—the Northern,
Southern, and Montreal—the Northern remained as the most important. In 1821 it provided 8,995 whole beaver against 5,312 from the
Southern department, 36,937 marten against 31,528, 2,660 otter
against 1,528, and 82,312 muskrats against 30,602 and its furs were
valued at £48,050. In 1828[9] this department showed an apparent
gain of £73,000 compared with £26,000 from the Southern department[10] and £6,000 from Montreal department.[11] The disparity was
even more obvious in the following year with £96,515, £30,593,
and £4,962 as respective gains.

In the Northern department the amalgamated Company began the
task of reorganizing the trade. This department became an excellent
example of the economies of monopoly in the fur trade. The personnel
was efficiently organized. Expenses were eliminated in every possible
direction and control of the supply of furs was adjusted to price levels.
The supply of provisions[12] and supplies was developed with reference
to the lowest possible cost in the self-sufficiency of each post, of the
departments, and of the organization as a whole. Goods were imported, distributed, and handled with the greatest possible economy.
Seldom has there existed an instance in which monopoly control was

[8]The Company secured exclusive trade in the country outside the Hudson Bay
drainage basin in 1821 for 21 years. Anxiety to have this renewed led to the
great interest in exploration as a means of impressing the British government.
P. W. Dease and T. Simpson were sent out in 1836. A. Simpson, *Life of Thomas
Simpson*, pp. 176–183.

[9]The returns for 1828 were estimated at $894,879 and for 1829 at £132,070
from which was deducted a loss of 5d. per skin on 7,000,000 muskrats shipped
in 1828 or £20,833 giving net returns of £111,327 or £523 for 1/85 share.

[10]Including £5,821 from Michipicoten district in 1828 and £5,200 in 1829.

[11]One hundred per cent increase over the preceding year.

[12]For a description of pemmican, see A. Simpson, *Life of Thomas Simpson*,
p. 204.

exercised over a wide area through such a long period of history in a single industry as in the Northern department from 1821 to 1869. And seldom has it been the fortune of an institution to be linked throughout its history to the life of one man, as in the case of Governor Sir George Simpson. The activities of the Hudson's Bay Company in the period 1821 to 1869 deserve an important place in the history of monopolies.

A problem of immediate importance in the rearrangements of the interior was the elimination of bitterness which had been a part of the competition of the preceding period. The men of the Hudson's Bay Company complained that the "comfortable districts were set aside for friends of the N. W. C." Colin Robertson wrote:

> It never occurred to the new concern that such men as John Clarke and Colin Robertson were in existence. . . . The N. W. C. have gained a complete victory for the best places. John George McTavish becomes superintendent of York. McLoughlin goes to the Columbia. I am to have Norway House. Mr. John Clarke, full of health and vigor, was represented as compelled to go to Montreal for his health for a time.[13]

The diary of Nicholas Garry is most illuminating on the necessity for tact. The diplomacy of Governor Simpson was vital to success during the early years of amalgamation.

A further problem of immediate importance was the introduction of the Indians to the new *régime*.[14] The Indians were assured of the supremacy of the Hudson's Bay Company and brought under the control of monopoly. An unsigned letter, the author of which would be suggested to anyone with a knowledge of the history of the period, dated Red River, Fort Garry, May 20, 1822, was eloquent on this point.

> Their immediate wants have been fully supplied, but of course the scenes of extravagance are at an end, and it will be a work of time to reconcile them to the new order of things. . . . I have made it my study to examine the nature and character of Indians and however repugnant it may be to our feelings, I am convinced they must be ruled with a rod of Iron to bring and keep them in a proper state of subordination, and the most certain way to effect this is by letting them feel their dependence upon us. . . . In the woods and northern barren grounds this measure ought to be pursued rigidly next year if they do not improve, and no credit, not so much as a load of ammunition, given them until they exhibit an inclination to renew their habits of industry. In the plains however this system will not do, as they can live independent of us, and by withholding ammunition,

[13]A. C. Laut, *Conquest of the Great Northwest*, II, 237.
[14]As to a serious smallpox epidemic among the prairie tribes tributary to Carlton, see A. Simpson, *Life of Thomas Simpson*, p. 201.

tobacco and spirits, the Staple articles of Trade, for one year, they will recover the use of their Bows and spears, and lose sight of their smoking and drinking habits; it will therefore be necessary to bring those Tribes round by mild and cautious measure which may soon be effected.[15]

The difficulties involved in abandoning posts in the interests of economy and of handling the Indians were shown in the murder of the Company's men at St. John on Peace River in 1823 and in the abandonment of that post and Fort Dunvegan in 1824.[16] But eventually the natives were brought under control.

Again the large personnel of both companies incidental to competitive conditions was reduced and arrangements made for settling those who had been discharged, at Red River. A letter of February 27, 1822, stated:

It has become a matter of serious importance to determine on the most proper measures to be adopted with regard to the men who have large families and who must be discharged, and with the numerous halfbreed children whose parents have died or deserted them. These people form a burden which cannot be got rid of without expense, and, if allowed to remain in their present condition, they will become dangerous to the Peace of the Country and safety of the Trading Posts. It will therefore be both prudent and economical to incur some expense in placing these people where they may maintain themselves and be civilized and instructed in Religion.

We consider that all these people ought to be removed to Red River. . . .[17]

A later writer noted that

The number of servants employed by the contending parties was triple the number required in quiet . . . times, and, more especially, when the business came to be managed by one firm. . . . The influx of families, from the fur trade, in 1822, and the following summer, exceeded in number those who represented the original colonists brought in from all quarters by his Lordship.[18]

The problem of settling the surplus population was closely related

[15]Can. Arch., Selkirk Papers, XXIV, 72.

[16]See Journal of Archibald McDonald, *Peace River: A Canoe Voyage from Hudson's Bay to Pacific by the Late Sir George Simpson in 1828*, ed. M. McLeod, p. 16. See "Correspondence, J. B. Tyrrell and H. A. Innis," *Can. Hist. Rev.*, June, 1928, p. 157.

[17]Oliver, *The Canadian North-West*, I, 638.

[18]D. Gunn and C. R. Tuttle, *History of Manitoba*, pp. 225–226.

to the organization of transport. As already pointed out, the effectiveness of the competition of the Hudson's Bay Company was dependent in part on the shorter route from Hudson Bay to the interior and on the use of the York boat. The Northwest Company route from Fort William to Lake Winnipeg dependent on the expensive canoe[19] was abandoned and the York boat was supreme. Nicholas Garry wrote in his diary for 1821, "The whole country may now be supplied with boats. . . ."[20] Fort William declined and Garry wrote of Rainy Lake:

The Post of Lac la Pluie or Rainy Lake before the Union of the two Companies was one of great Importance. Here the People from Montreal came to meet those who arrived from the Athabascan Country and exchange Lading with them receiving the Furs and giving the Goods to trade in Return. It will now become a mere trading Post as the Athabascans will be supplied from York Fort.[21]

Concerning Bas de la Rivière, formerly the Northwest Company's provision depot, he wrote:

At the Moment we were there, there were 50 Women and Children living at the Expense of the Company. This is an immense Expense and some Steps should be taken to avoid it.[22]

The development of Red River settlement was an immediate solution of the reduction of personnel.

The problems of transportation which had dominated the policy of the Hudson's Bay Company on Hudson Bay continued with monopoly control in the interior. In the evidence given in 1857 it was reported that two ships were generally sent to York, one ship to Moose and another to East Main.

The home cargo is not nearly so bulky as the outward cargo, generally speaking. . . . This ship which is now sent is seven years old. She is, perhaps, what you would call full, but sailors would not call her full, perhaps, once out of those seven years. Of course it greatly depends on how you

[19]The expense of a canoe varied from £300 to £500; see a detailed list of expenses of a light canoe from Montreal to Fort William, in which £300 is given, in "Diary of Nicholas Garry," pp. 197–198. There appears to be little evidence that the supply of birch bark on the Northwest Company route was becoming exhausted but this might reasonably be expected.

[20]*Ibid.*, p. 151.

[21]*Ibid.*, p. 125.

[22]*Ibid.*, p. 133.

stow a ship. . . . We have about 200 tons of stone ballast; we take in stone ballast at York [for a vessel of 524 tons].[23]

The long and difficult haul upstream on the Nelson and the Saskatchewan of heavy and bulky goods and the return downstream of furs and the shortness of the season accentuated the problem of overhead cost incidental to an unbalanced cargo. The problem was more serious with the marked increase in capital necessary to carry on trade in the more remote interior. The average turnover was three and four years and the proportion of assets to capital very large, for example, in 1856, capital totalled £500,000 while assets in June of that year were £1,468,301 and liabilities £203,233.18.11.

York Factory was the terminus of vessels from England. Regarding the external transport Garry suggested in 1821:

Two small Vessels of 150 to 200 Tons each would be more desirable at York than the *Prince*. . . . It will be necessary to have a Vessel of 40 to 50 Tons to run between York, Severn, Albany and Moose. It appears expedient a Vessel should run to the United States or Canada to convey Buffalo Robes, Moose Skins, &c., and to take returns of such goods as may be cheaper than in England.[24]

Goods were unloaded, stored, and packed for the voyage to the interior. A trunk-line system was developed from York Factory to Norway House and feeders were attached to Red River and to the posts on the Saskatchewan. Direct transportation was provided for goods from York Factory to Red River.

The brigade that carries the furs from Fort Douglas to York Factory . . . passes to the west of Elk Island. It performs its voyage in about fifteen or twenty days. On its return, the voyage requires from thirty to thirty-five days, on account of the length of time consumed in ascending the streams. It is usual for the Company's ships to leave England together, with supplies of goods; they generally sail about the last of June, arrive at York Factory about the middle of August, and return to England with the furs brought down in the spring. The brigade does not

---

[23]Evidence of Capt. D. Herd, *Report from the Select Committee on the Hudson's Bay Company*, 1857, pp. 256–257. For dates of arrival of vessels at York Factory between 1789 and 1880, see R. Bell, "Report on Hudson's Bay" (Geological Survey) and between 1870 and 1883 C. R. Tuttle, *Our North Land*, p. 31; also I. Cowie, *The Company of Adventurers*, pp. 96–97. Cowie suggests an average for York Factory of July 31 for date of arrival and August 13 for date of departure. In one or two instances boats were unable to arrive or to depart but see also W. Coats, *Geography of Hudson Bay*, pp. 18–19.

[24]"Diary of Nicholas Garry," pp. 198–199.

wait their arrival, but carries and distributes at all the posts, the goods imported the preceding year, so that there is always one year's supply in advance at York Factory.[25]

For the transport of goods to the remote districts of Athabasca and Mackenzie River, Norway House became a second depot. Goods were brought from York Factory to Norway House and dispatched to Mackenzie River about the middle of June in the following year by the Portage la Loche brigade.[26] The brigade arrived at Portage la Loche (thirteen miles—the height of land between the Hudson Bay drainage basin and Mackenzie River drainage basin), discharged its trading goods and provisions, and loaded the furs brought to this point by the Mackenzie River brigade. The latter usually began at Fort Simpson in the latter part of May, went downstream to Fort Good Hope and collected the furs of that post as well as of Fort Norman on the return. At Simpson the returns of Liard River were also collected, and leaving about the middle of June the whole was taken up the Mackenzie arriving at Portage la Loche about the end of July. The trading goods were loaded and leaving Portage la Loche early in August, were floated downstream, and distributed to the Mackenzie River posts. With the discoveries on the Yukon, goods were taken up the Liard to Dease Lake and later to Fort Selkirk. Further discoveries in 1851 by Robert Campbell, as that the Porcupine River was a tributary of the Yukon, led to the abandoning of the difficult Liard River and Frances Lake approach to the Yukon and its tributaries, and goods were taken down the Mackenzie to the mouth of the Peel River over the portage to La Pierre's house and down the Porcupine to Fort Yukon.[27] The furs were taken downstream from Portage la

[25]W. H. Keating, *Narrative of an Expedition to the Source of St. Peter's River, Lake Winnepeek, Lake of the Woods &c., . . ., 1823*, II, 79. For descriptions of journeys from England to York Factory, see John West, *Substance of a Journal during a Residence at the Red River Colony . . . in the Years 1820, 1821, 1822, 1823, passim*; R. M. Ballantyne, *Hudson's Bay; or, Every-Day Life in the Wilds of North America*. Isaac Cowie, *The Company of Adventurers*, chaps. ii, iv.

[26]See Journal of Archibald McDonald, pp. 11–12, also *passim*. For other detailed descriptions of the routes from Norway House to Great Slave Lake, York Fort to Athabasca Lake, and York Fort to Red River, as well as for suggestions of improvements in these routes, see "Diary of Nicholas Garry," Appendix B, pp. 183–191; also [Wilcocke], *A Narrative of Occurrences*, Appendix III. For an excellent description and history of the work of the Portage la Loche brigade see J. J. Hargrave, *Red River*, pp. 160–167.

[27]See A. H. Murray, *Journal of the Yukon, 1847–48*, ed. L. J. Burpee, Introduction, *passim*.

Loche to York Fort and sent to England, the Portage la Loche brigade returning to Red River from York Fort in the late autumn. The Athabasca brigade brought its furs to Norway House and returned with the supply of goods from that depot. Boats were constructed at Chipewyan in 1823 and an entry in the journal dated May 21 of that year refers to "the first boats of the kind that ever sailed on Athabasca Lake—fired two shots with our cohorn on the occasion." The Saskatchewan brigades and other brigades such as those from Swan River and Rainy Lake brought their furs and supplies to York Fort and returned with their supplies of trading goods. The route from York Fort to Norway House was the basic short trunk line from which other routes branched to various departments.

New recruits for the service were taken on board by outgoing ships from England at Stromness. On arrival at York Fort, these men were taken inland by a boat and two men left by the Saskatchewan River brigade. In the following spring they were brought back to the depot for distribution among the various departments, to take the place of servants returning to Canada or to England. For Mackenzie River these recruits helped to take the outfit to Portage la Loche. In 1836 it was resolved that only European servants should be sent to Mackenzie River since retiring servants were able to get the boat for England at York Factory immediately on coming out,[28] while Canadian servants were obliged to wait until the following year to get to Canada. At Norway House outgoing brigade servants for the New Caledonia and Columbia districts made up the crews for the Saskatchewan outfit. This outfit was left at Edmonton and the crews continued the journey to their respective districts.

In the reduction of overhead costs of transportation, careful planning of the brigades was accompanied by steady improvement of transportation facilities. Improvements noted in the construction of boats in the early period were continued. In 1822 these boats carried 50 pieces; in 1825 according to regulations, 60 pieces; in 1833 the regulations provided "the lading of each Boat upwards [York Fort to Norway House] per Trip to be 80 and downwards 70 pieces; 5 of which to be left at Oxford House and the remaining 65 ps. per Boat to be delivered at York,"[29] and in 1836, "70 pieces goods of full weight or measurement; exclusive of the usual allowance for passengers, viz.— 10 pieces for each Commissioned Gentleman, 5 pieces for first class Clerks, 3 pieces for junior Clerks, and Postmasters."[30] In the same

[28]Oliver, *The Canadian North-West*, II, 728.
[29]*Ibid.*, p. 700.   [30]*Ibid.*, p. 746.

year following the regulation boats were ordered to be built with 28–foot keel. A description of 1848 stated:

Our boat, which was the counterpart of the rest, was long, broad, and shallow, capable of carrying forty hundredweight, and nine men, besides three or four passengers, with provisions for themselves and the crew. It did not, I suppose, draw more than three feet of water when loaded, perhaps less, and was moreover very light for its size.[31]

At a later date Ryerson wrote: "Each boat will carry two or three tons weight, and costs from £20 to £25, and is usually manned by eight, ten, or twelve voyageurs. . . . It requires all the crews of the brigade—that is thirty men—to carry or take over [the portage] one boat. . . ."[32] The boats were expected to last two seasons, although the main line, the painter, and some other parts of the *agrets* lasted only one year. The sails were serviceable for four years.

Every effort was made to increase the size of the boats, to reduce the number of boats in a brigade, to prevent destruction through carelessness of the men, and to improve transportation routes. To reduce the costs of boat transportation on the difficult trunk route between York Factory and Norway House attempts were made to build a winter road[33] between York Fort and Norway House but they were unsuccessful.[34] On Lake Winnipeg marked improvement was made in the construction in 1831–32 of two decked boats of 12 tons each, the *George* and the *Alexandra*.[35] These boats carried 300 pieces each and were used to transport freight between Norway House and Red River, to meet the Saskatchewan brigade at Grand Rapids, and to bring provisions from Red River settlement. Following the use of these boats the returns in 1834 from Fort Pelly and Fort Ellice of the Swan River districts[36] were sent out by the Assiniboine River and of the other establishments by the Dauphin River. After this year one-half the outfit for the district was taken in to Fort Pelly, Manitoba, and Shoal River posts and the remainder for Fort Ellice by Red River settlement.[37]

[31]R. M. Ballantyne, *Hudson's Bay*, pp. 71–72.

[32]John Ryerson, *Hudson's Bay*, pp. 91–95.

[33]Oliver, *The Canadian North-West*, I, 649 f.

[34]March 7, 1834: "that d——d winter road that has been conceiving for the last seven years, but has as yet brought forth nothing"; A. Simpson, *Life of Thomas Simpson*, p. 94. For a general criticism of company management of Red River, see *ibid.*, chap. vii. Thomas Simpson apparently annoyed the half-breeds by his efficiency methods; *ibid.*, chap. viii.

[35]*The Canadian North-West*, I, 664.

[36]*Ibid.*, II, 695.　　　　　[37]*Ibid.*, p. 714.

The movement of settlement to the northwest in the United States following the development of transportation facilities in that area had an important effect on the later organization of transport of the Company. Red River carts began to freight supplies from St. Paul, the head of steamboat navigation on the Mississippi. On July 10, 1847, 120 carts arrived at St. Paul from Red River[38] and in 1856 it was claimed that 500 carts[39] (an estimate of 200 carts[40] appears safe) left Pembina or Red River settlement with wheat, tallow, beef, and other produce for St. Paul or St. Anthony. Freight from England to York was £5 plus £1 for lighterage and storage per ton and from York Fort to Red River, £20—a total of £26—whereas freight from St. Paul to Red River was £18 per ton.[41]

The increasing quantity of goods demanded by the Company for the trade and for the settlement hastened these new arrangements. In 1849 the Company's boat to Hudson Bay (the *Graham*) was lost and this loss was followed by that of the *Baroness* in 1858 and of the *Kitty* in 1859. These serious losses, held to be the result of loading too much freight on lightly constructed boats, led to a demand for improvement of the southern route through the United States. The superiority of certain American and Canadian goods was an additional factor leading to an increase of trade from the south. In a letter to W. McTavish dated Norway House, December 20, 1859, W. Sinclair wrote:

As the American steel traps are much superior to any we can get made I would be much obliged if you would get a case of beaver traps for this place. . . . Our axes ought also to be from Canada made the same as our felling axes—these made in the country are really not worth carrying up into the interior. [Can. Arch., Norway House Letter Book, 1859–1862.]

In the winter of 1858–59 Anson Northup took a boat up the Crow Wing River, dismantled it and packed the cabin, machinery, and hull timbers on sleighs and took them by horses and oxen to the mouth of the Cheyenne River, a tributary of the Red River. With the financial assistance of the St. Paul Chamber of Commerce the boat was rebuilt, christened the *Anson Northup*, and launched on May 19. The crew was obliged to cut timber for firewood all the way down to Fort Garry and to lie to by night, but in spite of these handicaps she was able to make a return trip in eight days. The addition of steamboats greatly increased the extent of the trade and reduced the Company's cost of

[38]See a notice of *Wisconsin Herald*, Sept. 15, 1847, in *Beaver*, Jan., 1921.
[39]*Report from the Select Committee on the Hudson's Bay Company*, 1857, p. 108.
[40]*Ibid.*, p. 142.   [41]*Ibid.*, pp. 71–72.

transportation.[42] Heavy bulky goods could be floated down the Red River to the colony. A letter from W. Sinclair to Sir George Simpson[43] dated September 18, 1860, reported that the season had ended satisfactorily in spite of the change inaugurated in importing from the United States. With this arrangement the Saskatchewan brigade no longer went to York Factory but left all its returns at Norway House, proceeded to Fort Garry, and returned with goods and provisions to Grand Rapids on the opposite side of the lake to Norway House. The revolution in transport had begun and the old order began to lose ground.

The evolution in the transport of goods to Fort Garry which began with the steamboats had an immediate effect on the transport of the interior. For winter and for overland transport in the more remote districts in which a relatively small amount of goods was handled, horses and dogs were an important supplement to the boats. The packsaddle became an important part of the equipment with plenty of shaganappi[44] for diamond hitches and knots. Horses were supplied at Edmonton by the Saskatchewan department to transport goods to Fort Assiniboine for the Columbia department. This trade was handled at a fixed rate of 5/ for each piece of 90 pounds.[45] According to the journal of 1823–24, horses were used at Fort Chipewyan but the expenses for hay were heavy. In 1843, horses were employed at Portage la Loche, half-breeds from the Saskatchewan bringing them to this point[46] and hiring them to the men engaged in transportation. Later oxen and horses were employed by the Company to haul goods over the portage[47] but proved a constant source of trouble.

The packsaddle had decided limitations since a horse could carry only from 100 to 200 pounds. It was not until the freighters between

[42]The American and Canadian goods shipped to Fort Ellice between June 1, 1864, and May 31, 1865, included large and middling felling axes, as well as half-size, small, and large round head axes. It was found that iron axes made at York Factory were much inferior. There were also narrow and broad L'Assomption belts, and matches which came from St. Paul, each box containing about 200 matches and selling at 60 cents a box. The Company doled them out to employees only in cases where flint and steel failed. Steel traps for beaver, fox, and muskrat increased very rapidly. Perry Davis Pain Killer and earthenware pipe bowls largely completed the list.

[43]Simpson died in 1860.

[44]G. M. Grant, *Ocean to Ocean*, pp. 187–188.

[45]H. A. Innis, "Rupert's Land in 1825," p. 308.

[46]John McLean, *Notes of a Twenty-five Years' Service in the Hudson's Bay Territory*, II, 199–200.

[47]J. J. Hargrave, *Red River*, pp. 238–239.

St. Paul and Fort Garry were displaced by the steamboat and began to haul goods in Red River carts from Fort Garry to Portage la Prairie, Fort Ellice, and Fort Carlton on the Saskatchewan and to Edmonton that the horse became important to the Company's transport. The Indian ponies (shaganappies) were popular for light freight. Oxen and Red River carts carrying about 800 pounds of freight per cart and travelling 15 to 20 miles per day travelled to Edmonton and returned (approximately 2,000 miles) during the summer. The Red River cart which apparently made its appearance in the French *régime* and was revived by Alexander Henry became a central part of the equipment. Grant wrote:

It was a marvel how well those Red River carts stood out all the jolting they got. When any part broke before, a thong of Shaganappi had united the pieces. Shaganappi in this part of the world does all that leather, cloth, rope, nails, glue, straps, cord, tape, and a number of other articles are used for elsewhere. Without it the Red River cart, which is simply a clumsy looking, but really light, box cart with wheels six or seven feet in diameter, and not a bit of iron about the whole concern, would be an impossibility. These high wheeled carts cross the miry creeks, borne up by the grass roots, when ordinary waggons would sink to the hubs.[48]

In 1873, it was estimated 150 carts left Fort Garry for Edmonton.[49]

The Hudson's Bay Company also found it necessary to keep large numbers of horses. Grant on his journey across the prairies in 1870 wrote:

Every station of the Hudson's Bay Company has a "guard," or judiciously selected spot, well supplied with good water, wood, pasturage, and shelter, where the horses are kept. . . .

This was the first "guard" we had seen. They are usually at a distance from the Forts, but it so happened that this one although ten miles from the Fort was by the roadside. We could not have seen a better specimen, for, on account of the grasses being so good, more horses are kept at Fort

[48]G. M. Grant, *Ocean to Ocean*, p. 122.

[49]See *Catalogue of the Hudson's Bay Company's Historical Exhibit* at Winnipeg (4th ed., 1924), p. 55. For further description see Hon. John Schultz, *The Old Crow Wing Trail*; also W. G. Fonseca, *On the St. Paul Trail in the Sixties*; also W. J. Carter, "Reminiscences regarding the West," unpublished manuscript in the University of Toronto Library. Valuable works on the development of the American trade include H. M. Chittenden, *The American Fur Trade of the Far West*; Isaac Lippincott, "A Century and a Half of Fur Trade at St. Louis"; F. J. Turner, *The Character and Influence of the Indian Trade in Wisconsin*; W. P. Shortridge, *The Transition of a Typical Frontier*; K. W. Porter, *John Jacob Astor*.

Pitt than at any other post on the Saskatchewan. There are 300 now, and they increase rapidly though the prairie wolves destroy many of the foals. . . . When weak or sickly, or returned from a "trip," knocked up with hard driving and cudgelling, for the half-breed looks upon cudgelling as an essential and inevitable part of driving, they may be taken into the barn at the Fort for a time and fed on hay, but not otherwise. At the "guard," only one Indian is in charge of the whole herd. The horses keep together and do not stray, so fond are they of one another. The chief difficulty in selecting some for your journey is, to get those you want away from the pack. There is a thick grove of aspens where they take shelter in the coldest weather, and near it is the tent of the keeper. His chief work seems to be making little inclosures of green logs or sticks, and building fires of green wood inside to smoke off the mosquitoes. Round these fires the horses often stand in groups, enjoying the smoke that keeps their active tormentors at a little distance.[50]

The men about the Company's posts were engaged to an increasing extent in freighting, making carts and sleds, hauling hay, and similar activities.

In the remote northern districts horses could not be used and dogs were employed during the winter. Goods were brought from Yukon territory across the portage to the Mackenzie River. In Peel River district large numbers of dogs and supplies of birch wood for sleighs were imported. Toboggans were not suited to the Arctic coast with its harder ice and snow. In the maintenance of communications throughout the northern districts dogs were also extremely important.

On the Pacific coast[51] or in the Western department goods were brought from England by Cape Horn to the depot at Fort Vancouver (later, 1843, Victoria). After the amalgamation they were taken up the Columbia to various posts and up the Okanagan to Kamloops. From Kamloops a pack train transferred the goods to a new depot at Alexandria whence they were taken by boats up the Fraser to the New Caledonia department. With the establishment of a new boundary line in 1846 the Okanagan route was abandoned and goods were taken in by the Lower Fraser and Yale and Hope to the North.[52] With the

---

[50]G. M. Grant, *Ocean to Ocean*, pp. 148–151. For illuminating evidence of this change see Can. Arch., Journal of Fort Ellice, May 1, 1858, to April 27, 1859; also I. Cowie, *The Company of Adventurers*, p. 187.

[51]See Canada, Dept. of the Interior, *Certain Correspondence of the Foreign Office and of the Hudson's Bay Company* on development along the coast.

[52]See F. W. Howay, "The *Raison d'être* of Forts Yale and Hope." For a full description of the situation in the interior see A. G. Morice, *History of the Northern Interior of British Columbia*, and W. N. Sage, *Sir James Douglas and British Columbia*.

development of a coasting trade the organization became more complex. For this trade it was necessary to have the outfit one year in advance and to increase the number of ships. In 1827 the *Cadboro* (72 tons) arrived from England[53] and assisted in establishing Fort Langley on the Lower Fraser. In 1829 two brigs were sent out from London for the coasting trade and one for the inland trade. In 1833 a new coppered brig of 150 tons was purchased for £1,250 from the Sandwich Islands for the coasting trade. In 1836 the *Beaver*, the first steam vessel, costing £15,000, arrived at Fort Vancouver.[54] Coasting vessels called at temporary and permanent posts along the coast distributing goods and collecting furs in the summer.[55] These vessels were also used to develop trade with the Sandwich Islands and the southern coast of California.

The organization of transport over wide and diverse territory was accompanied by general improvements in the technique of packing. In new districts Indians were instructed in the methods of preparing skins, for example, drying lynx skins with the fur outside, and removing the genitals of marten. At the posts the claws of marten were clipped to prevent injury to the skins after they had been packed. Beaver and bearskins were well beaten and dusted. Instructions were issued emphasizing the necessity of careful handling and packing for transport over long distances. Packs were made up with considerable uniformity—250 or 300 marten and some fox carefully covered with 10 large beaver and 2 bearskins or bear and beaver on the top and bottom of the pack, and deerskin on the sides. With high prices regulations were issued forbidding the use of these skins as wrappers. Rats were made up into uniform packages of 600 rats and 2 large beaver. From the Yukon, marten, silver, and cross fox were carefully packed in 60- to 84-pound bales with dressed leather and sent out with the Peel River returns thus saving the interest on the more valuable furs. Especial care was taken on the difficult part of the trip from La Pierre's house to Peel River. Yukon furs were packed in smaller weights and in different moulds since they were taken on Yukon sleds and the pack frames were adjusted to turn out packs of 26 inches in length by 18 inches in breadth. In the Mackenzie River district elaborate care was taken in handling furs and special regulations were frequent. Inside the cover of each bale was placed a list of contents

[53]Sir Charles Piers, "Pioneer Ships on the Pacific Coast."

[54]C. W. McCain, *The History of the S.S. "Beaver."*

[55]For a description of the difficulties of trading with Indians on the Pacific coast see *Traits of American Indian Life*, by a Fur Trader.

written on parchment or deerskin. At Resolution running numbers were burned on wooden tallies on the bales to allow no chance of loss. Furs were carefully baled and each bale marked with letters representing the district and showing the outfit and number of the bale. The fur presses were designed to give the bale the correct shape and to permit the use of levers to secure the greatest compactness. Also the packing of goods for the interior required skill of a high order.[56] Valuable commodities were distributed throughout the bale to give each bale an approximately equal value. They were arranged in pieces of 90 to 100 pounds and in shapes which could be carried without difficulty or fear of breakage.

Continuation of a policy of self-sufficiency[57] in provisions and supplies in the posts, the districts, and the Company's trading territory generally was essential to a reduction of incoming cargo. Economy in the transport of supplies and provisions through the growth of local produce was especially evident in the more distant departments and posts. Potatoes were a staple crop grown at most of the posts. Fish was important for men and dogs—at Norway House 12,000 fish were taken in the autumn of 1828, a supply for four months, and in 1861, 20,000 fish were taken. Fishing was carried on extensively in the Mackenzie River district at Big Island at the entrance of Mackenzie River, at Resolution, Fort Rae, and other points on Slave Lake and on the river as well as on lakes in the interior. Reports indicated as high a catch as 1,300 fish per day from the latter sources. At Big Island and other fishing points the catch varied appreciably from season to season. The former point was regarded as the important source of supply of fish for posts down the river such as at Simpson and as many as four boats with five oarsmen and a steersman per boat were engaged at this fishery. With five nets this fishery yielded about 150 fish per day. Numerous complaints indicated its importance: boats were unsatisfactory, timber was difficult to secure for building drying frames, nets of No. 9 and even of No. 10 twine were found too weak, fishermen were unable to handle more than 6 or 7 nets per day each, and nets were changed only three times per month. Fluctuations and many failures had serious consequences.

Other sources of food supply were drawn upon in Mackenzie River. Letter books reveal a constant dependence on rabbits. Moose con-

---

[56]See I. Cowie, *The Company of Adventurers*, pp. 106–107, 277–278, for details on packing of goods and furs; also Oliver, *The Canadian North-West*, II, 812.

[57]Journal of the Hudson's Bay Company's post at Fort Chipewyan, April, 1822, to January, 1824, University of Toronto Library copy.

stituted another source and skilled moose hunters, often in great demand, were sent from more favourable districts to poorer hunting territory. This animal was also used for making pemmican as among the Sikannies trading at Fort Liard. Caribou became more important with the opening of posts in the vicinity of Fort Rae and Fond du Lac. For example the inventory at Fort Rae for March 19, 1853, showed on hand 1,583 lb. dry meat, 10,000 lb. half-dried meat, 785 lb. pounded meat, 540 lb. grease, 2,000 tongues, and 600 lb. fresh meat. Fort Chipewyan depended on a supply of buffalo, moose, and caribou meat and especially on the fisheries.

These provisions fluctuated widely and seasons in which caribou did not migrate from the barren grounds to the woods brought considerable hardship. Moreover it was difficult to secure the correct proportion of grease to meat for the manufacture of pemmican. At Simpson it became necessary at times to change the ratio of 35 lb. grease, 55 lb. pounded meat to 33 lb. grease and 57 lb. meat and the tariff was arranged to encourage trade in grease (1 Made Beaver = 5 lb. grease or 8 lb. pounded meat or 2 large or 3 small side ribs). Fluctuations, dependent on seasons, climate, and periodic cycles, were characteristic of all the supplies, fish, rabbits, moose, and caribou.

Resolution, Simpson, and Liard were important centres for agriculture. Potatoes and butter were sent from Resolution. In 1852 the crops at Fort Simpson included 700 bu. potatoes, 120 bu. turnips, 180 bu. barley; at Resolution, 90 kegs potatoes, 50 kegs turnips; at Fort Halkett, 20 kegs barley, 20 kegs potatoes and cabbage and turnips; at Fort Liard, 700 kegs potatoes, 500 kegs Swedish turnips—an increase in the latter post from 200 kegs potatoes and 60 kegs barley in 1851. Barley yielded in the ratio of 1 to 12. Simpson as headquarters for the district was the general clearing house for surplus products.

In most departments agriculture became a more important source of supply for provisions. A minute of council resolved that,

In order to save the expense of transporting Flour from the Depot to Athabasca or McKenzie's River Districts it is [recommended] that the Gentlemen in charge of Posts in Peace River where the climate and soil are favorable to cultivation, be directed to devote their attention to that important object forthwith; as it is intended that those Districts shall depend on Peace River alone for their Flour after the close of Outfits 1834.[58]

[58]Oliver, *The Canadian North-West*, II, 692; also Dunvegan Journal 1839–42, 1853–55, University of Toronto Library copy.

Fort Langley had a stock of cattle and swine. New Caledonia had its fisheries. The settlement at Fort Vancouver began in 1824 with 17 cows and by 1832 had over 400 cattle. The production of farm products was rapidly extended and in 1832[59] the crops at this point brought returns of 3,500 bu. wheat, 3,000 bu. barley, 3,000 bu. peas, 15,000 bu. potatoes, and 2,000 bu. oats.

Although the self-sufficiency of posts was important in the reduction of incoming cargo and of transportation costs, the problem of securing an adequate supply of provisions suitable to the unavoidable outlay for transportation continued from the earlier period. The demand for supplies of food of slight bulk and high food value such as pemmican remained. In contrast with the Northwest Company pemmican was dispatched from the Red River and the Saskatchewan territory to Norway House and Cumberland House rather than to Fort Alexander and Cumberland House. At these points it was picked up by the in-going Portage la Loche and Athabasca and other bridages. The location of the depots and the areas from which food was taken partially solved the problem incidental to an unbalanced, heavy upstream cargo. On the Saskatchewan furs and pemmican were moved downstream to equalize the movement of goods upstream. In 1827, 500 pieces of provisions were required for the posts, including Cumberland, 93; Bas de la Rivière, 50; Norway House, 120; Oxford House, 70; and York Factory, 167. Provisions in New Caledonia were supplemented by supplies of grease first from the Saskatchewan district and later, about 1830, from Dunvegan on Peace River. In 1832, 600 pieces of common pemmican and 50 bags of fine pemmican (45 pounds each) were used at Norway House and the lower establishments and 80 pieces at English River. Pemmican was supplied at 2d. per pound common and 3d. per pound fine. Throughout the next decade the supply changed slightly. The demands of Cumberland House varied from 100 to 140 bags. In 1840, 3,500 pounds grease, 450 bales common pemmican, 150 bales dried meat, and 500 buffalo tongues were asked for.[60] Requisitions for common pemmican to Norway House continued to decrease, 400 bags in 1842, 300 bags, 1843, and 100 bags in 1844. Dried-meat requisitions declined from 150 bales in 1841 to 100 bales in 1842 and 50 bales in 1844. Tongues ceased to

[59]For detailed information on later agricultural activities of the Company, see memorial submitted to British and American Joint Commission for the Final Settlement of the Claims of the Hudson's Bay and Puget's Sound Agricultural Companies.

[60]See F. G. Roe, "The Extermination of the Buffalo in Western Canada" and W. Hough, "The Bison as a Factor in Ancient American Culture History."

be exported after 1843. In the Mackenzie River department, provisions, especially pemmican, were supplied from Saskatchewan and Dunvegan. The requisition of Fort Simpson headquarters from Chipewyan included 48 bags of pemmican, or 40 bags pemmican and dried meat equal to 8 bags, 2 bags of fine pemmican and "as much butter as can be spared." In 1857 it was estimated that 2,000 to 3,000 hundredweight of pemmican were manufactured annually.

In the latter part of the period, the production of pemmican on the Saskatchewan declined. After 1852, with increasing scarcity of pemmican and supplies from Saskatchewan and other districts, pemmican was no longer sent to Mackenzie River department. Its production tended to fall off at certain posts and Milton and Cheadle wrote:

Fort Pitt stands, like Carlton, on the flat below the high old bank of the river Saskatchewan, and is a similar building, but of smaller size. This establishment furnishes the largest quantity of pemmican and dry meat for the posts more distant from the plains. The buffalo are seldom far from Fort Pitt, and often whilst there is a famine at Carlton and Edmonton, the people of the "Little Fort," as it is called, are feasting on fresh meat every day.[61]

In 1859 the Swan River and Saskatchewan brigades were short of provisions and the pemmican was badly prepared because of a scarcity of tallow. Milton and Cheadle on their journey in 1862–63 wrote:

The buffalo have receded so far from the forts, and the quantity of white fish from the lakes, one of the principal sources of supply, has decreased so greatly, that now a winter rarely passes without serious suffering from want of food. This deficiency has become so urgent, that the Hudson's Bay Company contemplate the immediate establishment of extensive farms in the Saskatchewan district, which is so admirably adapted for agricultural and grazing purposes.[62]

Following the decline of the supply of pemmican from the Saskatchewan district, Swan River and Red River districts exported larger

[61]Viscount Milton and W. B. Cheadle, *The North-West Passage by Land*, p. 169.

[62]*Ibid.*, p. 157. For descriptions of agriculture carried on at different posts of the Hudson's Bay Company, especially along the Saskatchewan, see *ibid.*, *passim*; M. McNaughton, *Overland to Cariboo*; G. M. Grant, *Ocean to Ocean*; P. Kane, *Wanderings of an Artist among the Indians of North America*; J. McDougall, *Pathfinding on Plain and Prairie* and *Saddle, Sled, and Snowshoe*; H. J. Moberly and W. B. Cameron, *When Fur was King*; and Hudson's Bay Company, Diary of Fort Edmonton, October 1854 to May 1856, University of Toronto Library copy.

quantities. Swan River began to supply grease in 1841 and pemmican and dried meat in 1842 sending out 3 cwt. soft grease, 20 bales dried meat, and 70 bags of pemmican in 1845. Red River exported larger quantities of pemmican and dried meat after 1840. With the decline in the supply of pemmican and its shift to other areas flour became a more important export from Red River. Flour requisitions from Red River increased from 200 cwt. in 1825 to 1,200 cwt. in 1833 and declined from 1,000 cwt. in 1838 to 750 cwt. in 1845. The price was reduced from 20/ per cwt. in 1823 to 10/ in 1832 but increased again to 12/ in 1836 and remained at that price to 1838. Requisitions for pork, beef, and ham remained very stable throughout the period, declining slightly from 1832 to 1838 but rising throughout the period 1840 to 1845. Butter steadily increased. Indian corn, peas, and barley practically disappeared in the first two or three years. Prices were remarkably steady with a tendency to increase. Cheese, eggs, suet, French beans, assortments of garden seeds, and even potatoes were added to the requisition after 1837 and especially after 1840. Red River settlement with its favourable climate became the chief source of agricultural products which were shipped downstream and across the lake to Norway House.

The policy of the Company with regard to supplies was similar to that which had been adopted for provisions. The organization, the department, and the post as far as possible were self-sufficient. Minutes of Council for 1830 directed,

That Gentlemen in charge of Districts & Posts be directed to use their utmost endeavors to collect large quantities of Leathers dressed, and Parchment, Buffalo Robes, Pack Cords, Snow Shoe line, Sinews, tracking Shoes, Leather tents etc. etc., are these are articles absolutely necessary for the trade in many parts of the Country and cannot be purchased in Europe or Canada.[63]

These commodities were exchanged between various departments and posts. Leather, parchment, pack cords, and babiche were furnished from Saskatchewan district *via* Edmonton, Fort Assiniboine, and the Leather Pass, and after 1831 from Dunvegan, to New Caledonia. In that year 650 dressed moose skins, 100 pounds babiche snares and beaver nets, and 2,000 fathoms pack cords were sent from Dunvegan. The amounts varied and generally included sinews and grease to the extent of two canoes or 50 pieces. Leather was apparently sent to this district in 1835 and in other years by Jasper House and Tête Jaune Cache, meeting a canoe at the latter point from New Caledonia, or by

[63]Minutes of Council, 1830, in Oliver, *The Canadian North-West*, I, 654.

Okanagan and return by Fort Alexandria. The Saskatchewan department also furnished boats, tracking shoes, leather tents, and other
products. Milton and Cheadle wrote:

The establishment at Edmonton is the most important one in the
Saskatchewan district, and is the residence of a chief factor, who has
charge of all the minor posts. It boasts of a windmill, a blacksmith's
forge, and carpenter's shop. The boats required for the annual voyage
to York Factory in Hudson's Bay are built and mended here; carts, sleighs,
and harness made, and all appliances required for the Company's traffic
between the different posts.[64]

Agrets including whale line, oilcloth, sails, blocks, nails, iron, pitch,
tar, and stern-plate nails were sent to Edmonton with the Saskatchewan brigade in the fall and the boats constructed during the
winter. From 8 to 14 boats of 24-foot keel (later 28-foot) were sent
to Norway House for distribution annually—a convenient arrangement for taking the department's supply of surplus pemmican down
the Saskatchewan. From 100 to 120 pairs of tracking shoes were sent
infrequently before 1840. After that date the number increased from
500 to 1,000 pairs. From 20 to 30 leather tents were sent after 1839.
Swan River department supplied 200 to 300 bushels of salt at 5s. per
bushel in 1831 and at a uniform price of 8/ per bushel from 1835 to
1842, chiefly for Red River, being found unsatisfactory for preserving
meat. After 1840 the same department supplied from 15 to 20 leather
tents, and in 1840 and 1843, 300 pounds of gum. The supply of leather
was affected by the decrease of buffalo as in the case of pemmican.
In 1859 complaints were made regarding the Saskatchewan and Swan
River districts. The Mackenzie and Athabasca districts became more
important as sources for this commodity.

Rainy Lake supplied 5 new bark canoes in 1825, 3 for Fort Alexander and 2, together with 50 fathoms of best bottom and side bark,
for Norway House. Birch bark, cedar canoe splinters, and timbers were
also supplied. In 1825 Winnipeg district supplied ten sets of cedar
canoe timbers and *lisses* and 3 kegs of gum for Norway House. Nelson
River supplied 6 kegs of gum and 20 bales of watap for York Factory.
Red River department supplied 400 portage slings at 2/8 in 1832. The
number declined and the price was reduced to 2/-. After 1840, from
150 to 250 were sent. Tracking shoes were sent in large numbers in
1840 and 1841. Oak staves, boards, and headings for barrels and sleds

[64]Viscount Milton and W. B. Cheadle, *North-West Passage by Land*, pp.
179–180.

became an important export after 1841. "Country made articles" produced at York included Indian axes, ice chisels, fish and muskrat spears, ironwork for boats, articles made from tin, drinking pots, pans, kettles, kegs, and firkins.[65] In Mackenzie River district, tracking shoes and moccasins were ordered, 120 pairs (60 with tops) in one year. Resolution and Big Island supplied boards and planks for other posts. Oars, pack cords, and snowshoe laces cut from moose skin, moose and deerskins were ordered from Big Island. Fort Liard supplied grindstones, sledges, axe handles, lodges, canoes, and oars. Deerskin robes and babiche were obtained from Fort Rae. Leather was sent from the Yukon. Salt was distributed to various posts from Norman. In one year the blacksmith at Fort Simpson manufactured 500 traps. Between departments similar specialization and exchange were carried out. Leather was furnished on a large scale to the Southern department. Requisitions for leather collectively from the districts in 1825 included 1,000 dressed skins, 200 clean parchment, and 200 buffalo robes from Red River. Accounts between the various departments were adjusted according to a schedule of prices drawn up by the Council.[66]

Economy was enforced in all departments. Old spirit kegs were taken on to the depot in parcels, or filled with grease, and rebuilt. The available letter books of the departments leave a distinct impression of constant enforcement of economy measures by the department heads. In Mackenzie River district old ironworks were sent from various posts to Simpson to be repaired by the blacksmith. Old ironworks and unsalable goods were sent to new districts in which the natives were as yet unacquainted with European products, as from York Factory to the Eskimo in Ungava.[67] Tobacco covers were collected from various posts for packing fur in remote districts. Pack cords were handled in a similar fashion and twisted babiche used as a substitute for cross lashing. Old tracking line or bale cords were used for buoy lines, for trout lines, and for mending nets. Sugar kegs were made into water buckets. Old boats were burned for the nails. Instructions regarding the erection of new posts[68] illustrated the demands for economy: buildings must be placed (1) beyond reach of inundation, (2) in vicinity of firewood and wood for buildings (logs at least

[65]I. Cowie, *The Company of Adventurers*, pp. 105–106.

[66]Minutes of Council for 1825, H. A. Innis, "Rupert's Land in 1825," also for 1841, Oliver, *The Canadian North-West*, II, 834–835.

[67]Oliver, *The Canadian North-West*, II, 739.

[68]Can. Arch., Anderson Letter Books—see especially the long arguments on the relative advantages of Simpson and Big Island as a site for headquarters.

8″ × 6″), (3) near a good summer and winter fishery, (4) with a good harbour for boats, (5) if possible where soil is good. At Lac Brochet three buildings were erected: one store 25′ × 18′, one men's house 20′ × 16′, one master's house 15′ × 15′—all of round logs and 40′ apart to avoid loss from fire; at Norman, one store 30′ × 20′ with 10′ posts; house for manager, 25′ × 16′—two rooms 8′ × 16′ and 17′ × 16′; men's house 20′ × 15′.

In the persistent problem of reducing the overhead incidental to a heavy one-way traffic, control over the incoming supply of goods was important. Goods of high value and low weight and bulk were stressed. The Northern department consumed annually over 100,000 pounds of tea and 50,000 pounds of tobacco.[69] Hardware and equipment essential to the pursuit of the fur trade were difficult to reduce in quantity as was shown in the cargoes of the boats. The cargo of the *Prince Rupert* bound for York Factory, 1867, included 60 tons of gunpowder, bullets, and shot in proportion, cases of flintlock, Indian guns, twine for fishing nets, tea, sugar, tobacco, rum, brandy, wines, axes, files, traps, knives, needles, awls, frying pans, pots, copper kettles, flints, fire steels, blankets, and clothing.[70] The quantity of goods arriving each year was remarkably constant and the value of the indents was controlled with unusual directness.[71] Reduction in the importation of various commodities was carried out with relatively slight difficulty. Liquors were gradually prohibited in various posts throughout the district.[72] In 1825 liquors supplied to Red River were limited to 150

[69]J. J. Hargrave, *Red River*, p. 370.

[70]I. Cowie, *The Company of Adventurers*, pp. 76–77.

[71]See an estimated requisition of country produce for outfit 1845 from various posts on Norway House, in Oliver, *The Canadian North-West*, II, 870. The indents for outfits in 1833, 1835, 1842, 1844, 1845 were £15,000. In 1834 they were £10,000; in 1837, £28,000; in 1838, £25,000; in 1839, £17,000; in 1840, £20,000; in 1843, £17,500. In 1843, £4,500 went to Red River; and in 1844, £4,000. The number of pieces of trading goods sent to Athabasca in 1830 was 220; from 1831 to 1833 annually, 200; from 1835 to 1841 annually, 250; in 1842, 190; and in 1843, 180. Mackenzie River received 250 pieces in 1830, 1832, and 1833, 1836 to 1839, 280 pieces in 1831, 200 in 1835, 220 in 1840, and 300 annually from 1835 to 1837 and in 1842 and 1843, 150 in 1839 and 1841, and 140 in 1840. In contrast with these shipments, 550 pieces were sent to this department in 1878 in a competitive period. Saskatchewan received 240 pieces in 1825, 360 in 1830, 250 in 1831 and 1832, 550 in 1833, 1837, 1839, and 1841, 500 in 1835, 1836, and 1840, 450 in 1842 and 1843. In 1878 Edmonton received 800 pieces. *Ibid.*, I, II.

[72]*Report from the Select Committee on the Hudson's Bay Company*, 1857, pp. 79–80, 368.

kegs of 9 gal. each annually, and in 1837, 3,800 gal. of spirits were imported in Hudson Bay territory, and the average from 1847 to 1857 was 4,911 gal., of which two-thirds was sent to Red River and one-third allotted to servants and Indians.[73] The amount of sugar imported was reduced.[74]

Attempts were also made to increase the outgoing cargo by developing trade in other commodities. According to Ballantyne:

The trade carried on by the Company is in peltries of all sorts, oil, dried and salted fish, feathers, quills, &c.; and a list of some of their principal articles of commerce is subjoined:—

Beaver-skins.	Fox-skins, Cross
Bear-skins, Black.	Ditto, Red.
Ditto, Brown.	Ditto, White.
Ditto, White or Polar.	Ditto, Blue.
Ditto, Grizly.	Ivory (tusks of the Walrus.)
Badger-skins.	Lynx-skins.
Buffalo or Bison Robes.*	Marten-skins.
Castorum.	Musquash-skins.
Deer-skins, Rein.	Otter-skins.
Ditto, Red.	Oil, Seal.
Ditto, Moose or Elk.	Ditto, Whale.
Ditto, parchment.	Swan-skins.
Feathers of all kinds.	Salmon, salted.
Fisher-skins.	Seal-skins.
Goose-skins.	Wolf-skins.
Fox-skins, Black.	Wolverine-skins.
Ditto, Silver.	

*The hide of the bison—or, as it is called by the fur-traders, the buffalo—when dressed on one side and the hair left on the other, is called a robe. Great numbers are sent to Canada, where they are used for sleigh wrappers in winter. In the Indian country they are often used instead of blankets.

The most valuable of the furs mentioned in the above list is that of the *black fox.* This beautiful animal resembles in shape the common fox of England, but it is much larger, and jet black, with the exception of one or two white hairs along the back bone, and a pure white tuft on the end of the tail. A single skin sometimes brings from twenty-five to thirty guineas in the British market. . . .

The most profitable fur in the country is that of the marten. It somewhat resembles the Russian sable, and generally maintains a steady

[73]*Ibid.*, pp. 60–61.

[74]For a description of goods traded, see Can. Arch., Accounts of merchandise for trade and stores for use of Fort Ellice supplied June 1, 1864, to May 31, 1865, 1864 outfit; totals of quantities entered for coming year; Inventory June 1, 1864; Invoices, transfers from other posts.

price. These animals, moreover, are very numerous throughout most part of the Company's territories, particularly in M'Kenzie's River, whence great numbers are annually sent to England.[75]

On the Pacific coast, Fort Langley in 1830 prepared 220 barrels of salmon and in 1831 nearly 300 barrels. The district developed an export trade in salmon and timber with California and the Sandwich Islands.[76] Experiments were constantly made in the development of new lines of trade. In 1830 orders were given that bears' grease should be collected at 2/ per pound. An experimental farm and other organizations were devised partly to increase the supply of provisions for the department but also to develop an export of wool, hemp, and flax to England. Instructions were sent with the object of developing a trade in caviare.[77]

The problem of personnel and wage costs was closely related to the general problem of overhead costs in transportation. Large numbers of men were engaged during the open season moving freight up the rivers to the various posts and furs down the rivers to the depot at York Factory. For the handling of freight on the trunk route from York Factory to Norway House overhead was shifted to an increasing extent to the Indians and later to Red River settlement. In 1832 Indians of the Island Lake district were employed in the transport of 640 pieces from York Factory to Norway House and in the transport of 400 pieces, provisions, leather, furs, etc. from Norway House to York Factory by 80-piece boats in two trips and it was resolved that "the said Indians be paid after the rate of 60 Made Beaver for Middlemen, 65 M. B. for Bowsmen and 70 M. B. for steersmen for their service during the season."[78] In 1836 crews of 4 boats—say 28 men—were to be engaged

for two Trips to York Factory (returning from Norway House) with ladings of 75 piece p. Boat, at £12 for Steersmen, £10.10 for Bowsmen and £9 for Middlemen, and . . . the remainder of the Outfit [was to] be freighted from York on Contract with Settlers at 18/ p. piece to Red River and 14/ to Norway House.[79]

Two years later settlers were hired for the transport of goods from

[75]R. M. Ballantyne, *Hudson's Bay*, pp. 35–37. For interesting details on various aspects of the trade see H. M. Robinson, *The Great Fur Land; or, Sketches of Life in the Hudson's Bay Territory.*

[76]G. V. Bennett, "Early Relations of the Sandwich Islands to the Old Oregon Territory"; K. W. Porter, *John Jacob Astor.*

[77]Oliver, *The Canadian North-West*, II, 798; see D. Gunn and C. R. Tuttle, *History of Manitoba*, chaps. viii, ix, and Can. Arch., Journal of Robert Campbell.

[78]*The Canadian North-West*, I, 665.   [79]*Ibid.*, II, 732.

York to Norway House and Red River but under "the express con-dition that no Indians are to be employed in such transport."[80] This freight was contracted for by settlers by the piece. The burden of over-head was materially reduced through hiring temporary employees rather than a permanent force throughout the year. Effective control over this route was shown in the reduction in freight charges. The freight per piece from York Fort to Red River declined from 25/ in 1825, to 20/ in 1830, 18/ in 1831, 17/ in 1838, and 16/ in 1840— a reduction for the period of 9/; from York Fort to Norway House it declined from 15/ in 1830 to 14/ in 1831 and 13/ in 1838; from Norway House to Red River, from 5/ in 1830 to 4/ in 1831 and 3/ in 1833. The substantial reduction on the route from Norway House to Red River and from York Fort to Red River was the result of the employment of larger boats on Lake Winnipeg. The remaining rates varied as a result of several factors. Upstream rates were higher than downstream in proportion to the swiftness and difficulty of the water. Oxford House to Norway House was twice as high, 4/ (1831), as in the opposite direction, 2/, but York Factory to Oxford House was over three times as high, 10/, as in the opposite direction 3/. Rates were also adjusted according to the amount and character of the traffic —traffic downstream from Red River to Norway House was one-quarter as expensive as heavy traffic in the opposite direction. On the other hand freight on this route in either direction tended to become equal as in 1833. Rates were also determined by the application of the long- and short-haul principle as shown in rates charged to other points—York Factory to Mackenzie River, 50/; to Athabasca, 40/; to Saskatchewan, English River, Rainy Lake, Upper Red River, and Swan River, 30/; to Churchill and Severn, 2/.[81] Evidence of the de-cline in wages is shown as early as 1832 in a letter written by W. Sin-clair to Ermatinger dated Norway House, June 22.

Money is an article that is getting scarce at least its the Case with some in this Country, the *Wigs* or Nabobs are getting so avaricious— that they are getting into a System of economy that ere long they Will starve themselves to death. altho the returns are still increasing, The Outfits are courtailed; No increase of Wages, More Work got out of the Men than usual & at this place alone upwards of 50 Indians are employed in Working up goods all Summer at the rate of £4. p. Man: in the Course of the Summer three Trips is made from the Factory with 80 pieces p. Boat, the Boats are larger than usual, for this Tripping Business only.[82]

[80]*Ibid.*, p. 780.   [81]Cf. rates given *ibid.*, pp. 705–706.
[82]Can. Arch., Ermatinger–Tod Papers, p. 273.

Further evidence that this policy was continued was shown in the complaints of settlers that each piece had been increased in weight from 90 to 100 and 105 pounds.

On other portions of the transport routes a similar policy was followed. Wentzel wrote in 1824: "Engagés' prices are now reduced to twenty-five pounds annually to a *boute* and twenty pounds to middlemen, without equipments or any other perquisites whatever. . . . In short, the North-West is now beginning to be ruled with an iron rod."[83]

For the main routes from Red River to York Factory and from Norway House to Portage la Loche in which the cost of transportation was the significant item, Red River settlement was a reserve from which men could be taken in the open season and brought back to be discharged in the winter. On tributary routes the men employed at the posts throughout the year were engaged in transportation during the open season. In most cases these men were aided by Indians employed for the season. In 1834 the voyaging complement of servants was reduced from Rainy Lake and six Indians were hired for the summer at £5 per man to make up the crews, and in 1837 three Indians were hired for the English River voyage. Indians were also trained as *voyageurs* between Simpson and Portage la Loche to reduce expenses. Good Hope, as the terminus of the route on Mackenzie River, supplied an important complement. Wages of the trippers were reduced throughout the period. Wages of the Mackenzie River transport declined for steersmen from £22 in 1825 to £21 in 1831; to £18 in 1832; and to £16 in 1833; for bowsmen for the same dates, from £20, to £18, to £16, and to £14; and for the middlemen, from £17 to £15, to £14, and to £12. Guides were paid £5 more than the wages of steersmen and later £25 for the season. In the construction of the winter road, men were hired throughout the year but generally the transportation schedule provided for their return to Red River for the winter.

The personnel of the Company included three classes: (1) settlers contracting to freight goods by the piece, engaged, as shown, chiefly on the main route, (2) trippers engaged for the season by the Company as on the Portage la Loche brigade, (3) the staff engaged throughout the year on various minor routes. The importance of the permanent staff is suggested in the following statistics for 1857. In that year the Company employed 16 chief factors, 29 chief traders, 5 surgeons, 87 clerks, 67 postmasters, 1,200 permanent servants, 500

[83]L.-R. Masson, *Les Bourgeois*, I, 150.

voyageurs and temporary servants, 150 officers and crews of vessels—
a total of about 3,000, including Indian labourers.[84]

Wages of men hired throughout the year were closely dependent
on the rates paid for transport but provisions were included to reduce
the turnover of this labour and to keep it under close control. In 1825
wages in Athabasca and New Caledonia were for steersmen, £24;
bowsmen, £22; and middlemen, £19; and the same rates prevailed
in 1836 for Athabasca and Mackenzie River. At the latter date, however, New Caledonia was included with Millbank, Nass, and Stikine,
and bowsmen were reduced to £19. In districts of the Northern department excluding Athabasca and Mackenzie River the rates were lower
and in 1836 steersmen, bowsmen, and middlemen were paid £22,
£20, and £17 respectively. Fishermen's wages were raised from £17
to £19 in 1836 and to £3 more than the wages of middlemen in
1837. Gentlemen's waiting men were paid middlemen's wages, or
£17. In 1851 in the Mackenzie River district steersmen were paid
£27; bowsmen, £25; and fishermen, £22. In 1857 fishermen were
paid as high as £30, £35, and £40. For various trades, wages[85]
tended to vary from transport rates. Wages of interpreters varied and
were especially high, and in new territories in which the acquaintance
of new tribes rendered their service extremely valuable, rose as high as
£32 per year on the Yukon. Skilled labourers and servants were
brought from England and Scotland on five-year contracts at fixed
rates of pay. Sloop men were paid £20 *per annum*, boat builders,
coopers, blacksmiths, masons, joiners, and plasterers, £25 to £30
per annum, and labourers, £16 to £17. In 1857 wages of labourers
were increased to £20. Servants brought from Canada were hired
generally on a three-year basis, a small number of skilled workmen
at the same rate of pay as those from Europe and the unskilled

[84]Evidence of Sir George Simpson, *Report from the Select Committee on the
Hudson's Bay Company*, 1857, p. 57. For a description of the personnel see R.
M. Ballantyne, *Hudson's Bay*, pp. 29–30; A. G. Morice, *Northern Interior of
British Columbia*, chap vii; I. Cowie, *The Company of Adventurers*, pp. 137 ff.

[85]In the period from 1836 to 1843 excluding 1838, 152 labourers (Orkneymen) at £16 or £17 per year, 23 sloopers at £20 per year, 11 boat builders
at £25 to £30 per year, 8 coopers at £25 to £30, 13 blacksmiths at £25 to
£30, 1 plasterer at £30, 3 joiners at £25 to £30, and 3 masons at £25 to
£30 came out from Europe on a five-year contract. In the same period 234
labourers at £16 to £17, or *prix de poste*, 3 blacksmiths at £25, 1 joiner
at £30, 1 carpenter at £30, 1 cooper at £25 came from Canada on a three-
year contract. From 1841 to 1843, 60 servants were hired from Red River on a
three-year contract at *prix de poste* and £16 to £17. A runner and labourer
at Michipicoten was paid $146 per year in 1868.

labourers at a slightly higher rate than those from Europe. As a rule
Canadians were better axmen and were accustomed to pioneer conditions. Single men were preferred to married men although a certain
number of women was regarded as essential. Red River became an
increasingly important reserve and labourers from this colony were
also hired on a three-year basis. Native labour was encouraged.
"Strong, healthy half-breed lads not under 14 years of age" were
engaged as apprentices to tradesmen for terms of seven years, and
were paid for first two years, £8 *per annum*, next two years at £10
per annum, following two years at £12 *per annum*, and last year at
£15—a total of £75; "such lads not to be employed with their fathers
nor in the Districts where their fathers or family reside."[86]

Wages were regulated by the Council, and control was exercised
effectively. Variations from the schedules in the districts were charged
to the accounts of the chief factors in charge of the district. Unskilled
labourers from Canada were paid during the early period at wages
fixed at the posts (*prix de poste*) but later these wages appear to have
also been fixed by the Council.

The higher ranks were paid according to a fixed schedule.
Apprentice postmasters were hired at £20 to £30 per year from
three to five years. Postmasters were hired for three years at salaries
ranging from £25 to £75 depending on ability and length of service.
Apprentice clerks[87] were hired for five years at £20, 25, 30, 40,
and 50 for each consecutive year. Clerks contracted for three years
at £100 per year but junior men were occasionally paid lower wages
varying from £50 to £75. The agent at Quebec received £250 *per
annum* for three years. Encouragement was given to natives of the
country educated at Red River in a schedule of payments as apprentice
clerks £30, £40, £50, for three years, £75 per year for three years,
and finally £100 per year. On the other hand few of the natives of
Red River were appointed as apprentice clerks, but rather as apprentice postmasters. Chief Factor Anderson claimed that the rule
of appointing men educated in Red River as assistant postmasters and
European men as apprentice clerks, was unfair. For example, an
apprentice clerk from Europe received for his first engagement of five
years, £165; his second engagement, three years, £225; his third
engagement, three years, £300; giving a total for eleven years of
£690, or £63 per year, whereas an apprentice postmaster educated
in Red River received for the three engagements £100, £120, and

[86]Oliver, *The Canadian North-West*, I, 653.

[87]See a copy of form of contract, I. Cowie, *The Company of Adventurers*, pp.
69–72.

£225 respectively, or a total of £445 and an average of £40 per year. There were other complaints of discriminations against Canadians. John McLean mentions Deschambault as a clerk who had seen thirty years' service without promotion although Chief Factor Anderson claimed that he was useless as a trader and that even McLean while in charge of the district never trusted him.[88] Men in the upper ranks were not encouraged to marry until late. The advice of Sir George Simpson to Robert Campbell was typical.[89] "Now Campbell don't you get married as we want you for active service."

Allowances were made to the various members of the service in such luxuries as tea and other articles. The supply was very limited and smuggling was in many cases the result. Servants were given advantages in cheaper prices for their purchases. Private trade among the servants or officers in furs or leather was rigidly prohibited. Fines were imposed for misconduct and the returns added to a benefit fund in aid of disabled, aged, and retired servants—below the rank of clerks. Annual levies were made—chief factor, 40/; chief trader, 20/; clerk of £100 and upward, 5/; clerk under £100, 2/6; apprentice clerks and postmasters, 2/; labourer or mechanic of £20 and upward, 1/6; labourer or mechanic under £20, 1/. This arrangement was made in 1840, but the payments were increased in 1841 to 4/ on all salaries of £20 and under, and 1/ additional for every £10 of salary above £20. In 1840 an annual sum of £300 was set aside as a pension for clerks. Provision was made in the Deed Poll for retired partners and cases existed in which old and destitute partners were re-hired as clerks as in the case of James Hughes.[90] Interest was paid on moneys left with the Company of from 2½ to 3 per cent. Donations were made to missions and educational institutions from year to year and the governmental policy of the Company toward Red River was to an appreciable extent determined by these personnel considerations. On retiring from the service, men were encouraged to settle at Red River and various arrangements[91] were made in grants of land to retiring servants. It was estimated that six out of eight remained after the five-year contract expired, some remaining in the service for twenty-five to thirty years.[92]

[88]John McLean, *Twenty-five Years' Service*, II, 252.

[89]Robert Campbell, *Discovery and Exploration of the Youcon*; Can. Arch., Journal of Robert Campbell.

[90]Oliver, *The Canadian North-West*, I, 655.

[91]See a full description, Archer Martin, *The Hudson's Bay Company's Land Tenures, passim*; also I. Cowie, *The Company of Adventurers*, p. 73.

[92]Evidence of Sir George Simpson, *Report from the Select Committee on the Hudson's Bay Company*, 1857, pp. 69–70.

The problem of personnel on the Pacific coast was less complicated, but followed similar lines. After the amalgamation the posts were not reduced as in the east since the Hudson's Bay Company had not penetrated to this district and there was no duplication such as accompanied competition. Posts were established along the coast at Fort Langley, at Millbank Sound, and (after the lease of the Russian territory) at the mouths of the more important northern rivers. This expansion involved an increase in personnel and a shifting from the east. It was claimed that most of the new hands from Canada were sent to this district because of its difficulties. McLoughlin in a letter to Simpson dated March 20, 1844, wrote:

As you say the *Boutes* must be trained in the country, but the truth is the men are so miserably small and weak for years past we cannot find men of sufficient physical strength among the recruits to make efficient Boutes to replace our old hands. At present we have some Boutes who ten years ago were considered old and so little attention is paid to the selection of the men that in 1839 a man was sent here from Montreal who had only one finger and a thumb remaining on his hand; in 1840 we received another who has one of his arms withered . . . and among the recruits who have come here from 1839 to 1843 both inclusive, there is only one man who can serve for a Boute.[93]

The abandonment of the coast posts and the establishment of a coastal steamer led to the retirement of a number of men and as in Red River, the Company encouraged the settlement of its retired and discharged servants at Fort Vancouver.

Esprit de corps was evident as in the earlier periods especially among the transport brigades. A trip to the "Long Portage" entitled a *voyageur* to say, "Je suis un homme." In the latter part of the period demoralization of the service became conspicuous.[94] Larger quantities of goods were imported, population increased, wages increased in the settlement, and larger numbers were employed in freighting from the south. In 1851 Anderson complained that wages were too low to get good men. For the Portage la Loche brigade only boys and old men were available. In that year, low water, heavily loaded boats which broke easily on touching the shores, and a crew out of which only six men could carry two pieces, were factors demoralizing transportation. It was

[93]"Letter from Doctor John McLoughlin to Sir George Simpson, March 20, 1844," ed. K. B. Judson.

[94]For an excellent description of the demoralization see J. J. Hargrave, *Red River*, pp. 165–167; for a description of the importance and position of the guides in the Portage la Loche brigade, see *ibid.*, pp. 236–237.

necessary to break young men into the "line, collar and oar" and pay gratuities to the better hands. At the portage the men refused to work when horses and oxen were available, the neighbouring Indians were demoralized, and private trading was prevalent.[95] On the return trip from Portage la Loche to York Factory further difficulties were in evidence. In a letter to Robert Campbell dated Norway House, December 21, 1859, W. Sinclair wrote: "Many of them will come this far [Norway House] that will not go as far as York, it's the Lower River that is the stumbling block for procuring freighters." In the same year he wrote to Sir George Simpson in a letter dated November 14.[96]

The fall freight did not turn out so satisfactorily as could be wished for at York the Portage brigades refused to take the cargo offered them, 60 pieces, in the present state of water which was low, being 15 pieces less than they were bound to take. Some of the boats at that season came up from York in 18 days with forty pieces so that it could not have been so low as the year the rifles came up, a good deal of this is sheer insubordination and I have written Chief Factor McTavish about it, not to let it pass unnoticed as such conduct is becoming too frequent.

These difficulties hastened the movement in which goods were brought in from the south rather than York Factory. In a letter to Ermatinger date La Cloche, August 5, 1859, Robert Miles wrote: "The Red River freighters had agreed among themselves to make the Company pay a much higher freight in which they were disappointed by seeing that it is taken out of their hand via St. Pauls and I doubt not in a short time will rue the day of their abuse to the Company."[97]

The problem was not limited to the transport personnel. It became increasingly difficult to get men for the permanent staff. W. Sinclair in a letter to J. A. Clare, dated June 21, 1860, wrote:

I have intimated to you during the winter that it was rumored that the new hands intended refusing to go to Mackenzie River. Such is the case, five of them rebelled and would not go. I would not go to extremities to enforce them to go at the time but we shall find other means to thwart their intention of getting home or choosing to go where they think proper; upon no consideration are they to be permitted to return to Europe. My intention now is they be dispersed and sent to the distant posts, Trout

[95]See Can. Arch., Anderson Letter Books, Diary of Anderson's voyages from Simpson to Portage la Loche and return in 1856 and 1857; also Simpson to Good Hope and return and out *via* Portage la Loche to Norway House and Red River in 1858.

[96]Can. Arch., Norway House Letter Book, 1859–1862.

[97]Can. Arch., Ermatinger–Tod Papers, p. 321.

Lake, Dunvegan, Nelson's River, and some other place. None of them must be kept where flour, pork or pemmican are issued out in rations. One of the ringleaders I sent down to be sent out of the way of planning mischief. The Blacksmith murmured about doing any other duty excepting his trade, and refused to go to Mackenzie River unless to get a passage and not work. I was obliged to consent to his demands, tho' it is particularly contrary to the rules of the service. Tradesmen are subject to work on the passage from place to place and do what they can. By this opportunity four other servants are sent down. I cannot recommend any of them to be re-engaged. The only one worth engaging . . . asks for higher wages than he is worth.[98]

With poorer men, difficulties arose as to the allocation of the men between the posts. York Factory chose the best men, Norway House the next best, and the other departments received the remnant of lazy men and cripples. Selection on the basis of alphabetical order was suggested as a solution. The introduction of trade from the south necessitated a reorganization of the Company's arrangements all along the line.

An effective policy of monopoly control in the reduction of costs in the department necessitated the constant improvement of the communication system. The improvement of transport facilitated the extension of the express system of the preceding companies by which information on the activities of various districts could be immediately forwarded to headquarters and by which orders from headquarters could be dispatched to the districts. Within a department letters were sent and dispatched from various posts to headquarters on information respecting various needs of posts and their activities, on personnel, engagements, advances, requisitions, and so on. In the Mackenzie River department an express was dispatched as follows:

Posts	Arrival	Departure
Simpson	....	22 Jan. before daybreak
Norman	6 Feb. afternoon longer than usual because of snow.	7 Feb. daybreak
Good Hope	13 Feb. after sunset.	14 Feb. "
Peel River	27 Feb. forenoon	28 Feb. "
La Pierre's House	3 March after sunset	5 March "
Youcon	19 March noon	24 March early.

From information received at headquarters the chief factor made recommendation to the governor in chief regarding appointments,

[98]Can. Arch., Norway House Letter Book.

establishments, and general regulations. In the Northern department a winter express was sent from the depot and the interior, meeting at Carlton House. One proceeded northward *via* Isle à la Crosse and Athabasca and the other south *via* Cumberland and Norway House. In 1832 the southern express went *via* Fort Pelly and Norway House. Private letters brought by ship were sent from the depot to Norway House or Cumberland before the closing of navigation and forwarded to their destinations before the returns were brought down in the spring. Between departments a packet was sent from Sault Ste Marie to Red River on February 1 and a packet from Red River to the Southern department, Canada, and England on December 1. In 1836 a packet from Red River *via* St. Peters to England was sent on November 1. The following year one packet *via* St. Peters left October 21 and another packet (including duplicates of the earlier one) *via* Rainy Lake, December 21. In 1841 the usual winter packet between the Northern and Southern departments was discontinued and papers were sent from York to Red River and dispatched to Sault Ste Marie by Rainy Lake on January 20. Papers from Moose Factory were sent to Michipicoten arriving February 1. Michipicoten became the exchange point for communications between the Northern and the Southern departments.[99] In Hudson Bay a packet passed regularly between York Factory, Severn, Albany, and Moose Factory. From Columbia an express left Fort Vancouver about March 20, arrived at Norway House June 16, and returned from York Factory July 14. In 1827 this express proceeded to Edmonton, overland to Fort Assiniboine, and upstream with the leather brigade for New Caledonia and Jasper House to Athabasca Pass and Boat Encampment on the Columbia.[100]

In addition to the organization of expresses for communication between departments and posts, the affairs of the Company were regulated by inspection journeys which became more effective and numerous with improved transport.[101] From year to year Governor Simpson made his round of visits to the Councils and to the more important posts in the Eastern districts. Less frequently he visted the more remote department on the Pacific coast. He travelled at remarkable speed, leaving Lachine each year and proceeding by canoe with a picked crew up the Ottawa to Fort William and Norway House where

[99]Oliver, *The Canadian North-West*, I, 654.

[100]For an excellent description of the system of expresses and their improvement, see J. J. Hargrave, *Red River*, pp. 99–101, 155–159.

[101]See the detailed description of the journeys in Edward Ermatinger, "York Factory Express Journal . . . 1827–1828"; also David Douglas, *Journal . . . 1823–1827.*

he presided at the Council meetings. With the construction of the railroad to Chicago he went to Red River by that point and St. Paul. By these visits of inspection[102] he was able to gain a remarkable knowledge of the demands of the trade and to bring the trade under the control of a central organization.

The accounting methods of the Company were extended to provide more adequate control over the territory. At the depot (York Factory) control systems of accounts were kept for the interior districts. Accounts[103] of every district and of every officer and man were made out annually. Inventories were made out at every post on May 31— the closing date for each outfit. With these were included transfers from other posts and the invoices of goods received to show total receipts. Transfers to other posts and inventory of the following spring gave expenditures. Upon this was based, after allowing for competition in various areas, the indents or requisitions for the later years. Fur receipts were entered from day to day and the total was required to balance with the amount shipped. Provisions were handled in a similar way but with a wide margin. Each post was charged with its expenses of transportation, wages, interest, and other costs. The activities of each post from day to day were noted in journals[104] and an elaborate check was kept on each post manager and on each district manager.

Barter was carried on by a unit referred to as Made Beaver or M. B. The changing value of the beaver, especially the later decline in its importance and the fall in price (from 30s. to 32s. per pound in 1837 to 7s. or 8s. in 1854), necessitated the establishment of a unit other than the large beaver skin which was called Made Beaver. Other furs were sold by the Indian on the basis of a relatively fixed tariff. The changes were slight but with cheaper manufactured goods the tariff was reduced favourably to the Indian. Garry described the trade[105] in 1821:

---

[102]See the journal of Archibald McDonald, *Peace River*, ed. M. McLeod, for details of his journey in 1828; also Sir George Simpson, *Narrative of a Journey round the World during the Years 1841 and 1842*, I; "Letters of Sir George Simpson 1841–43," ed. J. Schafer; The Earl of Southesk, *Saskatchewan and the Rocky Mountains*, chaps. i, ii; J. J. Hargrave, *Red River*, chaps. i–vi. See other tours of inspection by Governor Dallas through the Northwest in 1862, *Red River*, pp. 237–241, and through Eastern territory in 1863, *ibid.*, pp. 293–296.

[103]See I. Cowie, *The Company of Adventurers*, pp. 225–227, for a discussion of the difficulties of a fixed tariff for the posts.

[104]*Ibid.*, pp. 280–283.

[105]"Diary of Nicholas Garry," pp. 199–200. For a description of trading see also R. M. Ballantyne, *Hudson's Bay*, pp. 38–39.

Beaver is the Standard to which all other skins are reduced and by which the Indians trade. For Instance should an Indian have the following Skins:—

Beaver, Whole or full grown	30 = 30	Whole Beaver
" , Half or cub	11 = 5½	" "
Otters, Prime, large	1 = 2	" "
" " , small	1 = 1	" "
Fox, Black, prime	1 = 2	" "
" , Red	3 = 1½	" "
" , White	4 = 2	" "
Martens	9 = 3	" "

After the Trader has examined the Skins he tells the Indian his Trade amounts to 4 Tens and 7 mores [sic] at the same Time gives the Indian 47 quils, signifying that he will give him Goods. The Indian will perhaps take:

A Gun	= 11	Quils
3 Yards Cloth	= 9	"
3 lb. of Powder	= 6	"
8 lb. of Shot	= 4	"
1 large Blanket	= 8	"
1 Hatchet	= 2	"
1 File	= 1	"
1 3-Gallon Kettle	= 6	"
	47	"

The Made Beaver[106] was valued at from one to two shillings and was perfected as a method of controlling accounts and as an index of efficiency. In competitive districts money displaced barter and weakened the Company's control over the trade.[107]

[106]See *The Fur Trade and the Hudson's Bay Company* (Chambers's Repository), p. 25. Anderson gives corrections and additions to the tariff cited in his Letter Books showing that the Company's actual tariff was much more favourable to the Indians. Anderson estimated that from 1850 to 1853 the cost of a Made Beaver being the expenses divided by the number of Made Beaver in the returns was about 7/11 on an average, and the value of a Made Beaver being the amount of the returns divided by the number of Made Beaver in them was on an average about 14/11. The objective of the manager was to decrease the cost of Made Beaver in goods and increase the value in furs.

[107]"Mildness and conciliation . . . with Indians . . .; an absence of interference in the quarrels of individuals, . . . and an invariable rule of avenging the murder by Indians of any of its servants, blood for blood, . . . are the three and only *principles* followed out by the Hudson's Bay Company . . .; and its sole *aim* is to derive the greatest possible revenue from that territory." In "*protected* territories, the value of goods bartered for furs is . . . under one twentieth of the value of those furs in England" and in unprotected territories with com-

In 1826 the Keith system of equipping Indians was adopted in various posts and a regular and fixed standard of debts given to the Indians was applied. Difficulties arose in the establishment of new posts, since the Indians occasionally left the old posts to trade with the new ones—for example, Peel River complained of the desertion of Indians to Good Hope, but these complaints were not numerous and were effectively met. The Indians' hunt varied from 50 to 200 beaver, the largest of which Ballantyne had heard being 250. As a general rule furs were brought twice yearly, October (autumn hunt) and March (winter hunt). Goods were given to the Indian to the extent of a certain number of skins dependent on his abilities as a hunter. The furs caught were brought in to cancel the debt. An excess in the value of the furs over the debt was paid by the Company in goods which the Indian demanded according to the fixed tariff. In addition, rewards were given to hunters as gratuities—such commodities as beads, knives, gun flints, gun worms, hooks, needles, thread, awls, gartering ribbons, and so on. Sir George Simpson estimated that 20 per cent of the outfit was made up of gratuities. In certain territories ammunition was sold only in exchange for provisions or was given as a gratuity. At Simpson gratuities included a few inches of tobacco, a fish, a few flints, awls, hooks, and a trifle of ammunition in proportion to their hunts.

Concentration of authority became evident even within the Northern Council. A new Deed Poll[108] was made out on June 6, 1834, which made no provision for a specified number of chief factors and chief traders but reduced the number of chief factors to 16 with 32 shares and raised the number of chief traders to 29 with 29 shares—a total of 61 shares.[109] Provision was made that any possible deficit should not be charged to an individual wintering partner. Throughout the period the number of active chief factors declined and the number of chief traders increased. In 1863 the shares were distributed among 15 chief factors, 30 shares; 37 chief traders, 37 shares; 10 retired chief factors, 13 shares, 10 retired chief traders, 5 shares; total 85 shares.[110]

---

petitive prices of furs, two to ten times greater than in protected regions. A. Simpson, *Life of Thomas Simpson*, pp. 418–419. The entire value of furs traded averaged less than £200,000 per annum. In one year it was £211,000 and the net profits for that year were £119,000. *Ibid.*, p. 420.

[108]For further details and a list of chief factors and chief traders appointed and promoted under the old and new Deed Polls with the date of their appointments see Oliver, *The Canadian North-West*, I, 624–625.

[109]Cf. "Diary of Nicholas Garry," p. 182.

[110]Beckles Willson, *The Great Company*, II, 281.

The increasing importance of the lower ranks is shown in the period from 1830 to 1843 for the Northern department.[111] The number of chief factors declined from 13 to 11 but was as low as 7 in 1837; the number of chief traders declined from 15 to 13 but was as low as 9 in 1841, and the number of clerks increased from 39 in 1830 to 43 in 1843 and reached a high point of 49 in 1840; the number of postmasters increased from 8 to 23 and the number of interpreters from 5 to 8. The number attending the council meetings and the number of chief factors and chief traders allocated to posts and districts are valuable indices of the trend toward concentration. The number of chief factors attending the Council meetings declined from 12 in 1830 to 3 in 1843 and the total attendance including chief traders declined from 15 in 1830 to 5 in 1843. The reaction of the partners is suggestive as shown in the following extracts. Regarding the Deed Poll of 1834 a letter written by Tod to Ermatinger dated York Factory, July 21, 1834 notes:

The return of Govr. Simpson once more to the Indn. Country, You must know, has introduced a very considerable change into the Concern, which is now extended to an indefinite period of time. The number of C.F.'s are to be reduced to Sixteen & that of C.T.'s increased in proportion (so much more in favour of clerks) but the power of nomination is entirely taken from the former & vested solely in the hands of the Company, the latter have also assumed the right of dismissing from their employ (commissioned or non commissioned) all or any who may hereafter become either incapacitated or troublesome whether disposed to retire or not—such, however, are to be allowed an interest in the Concern Six years after retiring.[112]

The declining importance of the Council was described in a letter from Robert Miles to Ermatinger dated La Cloche, August 5, 1859:

Sir George & Hopkins I hear reached Montreal the 16th July—the Western Brigades being detained by Ice at the Grand Rapid, he was waiting at Norway House for them Seven days, consequently he did their business for them before hand & Settled their Council in one day.—This is brisk work & must fully carry out the terms of the Deed Poll with respect to the business assigned therein to the Councillors—Bah![113]

Not only did the Council decline in importance but there were complaints that the Governor promoted those who were most likely

111Extracted from Oliver, *The Canadian North-West.*
112Can. Arch., Ermatinger–Tod Papers.
113*Ibid.*

to submit to centralized control. Wintering partners trained in the organization of the Northwest Company were gradually replaced by younger partners trained in the methods of the new discipline. Sir George Simpson's control over Robert Campbell contrasted strikingly with his lack of control over the old partners. The biographies of John McLoughlin and Sir James Douglas are interesting parallels. The bitterness incidental to the old rivalry of the Northwest Company disappeared with the elimination of the more discontented partners. The complaints of patronage were evidence of the increasing power of the Governor. Sinclair in a letter to Ermatinger dated Fort Frances, Rainy Lake, August 1, 1835, wrote:

One of Mr. Logan's Daughters dead as also a Son of Gov. Simpson for which some of the Gentlemen are wearing Black Crap.—on their hats, Mr. Stuart to distinguish himself from the other Mourners has for Want of Blac Crap an Old sooty Coloured, Canton Crape scarf, with half a yard of it dangling at his back, he looks More like a Wolf, than a human being—all this is in the way of Courting favor.[114]

In a letter to Ermatinger dated Columbia, Cowlitz Plain, February, 1840, Tod wrote:

But the Service is at present absolutely swarming with Finlaysons, Simpsons,[115] & Mackenzies, so that few others, no matter what their qualifications may be, stand any chance—Friend Work on his way to Vancouver last fall was induced to remain here with me two Nights during which many a long philipic was held forth on the privations of the Service & this "Cursed Country" but he is as far as ever from coming to any determination about quitting it.[116]

The tendency was in the direction of close control such as had characterized the policy of the Hudson's Bay Company in Hudson

[114]*Ibid.*

[115]Aemilius Simpson died at Nass, September 2, 1831; Alexander Simpson was in the service; Thomas Simpson complained of lack of promotion. A. Simpson, *Life of Thomas Simpson*, p. 81. Clerks' salaries were £20 to £100 per year. Chief traders received $\frac{1}{850}$ of the whole profits of the Company, chief factors $\frac{8}{850}$. Thomas Simpson joined the company in 1829, his apprenticeship to last two years (*ibid.*, p. 51); he was to receive £40 for the first year and £50 for the second year. He went to Norway House as Governor Simpson's secretary, returning to Lachine. Wages in the Hudson's Bay Company were £17 per year for labouring men and they could purchase supplies from its stores at moderate prices. French Canadians "of the old voyageur parishes" refused to work for such terms; Thomas Simpson took nearly a hundred recruits from Lachine in 1830; he went to York Factory. He went to Red River in February, 1831, and spent the next five years there making annual trips to York Factory.

[116]Can. Arch., Ermatinger–Tod Papers.

Bay. In 1821 Nicholas Garry wrote, "I fear the old Hudson's Bay servants are too fond of old regulations to encourage a new branch of trade and innovations." This attitude was encouraged by the policy of the Company throughout the period.

The effectiveness with which the trading territory was brought under the control of the central authorities was the cause of dissatisfaction among the partners of the interior who had been accustomed to Northwest Company methods which gave the individual partner control of his territory and stimulated interest in the trade. The fur trade continued to depend on an aggressive personnel and on the ability of the individual trader. The possibilities of expansion had largely disappeared and aggressiveness became less important but it remained essential to the successful conduct of the trade especially in remote areas. In these areas and in areas under the control of individuals trained in the Northwest Company the struggle between the old and the new disciplines was waged. In the Mackenzie River and the Yukon, the Columbia, and Labrador, the victory was in many cases with the old.

In the opening of new districts in which increasing costs, possibilities of competition, and heavy interest charges were appreciable factors, central control was not conducive to effective prosecution of the trade. Friction which existed between John McLoughlin as chief factor of the Columbia department and Sir George Simpson[117] was partly a result of conflict between Northwest Company methods and the Hudson's Bay Company's methods, and partly a result of personal animosity but these were undoubtedly accentuated by geographic considerations. John McLean's difficulties in opening up the Ungava and Labrador districts, his resignation from the Company, and his later hostility were largely the result of friction with Governor Simpson and the Council intensified by geographic factors.[118] The Mackenzie River district may be chosen as a specific example of the general problem. Numerous complaints came from this district of discrimination. In the long journeys goods arrived in bad condition and there were protests against pilfering for which it was difficult to fix responsibility, since the goods had been transferred through many hands. There were complaints of broken crockery, of the loss of a bale of valuable dry goods (the valuable goods had not been packed equally

---

[117]See "Dr. John McLoughlin's Last Letter to the Hudson's Bay Company, 1845," ed. K. B. Judson, and "Letter from Doctor John McLoughlin to Sir George Simpson, March 20, 1844," ed. K. B. Judson.

[118]See complaints regarding Simpson's arbitrary measures in John McLean, *Twenty-five Years' Service*, especially II, chap. xvi, and letter to Sir George Simpson, Portage la Loche, August 3, 1844, pp. 237 f.

among the other bales), axes sent from York Factory were bad, provisions were inadequate, Red River portage straps and oxhide shoes were of poor quality. The controversy over the management of the Yukon Territory from Mackenzie River between Governor Simpson and Chief Factor Anderson illustrates more specifically the problem of central control. Robert Campbell received every encouragement through letters and promotion in establishing posts in the Yukon district from Governor Simpson, whereas Anderson consistently advocated their abandonment. Anderson reported a loss for Frances Lake, Pelly Banks, and Fork Selkirk for the outfits of 1848–49–50 of £1,467 and on the 1851 outfit for Fort Selkirk of £383.10.2. The post had never paid and the loss was largely occasioned by transport costs. On the 1851 outfit for Fort Selkirk the goods cost £147.3.0, Youcon and Peel River transferred to it, £87.17.6, and wages totalled £387.0.0 making a total expenditure of £622.0.6 for which there were returns in fur and leather of £238.10.4 and a loss of £383.10.2. In a letter from Fort Simpson dated November 30, 1852, Anderson advised the abandonment of Fort Selkirk on the following grounds: (1) If the fort were re-established the Indians would have to be punished and this would require a large complement of men. (2) The post could never pay because of the distance from the market and it would be necessary to send out the most valuable fur (fox and marten) first, to prevent a loss of interest. Returns reached the market in the seventh year and in some cases in the tenth year, and six years' interest was added to cost of goods as well as to wages. (3) Competition with the low tariff of the Chilcats. He complained that goods were actually bought by Indian middlemen at Lynn Canal from the Hudson's Bay Company coast steamer and sold in competition with Fort Selkirk goods. With persistent agitation of this character Anderson was able to write that the governor had yielded to his views in abandoning Frances Lake and other posts. The complaints of A. H. Murray[119] as to his difficulties in competing with the Russians at Fort Yukon[120] further illustrate the problem of control in distant areas. Requisitions for commodities in great demand, such as guns and beads, could be filled only after a long period of time had elapsed. Beaver and marten alone could be purchased, and muskrats were refused because of the low value and heavy transportation costs, with serious results to the Indian trade. Resort to questionable methods of trade was essential.

[119]A. H. Murray, *Journal of the Yukon, 1847–48.*
[120]See Canada, Dept. of the Interior, *Certain Correspondence of the Foreign Office and of the Hudson's Bay Company* on the problem of the Yukon.

Hostilities with Indian middlemen, more expensive provisioning, and higher prices were important considerations. The Indians insisted on commissioned officers for their posts and a more expensive personnel. The Chilcats (coast Indians and middlemen) preferred leather par dressed with the result that the Company was also obliged to accept it. Robert Campbell's difficulties with these middlemen in the destruction of Dease Lake and Fort Selkirk were notorious. The gains of the Company which were incidental to monopoly control were offset in part by losses which followed too rigid an application of methods of control especially in the more remote districts. A decline in morale was accompanied by unwise and expensive decisions of the central body.

The success of monopoly control over costs was measured from the pecuniary point of view in terms of net profits and of dividends to the shareholders and wintering partners. But net profits were also dependent on the number of furs sold and the price for which they were sold. If the Company was in a position to restrict the supply of furs on the European market and to raise the price, net profits were increased. If the Company could increase the supply of furs with a stable price, net profits would again be increased. It is possible that the Company through attempts to determine fashions and in other ways was able to increase the price of furs but the evidence of these activities is extremely slight and it is probable as a result of competition from fur produced in Russia and other areas that its control over the market was not material.

In the production of furs the Company was not in a position to expand its territory to any great extent. New posts were established on the fringes of the earlier territory in the Yukon and Labrador[121] but the contributions were not significant.[122] The Company was mainly concerned therefore with the territory previously covered by the two separate companies and especially by the Northwest Company. After the amalgamation steps were taken to nurse back the beaver supply

[121]Samuel Robertson at Sparr Point and French Canadians were sending furs and seal oil to Quebec about 1833. Agents of the Fur and Fish Company received food, clothing, and $80 per year. See *Audubon and his Journals*, I, Labrador Journal, 1833, pp. 343–445.

[122]On the journey of Samuel Black up the Finlay River in 1824, see J. N. Wallace, "The Explorer of Finlay River in 1824," *Can. Hist. Rev.*, March, 1928, pp. 25–32; also correspondence, *ibid.*, June, 1928, pp. 156–160; and extracts of the diary, P. L. Haworth, *On the Headwaters of Peace River*; and G. Bryce, *Remarkable History*, pp. 291–294. On the death of Black see *Traits of American Indian Life and Character*, by a Fur Trader, chap. xii.

in territories which had been exhausted in the period of competition. In the Minutes of Council, 1825, it was directed: "Indians—Beaver hunting in summer discouraged; Nelson Lake Indians to be discouraged hunting beaver." Five years later it was ordered[123]

that the different District in the Northern Department be restricted to not exceeding the following number of Beaver for the Current Outfit, founded on an average list of returns for three years as expressed in number 131.

Minutes of Council 1826, viz.:—

Athabasca	5000	Winnipeg	50
Saskatchewan	5500	Norway Ho.	120
English River	650	Island Lake	100
Cumberland	150	Nelson River	400
Swan River	400	York & Churchill	300

[total 12670]

In the regulations of 1833 it was urged

that Gentlemen in charge of Districts and Posts, except such as are exposed to opposition, exert their utmost efforts in discouraging the hunting of Cub Beaver and beaver out of season, and that no Beaver traps be issued from the Depot, except for sale to the Piegan Indians, and that in any cases where an unusual proportion of Cub or unseasoned Beaver appears the same be particularly represented to the Governor & Committee.[124]

Similar regulations were passed in the next decade. The Company's measures were apparently not wholly successful, chiefly, it was stated,[125] because the Indians converted the beaver skins into clothing when they were not allowed to sell them. In 1841 the situation was serious:

The impoverishment of the Country in the article of Beaver is increasing to such an alarming extent that it becomes necessary to take effectual measures for providing an immediate remedy; to that end it is Resolved
90. That the Gentlemen in charge of Districts and Posts be strictly enjoined to discourage the Hunting of Beaver by every means in their power; and that not more than half the number collected Outfit 1839 be traded during the Current and two ensuing Outfits at the undermentioned Districts and Posts [25 posts Northern department, 7 posts Southern de-

123Minutes of Council, 1830, in Oliver, *The Canadian North-West*, I, 654.
124Minutes of Council, 1833, *ibid.*, II, 704; see also "Standing Rules and Regulations XIII," No. 41, 1836, *ibid.*, p. 754.
125John McLean, *Twenty-Fve Years' Service*, II, 265 f.

partment] and as a further remedy for the evil; if it be found that Gentlemen disregard this instruction as they have done many others issued from time to time for the same object, it is Resolved

91. That the Governors and Committee be respectfully advised to give notice of retirement from the Service to such Gentlemen as may not give effect to the spirit and letter of the Resolutions . . .

92. That all Indians at Posts where this restriction exists and who do not kill Beaver be paid in Goods the value of 10 Skins of Made Beaver for every 9 Skins in small Furs they trade in course of the year.[126]

According to Governor Simpson, in the latter part of the period the exchange of goods for furs was arranged to encourage the production of cheaper furs. These furs—muskrat and others—were paid for at a higher rate in proportion to value than the finer furs. Consequently the finer fur-bearing animals were protected and the cheaper and more abundant fur-bearing animals were exploited.

The Company not only attempted to conserve its supply of furs by direct regulations but was also in a position to carry into effect regulations providing for the largest returns from sales. In 1836 it was resolved that no common cub skins be traded because of the high duties in England. In 1839 with the low price of muskrat in England, prices were reduced throughout the whole Northern department; no small rats were taken and 12 large rats were made equal to 1 Made Beaver. In Red River[127] competition necessitated a higher price and 10 large rats were equal to 1 Made Beaver. In 1840 only half the quantities of lynx and musquash sent to England in 1839 were forwarded. In 1841 regulations permitted the purchase of spring rats only at 12 per Made Beaver in both the Northern and Southern departments and only half of the rats retained at York Fort in 1840 together with the Mackenzie River outfit were sent. In 1842 only spring rats were to be purchased at 10 per Made Beaver in the Northern department. No small or damaged rats were purchased, and only 500,000 were sent to England (Southern department, 1839–40 outfits, 183,000, and 1841 outfit, 90,000; Mackenzie River, 1841 outfit, 30,000; Northern department, outfits 1839–40 at York Factory, 234,000). Monopoly control was effective in controlling the production and sale of the cheaper furs as in the case of muskrat. In the remote districts, to which costs of

[126]Minutes of Council, 1841, *The Canadian North-West*, II, 831–833; Minutes of Council, 1842, *ibid.*, pp. 849–850; Minutes of Council, 1843, *ibid.*, pp. 865–866.

[127]G.-A. Belcourt, *Mon Itinéraire du Lac des Deux-Montagnes à la Rivière Rouge.*

transportation were high, the cheaper, bulkier furs were restricted and the lighter, dearer furs encouraged through adjustments of the tariff and other regulations. In the Yukon guns alone were given in exchange for marten and black fox. Other commodities were sold at high prices, traps at 15 Made Beaver each. Ammunition and tobacco were only allowed for trade and not for debt. The difficulties of transporting dressed moose leather led to restrictions as to the quantity traded. Only cheap articles such as ammunition and tobacco could be exchanged for leather. Rats and beaver were not accepted at Fort Norman and the Indians were directed to hunt marten and fox. At Fort Rae only prime spring rats were taken and in limited numbers. Provisions were accepted in 1851 at a definitely lower rate—1 Made Beaver in furs, 2/, and in provisions, 1/. But these ratios varied in different areas. In 1853 at Fort Simpson 1 pt. of powder = 7 Made Beaver of furs or 12 Made Beaver of meat; 12 balls = 1 Made Beaver of furs; 8 balls = 1 Made Beaver of meat. These rates were found to stifle the industry of the Indian and to lead to recklessness. New rates were 7 Made Beaver = 2 lb. powder, 1 lb. shot, and 20 balls. On the Yukon where animals were more numerous 7 Made Beaver = 1¾ lb. powder, 5¼ lb. shot, and 15 balls.

The policy of controlling production became more effective through a careful study of the needs of the trade and of particular tribes. Eskimos demanded files and axes. Shells, beads, and special types of knives were imported for the Yukon trade. The trade followed cyclical fluctuations—in a poor rabbit season demands for blankets, cloth, and capotes were much greater. Fox and marten because of their value and lightness were in greatest demand and the staple trading articles, ammunition, flint, knives, steels, and axes, were reserved for these furs. Rats were not accepted, accepted in limited quantities, or sold to the servants for clothing.

The tariff was a mechanism by which the Company was able to carry out its policies in conserving furs, in controlling the supply marketed, and in making the largest possible returns.[128] Its effectiveness was seriously impaired with increase in trade from the south and the weakening of the Company's monopoly position. Following the amalgamation, the charter of the Company gave control over the Hudson Bay drainage basin, with the exception of territory which had been sold to Lord Selkirk. The Pacific coast drainage basin and the territory beyond the Hudson Bay drainage basin was controlled under a grant

[128]John McLean, *Twenty-five Years' Service*, II, 227.

dated December 5, 1821, which gave exclusive rights to trade with the Indians

in all such parts of North America to the northward and the westward of the lands and territories belonging to the United States of America as shall not form part of any of our provinces in North America, or of any lands or territories belonging to the said United States of America, or to any European government, state or power . . . for the full period of 21 years. . . .[129]

This grant was extended in 1838 for an additional twenty years.[130]

The territory which had been sold to Lord Selkirk in the Red River district and which became the centre of Red River settlement was the cause of considerable difficulty. Nicholas Garry pointed out numerous problems[131] in the "control of the Selkirk estate." "The Hudson Bay service is put to much inconvenience by the arrival of the colonists." "Military protection and laws must be introduced at the colony." These were typical comments. John West, a missionary to Red River, wrote on May 24, 1822:

It was now hinted to me that the interest I was taking in the education of the native children had already excited the fears of some of the chief factors and traders to the extent to which it might be carried. Though a few conversed liberally with me on the subject there were others who were apprehensive that the extension of knowledge among the natives and the locating them in agricultural pursuits where practicable would operate as an injury to the fur trade.[132]

These fears were justified as competition and petty trade were in evidence at an early date. A letter of March 27, 1822, ordered

that Mr. Clarke be directed to exert himself to the utmost in putting an immediate and complete stop to the Petty Traders from Canada or from the United States, who have for some time past been carrying on an unauthorized Traffic in Furs upon the Red River with the Indians and other persons within the Company's Territories.[133]

[129]*Report from the Select Committee on the Hudson's Bay Company*, 1857, pp. 425–427.

[130]See the correspondence in *Papers relating to the Hudson's Bay Company 1842–70*.

[131]"Diary of Nicholas Garry," *passim*.

[132]John West, *Journal*, p. 92.

[133]Oliver, *The Canadian North-West*, I, 640; see a letter on the difficulties of jurisdiction between the Company and the colony on the suppression of petty trade from the Governor, Deputy Governor, and Committee of Hudson's Bay Company to George Simpson, May 21, 1823, *ibid.*, p. 240, also p. 633.

To obtain more complete control the Company acquired[134] the territory of Assiniboia from the Selkirk estate in 1834. Control of the supply of furs in the face of competition from the south was strengthened through an agreement dated March 21, 1833, in which the Hudson's Bay Company paid £300 annually to the American Fur Company for withdrawing from Rainy Lake, Winnipeg, and Red River districts.[135] In 1840 the two companies agreed to oppose a third party in the same districts.[136] Through these arrangements the Hudson's Bay Company reduced its complement of servants in the district and carried on the trade more economically.[137]

The Red River settlement was a vulnerable point in the defences of the Company and these arrangements were eventually doomed to failure. Petty trade proved difficult to check and in spite of drastic measures continued to increase. Methods of checking private trade in Red River have been an important subject in most of the histories of western Canada.[138] Improvement of transportation facilities to the south made control impossible and it became necessary to meet competition—as in the territory subordinate to Missouri, in buffalo robes—with the informal weapon of a higher price.[139] In 1847 large numbers of buffalo robes[140] were sold in St. Paul at $3.50 each by settlers from Red River. Exports of furs in 1856 from Pembina and Red River through St. Paul, according to one statement,[141] included "64,292 rats; 8,276 minks; 1,428 martens; 876 foxes; 3,600 coons; 1,045 fishers; . . . 2,542 rit foxes; . . . 7,500 buffalo robes" and other furs,

---

[134]June 6, 1834, Chester Martin, *Lord Selkirk's Work in Canada*, p. 223. For a description of the activities of the colony under the Selkirk *régime*, see *The Canadian North-West*, I, 154.

[135]*The Canadian North-West*, II, 716.

[136]*Ibid.*, pp. 805–806.

[137]*Ibid.*, p. 698.

[138]For a discussion of the development of free trade see D. Gunn and C. R. Tuttle, *History of Manitoba*, chaps. x f.; also an excellent account given by H. G. Gunn, "The Fight for Free Trade in Rupert's Land"; Evidence of Sir George Simpson, *Report from the Select Committee on the Hudson's Bay Company*, 1857, pp. 80–81; Evidence of Lieut. Col. W. Caldwell, *ibid.*, especially pp. 305 f.; Evidence of Mr. John McLaughlin, *ibid.*, pp. 262 f.; Evidence of Rev. Griffith Owen Corbett, *ibid.*, pp. 146 f.; also John P. Pritchett, "Some Red River Fur-Trade Activities"; and Clarence W. Rife, "Norman W. Kittson, a Fur-Trader at Pembina."

[139]Minutes of Council, 1833, in Oliver, *The Canadian North-West*, II, 695; also 1836, p. 731.

[140]*Beaver*, January, 1921.

[141]*Report from the Select Committee on the Hudson's Bay Company*, 1857, p. 125.

valued at $97,000. Prices paid by competitors were responsible.[142] The American Fur Company, for example, paid for otter skins $3.50 compared with 6/ from the Hudson's Bay Company; $2.00 for fisher compared with 2/; $3.25 for beaver compared with 6/; $15.00 for silver fox compared with 10/, and in the case of summer and yearling buffalo robes the latter company refused to purchase them.

Competition spread to the interior. In 1859 free traders Whitway and Harper outfitted at Red River and traded at Norway House. After 1861 the free trader[143] began to penetrate the Saskatchewan area[144] and in 1862 he was trading at Cumberland House. At Norway House the free trader competed effectively with such commodities as tea, sugar, and fancy light and pink cottons and the villagers began to take furs to Red River.[145] W. Sinclair wrote to Sir George Simpson on July 11, 1860: "They come and trade with the York and Oxford House Indians during the time of tripping in the summer—this arises from the high prices given for furs at Red River." In 1862 the free trader was threatening the Nelson River district. Complaints arose of independent trading between the trippers of the Mackenzie River brigade and the Portage brigade and the guide was accused of trading. To check this competition the Company found it necessary to raise the tariff at competitive points. Further, the number of traders at these points was increased and a personnel built up to hold subposts and to travel to various points for furs. A report on the causes of a decline in profits from 1858 to 1860 at Norway House was illuminating. These causes included an increase of the fur tariff in 1859 in which the price of marten was doubled, an increase in trippers' wages to equal the wages of Red River settlement, an increase in the consumption of colonial produce which in turn had increased in price, a decline in the most important post, Nelson River, through greater consumption of produce and the additional expense, including a boat in which to import this produce, and a loss on tea, sugar, tobacco—low-priced bulky commodities which could not be sold to pay the freight in the sales shop. For the men a 50 per cent tariff was not adequate to pay

[142]*Ibid.*, p. 283.

[143]J. J. Hargrave, *Red River*, pp. 232–233; I. Cowie, *The Company of Adventurers*, pp. 361–362.

[144]"Three Wesleyan missionaries have come in for Lac la Pluie and the Saskatchewan; and furs have fallen 15 to 20 per cent. in price. Ominous signs these." Letter of Thomas Simpson, Red River, June 5, 1840, in A. Simpson, *Life of Thomas Simpson*, p. 351.

[145]See a description of Red River, *ibid.*, pp. 86–87. Firewood was becoming scarce and the cast-iron stove being used.

33⅓ per cent on the York Factory cost and 15/ freight on each piece, and for the officers a 33⅓ per cent tariff involved a loss. Finally a larger number of men were employed in providing buildings as a result of the new policy of importing from the United States.

A contributing factor to the development of competition was the constant decline in the supply of valuable furs in the more southern districts.[146] The decrease of the fur trade from 1803–1804 to 1857 in the southern district of the Hudson Bay territory and the northern states was estimated by Ellice at one-half or two-thirds. An increase in the number of trappers and more effective methods of trapping[147] were responsible for the persistent decline. According to John McLean[148] the Company met competition by general instructions to destroy fur-bearing animals along the frontier "so as to offer no inducement to petty traders to encroachment on the Company's limits." But these devices probably defeated their own ends. Increase in settlement was fatal to monopoly control of furs and indeed to the large supply of furs.

On the Pacific coast similar tendencies were in evidence. The licence agreement of 1821 and the renewal of 1838 were supported by various arrangements in the attempts to prevent competition. In this field the advantages of a large central organization, such as the Hudson's Bay Company, were evident in the diplomatic negotiations[149] with the home government. The close relationship between the large central organizations of the fur trade and the home government was still a characteristic feature. In securing the licence and its extension, in the arrangements for leasing Russian territory, in the grant of Vancouver Island, in the investigation of 1857, and in the numerous boundary disputes in the Oregon territory, the position of the Company was greatly strengthened by its diplomatic representatives.[150]

[146]*Report from the Select Committee on the Hudson's Bay Company*, 1857, pp. 32–37. On the decline in beaver see *ibid.*, p. 316. For evidence on the decrease in shipments from the United States of finer furs and increase in the cheaper furs, see H. Poland, *Fur-bearing Animals*, pp. xxviii–xxxiii.

[147]See a description of various fur-bearing animals and of methods of trapping in the vicinity of Fort Carlton, Viscount Milton and W. B. Cheadle, *North-West Passage by Land*, pp. 98–102, 161–162.

[148]J. McLean, *Twenty-Five Years' Service*, II, 262–263.

[149]See *Papers relating to the Hudson's Bay Company 1842–1870*. See a most interesting description of the diplomacy exercised in securing a renewal of the licence in 1838. Extracts from James Douglas's notebook, 1841, relating to his conversations with Sir George Simpson, W. N. Sage, *Sir James Douglas and British Columbia*.

[150]Oliver, *The Canadian North-West*, II, 791–797.

As a result of negotiations with the home government and Russia an agreement dated February 6, 1839,[151] with the Russian American Company gave the Hudson's Bay Company a lease for ten years of the coast and the interior country between Cape Spencer and latitude 54°40′ for an annual rental of 2,000 seasoned land otter skins taken from the west side of the Rocky Mountains. The Hudson's Bay Company also agreed to sell all the seasoned land otter skins collected in the west side (not exceeding 2,000 skins at 23/ sterling per skin), 3,000 seasoned land otter skins taken on the east side of the mountains at 32/ per skin; 2,000 Fenagos (126 lb. each) of wheat in 1840 and 4,000 Fenagos each year thereafter at 10/9; 160 cwt. wheat flour, 18/5; 130 cwt. peas, 13/; 130 cwt. grits and hulled pot barley, 13/; 300 cwt. salted beef, 20/; 160 cwt. salted butter, 56/; 30 cwt. pork hams 6d. per lb. for 9 years. British manufactured goods for the Russian American Company were brought from England at £13 per ton. Later the rental paid in otter skins was changed to £1,500 per year. These companies also made agreements restricting the sale of liquor to the Indians.[152] The arrangements were important to the Company in supplying a steady market for furs and for the surplus agricultural produce of the Columbia district. In 1842, 3,000 prime otter and 150 fisher were sold to the Russian American Company. Otter skins were brought from the Montreal department and from Albany and disposed of in this market.

But competition was inevitable. In the early part of the period traders in the southern territory[153] led hunting expeditions to the interior in search of beaver and followed the methods used before 1821. In 1826 the Snake expedition brought in 2,188 beaver skins or 2,817 pounds, and 79 other skins at a total cost of £1,513.9.15, or 13/4 per Made Beaver. If the beaver sold at 20/ it was estimated the transaction would clear 100 per cent. But this was exceptional. In 1827 Americans were competing near Fort Colville and competition along the Columbia was regarded as serious since Columbia beaver sold at the highest prices and commanded 5/ more per skin than that of New Caledonia. Competition was also in evidence on the coast and necessitated the establishment of posts to the north. In 1831 the coast returns of the

---

[151]Sir George Simpson, *Narrative of a Journey round the World*, I, 226; also agreement prohibiting use of spirituous liquors on the Northwest coast, May 13, 1842, *Report from the Select Committee on the Hudson's Bay Company*, 1857, pp. 368–369.

[152]H. A. Innis, "Rupert's Land in 1825," pp. 310, 316.

[153]Can. Arch., McLeod Papers.

Company were 3,000 beaver skins costing £1,600 and of these Fort Langley produced more than one-half. In 1832, three American vessels were competing along the coast but in that year for the first time 2,000 skins brought a gain of £1,613. Of the different units in the Columbia department the Vancouver sale shop was the most profitable, giving returns of £3,147.13.11 out of a total of £17,481.5 in outfit 1843, and of £3,838.2.5 out of a total of £14,503.17.2 in outfit 1842. Other valuable units were the Snake expedition in 1842, £2,405.12.8, but this declined to £1,225.6.10 in 1843; Langley Fort, £1,702.16.10 in 1842 and £1,892.10.4 in 1843; Simpson Fort, £1,486.2.4 in 1842 and £2,566.10.1 in 1843; McLoughlin Fort declined from £1,465.9.3 in 1842 to £748.12.6 in 1843. The Russian Transfer brought £1,460.17.9 in 1842 and £1,430.5.0 in 1843. The Vancouver Indian trade increased from £1,186.16.10 to £2,273.14.6. The California establishment was changed from a loss of £2,813.8.11 in 1842 to a gain of £1,848.5.7 in 1843. The steamer *Beaver* brought returns of £1,153.17.5 in the latter year. The Vancouver depot was carried at a loss of £1,213.3.1 in 1842 and of £991.18.11 in 1843. The total profit increased from £7,687.6 in 1842 to £13,706.6 in 1843. The value of the Columbia department as a whole is difficult to determine. McLoughlin reported a gain of £22,974 for outfit 1841 but Simpson held that actual profits were £1,474; from a gain of £16,982 in 1842 he made out a loss of £4,003, and from a gain of £21,726 in 1843 he made a loss of £3,136, the discrepancy being the result, according to Simpson, of an overvaluation of 25 per cent. Simpson's estimate probably represented a more accurate survey of the situation. Settlement as at Red River was responsible for the breakdown of monopoly. Settlers from the United States occasioned the loss of Oregon in 1846. The gold rush led to a constant northern migration from California after 1849 and to British Columbia in 1857. With the rush of immigration the monopoly agreements of the Company disappeared.

The net results of the Company's policies were shown in the supply of furs. Statistics[154] of the sales of furs by the Hudson's Bay Company are suggestive of general tendencies. The sale of beaver decreased gradually to 1844 and 1850 as a result of the policy of nursing the beaver territories and of the substitution of silk hats which became more marked after 1839. After 1859 beaver ceased to be sold by the

[154]E. T. Seton, *The Arctic Prairies*, p. 110; also statistics in H. Poland, *Fur-bearing Animals*; and H. A. Innis, *The Fur Trade of Canada*, pp. 77–79. For statistics of Canadian production, 1830–31, see Henry Bliss, *The Colonial System*.

pound—conclusive evidence of the disappearance in the consumption of beaver for beaver hats. Exports of beaver, however, increased steadily to 1869 as a result of competition from the south. With allowances for varying regulations and their enforcement, for uncertain transportation facilities (returns from York Factory and Main River not arriving one year and two years' returns coming the following year), and for natural fluctuations of beaver, the effects of monopoly control were conspicuous. A decline in control led to increase in exports. With marten, production was closely related to expansion in the Mackenzie, the Yukon territories, and remote areas in which the Company exercised an effective monopoly control. A steady demand accounted for a steady supply with the usual periodic fluctuations. Fluctuations in beaver returns possibly influenced the returns in marten but the supply was remarkably steady. Fox on the other hand increased steadily throughout the period reaching the highest point in 1868, again as a result of increasing competition in the southern territories. Wolf fluctuated in a more pronounced fashion, the exports increasing to a marked extent from 1839 to 1860, largely the result of competition in the plains areas. Fisher increased steadily to the highest point in 1869. Otter fluctuated violently from 1821 to 1838 and increased steadily from that date to the highest point in 1865. Bear increased steadily throughout the period. Lynx remained steady with the typical cyclical fluctuations. Skunk appeared in the returns after 1850. Raccoon became more important from 1860 to 1870, badger appeared after 1840, and rabbit was uncertain until 1845. Muskrat increased in importance but was definitely controlled. During the latter part of the period cheaper southern furs assumed a more important position and furs in which the company exercised a monopoly tended to remain stationary.

Estimates of the production of districts are scarce but the existing evidence points to the effectiveness of monopoly control. In 1821 the Mackenzie River district (a monopoly district) supplied 111 packs; in 1822, 122 packs and 3 kegs of castoreum valued on 1820 prices at £12,000; in 1823, 134 packs, 3 kegs castoreum, 12 packs of leather; and in 1827, 157 packs of fur. The district produced 154 packs in 1831 at a profit of £1,263. In 1852 Liard River returns totalled 32 packs of fur including 4,200 marten, 1,582 beaver, and 85 bear. McLean estimated the annual returns of Mackenzie River district as £12,000 and the outfit about £1,200.[155] In 1844 the returns of the

[155]John McLean, *Twenty-five Years' Service*, II, 254.

district exceeded £15,000.[156] Returns for outfits 1844–45–46 (the largest to that period) were £77,622 with a sale of 120,569 marten. For the period 1853–54–55, the returns had increased to £90,027 with 137,132 marten. The increase was the result of monopoly control as shown in the energetic direction of Anderson and necessitated by the increasing competition in the southern districts. Profits from non-competitive departments offset losses in competitive areas. Anderson reduced his personnel as far as was consistent with the largest returns, selected and trained the men under his control, and determined the policy of his department in spite of the views of the Governor and Council. The results were shown, for example, in the returns of furs. From a seven-year average (1844–50) in the Mackenzie River district to a six-year average (1851–56) cross fox increased from 1,244 to 2,125, red fox from 1,411 to 2,509, white fox from 258 to 1,583, silver fox from 488 to 635, and blue fox from 0 to 50. Beaver increased from 5,040 to 7,965 in 1856 and marten from 16,012 in 1851 to 40,294 in 1856. Marten increased in the Yukon department through 1854, 1855, and 1856 from 1,901 to 4,765 and 6,176 respectively, making the returns from that department £2,108.15.8, £2,379.17.4, and £4,196.4.8 for those years. In Peel River for the same dates, marten increased from 1,501 to 1,969 and 2,763 and returns from £1,506.13.1 to £1,920.10.4 and £2,030.12.6. New Caledonia, which was also a monopoly district, gained materially. In 1822 it registered a gain of 2,000 beaver and exported 103 packs and 6 kegs castoreum. In 1823 exports were 112 packs and 8 kegs castoreum. It became "one of the richest districts in the Company's domain; its returns average about 8,000 beavers with a fair proportion of other valuable furs."[157] In 1826 the Columbia department produced (presumably before New Caledonia returns were included) an apparent gain of £2,553.18 from 2,740 large beaver weighing 4,255 lb., 837 small beaver weighing 551 lb., 114 large otter, 9 small otter, and 3 musquash. With the addition of New Caledonia and the reorganization of the district the 1828 outfit showed an apparent gain of £31,739 including £3,141.3.5 cleared on Ogden's outfit. In 1831 the apparent gain was £33,700, an increase of £6,000 over the preceding year. In 1833 the district produced 20,000 beaver and an apparent gain of £20,000 of which it was estimated that New Caledonia sent returns of £11,000 to Fort Vancouver from which a deduction of the value of the outfit, wages, and expenses (£3,000) left £8,000 profit.[158] Fort

---

156*Ibid.*, p. 232.   157*Ibid.*, p. 306.
158*Ibid.*, p. 250.

Alexandria alone produced 1,832 beaver skins in 1820. In 1836 to 1839 the profits of New Caledonia were estimated at £10,000. In 1848 they had declined to £6,914.12.11. The more remote non-competitive areas began to show the effects of competition in the south.[159]

The final results of monopoly control during the period were shown in the returns of the Company. The shares of the wintering partners were crucial indices, since these officers were primarily responsible for the conduct of the trade. The average annual return for $\frac{1}{85}$ share from 1821 to 1872 was estimated at £360.[160] Returns to 1833 averaged £393.8.4 per share and to 1840 averaged £400. Profits fluctuated greatly and declined after that date. In 1841 the returns were £120.[161] Total profits for the period 1840 to 1857 averaged £65,573.2.7 of which £39,343.17.6 were appropriated to the Company and £26,229.5.1 to the chief factors and traders. From these profits the returns of chief factors averaged £617.3.2 and of the chief trader £308.11.7.[162] In the decade from 1853 to 1862 average profits increased apparently as a result of competition and the abandonment of the policy of protection to the fur-bearing animals. Dividends[163] were being paid out of capital. The average return[164] on $\frac{1}{85}$ share from 1853 to 1862 was £466.5.6½. The returns fluctuated violently throughout the period increasing from £334.12.3 in 1853 to £690.18.2 in 1854 and to the highest point of £872.10.1 in 1855. They declined sharply to £339.9.5½ in 1856 and recovered to £479.39 in 1857 and £475.15.1½ in 1858. But further decline followed to £259.11.3½ in 1859, to £248.1.8 in 1860, and £207.8.6 in 1861. The rally in 1862 brought them to £353.5.1.

The final blow[165] to the monopoly followed increase in settlement on the Pacific coast and in the Red River district. In eastern Canada industrialism was following the path of the fur trade. Directors of the

[159]See *Journal of John Work*, passim; also A. C. Laut, *Conquest of the Great Northwest*, II, 239 ff.

[160]A. G. Morice, *Northern Interior of British Columbia*, p. 107.

[161]J. McLean, *Twenty-five Years' Service*, II, 257 f.

[162]Evidence of the Rt. Hon. Edward Ellice, *Report from the Select Committee on the Hudson's Bay Company*, 1857, p. 326.

[163]For a list of dividends declared and market prices of stock from 1847 to 1856, see *ibid.*, pp. 446–449.

[164]M. MacLeod, *Oregon Indemnity: Claim of Chief Factors and Chief Traders* (1892), p. 45; also Sir E. W. Watkin, *Canada and the States*, pp. 154 ff.

[165]For a description of a competitive voyage along the Pacific coast see R. B. Johnson, *Very Far West Indeed*, chaps. xv–xvi.

Grand Trunk planned the extension of the railway to the prairies and to the Pacific coast. The centralized organization of the Hudson's Bay Company made possible the acquisition of control by other interests in 1863 as it had in 1811 by Lord Selkirk. Since the amalgamation the stock of the Company had been concentrated in a small number of controlling hands. The Hon. Edward Ellice, who had been connected with the trade since 1803 and who was influential in the promotion of the amalgamation, remained an important shareholder and became deputy governor from 1858 to 1863.[166] In 1856 there were 268 "proprietors" of whom 85 held 2 votes or more. Six members of the Ellice family had 2 votes or more and 2 members 1 vote. The stock of the Company had increased very slightly from £400,000 to £500,000. This arrangement disappeared at one stroke in the face of the new finance, imperial pressure, and industrialism symbolized in railroads. Negotiations provided for an increase of capital stock from £500,000 to £2,00,000 in 1863 and the control by financial interests friendly to the Grand Trunk. Finally in 1869 the last bulwark of the Company was surrendered and the land over which it had control was sold to Canada. With the sale of its rights to Prince Rupert's land to Canada, the Company definitely abandoned the claim to legal[167] protection in exclusive trade as a weapon against competition from outside areas and competition forged ahead with even greater intensity.

[166]Sir William Schooling, *The Governor and Company of Adventurers of England Trading into Hudson's Bay.*

[167]The Hudson's Bay Company's right to exclusive trade was generally regarded as dubious. For a full description of various powers granted under the charter see James Dodds, *The Hudson's Bay Company, Its Position and Prospects, passim.*

PART FIVE

THE INDUSTRIAL REVOLUTION AND THE FUR TRADE (1869-1929)

11. The Decline of Monopoly

[The reader of this edition is asked to note that the final year of reference for this chapter is 1929. The present tense should be read with this date in mind. A few footnote references, added for this edition from the author's MS notes, which take the account past 1929, have been dated.]

THE effects of machine industry on the fur trade had been pronounced in securing a cheaper supply of goods from Great Britain. Silk had been substituted to a large extent for beaver in the making of hats and fancy fur had taken the place of beaver. More immediate effects of the Industrial Revolution on the fur trade of Canada followed improvements in transportation. The change in transport organization of the Hudson's Bay Company which began in the latter part of the preceding period, and which made the York boat and the depots at York Factory and Norway House obsolete in the face of the strategic importance of Fort Garry, was soon completed. The Swan River district sent its last run of boats to York Factory in 1874 and goods practically ceased to be sent through York Factory after 1874–75. Freighting was limited to gunpowder. With the change in Company headquarters from York Factory to Fort Garry in 1878 country produce at York Factory was gradually brought to Norway House. On the return trips country produce for Island Lake and York Factory, as well as castoreum, buffalo tongues, and quills for London, were sent down. Island Lake continued to receive its goods from York Factory and Oxford House became a central transport depot. The annual vessel from London continued to call at Churchill and later at York Factory, but its vital importance to the Northwest had disappeared.

At the beginning of the period goods were sent from the depot at Fort Garry by Red River carts to posts on the Plains and on the Saskatchewan at very high cost. Grant wrote:

The expense of bringing anything into or sending anything out of the country by this old fashioned way is of course enormous. The prime cost of the articles is a bagatelle. Transport swallows up everything. No wonder

¹G. M. Grant, *Ocean to Ocean*, p. 159. Captain Butler's trip of inspection in 1870 along the Saskatchewan from November 14 to February 2, 1871, cost $1,032. See also Julian Ralph, *On Canada's Frontier*. For a description of the

that the price of a pound of tea, sugar, or salt, is here exactly the same. They weigh the same, and cost the same for carriage.[1]

The difficulties of the Portage la Loche brigade in the early part of the period continued and demoralization became more evident. Affidavits were taken with the men's contracts to make desertion punishable. *Voyageurs* learning of the high wages outside were anxious to leave the service. The new Rainy Lake brigade to Portage la Loche was the cause of complaints of delay. Goods and furs were lost in transport. Guides were obliged to keep a diary to be sent to the head office in order to check the cause of losses. Directions were issued as to methods of packing furs to prevent loss. The maintenance of oxen and transport equipments at Portage la Loche involved a heavy expense.

The expenses involved in sending goods to Mackenzie River[2] were the occasion for numerous suggestions of economy. In a memorandum to D. A. Smith dated Fort Simpson, November 21, 1872, Hardisty advocated the use of the Yukon River and a portage of thirty-five and a half miles from the Bell River to the East Rat River and Peel River to bring all the freight for Mackenzie and Athabasca districts. This change would reduce expenses one-half and make possible the discharge of all Indian *voyageurs*, all expensive servants (guides, steersmen, bowsmen), and all those married with families. It was estimated that the goods paid to Indian tripmen equalled one-fifteenth of the whole outfit—two boatloads of ammunition, tobacco, ironworks, etc., paid annually for provisions for transport. These goods would be available for trade in furs. A saving in wages, provisions, equipment (boats, sails, rigging, oilcloth, leather covering, tracking shoes) would result. One half the able-bodied men of the district engaged in transport would be released to hunt furs and increase the returns. It was estimated that the trip to the portage cost in provisions twenty-three bales good summer meat, seven bales (ninety pounds each) for officers, eight bags common pemmican for the Fort Rae boat to the portage, five bags fine pemmican (forty-five pounds each) for the officers, and one keg of grease. The necessity for the strictest economy in transportation expenses was constantly urged. In a letter to Chief Factor Archibald Macdonald dated January, 1875, D. A. Smith wrote: "Without strict economy in . . . outfits, officers, men, and posts in every item to the

fur trade in New Brunswick, see R. L. Dashwood, *Chiploquorgan; or, Life by the Camp Fire*. On the fur trade in New Brunswick, 1764–75, see J. B. Brebner, *The Neutral Yankees of Nova Scotia*, p. 132.

[2]For a description of numerous details of the fur trade of the seventies from Mackenzie River to Red River, see A. C. Garrioch, *The Far and Furry North*.

lowest possible degree, dividends cannot be expected. . . . The difficulty of freighting in such large, bulky outfits, as well as the very heavy cost of freight, must always be borne in mind."[3]

The demand for improvements in transportation became more urgent with the increase in cheaper goods at Red River and the competition which followed. A solution to the problem of heavy costs of transportation in the country beyond Fort Garry was found in the use of steamboats below Fort Garry and on Lake Winnipeg to Grand Rapids and on the Saskatchewan above that point. The steamer *Colville*, a round-bottomed boat, was engaged to transport freight from Lower Fort Garry to Grand Rapids. A light tramway[4] was completed at Grand Rapids in 1877 and goods were carried over the portage. In 1874 the steamer *Northcote* ($2\frac{1}{2}'$ to 3' draft, 150' in length and 30' beam) was built above Grand Rapids and goods were loaded on this boat and sent upstream to points on the Saskatchewan. After one year's difficulties and experience had been acquired in navigating the Saskatchewan, goods were taken annually by this route. The *Lily* was added for the South Saskatchewan at a later date and the *Northwest* and the *Manitoba* (no longer in use on the Red River following the completion of the St. Paul and Manitoba Railway) were "warped" over Grand Rapids and also used on the Saskatchewan. Finally the *Marquis* was built at Grand Rapids—of deeper draft, greater engine power, and able to go up any of the rapids without the aid of warping lines. These boats were flat-bottomed sternwheelers designed for river transportation. The *Lily* alone had a steel hull built in England, brought out in sections, and assembled above Grand Rapids. With high water all the boats went to Edmonton but generally only the lighter draft boats were used on the upper river. The captains and mates were largely Americans trained in the Mississippi steamboat school who migrated to the North with the falling off of Mississippi traffic which followed the railroads. The great difficulties on the Saskatchewan were the rapids, the swift water, and a sandy gravel bottom which caused rapid changes in the channel. The sand and swift water were said to have serious effects on the hull of the steamboat, especially on the South Saskatchewan.

With these improvements goods were sent to Fort Carlton and taken by Green Lake to Isle à la Crosse Lake and Portage la Loche and the northern districts. A cart road was built from Fort Carlton to

[3]Beckles Willson, *Life of Lord Strathcona*, p. 353.

[4]Walter Moberly, *The Rocks and Rivers of British Columbia*, p. 99. Lady Dufferin drove the last spike, September 11, 1877.

Green Lake in 1875 and this was in use in 1876. Later a route by Lac la Biche was improved and finally a route north of Edmonton to Athabasca Landing, ninety miles, was adopted.[5] From this point goods were sent down the Athabasca to the Mackenzie. From the same depot goods were taken up the Athabasca to a point on Lesser Slave Lake (now Grouard) and freighted to Peace River Crossing. In 1878 plans were made to forward 800 pieces of outfit 1879 for Peace River and Athabasca to Lesser Slave Lake and the Smoky River. Supplies for New Caledonia were also taken in by this route to Peace River and Hudson's Hope and large numbers of oxen were kept at Lesser Slave Lake for this expensive portage. Goods for Athabasca continued to be sent in *via* Portage la Loche as in 1878 eight boatloads (seventy-five pieces each) followed the old route from Cumberland House on the Saskatchewan and returned with furs (fifty pieces each). Goods were sent, therefore, from three points on the Saskatchewan to the interior, Cumberland House, Fort Carlton, and Edmonton. The Saskatchewan became a base line of transportation.

As a result of the construction of the Canadian Pacific and its branch lines to Prince Albert and Edmonton, further changes developed. Prince Albert displaced Fort Carlton as a base after the Northwest Rebellion until 1890 when Edmonton[6] came into prominence through the construction of the railroad from Calgary. The Saskatchewan boat service ceased about 1893.

Following improvements in transportation in the prairie districts plans were laid at an early date for steamboats on the Athabasca and the Mackenzie. In a letter to Hardisty dated Fort Garry, December 20, 1875, J. Grahame wrote of "the great difficulty to import a sufficient quantity of goods to meet the increased price of furs and you will be glad to learn that initiatory steps have been taken to place steam above the Cassette rapids." A steamboat (the *Athabasca*) was built to run from Athabasca Landing to Grand Rapids on the Athabasca River.[7] This connected with a small tramway on Grand Rapids Island in the center of the rapids and a steamer (the *Grahame*, 1882)[8] which ran

---

[5]F. J. Alcock, "Past and Present Trade Routes to the Canadian Northwest."

[6]The *Northwest* (steamer) came to Edmonton in 1896 (*Edmonton Bulletin*).

[7]For some years later see H. A. Cody, *An Apostle of the North: Memoirs of the Right Reverend Bishop William C. Bompas*, p. 204. On Anglican farms at Vermilion and Dunvegan as a result of famine see *ibid.*, pp. 202–203; also *A Heroine of the North: Memoirs of Charlotte Selina Bompas.*

[8]The *Grahame* was launched at Chipewyan in 1883, according to A. C. Garrioch, *A Hatchet Mark in Duplicate*, p. 164. She ran to McMurray and up the Clearwater to Portage la Loche whence the route led to Isle à la Crosse

to Fort Fitzgerald. In 1885 the *Wrigley* was built on the other side of the sixteen-mile portage at Fort Smith and access was given by steamboat to all the forts on the Lower Slave River, Slave Lake, and the Mackenzie.

Railroad construction to Peace River Crossing in 1914 changed the route to that point—goods going down the Peace River being freighted over Vermilion Falls (Western Cartage & Storage Company) and transshipped to a steamer for Fort Fitzgerald. Later (1916) with completion of a railway to Athabasca Landing the route was brought back to this point. In 1920 the railway was extended to Waterways, the last scows were taken from Athabasca Landing that year,[9] and the tramway on the island in Grand Rapids was taken up. In 1925 the Alberta and Great Waterways railway was improved with an extension to McMurray. The route to the Arctic has been improved with the addition of larger steamboats and the acquisition of the Alberta & Arctic Transportation Company in 1924 gave the Company control of the important steamship (*D. A. Thomas*) on Peace River from Hudson's Hope to Red River (goods being freighted four miles over Vermilion Chutes) as well as the *Distributor* (built in 1920) on the Mackenzie River. The Company was consequently in possession of efficient transportation equipment in the newer boats and of ample reserve in the older boats which were displaced on Peace River and on Mackenzie River.[10]

The extent of the penetration of machine industry may be shown in a more detailed study of transportation in the Mackenzie River territory. In the northern districts transportation remains dependent on the rivers and is consequently distinctly seasonal in character. Transportation during the winter months is extremely limited and ex-

---

Lake and Beaver River at least as late as 1885. The *Grahame* was probably shifted to Athabasca Landing with the coming of the railway to Edmonton. *Ibid.*, pp. 178–179.

[9]*Beaver*, December, 1920.

[10]In 1924 the Alberta & Arctic Transportation Co. operated the *Athabasca River*, capacity 200 tons, 58 passengers, Waterways to Fitzgerald and return, weekly; the *Fond du Lac* (motorboat), Chipewyan or Fond du Lac and return (in July), and assisting the *Athabasca River* in low water; the *Distributor*, Fort Smith to Aklavik and return, twice, and a third time to Fort Norman; the *Liard River* (motor tug), Resolution to Rae and return, twice, and Simpson to Nelson and return, once, and Aklavik and return; the *Lady Mackworth* (inspection boat), the *D. A. Thomas*, Vermilion Chutes to Hudson's Hope, *Weenusk* (motorboat) assisting *D. A. Thomas*; *Mackenzie River*, *Slave River*, *Canadusa*, in reserve. With increasing traffic the *Mackenzie River* was placed in operation in 1929.

pensive. It is estimated that the cost of carrying mail between two posts —say 150 miles—(two men and a dog team)is about $150. A trip with furs from Resolution to Edmonton in the winter would cost up to $500 and $1,000. Dogs are valued at $20 to $25 in summer and up to $100 in winter. Dog harness of the best manufacture, lined with elk skin, is sold at $40 a set for four dogs, or $10 apiece, although plain leather harness, more difficult to handle in winter, is much cheaper. Sleds are sold at $35 to $37, unlaced. The limit of travel is forty to fifty miles per day—only the very best dog runners under unusually favourable circumstances travelling beyond this distance. Long winter nights and the difficult work of dog driving restricts the number of hours. Dogs will haul up to five hundred pounds and regulation loads with four dogs weigh four hundred pounds, with blankets, provisions, and dog feed extra. This necessity of carrying a supply of provisions and dog feed limits the amount of freight and the distance travelled. Dogs are highly expensive in other ways. They must be raised and trained by skilled drivers. They must be fed throughout the summer for the work done in winter. In localities in which fish is available in large quantities this problem is simplified but in other localities as at Fort Vermilion where coarse bread, corn meal, or oatmeal mixed with tallow must be bought in large quantities the expense is appreciable. Moreover, loss follows from the heavy over-head of summer feeding. The overhead is shifted in many cases to the dog and death is frequently the result of lack of food or of attempts on the part of the dog to get food. From the comments of numerous travellers one would gather that the north country offered vast fields for the activities of the Humane Society.[11] Oxen are used by the missions and horses have been used at Fort Simpson but not below that point.

Not only is transportation seasonal in character but the traffic continues as a predominantly one-way traffic. Downstream it is estimated that freight for the posts would vary in proportion to the fur taken out—10 tons of fur upstream to 230 to 370 tons of freight downstream. The large steamboats with barges handle from 140 to 200 tons. A much longer time is taken on the journey upstream than downstream. Peak-load costs are unusually high since labour and its supply of provisions must be carried for the difficult work of loading and unloading. Moreover, the Mackenzie River drainage basin has certain distinct characteristics which seriously interfere with transport organ-

[11]Fullerton Waldo, *Down the Mackenzie through the Great Lone Land*, pp. 48 ff., and *passim*.

ization though it is admirably adapted in many ways to the extension of the fur trade. Flowing to the north and draining comparatively well-wooded territory, heavy goods can be floated down and the lighter furs brought back with the least possible cost. At Smith Portage heavy freight is unloaded at Fitzgerald at water level and taken down the steep sandy hill at Fort Smith. Light furs are brought out in the opposite direction. The beds of the rivers change frequently and the water changes with remarkable rapidity especially with the spring floods and the decline in flow throughout the summer. Great dependence must be placed on pilots and on their ability to read water. The old *Liard River*, for example, caught on a rock in the Liard River and before she could be taken off the water had fallen, making salvage impossible. The *Mackenzie River* was left for over a month on Dry Island in 1923 through similar circumstances. The large steamboats find great difficulty in making more than two trips to Aklavik in the Mackenzie delta. The third trip until 1928 did not proceed beyond Norman because of low water in the Ramparts area. The length of the season has been increased by the use of smaller boats able to operate in much lower water characteristic of the late summer and early fall, and a gas boat and a barge were used to continue the third journey from Norman to Aklavik. The *Liard River* left Aklavik in 1924 at the latest date on record, September 24. In 1928 the *Distributor* made a third trip, for the first time leaving Fort Smith on August 30, arriving at Aklavik in twelve days but requiring six weeks for the return trip because of low water at the Ramparts and storms on Slave Lake. Further disadvantages arise from the deposit of sediment carried down by the swift water to the deltas. Channels must be carefully marked with beacons and buoys. Posts located near the deltas as at Resolution on Slave Lake and Chipewyan on Lake Athabasca become more difficult to approach with the filling in along the shore. Heavy stone piers are run out at Chipewyan and an extension of the pier at Resolution has been made. Buoys must be replaced every season because of the ice and usually this has been done at a late date or not at all. Boats commonly run aground and considerable inconvenience follows from the waste of time and energy employed in getting them into deep water. As yet the government has done little in the direction of improving navigation facilities beyond charting the river which frequently changes its bed, and the erecting of beacons at the entrance of Mackenzie River and the mouth of Slave River.

Other difficulties follow from the existence of a very long stretch of river and a short stretch of intervening lake. Boats adapted to river navigation are not adapted to deep-water navigation. Flat-bottomed boats in which the fire box is located forward and the engine aft near the large stern wheels, the whole held together by the main hogchain, and having neither keel nor hold, cannot be built to withstand heavy seas. On the other hand the boats must be built with light draft giving ability to put in at various places along the river bank for freight and for wood. In the early spring or early fall boats may be held up on Slave Lake for two weeks or more. In a very late spring, as in 1927, boats may not be able to reach Aklavik before the middle of July. The companies have not been in a position in all parts of their transportation service to solicit passenger traffic because of the difficulties in arranging for a fixed schedule.

The character of the river has other problems incidental to seasonal changes. Boats are hauled out of the water in the autumn and launched in the spring to prevent damage from ice. Fort Smith and vicinity (Bell Rock and Gravel Point) are equipped with the necessary machinery for this work as well as for repairing. Ice does not go out of the lakes as quickly as it does out of the rivers. Consequently goods are rushed down from Fort Smith with the launching of the boats toward the end of May and deposited in a warehouse at the mouth of Slave River. Finally, on the disappearance of ice on the lake, steamboats rush goods from Smith and the warehouse in Slave River to the posts on Slave Lake and the Mackenzie River.

The relative shortness of the season, the length of the trip, the long upstream pull, the necessity of getting down at the earliest possible moment since the earliest boat secures the largest share of passenger traffic going in and coming out, and the large quantities of freight sent down necessitate a type of boat with ample supplies of steam power. The fuel problem is consequently important. The large steamers consume from three-fourths to one cord of wood per hour. This wood requires ample space in the boat and a heavy freight load involves frequent landing at woodpiles. The relative scarcity of wood farther down the river requires a heavy load on the latter part of the trip to Aklavik and return. Arrangements are made for placing the wood at convenient intervals along the river bank. Woodcutters are imported for the winter season and their outfits are taken down the river free of charge from Smith. In spite of the companies' precautions these men are usually trappers on an important scale as well. They were paid in 1924, $5.00 a cord above Resolution and $6.00 a cord below and it was estimated that two men would cut two hundred to three hundred cords in a season. Spruce, a small quantity of birch, poplar, balm of Gilead, and driftwood are cut into three-foot lengths and piled conveniently along the river banks but sufficiently high to be beyond the reach of floods in the spring. For best results the wood should be cut a year to allow it to dry. The wood must be thrown from the banks, thrown down plank chutes, or hauled aboard the steamboat with the capstan. Labour and time[12] are consumed in cutting, piling, loading, and firing and each boat must carry a large number of deck hands for this work. The deck hands must live directly over the engine and in crowded conditions, in spite of every effort of the companies, and they must be called out at all hours and on short notice. Possibilities of economy exist in the use of compound engines, careful planning of wood yards, and in the use of oil burners and the consumption of oil produced at Fort Norman. The advantages of oil as supplied at Fort Norman have been under advisement but the heavy barges for carrying oil are an important drawback.

The use of gasoline engines, as already suggested, has been responsible for various improvements in the transport. The first small gasoline boat, the *Lady of the Lake*, was brought down in 1920 although "kickers" had been numerous before that date. The use of gasoline in smaller motor boats involved the employment of large flat-bottomed barges and scows carrying, when well stowed, forty-five to eighty tons. These arrangements have been important in the improvement of subsidiary routes. For inspection boats and for making trips on the shallower tributaries which are impossible for the larger steamboats, the gasoline tugboat has revolutionized transport. On the Liard River, goods were tracked up the difficult rapids about thirty miles above Fort Simpson and the swift water for four hundred miles to Fort Nelson. It is estimated that one man can handle two tons of freight on a line. The average trip up the river was twenty-one days although it has taken forty-seven days. The consumption of provisions, the wearing out of from one to three pairs of moccasins per day, and the heavy wage item made these posts expensive. Stiff rapids complicated the problem of adapting gas boats to this river. Expert pilots are a prerequisite and only one barge can be taken through the rapids at a time. A consumption of six to six and one-half gallons of gasoline

[12]The length of time required for loading wood has been reduced recently by sending a man and a team of horses down the river before the ice breaks on the lake to haul out wood to the bank, as well as by the use of new methods of loading. In an average trip from Simpson to Aklavik and return to Smith 414 hours would be required of which 66 would be employed loading 225 cords of wood, 91 in loading and unloading goods, tying up for darkness and for wind, and the remaining 257 hours in running.

per hour necessitates the transport of a heavy load of this commodity and the use of caches along the route. With one engineer the boat must be tied up at intervals for rest but these intervals are not frequent. But in spite of these handicaps it is possible for a motor boat to take two barges to Fort Liard and one barge to Fort Nelson making a return trip to Simpson in eleven days. In the Mackenzie River district the *Liard River*, valued at $12,000, is used to transport freight from Fort Smith to the warehouse at the mouth of the Slave River, and from this warehouse to Fort Rae, on the north arm of Slave Lake, to Fort Liard and Fort Nelson on the Liard River, and finally, in the latter part of the season, from Norman to Aklavik in the Mackenzie delta.

Further improvements on the Mackenzie River route have been adopted or are under experiment. Boats leave McMurray at the end of steel early in May rushing goods down from that point to Fort Fitzgerald for transport across the portage. These goods are checked and stored in a large warehouse preparatory to freighting to Fort Smith, where they are again checked and stored preparatory to loading on the Mackenzie River barges and boats. The Smith portage (fourteen miles) at the entrance of the Northwest Territories has been greatly improved with new roads and the addition of motor cars beginning in 1921. The Hudson's Bay Company acquired from the Alberta & Arctic Transportation Company in 1924 two large caterpillar tractors (about $15,000 each) with trucks capable of carrying eight to ten tons each. Each tractor hauls twenty to thirty tons travelling at about two miles per hour and consuming five gallons of gasoline per hour or about seventy-five gallons per round trip. These tractors have not been found altogether successful in the sandy road near Fort Smith; the sand wears out the rollers and the heavy tractors break down the roads for the freighters.[13] They were supplementary to the organization of the chief methods of transport for the portage. In 1924 the Hudson's Bay Company contracted to have freight moved over the portage at $1.00 per hundredweight. The contractors imported annually teams and "skinners," the later being paid at $45 to $65 per month. Hay was brought in and sold at $25 a ton. Fourteen teams were engaged on Hudson's Bay Company freight, seven going in and seven returning. Freight was taken to the half-way house and from there forwarded to Fort Smith. In hot weather the work could be carried on only at night on account of the "bull flies." The tremendous increase in the number of goods consumed (about 1,500 tons in 1928)

[13]Fullerton Waldo, *Down the Mackenzie*, chap. v.

in the remote districts is an indication of the highly organized transport. In 1928 three Gotfredson trucks were added, having a capacity of forty tons per day.

Attempts have been made to avoid the portage and the late seasons occasioned by ice on Slave Lake and on the long reach of slack water above the head of the line, by sending a part of the goods for the Mackenzie River by a road built by the British Columbia government from St. John on Peace River to Fort Nelson on Nelson River. Freight taken over this road is sent down the Liard and Mackenzie rivers before the ice has left Slave Lake and before the large steamboats can get down. Outfits have been taken in by this route by competitors K. Mackenzie and others in 1924 and later years. An experiment conducted by the Hudson's Bay Company in 1924–25, however, was not a success.[14]

With improvements in transportation the handling of freight has reached a high degree of organization. From Edmonton to the posts on the Mackenzie River most of the freight must be handled at least nine times because of the portages and transshipments from rail to boat. Goods must be carefully packed—boxes with strap iron, double bags for flour and sugar—and in sizes convenient for hand labour. Formerly surprising breakages occurred with boxes of candy and products of this character. Loading machinery is not feasible on an extensive scale with flat-bottomed river steamboats. Checking and stowing of freight are important tasks. Pieces must be marked with weight, outfit, number, district, post, and in some cases, places of shipment, and these must be checked at every point of transshipment by checkers and pursers. In stowing, freight for the last posts is loaded first and freight for other posts added in order of distance with careful attention to the effects of the load on the list of the boat. Unloading is accomplished with the least possible difficulty. To facilitate arrangements freight for the most distant post in the district is numbered 1 and the remainder in order 2, 3, 4, and so on.[15] The location of the post buildings at the top of high banks along the river necessitates the use of capstans, windlasses, and other arrangements, or dependence on manual labour. Inadequate arrangements at the posts in the lack of "deadmen" for mooring the boats are serious and in some cases dangerous handicaps. But these are difficulties indicating that the Industrial Revolution is still in progress.

[14]See E. M. Kindle, "Arrival and Departure of Winter Conditions in the Mackenzie River Basin," p. 392.

[15]A typical marking, R. 7, 256, 120, 33 = R (district), 7 (post), 256 (outfit 1926), 120 (weight), 33 (number of piece).

The revolution in transport in other areas has been equally in evidence. Territory which had not been penetrated has yielded to the inroads of machine industry. In 1914 the *Fort McPherson*, a gas schooner of fifty tons, and the *Ruby* left Vancouver with provisions for Western Arctic posts and lumber for posts at Herschel Island and at Baillie Island. Unable to get in that year, the *Ruby* discharged her cargo and the *Fort McPherson* was beached for the winter. In 1915 they were successful in reaching Herschel Island. Posts have been established since at Herschel Island, Baillie Island, Kittigazuit, Bernard Harbour (1916), King William Land (1923), Bathurst Inlet (1925), Fort Hearne (1928), Fort Collinson (1923), and Cambridge Bay (1921). In 1921 the *Lady Kindersley* was launched as an auxiliary schooner to take goods from Vancouver to these posts but she was lost with all her freight in 1924. In 1925 a successful trip was made with the *Baychimo* from Vancouver and in the following year the *Bay Maude*, a smaller vessel, was added. The latter is able to winter in the Arctic and to visit posts impossible to the larger boat because of the necessity of returning at an early date through Bering Strait. Plans are under consideration for the establishment of a depot on the Mackenzie delta at which the river steamboat could deposit freight and from which an ocean-going boat could distribute to Western Arctic posts. With these improvements the Western Arctic district has been created and includes eighteen posts extending east from the boundary of Alaska to King William Land.

On the Atlantic side steamers came into use for the first time with the purchase of a steam auxiliary in England for work on the Labrador and Ungava coast in 1860.[16] Steam was employed in the transport of York Factory supplies on the *Erick*, an old Greenland whaler, in 1892. The *Pelican* replaced the *Erick* in 1901. In 1906 the first steam vessel went to James Bay when the *Discovery*, Captain Scott's vessel, was purchased. Later the *Nascopie* was used to take supplies to Labrador, Ungava, and the Bay posts from Montreal and St. John's. Charlton Island still remains a depot at which small schooners and motor boats call to distribute goods to subsidiary posts. The steamer *Inenew* and the schooners *Fort Charles* and *Fort George* are important subsidiaries.[17] The motor tug *Caribou* and the schooners *York Factory* and *Nannuck* were employed in distributing supplies to the posts at Coats Island, York Factory, and Chesterfield Inlet. The *Baychimo* completed her first season in 1921, establishing two new posts at Pond

[16]*Beaver*, May, 1921.
[17]See Moose Factory Post Journal, 1920, *ibid.*, January, 1921.

Inlet and Netchalik in Baffin Land in that year and arriving in St. John's, September 21. In 1925 she was transferred to Vancouver for the Western Arctic trade. The *Bayeskimo*, a distributing boat for Ungava district, was wrecked in 1925 and the *Bayrupert* left Gravesend on her maiden voyage on June 13, 1926, but was wrecked on the Labrador coast in 1927. The completion of the Hudson's Bay Railway will bring new changes in transport organization (1930). Throughout the whole of the fur-producing areas of Canada, a revolution in transport has occurred since 1869 in which the steamboat, the railroad, and the gasoline motor have been chiefly concerned.

Machine industry has effected communication as well as transportation. The Hudson's Bay Company has a private telephone from Fort Smith to Fitzgerald. Postal communication limited to registered mail and letters brought in once or twice during the winter, has been supplemented with the development of the radio. Receiving sets have become common. A sending outfit was established at Fort Simpson in 1924 and at Aklavik in 1925 to connect with the Canadian National Telegraphs, with most satisfactory results.[18]

Improved transportation and communication had important effects on personnel policy. The industrial and agricultural development of southern districts became an important base for a supply of labour. During the navigation season the lower ranks of the service are recruited chiefly from half-breeds and Indians in the country. These labourers are hired by the day or by the trip for the heavy work of loading and unloading. As a result no adequate personnel policy has been followed. Deck hands hire for one trip for the experience, for odd things which may be picked up in the freight, and for the wages. In many instances the results are not in the best interests of efficient transportation but on the other hand efficient mates do perform miracles in the work accomplished. Half-breed labour responds with unusual alacrity to leadership. Semiskilled labour is obtained from trappers idle during the summer, miners from Alberta, and students acting as pursers. An unusual shift in occupation is inevitable with seasonal changes and the burden is borne partly by the company in higher wages, especially for skilled labour, partly by the labourer, and partly by the community of British Columbia and Alberta. Mates, captains, and engineers commonly go to British Columbia for the winter. In highly skilled labour, the unions have had little effect. The Pilots and Mates Association and the Engineers Association have not been uniformly successful in securing the adoption of a scale of wages. It is a

[18]W. A. Steel, "The Northwest Territories Radio System."

matter of dispute as to how far this policy has resulted in efficient management.[19] Certainly there exists room for improvement but the problem is undoubtedly complicated with difficulties of developing a well-rounded policy for unskilled labour. An unskilled pilot may be the occasion for very serious losses. The *esprit de corps* of the old Portage la Loche brigades persists with difficulty in the face of the new demands of machine industry. The overhead of high peak-load costs of transport labour can be shifted without difficulty to the southern districts.

Similar changes have followed in the permanent staff. Increasing competition and economy measures led to a reduction of wages in the early part of the period. On June 1, 1873, regulations were issued giving a married man and wife, one and one-half ration of country provisions; wife and child, one and three-fourths rations; wife and two children, two rations. No rations were given to any family above this. In a letter dated Carlton House, July 10, 1875, Grahame wrote to Hardisty: "It is very desirable that you should succeed in inducing good European servants to renew their contracts for there is not only great expense incurred in sending them home and bringing out recruits, but also great difficulty in obtaining the latter by last accounts." Beginning in 1876 skilled labour (servants and wheelwrights) was brought from Scotland by Montreal to Fort Garry rather than by York Factory. At this date carpenters, as representatives of skilled labour, were paid £35 and £40 per year and unskilled labourers £20 per year with gratuities of £2 for tea and sugar. Skilled labour on the permanent staff became much less important with the increasing importation of manufactured products.

The chief problem which followed from competition and the increasing centralization of control was a continued decline in initiative among the traders in the interior. During the period of monopoly control this decline had been in evidence. A complaint against Shaw at Dunvegan in 1860 regarding "the old thing over of squandering provisions amongst his relations and starving the Company's servants and wasting the Company's property," was typical. Complaints were numerous that young men no longer found any inducement to enter the service because of the low returns. Finally more direct control

[19]For a description, 1893, of the weakening of morale especially after following the policy of appointing a commissioner every five years, see H. S. Somerset, *The Land of the Muskeg*. It is a story of a trip from Edmonton to Athabasca Landing, up to Little Slave Lake, across to the Peace River and out by Giscome Portage.

which followed improved transportation tended to disregard the interests of the individual trader. The net result was the abandonment of the old partnership arrangements and the appointment of the personnel on a contract basis. The arrangements which had characterized the fur trade from its beginning in New France, by which inland traders were stimulated to greater activities through a share of the profits, disappeared with the development of transportation facilities, and the new discipline held sway. No new areas remained to be explored, no necessity existed for the stress which was placed on the partners in the days of the Northwest Company. No change has been more significant of the new era of the fur trade.

The disappearance of control of the wintering partners began in the centralization policy of Sir George Simpson but it was not until after his death and the reorganization of the Company in England in 1863 that the change became pronounced.[20] The increase in capital was carried out without the consent of the wintering partners, and was the occasion for considerable protest and alarm.[21] D. A. Smith as an unofficial representative conferred with the London authorities but returned with slight hopes. He wrote to Barnston, "We must be prepared not to receive very much sympathy from the new shareholders or the new Board."[22] After various suggestions and the sale of the Northwest territory to Canada for £300,000, he was dispatched to represent the wintering partners. Their claims were met by the payment of £107,055. The Deed Poll of 1834 was revoked and a new Deed Poll of 1871 was arranged. In this Deed Poll the wintering partners were given 40 per cent of the returns from the fur trade as before but no reference was made to the returns from land. The number of shares was increased from eighty-five to one hundred and the number of grades to five. Inspecting chief factors held three shares; chief factors, two and one-half shares; factors, two shares; chief traders, one and one-half, and junior chief traders, one share.[23]

Following transportation improvements the last meeting of the Council at Norway House was held in 1870 with D. A. Smith as chief commissioner. Later meetings were held at Fort Carlton and the last

[20]See *The Reflections of Inkyo on the Great Company* which emphasizes the change after 1863 but especially during and after the war in the Company's finance.

[21]See J. J. Hargrave, *Red River*, p. 298; also Beckles Willson, *Life of Lord Strathcona*, chap. vi, *passim*.

[22]Beckles Willson, *Life of Lord Strathcona*, p. 134.

[23]Beckles Willson, *The Great Company*, chap. xxxv; also A. G. Morice, *The History of the Northern Interior of British Columbia*, chap. vii.

meeting of the Council was held in the Queen's Hotel, Winnipeg, in 1887. At this meeting announcement was made to the effect that no new commissions would be issued to clerks or servants who had entered since the transfer in 1870.[24] In 1893 the Deed Poll for trade rights was acquired by the Home Board. The last commission was issued in 1905. Mr. D. A. Smith was chief commissioner to 1874, Mr. James A. Grahame to 1884, Mr. Joseph Wrigley to 1891, and Mr. C. C. Chipman to 1911. Mr. Chipman had control of all the activities of the Company but in 1911 a change was made in which a separate fur commissioner was appointed.[25] Mr. R. H. Hall was fur trade commissioner to 1913, when Mr. N. H. Bacon from London was appointed. He was succeeded by Mr. J. Thomson (1918), and Mr. A. Brabant was appointed in 1920. In 1927 Mr. Brabant retired and was succeeded by Mr. C. H. French.

The disappearance of the partnership arrangements in the Deed Poll contributed to the general decline of initiative in the service. An old officer of the Company wrote:

This very startling information threw a wet blanket over the entire service, and produced in many cases very unfavourable results in the Company's interests. These I need not here rehearse, further than to say that it always has been, and is today, conceded by all in the service who are in a position to know, that it was one of the biggest mistakes the Company ever made when they decided to cut out granting commissions. The only interest the majority of their servants have had in the service since then was their weekly, monthly, or annual salary. I have been through it; from one end to the other I have seen it; I know it to be so, and closing this subject, I will leave it at that.[26]

The disappearance of commissions left many servants of the Company dissatisfied, promoted disloyalty, and furthered competitive efforts.

A further change was made in 1902 with the discontinuance of the apprenticeship system. Post managers became to a large extent men chosen from various fields of business or men who were raised and

---

[24]N. M. W. J. McKenzie, *The Men of the Hudson's Bay Company*, p. 46; also Alexander Begg, *History of the North-West*, II, chap. xxvi. For an interesting discussion of the relation between the wintering partners and the Company, see Beckles Willson, *Life of Lord Strathcona*, chaps. xv, xvi, xx, *passim*, and M. Mac-Leod, *Oregon Indemnity, passim*.

[25]*Report of the Governor and Committee of the Hudson's Bay Company . . . 10th July, 1911*. See also *The Hudson's Bay Company—What is it?* (1864) which claims that the Company brought together the agent of the Northwest Transit Co., the head of the Grand Trunk, and ex-Governor General of Canada and silenced them by admitting them to the Company.

[26]N. M. W. J. McKenzie, *Men of the Hudson's Bay Company*, p. 46.

educated in the country, in many cases half-breeds. The fur trade was placed on a level with other lines of trade. This change did not improve the service although it produced a number of capable traders. Intense loyalty was a result of promoting men who had been educated in the country. Families of three and four generations have seen service with the Company. On the other hand results of the policy were alleged to be shown in favouritism to members of the manager's family, in family feuds, and in difficulties of control over post managers.

Increasing competition, especially during the World War, necessitated further changes. The rise in prices of fine fur throughout the period following 1900 and especially after 1914 revolutionized the trade. With the war the increasing purchasing power of the United States and the decline in export of furs from Russia caused a further pronounced rise in prices, especially from 1916 to 1919, an increase in the number of traders and trappers, new transportation improvements, and general demoralization of the trade. The growth of large competitive organizations followed the penetration of more remote territory and the necessity of expensive transportation facilities. It is claimed that competition from Lamson-Hubbard Company increased wages materially—although this increase was possibly less than is ordinarily supposed. Hudson's Bay Company managers with large families could not be compared with single men who were managers of competing companies. Wages of interpreters have increased and in many instances the interpreter is hired to manage subposts established in winter or to go *en derouine*. Wages were higher partly as a result of the character of the work and partly as a result of their existence as potential competitors. The Company has established a reputation in fair treatment, and free traders or rival companies are said to follow the rule of avoiding the Company's "discards." Men are discharged only after great provocation. Complaints have arisen that post managers located at most distant points who undergo the greatest hardships receive no higher pay although these posts are usually the most remunerative, but on the other hand post managers are given supplies at prices below cost and these prices, though previously varying with the distance of the post from headquarters, are at present all on the same basis. Supplies have increased materially as a result of competition and improved transportation.[27] The Company has followed the policy of paying 5 per cent on employees' deposits. It is even contended in some quarters that the Company permits the existence of rival companies to stimulate the activities of the post managers.

[27]See Martin Hunter, *Canadian Wilds*, chap. ix on Officers' Allowances.

These changes were hastened by rearrangements in London. Lord Strathcona, formerly D. A. Smith, was governor of the Company from 1889 to 1914 and with his resignation and death there disappeared one of the last links with the old order. His *régime* bridged the uncertain period between the old and the new. The appointment of Sir Robert Kindersley (1916) as successor, and, in turn, of Mr. C. V. Sale (1925), marked the beginning of a new era for the Hudson's Bay Company.

Significant indications of the new period are seen in several directions. After the war the Company returned to the system of importing apprentices from Scotland (chiefly from Aberdeen and latterly from Inverness). Young men are selected from among a large number of applicants. Their expenses are borne by the head office and they are shifted about to different posts to gain a thorough knowledge of widely varying trading conditions and customs of the Indians. The abler post managers are chosen to give instruction. At the end of the five-year contract apprentices in many cases have married women of the country, and with the possibilities of promotion the men have generally taken a keen interest in the business.

The Company has followed more consistently the policy of selecting and hiring the more effective traders of competitive organizations. On the amalgamation with Lamson-Hubbard the abler men were retained. It has also given recognition on a larger scale to the principle of promotions in the service. In the earlier part of the period appointments to the higher ranks of the service of men from outside occasioned considerable disappointment. The promotions of Mr. A. Brabant and of Mr. C. H. French to fur trade commissioner are a recognition that emphasis is placed on long apprenticeship in the service.

New devices were developed to stimulate the interest of the personnel and to strengthen the position of the central authorities. The new discipline was brought eventually to an industry which in its preceding history had shown strikingly divergent characteristics. It was only necessary to compare the modern methods adopted by the Company to improve *esprit de corps* in the personnel with the whole-souled interest of the wintering partners of the Northwest Company. There is a great gulf fixed between the old Beaver Club of Montreal and the *Beaver* edited by a trained writer who solicits reminiscences and photographs of old fur traders to stimulate interest in the trade. The establishment of the *Beaver* in 1920, the elaborate celebration of the 250th anniversary, the establishment of an unofficial censorship over publications which include references to the Company, the inauguration of a pension system, and periodic bonuses are part of the new order. The latest change has come with the revival of the rank of chief factor.[28]

Improvements in transportation and communication materially altered the problem of supplies and provisions. In the agricultural districts, to the south, a tremendous increase in the production of foodstuffs, and improvements in methods of canning and conserving food had provided a base of provisions and supplies. Decline and violent fluctuations in the supply of country produce especially pemmican and the larger game animals necessitated an increasing dependence on agriculture. In 1871 the Saskatchewan district was unable to supply pemmican, and the Athabascan department found it necessary to furnish its own provisions for the entire distance to Norway House instead of to Isle à la Crosse. With the decline in the production of pemmican on the plains, the Mackenzie River district depended to an increasing extent on the caribou meat obtained at Fort Rae or at Good Hope and Bear Lake. In 1878 requisitions on the Saskatchewan district were made for outfit 1879 for provisions and supplies on the following basis. Edmonton was required to send 30 bags of pemmican, 50 buffalo skins and 30 bags of flour to Lesser Slave Lake for the transport service between that point and Smoky River; and 300 pounds common pemmican, 350 whole buffalo skins and 20 pounds sinew to Peace River for the New Caledonia outfit at Hudson's Hope. Saskatchewan district deposited at Cumberland House 200 bags common pemmican, 400 whole dressed buffalo skins, 50 large moose skins, and 8 leather tents (10 skins each), and at Grand Rapids for Norway House, York Factory, and Island Lake, 300 bags common pemmican, 20 leather tents (10 or 12 skins), 600 buffalo skins, 400 half buffalo skins.[29] Specialization within the department in the production of provisions and supplies continued but became of less importance. In 1878 Cumberland House forwarded to Norway House 50 pounds large snowshoe netting and 50 pounds small snowshoe netting; 20 fathoms of birch bark for canoe bottoms and an equal amount for canoe sides were ordered from Fairford for Norway House. Country produce was supplied to an increasing extent from Fort Garry. At present the posts are as far as possible independent in the supply of such provisions as potatoes. Dried fish are sent from Arctic Red River to Good Hope and are put up in large numbers especially for dog feed

[28]*Beaver*, March, 1927, p. 58; Hudson's Bay Company, *Report*, 1927.

[29]Minutes of Council, 1878, Fort Carlton, *Beaver*, July, 1921. For a description of the trade in buffalo hides, see Sir C. E. Denny, *The Law Marches West*, pp. 29, 60.

at Resolution, Rae, and Big Island. Occasionally posts enter farming on a large scale as at Fort Vermilion but the tendency has been to import larger quantities of such staples as flour and bacon and to depend to a less extent on the country. Even Fort Vermilion post has closed its flour mill more recently and since the war canned goods have become more prominent. In the face of transportation improvements the organization for the supply of provisions in the early period was revolutionized.

Improvements in transportation[30] and communication have been accompanied by improved methods of control. An old fur trader of the Hudson's Bay Company described the important changes:

In my early years, the Annual Indent or Requisition on London covered everything for the year, and that was all you received. Then came additional requisitions on Winnipeg followed by monthly, weekly and daily requisitions. Next came telegraphing requisitions to be sent by express, perhaps two or three times a day, then wireless requisitions and other communications from remote and inland Posts. At the present time the Governor and Committee are considering the advisability of an airship transport service for passengers and freight, to the more remote and inland Posts and Districts, which no doubt will be an accomplished fact before what I am writing reaches the Public, and this all within the past forty-four years.[31]

Control from a central headquarters became more pronounced under these conditions. Districts were enlarged. Inspection visits were carried out with greater frequency and effectiveness. The reliance placed upon the trader in remote districts became less.

[1889] During, prior, and for a few years subsequent, a regular reorganization was being inaugurated throughout the whole service, which involved the transferring of many of the men and officers to other charges, as well as the enlarging of Districts, by the merging of several small ones into one large District under one management. This was evidently necessary as there were no more Commissions being granted.[32]

These changes have continued. In 1914 headquarters for Keewatin district was moved from Norway House to Winnipeg. Mackenzie River

[30]A canoe factory was in operation in the 1930's at Rupert's House to makes canoes for posts in James Bay and beyond. R. H. H. Macaulay, *Trading into Hudson's Bay* (1934), p. 73.

[31]N. M. W. J. McKenzie, *Men of the Hudson's Bay Company*, pp. 104–105. Latest reports show that the aeroplane is actually being used to bring out furs in winter and to carry mail.

[32]*Ibid.*, p. 136.

and Athabasca districts have been amalgamated and headquarters for Mackenzie River district have changed successively from Fort Simpson to Fort Smith and to McMurray (1915). The latest arrangements have placed the two districts, Athabasca and Mackenzie River, under one district manager with headquarters at Edmonton. Fewer difficulties have arisen as to the jurisdiction of various posts and of various districts. Inspection visits were made twice yearly.[33] In 1924 in the Mackenzie River district the *Lady Mackworth* was employed as an inspecting boat. The district manager was in a position to visit each post, go over the accounts, and discuss general problems of the trade and he was in turn in close touch with the fur trade commissioner.

Changes in accounting following the spread of the price system have also made control more effective. The penetration of money in remote territories followed the payment of treaty to the Indians.[34] Treaty was made with large numbers of Indians after 1870 and they became accustomed to the use of cash. In 1900 treaty was made with the Dog-ribs and the Yellow-knives involving the cession of 372,000 square miles in the Mackenzie River district. Since that date practically all the Indians of the Mackenzie River drainage basin[35] have made treaty. Consequently every year each Indian receives $5, each counsellor, $15, and each chief, $25. The inrush of miners to the Yukon in 1898 and of trappers, prospectors, and competing traders since 1900 increased the supply of money. The one-dollar note has taken the place of the "skin" and poker games are conducted entirely with that denomination. Smaller units have not as yet become of any importance. In 1873 changes were begun leading to the adoption of Dominion currency in the accounts of the Company. As late as 1893[36] the skin "MB" was valued at about 50 cents and all trade north of

[33]See descriptions of inspection trips in 1872–73, Can. Arch., W. J. Christie, Journal of a voyage from Fort Garry to Fort Simpson and return to Carlton, August 22, 1872 to January 28, 1873; Inspection trip in British Columbia, by C. H. French, *Beaver*, January, 1921; Inspection trip of P. H. Godsell in winter of 1921, Mackenzie River, *ibid.*, May, 1921.

[34]See Hon. Alex. Morris, *The Treaties of Canada with the Indians of Manitoba and the Northwest Territories including the Negotiations on which they are based and Other information relating thereto, passim.* Treaty No. 8, involving a large portion of northern Alberta, was made in 1899; see Charles Mair, *Through the Mackenzie Basin: A Narrative of the Athabasca and Peace River Treaty Expedition of 1899,* pp. 1–149, *passim.*

[35]See an interesting account of a winter spent among the Loucheux Indians near Fort McPherson at Wind City in 1898–99. A. Graham, *The Golden Grindstone,* pp. 86 ff.

[36]Frank Russell, *Explorations in the Far North,* p. 59.

Athabasca Landing was carried on through this medium. Coins were in use as ¼ MB, MB, 5 MB, 10 MB. Various posts have continued to change their currency.[37] Fond du Lac ceased to use the skin after 1906. In 1923 the Eskimo still used tokens: white fox, 1 token; blue fox, 2 tokens; cross fox, 5–15; silver fox, 15–40; otter, 4–8; mink, 1; marten, 2; white bear, 4–10; deerskin, ½.[38] On the whole cash accounts have been gradually adopted over a wider area. Education of the Indians at mission schools[39] has prepared the way for the spread of the price system.

In the more important companies requisitions are sent in by the post manager based on the preceding year's turnover. These are inspected by the district manager and the head office. Goods are purchased and sent to various posts—the invoice accompanying them showing prime cost, freight, insurance, and other charges. The charges are allocated evenly on the bales and each bale is made up of expensive and cheaper goods leaving the percentage of incidental charges to the prime cost as far as possible at the same level. Head-office and district expenses are apparently allocated to the posts on the basis of capital investment and transportation expenses on the basis of the weight of goods imported. A general loss on the transportation business which appears to be the rule is met by allocation to the posts. On the furs sold through London a charge of 10 per cent is made to the district for freight and warehouse charges by the London office.

With capital accounts a conservative policy is followed. Buildings[40] are constructed substantially with squared logs, whitewashed, and kept in excellent condition. They include sales shop and office, store, house, warehouse, fur press, drying frames and the ubiquitous flagpoles, the whole costing at least $3,000. Depreciation for buildings is written off at a very rapid rate as is also the case with vessels. The Company has established its own insurance fund and the loss from fires is relatively slight.[41] The inventory is conservatively valued. It is said, for example,

[37]See the *Beaver*, June, 1921.

[38]Canada, Dept. of the Interior, Natural Resources Intelligence Branch, *The Hudson Bay Railway Belt and Hudson Bay*, p. 22.

[39]Regarding the death of Indian students at a mission school at Vermilion in the eighties, see A. C. Garrioch, *A Hatchet Mark in Duplicate*, p. 161. "Which is it better to do, to persevere in his education at the risk of his life, or to permit of his return to the meat diet and outdoor life of his own people?"

[40]See a description of buildings at Fort Ellice, in N. M. W. J. McKenzie, *Men of the Hudson's Bay Company*, pp. 21 f., and of other posts, Martin Hunter, *Canadian Wilds*, chap. vi.

[41]Martin Hunter, *Canadian Wilds*, chap. x.

that dogs are carried at $4.00. To cover these various items of expense, goods are sold roughly on a tariff of 100 per cent on cost landed. Expenses of operating a post vary from $5,000 to $15,000. The district and the post are the control units of the companies' accounting systems.

On the other hand control of interior posts involves numerous problems. The character of the trade limits the effectiveness of supervision over increasingly large districts. The fur trade still depends inherently on the ability of the trader. Requisitions of the post manager in the best interests of trade at a particular post may be blue-pencilled by the district manager on general principles and lack of elasticity in directing the fur trade has notoriously serious consequences. These problems are especially evident in the appointment of a new district manager and are less serious with long acquaintance with the peculiarities of each post in the district. On the other hand long experience of the Company enables it to restrict the stock to goods actually in demand. The crucial points in an adequate control system of accounting are the interior posts. Furs are caught during the winter season. Transportation to outside markets at that time is limited and largely impossible. During the season in which furs are caught the post managers are placed beyond the control of the district manager. Prices may fall on the outside market and the post manager continues to purchase on his old tariff at a loss. Post managers will be able to follow market fluctuations more closely with the development of the radio but even this method of communication has its limitations.

These problems are seriously intensified as a result of the increase in competition. Machine industry and its effect on transportation was not limited to the Hudson's Bay Company. Railroad construction on the plains led to a marked increase in competition. Large numbers of half-breeds and former servants of the Company deserted to join the ranks of competitors. The returns were materially increased but the supply of furs was rapidly exhausted. American firms from St. Paul and the American West, and new firms from Winnipeg, Edmonton, Vancouver, and the new railroad towns took a more active part in the trade. Large numbers of miners in the gold rush of 1898 went down the Mackenzie and across the headwaters of its tributaries to the Yukon. Many of these remained in the Mackenzie district to become traders.

In British Columbia and on the Pacific coast drainage basin, the gold rush beginning on the Fraser in 1857 and extending to the Cariboo district and beyond in the sixties increased the number of free traders.

Americans rapidly followed up the retreat of the Russians after the cession of Alaska to the United States in 1867. Traders penetrated the Peace River territory[42] by Giscome Portage and the Parsnip River.[43] Elmore,[44] one of the early traders, was financed by Dunlevy[45] and other houses in Vancouver. Davis (Twelve-Foot Davis—so named because of a canoe he possessed of that dimension[46]) was another important trader. Brick Brothers,[47] sons of a missionary at Shaftesbury, brought in goods for trading purposes from Edmonton by Athabasca Landing[48] and it is claimed were the first competitors to use this trail to Peace River in 1886. Later with increasing numbers the traders were organized under Bredin, Cornwall, and Roberts. This firm sold out in 1906 to Revillon Frères—the members agreeing not to trade in certain districts for a certain period of time. The completion of the railroad to Peace River in 1914 materially changed the situation by increasing competition from cash buyers with centres in Edmonton. Furs are sent outside, sold to visiting buyers or to established firms, the Hudson's Bay Company, Revillon Frères, or smaller firms. Competition as a result is severe. Arrangements have been made in which trappers have sold their furs through a small fur exchange by sealed bids but this has not been entirely successful because of charges of collusion among the buyers.

At Fort Vermilion the development of farming and the restriction of markets had interesting effects on competition. The Hudson's Bay

[42]There was a severe epidemic and loss of life among the Beaver Indians at Dunvegan in 1886; Garrioch, *A Hatchet Mark in Duplicate*, p. 236. Garrioch mentions goldmining on the upper waters of the Peace in 1871, and a plague of mice on Peace River in 1887. The brothers E. J. and H. Lawrence went in in 1879, one on Peace River, the other at Vermilion. Garrioch took cattle to Vermilion from Edmonton in 1880.

[43]See H. J. Moberly, *When Fur was King*.

[44]Elmore traded as far down as Fort Vermilion in 1882. Garrioch, *A Hatchet Mark*, p. 189.

[45]Soda Creek.

[46]According to Somerset, *Land of the Muskeg*, pp. 51–52, Twelve-foot Davis was so called because of the size of the claim he held on the Cariboo; see Somerset for a description and sketch of Davis.

[47]For an unflattering description of J. G. Brick see Somerset, *ibid.*, pp. 35–38. Brick went in in 1882.

[48]Goods were sent to Athabasca Landing, taken up the river by steamboat and then hauled in a sturgeon-head to Lesser Slave Lake post and carried by trail to Peace River. For a valuable description of a sturgeon-head and methods of towing it, see Somerset, *ibid.*, pp. 5–7. Fort Alexandria to Fort St. James route was abandoned in 1878 and goods taken to the mouth of the Skeena, up the Skeena to Babine, and by wagon to Stuart Lake.

Company ceased its farming operations and purchased directly from the settlers, selling the produce purchased to the Indians and trappers. With increased farming operations and the high prices of furs during the war, prominent settlers disposed of their surplus produce directly to the trappers for fur. This competition began in 1916 and became increasingly serious after the war. In retaliation the Company refused to buy farm produce and imported corn meal. Mr. Sheridan Lawrence,[49] an important competitor, has been forced consequently to dispose of larger quantities of produce for furs. A later move of the Company in 1924 in reduction of steamboat rates upstream from Vermilion to Peace River may give the surplus produce a market and lessen the competition for furs. Estimates of competitors' purchases of furs at this point vary from $10,000 to $20,000. It is alleged that pressure has been brought on the government by the settlers to weaken the Company in the removal of the ferry and in other ways but the heavy capital investment of the Company in a heavily stocked store, and its long experience in handling furs together with the possession of an efficient manager would appear to count for much. Sealed bids have been used in which Lawrence, Revillon Frères, and the Hudson's Bay Company are the chief competitors but the problem has not been solved. Personal relationship and experience in judging character remains an important asset. At Red River below Vermilion Chutes, an outpost of Fort Vermilion, competition was confined to two firms, the Hudson's Bay Company and Revillon Frères—Lamson-Hubbard having been purchased by the former in 1924.

The influence of transportation improvement on competition is clearly shown on Athabasca and the Mackenzie River. With the completion of a railroad to Athabasca Landing and later to Waterways competition increased rapidly. Outfits were taken to the railhead and floated downstream to various posts. Lumber can be imported to railhead, made into scows, the goods loaded, floated down, and unloaded, and the scows broken up for the lumber to be used for building. A scow of 8–foot bottom, 11–foot top, 50–foot length, weighing 2 tons, built with about 2,000 feet of 1¼-inch lumber, will carry up to 25 tons of freight. The lumber is bevelled, nailed to the framework, and oakum is hammered in and covered with hot tar to complete the construction. At McMurray large numbers of stores compete for furs, and at Chipewyan and Fort Smith several free traders have appeared. A smaller number of individual competitors have sent outfits downstream

[49]See H. A. Cody, *An Apostle of the North: Memoirs of Bishop Bompas*, pp. 202–203.

to Resolution and to Fort Rae. Below Slave Lake competition after 1924 with the purchase of the Lamson-Hubbard Company was largely restricted to the Hudson's Bay Company and the Northern Trading Company and, to a very slight extent, the missions. The penetration of the lower Mackenzie River district by large organizations has been of more recent date. Hislop & Nagel are said to have penetrated as far as Fort Rae in 1882. This firm sold out to the Northern Trading Company in 1913. The purchase by the latter of the *Northland Trader* from the Roman Catholic mission gave them independent transportation facilities throughout the whole Mackenzie district from Athabasca Landing to Aklavik, a post established by them in 1915. With the oil rush the *Northland Pioneer* was added. This company is reported to have floated a bond issue of $185,000 in 1921 and went into the hands of the receiver in 1924. It was bought out by Mr. Max Finkelstein in 1925 and reorganized as the Northern Traders Limited although the Edmonton directorship remained with Mr. J. K. Cornwall, Mr. Slater, and Mr. Sawle. The *Northland Trader* was wrecked off Loutit Island in Slave Lake in 1924 and transportation facilities were restricted to the *Northland Pioneer*. With the loss of the latter boat (1927) a four-year contract has been arranged with the Alberta & Arctic Transportation Company for the transportation of freight.

Competition from another large organization began with the high prices of furs in the war years. In 1914 Mr. J. Bryan began as a cash buyer and with substantial profits made in the years of rising fur prices was successful in interesting Boston capitalists. The Lamson-Hubbard Company was enlarged and newly incorporated with a capital of $1,500,000 in 1916.[50] In 1918 this organization became an effective competitor in co-operating with other interests to exploit the Mackenzie territory. On Peace River the Diamond P stores, said to have been controlled by Lord Grenfell, were transferred to Lord Rhondda's interests and a steamboat, the *D. A. Thomas*, was built for river service. This equipment was transferred to Lamson-Hubbard. On the Mackenzie River developments were similar to those on the Saskatchewan River. Railroads displaced the steamboat. Previous to the construction of the Grand Trunk Pacific in British Columbia the B. X. Company had operated a steamboat line in the Fraser Valley. With the construction of the railroad, steamboats became obsolete and were moved to the Mackenzie River. Arrangements were effected with the Lamson-Hubbard Company and a third independent line operated from McMurray to Aklavik. The Alberta & Arctic Transportation Company

[50]A. L. Belden, *The Fur Trade of America*, pp. 104–105.

operated the new line as a subsidiary company of Lamson-Hubbard. Consequently control was secured of the Peace River transportation service as well as of the Mackenzie River service. Cut-throat competition which inevitably followed the existence of three independent transportation systems led to the purchase of the Lamson-Hubbard and Alberta & Arctic companies by the Hudson's Bay Company in 1924.

Competition in the Mackenzie River district from the missions is limited. The Roman Catholic missions are apparently regarded with suspicion as furs coming into their possession by gifts or otherwise are sold outside. A general statement is commonly made that Roman Catholic Hudson's Bay post managers and resident Roman Catholic missionaries are not usually good friends. Arctic Red River is cited as an example of a post established through Roman Catholic competition. The Anglican missions apparently sell their furs through the Hudson's Bay Company and Anglican mission stores charge prices mutually agreed upon with the Company. Additional competition has followed the construction of the road from St. John to Fort Nelson but it has not been of serious importance. In the Athabasca and Mackenzie River districts competition varies directly with transportation facilities.

In other areas various companies and traders have increased competition. Revillon Frères was incorporated at Ottawa, May 16, 1906 (Revillon Frères Trading Company, 1911). The firm began its activities in Canada after the visit of Victor Revillon in 1901.[51] Five posts were established on the northwest of the St. Lawrence and later another was added at Northwest River. Posts were established on Hudson Bay and the *Stord* sent from Quebec. Unfortunately she ran aground in the Gulf of St. Lawrence as did also the *Eldorado* which relieved her in Hudson Bay. The first post was finally built through a fresh voyage of the *Stord* on the River Korsook. The *Violet* was later added to the fleet. In 1908 a fleet of schooners and two new vessels, one the *Adventurer*, 2,500 tons, and the other 500 tons, were added to the Hudson's Bay service. A depot was established at Stratton Island and small boats distributed to posts at Fort George, Rupert, Moose, and Albany. Other posts were added including Whale River, Port Harrison, Athawapiscat, and Veenisk. With the beginning of the war

[51]Romanet joined Revillon Frères in 1903. He apparently spent 1904–5 at Loon Island in Hudson Bay guarding the property of the wrecked *Eldorado* and then returned to Koksoak in Labrador. A very good account of his activities at the latter post, which mentions Butler, is to be found in Lowell Thomas, *Kabluk of the Eskimo* (1932).

and the requisitioning of the *Adventurer* goods were taken from Pagwa on the C.N.R. down the Albany in scows, and headquarters were transferred to Albany. At present scows are built at Pagwa, floated down in the spring at high water to the Albany, and towed down that river to Albany post by a gas boat. In 1899 the Company built its first warehouse at Edmonton. At the same time the Prince Albert district was organized (1901–1904), and in 1905 goods were sent into Peace River. Posts supervised from Edmonton included Sturgeon Lake, Prairie Lake, Fort St. John, Fort Vermilion, Hay River, Keg River, Wabiscond, and Trout Lake; and from Prince Albert—Isle à la Crosse, Buffalo River, Clear Lake, Montreal Lake, Lac la Ronge, Stanley, Le Pas, Cumberland House, Pelican Narrows, Pukitawagan, South Deer Lake, Lac du Brochet, Casimir, and Nuelton. The Company has penetrated Peace River, the Saskatchewan River, and Hudson Bay. At railroad towns competition has become severe as at Peace River and Le Pas. At the latter point traders from Winnipeg and small stores in Le Pas follow the railroad and purchase furs from the trapper throughout the winter. Sealed bids tried for two years have proved unsuccessful because of the usual charges of collusion. Revillon Frères closed their establishment at Le Pas in 1923 and competition has continued with large numbers of small traders. The Western Grocers Company, the American Hide & Fur Company (established 1920), M. H. Levinson & Company, Ltd. (established 1922), A. B. Shubert, Ltd. (1919), The Northwest Hide & Fur Company (1890 and 1902), Carruthers Hide & Fur Company, Ltd. (1893), the George Soudack Fur Company, and the Western Traders Company are important competitors.

In areas subsidiary to railroads the number of traders fluctuates rapidly and the turnover is relatively high. Small firms which were important as fur-buying companies in the beginning of western expansion have largely disappeared. The importance of the individual trader in the conduct of the trade renders this high turnover inevitable. Stobart, Eden & Company from Winnipeg began as important traders in the Saskatchewan region. The MacMillan Company from Minneapolis was also an important buyer in that area. Norris and Carey, formerly employees of the Hudson's Bay Company, began business in Edmonton shortly after 1870. John A. McDougall began as an independent buyer in Edmonton shortly after his arrival in 1876, joined with M. R. Secord in 1897 in a partnership, and conducted a large and important trade throughout the northern and surrounding district. This firm made arrangements with numerous buyers and firms throughout the northerly fur-producing areas and sold the furs chiefly to Lampson

& Company in London. It ceased to trade in furs in 1908. I. G. Baker & Company, as well as other smaller traders, freighted goods from Fort Benton in Montana to Calgary and the north. The difficulties attending the importation of liquor by large numbers of free traders from Montana and the south, led to the organization of the Northwest Mounted Police.[52]

The increasing accessibility of the northern areas and the possibilities of the white fox have led to competition at Herschel Island and east along the Arctic coast.[53] Captain Pedersen from San Francisco trades regularly to Herschel Island outfitting other traders as William Seymour at Herschel Island, O. Bergstrom, 250 miles east, Williams and Ostergaard at Anderson River, and S. McIntyre at Langton Bay. Liebes & Company from San Francisco are also traders to Herschel Island. Captain Klengenberg[54] outfits at Vancouver and trades at two posts, Cape Krusenstern at the western end of Coronation Gulf and on Bathurst Inlet. Small traders as in the expedition of Gus and Lyman de Steffany to the Western Arctic have been able to compete temporarily.

[52]See Lieutenant Butler's instructions and report, W. F. Butler, *The Great Lone Land*, pp. 353–383; also A. L. Haydon, *The Riders of the Plains . . . 1873–1910*, chaps. ii, iii; Col. S. B. Steele, *Forty Years in Canada*, chaps. v, vi.

[53]See a valuable article, "Aklavik, Capital of Canada's Western Arctic," *Toronto Star Weekly*, February 19, 1927, pp. 24, 31; also "Canada's Arctic Now Booms," by Ross Cameron, *ibid.*, September 10, 1927. References on the opening of the West include Mgr. A. Taché, *Esquisse sur le nord-ouest de l'Amérique*; Capt. W. F. Butler, *The Wild North Land*; D. M. Gordon, *Mountain and Prairie*; C. Horetzky, *Canada on the Pacific*; John Macoun, *Manitoba and the Great North-West*; Warburton Pike, *Through the Subarctic Forest* and *Barren Ground of Northern Canada*; J. W. Tyrrell, *Across the Sub-Arctics of Canada*; H. A. Auer, *The North Country*; A. H. Harrison, *In Search of a Polar Continent 1905–1907*; D. T. Hanbury, *Sport and Travel in the Northland of Canada*; A. D. Cameron, *The New North*; G. M. Douglas, *Lands Forlorn*; E. Stewart, *Down the Mackenzie and up the Yukon in 1906*; W. B. Cameron, *The War Trail of Big Bear*; V. Stefansson, *The Friendly Arctic*, also *My Life with the Eskimo* and *Hunters of the Great North*; and E. M. Kindle, "Canada North of Fifty-six Degrees." See also *A Heroine of the North: Memoirs of Charlotte Selina Bompas* and H. A. Cody, *An Apostle of the North: Memoirs of Bishop Bompas*.

[54]See further *Klengenberg of the Arctic: An Autobiography*, ed. Tom MacInnes (1932), *passim*. Klengenberg began with floor whaling, selling bone for corsets; Herschel Island was one of his early place of operation; he drifted into fur trade with the Eskimo. He established Rymer Point in 1919 and sold furs to Captain Peterson. He had great difficulties in getting through customs and regulations which prohibited American vessels from engaging in coast trading about 1924 or 1925. He helped to establish the Hudson's Bay Company post at Bernard Harbour in 1916 with the *McPherson*. He finally settled at Vancouver and the trade was carried on by his son Patsy.

Competition has become more serious in the Western Arctic with the sale of small schooners to the Eskimo. The schooners are 30 to 35 feet long and are valued at about $3,000 or $3,500 to $4,500 with gasoline power attached. In 1924 the Eskimo fleet at Aklavik totalled thirty-nine schooners, of which nineteen had auxiliary power, and twenty-eight whale and other boats, of which two had power. These were valued at a total of $128,000 and had been brought in within five years. The Eskimo are able to visit various points to secure highest prices for furs and lowest prices for goods. Latest reports (1928) show an increase in competition in the Mackenzie delta.

On Hudson Bay and the Eastern Arctic[55] competition also developed. Competitors have included the Harmony Company of the Moravian Missionaries on the Labrador coast and the Sabellum Trading Company from London in the Eastern Arctic. The Hudson's Bay Company purchased the trading rights of the Moravian Missionaries in 1926 and the report of the Company for 1927 states that arrangements have been made with Revillon Frères of Montreal "which will enable both companies to avoid undue competition in the establishment of new posts, to consolidate their efforts on transport routes, and at the same time to co-operate in measures for safeguarding the interests of the native population." Other companies have been bought out in the Eastern Arctic and at present the Hudson's Bay Company is in substantial control.[56] On the other hand throughout northern

[55]For an excellent account of the technique of trapping up the Grand River from North West River in the winter of 1930–31, see E. Merrick, *True North*.

[56]See a list of Hudson's Bay Company posts in the St. Lawrence-Labrador district, under the management of Ralph Parsons, Fur Trade Commissioner, 1909 to 1928. R. H. H. Macaulay, *Trading into Hudson's Bay* (1934), 106.

Northern Quebec Posts	Date of establishment	Baffin Land Posts	Date of establishment
Stupart's Bay	1914	Lake Harbour	1911
Sugluk West	1925	Amadjuak	1921
Sugluk East	1929	Cape Dorset	1913
Wolstenholme	1909	Frobisher Bay	1914
Cape Smith	1925	Pangnirtung	1921
Povungnetuk	1921	Blacklead Island	1921
Port Harrison	1920	Clyde	1923
Coat's Island	1918	Pond's Inlet	1921
Mansel Island	1928	Tukik	1926

Ungava Bay Section

Fort McKenzie	1917		
Payne Lake	1921	[List cont'd p. 371]	

Canada competition has become increasingly prominent and with the construction of a railway to Hudson Bay in 1929 there are no signs of abatement.

The effect of competition on the control devices of the Company has been serious. It has been necessary to organize the trade on a competitive basis, to provide "shock" arrangements at competitive points and reserves of competent traders who can be dispatched to hold the line in danger zones. The Company has been obliged to organize its position for purposes of defence and offence. With competition in the Plains following railroad construction the Company adopted the policy of equipping the more trustworthy free traders and securing the furs through them.[57] The later methods of combatting competitors may be illustrated with reference to the Mackenzie River district which may be regarded as a front-line trench in the present competitive struggle. Competition was checked in the early period by a control of the elaborate transport organization as illustrated in letters of Chief Commissioner Grahame to Hardisty. In a letter dated Fort Garry, May 11, 1875, he wrote: "If we improve communication we cannot prevent other parties making use of the facilities we may create and consequently add to your difficulties." Again in a letter dated Fort Garry, June 7, 1876, he wrote: "Should any boats arrive at Portage La Loche not employed by the Company but carrying passengers, priests, missionaries or freight intended for McKenzie's River you will decline furnishing any transportation for them beyond that point or assistance in any way whatever." The road *via* Lac la Biche to McMurray was not used because it might give access to

	Date of establishment		Date of establishment
North Somerset Island		*St. Lawrence Section*	
Sikinik	1926	Mutton Bay	1929
		Harve St. Pierre	1929
Chesterfield Section		Oskelaneo	1926
Padley	1926	Natashquan	1926
Southampton Island	1924	Chibougamau	1928
		Labrador Section	
		Frenchman's Island	1928

In addition the following were acquired in the same period:

From the Moravian Mission
Hopedale   Nain
Makkovik   Hebron
Nutak

From Job Bros. and Co.
Blanc Sablon

[57]I. Cowie, *The Company of Adventurers*, especially chaps. xiii ff.

Manitoba traders. More recently competitors have alleged that in the large river steamboats their goods were discriminated against by higher freight rates and judicious carelessness.[58]

High prices were another effective weapon. Instructions were given to purchase at Chipewyan furs being taken out by Lac la Biche by free traders at the tariff rates of Mackenzie River district. Miners at Dease Lake were the cause of considerable difficulty following reports of the large profits of the trade. Instructions were issued that traders should take no initiative in opening up the country. Strangers were not to be permitted to take up quarters inside the posts. Traders were "not employed to buy goods but to trade furs." In 1871, McQuesten and Davis were free traders interfering with the returns of Hay River. Sinclair, at that post, was directed from Simpson to take ammunition and tobacco and live with the Indians during the winter thereby reducing the cost of Hay River establishment and securing a supply of furs. He was sent from Hay River to act in concert with the Athabasca district officer from Fort Vermilion to drive out the opposition. To prevent a change in the tariff the Athabasca officer was instructed to trade all marten and the most valuable furs at the higher Athabasca rather than Mackenzie River prices. The greatest provocation having arisen, the tariff for marten was raised from one to one and one-half and two Made Beaver. In 1872, McQuesten had been driven from Hay River with only two small packages of common beaver but later he was found at a most inconvenient place below the Forks of the Nelson and West Branch rivers. Finally it was arranged that McQuesten should be transferred to Alaska and all his goods were made over to the Company for a similar amount in kind at La Pierre's house. He gave up 173 marten at 8/ payable in goods at 100 per cent on the invoice price of the district or 166 per cent on prime cost. It was claimed that the payment of a high price was cheaper than allowing the furs to go to Manitoba to stimulate further competition.[59] Buying out of competitors in the Mackenzie River district is said to have been carried out successively during the later years.[60] The latest purchase was that of the Lamson-Hubbard Company and its subsidiary, the Alberta & Arctic Transportation Company, in 1923–24. Other

[58]The description would not hold at the present time because of the marked improvement in arrangements.

[59]For evidence of severe competition at Le Pas 1873, at Green Lake 1874, at Rampart House 1880, in the Athabasca district and at Dease Lake 1881, see Beckles Willson, Life of Lord Strathcona, pp. 341 f.

[60]See a letter regarding the policy of buying out Sylvester at Dease Lake, ibid., pp. 364–365.

methods included that of concentrating on posts in which competitors threatened to become serious. The concentration of the best traders at these posts has had effective results. The squeezing out of competitors at isolated points was carried out more effectively through the advantages of extensive communication, large capital resources, and an elaborate selling organization. The Company has charged what the traffic would bear. More expensive dry goods are sold at a higher level and the prices of the posts vary with the amount of competition. Goods are sold at a much higher price at posts down the river. At Aklavik, however, prices are forced down because of competition from Vancouver. On the other hand this policy has tended to defeat its own ends. In the competition which followed the abolition of the monopoly in 1869, the Mackenzie River as a monopoly district became the object of numerous economies. In 1871 various regulations were designed to increase the turnover of goods. Goods which sold slowly were rigidly excluded from the stocks. To increase the supply of furs double-barrelled percussion guns were exchanged only for fine furs. Even at Fort Rae, a provision post, the Indians were obliged to accept the common Indian gun for half furs and half meat. Copper kettles and steel traps were exchanged for meat. But these efforts encouraged competition and more goods were demanded. Indians became specific —refused light-pattern print cloths and demanded dark-coloured prints. Through the competitors they learned of the use of double-barrelled percussion guns and refused to give furs for any others. Complaints were heard that Indians persistently claimed that the marten hunts were bad in the autumn in order to get more debt. The Eskimo along the Mackenzie delta began to demand American patent goods—stout cotton drill, patented American awls, oxhead gimlets, small saws, dovetail saws, rat-tail files, horse bells, dog bells—following the visits of American whalers to Herschel Island and Baillie Islands especially after 1890.

Further claims were made to the effect that the Company through its influence with the government secured legislation unfavourable to competitors. Licence fees and regulations and the setting aside of Indian reserves were held to be the result of the Company's activities as they seriously affected competitors.

Competition in remote fur-producing regions renders control over the post manager practically impossible. Competitors bring in an inelastic supply of goods during the open season and these must be exchanged for the largest possible supply of furs which in turn is relatively inelastic and under conditions of competition apt to decline. The necessity of having a permanent establishment at the numerous posts, of establishing outposts, and of constantly sending out runners to get furs greatly increases the overhead of the trade and stimulates further efforts "to get the furs." The Indians are in a position to gain temporarily from the situation but competition is destructive for all concerned. The situation becomes more serious at the most distant posts since the overhead incidental to transportation must be added.

The trade during the early period was carried on largely through the personal contact of the trader. Indians received a gratuity in ammunition and tobacco for the summer, corresponding to the amount of the hunts. Chiefs were selected and rewarded on the same basis. Ammunition was supplied to enable the Indian to get provisions more easily so that he could spend more time "chasing fur." Credit was given to the extent of an outfit in the autumn and paid during the winter. Bad debts were usually struck off and recoverable debts charged off at a certain rate until they were fully paid. Attempts were made to improve this situation by abolishing the credit system, and in 1872 the Company planned a determined attack. Chief Commissioner Grahame wrote to Hardisty in a letter dated June 7, 1876, "the credit system must be discontinued." The Company was not successful chiefly as a result of competition. Gratuities are given to the best hunter by the Company and these gratuities are increased by competitors.[61] "Departures" and "arrivals," modifications of the gratuity by which the Indian coming in during the winter was given flour and bacon or "grub" for himself and dogs while at the posts, were increased by competitors. Finally the Indian brings in his fur to pay for the debt and indirectly the gratuities. The Indian persists in regarding a skin as a skin and refuses to permit grading of his catch. Unskilled fur buyers are consequently not at a disadvantage and competition becomes more serious. Moreover, the Indian is a ward of the Crown and cannot be sued if he does not pay his debt. Repayment of his debt depends on "his good heart." Instead of paying the debt the Indian may sell his furs to a competitor. This game has limitations but it is not unknown. To protect themselves against these contingencies as well as against a fall in price in outside markets and against loss on furs the Company must take a wide margin on the price of the goods. Protection can only be gained by "whipsawing" the Indian on his credit and the results are inevitable. Under conditions of competition the debt is by no means totally recovered. Indeed 75 per cent of the total is regarded

[61]For a description of competition at Chipewyan see F. Russell, *Explorations in the Far North*, p. 58.

as a very favourable recovery. Further protection is essential in higher prices and the good hunter is forced to pay the poor hunter's debts. Fur trading becomes a game of poker. Large credit is given representing in many cases a small quantity of goods. With the arrival of furs large gratuities are given. This "generosity" is in many cases rewarded with the trade. Under these circumstances accounting control is impossible. The cost of fur is difficult to determine.

It has been aptly said by a well-known trader until recently engaged in the trade, "Lack of rapid transportation and communication in the north militates against safe cash buying."[62] Improved transportation and consequent competition has led to a marked decline at Peace River of the "credit" system and the grubstaking system. At Fitzgerald and Fort Smith and at other points the more recent competitors have usually given large credits to Indians who have ceased dealing with, or who have been unable to get credit from, the Company. In many cases the furs are taken to the Company in the spring with disastrous results to competitors. In still other cases the process is not completed until the end of the second year and a rise in the price of furs may further postpone disaster. Debts may represent twice the value of the goods but competition usually prevents this method of escape. Occasionally the competitor who has survived for two or three years is in a position to compete more effectively. Under these conditions as at Fitzgerald, Fort Smith, Resolution, and other posts competition becomes more serious and changes begin to appear. Arrangements are made between competitors to abolish the gratuity system. At Resolution the system was said to have been abolished in 1922. "Departures" are said to have also disappeared, but there remains the "arrival." At other posts where competition is less severe these institutions still persist. It is said that at Fort Simpson agreements are made at the beginning of the season as to the amount of credit to be given, as to the prices to be paid for fur, as to trading on Sunday, only to disappear when the trade opens. In 1924 Fort Norman was a notorious competitive point.

The changes have been hastened by the appearance of the white trapper. The white trapper is in a position to go outside to sell his furs. He demands cash for his furs and insists that they shall be graded. Several posts have as a result one price for the white trapper and one price for the Indian. At Resolution the credit price was held to be at least one and one-half times as high as the cash price. The establish-

[62] J. K. Cornwall, *Memorandum re fur trade* [1924], University of Toronto Library.

ment of a one-price system in some posts is an indication of the effects of cash buying. At outside points control has been made effective with the introduction of modern and improved accounting systems.[63] Along the frontier with lack of transportation facilities during the winter competition has made control impossible.

In spite of the difficulties incidental to competition the position of the Company has been greatly strengthened by its personnel, by its long acquaintance with the characteristics of the trade, and by its historical position. Its advantage in the possession of a large central organization and its effectiveness in dealing with governments, its reputation in the selling market, and its connection with other important capital interests in the London market, and consequently its control over important transportation developments, have been of material importance. Its control over land at strategic posts[64] provided in Rupert's Land Act of 1869 was also important. Each of these advantages has been used effectively and with excellent results. To illustrate its strength, the Company's position has been improved at competitive points through its selection of traders experienced in bargaining with individual trappers and traders in handling fur, and in judging the market. Lots of fur are brought in by traders and trappers. The Company's representative has the fur carefully graded and counted. After examining it an offer is made usually as a lump sum worked out on the value of each grade. In other cases the fur may be sold through an exchange or by sealed bids. The Company places its bid along with other competitors. The Hudson's Bay Company trader meets competitors effectively under the most difficult conditions.

Control of a marketing organization has been an important factor in the Company's favour and a long and reputable history in the London market has given a decided advantage. Furs sent to London from various districts are carefully graded according to district and quality.[65] The standards are maintained from year to year and the purchaser has been insured against loss by an old and well-established reputation. This reputation has been found to be of considerable value in the inauguration in 1921 of a policy of purchasing skins on con-

[63]For an invaluable description of the change see N. M. W. J. McKenzie, *Men of the Hudson's Bay Company, passim.* McKenzie was with the Company practically throughout the whole period, worked his way up from the ranks, was placed in a large number of competitive districts, and was responsible for some of the innovations in accounting.

[64]For a list of the number of acres ceded to the Hudson's Bay Company at the important posts see Beckles Willson, *The Great Company*, pp. 509–512.

[65]See the *Beaver*, October, 1921.

signment. For the posts at which furs are purchased for cash and at which competition is severe, the furs are sold to some extent at Montreal and other important North American auctions but for the interior posts at which furs are purchased on credit, they are dispatched from district headquarters to London. Considerable ill feeling has existed against London because of lack of interest in the problems of the districts. The difficulties have followed partly from the grading of furs— the London houses grading the furs lower than the grades of the post and district managers. Adjustments have been made in which the posts and districts have been given a flat average tariff but difficulties still exist.[66] The marketing organization has been generally adapted to the new demands of the fur trade to strengthen the Company's position. On the other hand the effects of increasing competition have been shown and will continue to be shown in the reorganization of the trade. Larger numbers of white trappers have pushed into new country. More effective trapping has had its effect on the supply of fur-bearing animals. The Indian and half-breed population has become accustomed to new methods of trading. Increase in the importation of goods has raised the standard of living. The effects of the war as shown in rising prices have placed the trade on a new and as yet unorganized footing. New alignments are in constant process of formation and the end of the change does not appear to be immediately in sight. The ability of the Hudson's Bay Company to meet competition is registered finally in returns from the fur trade. The general decline in fur returns during the early part of the period was unmistakable. The average for each share for the first 25 years under the Deed Poll of 1871 was £213.12.2½. Outfit 1872 yielded less than half this average, £102.3.9 per ¹⁄₁₀₀ share of the 40 per cent allotted to fur traders. An increase followed in 1873 to £373.2.7, when the total profit of the fur trade was approximately £93,250, but outfit 1875 brought no returns; outfit 1876, £100; outfit 1877, £150; and outfit 1878–79, £200. The more remote districts of the Northern department[67] maintained their returns and even increased them to offset the decline[68] in the more accessible districts following settlement and competition. Mackenzie River department produced £20,086.2.3 in 1872 and approximately the same in 1873, or $100,778.82. Fall in prices, duties on imports, high wages, increasing cost of provisions, disorganization of transport following

[66]N. M. W. J. McKenzie, *Men of the Hudson's Bay Company*, pp. 195–196.
[67]G. Bryce, *Remarkable History of the Hudson's Bay Company*, p. 471.
[68]See a comparison of the returns of each department in 1871 and 1872, Beckles Willson, *Life of Lord Strathcona*, p. 349.

the shift from York Factory to Red River, personal dislikes to new appointments as with Mr. Grahame, and discontent with the new Deed Poll contributed to the difficulties of competition.

For the later period comparison is difficult because of the arrangement of the accounts combining sales shops and the fur trade. Statistics on fur returns are available, unfortunately only for the war and post-war years. A decline in the early part of the century was evident in the increasing importance of returns from the sales shop. Disorganization of the fur trade following the war and competition in Canada were responsible for severe fluctuations in profits. In 1915 the Company sustained a loss of £33,536. In the following years an increasingly favourable balance was shown and in 1919 the profits totalled £160,382. A heavy loss of £84,086 in 1921 was followed by a marked improvement in the following year with profits of £237,100 and since that date the fur trade has remained an important item. The increase has followed expansion in new areas and the adjustment of the Company's policy to the new demands of the fur trade. The heavy investment of the fur trade is still a dominant factor. On May 31, 1925, the Company had as assets invested in the fur trade, £1,425,660.

The period after 1869 has been one of the most interesting periods in the history of the trade. The last new areas in the Arctic regions and the last new tribes have practically disappeared. The trade has gone through a period of remarkable transportation and communication changes. These changes, beginning with the disappearance of Hudson's Bay Company control, have gained momentum after 1900 and especially after 1914. The increased demand for furs following improvements in manufacturing and the importance of new fur-bearing animals like the white fox have been of pronounced importance.[69] The

[69]On changes in various aspects of the fur trade see the following. G. M. Sutton, *Eskimo Year* (1934): On Southampton Island one blue fox was taken to every 100 white foxes; Eskimos on the Island sometimes take 1500 white foxes a year; the Shugliamiut, the original Eskimos on Southampton Island, died out in the 1902 epidemic. P. H. Godsell, *Arctic Trader*, gives an account of the trade from 1906 to 1934 in the Hudson's Bay Company; see also Godsell, *The Vanishing Frontier* (1939). Grey Owl, *Pilgrims of the Wild* (1934), describes the wiping out of animal life in Ontario by white trappers especially those evading the draft in 1917–18. About 1928–29 the demand for silky "fur" of the newborn seal "cats" partly changed the character of the seal hunt; W. H. Greene, *The Wooden Walls among the Ice Floes*. See B. Brouillette, *La Chasse des animaux à fourrure au Canada* (1934), for an excellent account of geographic backgrounds, habitat of animals, transportation routes, life of trappers, current trade, and conservation measures, also an appendix on the

revolution is not complete. The drift has been unmistakable and one cannot predict for the production of wild fur in Canada, without an immediate and thorough investigation with consequent regulations, a happy future. It is significant that in 1927 the Hudson's Bay Company announced that it had acquired a strong interest in two fox farms on Prince Edward Island. Monopoly in the fur trade has made its last stand. Improvements in transportation[70] and communication will go on. The time would appear to have arrived for a competent survey of the problems of the trade looking to the conservation of one of Canada's important natural resources.

---

decline of furs from 1929 to 1932 (pp. 185–186) and a short bibliography. At Rupert's House by agreement with the Quebec government a sanctuary of 7000 sq. miles was set aside for beaver in the 1930's. R. H. H. Macaulay, *Trading into Hudson's Bay*, pp. 100–101. See also a description, *Canada's Eastern Arctic*, assembled by W. C. Bethune (1934).

[70]In 1932 planes are used extensively. Rapid increase in use of aeroplanes by Hudson's Bay Company particularly with depression and possible sharp reduction in costs. Expensive packing needed for portages unnecessary and goods, flour, etc. taken in bags without further cost. Freight from Churchill to Cariboo 60 lbs. at 9 cents a lb. Contract of company to numerous posts lowers costs materially.

PART SIX

CONCLUSION

Conclusion*

1. *The Importance of Staple Products*

FUNDAMENTALLY the civilization of North America is the civilization of Europe and the interest of this volume is primarily in the effects of a vast new land area on European civilization. The opening of a new continent distant from Europe has been responsible for the stress placed by modern students on the dissimilar features of what has been regarded as two separate civilizations. On the other hand communication and transportation facilities have always persisted between the two continents since the settlement of North America by Europeans, and have been subject to constant improvement.

Peoples who have become accustomed to the cultural traits of their civilization—what Mr. Graham Wallas calls the social heritage—on which they subsist, find it difficult to work out new cultural traits suitable to a new environment. The high death rate of the population of the earliest European settlements is evidence to that effect. The survivors live through borrowing cultural traits of peoples who have already worked out a civilization suitable to the new environment as in the case of the Indians of North America, through adapting their own cultural traits to the new environment, and through heavy material borrowing from the peoples of the old land. The process of adaptation is extremely painful in any case but the maintenance of cultural traits to which they have been accustomed is of primary importance. A sudden change of cultural traits can be made only with great difficulty and with the disappearance of many of the peoples concerned. Depreciation of the social heritage is serious.

The methods by which the cultural traits of a civilization may persist with the least possible depreciation involve an appreciable dependence on the peoples of the homeland. The migrant is not in a position immediately to supply all his needs and to maintain the same standard of living as that to which he has been accustomed, even with the assistance of Indians, an extremely fertile imagination, and a benevolent Providence such as would serve Robinson Crusoe or the

---

*The reader is referred to the statement in italic type at the head of chapter 11, p. 341.

Swiss Family Robinson on a tropical island. If those needs are to be supplied he will be forced to rely on goods which are obtainable from the mother country.

These goods were obtained from the homeland by direct transportation as in the movement of settlers' effects and household goods, involving no direct transfer of ownership, or through gifts and missionary supplies, but the most important device was trade. Goods were produced as rapidly as possible to be sold at the most advantageous price in the home market in order to purchase other goods essential to the maintenance and improvement of the current standard of living. In other words these goods supplied by the home country enabled the migrant to maintain his standard of living and to make his adjustments to the new environment without serious loss.

The migrant was consequently in search of goods which could be carried over long distances by small and expensive sailboats and which were in such demand in the home country as to yield the largest profit. These goods were essentially those in demand for the manufacture of luxuries, or goods which were not produced, or produced to a slight extent, in the home country as in the case of gold and of furs and fish. The latter was in some sense a luxury under the primitive conditions of agriculture in Europe and the demands of Catholic peoples. The importance of metropolitan centres in which luxury goods were in most demand was crucial to the development of colonial North America. In these centres goods were manufactured for the consumption of colonials and in these centres goods produced in the colonies were sold at the highest price. The number of goods produced in a north temperate climate in an area dominated by Pre-Cambrian formations, to be obtained with little difficulty in sufficient quantity and disposed of satisfactorily in the home market under prevailing transport conditions, was limited.

The most promising source of early trade was found in the abundance of fish, especially cod, to be caught off the Grand Banks of Newfoundland and in the territory adjacent to the Gulf of St. Lawrence. The abundance of cod led the peoples concerned to direct all their available energy to the prosecution of the fishing industry which developed extensively. In the interior, trade with the Indians offered the largest returns in the commodity which was available on a large scale and which yielded substantial profits, namely furs and especially beaver. With the disappearance of beaver in more accessible territory, lumber became the product which brought the largest returns. In British Columbia gold became the product following the fur trade but eventually lumber and fish came into prominence. The lumber industry has been supplemented by the development of the pulp and paper industry with its chief reliance on spruce. Agricultural products—as in the case of wheat—and later minerals—gold, nickel, and other metals—have followed the inroads of machine industry.

The economic history of Canada has been dominated by the discrepancy between the centre and the margin of western civilization. Energy has been directed toward the exploitation of staple products and the tendency has been cumulative. The raw material supplied to the mother country stimulated manufactures of the finished product and also of the products which were in demand in the colony. Large-scale production of raw materials was encouraged by improvement of technique of production, of marketing, and of transport as well as by improvement in the manufacture of the finished product. As a consequence, energy in the colony was drawn into the production of the staple commodity both directly and indirectly. Population was involved directly in the production of the staple and indirectly in the production of facilities promoting production. Agriculture, industry, transportation, trade, finance, and governmental activities tend to become subordinate to the production of the staple for a more highly specialized manufacturing community. These general tendencies may be strengthened by governmental policy as in the mercantile system but the importance of these policies varies in particular industries. Canada remained British in spite of free trade and chiefly because she continued as an exporter of staples to a progressively industrialized mother country.

The general tendencies in the industrial areas of western civilization, especially in the United States and Great Britain, have had a pronounced effect on Canada's export of staples. In these areas machine industry spread with rapidity through the accessibility of the all-year-round ocean ports and the existence of ample supplies of coal and iron. In Great Britain the nineteenth century was characterized by increasing industrialization[1] with greater dependence on the staple products of new countries for raw material and on the population of these countries for a market. Lumber, wheat, cotton, wool, and meat may be cited as examples of staple imports. In the United States[2] the Civil War and railroad construction gave a direct stimulus to the iron and steel industry and hastened industrial and capitalistic growth. These two areas began to draw increasingly on outside areas for staples and even continental

[1]C. R. Fay, *Great Britain: An Economic and Social Survey from Adam Smith to the Present Day.*

[2]See Chas. A. and Mary R. Beard, *The Rise of American Civilization.*

United States has found it necessary with the disappearance of free land, the decline of natural resources, and the demand for new industrial materials, notably rubber, to rely on outside areas as shown in her imperialistic policy of the twentieth century. Canada has participated in the industrial growth of the United States, becoming the gateway of that country to the markets of the British Empire. She has continued, however, chiefly as a producer of staples for the industrial centres of the United States even more than of Great Britain making her own contribution to the Industrial Revolution of North America and Europe and being in turn tremendously influenced thereby.

2. *The Fur Trade*

The history of the fur trade in North America has been shown as a retreat in the face of settlement. The strategic campaigns in that retreat include the Conquest of New France, the Quebec Act of 1774, the American Revolution, the Jay Treaty of 1794, the amalgamation of 1821, the Oregon Treaty of 1846, and the Rupert's Land Act of 1869. The struggle continues in the newly settled areas of the Dominion. The trade has been conducted by large organizations from the artificial and natural monopolies of New France to the Northwest Company and the Hudson's Bay Company which still occupies an important position. It has depended on the manufactures of Europe and the more efficient manufactures and cheaper transportation of England. Control of the fur trade was an index of world importance from the standpoint of efficient manufactures, control of markets, and consumption of luxuries. The shift from Paris to London of the fur trade was significant of the industrial growth of France and England—just as possession of Canada after the American Revolution was significant of the industrial limitations of the United States. The demands of the Indians for cheaper and greater quantities of goods were determining factors in the destiny of the northern half of North America.

The crises which disturbed the history of the fur trade were determined finally by various important factors including the geographic background and the industrial efficiency of England. These long-run factors were obscured by a complexity of causes which centred about each crisis. In the first half of the seventeenth century the Indian trading organization was essential to the trade. In the latter part of the century the French trading organization to the interior became more effective and the market became flooded with furs. Finally the geographic limits of the trade with the canoe were reached with the extension of the trade to the Saskatchewan in the first half of the eighteenth century. In the second half of the century transport became more efficient with the development of lake transport supplementary to the canoe and the trade was extended with increased capital resources and efficient business organization to the Pacific. With continued decline in the supply of beaver, the development of a more efficient transport and of a more elastic business organization from Hudson Bay, amalgamation became inevitable and the canoe disappeared as the dominant form of transport in the fur trade. Dependence on the York boat rather than the canoe was symbolic of the increasing importance of capitalism. After the amalgamation improved transport facilities from the south led to the disappearance of monopoly control in 1869 and to the reign of competition which has become increasingly severe since that date. The beaver became less important after the amalgamation and the trade more dependent on other varieties of furs. Supply decreased less rapidly and in spite of competition the trade continued on a more permanent basis. Severe fluctuations were the result, throughout the period, of the discoveries of new territory and new Indians but especially of wars. These fluctuations were more serious in the earlier period of the French *régime* and occasioned serious results for the colony and the mother country. They became less serious after the Conquest and were less disastrous to the mother country. With the disappearance of these fluctuations, business organization became more efficient. But in the long run improved transport combined with geographic advantages reigned supreme. It was significant, however, that business organization was of vital importance to the trade and, combined with geographic advantages, maintained a strong position. This combination favoured the growth of capitalism which became conspicuous in the later days of the Northwest Company and in the succeeding Hudson's Bay Company especially after 1869.

The early history of the fur trade is essentially a history of the trade in beaver fur. The beaver was found in large numbers throughout the northern half of North America. The better grades of fur came from the more northerly forested regions of North America and were obtained during the winter season when the fur was prime. A vast north temperate land area with a pronounced seasonal climate was a prerequisite to an extensive development of the trade. The animal was not highly reproductive and it was not a migrant. Its destruction in any locality necessitated the movement of hunters to new areas.

The existence of the animal in large numbers assumed a relatively scant population. It assumed an area in which population could not be increased by resort to agriculture. Limitations of geological formation, and climate and a cultural background dependent on these limitations precluded a dense population with consequent destruction of animal life. The culture was dependent on indigenous flora and fauna and the latter was of prime importance. Moose, caribou, beaver, rabbit or hare, and fish furnished the chief supplies of food and clothing. This culture assumed a thorough knowledge of animal habits and the ability of the peoples concerned to move over wide areas in pursuit of a supply of food. The devices which had been elaborated included the snowshoe and the toboggan for the winter and the birch-bark canoe for the summer. This wide area contained numerous lakes and difficult connecting waterways, to which the canoe was adapted for extensive travel. Movement over this area occasioned an extended knowledge of geography and a widespread similarity of cultural traits such as language.

The area which was crucial to the development of the fur trade was the Pre-Cambrian shield of the northern half of the North American continent. It extended northwesterly across the continent to the mouth of the Mackenzie River and was bounded on the north by the northwesterly isothermal lines which determined the limits of the northern forests and especially of the canoe birch (*B. papyrifera*). The fur trade followed the waterways along the southern edge of this formation from the St. Lawrence to the Mackenzie River. In its full bloom it spread beyond this area to the Pacific drainage basin.

The history of the fur trade is the history of contact between two civilizations, the European and the North American, with especial reference to the northern portion of the continent. The limited cultural background of the North American hunting peoples provided an insatiable demand for the products of the more elaborate cultural development of Europeans. The supply of European goods, the product of a more advanced and specialized technology, enabled the Indians to gain a livelihood more easily—to obtain their supply of food, as in the case of moose, more quickly, and to hunt the beaver more effectively. Unfortunately the rapid destruction of the food supply and the revolution in the methods of living accompanied by the increasing attention to the fur trade by which these products were secured, disturbed the balance which had grown up previous to the coming of the European. The new technology with its radical innovations brought about such a rapid shift in the prevailing Indian culture as to lead to wholesale destruction of the peoples concerned by warfare and disease. The disappearance of the beaver and of the Indians necessitated the extension of European organization to the interior. New tribes demanded

European goods in increasingly large amounts. The fur trade was the means by which this demand of the peoples of a more limited cultural development was met. Furs were the chief product suitable to European demands by which the North American peoples could secure European goods.

A rapid and extensive development of the trade followed accessibility to the vast areas of the Canadian Shield by the St. Lawrence and its numerous tributaries and by the rivers of the Hudson Bay drainage basin. Following a rapid decline in the supply of beaver in more accessible territory and the necessity of going to more remote areas, the trade began in the Maritime Provinces, extended rapidly by the Saguenay and later by the St. Lawrence and the Ottawa to the Great Lakes, and northwesterly across the headwaters of the rivers of Hudson Bay drainage basin from Lake Superior to Lake Winnipeg, the Saskatchewan, the Churchill, across the headwaters of the Mackenzie River drainage basin to Mackenzie and Peace rivers, and finally to the headwaters of rivers of the Pacific coast to New Caledonia and the Columbia. The waterways along the edge of the Canadian Shield tapped the rich fur lands of that area and in the smaller rivers of the headwaters of four drainage basins provided an environment to which the canoe could be adapted.

The extension of the trade across the northern half of the continent and the transportation of furs and goods over great distances involved the elaboration of an extensive organization of transport, of personnel, and of food supply. The development of transportation was based primarily on Indian cultural growth. The birch-bark canoe was borrowed and modified to suit the demands of the trade. Again, without Indian agriculture, Indian corn, and dependence on Indian methods of capturing buffalo and making pemmican, no extended organization of transport to the interior would have been possible in the early period. The organization of food supplies depended on agricultural development in the more favourable areas to the south and on the abundant fauna of the plains area. Limited transportation facilities, such as the canoe afforded, accentuated the organization and production of food supply in these areas. The extension of the fur trade was supported at convenient intervals by agricultural development as in the lower St. Lawrence basin, in southeastern Ontario, and areas centring about Detroit, and in Michilimackinac and Lake Michigan territory, in the west at Red River, though the buffalo were more important in the plains area in the beginning, and eventually in Peace River. On the Pacific coast an agricultural base was established on the Columbia.

The increasing distances over which the trade was carried on and the increasing capital investment and expense incidental to the elaborate organization of transport had a direct influence on its financial organization. Immediate trade with Europe from the St. Lawrence involved the export of large quantities of fur to meet the overhead costs of long ocean voyages and the imports of large quantities of heavy merchandise. Monopoly inevitably followed, and it was supported by the European institutional arrangements which involved the organization of monopolies for the conduct of foreign trade. On the other hand, internal trade, following its extension in the interior and the demand for larger numbers of *voyageurs* and canoes to undertake the difficult task of transportation and the increasing dependence on the initiative of the trader in carrying on trade with remote tribes, was, within certain limits, competitive. Trade from Quebec and Montreal with canoes up the Ottawa to Michilimackinac, La Baye, and Lake Superior could be financed with relatively small quantities of capital and was consequently competitive. Further extension of trade through Lake Superior by Grand Portage (later Kaministiquia) to Lake Winnipeg, the Saskatchewan, Athabasca, the Mackenzie River, and New Caledonia and the Pacific coast involved heavy overhead costs and an extensive organization of transportation. But the organization was of a type peculiar to the demands of the fur trade. Individual initiative was stressed in the partnership agreements which characterized the Northwest Company. The trade carried on over extended areas under conditions of limited transportation made close control of individual partners by a central organization impossible. The Northwest Company which extended its organization from the Atlantic to the Pacific developed along lines which were fundamentally linked to the technique of the fur trade. This organization was strengthened in the amalgamation of 1821 by control of a charter guaranteeing monopoly and by the advantages incidental to lower costs of transportation by Hudson Bay.

The effects of these large centralized organizations characteristic of the fur trade as shown in the monopolies of New France, in the Hudson's Bay Company, and in the Northwest Company were shown in the institutional development of Canada. In New France constant expansion of the trade to the interior had increased costs of transportation and extended the possibilities of competition from New England. The population of New France during the open season of navigation was increasingly engaged in carrying on the trade over longer distances to the neglect of agriculture and other phases of economic development. To offset the effects of competition from the English colonies in the south and the Hudson's Bay Company in the north, a military policy, involving Indian alliances, expenditure on strategic posts, expensive campaigns, and constant direct and indirect drains on the economic life of New France and old France, was essential. As a result of these developments control of political activities in New France was centralized and the paternalism of old France was strengthened by the fur trade. Centralized control as shown in the activities of the government, the church, the seigniorial system, and other institutions was in part a result of the overwhelming importance of the fur trade.

The institutional development of New France was an indication of the relation between the fur trade and the mercantile policy. The fur trade provided an ample supply of raw material for the manufacture of highly profitable luxury goods. A colony engaged in the fur trade was not in a position to develop industries to compete with manufactures of the mother country. Its weakness necessitated reliance upon the military support of the mother country. Finally the insatiable demands of the Indians for goods stimulated European manufactures.

The importance of manufactures in the fur trade gave England, with her more efficient industrial development, a decided advantage. The competition of cheaper goods contributed in a definite fashion to the downfall of New France and enabled Great Britain to prevail in the face of its pronounced militaristic development. Moreover, the importance of manufactured goods to the fur trade made inevitable the continuation of control by Great Britain in the northern half of North America. The participation of American and English merchants in the fur trade immediately following the Conquest led to the rapid growth of a new organization[3] which was instrumental in securing the Quebec Act and which contributed to the failure of the American Revolution so far as it affected Quebec and the St. Lawrence. These merchants were active in the negotiations prior to the Constitutional Act of 1791 and the Jay Treaty of 1794.[4] As prominent members of the government formed under the Quebec Act and the Constitutional Act, they did much to direct the general trend of legislation. The later growth of the Northwest Company assured a permanent attachment to Great Britain because of its dependence on English manufactures.

The northern half of North America remained British because of the importance of fur as a staple product. The continent of North America became divided into three areas: (1) to the north in what is now the

[3]See Mrs. K. B. Jackson (as M. G. Reid), "The Quebec Fur-Traders and Western Policy, 1763–1774."
[4]See W. E. Stevens, *The Northwest Fur Trade, 1763–1800.*

Dominion of Canada, producing furs, (2) to the south in what were during the Civil War the secession states, producing cotton, and (3) in the centre the widely diversified economic territory including the New England states and the coal and iron areas of the middle west demanding raw materials and a market. The staple-producing areas were closely dependent on industrial Europe, especially Great Britain. The fur-producing area was destined to remain British. The cotton-producing area was forced after the Civil War to become subordinate to the central territory just as the northern fur-producing area, at present producing the staples, wheat, pulp and paper, minerals, and lumber, tends to be brought under its influence.

The Northwest Company and its successor the Hudson's Bay Company established a centralized organization which covered the northern half of North America from the Atlantic to the Pacific. The importance of this organization was recognized in boundary disputes, and it played a large role[5] in the numerous negotiations responsible for the location of the present boundaries. It is no mere accident that the present Dominion coincides roughly with the fur-trading areas of northern North America. The bases of supplies for the trade in Quebec, in western Ontario, and in British Columbia represent the agricultural areas of the present Dominion. The Northwest Company was the forerunner of the present confederation.

There are other interesting by-products of the study which may be indicated briefly. Canada has had no serious problems with her native peoples since the fur trade depended primarily on these races. In the United States no point of contact of such magnitude was at hand and troubles with the Indians were a result. The existence of small and isolated sections of French half-breeds throughout Canada is another interesting survival of this contact.[6] The half-breed has never assumed such importance in the United States.

"The lords of the lakes and forest have passed away" but their work will endure in the boundaries of the Dominion of Canada and in Canadian institutional life. The place of the beaver in Canadian life has been fittingly noted in the coat of arms. We have given to the maple a prominence which was due to the birch. We have not yet realized that the Indian and his culture were fundamental to the growth of Canadian institutions. We are only beginning to realize the central position of the Canadian Shield.

[5]*Ibid.*
[6]See Marcel Giraud, *Le Métis canadien.*

3. *The Forest Industries*

Canada emerged as a political entity with boundaries largely determined by the fur trade. These boundaries included a vast north temperate land area extending from the Atlantic to the Pacific and dominated by the Canadian Shield. The present Dominion emerged not in spite of geography but because of it. The significance of the fur trade consisted in its determination of the geographic framework. Later economic developments in Canada were profoundly influenced by this background.

The decline of the fur trade in eastern Canada which followed the export of furs from the Northwest through Hudson Bay after 1821 necessitated increased dependence on other staple exports. Wheat and potash had become increasingly important but they were overshadowed by the rise of the lumber trade. The transport organization and personnel of the fur trade and its capitalistic beginnings were shifted to the development of new lines of trade.[7] An extended financial organization under the fur trade was attested by the plans for the first establishment of a bank in Canada with the strong support of Phyn and Ellice[8] and the establishment of the Bank of Montreal in 1817[9] with John Gray, an old fur trader, as president and John Richardson of Forsyth, Richardson & Company, as a strong supporter. McGill University persisted as a memorial to the wealth acquired by James McGill. Edward Ellice became an important figure in London with strong colonial interests and Simon McGillivray retained an interest in colonial activities. On this basis, with the advantages of preference in England and abundant and cheap shipping after the war, the lumber exports to Great Britain increased rapidly in the face of Baltic competition.

As with the fur trade the development of the lumber trade depended on water transportation. A bulky commodity, it was restricted in the early period to the large rivers. The buoyant softwoods could be floated in rafts down the St. Lawrence and the Ottawa to Quebec for shipment to England. The largest and best trees were in demand for the square-timber trade. Square timber was in demand in England for the wooden shipbuilding industry, exports of which reached a peak in 1845.[10] As

[7]F. W. Howay, "The Fur Trade in Northwestern Development."

[8]Appendix G. For an advertisement of the Canada Banking Company, R. M. Breckenridge, *The Canadian Banking System, 1817–1890*, p. 18.

[9]See *Centenary of the Bank of Montreal, 1817–1917.*

[10]See A. R. M. Lower, "A History of the Canadian Timber and Lumber Trade," Master's thesis (University of Toronto Library).

the largest trees were cleared out it became necessary to go farther from the large rivers for timber and with smaller streams the long, square timber was more difficult to handle. Moreover, the cutting off of the forests and destruction by fires caused a decline in the flow of water in the streams and enhanced the difficulties and cost of transport. Decline in the use of wooden sailing vessels and increase in the use of iron steamships had an important effect on the square-timber trade. The saw-log trade developed with the improvement of sawmills which sprang into existence at an early date in response to the local demands of settlements. With decline in the size of logs, improvement of sawmill technique, and the hastening of transport in steamships, deals became of greater importance and, in the period prior to 1867, reached a peak in 1862.

The lumber industry created an important problem of overhead costs. Ships sailing from Quebec with lumber were in search of a return cargo which emigration provided.[11] "Coffin ships" suitable for the lumber trade were employed to take out emigrants. Immigration and settlement brought an increase in imports of manufactured products and in exports of potash, wheat, lumber, and other products. With agricultural development, labour and supplies were available for the seasonal prosecution of the lumber industry. With the westward movement settlement increased in Upper Canada and the middle west, the forests were cleared, and the St. Lawrence and the Great Lakes became more important as a transport route. The export of commodities[12] from the territory above Niagara Falls and in Upper Canada and the western states was shown in an increase from 54,219 tons of traffic in 1836 to 1,045,821 tons in 1851 passing through the Erie Canal. Wheat exported through the Welland Canal increased from 210,105 bu. in 1831 to 1,579,966 bu. in 1841, and merchandise increased from 736 tons in 1831 to 4,051 tons in 1841. The completion of the Welland Canal made possible the export of timber from the territory above Niagara Falls. Exports of staves increased from 137,718 in 1831 to 2,776,161 in 1841, square timber (cu. ft.) from 75,992 in 1832 to 1,155,086 in 1841, lumber (ft.) 986,888 in 1831 to 3,580,911 in 1841, saw logs, 4,187 in 1831 to 11,300 in 1841.

With increase in exports and imports to Upper Canada the demand for improved communication on the upper St. Lawrence became more insistent. Rafts of timber could be floated down the rapids but loads of

[11]H. I. Cowan, *British Emigration to British North America, 1783–1837.*

[12]See J. L. McDougall, "The Welland Canal to 1841," Master's thesis (University of Toronto Library).

grain and merchandise both up- and downstream became more difficult to handle. The demand of settlers for cheaper transport was an important factor in the struggle over the control of revenue to finance the construction of canals. The Act of Union of 1840 offered a solution and was followed by rapid construction of canals in the decade to 1850. Improvements of waterways were rendered obsolete through the disadvantage of water transportation, especially on the St. Lawrence with its northerly direction and its long closed season, and the construction of railroads to the seaboard in the United States. Railway lines were built after 1850 to shorten the water routes as in the road from Toronto to Collingwood. The Grand Trunk was extended from Sarnia to Montreal and Portland on the open seaboard. These railways not only joined the important settlements along the waterways but provided for the settlement of territory distant from the lakes and rivers. They provided an all-year-round outlet for lumber and agricultural produce from Canada and the United States, and for the import of merchandise.

The improvement of transportation in canals and railways had important effects on the lumber trade in providing for an extension of the supply of raw material and of the market for the finished product. The increasing demand for lumber in the United States following the rapid development of settlement in the Middle West and the growth of towns, as Chicago, stimulated the production of planks and boards. Decline in the size of trees and an increase in the number of saw logs and of smaller logs facilitated the introduction of modern sawmill technique with gang saws and band saws adapted to mass production. More recently the decline in supplies of American lumber and the rise in price of lumber hastened production on a large scale. Machine industry became increasingly important to the lumber industry. Dependence on water transportation for the raw material and the finished product, and on water power for sawing (latterly on steam power), was responsible for concentration of the industry at the mouths of large rivers as in New Brunswick. Mills were located at points accessible to large vessels along the coast and the Great Lakes as on Georgian Bay and at important waterfalls on the large rivers of the interior—the Saguenay, the St. Maurice, and the Ottawa. With the concentration, railways increased the supply of raw material as in the construction of the Canada and Atlantic Railway from Ottawa to Parry Sound by J. R. Booth.

The increasing demand for paper in the United States and the exhaustion of more available supplies of pulpwood were factors responsible for the development of the pulp and paper industry especially after 1900. Machine industry in lumber production provided a basis for the pulp and paper industry with its demands for large quantities of capital. Lumber interests were in control of substantial timber limits, of large sources of power, of skilled labour especially in the woods sections, and of capital. The decline of white pine and the existence of large quantities of spruce on the limits facilitated the shift to pulp and paper production. The migration of capital, skill, and technique from the United States hastened the movement. The forest industries concentrated about the mouths of the large rivers of the Atlantic and later the Pacific coast, the pulp and paper industry being dependent on those tributaries of the Atlantic and the Pacific which furnished abundant supplies of power.

4. Capitalism and the Staples

The lumber industry of eastern Canada was largely responsible directly and indirectly for the improvement of waterways and for the construction of railways prior to Confederation. Canal and railway construction was synonymous with heavy capital investment. Capital was obtained through private enterprise and substantial guarantees and aid from the imperial and colonial governments. Heavy expenditures involved the development of a strong centralized government in Canada. Canada's financial organization had been greatly strengthened through the strains incidental to the lumber industry. The crises in Great Britain and the United States in 1825–26, 1837, 1847, and 1857 had serious effects on construction industries and on the trade of a country interested in the export of lumber. The collapse of weaker banks in these periods contributed to the centralization of banking structure which became conspicuous in the period after Confederation. The fur trade and the lumber industry contributed the basic features essential to expansion after Confederation.

Capital investment in the transport improvement of eastern Canada brought serious problems. Immigration, settlement, and agriculture were hastened by the railroads but these were not adequate to support the overhead costs incidental to the heavy initial outlay in railroad construction and early railroad finance. Railway materials had been supplied by the rapidly expanding industry of Great Britain, and English financiers, as well as the Canadian government, were anxious to promote measures increasing traffic and reducing overhead. Sir Edward Watkin with the concurrence of the Duke of Newcastle proposed to extend the Grand Trunk to the west as a means of guaranteeing the successful operation of the road and as an escape from bankruptcy. Capital expenditures on canals had been largely responsible for the Act of Union and the additional expenditures on railways were largely responsible for Confederation and its provisions for the inclusion of the area westward to the Pacific.

Grand Trunk interests[13] in 1863 acquired control of the Hudson's Bay Company in London. This step was followed by Confederation in 1867, the sale of Rupert's Land to Canada in 1869, and finally the construction of the Canadian Pacific Railway. At one stroke Imperial interests and Grand Trunk interests favourable to the new technique replaced Hudson's Bay Company interests favourable to the fur trade. The large central organization in the fur trade facilitated the transfer and the organization of the new technique over a wide area. The fur trade and its personnel[14] continued to be fundamentally important. The fur trade had not only produced a centralized organization but it had produced a succession of fur traders who were typically self-reliant, energetic, and possessed of keen bargaining ability and high organizing capacity. D. A. Smith, later Lord Strathcona,[15] was not only an important official in the Hudson's Bay Company, trained in the school of the fur trade, but he was an influential force in the construction and management of the Canadian Pacific Railway which heralded the new industry. The relationship which existed with the opening of western Canada, in which important officials of the Hudson's Bay Company were prominent in the activities of the Bank of Montreal, of the Canadian Pacific Railway Company, and of the Dominion government, was not accidental.

The superposition of machine industry on an institutional back-

[13]See Sir E. W. Watkin, *Canada and the States: Recollections, 1851 to 1886.* On the problems of the period see R. G. Trotter, *Canadian Federation* and "British Finance and Confederation."

[14]Professor O. D. Skelton in a review of *A History of the Canadian Pacific Railway* (*Can. Hist. Rev.*, June, 1923), has pointed out the neglect of personality in the development of the railroad. The importance of the fur trade would appear to strengthen his contention.

[15]It is an interesting conjecture that the dramatic episode in the House of Commons in which Mr. D. A. Smith was in a position to oust the Macdonald administration from the government in 1873 was in part related to his connection with the fur trade. Rumours were current that Sir Hugh Allan was engaged in promoting a rival fur company to operate in the Northwest and his position as president of the Canadian Pacific Company to whom the charter for the construction of the transcontinental road had been given made this possibility unusually alarming. Mr. D. A. Smith as fur trade commissioner of the Hudson's Bay Company may have found his task in deciding the fate of the project during the debate on the Pacific scandal somewhat easier than is ordinarily supposed. See B. Willson, *Life of Lord Strathcona*, p. 337. For a most suggestive biography of Lord Strathcona see John Macnaughton, *Lord Strathcona.*

ground characteristic of the fur trade was effected with remarkably little disturbance. The rapidity with which the Industrial Revolution has swept across the North American continent was a result of the centralized organization which had paved the way for immediate growth. The economic organization of the fur trade was dependent on the Canadian Shield for a supply of furs and on the development of agriculture at convenient intervals to support the heavy cost of transportation. The economic organization of modern industrial Canada has depended on these agriculturally developed areas and more recently on the Canadian Shield. Agriculture and other lines of economic activity were started in suitable territory south of the Canadian Shield under the direction of the fur trade. The organization of the fur trade occasioned the organization of other lines of trade. The forwarding of supplies to the interior and the heavy one-way, in most cases upstream, traffic of the trade stimulated the development of trade in exports other than furs. The Hudson's Bay Company shifted from the fur trade to the retail and wholesale trade as the large number of their department stores in western Canada attests. The development of transportation organization in the recent gold rush from Hudson to Red Lake along lines already opened by the Hudson's Bay Company is evidence to the same effect. Early agriculture in Red River paved the way for the extensive production of wheat on the plains following the construction of the railroads. The parallel between wheat and furs is significant. Both involve a trunk line of transportation from Montreal to Winnipeg and feeders, in the case of the fur trade, to the north, and, in the case of wheat, to the south. Both were staples dependent on industrialized Europe for a market.

The construction of the Canadian Pacific Railway to the Pacific implied a marked advance in technology such as characterized the construction of transcontinental roads in the United States, notably cheap production of iron and steel and high explosives and standardized methods of railroad construction. The westward movement in the United States which had been speeded up with the steamboat and the railroad, eventually reached the northern part of the plains area. The stretch of level and agricultural territory in western Canada was settled during the period at which industrialism had gained momentum on the North American continent. The construction of a railway across the Canadian Shield added to the overhead costs incidental to earlier construction in eastern Canada. Rapid settlement of the prairies, rapid increase in the export of wheat and in imports of manufactured products, were encouraged as a means of increasing traffic. Wheat became a new staple export demanded to an increasing extent by the industrially deficient countries and produced, transported, and manufactured on a large scale only through the efficiency of modern industrialism.[16] With the addition of other transcontinental lines the main framework of the railway system was completed and Canada came under the full swing of modern capitalism with its primary problems of reducing overhead costs.

The problems of wheat incidental to overhead costs are of primary importance. Wheat is a plant grown in a north temperate land area. Its production has increased at a rapid rate over a long period; it affords a pronounced seasonal traffic especially as it is largely dependent on seasonal navigation; it has decided variations in yield and it occasions a pronounced one-way traffic. Wheat is shipped to the elevators on Lake Superior, to Georgian Bay ports, to Port Colborne and down the St. Lawrence to Montreal, and to Buffalo and New York. Shipping in the Great Lakes is suspended during the closed season and overhead costs on grain boats and elevators contribute to the general problem of the railroads.[17] Numerous devices have been followed in solution of the problem. The tariff has been invoked for the encouragement of a return traffic from the industrial east. The rapid industrial growth of eastern Canada and the growth of its metropolitan centres hastened the development of mixed farming. Heavy one-way traffic of vessels calling for wheat at Montreal provides for cheap freights on imports of raw material. The production of power on the proposed St. Lawrence waterway will hasten the tendency toward increased manufactures. The wheat flow has been reduced by increasing shipments through the all-year-open port of Vancouver and the Panama Canal. Industries of the Canadian Shield including lumbering, pulp and paper, mining, power development, and agriculture have been stimulated. The tourist traffic has been fostered. At the western extremity of the railroads in British Columbia overhead costs have been reduced through the rapid increase in the production of lumber, pulp and paper, minerals, agricultural products, canned salmon and halibut, and the export of wheat. The early rapid progress of the colony resulting from gold discoveries, and its feverish later development, were stabilized through railway construction, steamship connections with the Orient, and machine industry.

[16]For an interesting description of the importance of machine industry in the United States, see T. B. Veblen, "Price of Wheat since 1867." Canada had the advantage of a young country in borrowing directly from the experience of the United States. The extent of this borrowing has been tremendous in all lines of economic growth but wheat may be cited as an example.

[17]The importance of wheat to the overhead problems of the Canadian Pacific Railway has been described in H. A. Innis, *History of the Canadian Pacific Railway.*

In the fundamental problem of reduction of overhead costs, mining has occupied an important position necessitating the importation of large quantities of mining supplies to the Canadian Shield and providing for constant operation without appreciable seasonal fluctuations. The location of the mines within relatively short distances from the railroads has been a factor minimizing the problem of overhead charges. The pulp and paper industry has also contributed in its constant export of the finished product and its constant demands for labour and supplies. The development of surplus power, chiefly a result of the pulp and paper industry, has stimulated manufactures as in the conspicuous example of Arvida on the Saguenay. The problems consequent to a decline in the mining towns and to the exhaustion of resources will in part be solved by a shift in the use of power in these industries to manufactures. The industries of the Canadian Shield represent a direct contribution to the reduction of overhead costs—a contribution which promises to become even more important with the opening of the Hudson Bay region. The Maritime Provinces have unfortunately been outside the main continental developments although they have contributed to the main task through exports of coal, iron and steel, brains, and brawn. It is quite probable that they will become more closely linked with the movements following the opening of the Hudson Bay route.

The relation of the government of Canada to general economic growth has been unique. The heavy expenditures on transport improvements, including railways and canals, have involved government grants, subsidies, and guarantees to an exceptional degree. The budget debates on the heavy debt of the Canadian National Railways are an annual reminder of the relation between transport and government. The Canadian government has been an important contributor to the prosperity of the Canadian Pacific Railway and to the maintenance of the Canadian National Railways. The unique character of this development has been largely a result of the sudden transfer of large areas tributary to the fur trade to the new industrialism. The British North America Act, like the Act of Union, has provided for a strong central government. The prairie provinces as producers of wheat were controlled from Montreal and Ottawa as they were controlled in the earlier period as producers of fur under the Northwest Company. With the United States, residuary powers[18] were left with the states whereas in Canada they remain with

[18]See O. D. Skelton, *The Life and Times of Sir A. T. Galt*, especially on Galt's place in the Confederation movement; also W. B. Munro, *American Influences on Canadian Government*, chap. i, and W. P. M. Kennedy, "Canada: Law and Custom in the Canadian Constitution."

the federal government or rather with eastern Canada. Canada came under the sweep of the Industrial Revolution at one stroke whereas the westward movement of the United States was a gradual development. There are no transcontinental railroads controlled by one organization in the United States. In Canada transcontinental roads are distinct entities controlled in eastern Canada. Similarly in financial institutions the branch bank system with headquarters in the east has been typical of Canada but not of the United States. No such tendency toward unity of structure in institutions and toward centralized control as found in Canada can be observed in the United States. The Canadian government has a closer relation to economic activities than most governments. The trade in staples, which characterizes an economically weak country, to the highly industrialized areas of Europe and latterly the United States, and especially the fur trade, has been responsible for various peculiar tendencies in Canadian development. The maintenance of connections with Europe, at first with France and later with Great Britain, has been a result. The diversity of institutions which has attended this relationship has made for greater elasticity in organization and for greater tolerance among her peoples. This elasticity of institutions facilitated the development of the compromise which evolved in responsible government[19] and the British Empire. Having failed in her own colonial policy England was able to build up an empire in Canada on the remarkable success of French colonial policy. The fur trade permitted the extension of the combination of authority and independence across the northern half of the continent. Moreover, the business structure shifted from the elastic organization characteristic of the Northwest Company along the St. Lawrence from the Atlantic to the Pacific, to the more permanent organization from Hudson Bay. The diversity of institutions has made possible the combination of government ownership and private enterprise which has been a further characteristic of Canadian development. Canada has remained fundamentally a product of Europe.

The importance of staple exports to Canadian economic development began with the fishing industry but more conspicuously on the continent with the fur trade. The present boundaries[20] were a result of

[19]See Georges Vattier, *Essai sur la mentalité canadienne-française.*

[20]David Thompson was probably recommended by Ogilvie to help in the boundary commission; see J. J. Bigsby, *The Shoe and Canoe*, I, chaps. ii and v. J. B. Tyrrell became interested in Thompson through his work on the Dominion survey. Tyrrell bridges the gap between the fur trade, settlement (survey), and mining, the most recent development. See biography of Tyrrell by W. J. Loudon, *A Canadian Geologist* (1930).

the dominance of furs. The exploitation of lumber in the more accessible areas followed the decline of furs. The geographic unity of Canada which resulted from the fur trade became less noticeable with the introduction of capitalism and the railroads. Her economic development has been one of gradual adjustment of machine industry to the framework incidental to the fur trade. The sudden growth occasioned by the production of wheat and the development of subsequent staples in the Canadian Shield have been the result of machine industry. It is probable that these sudden changes will become less conspicuous as a result of a more closely knit unity and of the constant pressure of heavy overhead costs, and that Canadian growth will proceed on a more even keel. Revolutions in transport, which have such devastating effects on new countries producing raw materials, will become less disturbing even though full allowance is made for the effects of the Hudson Bay railway.

APPENDICES

Appendix A

*A Description of Hunting and Fishing, Extracted from a Manuscript
Mémoire, dated 1723, in the Public Archives of Canada*[1]

The principle of the Indians is to mark off the hunting ground selected by
them by blazing the trees with their crests, so that they may never encroach
on each other.

When the hunting season comes, each family pitches its tents in the
neighbourhood of its chosen district, and having reconnoitred the paths
taken by the beavers to their feeding ground, the traps are made in the
following manner.

They make a sort of barrier by means of stakes driven into the ground
on either side of the path, close to the pond, leaving only enough space for
the passage of the beaver or otter. There, they arrange two large levers of
about the thickness of an arm and from 8 to 10 feet long, called "saumiers,"
one of which is made fast in the ground, the other raised at one end, bears
upon the first and forms a triangular opening large enough for the passage
of the beaver; the top is closed by branches which support the "saumier."
They make a snare to the end of which is attached a piece of the beavers'
favourite wood. To give sufficient weight to the raised "saumier," they cross
over it two or more logs. When the animal starts to eat the bait, which it
can only do by passing between the levers, the "saumier" falls on its body, and
holds it. If there are several traps around the pond, and a number of beavers
have been caught, the hunters take them out, and carefully remove all traces
of blood; return to their tents and send the women to collect the spoils of
the hunt. It is the duty of the women to skin them and spread out the pelts
on a kind of circle used for that purpose, where they leave them till they
are dry. They fold them twice, the fur side in, and tie them in packages of
40 or 50. The small pelts, called "orachinées," are only folded once.

As these animals are very cunning, the hunters must use great caution.
Should the beavers not fall into these traps, the Indians set more on their
trail, made in the same way, except that two of them are placed a foot and
a half apart, with the snare supporting them both, in the middle. Thus, from
whichever side the beaver comes, it cannot avoid being caught.

The winter hunting is more cruel. The Indians break the ice opposite
the spot where the beavers come out of their huts, and surround it with
stakes driven into the ground. They leave a small opening which a hunter
covers with a net, while another destroys the hut. The beaver, trying to
escape, falls into the net, which is swiftly pulled across the ice, and the
hunter kills it with a blow on the head. Should he delay a second, it would

[1]C11A, CXXII, 307 ff.

gnaw the net to pieces. The hunters make other openings around the pond where they proceed in the same manner. This hunt is called the "chasse à la tranche," because, to break through the ice, sometimes two feet thick, they use an iron instrument, like a carpenter's chisel, called "tranche" at the end of a thick stick which serves as a handle.

The spring hunting is the most destructive. The hunters break the dams so as to drain the ponds. As the water runs off, they make entrenchments with stakes in the water, where the animals are caught; some try to escape through their holes from where the dogs chase them out and strangle them. The bite of the beavers is dangerous as they can cut through a man's arm.

The Indians eat their meat (or fish, according to a decision of the Sorbonne) which is similar to mutton, except for the flesh being red.

Appendix B

Report on the Price of Beaver 1670[1]

The only means of enabling the colony of Quebec in Canada to exist and thrive is to establish the beaver trade, its only source of income and money. Formerly, when the trade of this place was carried on by very few persons or by one company only, beaver was taken in payment, here, at the rate of 14 livres the pound, and in France, was worth 20l. and more.

In the last 5 or 6 years, competition between the numerous dealers has lowered the price to 4l. the pound. This reduction from so high to so low a price led everyone to believe that it could drop no lower. Consequently, several traders bought up a large stock of pelts, hoping for future consumption and a large profit. They were mistaken, however, there being still beaver on hand in various quarters. The vessels from Quebec returned, this year, with their cargoes for different private concerns who, as in previous years, had sought to sell their beaver, each man for himself, thus achieving the ruin of the trade and consequently of Canada, because all these merchants losing on their returns from France compensate their losses by raising the price of their produce in Canada.

Most of the habitants, having a large quantity of beaver, and receiving very little merchandise in exchange, are greatly hampered and unable to undertake anything for their own advancement. This would not occur should the King demand that all the habitants of this country, all merchants and dealers of Quebec place in the hands of a Company (formed for this purpose) all beaver *neufs* and *gras* received by them in exchange for their merchandise at the rate of 4l. the pound only the first year and 100 sols the pound the following years. The said Company would give them in exchange,

[1]Can. Arch., C11A, III, 162–166.

notes on solvent persons and would take upon itself all shipping risks, expenses and import duties into France of the said pelts, shipping them to France should it think best or leaving them in the country to await the highest prices. By means of these regulations, the Company thus formed would pledge itself to enter into relationship with the French and English of Acadia and establish a trade which might prove very advantageous both to the colony in Canada and to France herself.

His Lordship the Bishop of Canada, the Reverend Jesuit Fathers and Messieurs de Courcelles and Talon will bear testimony, if necessary, that the people of Canada will benefit by these regulations by which means the said Company would pledge itself to supply them with merchandise from France at a lower price than heretofore. This would encourage the various habitants of the country to penetrate further inland and up the rivers to seek beaver, as they would be assured of having money in France or merchandise at a reasonable price. Besides, all merchants dealing in Canada would benefit by this order of the King, having experienced, for the past four or five years, the impossibility of selling their beaver at 4l. the pound, after assuming the risks from Canada to France. In time, the people and the merchants would profit by the reasonable increase in price, and granting favours to no one, all would be free to enter the Company, or to sell their merchandise through it.

The said increase would particularly affect the Dutch who buy much more than half the *sec* or *neufs* beaver from Canada which is suitable for their Moscovie trade. For the surplus, it would affect the Spaniards to whom are sold, from France, the quantity of beaver hats necessary for Spain and the Indies, where the demand for "castor gras" hats is great, the least demand for these being in France.—It might be objected that to put all the beaver in the hands of one Company only is to create a monopoly, and that the increase in price would be to the detriment of the public, to which it may be answered that this change being made between the people of Canada and those of France, who are equally subjects of his Majesty, it follows that, far from any prejudice to the State, it will be, on the contrary, to its advantage: as one part of it, poor and weak, will be relieved and later enriched by the other parts of the State without their being inconvenienced; because the Company through whom the beaver trade would be carried on could be forbidden to sell the pelts for more than 7l. the pound the first year, and the following years 8l. the pound, in which case the increase in the price of manufactured beaver hats would hardly be perceptible.

The trade in all other skins in Canada, such as elk, otter, marten, muskrat and fox would be absolutely free, as only in the case of beaver is it necessary to centralize the trade, so as to make it profitable. Otherwise, it is likely that the colony of Canada will greatly suffer.

CHARLES AUBERT DE LA CHESNAYE

Jacques Lamothe

Appendix C

Report on the Price and Consumption of Beaver[1]

It is evident that the *ferme* is at present loaded with a stock of beaver for the payment of which it has disbursed . . . 1,433,242:2:6: ll. On the basis of the purchase price only, not including interest, cost of freight and carriage, depreciation, the value is estimated at . . . 400,624:13: ll.

The stock of beaver of the *ferme* today is worth . . . 2,760,048:5: ll. Of this quantity of beaver, it must be noted that for the current year 1694, in December last, 615,273:15: ll. worth has been received. According to letters received from Canada this year, we are assured that at least the same quantity of beaver will be received next December for the year 1695. Should this continue in the same proportion for the next few years, the Council may foresee the consequences. The merchants' profit on the high prices, fixed for beaver, and the ready cash which the *ferme* pays, have been responsible for increasing this trade to its present standard. However, there is no market for beaver, the demand for which is limited and cannot be forced. And judging by the amount of pelts received from Canada and the state of the market since the beginning of Pointeau's Lease, he will find himself, by the end of his term, with over 4,000,000 pounds on his hands. Which is shown by the following statement.

Amount of beaver sold:

During the first year

For home consumption, only	200,000:livres
" foreign " "	40,119:

During the second year

For home consumption	Nil
" foreign " , only	146,464:

Thus the amount of sales for two whole years will be barely 350,000:

The foreign trade is practically extinct. Merchants from Holland to whom Domergue had sold, during the year 1690, about 400,000 pounds' worth of beaver have still half of it on their hands which they are selling at a loss in order to get rid of it, and forcing prices down. And when they consider buying, it is only in small quantities, and on condition that the Company take back the *castors coupés* at half the value.

[1]Can. Arch., C11A, XII, Pt. I, 347–353.

Home consumption decreases daily, as shown in the falling off of the hat industry, reduced to half its former production.

Thus, the principal trade and the most profitable to the *fermier* is that carried on through France, with Spain for the consumption of the Indies. This has been stopped by the disorder in Mavalde and by the cessation of commerce on account of the war.

There is little hope for trade during the remainder of the Lease.

As regards Paris, the Company has, on several occasions, communicated with the principal hatmakers, both in general and in particular, offering them all possible credit facilities. But it has been unable to sell them 10,000 écus worth of merchandise, no matter what conditions it proposed to them. The shortest term they ask is three years. Three quarters of the hatmakers are ruined.

It is certain that the best market for this trade is that of the Kingdom and the Indies, as the sales price is the same, in the trade of Mavalde. The fixed assortment for their consumption consists of one quarter *castor gras* to three quarters *sec*. Beaver only costs the *fermier* 5l. 10 sols, and he sells it at 10l. the pound, which would bring him a considerable profit, but for his being overstocked to the extent of 17,000,000 and Home consumption never exceeds 150,000.

It may be estimated that one-half of the receipts from Canada consists of *castor gras* so that it is inevitable that at the end of the lease the *ferme* will be overstocked with more than two million, other things being equal. Most of the pelts at La Rochelle are damaged by vermine, and the experts who have inspected them say they will barely last a year. To save those in Paris, it has been necessary to clip the extremities of the pelts, with considerable waste.

The other kinds are exorbitant in price.

Castor sec for which the *fermier* pays 3l. 10 sols (one quarter deducted) can only be sold for 3l. 5 sols after the expenditure of freight and carriage and loss from waste and depreciation. There is therefore no profit.

The "Moscovie" for which he pays 4l. 10 sols cannot be sold at more than 6l. 10 sols the pelt up to 1½ pounds in weight, which brings it to the same price as the *sec*. The Company has offered lately to sell the skins at 3l. to 6l. and even then, cannot find buyers. This trade is being ruined.

From the above, two things result. Firstly, that the price set for the inhabitants of Canada is too high. Secondly, that the quantity being unlimited, the supply will always exceed the demand to such an extent that, at the end of this lease, the *ferme* will be stocked with a sufficient quantity of beaver to last the whole of the next lease. From which will result two drawbacks: either the *ferme* will not be able to dispose of the stock or Canadian trade will have to be abandoned. The only remedy is to make this a free trade so as to take it out of the *fermier*'s hands, to accept only beaver of good quality, both *gras* and *sec*, and also to reduce the purchase price in Canada.

Appendix D

Arrangements of the Hudson's Bay Company[1]

Resolved

1. That the Trade shall continue to be carried on for Account of the Company by servants entirely under the Control and removal at pleasure of the Committee.
2. That in place of the premia heretofore allowed to the servants at the Bay, certain shares of the net Profits of the Trade shall be allotted to the officers of the several Establishments, in the manner after specified.
3. That the Territories of the Company shall be divided by fixed limits so as to allot a specified District to each Factory.
4. That two new Factories shall be established one to comprehend the Country on the waters of the Saskatchewan above Cumberland, the other the remainder of the Country lying upon the waters which run into Lake Winipig.
5. That the general regulation of the affairs of the Company in the Bay shall be entrusted to two superintendants, one for the 5 northern Factories the other for the 3 Southern: to each of whom an adequate number of clerks shall be allowed.
6. That each Factory or District shall be in the immediate charge of a chief Factor, who shall have subordinate Traders under his Command.
7. That to each Factory there shall be appointed an Accountant, who shall also act as Storekeeper; and who shall be next in Authority to the Factor.
8. That the goods sent out by the Company for each Factory shall be consigned to the Factor, who shall be responsible for them; and for those intrusted to the subordinate Traders, as well as those which remain under his own more immediate management.
9. That each Factor shall be authorized to trade with the Indians within his limits, according to any rate or standard, which he shall judge most advisable, and suitable to local circumstances.
10. That each Factor shall have power to direct the proceedings of the Traders in his district, and to suspend from his functions any Trader, who is guilty of malversation, neglect or disobedience.
11. That all transactions both of the Factor and the subordinate Traders, shall be communicated to the Accountant, who shall make up regular Accounts for the accuracy of which he shall be responsible.
12. That the Accountant shall be particularly charged to make up annually a correct Inventory of the goods on hand at every Trading house within the limits of the Factory, as also of the outstanding Debts due by In-

[1]Can. Arch., Selkirk Papers, I, 29–36.

dians and by the Company's servants at the period of closing the Accounts of the year.

. . . .

16. That it shall be the duty of the Superintendant to direct and inspect the shipment of the Trade from the several Factories, as also the delivery and transmission of the goods consigned to each; to examine the Accounts of the several Factories in his Department their Indents, and the journals of the Factors and Traders, before they are transmitted to the Committee, to whom he shall report his observations on their contents: also to inform the Committee of the conduct and character of every officer in his department, generally to suggest every error, which may require to be rectified, and every improvement which he thinks advisable, in the mode of conducting the Company's affairs.

17. That the Accounts shall hereafter be kept in sterling money.

18. That in the Invoice of goods annually consigned to each Factory, every article shall be charged at an advance on the prime cost, sufficient to cover the expence of freight, insurance, interest of outlays, and charges of the Company's general Establishment.

19. That on Trading goods and Provisions this charge shall for the present be at the rate of 70 per cent advance on the prime cost, including in the cost all export duties and shipping charges.

20. That in the Inventories of stock on hand at the close of each year, the Factory shall value the goods remaining in store at an advance on the Invoice prices, which shall be calculated, to reimburse the expenses of storage and transport inland and which for the present shall be at the rate of   per cent on goods in the principal Factories of Churchill, York, Severn, Albany, Moose, and Eastmaines at   per cent on goods in store at the Trading houses within the districts of these Factories; and at the rate of   on goods in store at any post beyond the Outlet of Lake Winipig.

21. That in the Inventories of stock on hand, the Factories shall value the outstanding Debts due by Indians, according to the price of the goods advanced to them, calculated at the above rates and deducting one half of the total amount on account of the chance of bad debts.

22. That the servants of the Company shall be charged, for any goods which they may receive from the Trading stores, at the rate stated in the Inventory of the Post where they are taken up; but that each man may indent for such stores as he wants which shall be sent out with the next shipments: that the goods so indented for by the servants shall be stated separately in the Invoice, and charged at an advance of only 40 per cent on the prime cost and shall be delivered to the men at the Invoice price free from any additional charge for storage or Inland transport.

23. That an account shall be stated annually between the Company and each Factory in which the Factory shall be debited with

i. the stock on hand, remaining from the preceding year valued as specified in Resol: 20 and 21.

ii. the provisions, trading goods, and shops consigned to the Factory, charged at their Invoice prices.

iii. the whole yearly wages of the servants on the establishment of the Factory;

and on the other hand the Factory shall be credited with:

i. the stock on hand at the close of the year.

ii. the goods furnished to the Company's servants at the rates at which they are charged to the men and deducted from their wages.

iii. the net returns of the Trade of the Factory which shall be calculated from the price received at the Company's sales, deducting therefrom the Import Duties, and   per cent for freight and insurance:—the balance of this account to be reckoned the net Profit or Loss of the Factory.

24. That one half of the Net Profit of each Factory shall be distributed among the servants of the Company in the following proportions:

⅓ to the chief Factor

⅓ to be divided in equal shares among the masters of Trading Houses belonging to the Factory

⅓ to go to a General Fund contributed to by all the different Factories.

25. That the General Fund shall be divided among the two Superintendants, their Clerks, the Accountants of the Factories, and the Surveyor in proportions to be hereafter determined.

26. That besides the above premia the company shall allow fixed Salaries, not exceeding.

£ 150 to the Superintendants

£ 100 to the Factors

£ 60 to the Accountants

£ 50 to the Traders

£ 50 to the Superintendants Clerks

£ 60 to the Surveyor

27. That the Salaries of the Superintendants, their clerks, the Accountants and the surveyor shall be charged to the General Establishment of the Company and that the salaries of the Factors and Traders shall be charged to the Factory accounts.

28. That in case the shares of profit to be allowed to the servants in the Bay shall not amount altogether to £ 3,600 the Committee will take the cases of the several officers into consideration and where the individual appears to have conducted himself with zeal and ability, will make up his allowances to a sum not less than his emoluments have hitherto been.

That as the new system may not immediately produce all the effects, which are ultimately to be expected from it, the Committee will for the present allow the following salaries and insure the following premia to the respective Factors.

Salary		Prem.	Total	Former emol[ts]	
C. R.	100	150	£250	Auld	210
T. R.	80	100	180	{McNab	330
S. R.	80	100	180	{Cook	110
A. R.	100	150	250	Thomas	174
N. R.	100	120	220	Hodgson	300
E. N.	80	100	180	Thomas	210
Sask[n].	80	80	160	Gladmaint	180
Winipig	80	100	180	Bird	150

29. That after deducting £30 from the whole present emoluments of the Traders the remainder be allowed them respectively as paid salaries, and a premium of £30 be insured to them for the present thus securing to them at least the same emoluments as they at present enjoy.

Appendix E

An Estimate of the Furr and Peltry Trade in the District of Michilimakinac according to the Bounds and Limits Assigned to It by the French when under Their Government, with Their Names and Situations of Its Several Outposts Written by Major Robert Rogers Dated 27th of May, 1767[1]

To Fowler Walker:
List of Posts and the number of Canoes necessary to supply them.

In Lake Huron

Saguinau Bay	3
Machidach and Riviere au Sable	3

In Lake Michigan

La Grand Riviere and a few small Posts depending on it	6
St. Joseph and it's dependancies	8
Milwayte	8
La Baye and its Dependancies	30

In Lake Superior on the South Side

St. Marys	2
La Point, Chaguamigon, including St. Ance La Fonde du Lac } La Riviere Serpent and petite ouinipeck . . . . . . }	8

[1]Can. Arch., Hardwicke Papers, 35915, Pt. II, 219–222; also "Rogers's Michillimackinac Journal," *Proceedings of the American Antiquarian Society*, XXVIII, 224 ff.

On the north Side

Michipicoton 1
Changuina, Camanistiquoia or three Rivers 3
Nipigon and it's Dependancies one large one and five ⎰
    small ones which is equal to . . . . . . ⎱ 4

For the interior parts of the country
To West and North West of Lake Superior

Lake La pluye Six small canoes equal to 3
Lake du Bois Two Do   Do 1
Riviere de Boeuf and La Riviere Ouinipeck three small ⎰
    canoes equal to . . . . ⎱ . . . 1½
Fort la Reine on Lake Ouinipeck five small Canoes equal to 2½
Fort la Biche Three small canoes equal to 1½
Fort Dauphin Three small Canoes equal to 1½
Fort depee Five small Canoes equal to 2½
La prairie Five small canoes equal to 2½
The Scioux 2
If the foregoing parts are supply'd agreable to the above ⎫
plan I'm well informed that no more than about six canoes ⎬ 6
would be annually consumed at Michilimakinac . . . ⎭

Large canoes 100

One hundred canoes will not be more than sufficient for the annual consumption, if this trade be extended under proper Regulations to the Outposts, the Load for one of which when made up in Montreal into Bales of about Ninety Pounds French weight, for the conveniency of carrying them round the falls of Rapids, on the Awawa or North River, on the route of Michilimakinac is as follows. Eighteen Bales containing strouds, Blankets, Frize Coats, callimanco Bed Gowns, coarse callicoes, Linnen shirts, Leggings, Ribbons, Beads, Vermilion, Gartering, and many other such articles, also the following Pieces of about the same weight
Nine Kegs of Gun Powder
One Keg of Flints steels and Gun Screws
Ten Kegs of British Brandy
Four cases of Iron Work and cutlery ware
Two cases of Guns
Two bales of Brass Kettles
Two cases of looking Glasses and combs
Five Bales of manufactur'd carrot Tobacco
Twelve Baggs of Shot and Ball
One Box of silver Work and Wampum
Which goods at the lowest value at Quebec amount to £450 Sterling ⎰
    p. canoe . . . prime cost of 100 Canoes . . . ⎱ £45,000
To which I may add the price of the canoes together with the ⎫
wages of upwards of 1,000 Men, which are annually employ'd in ⎮
this Trade between spring and Harvest to navigate said canoes ⎬ 9,550
at £95 10ˢ p. canoe . . . . ⎭
Wages of clerks on Commissioners employ'd in sᵈ Trade com- ⎰
    puted at about . . . . ⎱ 3,888

I may also allow for Money annually paid to Mechanicks such as ⎫
Blacksmiths carpenters coopers and Taylors to make up cloaths ⎪
shirts and other things necessary for this trade together with ⎪ 1,740
the charges of carrying the said goods from Montreal to La Chine ⎬
and from Shenectady five leagues from Albany in order to be ⎪
embark'd . . . . ⎭
Provisions such as Beef Pork Biscuit Pease etc.   720

Prime cost and total expence of One hundred canoes to Michilimakinac £60,898

So that the total amount of the Merchandize with the outfitt and expences come
to £60,898 sterling in case the trade be open and free to the different Outposts
and these properly regulated by the commandant or Governor of Michilimakinac so that the whole may be equally divided as in the time of the French
which I have reason to think is not exaggerated.

Appendix F

Tariff Schedule of the North West Company[1]

And it appearing to the Concern by correct calculation that the present
Freight and advance are inadequate to form the just value of Goods at the
place of Rendezvous and in the Posts of the Interior:—The undersigned
Proprietors, forming a legal majority of the North west Company; at a
meeting held at Kamanitiquia this tenth day of July in the year of our Lord,
One thousand eight hundred and four . . . RESOLVED UNANIMOUSLY,
that the property belonging to this Concern shall henceforth be valued, at
all the Posts and settlements of the Company in the North West, and on
Lake Superior, according to, and at the rates of advance or percentage of
THE TARIFF OR SCHEDULE hereunto annexed, and not otherwise; The
said evaluation and advance to commence with the Inventories assumed by,
and composing part of the present Outfit 1804 and henceforward to be continued, . . . All Proprietors (and by their Order's) persons having Goods in
charge to class or assort their Inventories conformable to said Schedule. . . .
TARIFF or SCHEDULE[2] *referred to in the annexed RESOLVE of the
NORTH WEST COMPANY.*
at Batchiwina . . . Michipicoton and the Pic: Twenty percent advance
on the Cost at Montreal of all Goods as imported, *without distinction of
pieces*; at Kaminitiquia, twenty three per cent advance on the Montreal
Cost of all Goods without reserve.

[1]Can. Arch., Northwest Company Minutes.
[2]In the interior the percentages were based on the cost and advance to
Kaministiquia and varied with distance and the character of the goods. Dry

Appendix G

Articles of Agreement for Establishing a Bank at Montreal in Canada[1]

The parties of this Agreement, having come to a determination of forming a Bank at Montreal in Canada, have agreed as follows:—

1st.   The said Todd, McGill & Co. and Forsyth, Richardson & Co. engage to procure as soon as possible a separate office or house for the purpose of carrying on the Banking Business, and with the assistance of a Clerk or Clerks or of a person holding a share in said business make and issue Promissory Notes or Bills for and in the name of the Canada Banking Company, and for the payment of which Notes or Bills the parties to this Agreement hereby become bound and liable.

2nd.   It is agreed that no Notes or Bills shall be considered valid or bonding on any of the parties to this Agreement unless the same be signed by one of the two Houses of Todd, McGill & Co. and Forsyth, Richardson & Co. and by the Manager or Director for the time.

The said Phyn, Ellice & Inglis engage to honor all Bills drawn on them in the name of the Canada Banking Company, provided said Bills be signed by either Todd, McGill & Co. or Forsyth, Richardson & Co. They the said Phyn, Ellice & Inglis also agree to negotiate Bills and generally to do and transact all and every branch of the necessary business regarding this establishment free of commission or

---

goods including cases of guns, knives, hats, and baskets of kettles paid on the Kaministiquia advance and cost; 26% to Fond du Lac department and its dependencies; 45% to Nipigon department, and Lac la Pluie, Lac Ouinipique, Upper and Lower Red Rivers and Fort Dauphin departments; 60% to Fort des Prairies or the Rivière Opas departments; 65% to English River and dependencies; 70% to the Upper Athabasca River; 80% to Athabasca and dependencies. Tobacco to the various departments in the above order was increased from 65% to 105%, to 150%, to 155%, to 175% and 210%; gunpowder from 53% to 90%, to 125%, to 130%, to 140%, and to 170%; ironworks from 105%, to 130%, to 165%, to 170%, to 190%, and to 230%; high wines from 130%, to 210%, to 305%, to 310%, to 350%, and 420%, and shot and ball from 167% to 375% but in contrast with other commodities declining to 350% to Fort des Prairies or the Rivière Opas departments, and increasing again to 360%, to 400%, and to 490%. The position of shot and ball was the result of its importance to the provision departments. An assorted average of these goods increased from 55%, to 87%, to 112%, to 113%, to 123%, and to 130%. The average freight of each piece was determined at £4.10 to Fond du Lac and to the others in order, to £7.10, to £10.15, to £11, to £12.5, and to £14.16 Halifax Currency.

[1]Wolford, Simcoe Papers, II [1792], 375.

other charge for their own personal trouble, the parties considering that the share each holds is a sufficient compensation for any personal trouble.

It is agreed that none of the parties to this agreement shall under any pretence make use of money belonging to the Bank but for the purpose of discounting Notes or Bills or applying its fund in any other manner than is usually done in Establishments of this nature, and that they shall make no purchase or purchases of any kind or species of merchandise nor of any fixed or landed property except it be judged for the advantage or credit of the Company to be possessed of a house for the purpose of transacting the business.

That this Establishment shall commence from the date of this Agreement and continue for seven years successively, during which time no dividend of profits is to be made nor are any of the parties to draw out any monies from the Stock or Capital of the Company.

And for the true performance of this Agreement the parties hereunto bind themselves, their Executors, Administrators and Assigns jointly and generally, the one unto the other in the penal sum of five thousand pounds Sterling money of Great Britain to be paid by the party or parties breaking or not complying with this Agreement unto the other or others of the said parties, their Executors, Administrators and Assigns performing or willing to perform the same.

In witness, etc.

(signed) Phyn, Ellice & Inglis.

Isaac Todd, on Behalf of Todd, McGill & Co.

Thomas Forsyth, on behalf of Forsyth, Richardson & Co.

Appendix H

Comments by Author on Text[1]

page

12 According to the late Professor Louis Allen of University College, the University of Toronto, these Indians, as far as could be gathered from the vocabulary left to Cartier, were not Hurons but possibly Onondagas or western Iroquoian group.

22 In this period did agricultural Indians of St. Lawrence carry on hunting and have their positions weakened as monopoly traders in

[1]For an explanation of this Appendix, see above, Preface to the Revised Edition, p. x.

the same way as the Hurons later?—i.e. hunting and agriculture and control over St. Lawrence exposed them to raids from Montagnais etc. and Hurons.—Should it [this section] be headed struggle for the St. Lawrence—[wherein] monopoly position of agricultural St. Lawrence Indians broken?—i.e. were St. Lawrence agricultural Indians middlemen as Hurons were later and did they hold monopoly position?

In favour of this [view, was the] monopoly asked for by Cartier's nephews in seventies.

40   Was this because Indians were forced by Iroquois to leave St. Lawrence and come down by old route to Saguenay?

40   Were the difficulties accentuated by Iroquois raids in 1650's and in 1661–2 which necessitated stronger govt. activity?

49   French checked from James Bay on Albany—Indians shifted to Lake Winnipeg and York Factory 1682.

109   Contrast with fisheries—character of set-up—imperfect competition vs. more imperfect competition.

119   Pull to north
French pulled to south by Mississippi weakened hold on north in competition with H.B. diversified empire.

119   Were Radisson and Groseilliers an illustration of forcing out of French by Iroquois?—i.e. pressure from Dutch and Iroquois forced French to back route to Saguenay and led to movement to Hudson Bay with English by Radisson and Groseilliers.

119   Problems of readjustment and reorganization, delay in meeting changed conditions, imperfect competition. Concentration of French on St. Lawrence and opposition to Radisson developing two routes.

120   Significance of Restoration—wealthy court favourites supported formation of H.B. Co. and provided market for furs. Government by wealthy class meant close control and character of commodity demanded strict supervision to prevent private trade—same problem as Spanish with gold—closely centralized government a result.

152   Effect of American Revolution in destruction of Churchill and forcing Americans under Pond to Northwest.

200   Significance of increased demand for capital for transport over long distance to amalgamation.

338   Significance of opposition of H.B. to U.S. in Columbia in compelling U.S. to press south to take California from Mexico. Stronger British opposition weakened U.S. except that Oregon boundary readjusted. But opening of gold mines and taking over of California relieved whole pressure on B.C. If gold rush earlier would Columbia have been saved?

393 Rôle of Edward Ellice [in] unifying XY Co. and N.W. N.W. and H.B. Co. important to bill of union 1822 and probable influence on Durham 1840.

Fur trade unifying trend followed by federal trend [to] confederation—i.e. Maritimes etc. Carry over fur trade tendencies to St. Lawrence [their] disappearance with divergent interests N.S.

397 The southern route followed by the C.P.R. may have been partly a result of Strathcona's influence and his attempt to keep ry. from northern fur trading area and near U.S. boundary to develop settlement.

398 H.B. Co. hampered Confederation and expansion of west evident in delay and struggle of settlers for assembly—Riel rebellion etc. and on other hand by sudden rush of settlement and building of C.P.R. along southern route.

N.W. Co. [tended to] centralization

but after 1821 H.B. Co. tended toward disunity—difficulty of buying them out, on other hand Strathcona a factor linking whole together.

406–7 Balance St. Lawrence and H.B. Co. destroyed 1821 tended to stress immediately new staple of timber trade. Thread had snapped necessitating emphasis on new developments.

Problem of H.B. route:

1. French war against it but military operations and surplus furs brought inflation.
2. La Vérendrye expansion with H.B. competition brought downfall of *régime*.
3. Over-expansion to B.C. of N. W. Co. and final supremacy [of H.B. route] 1821
4. Ry. Competition 1929

    Effects on finance—Prior to 1713 govt. expenditure—inflation

                      Prior to 1763 govt.   ”   ”

                      Prior to 1821 over-capitalization of N.W. Co. (esp.) amalgamation

                      Prior to 1929 [over-capitalization of railways] govt. ownership

References

THE FOLLOWING is a list of the published works to which reference is made in the text.

An account of a voyage. . . . By the clerk of the *California.* See [Drage, Theodore Swaine].

Albany, New York (county), Committee of Correspondence. *Minutes, 1775–1778.* Albany, 1923–1925. 2 vols. (Continental Congress, Committee of Safety, Protection and Correspondence at Albany.)

Alcock, F. J. "Past and present trade routes to the Canadian Northwest." *Geographical Review,* Aug. 1920, pp. 57–83.

Askin, John. *The John Askin papers;* I, *1747–1795,* II, *1796–1820.* Ed. Milo M. Quaife. Detroit, 1928, 1931.

Atcheson, Nathaniel. *American encroachments on British rights; or, Observations on the importance of the British North American colonies and on the late treaties with the United States.* London, 1808.

[Atcheson, Nathaniel]. *On the origin and progress of the North-West Company of Canada, with a history of the fur trade, as connected with that concern; and observations on the political importance of the Company's intercourse with, and influence over the Indians or savage nations of the interior, and on the necessity of maintaining and supporting the system from which that influence arises, and by which only it can be preserved.* London, 1811.

Audubon, J. J. *Audubon and his journals.* Ed. Maria R. Audubon, with zoölogical and other notes by Elliott Coues. London, 1898.

Auer, H. A. *The north country.* Cincinnati, 1906.

The Aulneau collection, 1734–1745. Ed. Arthur E. Jones. Montreal, 1893.

Babcock, H. L. "The beaver as a factor in the development of New England." *Americana,* XI, 1916, 181–196.

Bacqueville de la Potherie, Claude Charles Le Roy. *Histoire de l'Amérique Septentrionale.* Paris, 1722 (1716?), 1753. 4 vols.

Bailey, V. *Beaver habits, beaver control and possibilities in beaver farming.* United States, Department of Agriculture, Bulletin no. 1078. Washington, 1922.

Ballantyne, Robert M. *Hudson's Bay; or, Every-day life in the wilds of North America, during six years' residence in the territories of the Honourable Hudson's Bay Company.* Edinburgh, 1848.

Bancroft, H. H. *History of the Northwest coast, 1543–1846.* San Francisco, 1884. 2 vols.

Bank of Montreal. *The centenary of the Bank of Montreal, 1817–1917.* Montreal, 1917.

Barnes, F. W. "The fur traders of early Oswego." *Proceedings of the New York State Historical Association,* XIII, 1914, 128–137.

Baxter, James Phinney. *A memoir of Jacques Cartier, sieur de Limoilou; his voyages to the St. Lawrence; a bibliography.* . . . New York, 1906.

Beard, Charles A. and Mary R. *The rise of American civilization.* New York, 1927–42. 4 vols.

"Beaver trade agreement." *Report of the Public Archives for the year 1928*, pp. 32–44. Ottawa, 1929.

Begg, Alexander. *History of the North-West.* Toronto, 1894–95. 3 vols.

Belcourt, G.-A. *Mon itinéraire du lac des Deux-Montagnes à la rivière Rouge. Bulletin de la Société Historique de Saint-Boniface*, IV, 1913.

Belden, A. L. *The fur trade of America and some of the men who made it and maintain it.* . . . New York, 1917.

Bell, C. N. *The earliest fur traders on the upper Red River and Red Lake, Minnesota (1783–1810).* Transactions of the Historical and Scientific Society of Manitoba, no. 1 new series. Winnipeg, 1926.

—— ed. *The journal of Henry Kelsey, 1691–1692.* Transactions of the Historical and Scientific Society of Manitoba, no. 4 new series. Winnipeg, 1928.

—— *The old forts of Winnipeg (1738–1927).* Transactions of the Historical and Scientific Society of Manitoba, no. 3 new series. Winnipeg, 1927.

Bell, Robert. "Report on Hudson's Bay and some of the lakes and rivers lying to the west of it." Canada, Geological Survey, *Report of Progress*, 1879–80, pp. C1–113.

Bemis, S. F. *Jay's Treaty, a study in commerce and diplomacy.* New York, 1923.

Bennett, G. V. "Early relations of the Sandwich Islands to the Old Oregon Territory." *Washington Historical Quarterly*, IV, 1913, 116–127.

Benton, E. J. *The Wabash trade route in the development of the Old Northwest.* Johns Hopkins University Studies in Historical and Political Science, Series XXI, nos. 1–2. Baltimore, 1903.

Bethune, W. C. *Canada's eastern Arctic: Its history, resources, population and administration.* Ottawa, Department of the Interior; Lands, Northwest Territories and Yukon Branch, 1934.

Biggar, H. P. *The early trading companies of New France: A contribution to the history of commerce and discovery in North America.* University of Toronto, Studies in History. Toronto, 1901.

—— *The voyages of Jacques Cartier.* Published from the originals with translations, notes and appendices. Publications of the Public Archives of Canada, no. 11. Ottawa, 1924.

Bigsby, J. J. *The shoe and canoe; or, Pictures of travel in the Canadas illustrative of their scenery and of colonial life.* . . . London, 1850.

Blair, E. H., trans. and ed. *The Indian tribes of the upper Mississippi valley and region of the Great Lakes, as described by Nicholas Perrot,* . . ., *Bacqueville de la Potherie,* . . ., *Morrell Marston,* . . ., *and Thomas Forsyth.* . . . Cleveland, 1911. 2 vols.

Bliss, Henry. *The colonial system: Statistics of the trade, industry and resources of Canada and the other plantations in British America.* London, 1833.

Boit, John. "Log of the *Columbia*—1790–1793." Ed. F. G. Young and T. C. Elliott. *Oregon Historical Quarterly*, XXII, 1921, 257–356.

Bompas, Mrs. Charlotte Selina. *A heroine of the North: Memoirs of Charlotte Selina Bompas (1830–1917), wife of the first bishop of Selkirk (Yukon).* Ed. S. A. Archer. London, 1929.

Bond, Phineas. "Letters of Phineas Bond, British consul at Philadelphia, to the Foreign Office of Great Britain, 1787–1794." Ed. J. F. Jameson. *Report of the American Historical Association*, 1896–1897: *1896*, 513–659; *1897*, 454–568.

Boucher, Pierre. *Canada in the seventeenth century*. From the French of Pierre Boucher, by Edward Louis Montizambert. Montreal, 1883.

Boucherville, Thomas Verchères de. "Journal de M. Thomas Verchères de Boucherville dans ses voyages aux pays d'en haut, et durant la dernière guerre avec les Américains, 1812–13." *Canadian Antiquarian and Numismatic Journal*, Third Series, III, 1–167.

Bougainville, L.-A. de. "Memoir." *Wisconsin Historical Collections*, XVIII, 167–195. Part of "The French régime in Wisconsin," *q.v.*

Brebner, J. B. *The neutral Yankees of Nova Scotia*. New York, 1937.

Breckenridge, R. M. *The Canadian banking system, 1817–1890*. Toronto, 1894.

Breithaupt, W. H. "Some facts about the schooner 'Nancy' in the War of 1812." *Ontario Historical Society, Papers and Records*, XXIII, 1926, 5–7..

British and American Joint Commission for the Final Settlement of the Claims of the Hudson's Bay and Puget Sound Agricultural Companies. *The Governor and Company of Adventurers of England trading into Hudson's Bay . . . submit the following memorial and statement of their claims upon the United States*. N.p., [1865].

"The British régime in Wisconsin." *Wisconsin Historical Collections*, XVIII, 223–468.

Brodhead, J. R. *History of the state of New York*. New York, 1853–1871. 2 vols.

Brouillette, B. *La chasse des animaux à fourrure au Canada*. Paris, 1934.

Bryce, George. "The Assiniboine River and its forts." *Proceedings and Transactions of the Royal Society of Canada*, 1892, Section II, p. 69.

—— *The remarkable history of the Hudson's Bay Company, including that of the French traders of north-western Canada and of the North-West, XY, and Astor fur companies*. London, 1900.

Buck, S. J. "The story of Grand Portage." *Minnesota History Bulletin*, V, 1923–1924, 14–27.

Buffinton, A. H. "New England and the western fur trade, 1629–1675." *Publications of the Colonial Society of Massachusetts*, XVIII, 1917, 165.

Burpee, L. J. "The Beaver Club." *Canadian Historical Association Report*, 1924, 73–92.

—— *The search for the western sea: The story of the exploration of north-western America*. Toronto, 1908.

Burt, A. L. *The United States, Great Britain, and British North America from the Revolution to the establishment of peace after the War of 1812*. New Haven, 1940.

Butler, W. F. *The great lone land: A narrative of travel and adventure in the north-west of America*. London, 1875.

—— *The wild north land: Being the story of a winter journey, with dogs, across northern North America*. Montreal, 1874.

Butterfield, C. W. *History of Brulé's discoveries and explorations, 1610–1626*, ... Cleveland, 1898.

—— *History of the discovery of the Northwest by John Nicolet in 1634, with a sketch of his life.* Cincinnati, 1881.

Cameron, A. D. *The new North: Being some account of a woman's journey through Canada to the Arctic.* New York and London, 1912.

Cameron, W. B. *The war trail of Big Bear.* Toronto, 1926.

Campbell, Robert (1808–1894). *Discovery and Exploration of the Youcon.* Winnipeg, 1885.

Campbell, Robert (1835–1921). *A history of the Scotch Presbyterian Church, St. Gabriel Street, Montreal.* Montreal, 1887.

Canada, Department of the Interior. *Certain correspondence of the Foreign Office and of the Hudson's Bay Company, copied from original documents.* [Compiled by Otto Klotz.] Ottawa, 1899.

Canada, Department of the Interior, Natural Resources Intelligence Branch. *Hudson Bay Railway belt and Hudson Bay.* Ottawa, 1923.

Canada, Geographic Board. *Handbook of Indians of Canada.* Ottawa, 1913.

Carter, C. E. *Great Britain and the Illinois country, 1763–1774.* Washington, 1910.

Carter, W. J. "Reminiscences regarding the West." Unpublished MS, University of Toronto Library.

Cartier, Jacques. *See* Baxter, J. P.; Biggar, H. P.

Cartwright, C E. *Life and letters of the late Hon. Richard Cartwright.* Toronto, 1876.

Cartwright, George. *Captain Cartwright and his Labrador journal.* Ed. Charles Wendell Townsend. Boston, 1911.

Carver, Jonathan. *Travels through the interior parts of North-America in the years 1766, 1767, and 1768.* London, 1781.

"Les chambres de commerce de France et la cession du Canada." *Rapport de l'archiviste de la Province de Québec pour 1924–1925,* pp. 199–228.

Champlain, Samuel de. *Œuvres.* Publiées sous le patronage de l'Université Laval par l'abbé C.-H. Laverdière. Québec, 1870. 6 vols. in 4.

—— *Voyages.* Ed. W. L. Grant. New York, 1907.

—— *Voyages.* Trans. Charles Pomeroy Otis, with a memoir by Edmund F. Slafter. Boston: Prince Society, 1878–1882. 3 vols.

—— *Voyages and explorations.* Ed. E. G. Bourne. Toronto, 1911. 2 vols.

—— *Works.* Trans. and annotated by six Canadian scholars under the general editorship of H. P. Biggar. Toronto: Champlain Society, 1922–1936. 6 vols.

Les chapeaux de castor. Paris, 1867.

Charlevoix, Pierre François Xavier de. *Journal of a voyage to North America.* Translated from the French. Ed. Louise Phelps Kellogg. Chicago, 1923. 2 vols.

Chittenden, Henry Martin. *The American fur trade of the Far West: A history of the pioneer trading posts and early fur companies of the Missouri valley and the Rocky Mountains. . . .* New York, 1902. 3 vols.

Clarke, Adèle. *Old Montreal: John Clarke, his adventures, friends and family.* Montreal, 1906.

Coats, William. *The geography of Hudson's Bay: Being the remarks of Captain W. Coats, in many voyages to that locality, between the years 1727 and 1751.* Ed. John Barrow. London: Hakluyt Society, 1852.

Cocking, Matthew. "An adventurer from Hudson Bay: Journal of Matthew

Cocking, from York Factory to the Blackfeet Country, 1772–73." Ed. L. J. Burpee. *Proceedings and Transactions of the Royal Society of Canada,* Third Series, vol. II, 1908, Section II, pp. 91–121.

Cody, H. A. *An apostle of the North: Memoirs of the Right Reverend Bishop William C. Bompas, D.D.* London, 1908.

Colden, Cadwallader. *The history of the Five Indian Nations of Canada, which are the barrier between the English and French in that part of the world....* London, 1747.

Cole, C. W. *Colbert and a century of French mercantilism.* New York, 1939. 2 vols.

Cook, James. *A voyage to the Pacific Ocean . . . for making discoveries in the Northern Hemisphere . . . in the years 1776, 1777, 1778, 1779 and 1780.* London, 1785. 3 vols.

Cornwall, J. K. *Memorandum re fur trade.* N.p., n.d. [1924]. [Item in University of Toronto Library.]

Coues, Elliott, ed. *New light on the early history of the greater Northwest: The manuscript journals of Alexander Henry* [the younger], *fur trader of the Northwest Company, and of David Thompson, official geographer and explorer of the same company, 1799–1814; exploration and adventure among the Indians on the Red, Saskatchewan, Missouri, and Columbia Rivers.* New York, 1897. 3 vols.

"Courts of justice for the Indian country." *Report on Canadian Archives,* 1892, pp. 136–146. [Includes App. D: "General return of the departments and posts occupied by the North West Company . . ." on p. 142; App. E: "Average number of peltries cleared at Quebec for England," 1793–1801, on p. 143; App. F: "Statement of furs exported from Quebec in the year 1801," p. 144.]

Cowan, Helen I. *British emigration to British North America, 1783–1837.* University of Toronto Studies, History and Economics, vol. IV, no. 2. Toronto, 1928.

Cowie, Isaac. *The company of adventurers: A narrative of seven years in the service of the Hudson's Bay Company during 1867–1874 on the great buffalo plains.* Toronto, 1913.

Cox, Ross. *Adventures on the Columbia River, including the narrative of a residence of six years on the western side of the Rocky Mountains, among various tribes of Indians hitherto unknown; together with a journey across the American continent.* New York, 1832.

Crouse, N. M. "The location of Fort Maurepas." *Canadian Historical Review,* IX, 1928, 206–222.

Cruikshank, E. A. "Early traders and trade-routes in Ontario and the West, 1760–1783." *Transactions of the Royal Canadian Institute,* III, 253–274; IV, 299–313.

——— "Notes on the history of shipbuilding and navigation on Lake Ontario to September, 1816." *Ontario Historical Society, Papers and Records,* XXIII, 1926, 33–44.

Cuthbertson, G. A. "Fur traders on fresh water." *The Beaver,* outfit 265, Dec. 1934, 26–30, 41.

Dashwood, R. L. *Chiploquorgan; or, Life by the camp fire in the Dominion of Canada and Newfoundland.* Dublin, 1871.

Davidson, G. C. *The North West Company.* University of California Publications in History, vol. VIII. Berkeley, Calif., 1918.

Denny, Sir Cecil E. *The law marches west.* Ed. and arranged by W. B. Cameron. Toronto, 1939.

Denys, Nicolas. *The description and natural history of the coasts of North America (Acadia) by Nicolas Denys.* Translated and edited, with . . . a reprint of the original, by William F. Ganong. Toronto: Champlain Society, 1908.

Devine, E. J. *Historic Caughnawaga.* Montreal, 1922.

Dixon, George. *A voyage round the world; but more particularly to the north-west coast of America: performed in 1785, 1786, 1787, and 1788, in the* King George *and* Queen Charlotte, *Captains Portlock and Dixon.* London, 1789. [Contains 49 letters by William Beresford.]

Dobbs, Arthur. *An account of the countries adjoining to Hudson's Bay, in the northwest part of America; containing a description of their lakes and rivers, the nature of the soil and climates, and their methods of commerce. . . .* London, 1744.

Documents historiques. Québec, 1893.

Dodds, James. *The Hudson's Bay Company, its position and prospects* [an address to the shareholders]. London, 1866.

Douglas, David. *Journal kept by David Douglas during his travels in North America 1823–1827. . . .* London, 1914.

Douglas, G. M. *Lands forlorn: A story of an expedition to Hearne's Coppermine River.* New York, 1914.

[Drage, Theodore Swaine]. *An account of a voyage for the discovery of a North-West Passage by Hudson's Streights to the western and southern ocean of America, performed in the year 1746 and 1747, in the ship* California, *Capt. Francis Smith, commander.* By the clerk of the *California.* London, 1748. 2 vols.

Dugas, G. *Un voyageur des pays d'en haut.* Montreal, 1890. [Jean-Baptiste Charbonneau in the West, 1812–1862.]

Dugmore, A. R. *The romance of the beaver: Being the history of the beaver in the Western Hemisphere. . . .* Philadelphia, [1914].

Dussieux, L. *Le Canada sous la domination française d'après les archives de la Marine et de la Guerre. . . .* Paris, 1862.

Early western travels, 1748–1846: A series of annotated reprints of some of the best and rarest contemporary volumes of travel, descriptive of the aborigines and social and economic conditions in the Middle and Far West, during the period of early American settlement. Ed. R. G. Thwaites. Cleveland, 1904–1907. 32 vols.

Eastman, Mack. *Church and state in early Canada.* Edinburgh, 1915.

Edits, ordonnances royaux, déclarations et arrêts du Conseil d'Etat du roi concernant le Canada. . . . Québec, 1803–1806. 2 vols.

Elliott, T. C. "The fur trade in the Columbia River basin prior to 1811." *Washington Historical Quarterly,* VI, 1915, 3–10.

———— "Jonathan Carver's source for the name Oregon." *Oregon Historical Quarterly,* XXIII, 1922, 53–69.

———— "The origin of the name Oregon." *Ibid.,* XXII, 1921, 91–115.

———— "The strange case of Jonathan Carver and the name Oregon." *Ibid.*, XXI, 1920, 341–368.

Ellis, Henry. *A voyage to Hudson's-Bay by the Dobbs galley and California in the years 1746 and 1747 for discovering a North West passage, with an accurate survey of the coast and a short natural history of the country.* London, 1748.

Ermatinger, Edward. "Edward Ermatinger's York Factory express journal, being a record of journeys made between Fort Vancouver and Hudson Bay in the years 1827–1828." Ed. Judge C. O. Ermatinger and James White. *Proceedings and Transactions of the Royal Society of Canada*, Third Series, vol. VI, 1912, Section II, pp. 67–132.

Faillon, E.-M. *Histoire de la colonie française en Canada.* Ville-Marie, 1865–1866. 3 vols.

Fay, C. R. *Great Britain from Adam Smith to the present day: An economic and social survey.* London, 1928.

Five fur traders of the Northwest, being the narrative of Peter Pond, and the diaries of John Macdonell, Archibald N. McLeod, Hugh Faries, and Thomas Connor. Ed. Charles M. Gates. University of Minnesota Press, 1933.

Fleming, R. Harvey. "McTavish, Frobisher and Company of Montreal." *Canadian Historical Review*, X, 1929, 136–152.

———— ed. *Minutes of the Council, Northern Department of Rupert's Land, 1821–31.* With an introduction by H. A. Innis. Toronto: Champlain Society, 1940.

———— "The origin of 'Sir Alexander Mackenzie and Company.'" *Canadian Historical Review*, IX, 1928, 137–155.

———— "Phyn, Ellice and Company of Schenectady." *Contributions to Canadian Economics*, IV, 1932, 7–41. University of Toronto Studies, History and Economics.

Fonseca, W. G. *On the St. Paul trail in the sixties.* Transactions of the Historical and Scientific Society of Manitoba, no. 56. Winnipeg, 1900.

Fortrey, S. *Englands interest and improvement, consisting in the increase of the store, and trade of this kingdom.* Cambridge, 1663.

Franchère, Gabriel. *Narrative of a voyage to the northwest coast of America in the years 1811, 1812, 1813 and 1814; or, The first American settlement on the Pacific.* New York, 1854.

Franklin, [Sir] John. *Narrative of a journey to the shores of the polar sea, in the years 1819, 20, 21, and 22.* London, 1824. 2 vols.

Fraser, Simon. "Journal of a voyage from the Rocky Mountains to the Pacific coast, 1808." In L. R. Masson, *Les bourgeois de la Compagnie du Nord-Ouest* (*q.v.*), I, pt. 2, 155–221.

"The French régime in Wisconsin, 1634–1760." *Wisconsin Historical Collections*, XVI; XVII; XVIII, 1–222.

The fur trade and the Hudson's Bay Company. Chambers's Repository of Instructive and Amusing Tracts, no. 65.

"Fur-trade on the Upper Lakes, 1778–1815." *Wisconsin Historical Collections*, XIX, 234–488.

Garrioch, A. C. *The far and furry north: A story of life and love and travel in the days of the Hudson's Bay Company.* Winnipeg, 1925.

——— A hatchet mark in duplicate. Toronto, 1929.

Garry, Nicholas. "Diary of Nicholas Garry, deputy-governor of the Hudson's Bay Company from 1822–1835: A detailed narrative of his travels in the Northwest territories of British North America in 1821. . . ." *Proceedings and Transactions of the Royal Society of Canada*, Second Series, vol. VII, 1900, Section II, pp. 3–204.

"General list of partners, clerks & interpreters who winter in the North West Company's service. . . ." *Report of the Public Archives of Canada for the year 1939*, pp. 53–56.

Gérin, Léon. "Le gentilhomme français et la colonisation du Canada." *Proceedings and Transactions of the Royal Society of Canada*, Second Series, 1896, Section I, 65–94.

Gipson, L. H. *The British Empire before the American Revolution: Provincial characteristics and sectional tendencies in the era preceding the American crisis.* Caldwell, Idaho, 1936.

Giraud, Marcel. *Le métis canadien: son rôle dans l'histoire des provinces de l'Ouest.* Université de Paris, Travaux et Mémoires de l'Institut d'Ethnologie, no XLIV. Paris, 1945.

Glazebrook, G. deT. "A document concerning the union of the Hudson's Bay Company and the North West Company." *Canadian Historical Review*, XIV, 1933, 183–188.

Godsell, P. H. *Arctic trader: The account of twenty years with the Hudson's Bay Company.* New York, 1934.

——— *The vanishing frontier: A saga of traders, Mounties and men of the last North West.* London, 1939.

Gordon, Daniel M. *Mountain and prairie: A journey from Victoria to Winnipeg via Peace River Pass.* Montreal, 1880.

Graham, A. *The golden grindstone: The adventures of George M. Mitchell.* Toronto, 1935.

Graham, G. S. "The Indian menace and the retention of the western posts." *Canadian Historical Review*, XV, 1934, 46–48.

Grant, Anne (MacVicar). *Memoirs of an American lady, with sketches of manners and scenery in America, as they existed previous to the Revolution.* New York, 1846.

Grant, George M. *Ocean to ocean: Sandford Fleming's expedition through Canada in 1872; being a diary kept during a journey from the Atlantic to the Pacific with the expedition of the Engineer-in-Chief of the Canadian Pacific and Intercolonial Railways. . . .* London and Toronto, 1873.

Great Britain, Colonial office. *Papers relating to the Red River Settlement; viz., Return to an address from the honourable House of Commons to His Royal Highness the Prince Regent . . . for copies or extracts of the official communications which may have taken place between the Secretary of State and the provincial government of Upper or Lower Canada relative to the destruction of the settlement on the Red River. . . .* London, 1819.

Great Britain, Parliament, House of Commons. *Papers presented to the Committee Appointed to Inquire into the State and Condition of the Countries adjoining to Hudson's Bay, and of the Trade carried on there.* London, 1749.

——— *Report from the Committee Appointed to Inquire into the State and Con-*

dition of the Countries adjoining to Hudson's Bay, and of the Trade carried on there. London, 1749.

———— *Report from the Select Committee on the Hudson's Bay Company. . . .* [London, 1857.]

Green, Ernest. "The Niagara portage road." *Ontario Historical Society, Papers and Records*, XXIII, 1926, 260–311.

Greene, W. H. *The wooden walls among the ice floes: Telling the romance of the Newfoundland seal fishery.* London, 1933.

Grey Owl. *Pilgrims of the wild.* Toronto, 1934.

Grimes, Eliah. "Letters on the northwest fur trade." Ed. S. E. Morison. *Washington Historical Quarterly*, XI, 1920, 174–177.

Gunn, Donald and Tuttle, Charles R. *History of Manitoba: From the earliest settlement to 1835* [Gunn], *and from 1835 to the admission of the province into the Dominion* [Tuttle]. Ottawa, 1880.

Gunn, H. G. "The fight for free trade in Rupert's Land." *Proceedings of the Mississippi Valley Historical Association*, 1910–1911, 73–90.

Hadfield, Joseph. *An Englishman in America 1785: Being the diary of Joseph Hadfield.* Ed. Douglas S. Robertson. Toronto, 1933.

"The Haldimand papers: Copies of papers on file in the Dominion Archives at Ottawa, Canada." *Report of the Pioneer Society of the State of Michigan*, IX, 343–658. 2nd ed., Lansing, 1908.

Hanbury, D. T. *Sport and travel in the Northland of Canada.* New York, 1904.

Hargrave, Joseph James. *Red River.* Montreal, 1871.

Harmon, Daniel Williams. *A journal of voyages and travels in the interior of North America . . . including an account of the principal occurrences, during a residence of nineteen years, in different parts of the country. . . .* Toronto, 1904.

Harrington, V. D. *The New York merchant on the eve of the Revolution.* New York, 1935.

Harrison, A. H. *In search of a polar continent, 1905–1907.* Toronto, 1908.

Hawkins, J. H. *History of the Worshipful Company of Feltmakers of London.* London, 1917.

Haworth, P. L. *On the headwaters of Peace River: A narrative of a thousand-mile canoe-trip to a little-known range of the Canadian Rockies.* New York, 1912.

Haydon, A. L. *The riders of the plains: A record of the Royal Northwest Mounted Police of Canada, 1873–1910.* London, 1910.

Hearne, Samuel and Turnor, Philip. *Journals.* Ed. J. B. Tyrrell. Toronto: Chamnorthern ocean . . . in the years 1769, 1770, 1771, and 1772. Ed. J. B. Tyrrell. Toronto: Champlain Society, 1911.

Hearne, Samuel and Turnor, Philip. *Journals.* Ed. J. B. Tyrrell. Toronto: Champlain Society, 1934.

Heaton, H. *The Yorkshire woollen and worsted industries from the earliest times up to the Industrial Revolution.* Oxford, 1920.

Henday [earlier Hendry], Anthony. "York Factory to the Blackfeet country: The journal of Anthony Hendry, 1754–55." Ed. L. J. Burpee. *Proceedings and Transactions of the Royal Society of Canada*, Third Series, vol. I, 1907, Section II, pp. 307–64.

Henry, Alexander. *Travels and adventures in Canada and the Indian territories, between the years 1760 and 1776 . . . by Alexander Henry, fur trader.* Ed. James Bain. Toronto, 1901.

Henry, Alexander [the younger]. *See* Coues, Elliott.

Heriot, George. *Travels through the Canadas, containing a description of the picturesque scenery on some of the rivers and lakes; with an account of the productions, commerce, and inhabitants of those provinces. . . .* London, 1807.

Horetzky, Charles. *Canada on the Pacific: Being an account of a journey from Edmonton to the Pacific by the Peace River valley, and of a winter voyage along the western coast of the Dominion.* Montreal, 1874.

Hough, W. "The bison as a factor in ancient American culture history." *Scientific Monthly*, XXX, 1930, pp. 315–319.

Howay, F. W. "David Thompson's account of his first attempt to cross the Rockies." *Queen's Quarterly*, XL, 1933, 333–356.

—— "Early days of the maritime fur-trade on the Northwest coast." *Canadian Historical Review*, IV, 1923, 26–44.

—— "The fur trade in northwestern development." In *The Pacific Ocean in history: Papers and addresses presented at the Panama-Pacific Historical Congress. . . .* New York, 1917.

—— "Indian attacks upon maritime traders of the North-West coast, 1785–1805." *Canadian Historical Review*, VI, 1925, 287–309.

—— ed., "Letters relating to the second voyage of the *Columbia*." *Oregon Historical Quarterly*, XXIV, 1923, 132–152.

—— "An outline sketch of the maritime fur trade." *Canadian Historical Association Report*, 1932, 5–14.

—— "The *raison d'être* of Forts Yale and Hope." *Proceedings and Transactions of the Royal Society of Canada*, Third Series, vol. XVI, 1922, Section II, 49–64.

Hudson's Bay Company. [Catalogue of the] *Hudson's Bay Company's historical exhibit at Winnipeg.* 4th ed., 1924.

—— *Copy of the deed poll under the seal of the Governor and Company of Adventurers of England trading into Hudson's Bay, bearing date the twenty-sixth day of March, 1821. . . .* London, 1821.

—— *Report of the Governor and Committee of the Hudson's Bay Company.* London, 1911, 1927.

The Hudson's Bay Company. What is it? London, 1864.

Humphreys, R. A. "Governor Murray's views on the plan of 1764 for the management of Indian affairs." *Canadian Historical Review*, XVI, 1935, 162–169.

Hunt, G. T. *The wars of the Iroquois: A study in intertribal trade relations.* Madison, Wisc., 1940.

Hunter, Martin. *Canadian wilds: Tells about the Hudson's Bay Company, northern Indians and their modes of hunting, trapping, etc.* Columbus, Ohio, [1907].

Hunter, Robert, Jr. *Quebec to Carolina in 1785–1786: Being the travel diary and observations of Robert Hunter, Jr., a young merchant of London.* Ed. Louis B. Wright and Marion Tinling. San Marino, Calif., 1943.

Inkyo [pseud.]. *The reflections of Inkyo on the great Company.* London, 1931.

Innis, H. A. "Correspondence, J. B. Tyrrell and H. A. Innis." *Canadian Historical Review*, IX, 1928, 156–160.

———— *The fur trade of Canada.* Toronto, 1927.

———— *A history of the Canadian Pacific Railway.* London, 1923.

———— "The North West Company." *Canadian Historical Review*, VIII, 1927, 308–321.

———— *Peter Pond: Fur trader and adventurer.* Toronto, 1930.

———— Review of J. P. Pritchett, *The Selkirk purchase of the Red River valley, 1811. North Dakota Historical Quarterly*, VI, 1932, 171–173.

———— "Rupert's Land in 1825." *Canadian Historical Review*, VII, 1926, 303–320.

———— *Select documents in Canadian economic history, 1497–1783.* Toronto, 1929.

Insh, G. P. *Scottish colonial schemes, 1620–1686.* Glasgow, 1922.

Irving, Washington. *Astoria.* New York, 1861.

Jérémie, [Nicolas]. *Relation du Détroit et de la baie d'Hudson.* Bulletin de la Société historique de Saint-Boniface, no 2. Saint-Boniface, 1912. [First published in Amsterdam in *Recueil de voyages au nord*, ed. Jean Frederic Bernard, 1715–1738.]

———— Nicolas. *Twenty years of York Factory, 1694–1714: Jérémie's account of Hudson Strait and Bay.* Translated from the French . . . with notes and introduction by R. Douglas and J. N. Wallace. Ottawa, 1926.

Jesuit relations and allied documents: Travels and explorations of the Jesuit missionaries in New France, 1610–1791. Ed. Reuben Gold Thwaites. Cleveland, 1896–1901. 74 vols.

Jewitt, John R. *The adventures of John Jewitt, only survivor of the crew of the ship* Boston *during a captivity of nearly three years among the Indians of Nootka Sound, in Vancouver Island.* Ed. R. Brown. London, 1896.

Johnson, I. A. *The Michigan fur trade.* Lansing, 1919.

Johnson, Richard Byron. *Very far west indeed: A few rough experiences on the north-west Pacific coast.* London, 1872.

Johnson, Sir William. *The papers of Sir William Johnson.* Ed. James Sullivan and Alexander C. Flick. Albany, N.Y., 1921–1951. 10 vols.

Jones, A. E. *Old Huronia. Fifth report of the Bureau of Archives for the Province of Ontario.* Toronto, 1909.

Kalm, Peter. *Travels into North America: Containing its natural history and a circumstantial account of its plantations and agriculture in general, with the civil, ecclesiastical and commercial state of the country, the manner of the inhabitants. . . .* 2nd ed., London, 1772. 2 vols.

Kane, Paul. *Wanderings of an artist among the Indians of North America, from Canada to Vancouver's Island and Oregon, through the Hudson's Bay Company's territory and back again.* London, 1859.

Keating, William H. *Narrative of an expedition to the source of St. Peter's River, Lake Winnepeek, Lake of the Woods, &c., . . . 1823, . . . under the command of Stephen H. Long, U.S.T.E.* London, 1825. 2 vols.

Kellogg, Louise Phelps. *Early narratives of the Northwest, 1634–1699.* Original Narratives of Early American History. New York, 1917.

———— *The French régime in Wisconsin and the Northwest.* Madison, 1925.

Kelsey, Henry. *The Kelsey papers*. With an introduction by Arthur G. Doughty and Chester Martin. Ottawa, 1929.
    See also Bell, C. N.
Kennedy, W. P. M. "Canada: Law and custom in the Canadian constitution." *Round Table*, Dec. 1929, pp. 143–160.
Kenney, J. F. "The career of Henry Kelsey." *Proceedings and Transactions of the Royal Society of Canada*, Third Series, vol. XXIII, 1929, Section II, 37–71.
Kindle, E. M. "Arrival and departure of winter conditions in the Mackenzie River basin." *Geographical Review*, Dec. 1920, pp. 388–399.
————— "Canada north of fifty-six degrees: The land of long summer days." *Canadian Field-Naturalist*, March 1928, pp. 53–86.
Klengenberg, C. *Klengenberg of the Arctic: An autobiography*. Ed. Tom Mac-Innes. London, 1932.
Knight, James. *The founding of Churchill, being the journal of Captain James Knight, governor-in-chief in Hudson Bay, from the 14th of July to the 13th of September, 1717*. Ed. James F. Kenney. Toronto, 1932.
Kohl, J. G. *Kitchi-Gami: Wanderings round Lake Superior*. . . . London, 1860.
Kuykendall, R. S. "A Northwest trader at the Hawaiian Islands." *Oregon Historical Quarterly*, XXIV, 1923, 111–131.
Lafitau, Joseph François. *Mœurs des sauvages ameriquains, comparées aux mœurs des premiers temps*. Paris, 1724. 2 vols.
Lahontan, Louis Armand de Lom d'Arce, baron de. *New voyages to North-America*. Ed. Reuben Gold Thwaites. Chicago, 1905. 2 vols.
Lanctot, G. "Les premiers budgets de la Nouvelle-France." *Canadian Historical Association Report*, 1928, pp. 27–33.
Landmann, George Thomas. *Adventures and recollections of Colonel Landmann, late of the Corps of Royal Engineers*. London, 1852. 2 vols.
La Rochefoucauld-Liancourt, F. A. F., duc de. *La Rochefoucault-Liancourt's travels in Canada 1795 with annotations and strictures by Sir David William Smith, Bart*. Ed. William Renwick Riddell. *Thirteenth Report of the Bureau of Archives for the Province of Ontario, 1916*. Toronto, 1917.
Lart, Charles E., ed. "Fur-trade returns, 1767." *Canadian Historical Review*, III, 1922, 351–358.
Laut, Agnes C. *The 'Adventurers of England' on Hudson Bay: A chronicle of the fur trade in the North*. Toronto, 1914.
————— *The conquest of the great Northwest, being the story of the Adventurers of England known as the Hudson's Bay Company: New pages in the history of the Canadian Northwest and western states*. New York, 1918. 2 vols. in 1.
————— *Pathfinders of the West, being the thrilling story of the adventures of the men who discovered the great Northwest, Radisson, La Vérendrye, Lewis and Clark*. Toronto, 1904.
La Vérendrye, Pierre Gaultier de Varennes, sieur de. *Journals and letters of Pierre Gaultier de Varennes de la Vérendrye and his sons with correspondence between the governors of Canada and the French court, touching the search for the western sea*. Ed. L. J. Burpee. Toronto: Champlain Society, 1927.
    See also Robinson, D., ed.
Le Clercq, Chrestien. *New relation of Gaspesia, with the customs and religion*

of the Gaspesian Indians. Ed. William F. Ganong. Toronto: Champlain Society, 1910.

[Lees, John]. *Journal of J. L., of Quebec, merchant.* Detroit, 1911.

Le Jeune, Paul. *Relation de ce qui s'est passé en la Nouvelle France en l'année 1638.* Paris, 1638.

Lescarbot, Marc. *The history of New France.* Trans. and ed. W. L. Grant; with an introduction by H. P. Biggar. Toronto: Champlain Society, 1907–1914. 3 vols.

Lespinasse, René de. *Les métiers et corporations de la ville de Paris,* tome III. Paris, 1897. "Histoire générale de Paris."

Levasseur, E. *Histoire des classes ouvrières en France depuis la conquête de Jules César jusqu'à la Révolution.* Paris, 1859.

Lewis, Lawrence. *The advertisements of The Spectator: Being a study of the literature, history and manners of Queen Anne's England as they are reflected therein. . . .* Boston, 1905.

Lewis, Oscar. *The effects of white contact upon Blackfoot culture, with special reference to the role of the fur trade.* American Ethnological Society Monographs, no. 6. New York, 1942.

Lippincott, Isaac. "A century and a half of fur trade at St. Louis." *Washington University Studies,* III, 1915–1916, pt. II, 205–42.

Long, D. E. "English interest in the fur-trade of Hudson Bay before 1670." *Canadian Historical Review,* XIV, 1933, 177–183.

Long, John. *John Long's voyages and travels in the years 1768–1788.* Ed. M. M. Quaife. Chicago, 1922.

Loudon, W. J. *A Canadian geologist.* Toronto, 1930.

Lower, A. R. M. "A history of the Canadian timber and lumber trade." M.A. thesis. University of Toronto, 1923.

McCain, Charles W. *The history of the S.S. "Beaver": Being a graphic and vivid sketch of this noted pioneer steamer . . . also containing a description of the Hudson's Bay Company from its formation in 1670 down to the present time.* Vancouver, 1894.

Macaulay, R. H. H. *Trading into Hudson's Bay: A narrative of the visit of Patrick Ashley Cooper, thirtieth governor of the Hudson's Bay Company, to Labrador, Hudson Strait, and Hudson Bay in the year 1934.* From the journal of R. H. H. Macaulay. Winnipeg: Hudson's Bay Company, 1934.

McComber, A. J. "Some early history of Thunder Bay and district." Thunder Bay Historical Society, *Papers of 1923–24,* pp. 13 ff.

McDonald, Archibald. *Peace River: A canoe voyage from Hudson's Bay to Pacific, by the late Sir George Simpson (governor, Hon. Hudson's Bay Company) in 1828; journal of the late Chief Factor, Archibald McDonald (Hon. Hudson's Bay Company), who accompanied him.* Ed. Malcolm McLeod. Ottawa, 1872.

McDougall, J. L. "The Welland Canal to 1841." Master's thesis. University of Toronto Library.

McDougall, John. *Pathfinding on plain and prairie: Stirring scenes of life in the Canadian North-West.* Toronto, 1898.

—— *Saddle, sled, and snowshoe: Pioneering on the Saskatchewan in the sixties.* Toronto, 1896.

M'Gillivray, Duncan. *The journal of Duncan M'Gillivray of the North West Company at Fort George on the Saskatchewan, 1794–5.* With introduction, notes and appendix by Arthur S. Morton. Toronto, 1929.

Mackay, James. "Extracts from Capt. Mackay's journal—and others" including "Notes on the above journals made by John Hay." *Proceedings of the State Historical Society of Wisconsin,* 1915, pp. 190–210.

Mackenzie, Alexander. *Voyages from Montreal through the continent of North America to the frozen and Pacific oceans in 1789 and 1793 with an account of the rise and state of the fur trade.* Toronto, n.d. 2 vols.

McKenzie, N. M. W. J. *The men of the Hudson's Bay Company, 1670 A.D.– 1920 A.D.* Fort William, 1921.

McLaughlin, A. C. "The western posts and the British debts." *Annual Report of the American Historical Association for the year 1894,* pp. 413–444.

McLean, John. *Notes of a twenty-five years' service in the Hudson's Bay territory.* London, 1849. 2 vols.

[MacLeod, M.]. *The Oregon indemnity: Claim of chief factors and chief traders of the Hudson's Bay Company, thereto, as partners under treaty of 1846.* N.p., 1892.

Macleod, W. C. "Trade restrictions in early society." *American Anthropologist,* XXIX, 1927, 271–278.

McLoughlin, John. "Dr. John McLoughlin's last letter to the Hudson's Bay Company, [1845]." Ed. K. B. Judson. *American Historical Review,* XXI, 104–134.

———— "Letter from Doctor John McLoughlin to Sir George Simpson, March 20, 1844." Ed. K. B. Judson. *Oregon Historical Quarterly,* XVII, 1916, 215–239.

Macnaughton, John. *Lord Strathcona.* Toronto, 1926.

McNaughton, Margaret. *Overland to Cariboo: An eventful journey of Canadian pioneers to the gold fields of British Columbia in 1862.* Toronto, 1896.

Macoun, John. *Manitoba and the great North-West . . . being a full and complete history of the country. . . .* Guelph, 1882.

Mair, Charles. *Through the Mackenzie basin: A narrative of the Athabasca and Peace River treaty expedition of 1899 . . .; also notes on the mammals and birds of northern Canada,* by Roderick MacFarlane. Toronto, 1908.

Marbois, François de. "Marbois on the fur trade, 1784." *American Historical Review,* XXIX, 1923–4, 725–740.

Margry, Pierre. *Découvertes et établissements des Français dans l'ouest et dans le sud de l'Amérique Septentrionale, 1614–[1754]: Mémoires et documents inédits.* Paris, 1879–1888. 6 vols.

Martin, Archer. *The Hudson's Bay Company's land tenures and the occupation of Assiniboia by Lord Selkirk's settlers, with a list of grantees under the Earl and the Company.* London, 1898.

Martin, Chester. *Lord Selkirk's work in Canada.* Oxford, 1916.

Martin, G. *La grande industrie sous le règne de Louis XIV.* Paris, 1898.

Martin, H. T. *Castorologia; or, The history and traditions of the Canadian beaver.* Montreal, 1892.

Maseres, Francis. *The Maseres letters, 1776–1768.* Ed. W. Stewart Wallace. Toronto, 1919.

Massicotte, E.-Z. "La Compagnie du Nord." *Bulletin des recherches historiques,* XXIV, 275–276.

———— "Dominique Rousseau, maître orfèvre et négociant en pelleteries." *Ibid.*, XLIX, 1943, 342–348.

Masson, L. R. *Les bourgeois de la Compagnie du Nord-Ouest: Récits de voyages, lettres et rapports inédits relatifs au Nord-Ouest canadien. . . .* Québec, 1889–1890. 2 vols.

[Maude, John]. *Visit to the falls of Niagara, in 1800.* London, 1826.

Meares, John. *Voyages made in the years 1788 and 1789, from China to the north west coast of America. . . .* London, 1790.

Melville, C. D., Lower, A. R. M. and Comeau, N. A. *Reports on fisheries investigations in Hudson and James Bays and tributary waters in 1914.* Ottawa, 1915.

Merrick, E. *True north.* New York, 1933.

Merriman, R. O. "The American bison as a source of food: A factor in Canadian economic history." Master's thesis. Queen's University, 1925.

Mills, E. A. *In beaver world.* Boston and New York, 1913.

Milton, W. F., Viscount, and Cheadle, W. B. *The north-west passage by land, being the narrative of an expedition from the Atlantic to the Pacific. . . .* London, 1901.

Moberly, Henry John, in collaboration with William Bleasdell Cameron. *When fur was king.* Toronto, 1929.

Moberly, Walter. *The rocks and rivers of British Columbia.* London, 1885.

Morgan, L. H. *The American beaver and his works.* Philadelphia, 1868.

Morice, A. G. *The history of the northern interior of British Columbia (formerly New Caledonia), 1660–1880.* London, 1906.

Morison, Samuel Eliot. *The maritime history of Massachusetts, 1783–1860.* Boston and New York, 1921.

Morris, Alexander. *The treaties of Canada with the Indians of Manitoba and the Northwest Territories, including the negotiations on which they are based. . . .* Toronto, 1880.

Morris, G. P. "Some letters from 1792–1800 on the China trade." *Oregon Historical Quarterly*, XLII, 1941, 48–87.

Morton, A. S. "La Vérendrye: Commandant, fur-trader and explorer." *Canadian Historical Review*, IX, 1928, 284–298.

———— "The place of the Red River settlement in the plans of the Hudson's Bay Co., 1812–1825." *Canadian Historical Association Report*, 1929, pp. 103–109.

Munro, W. B. *American influences on Canadian government.* Toronto, 1929.

———— "The Brandy Parliament of 1678." *Canadian Historical Review*, II, 1921, 172–189.

———— "The *coureurs de bois*." *Proceedings of the Massachusetts Historical Society*, LVII, 1923–4, 192–205.

Murray, Alexander Hunter. *Journal of the Yukon, 1847–48.* Ed. L. J. Burpee. Publications of the Canadian Archives, no. 4. Ottawa, 1910.

New France, Conseil supérieur de Québec. *Jugements et délibérations du Conseil souverain de la Nouvelle-France.* Publiés sous les auspices de la Législature de Québec. Quebec, 1885–1891. 6 vols.

"North-western explorations." *Report on the Canadian Archives*, 1890, pp. 48–66.

"The North West trade." *Report on the Canadian Archives*, 1888, pp. 59–72.

Nute, Grace Lee. "A British legal case and old Grand Portage." *Minnesota History*, XXI, 1940, 117–148.

—— *Caesars of the wilderness: Médard Chouart, Sieur des Groseilliers and Pierre Esprit Radisson, 1618–1710.* New York, 1943.

O'Callaghan, E. B. *History of New Netherland; or, New York under the Dutch.* New York, 1848. 2 vols.

O'Callaghan, E. B., ed. *Documents relative to the colonial history of the state of New-York, procured in Holland, England and France, by John Romeyn Brodhead, Esq., agent, under and by virtue of an act of the legislature. . . .* Albany, 1856–1857. 15 vols.

Oldmixon, John. *The British Empire in America, containing the history of the discovery, settlement, progress and state of the British colonies on the continent and islands of America.* 2nd ed., London, 1741. 2 vols.

—— "The history of Hudson's-Bay." In J. B. Tyrrell, ed., *Documents relating to the early history of Hudson Bay (q.v.),* pp. 373–410.

Oliver, E. H., ed. *The Canadian North-West, its early development and legislative records: Minutes of the Councils of the Red River colony and the Northern Department of Rupert's Land.* Publications of the Canadian Archives, no. 9. Ottawa, 1914–15. 2 vols.

O'Neil, M. "The Peace River journal, 1799–1800." *Washington Historical Quarterly,* Oct. 1928, 250–270.

Parkins, A. E. *The historical geography of Detroit.* Lansing, Mich., 1918.

Parkman, Francis. *La Salle and the discovery of the Great West. Boston,* 1918.

—— *The Old Régime in Canada.* London, 1909.

Perrot, Nicolas. *Mémoire sur les mœurs, coustumes et relligion des sauvages de l'Amérique Septentrionale.* Ed. le R.P. J. Tailhan. Paris, 1864.

Phillips, P. C. "The fur trade in the Maumee-Wabash country." *Studies in American history inscribed to James Albert Woodburn . . . by his former students,* pp. 94 ff. Bloomington: Indiana University, 1926.

Piers, Sir Charles. "Pioneer ships on the Pacific coast." *Beaver,* Dec. 1926, 6–7; March 1927, 74–75.

Pike, Warburton. *The barren ground of northern Canada.* London, 1892.

—— *Through the subarctic forest: A record of a canoe journey from Fort Wrangle to the Pelly Lakes and down the Yukon River to the Behring Sea.* London, 1896.

Pike, Zebulon M. *The expeditions of Zebulon Montgomery Pike to headwaters of the Mississippi River, through Louisiana territory, and in New Spain, during the years 1805–6–7.* Ed. Elliott Coues. New York, 1895. 3 vols.

Poland, H. *Fur-bearing animals in nature and commerce.* London, 1892.

Pond, Peter. "Journal of Peter Pond." Part of "The British régime in Wisconsin" *(q.v.),* pp. 315–354.

Poole, R. C. *A history of the Huguenots of the dispersion and the recall of the Edict of Nantes.* London, 1880.

Porter, K. W. *John Jacob Astor, business man.* Cambridge, Mass., 1931.

Pratt, J. W. "Fur trade strategy and the American left flank in the War of 1812." *American Historical Review,* XL, 1935, 246–273.

Preble, E. A. *A biological investigation of the Hudson Bay region.* Washington, 1902.

Pritchett, John P. "Some Red River fur-trade activities." *Minnesota History Bulletin*, V, 1923–4, 401–423.

Prud'homme, L.-A. "La baie d'Hudson." *Proceedings and Transactions of the Royal Society of Canada*, Third Series, vol. III, 1909, Section I, 3–36; vol. IV, 1910, Section I, 17–40; vol. IV, 1911, Section I, 119–165.

—— "Pierre Gaultier de Varennes, sieur de La Vérendrye, . . . , 1685–1749." *Ibid.*, Second Series, 1905, Section I, 9–57.

—— "Les successeurs de La Vérendrye sous la domination français. . . ." *Ibid.*, Second Series, 1906, Section I, 65–81.

Quebec, Province of, Provincial Archives. "Congés de traite conservés aux Archives de la Province de Québec." *Rapport de l'archiviste de la Province de Québec pour 1922–1923*, pp. 191–265.

—— "Congés et permis déposés ou enregistrés à Montréal sous le régime français." *Rapport de l'archiviste de la Province de Québec pour 1921–1922*, pp. 190–223.

Radisson, Pierre Esprit. *Voyages of Peter Esprit Radisson: Being an account of his travels and experiences among the North American Indians, from 1652 to 1684*. Transcribed and edited by Gideon D. Scull. Boston: Prince Society, 1885.

Ralph, Julian. *On Canada's frontier: Sketches of history, sport and adventure and of the Indians, missionaries, fur-traders, and newer settlers of western Canada*. New York, 1892.

Recueil d'arrests et autre pièces pour l'établissement de la Compagnie d'Occident. Amsterdam, 1720.

Reid, Marjorie G. "The Quebec fur-traders and western policy, 1763–1774." *Canadian Historical Review*, VI, 1925, 15–32.

Rife, Clarence W. "Norman W. Kittson, a fur-trader at Pembina." *Minnesota History*, VI, 1925, 225–252.

Robinson, Doane, ed. "Vérendrye." *South Dakota Historical Collections*, VII, 1914, 89–402.

Robinson, H. M. *The great fur land; or, Sketches of life in the Hudson's Bay territory*. London, 1879.

Robinson, P. J. *Toronto during the French régime: A history of the Toronto region from Brulé to Simcoe, 1615–1793*. Toronto, 1933.

Robson, Joseph. *An account of six years residence in Hudson's-Bay, from 1733 to 1736, and 1744 to 1747. . . .* London, 1752.

Roe, F. G. "The extermination of the buffalo in western Canada." *Canadian Historical Review*, XV, 1934, 1–23.

Rogers, Robert. "Rogers's Michillimackinac journal." Ed. William L. Clements. *Proceedings of the American Antiquarian Society*, N.S., XXVIII, 1918, 224–273.

Ross, Alexander. *Alexander Ross's Adventures of the first settlers on the Oregon or Columbia River, 1810–1813*. Early Western Travels, ed. R. G. Thwaites, vol. VII. Cleveland, 1904.

—— *The fur hunters of the far West: A narrative of adventures in the Oregon and Rocky Mountains*. London, 1855. 2 vols.

Roy, P.-G. *La famille Aubert de Gaspé*. Lévis, 1907.

Russell, Frank. *Explorations in the far North . . . being the report of an expedi-*

tion under the auspices of the University of Iowa during the years 1892, '93 and '94. University of Iowa, 1898.

Ryerson, John. *Hudson's Bay; or, A missionary tour in the territory of the Hon. Hudson's Bay Company.* Toronto, 1855.

Sagard-Théodat, Gabriel. *Le grand voyage du pays des Hurons situé en l'Amérique vers la Mer douce.* . . . Paris, 1865. 2 vols.

────── *Histoire du Canada et voyages que les Frères mineurs Recollects y ont faicts pour la conversion des infidèles depuis l'an 1615.* Paris, 1866. 4 vols.

Sage, W. N. *Sir James Douglas and British Columbia.* Toronto, 1930.

Salone, E. *La colonisation de la Nouvelle-France: Etude sur les origines de la nation canadienne française.* Paris, 1906.

Savary des Bruslons. *Dictionnaire universel de commerce.* 1723–30. 3 vols.

Schoolcraft, H. R. *The American Indians, their history, condition and prospects, from original notes and manuscripts.* Rochester, 1851.

Schooling, Sir William. *The Governor and Company of Adventurers of England trading into Hudson's Bay during two hundred and fifty years, 1670–1920.* London, 1920.

Schultz, [Sir] John. *Old Crow Wing Trail.* Transactions of the Historical and Scientific Society of Manitoba, no. 45. Winnipeg, 1894.

Scott, W. R. *The constitution and finance of English, Scottish and Irish joint-stock companies to 1720.* Cambridge, 1910–12. 3 vols.

Sée, Henri. *L'évolution commerciale et industrielle de la France sous l'ancien régime.* Paris, 1925.

Selkirk, Earl of. *A sketch of the British fur trade in North America, with observations relative to the North-West Company of Montreal.* London, 1816.

Seton, E. T. *The Arctic prairies: A canoe-journey of 2,000 miles in search of the caribou; being the account of a voyage to the region north of Aylmer Lake.* Toronto, 1911.

────── *Life histories of northern animals: An account of the mammals of Manitoba.* New York, 1909. 2 vols.

Severance, F. H. *An old frontier of France: The Niagara region and adjacent lakes under French control.* New York, 1917. 2 vols.

Shortridge, W. P. *The transition of a typical frontier, with illustrations from the life of Henry Hastings Sibley, fur trader.* . . . Menasha, Minn., 1922.

Shortt, Adam. *Documents relating to Canadian currency, exchange, and finance during the French period.* Ottawa, 1925.

[Silvy, Antoine]. *Relation par lettres de l'Amérique Septentrionalle (années 1709 et 1710).* Ed. Le P. Camille de Rochemonteix. Paris, 1904.

Simcoe, John Graves. *The correspondence of Lieut. Governor John Graves Simcoe, with allied documents relating to his administration of the government of Upper Canada.* Ed. E. A. Cruikshank. Toronto, 1923–31. 4 vols.

Simpson, Alexander. *The life and travels of Thomas Simpson, the Arctic discoverer.* London, 1845.

Simpson, Sir George. "Letters of Sir George Simpson, 1841–1843." Ed. J. Schafer. *American Historical Review*, XIV, 1908, 70–94.

────── *Narrative of a journey round the world during the years 1841 and 1842.* London, 1847. 2 vols.

Skelton, O. D. *The life and times of Sir Alexander Tilloch Galt.* Toronto, 1920.

———— Review of H. A. Innis, *A history of the Canadian Pacific Railway*. *Canadian Historical Review*, IV, 1923, 179–181.

"Sketch of the fur trade of Canada, 1809." *Report of the Public Archives of Canada*, 1928, pp. 56–73.

Somerset, H. Somers. *The land of the muskeg*. London, 1895.

Southesk, James Carnegie, Earl of. *Saskatchewan and the Rocky Mountains: A diary and narrative of travel, sport, and adventure, during a journey through the Hudson's Bay Company's territories, in 1859 and 1860*. Toronto and Edinburgh, 1875.

Speck, F. G. *Family hunting territories and social life of various Algonkian bands of the Ottawa valley*. Memoir 70; Anthropological series, no. 8. Ottawa: Geological Survey, 1915.

Stanley, George F. G. *The birth of western Canada: A history of the Riel rebellions*. Toronto, 1936.

Steel, W. A. "The Northwest Territories radio system." *Canadian Defence Quarterly*, April 1927, 325–328.

Steele, [Sir] S. B. *Forty years in Canada: Reminiscences of the great North-West. . . .* Toronto, 1915.

Stefansson, Vilhjalmur. *The friendly Arctic: The story of five years in polar regions*. New York, 1921.

———— *Hunters of the great North*. London, 1923.

———— *My life with the Eskimo*. New York, 1913.

Stevens, Wayne E. *The Northwest fur trade, 1763–1800*. Urbana, Ill., 1928.

———— "The organization of the British fur trade, 1760–1800." *Mississippi Valley Historical Review*, III, 1916, 172–202.

Stewart, Elihu. *Down the Mackenzie and up the Yukon in 1906*. Toronto, 1912.

Sulte, Benjamin. "Canot d'écorce." *Bulletin des recherches historiques*, vol. XXII, 1916, 236–241.

———— "Le commerce de France avec le Canada avant 1760." *Proceedings and Transactions of the Royal Society of Canada*, Second Series, vol. XII, 1906, Section I, 45–63.

———— "Les coureurs de bois au lac Supérieur, 1660." *Ibid.*, Third Series, vol. V, 1911, Section I, 249–266.

———— "Le fort de Frontenac, 1668–1678." *Ibid.*, Second Series, vol. VII, 1901, Section I, 47–96.

———— "Les Français dans l'Ouest en 1671." *Ibid.*, Third Series, vol. XII, 1918, Section I, 1–31.

———— "Guerres des Iroquois, 1670–1673." *Ibid.*, vol. XV, 1921, Section I, 85–95.

———— "Le Haut-Canada avant 1615." *Ibid.*, Second Series, vol. X, 1904, Section I, 63–90.

———— *Histoire des Canadiens-français, 1608–1880: Origine, histoire, religion, guerres, découvertes, colonisation, coutumes, vie domestique, sociale et politique, développement, avenir*. Montréal, 1882–1884. 8 vols.

———— *Mélanges historiques: Etudes éparses et inédites de Benjamin Sulte*. Comp., annotées et pub. par Gérard Malchelosse. Montréal, 1918–34. 21 vols.

Surrey, N. M. M. *The commerce of Louisiana during the French régime, 1699–1763*. New York, 1916.

Sutton, G. M. *Eskimo year: A naturalist's adventures in the far North.* New York, 1934.

Taché, A. *Esquisse sur le Nord-Ouest de l'Amérique.* Montréal, 1869.

Tanner, John. *A narrative of the captivity and adventures of John Tanner, (U.S. interpreter at the Saut de Ste. Marie,) during thirty years residence among the Indians in the interior of North America.* Prepared by Edwin James. New York, 1830.

Thomas, Lowell. *Kabluk of the Eskimo.* Boston, 1932.

Thompson, David. *David Thompson's narrative of his explorations in western America, 1784–1812.* Ed. J. B. Tyrrell. Toronto: Champlain Society. 1916.

——— *See* Coues, Elliott.

Tohill, L. A. *Robert Dickson, British fur trader on the Upper Mississippi: A story of trade, war, and diplomacy.* Ann Arbor, Mich., 1927.

Tomison, William. "Journal." *Beaver,* Oct., 1920, p. 31; Dec., 1920, p. 7.

Traits of American Indian life and character. By a Fur Trader. San Francisco, 1933.

Trotter, R. G. "British finance and Confederation." *Canadian Historical Association Report,* 1927, pp. 89–96.

——— *Canadian federation, its origins and achievements: A study in nation building.* Toronto, 1924.

Turner, F. J. *The character and influence of the Indian trade in Wisconsin: A study of the trading post as an institution.* Johns Hopkins University Studies in Historical and Political Science. Baltimore, 1891.

Turnor, Philip. *See* Hearne, Samuel and Turnor, Philip.

Tuttle, Charles R. *Our north land, being a full account of the Canadian North-West and Hudson's Bay route, together with a narrative of the experiences of the Hudson's Bay expedition of 1884. . . .* Toronto, 1885.

Tyrrell, J. B. "Arrivals and departures of ships, Moose Factory, Hudson Bay, Province of Ontario, 1751–1880" *Ontario Historical Society, Papers and Records,* XIV, 163 ff.

——— "Correspondence, J. B. Tyrrell and H. A. Innis." *Canadian Historical Review,* IX, 1928, 156–160.

——— ed. "David Thompson and the Rocky Mountains." *Ibid.,* XV, 1934, 39–45.

——— ed. *Documents relating to the early history of Hudson Bay.* Toronto: Champlain Society, 1931.

——— "Peter Fidler, trader and surveyor, 1769–1822." *Proceedings and Transactions of the Royal Society of Canada,* Third Series, vol. VII, 1913, 117–127.

Tyrrell, James W. *Across the sub-Arctics of Canada: A journey of 3200 miles by canoe and snowshoe through the Hudson Bay region.* Toronto, 1908.

Umfreville, Edward. *Nipigon to Winnipeg: A canoe voyage through western Ontario by Edward Umfreville in 1784; with extracts from the writings of other early travellers through the region.* Ottawa, 1929.

——— *The present state of Hudson's Bay, containing a full description of that settlement, and the adjacent country, and likewise of the fur trade, with hints for its improvement . . . and a journal of a journey from Montreal to New-York.* London, 1790.

Unwin, George. *Industrial organization in the sixteenth and seventeenth centuries.* Oxford, 1922.

Vattier, Georges. *Essai sur la mentalité canadienne-française.* Paris, 1928.

Veblen, T. B. "The price of wheat since 1867." *Journal of Political Economy,* I, 1892, 69–103.

The Victoria history of the county of Surrey. Ed. H. E. Malden. Vol. II. [London], 1905. In "The Victoria History of the Counties of England."

Waldo, Fullerton. *Down the Mackenzie through the Great Lone Land.* New York, 1923.

Wallace, J. N. "The explorer of Finlay River in 1824." *Canadian Historical Review,* IX, 1928, 25–32, 156–160.

—— *The wintering partners on Peace River from the earliest records to the union in 1821; with a summary of the Dunvegan journal, 1806.* Ottawa, 1929.

Wallace, W. S. "The pedlars from Quebec." *Canadian Historical Review,* XIII, 1932, 387–402.

Warren, E. R. *The beaver: Its work and its ways.* Baltimore, 1927.

Watkin, Sir E. W. *Canada and the States: Recollections, 1851 to 1886.* London, 1887.

Weld, Isaac. *Travels through the states of North America, and the provinces of Upper and Lower Canada, during the years 1795, 1796, and 1797.* London, 1799.

West, John. *The substance of a journal during a residence at the Red River colony, British North America, and frequent excursions among the northwest American Indians, in the years 1820, 1821, 1822, 1823.* London, 1824.

[Wilcocke, Samuel Hull]. *A narrative of occurrences in the Indian countries of North America, since the connexion of the Right Hon. the Earl of Selkirk with the Hudson's Bay Company, and his attempt to establish a colony on the Red River. . . .* London, 1817.

Willson, Beckles. *The great Company, being a history of the Honourable Company of Merchant-Adventurers, trading into Hudson's Bay.* London, 1900. 2 vols.

—— *The life of Lord Strathcona and Mount Royal . . . (1820–1914).* Toronto, 1915.

Wintemberg, W. J. "Was Hochelaga destroyed or abandoned?" *American Anthropologist,* XXIX, 1927, 251–254.

Wissler, Clark. *The American Indian: An introduction to the anthropology of the New World.* 2nd ed., New York, 1922.

—— "The influence of the horse in the development of Plains culture." *American Anthropologist,* new series, XVI, 1–25.

Work, John. *The journal of John Work, a chief-trader of the Hudson's Bay Co., during his expedition from Vancouver to the Flatheads and Blackfeet of the Pacific Northwest.* Ed. William S. Lewis and Paul C. Phillips. Cleveland, 1923.

Wraxall, Peter. *An abridgment of the Indian affairs contained in four folio volumes, transacted in the colony of New York, from the year 1678 to the year 1751.* Ed. Charles Howard McIlwain. Cambridge, Mass., 1915.

Index

ABERDEEN, 358
Abitibi River, 48, 50
Acadia, 18–19
Accounting, 360–361; H.B. Co., 128, 318–320, 360–361; recommendation of Robertson, 162–163; N.W. Co., 243–244
Act of Union, relation to canals, 395, 400
Adhemar, J. Bte., fort of, 191; licences of, 193, 193n, 195–196
Adventurer, 367, 368
Agreements, N.W. Co., 199–200, 248–250
Agriculture: corn, 11–19, 26–28, 33, 36–37, 61, 143, 167–168, 183, 224; flour, from Niagara, 225, from Red River, 303; at posts, 299–301
Aigremont, F.-Clairambault, Sr. d', 59
Airplane, use of, 360n, 380n
Aix-la-Chapelle, treaty of, 116
Aklavik, 345n, 347–348, 349n, 350, 366, 370; wireless station, 353; competition with Vancouver, 373
Alaska, 352, 373; ceded to U.S., 364
Albanel, Father, 49
Albany (N.Y.): competition from, 84, 100, 174–176, 174n, 178n, 219–221, 252; boats on route, 159; trade at, 169, 177n, 180–182, 221n
Albany River (H.B.), 45, 49, 290; fort on, 119–120, 139, 142; posts on, 149, 154, 367; goods sent down, 317, 333, 368
Albermarle, 1st Duke of, 124
Alberta, 353
Alberta and Arctic Transportation Co.: acquired by H.B. Co., 345, 345n, 350; contract with Northern Trading Co., 366–367; subsidiary to Lamson-Hubbard, 373

Alberta and Great Waterways Railway, 345
Alexandra, 293
Algonquin Indians: wars with Iroquois, 12, 23–28, 30, 37; trade, 12, 14–15, 21–22, 45, 71; attempts to control trade, 28–29
Allan, Sir Hugh, 397n
Allegheny River, 88
Allouez, Father, 46
Allsopp, George, 175n
Amadjuak, 370n
American Fur Co., 187, 330–331
American Hide and Fur Co., 368
American Revolution, 178–180, 184–187, 219, 286, 386, 391; effect on movement of trade to north, 252
Amsterdam, 77
Anderson, Chief Factor, on apprenticeships, 312–313; on Portage La Loche Brigade, 314; on tariffs, 319n; against expansion to Yukon, 324; in Mackenzie River district, 336
Anderson River, 369
Andriani, Count, 240n, 241n, 266n
Anglican missions, 362, 364, 367
Anson Northrup, 294
Apprenticeship, 312–313, 356–368
Archithinue Indians (Blackfoot), 122, 139
Arctic Ocean, 285, 297, 369, 378
Arctic Red River, 359, 367
Arlington, Earl of, 124
Arvida, 400
Askin, John: loss on trade, 187; owner of lake vessel, 220; farming of, 225n; contractor, 225; on loss of XY Co., 257
Assiniboine Indians, 59; competition for furs, 46–50, 89–92, 99, 151, 188; trading by Kaministiquia, 94, 190; as middlemen, 121, 137; smallpox, 192

Assiniboine River, 120, 293; Indians from, 46, 48; La Vérendrye on, 94–95; competition on, 154, 158, 160, 269; forts on, 191, 233–234

Astor, J. J., 164n, 187, 187n, 261, 261n

Atcheson, Nathaniel, 261n

Athabasca, 344

Athabasca district: Indians from, 151; Pond in, 152, 196, 199; H.B. Co., 153–154, 164–165, 200; trade in, 192–195, 253; effect of trade expansion on transport to, 206, 236–241, 248, 261, 291–292, 309, 342, 361, 390; communication with, 226, 244–245; importance of, 229–230, 267, 275; supplies from, 232, 237, 304–305; effect of competition on, 274–275, 372; goods sent to, 291, 301; management of, 311, 326, 361–362

Athabasca Indians, 149–150; smallpox, 152, 192; trade to Hudson Bay, 202

Athabasca Landing, 344, 345n, 361, 364–366, 364n

Athabasca Pass, 317

Athabasca River: Pond on, 19; Thompson on, 204; posts on, 229, 317

Athabasca River, 345n

Athabaska, 222

Athawapiscat, 367

Attikamegue Indians, 47

Aubert, Neret and Gayot (Company), 73, 103

Aubert de la Chesnaye, Charles, 63

Aubry-bouché (rue), 18

Auld, W., 159, 270

Auldjo, A., 184

Aulneau, Father, 92

BABINE, 364n

Bacon, N. H., 356

Bacqueville de la Potherie, C. C. Le Roy, 54, 56, 60, 115

Bad Lake, 279

Baffin Land, 353, 370n

Bailey, Mr. (H.B. Co.), 123–124

Baillie Island, 352, 373

Baker, I. G., and Co., 369

Ballantyne, R. M., 307, 320

Bank of Montreal, 393, 396

Bannerman (fur trader), 196–197

Baroness, 294

Basques, 9, 31

Bathurst Inlet, 352, 369–370

Baxter, Alexander, 190

Bay Maude, 352

Baychimo, 352

Bayeskimo, 353

Bayrupert, 353

Bear Lake, 201–202, 256, 262, 275, 359

Bear River, 202

Bearskins, 96, 265, 298

Beaubien (fur trader), 255

Beaumois (fur trader), 98

Beaver: general, 3–6; importance to Indian, 12–14; hunting of, 14n, 19; extermination of, 28, 28n, 109, 113, 188, 263–264, 266–267, 332, 332n; trade in, 35–36, 42, 61, 139, 150, 168–169, 270; regulations of trade, 40, 68–69, 74; sources of, 47–49; grades, 64–68, 104–105, 126; production of, 70–71, 99–100, 116–117, 136–138, 260–261, 265–266, 286; consumption, 101, 245–246; cost of handling, 103; prices, 104–105, 138, 161–162, 194–195, 264–265, 318–319, 328; conservation of, 328, 378n

Beaver (magazine), 358

Beaver (sloop), 222, 259

Beaver (steamer), 298, 334

Beaver Club, 251, 251n, 358

Beaver hats: 4, 4n, 11, 12, 23, 71, 74–76, 74n, 76n, 83, 90, 334–335; fashions in, 11–12, 74–77, 341; cost of manufacturing, 76, 264n; marketing, 77, 80, 81; manufacture prohibited in colony, 114n, 117n

Beaver Indians, 45, 201–203, 231, 364n

Beaver Lake, 195

Bedford House, 154

Bégon, M., Sr. de la Picardière, 79, 88

Bell River, 342

Bell Rock, 348

Bergstrom, O., 369

Bering Strait, 352

Bernard Harbour, 352, 369n
Bernon, Sr. Samuel, 58
Berrenger (Co. of New France), 39
Bersiamite Indians, 30
Big Falls, 279
Big Island, fishing at, 299, 360; supplies from, 305, 305n
Bigot, François, 85
Bigras, J. B., 211
Bilbao, 78
Birmingham, 167
Black, Samuel, 325n
Blackfoot Indians, 138, 139, 151, 235
Blacklead Island, 370n
Blanc Sablon, 371n
Blondeau, Jr., 190
Blondeau, Barthélemi, 196n, 197n
Blondeau, Maurice, 189–194, 193n
Blue Fish River, 202
Board of Trade, 170, 178
Boat brigades, 292–293
Boat Encampment, 317
Boats, size of, H.B. Co., 154, 158–160, 292–293, 304, 309
Bonssel, Pierre, 211
Booth, J. R., 395
Boston: competition from, 51, 81; communication through, 208; export of furs through, 243; Lamson-Hubbard from, 366
Bostwick (fur trader), 168
Boucherville, Thomas Verchères de, 256n, 257n
Bougainville, L.-A., Comte de, 225n
Boulard, 39
Bourbonnois, Antoine, 191
Bourbonois, Lafrance, 189
Bourdignon, Henry, 193
Bouthillier, André, 211
Bouvier, 30
Bow River, 234
Boyer (fur trader), 98
Boyer, Charles, 198n
Boyer and Bisonett, 209n
Brabant, A., 356–358
Brandon House, 154
Brassy Hill River, 192
Bredin, Cornwall and Roberts, 364
Brick Brothers, 364, 364n
Brickwood, Pattle and Co., 250

British Columbia, 363, 366, 392, 399; gold rush to, 334, 384; road to Nelson built by, 351; labour from, 353–354; competition from, 366
British North America Act, 400
Bruce (William), 193n, 196n, 198n
Brulé, Etienne, 28–31
Brunnet, J. B. E., 211
Bryan, J., 366
Bryce, G., 140, 154, 285
Buffalo: trade in skins of, 27, 163, 290, 303–307, 330, 359n; dependence of Indians on, 139, 163, 235; consumption of meat of, 235, 235n
Buffalo (N.Y.), 399
Buffalo River, 368
Burnet, Governor, 88
Burpee, L. J., 224n
Butler, Capt., 341n, 369n
B.X. Co., 366

Cadboro, 298
Cadillac, Antoine de Lamothe, 67n
Cadotte, J. B., 186, 249
Cadotte, J. B. (partner of Alexander Henry), 168, 194, 194n
Cadotte, M., 186
Caledonia, 257n
Calgary, 95, 344, 369
California, 298, 308, 334
Callander, 163
Cambridge Bay, 352
Cameron, Duncan, 154, 271, 275
Campbell, J. D., 250, 279
Campbell, Robert, 313, 315, 322; on the Yukon, 291, 324–325
Campion, Etienne, 167, 190
Canada and Atlantic Railway, 395
Canada Banking Co., 393n
Canadian National Railways, 368, 400
Canadian National Telegraphs, 353
Canadian Pacific Railway, 344, 397–400, 399n
Canadusa, 345n
Canoe, birch-bark, 13, 13n, 19, 20, 24, 81, 143, 159–161, 195–199; importance to Europeans, 20, 167–168, 179, to Indian middlemen, 44, 82, 97, 143, 151; size and use of, 60, 111, 207–210, 215–218, 216n, 238;

expense of, 219–223, 238, 276, 289; manufacture of, 222, 222n, 223n; *canot du Nord*, 226–229, 226n, 231
Canton, 243
Cap de Victoire, 28
Cape Dorset, 370n
Cape Horn, 297
Cape Krusenstern, 369
Cape Smith, 370n
Cape Spencer, 333
Capital, 247–248, 251–252, 258–259, 290
Carcajou, 201
Caribou, 352
Cariboo district, 363, 364n
Carillon, 171
Carillon rapids, 239n
Carleton, Sir Guy, 173, 173n, 217
Carleton Island, 184n
Carlton House (Ass.), 154
Carolina, 87, 124
Carrot River, 95
Carruthers Hide and Fur Co., 368
Carteret, Sir George, 124
Cartier, Sr., 92
Cartier, Jacques, 9–12, 14, 16, 17
Carver, Jonathan, 168, 190
Casimir, 368
Cassette Rapids, 344
Castillon, Sr. (Co. of New France), 39
Castor gras, 14; competition with Hudson Bay for, 48–49, 69–70, 94–95; problem of regulating supply, 75, 78, 80–81, 90, 104–106; disappearance of, 264
Catapoi River, 254n
Cedar Lake, 95, 137, 151, 192
Cedars, 171
Chaboillez, C., 195–196, 259
Chaffault (Co. of New France), 39
Chaleur Bay, 10
Chamailant (fur trader), 198
Chambly, 211
Champigny, J. B. de, 70, 75, 116
Champlain, Samuel de, 3, 12, 14, 17, 20–26, 30–37
Chaouanons Indians, 56
Charlebois (fur trader), 198

Charlotte, 257n
Charlton Island, 128, 259, 352
Chatelets, Sr., 39
Cheadle, W. B., 302–304
Chequamegon, 51, 56, 168; Saulteurs at, 43–44; returns from, 100, 102; lease of, 108–109, 186; Alexander Henry at, 172
Chesterfield House, 153
Chesterfield Inlet, 153n, 352, 371n
Cheveux Relevés Indians, 17
Cheyenne River, 294
Chibougamau, 371n
Chicago, 55, 318, 395
Chief factors, 320–321, 320n, 337
Chilcat Indians, 324–325
China, 205n, 243, 246, 265
Chinn, Edward, 193
Chipewyan Indians, 153, 201–203, 231
Chipman, C. C., 356
Chippewa Indians, 45, 168, 181
Chiswick House, 154
Churchill River, 5, 96, 120, 135–137, 141–142, 144, 150–152, 158, 309, 389; Montreal traders on, 195, 199, 202
Civil War (U.S.), 392
Clare, J. A., 315
Clarke, John, 164, 164n, 287, 329
Clarke, Jonas, 208
Clark's Fork River, 204
Clause (fur trader), 190
Clear Lake, 199, 368
Clyde (Baffin Land), 370n
Coats, Capt., 131
Coats Island, 352, 370n
Cocking, Matthew, 151–152, 151n, 188–189, 192
Colden, Cadwallader, 84
Cole, John, 197n, 199n
Colen, Joseph, 155
Colleton (shareholder, 1667), 124
Collingwood, 395
Coltman, W. B., 163
Columbia department, 204–205, 243, 261, 287, 292, 295, 389; transport in, 297, 317; control of, 322, 333–336; returns of, 333, 336

Colville, 343
Compagnie du Nord, 50
Compagnie d'Occident, 103–104
Company of Canada, 72–73
Company of the Habitans, 39, 40, 63
Company of New France, 38–40
Company of Normandy, 40
Company of West Indies, 63, 103
Competition, 138, 254–257, 269–274, 356–357, 362–374
Congés, 62, 62n, 97–99
Congress (U.S.), 247, 252
Conseil Souverain, 63
Constitutional Act (1791), 391
Conway, H. S., 171n
Cook, Capt. James, 203
Cook's Inlet, 200
Copper, 11, 14, 31, 149–150
Copper Indians, 149–150, 152, 200; treaty with, 361
Coppermine River, 149
Cornwall, J. K., 366
Coronation Gulf, 369
Corry, Thomas, 151, 151n, 190, 192, 196
Coulonges, Sr. de, 92
Courcelles, Rémy, Sr. de, 51, 65, 407
Coureurs de bois, 115n; work of, 58–62; regulations for, 67–69, 107
Craven, William, Earl of, 124
Cree Indians: Montreal trade with, 44–49, 89–94, 99, 102, 150–151, 190, 231; English trade with, 48, 121, 137, 158; as traders, 202–203, 235
Cross Lake, 272
Crow Wing River, 294
Cumberland House, 144n, 152, 152n, 153, 157n, 158, 159n, 190, 194, 197n, 232, 317; N.W. Co., depot at, 234–235; H.B. Co. depot at, 301, 317, 326, 344, 359; free trade at, 331, 368
Cumberland Lake, 96

DALLAS, Governor, 318n
Dassu (fur trader), 198
D. A. Thomas, 345, 345n, 366

Dauphin River, 293
Davidson, G. C., 233
Davis ("Twelve-foot"), 364, 364n, 372
Davis, Strachan and Co., 208
Dease, P. W., 286n
Dease Lake, 291, 325, 372, 372n
Debt, 374–375
Deed Poll (1821), 284–286, 313, 320n; (1834), 320–321, 355; (1871), 355–356, 377–378
Deering's Point, 121–122
Deerskins, 264–265
Deloge, Joseph, 191
Denmark, 73
Denonville, J.-R. de B., Marquis de, 50, 54n
Denys, Nicolas, 3, 10, 18, 74, 76
Deschaillons, Sr., 91
Deschambault (clerk), 313
Desfonds, Joseph, 191–192
Desjerlais (fur trader), 198
De Steffany, Gus and Lyman, 369
Detroit River, 55
Diamond P stores, 366
Discovery, 352
Distributor, 345, 345n, 347
Dividends, H.B. Co., 120, 142, 158
Dobbs, A., 137
Dobie, R., 171n, 191, 196, 215
Dobie and Badgeley, 184
Dog Lake, 89
Dog-rib Indians, 149, 150, 152, 201, 361
Domergue (controller of trade), 70, 408
Donnaconna, 11, 14
Douglas, Sir James, 322
Douglas and Symington, 182n
Doyle, Capt. (24th Regt.), 185
Drax, Lady Margaret, 124
Dreuillettes, Father Gabriel, 46
Dry Island, 347
Du Chesneau, Jacques, 45, 59, 63, 65, 66
Duchesneau, Joseph, 193
Duck Lake, 272
Duluth, D. G., 49, 51
Dumay, Pierre, 191

Dunlevy (trader), 364
Du Pont, F. G., Sr. de, 30
Durand (fur trader), 193
Durivage, J., 98, 111
Durocher, J. B., 196
Dutch, competition with, 21, 31, 34–35, 45, 51–54, 65, 86
Duties on beaver, 170, 246–247; revenue from, 178
Dyer, Allen and Co., 250

EAGLE HILLS, 252
Eagle Indians, 139
East India Co., 205, 243, 246
East Main, 130, 142, 278, 289, 335
Eastern Arctic, 370
Edgar, William, 178n, 187, 203
Edmonton, 154, 234, 292, 295–296, 302–304, 317, 343–344, 346, 351, 359–361, 363–364, 368
Eldorado, 367, 367n
Elizabeth, 208
Elk Island, 290
Elk River, 231
Ellice, Alexander, 195
Ellice, Edward, 219, 251, 278, 283n 283–284, 332, 338
Ellis, H., 138
Elmore (fur trader), 364, 364n
Engineers' Association, 353
English Chief (with Alex. Mackenzie), 201
English River district, 202, 229, 234, 238–239, 241, 245, 253, 261, 267, 301, 309–310, 326
Erick, 352
Erie Canal, 394
Ermatinger, Edward, 309, 315, 321–322
Ermatinger, Lawrence, 191–196, 207–208, 208n, 210–215, 210n, 218–219
Eskimos, 144, 149, 201, 305, 362, 369n, 370, 373, 378n
Etechemin Indians, 12, 25
European goods, 70, 84, 96, 109–110, 118, 121, 271, 388–389
Evans, John, 233n

FACTORS, chief, 320–321, 320n, 337
Fairford House, 154, 359
Fairs, 57–58
Faubourg St. Antoine, 74n
Fauconnet (controller of trade), 70
Felt-makers Co., 131
Fermier, 64–78, 98–99, 107–109
Fidler, Peter, 154, 162
Finkelstein, Max, 366
Finlay, Hugh, 184n
Finlay, James (d. 1797), 189–190, 192, 194, 189n, 206
Finlay, James (1766–1830), 234, 250
Finlay River, 202, 325n
Fishing, 9, 23, 26, 132–133, 156, 299–301, 384–385
Fishing Lake, 256
Folle Avoine country, 240n
Fond du Lac, 345n
Fond du Lac (Lake Athabasca), 303, 345n
Fond du Lac (Lake Superior), 168, 186, 209n, 241, 254n, 266n, 267
Forks (Peace River), 202, 256
Forsyth, James, 284
Forsyth, Thomas, 186n, 187n, 278
Forsyth, Richardson and Co., 184, 186n, 221, 255, 255n, 257n, 393
Fort Albany, 164, 167, 290, 317; capture by French, 49; in hands of English, 122; supplies for, 130; fortification, 130; local supplies, 132–133; tariff for, 139, 141; beaver from, 142, 164; otter from, 333
Fort à la Corne, 95–97, 189
Fort Alexander (Winnipeg River) 232–235, 232n, 301, 304
Fort Alexandria (Swan River), 245, 256
Fort Alexandria (B.C.), 297, 304, 336–337, 364n
Fort Assiniboine, 295, 303, 317
Fort Astoria, 204
Fort Augustus, 234, 245
Fort aux Trembles, 191, 198n, 249, 255n
Fort Bas de la Rivière, *see* Fort Alexander
Fort Benton (Montana), 369

Fort Bourbon, 95–96, 98–99
Fort Bourbon (Nelson River), 89
Fort Carlton (Sask.), 287n, 296, 302, 317, 332n, 343–344, 354–355, 361n
Fort Chambly, 53
Fort Charles, 352
Fort Charles, 119
Fort Charlotte, 227, 227n, 229n
Fort Chipewyan, 200–201, 230, 244–245, 255, 274–275, 292, 295, 300, 347, 365, 372, 374n
Fort Churchill, 120, 130–132, 143, 149, 152n, 153n, 164, 309, 341; production of, 142, 326; Indians at, 143, 203; Hearne at, 150–153
Fort Collinson, 352
Fort Colville, 333
Fort Dauphin, 95, 98–99, 190–191, 194, 240n, 257n
Fort de Français, 49
Fort de l'Isle, 234
Fort des Prairies, 194, 234, 238, 240n, 245, 253, 267
Fort Detroit, 55, 89, 100, 102, 111–112, 224–226; depot at, 61, 111–112, 183–188, 212, 219–222, 253, 262, 389; returns from, 73, 100, 262; licences granted to, 108–109; prices at, 244n, 267
Fort Douglas, 290
Fort Dunvegan, 230n, 275, 288, 316, 344n, 354, 364n; goods at, 230; transport, 234; supplies from, 301–303
Fort Ellice, 293, 295n, 296, 307n, 362n
Fort Epinette, 192n, 233
Fort Erie, 183, 184, 224, 224n
Fort Espérance, 233
Fort Fitzgerald, 345–346, 345n, 350, 353, 375
Fort Frances, 322
Fort Frontenac, 46, 46n, 53, 55, 73, 87, 89, 108
Fort Garry, 287, 294–296, 341–344, 354, 359, 371
Fort George, 352
Fort George (B.C.), 204
Fort George (H.B.), 367

Fort George (Sask.), 234
Fort Good Hope, 202, 274, 291, 310, 316, 320, 359
Fort Halkett, 300
Fort Hearne, 352
Fort Hope, 297
Fort La Jonquière, 95, 111
Fort Langley, 298, 301, 308, 314, 333–334
Fort La Reine, 93–94, 98–99, 154, 154n, 190–191
Fort La Toruette, 49
Fort Levis, 167
Fort Liard, 202, 300, 305, 350
Fort McKenzie, 370n
Fort McLeod, 204
Fort McPherson, 352, 316n
Fort Maurepas, 92–94, 98
Fort Nelson (Liard River), 202, 274, 345n, 349–350, 367
Fort Nelson (Nelson River), 48–50, 71, 89, 120, 122, 126, 128, 130, 132, 140, 143, 351, 367; *see also* York Factory
Fort Norman, 291, 305, 316, 328, 345n, 347, 349–350, 375
Fort Ombabika, 49
Fort Orange, 35, 79
Fort Paskoyac, 95–97
Fort Pelly, 293, 317
Fort Pitt, 297, 302
Fort Rae, 299–300, 304, 328, 342, 345n, 350, 359–360, 366, 373
Fort Resolution, 299–300, 305, 345n, 346–348, 360, 366, 375
Fort Richlieu, 38
Fort Rouge, 94
Fort Rouillé, 89
Fort St. Charles, 91–93, 98
Fort St. James, 204, 364n
Fort St. Joseph, 55, 100
Fort St. Louis, 56
Fort St. Louis (Sask.), 95, 245
Fort Saint Pierre, 91
Fort Schlosser, 177n, 220n
Fort Selkirk, 291, 324–325
Fort Simpson, 202, 324, 334, 342, 372, 375; transport to, 291, 310, 316, 345n, 346–348; supplies for,

299–302, 305, 305n, 328; communication at, 346
Fort Smith, 345–350, 345n, 353, 361, 365, 375
Fort Vancouver, 297–298, 301, 314, 317, 334, 336
Fort Vermilion, 92
Fort Vermilion (Peace R.), 201, 230, 275, 344, 346, 360, 364–365, 364n, 368, 372
Fort Vermilion (Sask.), 232, 245
Fort Vincennes, 89
Fort William (*see* Kaministiquia), 228–229, 232, 289, 317
Fort Yale, 297
Fort Yukon, 291, 316, 324
Fouquet (Co. of New France), 39
Fox farms, 380
Fox Indians, 44, 51, 54, 89–94, 99, 102, 107, 110; trade of, 44–51, 53, 89; wars, 90–94, 99, 102, 106–110
Fox River, 91, 94, 99
Frances Lake (Yukon), 291, 324
François (fur trader), 152n, 188–189, 192, 193n
Franklin, Capt. John, 237, 273
Fraser, J., 284
Fraser, Simon, 204, 248n, 249–250
Fraser Lake, 204
Fraser River, 204, 297–298, 363, 366
French, C. H., 356–358
French Revolution, 212, 242, 246, 264n
Frenchman's Island, 371n
Frobisher, B. and J., 152–153, 189–193, 197–198, 213, 247, 250
Frobisher, Benjamin, 174, 191, 193–194, 196, 200, 206, 250
Frobisher, Joseph, 152n, 191, 194–196, 246, 249, 256n
Frobisher, Thomas, 194–198
Frobisher Bay, 370n
Fur and Fish Company, 325n
Furs: fancy, 12, 265n; production, H.B. Co., 120, 142, 307–308, 327–332; production and prices in Canada, 264–268, 334–337

GALINÉE, Father R. de B. de, 60

Gamelin, Ignace, 97–98, 177n
Garry, Nicholas, inspection trip of, 285, 287, 289–290, 318, 323, 329
Gasoline boats, 349, 352, 368
Gaspé, 11–12, 78, 266n
Gatineau, 23
Gautiot (fur trader), 193
Gayot, Bouélet and Pasquier, 73
Geanne, Robert, 211
Genoa, 127
George, 293
Georgian Bay: from the Ottawa to, 21, 24, 26; Indians driven from, 36, 43; Toronto to, 223; lumber from, 395; wheat exported by, 399
Germain, Lord George, 181, 189n
Germany, 71, 76, 80–81, 101, 246n
Geyer, George (Governor), 121–122
Giffard, Sr. Robert, 39
Gillam, Capt., 122
Giscombe Portage, 354n, 364
Goddard, J. Stanley, 168
Godefroy, Sr., 39
Gold rush, 334, 362–363
Gonneville, 98–99
Goodwin, Mr. (H.B. Co.), 254n
Gorst, Mr. (H.B. Co.), 123
Graham, 294
Graham, Andrew, 144n, 151n
Grahame, James A. (chief commissioner), 344, 354, 356, 371, 374, 378
Grahame, 344, 344n, 345n
Grand Banks, 384
Grand Portage, 235, 267, 390; French trade through, 89–111; Canadian trade through, 151, 152n, 158, 168, 183, 188–195, 199–201, 211–220, 222–228, 231–232, 237–253
Grand Rapids (Ath.), 344–345
Grand Rapids (Sask.), 160n, 293, 295, 321, 343, 359
Grand Trunk Pacific, 366
Grand Trunk Railway, 338, 356n, 395–397
Grant, A., 220
Grant, Charles, 197–198, 213–214
Grant, Cuthbert, 199, 199n, 229n, 249–250, 249n
Grant, D. A., 242, 255, 255n

Grant, George M., 296, 341
Grant, Peter, 250, 255n
Grant, Robert, 196n, 197n, 199n, 200, 253, 253n
Grant, Hon. W., 184
Grassy Lake, 254n
Gratuities, 376
Gravel Point, 348
Graves, Booty, 196n, 197n, 198, 198n
Gravesend, 129, 353
Gray, John, 393
Green, Lieut. Col., 258, 273n
Green Bay: Nicolet at, 31; growth of trade at, 43, 48, 51, 55, 61, 89, 91, 100, 102, 172, 267, 390; leasing of, 106–108
Green Lake, 343–344, 372n
Gregory, John, 199–200, 249–250, 255
Gregory and McLeod, 199n, 250, 253, 258
Grenfell, Lord, 366
Griffin, 46, 54
Groesbeeke (fur trader), 190
Groseilliers, M. C. des, 31, 36–37; with H.B. Co., 47, 49, 56, 119, 122–123
Grouard, 344
Guigues (holder of *ferme*), 74

HALDANE, John, 279
Haldimand, Sir Frederick, 181–182, 189, 213, 247
Hall, R. H., 356
Hallowell, James, 246, 250
Hamilton, Hon. Henry, 184n
Hamilton and Cartwright, 182n
Hammond, George, 185n
Hance, M., 212
Hardisty, Richard (chief factor), 342, 344, 354, 371, 374
Hare Indians, 201
Harmon, Daniel, 155, 222, 230–231, 231n, 236–237, 245, 248, 255–256, 264, 271, 273
Harmony Co., 370
Harper (trader), 331
Hatmakers, 75, 81, 170; complaints regarding poor beaver, 71, 105–106; migration of, 145n
Hatters Corporation, 16n, 74
Havre St. Pierre, 371n

Hay, John, 254n, 255n
Hay River, 230, 275, 368, 372
Hayes, Sir James, 124
Hayes Island, 130
Hayes River, 158, 278
Hearne, Samuel, 134, 143n, 149–152, 159n, 202
Heatley, Mr. (H.B. Co.), 123
Hebron, 371n
Henday, Anthony, 95–97, 122, 131, 134, 138–139, 151
Henley House, 139, 142, 144n
Henry, Alexander, the elder, 152, 167, 170, 187–189, 194–195, 198, 203, 206, 215–216
Henry, Alexander, the younger, 154, 160, 196n, 228–229, 232, 235, 245, 249, 251, 255, 255n, 256n, 257, 267n, 270–274, 296
Heriot, George, 223n, 226, 240n, 244n
Herschel Island, 352, 369, 369n, 373
Hislop and Nagel, 366
Hochelaga, 11, 14, 22n
Hocquart, Gilles, 115n
Holland: sale of beaver in, 64, 70, 73, 77, 80, 86, 101, 246; escarlatines imported through, 86
Holmes, William, 193n, 194, 196–198, 196n, 197n, 199n, 200, 242n
Honqueronon Indians, 28
Hopedale, 371n
Howard, Joseph, 192–193, 212
Hudson, Mr. (H.B. Co.) 255n
Hudson, Ont., 398
Hudson Bay: competition through, 45–51, 59, 63, 69, 73, 84, 89–91, 96–99, 101, 109–110, 114, 168–169, 194–195, 199–202; *castor gras* from, 70–71; wars with English, 122; English trade to, 119, 122, 124, 128–130, 137–138, 155, 142–163, 264; N.W. Co. on, 237; N.W. Co. attempt to purchase outlet, 278–279; transportation from, 285–294; express through, 317–318, 317n; competition on, 367–371
Hudson Bay Railway, 353, 400, 402
Hudson River, 34, 45, 53, 114
Hudson's Hope, 344–345, 345n, 359
Hudson's House, 153

Hughes, James, 260n, 313
Huguenots, 38
Hungerford, Sir Edward, 124
Huno, J., 98
Hunter and Bailey, 189n
Huron Indians: cultural traits, 11–12; trade of, 17, 20–38, 43–46, 51–52, 54, 56; effect of European goods on culture of, 18–20; war with Iroquois, 35–38

ILE PERCÉE, 9, 40, 78
Illinois Indians: beaver from, 3, 70; trade with, 44, 55, 60–61, 100; war with Iroquois, 56
Illinois River, 172, 185–186
Inenew, 352
Inglis, John, 248
Inglis, Ellice and Co., 186n, 261, 261n
Inspection, 317, 361, 361n
Insurance, 126, 362
Inverness, 358
Invincible, 222
Iroquois: wars, 12, 17, 20–26, 31–43, 63, 102; competition with, 45–46, 51–56, 65, 84–89, 116; hunters, 237, 264
Isaac Todd, 204
Island Lake, 308, 326, 341, 359
Isle à la Grosse, 245, 317, 359, 368
Isle à la Grosse Lake, 152, 162, 195, 274n, 343
Isle Jesus, 211
Italy, 101

JACOBS, Ferdinand, 197n
James Bay: posts on, 48–49, 120–122, 285; wages in, 125–126; organization in, 130–133, 285, 352; competition, 139, 149
Jasper House, 303, 317
Jay Treaty, 179–180, 185–186, 386, 391
Jeannott, Henry (fur trader), 192
Jérémie, Nicolas, 89, 132
Jesuits, 38
Job Bros. and Co., 371n
Johnson, Sir William, 170, 171n, 175, 175n
Jolliet, Louis, 51

Joseph, Père, 29
Judge, Capt., 208

KALM, Peter, 109
Kaministiquia, 257; French trade at, 49–51; La Vérendrye at, 89–92, 98; leasing of, 99–100, 107–109; Canadian trade to, 190, 260, 276–278; terminus at, 228–229, 260, 276–278, 390; wages at, 239–243; prices at, 244–245
Kamloops, 297
Kay, John, 195–198
Kay, William, 195–198
Keewatin district, 360
Keg River, 368
Keith system, 320
Kelsey, Henry, 120–134, 137–138, 144n, 151
Kenogami River, 49
Keweenaw, 266n
Kikabou Indians, 55–56
Kindersley, Sir Robert, 358
King, James, 273n
King William Land, 352
King's Posts, 81n, 106–108, 259–260, 285
Kingston, 219
Kirke, Sir John, 124
Kishkakon Indians, 45
Kittigazuit, 352
Kitty, 294
Klengenberg, Capt. C., 369, 369n
Knight, Capt. James, 131, 136n
Knistenaux Indians, see Crees
Koksoak, 367n
Kootenay House, 204
Kootenay River, 204
Korsook River, 367
Kullyspell House, 204

LA BARRE, J. A. L. de, 52
La Baye, 206, 390
Labour
  Hudson Bay Co., 134–136; wages, 125–126, 140, 154–155, 160–164, 310–316, 354, 357; labour conditions, 135; employés, 141–142, 310–311, 310n, 353
  Montreal trade, wages, 217–219,

237–240, 240n, 243n, 276–278; employés, 240–241

Labrador, 164n, 266n, 285, 367, 370; organization of, 322, 325; transport to, 352–353

Lac Bourbon, 95, 98

Lac des Courts Oreilles, 186

Lac des Isles, 240n

Lac d'Orignal, 153, 203, 245

Lac des Prairies, 93, 95

Lac du Brochet, 306, 368

Lachine, terminus of trade, 55, 167, 181n, 207, 209, 209n, 215–216, 317

Lachine Rapids, 20, 29; trade at, 32–33, 41, 55

Lac la Biche, 344, 372–373

Lac la Martre, 200

Lac la Pluie, 190, 200, 227

Lac la Ronge, 199, 368

La Cloche, 315, 321

Lacorne, St. Louis, 215

La Croix, Hubert, 182

Ladouceur, J. Bte., 98–99, 111

Lady Kindersley, 352

Lady Mackworth, 345n, 361

Lady of the Lake, 349

Lafitau, Father, J. F., 83n

La France, Joseph, 137–138, 140

La Galissonière, R. M. B., Comte de, 85

Lahontan, L. A. de L. d'A., Baron de, 4, 52–54, 58, 60–61

La Jemeraye (fur trader), 91–92

Lake Athabasca: Turnor at, 154; posts on, 196–202, 291–292, 347

Lake Champlain, 25, 182

Lake Erie, 25, 51, 53, 81n, 184, 218, 220, 222, 266n

Lake Harbour, 370n

Lake Huron, 26–27, 56, 87, 89, 102, 184, 207, 218–220, 222–224, 266n

Lake Manitoba, 234, 237n

Lake Michigan, 31, 36, 43–59, 89, 100, 167–168, 206–207, 222, 389

Lake Nipigon, 95, 190; trade to, 44, 209; competition with H.B. Co., 49–51; wages, 240n

Lake Nipissing, 24, 27

Lake of the Woods, 154; La Vérendrye on, 91–94; lease of, 99; route through, 190, 214; boundary to, 252

Lake Ontario, 25, 46–53, 86–89, 184, 219–220, 266n

Lake Pend d'Oreille, 204

Lake St. John, 15, 47, 259

Lake Simcoe, 223n

Lake Superior, 14, 31, 36, 43–51, 59–60, 89–92, 99–101, 167–168, 181, 183, 189, 222, 226, 252–254, 260, 267, 389–390, 399; production of furs, 206–207, 214, 218, 220, 242, 245

Lake Windermere, 204

Lake Winnipeg, 48, 50, 164n, 390; La Vérendrye at, 89–94, 99; French trade, 111, 138; H.B. Co. trade, 160, 165, 240n, 326, 330; Canadian trade, 189, 191–194, 226, 234, 267, 278–279; prices, 244n; transport on, 289, 293, 309, 389

Lake Winnipegosis, 95–96

La Lande, Antoine, 211

La Marque, Sr., 92–93, 98

Lampson and Co., 368

Lamson-Hubbard Co., 357–358, 365–367, 369, 372

Langton Bay, 369

Languedoc, 79

La Pérouse, Admiral, 152

La Pierre's House, 291, 298, 316, 372

L'Arbe Croche, 167

Laroche, Mathurin, 98, 111

La Rochefoucauld-Liancourt, F. A. F., Duc de, 222n, 244n, 266n

La Rochelle, 58, 62; centre of beaver trade, 73, 75–76, 103

Larocque, F. A., 259

La Salle, R. R. C., Sr. de, 46, 51, 54, 64

Laut, A. C., 142

Lauzon (Co. of New France), 39

La Vérendrye, François, Chevalier, 94, 95

La Vérendrye, Jean Baptiste de, 91–92, 99

La Vérendrye, Pierre Gaultier de, 92, 94, 99

La Vérendrye, Pierre Gaultier de Varennes, Sr. de, 90–95, 97–100, 118, 138, 190

Laviolette (fur trader), 254n, 255, 255n
Laviolette, Joseph, 98
Lawrence, E. J. and H., 364n
Lawrence, Sheridan, 365
Lead mining, 111
Leases, 106–109, 112; H.B. Co. lease (1821), 328–329
Leather Pass, 303
Le Blanc (fur trader), 190, 190n
L'Echelle, Sr., 99
Le Clair, Joseph, 193
Le Clercq, Chréstien, 3
Lecuyer, J., 198
Leduc, M., 167
Leduc, Phillippe, 98
Lees, John, 176n, 177n, 178n, 193n
LeGardeur de St. Pierre, 94, 99
Le Gras, Sr., 92, 98
Leith, Jamieson and Co., 255
Le Jeune, Paul, 27
Le Pas, 234, 368, 372n
Le Roux, Hubert, 191
Leroux, Laurent, 199–200, 199n
Lescarbot, Marc, 11
Lesieur, Toussaint, 249
Lesser Slave Lake, 202, 261, 344, 359
Levinson, M. H. and Co. Ltd., 368
Lewis and Clark expedition, 203
Liard River, trade at, 202–203, 291; Indian troubles on, 274; route to Yukon, 291, 335; transport, 347–348, 350–351
Liard River (1st), 347; (2nd), 345n, 347, 350
Licences, 175n, 332; limitation of, 67; character of, 106–109, 111–112; Canadian policy, 170–173; effect of American Revolution on, 182–183; to Grand Portage, 189–196, 253
Liebes and Co., 369
Lily, 343
Limbourg, 79
Lisbon, 76, 207
Livingston, Duncan, 201
Logan, Mr., 322
Long, John, 154
Long Sault Rapids, 60, 215
Longmoor, Robert, 197n
Longueuil, Sr., 87

Loon Island (H.B.), 367n
Lorme, F. M. S. de, 92
Loucheux Indians, 361n
Louisiana, 88
Louisiana Purchase, 187
Loutit Island, 366
Louvière, M. de, 93
Lynn, Canal, 324
Lynx, 93–94
Lyons, 73

McBEATH, George, 195–198, 200, 220
McCormick, Charles, 196n, 197n
MacDonald, Alexander, 163
Macdonald, Archibald, 342
MacDonald, John, 255
Macdonell, John, 158, 191, 222n, 224n, 229n, 234, 239n, 241n, 248n, 269
MacDonnell, Miles, 163
McDougall, John A., 368
McGill, James, 184, 193–198, 206, 393
McGill, James and Andrew, and Co., 186n
McGill, John, 196–197
McGill, John and Andrew, 184
McGill University, 393
McGillis, Hugh, 249
McGillivray, Duncan, 219, 235, 245, 251, 255n, 259n, 260n, 271, 278
McGillivray, Joseph, 249, 251
McGillivray, Simon, 261n, 283–285, 283n, 393
McGillivray, William, 248–249, 251, 253, 283–284, 283n
McIntyre, S., 369
Mackay, Capt. James, 233n
Mackenzie, Alexander, 153, 158, 196, 199, 224, 230–231, 234, 238, 242, 257n, 258, 261n; in Athabasca district, 200–203; as agent, 248–249; relations with N.W. Co., 252–256, 256n, 261, 283
Mackenzie, Alexander, and Co.: employés of, 238; amalgamation of, 258–261
McKenzie, H., 284
McKenzie, James, 249, 260
Mackenzie, K., 351

McKenzie, N. M. W. J., 376n

Mackenzie, Roderic, 245, 258, 262; in Athabasca district, 200–203; in N.W. Co., 248–250; in competition, 253–254

Mackenzie River, 345n, 347

Mackenzie River district, 5, 151, 298–299, 345, 360–361, 366–367; trade on, 200–203, 230–231, 260, 323; labour in, 237, 310–311; influence of monopoly on, 274, 335–336; transport to, 291–292, 297, 346–352; supplies and provisions in, 299–305, 342, 359; competition on, 331, 370–373, 377, 389–390

McKindlay, J., 196

McLean, John, 313, 323, 323n, 332, 335

McLeod, A. N., 284

McLeod, Alexander, 249, 250, 249n

McLeod, Normand, 199–200

McLeod Lake, 204, 230

McLoughlin, Dr. John, 287, 314, 322, 323, 334

McLoughlin Fort, 334

MacMillan Co., 368

McMurray, 345, 350, 361, 365–366, 371

Macomb, Edgar and Macomb, 184n

McQuesten (fur trader), 372

McTavish, John George, 287, 315

McTavish, Simon, 174n, 180, 219–220, 226, 242, 246; in northwest trade, 196–200, 249–256, 256n

McTavish, W., 294, 315

McTavish and Co., 268n, 280

McTavish, Fraser and Co., 261, 261n

McTavish, Frobisher and Co., 184, 221; in N.W. Co., 200, 227, 249–250, 250n, 259

McTavish, McGillivray and Co., 186n, 236, 261, 261n, 280n, 284n

Makkovik, 371n

Manchester, 166

Manchester House, 153

Mandan Indians, 154, 190–192, 192n, 233, 233n, 259

Manhattan, 51–53, 81

Manitoba, 373

Manitoba, 343

Manitoulin Island, 43

Mansel Island, 370n

Mansfield House, 154

Marchessau (fur trader), 209n

Marquette, Father Jacques, 51

Marquis, 343

Marseilles, 73

Marten: French trade in, 90–97; H.B. Co. trade in, 120, 127, 138, 150, 286, 298, 308, 319, 332, 336; Canadian trade in, 168, 201, 267; prices of, 264–265

Marten Lake, 201

Martin's Falls, 154

Martin's Falls House, 154

Maskoutech Indians, 54–57

Massacre Island, 92

Matonabbee, 149, 152

Mattawa River, 24

Maugras, Sr., 98–99

Maurepas, Marquis de, 93

Mayrand, M. (trader), 211

Me-caw-baw-nish Lake, 196n

Meinard, Louis, 211

Mercantile policy, 114–115, 114n, 177–179

Mer de l'Ouest, 98–100, 108–111, 191

Meulles, Jacques de, 57

Miami Indians: trade with, 44, 55–56, 60–61, 70, 87, 100; wars, 51, 102; lease of trade, 107

Michigan, trade in, 185n

Michilimackinac, 43, 56, 389–390; English at, 54; depot at, 59–61, 91–93, 99, 111, 167–168, 172–174, 177, 183–189, 191, 206–219, 215n, 222–227; trade of, 251, 255n, 267n; prices at, 244n

Michimilimackinac Co., 187

Michipicoten: lease of, 107; trade of, 166n, 196n, 198n, 266n, 268n; wages at, 311n; express to, 317

Micmac Indians, 10, 16

Miles, Robert, 315, 321

Millbank, 311, 314

Millington, Mr. (H.B. Co.), 123

Milton, Viscount, 302–304

Milwaukee, 225

Minneapolis, 368

Minnesota, 279

Missisauga Indians, 45

Mississippi River, 91, 99, 343; French trade on, 43, 61; exploration of, 51; English trade on, 88–91, 185–186, 206; competition from, 110, 167, 172–173, 180–181, 254, 294

Missouri River, 154, 259, 330

Mistassini, 47, 259

Mohawk River, 221

Monière, Sr., 99

Monontague, 240n

Monsoni Indians, 93

Montagnais Indians, 12, 15, 21–22, 24–25, 28

Montagne à la Bosse, 233

Montana, 369

Montée (Sask.), 232, 237

Montour, Nicholas, 196n, 198, 200, 256n

Montreal, 22n, 267, 277, 358, 390; establishment of, 37–38; trade at, 44–45, 50, 54–59, 84–85, 91–95, 101, 116–117; transport to, 52n, 289n; terminus at, 59, 78–79, 99–101, 109–112, 151, 167–189, 210–217, 239–267, 354; auction sales at, 376–377

Montreal department, 285–287, 333–334, 352–353

Montreal Lake, 368

Monts, P. du G., Sr. de, 32

Moose Factory, 49, 122, 130, 285, 367; establishment of, 120; arrival of ships at, 129n; tariff at, 141–142; depot at, 285, 289, 317

Moose Island (Slave Lake), 154

Moose Lake, 192

Moose River, 45; competition on, 149, 237, 259, 278, 290

Moravian missionaries, 370, 371n

Morel (fur trader), 198

Mountain Portage, 229

Mure (Muir), John, 255, 256n, 283

Murray, A. H., 324

Murray, J., 171n

Muskrat, 264–265, 286, 327

Mutton Bay, 371n

NAIN, 371n

Nancy, 257n

Nannuck, 352

Nantes, 73, 75

Nascopie, 352

Nass, 311

Natashquam, 371n

Naywatamee Poets, 121–122, 138

Nechako River, 204

Nelson Lake, 326

Nelson River, 278, 290, 316, 326, 351; competition on, 94–96, 151, 331, 367; trade on, 137–138, 142; supplies from, 304

Nelson River (Liard), 350, 372

Nepawi, 234, 255

Nepean, Evan, 185, 189n

Néret and Gayot, 70

Netchalik, 353

Nettley Creek, 191

Neutral Indians, 29, 31

Neveu, Sr., 98

New Brunswick, 395

New Caledonia, 389–390; posts in, 204, 240; trade in, 230, 244, 260, 333, 336–337; supplies in, 237, 301–303, 317, 359; transport to, 292, 317, 344; wages in, 311

New England, 10, 70, 79–81, 390–391

New Orleans, 172, 172n, 185–186

New Severn, 120, 122, 130, 142, 290, 309, 317

New York: competition from, 54, 84–87, 166, 174–177, 180, 221, 261, 399; imports from, 208

Newcastle, Duke of, 396

Niagara, 86, 219–220; trade at, 46, 100, 108, 266n; competition at, 87–89; route through, 183–186, 212, 220, 394–395; supplies from, 225

Nicolet, Jean, 31

Nipigon district, 91, 209; trade of, 100, 266n, 279; lease of, 108–109; competition in, 122, 154, 275

Nipissing Indians, 26–27, 44, 54, 87

Nolan, Sr., 93

Nolin, J. B., 196n, 222n, 257n

Non-Intercourse Act, 187

Nootka Sound, 261

Norris and Carey, 368
North Somerset Island, 371n
North West River, 370n
Northcote, 343
Northern Trading Co., 366
Northland Pioneer, 366
Northland Trader, 366
Northrup, Anson, 294
Northwest, 343, 344n
Northwest Hide and Fur Co., 368
Northwest Mounted Police, 369
Northwest Passage, 130–133, 130n
Northwest Rebellion, 344
Norton, Richard, 132, 136
Norway House, 287, 355, 359–360;
    depot at, 290–295, 299–310, 306n,
    315–326, 341; competition at, 331
Nottingham House, 154
Noüe, Sr. de la, 91
Nouvel, Father, 47
Noyelles, N. J. F. de, 98
Noyon (fur trader), 50
Nuelton, 368
Nutak, 371n

OAKES, Forrest, 195–198, 206, 209n,
    210–212, 210n, 215, 219
Ogden, P. S., 336
Ogilvy, John, 236, 255n, 256n, 261n
Ohio River, 53, 89, 179
Okanagan, 297, 304
Oldmixon, John, 119n
Onondague Indians, 88
Ontario, 286, 389, 392
Orange, 35, 51–53, 81
Oregon territory, 264, 332, 334
Oregon Treaty (1846), 386
Orkney Islands, 160
Orkneymen, 126, 160–161, 311n
Oskelaneo, 371n
Osnaburg House, 154
Oswego: competition from, 86–88,
    102; route, 160, 167, 177n, 182, 221
Ottawa Indians, 43–47, 50–58, 102
Ottawa River, 14–15, 21–28, 37–38,
    41–45, 167–171, 207, 209–212, 218,
    223, 225, 237, 267, 317, 389–390,
    395; lumbering on, 393–395
Otter, 97, 120, 265, 319, 333

Otter, 222, 222n
Oudiette, Nicolas, 64–65, 70
Ouatonon Indians, 87, 100, 107
Outagami Indians, 55–56
Overhead costs, relation to trade,
    15–16, 30–31, 58–59, 127–129, 205,
    290, 301–309, 346–348
Oxford House, 292, 301, 309, 331,
    341

PACHOT, M., 90
Pacific Coast district, 202–207, 247–
    248, 260–262, 308, 314–315, 318,
    328–329, 332–338, 366
Pacific Fur Co., 204, 206n
Padley, 371n
Pagwa, 368
Panama Canal, 399
Pangman, Peter, 193n, 196n, 197n,
    198–199, 200, 253, 253n
Pangnirtung, 370n
Papinachois Indians, 30, 47
Paris, 62, 74, 77, 103–104, 386
Parker, Gerrard, Ogilvy and Co., 186n,
    255, 256n
Parrent, Pierre, 211
Parry Sound, 395
Parsnip River, 202, 364
Parsons, Ralph (Commissioner), 370n
Pasquia, 192
Paterson, Charles, 193n, 193–198
Payne Lake, 370n
Peace Point, 202
Peace River, 154, 200–204, 230–231,
    237, 245, 256, 300, 344, 351, 359,
    364–368, 375, 389
Peace River Crossing, 344–345
Pedersen, Capt., 369
Peel River, 291, 297–298, 316, 320,
    324, 336, 342
Pelican, 352
Pelican Narrows, 368
Pelly Banks, 324
Pembina, 294, 330
Penetanguishene, 223, 223n
Perrot, Nicolas, 21, 43–44, 54
Perseverance, 257n
Peru, *vigogne* from, 75
Petite Nation, 60

Philadelphia, 208
Phyn, G., 196
Phyn and Ellice, 180, 184, 219, 393
Phyn, Ellice and Inglis, 250, 266n, 268n
Phyn, Inglis and Co., 255
Pic, 266n
Piegan Indians, 204, 326
Pierre au Calumet, 275
Pilots and Mates Association, 353
Pine Fort, 223n
Pine Island Lake, 196n
Pine Point, 223n
Pink, William, 151n
Pistol Bay, 136
Plains Indians, 138, 190–191, 235–236, 252, 269
Plante (fur trader), 198
Pointeau (*fermier*), 68, 70
Poland, 76
Pollock, Mr. (clerk), 253
Pomainville, Baptiste, 98
Pond, Peter, 152, 172n, 177, 180, 191, 194, 194n, 195–203, 196n, 197n, 199n, 221n, 252–253, 257, 267
Pond Inlet, 352–353, 370n
Pontchartrain, M. de, 59, 78
Pontiac, 188
Pont-Gravé, *see* Du Pont, F. G., Sr. de
Porcupine River, 291
Port Colborne, 399
Port Harrison, 367, 370n
Portage de l'Isle, 249
Portage du Traite, 152, 195
Portage la Loche, 151, 196–199, 202–203, 295, 342–344, 371; brigade, 291–292, 301, 310, 314–315; 314n, 315n, 354
Portage la Prairie, 296
Porteous (fur trader), 196
Porteous, Sutherland and Co., 197–198
Portland, 395
Portugal, 76, 80–81, 101
Potawatomi Indians, 43, 54–55
Povungnetuk, 370n
Prairie du Chien, 172n, 180n, 184, 254, 266n
Prairie Lake, 368

Prevost, Sir George, 262
Price, Benjamin, 208
Price and Morland, 207
Prices of beaver, 63–66, 68–70, 72–73, 85, 104–106; of fur, 194–195, 243–244, 264–265, 335
Primeau, Louis, 151, 152n
Primot, Pierre, 98
Prince Albert, 153, 344, 368
Prince Edward Island, 379
Prince of Wales Fort, 130, 132, 136, 141
Prince Rupert, 306
Prince Rupert, 124
Prince Rupert's Land, sale of, 338
Private trade, 127–128, 155
Profits, 336–337, 377–378
Provisions: general, 12–13, 130, 160n, 224–226, 232–236, 299–303, 331; on Hudson Bay: partridge, 132–134, 156, geese, 132–134, 156, fish, 132–134, 156, rabbits, 132–134, 156; on Mackenzie River: caribou, 300, moose, 299, rabbits, 299, fish, 299, potatoes, 299; New Caledonia: salmon, 206, 236–237; Pacific coast, 308, 333; Peace River, 359–60; Plains area: pemmican, 198–199, 235, 263–264, 301–302, 359; *see also* Agriculture
Prud'homme, L.-A., 95
Pukitawagan, 368

Qu'Appelle River, 233, 245, 256
Quebec, 68, 103–104, 111–112, 116, 208–212; trade at, 17, 24–29, 31, 34–39, 42, 48–50, 57–58, 72–73, 78–79, 85, 90, 170, 174–180, 183, 215, 260, 312, 367, 390; military importance of, 34–38; exports of fur, 265–266; lumber from, 393–395
Quebec, province, 174–175, 179, 286
Quebec Act (1774), 176, 176n, 179, 386, 391
Quebec Gazette, 169, 172

Raccoons, 208, 266–267
Radio, 353
Radisson Pierre Esprit, 45; with the

French, 24, 26, 31, 36–37, 45, 56; with H.B. Co., 49, 119, 122–123
Rainy Lake, 50, 90–91, 98, 154, 292, 304, 309–310, 330, 342; French trade at, 188–190; Canadian trade at, 188–190; depot for Athabasca, 226, 229–232, 237, 241–243, 289–291, 317; wages at, 240n
Rampart House, 372n
Ramparts, 347
Rankin, D., 196
Rapin, J. B., 99, 191
Rasilly, I. de, 18
Rastel, Mr., 124
Rat River, 240, 279, 342
Reaume, J., 254n, 255n
Red Deer River, 95, 234
Red Lake, 154, 279, 398
Red River, 4n; French traders on, 92–95; H.B. Co. traders on, 154, 161, 164; Canadian traders on, 191, 228, 232–234, 253–256, 267, 279; wages on, 239–241; communication to, 245, 294–295, 317–318; competition on, 263, 269–271, 329–334; settlement, 287–294, 302–313, 334–337, 389, 398; provisions from, 302–306; prices at, 327
Red River (Peace River), 343, 365
Reilhe, Antoine, 192
Reindeer Lake, 154, 279
Repentigny, de, 39
Revillon, Victor, 367
Revillon Frères, 364–365, 367, 367n, 368, 370
Rhondda, Lord, 366
Richardson, John, 186n, 187n, 284, 393
Richelieu River, 25, 29, 45
Richmond Fort, 130
Ricollet, A. R. F. de, 211
River la Coquille, 233
Rivière à la Biche, 95, 249
Rivière du Sauteux, 186
Rivière Maligne, 154
Rivière Tremblante, 158, 234, 249
Roberts, B., 169n, 172n, 189, 189n
Robertson, Colin, 161, 164–165, 260, 287

Robertson, Samuel, 325n
Robertson, William, 184, 184n
Robinson (of Montreal), 255
Robinson, Sir John, 125
Robson, Joseph, 96, 140, 144
Rocheblave, Pierre R. de, 257n, 280n, 284
Rocky Mountain Fort (Peace River), 204, 236n
Rocky Mountain House (Sask.), 234
Rocky Mountain Indians, 201, 231
Rogers, Robert, 171n
Roman Catholic Missions, 367
Romanet (of Revillon Frères), 367n
Roseaux, 92
Ross, John, 197–200, 200n, 253–254
Rotterdam, 77
Rowley, John, 212
Royer, Pierre, 99
Rozée (Co. of New France), 39
Ruby, 352
Rupert River, 45, 48, 119–120, 125
Rupert's House, 49, 119–120, 125, 130, 379n
Rupert's Land, 397
Rupert's Land Act (1869), 376, 386
Russia, 66, 71, 73, 76–77, 127, 201, 246, 332–334, 357, 364
Russian American Co., 333
Ryerson, John, 293
Rymer Point, 369n

Sabellum Trading Co., 370
Sagard-Théodat, Gabriel, 17, 20–21, 24, 26–28, 30–31, 37
Saguenay River, 400; trade at, 11–12, 21–22; route, 13–15, 23–24, 29, 37, 47–48, 389, 395
St. Anthony, 294
St. Clair River, 220
St. Genevieve, 211
St. Germain, Venant Lemaire, 195–198, 196n, 200, 249
St. Helen, 242
St. John (Peace River), 230, 288, 351, 367–368
St. John's (Newfoundland), 352
St. Joseph, 100, 172, 222
St. Leger, Brigadier General, 182

St. Louis fort, 34
St. Louis (Mississ.) 185–186
St. Louis Rapids, 32, 207, 215
Saint Malo, 73
St. Maurice River, 15, 21–22, 24, 37, 237, 395
St. Paul, 294, 295n, 296, 315, 318, 330, 361
St. Paul and Manitoba Railway, 343
St. Peters, 317
St. Petersburgh, 246
Saint Pierre, M. de, 99
St. Pierre, Leonard, 211–212
Saint Pierre River, 168, 186
St. Sulpice, 211
Sale, C. V., 358
Saleesh House, 204
Sales, 123, 126–127, 131, 245–247, 326–327, 376–377
San Francisco, 369
Sandwich Islands, 298, 308
Sanguinet, Charles, 193
Sanguinet, Christopher, 208
Sanschagrin, 95
Sanscrainte, Romant, 193
Sarjeant, Matthew, 142
Sarnia, 395
Saskatchewan River, 389–390; French on, 95–96, 109–111; H.B. Co. on, 121, 159–160, 290–295, 301–304, 309, 326, 341, 360; Canadians on, 151, 188–199, 233–234, 238, 251–256, 262, 278–279; competition on, 138, 270–279, 331, 368; steamboats on, 343–345
Saskeram Lake, 192
Sassevillet, François, 189
Sauk Indians, 44, 173
Sault Ste Marie, 232, 245, 257, 317; Indians at, 43, 56, 60; competition at, 47, 89; trade at, 168, 194n; portage at, 183, 218–223, 223n, 232, 247n, 257; canal, 222
Saulteur Indians, 43–45, 47, 87, 102, 228
Sauvage, F., 98
Sawle, Mr. (Northern Traders Ltd.), 366
Schenectady, 182n, 221, 226

Scotland, 311, 354, 358
Scott, Capt. R. F., 352
Sea otter, 205
Seal River, 137
Secord, M. R., 368
Seignelay, M. de, 59, 63
Selkirk, Earl of, 161, 164, 251, 279, 338; estate of, 328–330
Seven Oaks, 279
Severn River, 130
Seymour, Wm., 369
Shaftesbury, 1st Earl of, 124
Shaftesbury (Peace River), 364
Shaganappi, 296–297
Shallow Lake, see Saskeram Lake
Shaw (of Dunvegan), 354
Shaw, Angus, 153–154, 203, 234, 245, 249, 260, 284
Shoal River, 293
Shubert, A. B., Ltd., 368
Sikanni Indians, 300
Sikinik, 371n
Silk, replacing fur for hats, 341
Silvy, Père de, 131–132
Simcoe, John Graves, 178, 185, 221
Simpson, Aemilius, 322n
Simpson, Alexander, 322n
Simpson, Sir George, 285–287, 285n, 295, 313–327, 331, 334; inspection trips of, 317–318; increased authority of, 321–327, 355
Simpson, Thomas, 286n, 293n, 322n
Sinclair (of Hay River), 372
Sinclair, W., 295, 309, 315, 322, 331
Sioux Indians, 43–49, 51, 54, 58, 89–90, 92, 94, 99–102, 168, 181
Sipiwisk, 272
Skeena River, 364n
Skinners Company, 131
Slater, Mr. (Northern Traders Ltd.), 366
Slave Indians, 200
Slave Lake, 150; Canadian trade to, 152, 200–202, 229–231, 275; H.B. Co. trade, 154, 291n, 299, 345, 347–351; competition on, 365–366
Slave River, 154, 199–201, 231, 345, 350
Slave River, 345n

Small, Patrick, 200, 234n, 253, 254n
Smallpox, 152, 192, 199, 252, 287n
Smith, D. A. (Lord Strathcona), 342, 355–358, 397, 397n
Smith Portage, 347, 350
Smoky River, 201, 344, 359
Smuggling, 53, 77–81, 84, 86, 104, 166, 178, 205, 329–331
Snake expedition, 333–334
Solomons, Ezekiel, 168
Sorel River, 38
Soudack, George, Fur Co., 368
Souris River, 154, 233, 254n, 255
South Branch House, 153, 234
South Deer Lake, 368
South Saskatchewan, 153
Southampton Island, 371n
Southern department, 285–286, 305, 317, 327
Spain, 37, 71, 76–77, 80–81, 101, 172, 175n, 180, 185–186, 246
Sparr Point, 325n
Spiesmacker, F. C., 190, 190n
Spokane House, 204
Stadacona, 11
Standards of trade, 140–143, 140n, 318–319
Stanley, 368
Stedman, John, 177n, 178n
Stedman, Philip, 220n
Stevenson, Charles, 185n
Stikine River, 311
Stobart, Eden and Co., 368
Stord, 367
Strathcona, Lord, see Smith, D. A.
Stratton Island, 367
Street, Samuel, and Co., 182n
Stromness, 292
Stuart, Mr. (H.B. Co.), 322
Stuart Lake, 204, 364n
Stupart's Bay, 370n
Sturgeon-head, 364n
Sturgeon Lake, 368
Sturgeon River, 27, 255
Sturgeon River Fort, 196n
Sugluk East, 370n
Sugluk West, 370n
Supplies, 236–237, 303–307, 359–360
Susquehannah River, 88

Sutherland, Daniel, 197–198, 251
Sutherland, George, 159
Swan River district: H.B. Co. in, 155, 158, 254n, 292–293, 302–304, 309, 326, 341; Canadian traders in, 256
Sweden, 73
Sylvester (of Dease Lake), 372

TADOUSSAC, 12, 14, 22–23, 27–30, 32–33, 40, 48, 100; monopoly of, 63, 72
Talon, J. B., 51, 63, 65, 115n
T. Association, 255
Telephone, 353
Temiskaming, 48, 100, 107–108, 122, 237
Terre Blanche Portage, 272
Terrebonne, 165
Tête Jaune Cache, 303
Thain, Thomas, 236, 257n, 261n, 280n, 284
Thomas, Dr., 155
Thompson, David, 4–5, 154–155, 160, 204, 218, 250, 259n, 260n, 263, 401n
Thompson, John, 182n
Thomson, J., 356
Thorburn, William, 249–250
Three Rivers, trade at, 22, 24, 29, 35–38, 57; decline of beaver at, 28; canoes manufactured at, 222
Tobacco Indians, 31
Tod (H.B. Co.), 321–322
Todd, Isaac, 197–198, 206, 256n, 258
Todd, McGill and Co., 190, 198, 221, 225
Tomison, William, 155n, 159, 160n
Tongue River, 272
Toronto, 89, 223, 223n, 395
Tough, Mr. (clerk), 255n, 256n
Tracey, Mr. (fur trader), 168
Tracy, A. de P., Sr. de, 65
Trade, 10, 12, 40–44, 56–7, 61–63, 88, 114, 168–175, 177–178, 181–188, 206–207, 210–213, 307, 318–320, 331, 361–363
Trade goods: general, 6, 14–21, 43–44, 82, 97, 101–110, 129, 141–142, 156–160, 166, 169–173, 191–195,

207, 209, 216, 219, 228, 306, 320; cloth, 16, 33, 53, 78–79, 85–86, 129, 152n, 166, 185, 209n, 219, 236, 240; guns, 6, 18–20,35, 53–57, 93, 96–97, 110, 121, 123, 129, 135, 141, 152n, 156, 166, 173–174, 191–195, 228, 235, 253, 271, 306, 373; hatchets, 16–20, 33, 43, 48, 48n, 57, 97, 110, 123, 129, 150, 156, 295n; iron, 6, 16–18, 44, 97, 109–110, 149–150, 193, 201; kettles, 17–20, 33, 44, 56–57, 85, 93, 96, 110, 123, 129, 150, 152n, 157, 166, 193–195, 209n, 216, 228, 306, 373; knives, 17, 20, 33, 43, 57, 110, 129, 150, 152n, 195, 235, 240, 271, 306; liquor, 19, 82–87, 97, 102, 175, 176n, 181, 191–195, 216, 228–229, 235, 253, 268–269, 271–272, 287–288, 306–307, 333; sugar, 212, 220, 228, 307; tobacco, 24, 48n, 93, 96–97, 129, 141, 157, 163, 193–195, 209n, 210n, 216, 219, 228–229, 235, 240, 287–288, 306

Transportation
general, 15–16, 29, 219–222, 276–278, 292–298, 341–353
communication: by express, 244–245, 316–317, 317n, 360–361; telephone, 353; radio 353
freight: packing, 209–210, 217–218, 298–299; loading, 351; freighting, 309–310, 314–315
methods by land: pack line, 13, 19; snow-shoes, 13, 134; toboggan, 13, 297; horses, 139, 295–297, 350; Red River carts, 294–296, 341; dogs, 297, 346; trucks, 350–351
methods by water: York boats, 158–160, 289, 341, 387; sailing vessels on Great Lakes, 219–222, 252; river steamboats, on Red River, 294–296, on Saskatchewan, 341–342, on Mackenzie, 345–351; in Arctic, 352–353; steamships, 352–353; *see also* Canoe
routes: Grand Portage and Kaministiquia, 226–231, 242–243; Hudson Bay, 290, 352–353; Pacific Coast, 298–299, 300–302, 324–325

Traps, steel, 263–264, 264n, 294–295, 295n, 332n, 374
Trout Lake, 316, 368
Trudeau, Zenon, 233n
Tukik, 370n
Turks, 246
Turnor, Philip, 143n, 153n, 154, 157n, 164n, 196n, 202n, 234n
Tute, James, 193n, 197n, 198n
Tyrrell, J. B., 401n

Umfreville, E., 155, 252
Ungava, 305, 323, 352–353, 370n
United States, 179, 182, 187, 237–238, 252, 285, 290, 332, 332n, 334, 364, 385–386, 392, 395–398, 399n, 400–401; trade during American Revolution, 179–182, 187, 198; exports of fur through, 246, 265–267; imports through, 295
Upper Canada, 178
Upper Establishment, 234
Utrecht, Treaty of, 70, 84, 89–90, 122

Valorization, 64–66, 77
Vancouver, 352–353, 363, 369, 369n, 373, 399
Vancouver Island, 332
Van der Heyden, Dick, 169
Vaudreuil, P. de R., Marquis de, 79, 86, 90
Veenisk, 367
Verchères, Mme, 91
Verchères, Sr. de, 91, 98
Vermilion Falls, 201, 345, 365
Versailles, 78, 93
Vialars, Mr. (merchant), 208
Victoria, 297
Vignau (with Champlain), 30
Vigogne, 75, 81
Viner, Sir Robert, 124
Violet, 367
Virginia, 129

Wabash River, 53, 87, 89
Wabiscond, 368
Waden, Jean-Etienne, 193–199, 196n, 197n
Wager Inlet, 153n
Walker, Fowler, 170, 170n, 171n

Wallas, Graham, 383
Wappenassew, Chief, 191n
Waterways, 345, 345n, 365
Watkin, Sir Edward, 396
Weenusk, 345n
Welland Canal, 394
Wentzel, W. F., 262, 275, 310
West, John, 329
West Branch River, 372
West Indies, 53, 80, 85, 221
Western Arctic, 352, 369–370
Western Cartage and Storage Co., 345
Western department, 285, 297
Western Grocers Co., 368
Western Traders Co., 368
Whale Cove, 136
Whale River, 367
Whaling, 131
White fox, 369–370, 377–378, 378n
White Mud River, 255
Whitway, 331
Wilberforce, William, 235
Williams and Ostergaard, 369
Willson, Beckles, 139, 160
Wind City, 361n
Winnipeg, 356, 360, 363, 368, 398
Winnipeg River, 94, 154, 232, 304
Wintering partners, 242, 283n, 320–322, 337, 355
Wisconsin, 64, 102

Witney, 166
Woder, Thomas, 209n
Wolstenholme, 370n
Work, John, 322
Wright (fur trader), 196
Wrigley, Joseph, 356
Wrigley, 345

XY Co.: amalgamation of, 161, 202–203, 241, 245, 250–251, 256, 256n, 257n, 259, 279; competition of, 202, 269, 272, 279; at Grand Portage, 228n, 229

YELLOW-KNIFE INDIANS (*see also* Copper), 361
York, James, Duke of, 124
York Factory, 352
York Factory (*see also* Fort Nelson), 96, 121, 137–143, 151–156, 157n, 158–165, 159n, 192, 278, 289–295, 301–310, 315–318, 321–327, 331–335, 341, 352–354, 359, 378
Yorkshire, 166
Yukon River, 342
Yukon territory, 305, 323, 328, 335–336, 361–363, 369; transport to, 291–298; communication with, 297, 316; management of, 298–299, 324–325; wages, 311